THE U

# THE UNMAKING
# OF GOUGH

Paul Kelly

ALLEN & UNWIN

First published in 1976
Revised edition published in 1994
Allen & Unwin Pty Ltd
9 Atchison Street, St Leonards, NSW 2065 Australia

National Library of Australia
Cataloguing-in-Publication entry:

Kelly, Paul, 1947– .
 The unmaking of Gough.

 New ed.
 Includes index.
 ISBN 1 86373 788 X.

 1. Whitlam, Gough, 1916– . 2. Fraser, Malcolm, 1930– .
 3. Australia—Politics and government—1972–1975. I. Title.

320.994

Set in 10/11.5 pt Palatino 90% condensed by DOCUPRO, Sydney
Printed by McPherson's Printing Group, Australia

10 9 8 7 6 5 4 3 2 1

# CONTENTS

# PREFACE TO THE 1994 EDITION

This book tells the story of the most dramatic and turbulent eighteen months in Australia's political history. It is a detailed account of federal politics in the period from the May 1974 federal election to early 1976. It covers the upheavals within the Whitlam government, the loans affair, the rise of Malcolm Fraser, and the 1975 political and constitutional crisis involving Gough Whitlam, Malcolm Fraser, and Sir John Kerr, which climaxed in the dismissal of the Labor government.

I am grateful to Allen & Unwin for their decision to publish a new edition to coincide with the twentieth anniversary of these events. They will be a source of interest and controversy for as long as Australian politics is practised.

The original book has been given a light edit and trim to produce this new edition. I have retained as much as possible the spirit and letter of the original, which has its own value as a documentary perspective of events written at the time by a close observer in the press gallery. Some of my assessments and interpretations would be different if I wrote another account of these events now. I have also included a number of footnotes which were not in the original edition.

I thank my wife Margaret for her advice and assistance on the editing and her production of the index.

Paul Kelly
10 July 1994

# Preface to the 1976 edition

This book is both instant journalism and premature history. It deals with the events and factors underlying the fall of the Whitlam Labor government while not attempting to canvas in any way the achievements of that government. It also covers Malcolm Fraser's rise to power in the Liberal Party and his elevation to the prime ministership.

The author has drawn on material obtained while working in the parliamentary press gallery over this period. This has been supplemented by more than fifty conversations with politicians past and present, public servants, and ministerial staff, during the eleven week period in which the book was written. Many thanks to all those who helped. In particular thanks to Ros Kelly and Judy Sandry, without whose efforts the book would not have appeared.

Paul Kelly
5 April 1976

# PART I

# THE DISMISSAL

# 1

# SACKED

*What I will do as Governor-General is to pursue my interest in
law and politics. There are plenty of issues, many things I will
have the opportunity to express an opinion about.*

Sir John Kerr, 27 February 1974,
after the news of his appointment

There are few men who have either the power or the opportunity to
change the course of history. Australia's eighteenth Governor-General,
John Robert Kerr, had both in November 1975 and he was a man
prepared to exercise them. On the afternoon of Thursday 6 November,
inside his spacious study with its picture window overlooking the
tranquillity of Canberra's Lake Burley Griffin, Kerr began his serious
preparations for the most spectacular application of political power in
the nation's history. He moved towards his greatest judgement with all
the gravity which thirty years of law could muster, tinged with the thrill
of excitement bred into a man who had studied and practised the
exercise of power all his life in the military, industrial and legal com-
plexes of Australia.

Kerr was now at the full circle of his rich life and turbulent career.
Years before he had forsaken politics, his first and greatest love, for a
more noble and prestigious calling that eventually carried him by a
singular irony to the office of Governor-General, the very apex of
Australia's political structure. Having been guided in his early career
by the brilliant and erratic Dr Herbert Vere Evatt, who later assumed
leadership of the Labor Party, Kerr now found himself about to terminate the career of Evatt's most illustrious and flamboyant successor. In
so doing, he demonstrated that there is an ultimate political power in
Australia's system of government which other politicians either denied

outright or had forgotten about, and that this power accompanied the office of Governor-General, which the Labor Party ethic had assumed to be nothing more than a ceremonial figurehead, a pompous irrelevancy. Over the preceding weeks Kerr had used his tactical skills to outmanoeuvre Australia's Prime Minister, Edward Gough Whitlam, in a momentous game of political chess.

During the constitutional crisis the Governor-General displayed a highly developed sense of political ambivalence. Kerr was both for Whitlam and against him; for Whitlam if the Prime Minister's tactics proved successful, but inevitably against him if they failed.

In five weeks of crisis Kerr was sympathetic to the plight of the Labor government and uncritical to the Prime Minister of his tactics which were designed to crack the political nerve of the Opposition. Yet he was always aware that if Whitlam's political strategy failed then it would become the responsibility of the Governor-General himself to intervene. Kerr had recognised long before the budget was ever blocked in the Senate on 16 October 1975 that this might involve the dismissal of the Labor government.

The significance of 6 November is that on this day Kerr completed his last round of talks with Prime Minister Whitlam and the Leader of the Opposition Malcolm Fraser over the political deadlock. The crisis had been precipitated the previous month when, after a long period of deliberation, Fraser announced on 15 October that the Opposition would defer passage of the 1975–76 budget until the Labor government resigned or called a general election. The crisis was sealed when Whitlam announced the same evening, with the support of the Labor Party caucus, that he would remain in office and defy both the Senate and the Opposition, thereby forcing an historic confrontation.

Kerr now set his mind firmly on two fateful decisions, both inexorably linked, one crucial to the success of the other. He decided to dismiss Gough Whitlam as Prime Minister, and to keep this decision absolutely secret from Whitlam lest the leaking of the plan betray its swift execution.[1]

Kerr's decisions would not just extinguish the life of the Labor government. The crisis was not just a struggle between the Labor and coalition parties; it also represented the greatest test of strength between the House of Representatives and the Senate since Federation, the most profound test of the office of Governor-General and one of the most divisive political confrontations the nation had witnessed. The method and manner of its settlement would inevitably affect Australia's system of government into the twenty-first century and the psyche of Australia's two great political parties, the Labor Party and the Liberal Party, for decades.

On the evening of 6 November Kerr drove to Canberra airport to fly to Melbourne for an appointment. Just a few miles away, on the other side of the lake, Whitlam and a small group of friends were dining at Zorba's Restaurant in Canberra City, one of the local restaurants most frequented by the Prime Minister. Margaret Whitlam, speechwriter Graham Freudenberg, Whitlam's driver Bob Miller and his wife. and an old friend of the Whitlams from Cabramatta gathered in a 'family' dinner.

Whitlam's mood was of supreme confidence based upon the belief that he would prevail against Fraser. He was relaxed and expansive, reflecting on the crisis, the inevitable backdown which he believed Fraser now faced and his own plans for the future. Whitlam and Freudenberg discussed at length the consequences of such a backdown for Fraser. They both believed he would retain the Liberal leadership but they were certain that he would be permanently handicapped, that the electorate would never forgive his costly grab for power, and that henceforth Whitlam would hold a major advantage over his rival. Beyond this, and even more important, Whitlam would have defeated the Senate in such a thorough fashion that no Opposition party would ever again attempt to force an election through the Senate. Freudenberg put his beer on the table and said, 'Kerr is still the best appointment we've made.' Whitlam smiled. 'Too right,' he replied. Whitlam's confidence was based entirely upon his faith in Kerr. He toasted the man who was about to sack him.[2]

Why did Kerr keep his dismissal intentions a secret? A decisive clue is provided by an incident after the crisis, in early February 1976 when the Governor-General and Lady Kerr made an official visit to Tasmania. They arrived in Hobart from Canberra on Saturday 8 February and were guests of honour at a dinner given by the Governor of Tasmania and Lady Burbury. During this visit Kerr took the opportunity to go to the home of one of his oldest and best friends, the Professor of English at the University of Tasmania, Jim McAuley. The two men reflected on the events of the previous November-December. Kerr told McAuley that during the crisis he had been seriously thinking of telling Whitlam that he might have to dismiss him. But his wife, Lady Kerr, formerly Anne Robson, had said to him: 'No, don't do that. If you tell him, he'll sack you first.'

This is not to suggest that Kerr was dominated by his wife in his resolution of this crisis. But it highlights the extent to which Sir John and his wife felt there was a danger that Whitlam might seek to remove them in favour of a more compliant Governor-General. Sir John, ultimately, went to extraordinary lengths to conceal his decision from the Prime Minister. Whitlam was guilty of an appalling error: he completely misjudged his Governor-General. But, by the same token, he was lulled into this error by Kerr's determination to mislead his Prime Minister.[3]

Whitlam's entire political strategy during the four-week constitutional crisis that began in mid-October 1975 was based on one fundamental linchpin: that the Governor-General would act only on the advice of his Prime Minister and not without the advice of his Prime Minister. Whitlam always believed, not without reason, that Kerr was sympathetic to him personally as well as to the political goals for which he was fighting during the crisis. From the time Kerr accepted the position of Governor-General in 1974 he was fully aware that the potential existed for a major political upheaval. While the Labor government controlled the House of Representatives, it held only a minority in the Senate and the prospect of the Opposition blocking supply was ever-present.

According to Whitlam's recall, as early as June 1974 Whitlam and Kerr discussed the powers of the Senate at the Governor-General's Sydney residence, Admiralty House.[4] The former Prime Minister says that on this occasion Kerr entertained the idea of signing Appropriation Bills without prior passage through the Senate. Whitlam recalled that Kerr asked why the Senate, the House that could not initiate money bills or amend money bills, was thought to have the power to reject money bills. 'Wouldn't the power to reject be the ultimate form of amendment and therefore beyond the constitution?' Whitlam recalls Kerr asking him. This was taken by Whitlam as a clear indication of Kerr's scepticism about the Senate's money power and an indication of his doubt about whether, as Governor-General, he should accept the Senate's right to use such power.[5]

Whitlam told Kerr that he would investigate the ramifications of this position. According to Whitlam he informed Kerr later that, while there was legal backing for his argument, with which Whitlam himself sympathised, any move by a Governor-General along these lines could always be challenged in the High Court. Indeed, if Supply Bills received the Royal Assent without Senate passage, a High Court challenge would be inevitable; if the High Court declared the Governor-General's action invalid, only worse problems would be created. Whitlam put weight on this exchange and interpreted it, as the constitutional crisis loomed, as evidence of Kerr's sympathy towards his own view of the Senate's powers. This was naive given the extraordinarily radical nature of the idea—Royal Assent for bills that had not passed the Senate. If Whitlam's version is accurate then incredulity, not reassurance, would have seemed a better response.[6]

However it was during the period of the crisis, through to early November 1975, that the feedback which Whitlam received from Kerr most assured him that the Governor-General was favourably disposed to his position. Obviously, Whitlam made a false judgement overall; but there were signs of Kerr's approval of his position.

From the day the budget was first deferred, Whitlam stated and restated his views in forthright language, in public and in private. He adopted the position that the Senate must submit to him; he would never submit to the Senate. He demanded that the Senate vote either to accept or to reject the budget and made it clear that he would never succumb to an election at its behest. Whitlam's pronouncements, in public, in parliament and in private talks with his staff, journalists and politicians, were similar in substance to those he gave the Governor-General in private. In short, the Prime Minister's political stance was that he would not relent. As far as can be determined, at no stage, from 16 October to the afternoon of the sacking on 11 November, did Kerr indicate to Whitlam that the Prime Minister's stand was insufficient to resolve the deadlock between the Houses, nor did he ask Whitlam for advice which in the Governor-General's opinion would resolve the deadlock. Whitlam concluded that the Governor-General was tolerant of his position at this time. As far as is known, throughout this period Kerr never once told Whitlam he was unhappy with these tactics and never once sought alternative advice.[7]

The basis of the Fraser strategy depended upon an assessment of the situation which was given its strongest and clearest expression in an opinion by the former Solicitor-General Bob Ellicott, then a front bench Liberal and close adviser to the Opposition leader. Ellicott released his views in a press statement on 16 October—which was really a legal opinion—and sent a copy to the Governor-General. He argued that the Governor-General had not just the power but also the duty to dismiss his Ministers immediately if they were unable to obtain supply and offered no solution to the deadlock.

The Ellicott opinion was discussed between Whitlam and Kerr during the first week of the crisis. Kerr said Ellicott had sent him a copy of the opinion. 'It's bullshit isn't it?' he said to Whitlam. 'Is that what your people tell you?' The Prime Minister agreed saying he believed this was the view of the Law Officers. Kerr then asked whether he could speak with the government's advisers in the Attorney-General's Department himself. Whitlam said his view was that any opinions or advice given to the Governor-General should come from either himself or Ministers with his approval. He told Kerr he would have advice prepared by the government's Law Officers on the Ellicott opinion and sent to him. Whitlam asked the Attorney-General Kep Enderby to set this in train. The Prime Minister was deeply influenced by Kerr's apparent rejection of the Ellicott opinion. That opinion, of course, was similar to that given a few weeks later by the Chief Justice Sir Garfield Barwick and accepted by the Governor-General himself and included in his own letter when he dismissed the Prime Minister.[8]

Whitlam should have seen the straws in the wind. After all, Kerr was sufficiently interested in the opinion to want to talk with the government's legal advisers and then have a formal opinion on Ellicott's view. However, Whitlam had his confidence strengthened this day that Kerr took a dim view of the Ellicott opinion. This was of significance since the Ellicott assessment was fundamental to the Liberal strategy on which Malcolm Fraser had staked his political career. This assessment, which was released at the very start of the crisis, revealed the extent to which the Opposition had thought through the consequences before blocking the budget. Contrary to reports at the time, the Opposition had examined the possibility that Whitlam might try to 'tough it out' and remain in office when the budget was blocked. The Liberals had staked their strategy on an assumption opposite to Whitlam's: that eventually the Governor-General would intervene and dismiss the Prime Minister.

Another incident which bolstered the Prime Minister's confidence occurred on the weekend of 1–2 November in Melbourne when Kerr and Whitlam spoke with one another socially. During their talks Kerr put to Whitlam what appears to have been his only suggestion for a compromise during the period of the crisis. It was put on an informal and friendly basis confirming the view Whitlam had always held, namely that the Governor-General was anxious for a compromise political solution, not a dramatic vice-regal intervention.

Kerr suggested the solution could arise as a result of the Opposition's fear that the Government would call an early half-Senate election in the hope of winning control of the Upper House for a few months preceding 1 July 1976. (One of Fraser's tactical motives in blocking the budget to force a general election was his concern to prevent this situation. The possibility arose because at the next half-Senate election there would be four Senators elected for the first time representing the Northern Territory and the Australian Capital Territory. But these new Senators would take their Senate seats immediately rather than at 1 July 1976 when all other elected Senators took their places. This meant that there could be an interim Senate constituted for a few months before mid-1976 and there was an outside chance that Labor might control the Senate during this short period.) Kerr suggested that if Whitlam pledged that he would not resort to such an option—which meant that Whitlam would not hold an early Senate election—then, in return, the Opposition might agree to pass the budget and end the crisis.

Whitlam noted Kerr's suggestion and, although not over-impressed by it, decided to float the idea. On Tuesday 4 November Whitlam saw his Labour Minister Senator Jim McClelland in Canberra and, as they were talking, McClelland, off his own bat, suggested this compromise to Whitlam. 'You've been talking to Kerr,' Whitlam said immediately. McClelland acknowledged that he had indeed been talking to Kerr. Some time in the previous three days Kerr had rung McClelland at his Sydney home and spoken to him about the crisis. Kerr and McClelland were old friends and colleagues who had made their reputation as lawyers together and had enjoyed such a friendship for 25 years that, even after Kerr became Governor-General, he visited McClelland's Sydney home on several occasions. During their November discussion Kerr conveyed the same compromise proposal to McClelland which he had suggested to Whitlam at about the same time.

According to McClelland's recollection, Kerr told him: 'I believe that what is primarily on their [the Opposition's] mind is a worry that if you get a Senate majority for a short period you will introduce electoral reform that will put the Country Party out of business.' McClelland remembers Kerr saying: 'I believe that the best contribution that I could make in this crisis would be to call up Fraser and suggest to him that he could save face by agreeing to a suggestion such as that.' McClelland distinctly remembers Kerr saying that Fraser had 'painted himself into a corner'. He remembers Kerr saying that the real question was how to find a face-saving formula for the Opposition leader and that this proposal appeared to be the best one.[9]

Kerr's suggestion proves that he was anxious to find a compromise solution. But it was the spirit and manner with which he dealt with both Whitlam and McClelland that was important in shaping Labor's confidence. On Thursday 30 October, before he had floated this compromise, the Governor-General had lunch with both the Prime Minister and the Labour Minister at Government House after an Executive Council meeting. As the three men sat around the table at Yarralumla they chatted as friends, men who had dealt with each other for more than twenty-five years, in the law, in the Labor Party, and in political life. Kerr freely discussed the constitutional crisis over the lunch and the wine. Although there were no specific proposals put and the discussion was of a general nature, the Governor-General betrayed no sign that he was dissatisfied with Whitlam's approach, that he believed new measures were needed to resolve the crisis or that dismissal of the Government was an option in any sense.

Whitlam and McClelland, who were both men of considerable experience in worldly affairs, never had any doubt that the Governor-General would act with propriety and frankness in his dealings with his chief advisers. It was inconceivable to them that Kerr was only a few days away from sacking them from office.

The final and conclusive proof of Kerr's successful deception of his Prime Minister occurred on the morning of Tuesday 11 November. Whitlam phoned the Governor-General at 10 a.m. to seek an appointment with him and told Kerr he would be advising a half-Senate election for Saturday 13 December. He told Kerr he wanted to announce this decision to the Labor Party caucus which was meeting in a few minutes and then to the Parliament later. Kerr expressed no objection to Whitlam informing his caucus and, because of the Remembrance Day ceremonies, it was agreed that Whitlam's appointment at Government House should be set for the lunch break that day.

Before Kerr even took this call from the Prime Minister that morning, he had given instructions for the typing of a letter informing Whitlam of his dismissal. But Kerr wanted to be absolutely sure that Whitlam had no inkling of what was to come. When the Prime Minister drove to Government House that afternoon he had no idea he was driving to his own political execution. Whitlam was keyed up and in a buoyant mood, having delivered a strong speech in the party room, which backed him unanimously. That morning Labor members strode through Parliament House on top of the world, in contrast to their counterparts, the Opposition backbenchers, who were overwhelmingly worried about the course of events and who believed that a political compromise was almost certain.

Whitlam arrived at Government House just after 1 p.m. and saw the Governor-General. Before he had time to give Kerr the letter formally requesting a half-Senate election, the Governor-General asked him if he was prepared to recommend a general election. Whitlam, taken aback, replied that he wasn't. 'In that case I am withdrawing your commission,' Kerr said. 'I will contact the Queen,' Whitlam replied. 'It's too late,' the Governor-General said, handing the Prime Minister the letter notifying him that his commission was withdrawn. While this happened Malcolm Fraser was waiting in another room in Government House to be sworn-in as Prime Minister.[10]

Whitlam's dismissal was the biggest shock of his life. It stunned and amazed Labor MPs and Senators back at Parliament House when they heard of it, many of them refusing to believe the initial news. 'The bastard's sacked us,' Whitlam told his staff and senior Ministers at an urgent crisis meeting called at the Lodge just after 1.30 p.m.

The reasons for the Governor-General's action and his justification for that action have become a matter of high controversy. Kerr's motives were a mixture of self-interest combined with a determination to preserve the aloofness of the British monarch from Australian politics, thereby securing the maintenance of Australia's form of government. At the core of Kerr's action was an assessment of the Prime Minister. He believed that Whitlam would try to sack him, or at least approach the Queen in an effort to remove him, if the Prime Minister knew of his decision.[11]

The Governor-General was fully aware of the determination with which Whitlam had taken his stand and the sweeping nature of the Prime Minister's objectives. Whitlam had embarked on a strategy that would ensure the Senate's money power was broken for all time. He wanted to make certain that the constitutional provisions concerning the Senate's power over money bills became a mere debating point. If

Whitlam could succeed in a direct confrontation with the Senate and force the Opposition to abandon its election threat, a precedent would be set for all future Prime Ministers to do the same and for all future Senates to baulk at the deferral or rejection of a money bill. Whitlam was more committed to this task and this fight than to any other single issue in his political career. Within three short weeks he had single-handedly taken the Labor Party from the depths of despair when the budget was blocked to a position of euphoric over-confidence in early November as its standing rose in the opinion polls and pressure mounted on the Opposition parties to back down. Those people close to the Prime Minister said he had never been more resolute.

Whitlam was attempting to cement his own interpretation of the Constitution into history and ensure that the Senate's power, which he perceived as the greatest single obstacle to a reformist government in Australia, was dealt its severest blow since Federation. This was the origin of the Opposition allegation that Whitlam was putting himself above the Constitution.

The Governor-General remembered one conversation he had had with the Prime Minister in mid-1975 in which the dismissal of former NSW Labor Premier Jack Lang by the state governor Sir Philip Game was discussed. Whitlam had made the remark that, in this sort of situation, 'it's a race to see who gets rid of whom first'.[12] But more recently, an incident which stuck in Kerr's mind had occurred at a Government House dinner for the late Malaysian Prime Minister Tun Razak on the evening of 16 October—the day the Senate deferred the budget. The political situation was being discussed and Kerr later remembered Whitlam saying in a jovial fashion in front of Tun Razak when the three men were together: 'It depends whether I can get in and sack him before he sacks me.' Although the comment was lighthearted and made in a social situation in front of a third person, Kerr interpreted it as a clear sign of Whitlam's determination on this issue.[13]

The following weekend Whitlam appeared on the ABC's 'Four Corners' program and on the Monday evening was on 'A Current Affair'. In both interviews the Prime Minister stressed that the Governor-General had to rely on the advice of his Ministers, that it was inconceivable that he would act except on such advice, and that it would be a breach of the traditions of his office if he did otherwise. While Whitlam was merely repeating his concept of the role of the Viceroy, the message did not escape the notice of the Governor-General. For these reasons Kerr felt that his own position would be in jeopardy if his punches were telegraphed. So Kerr kept his decision secret for his own self-preservation—to ensure that his tenure as Governor-General was not abruptly terminated by a headstrong Prime Minister.

However, Kerr had other less base, more sophisticated reasons for his intervention. These relate directly to the Government House–Buckingham Palace connection during the five weeks of the crisis. Throughout this period Kerr was very careful to safeguard his rear. He wrote meticulous and lengthy letters to the Queen keeping her informed of developments in Australia, the political situation, the talks he was holding with both leaders, the prospects for settlement and how he personally viewed the crisis. The mailbag went to London twice weekly. There was hardly a delivery during this period that did not have a letter from Sir John to the Queen.[14]

From the start of the crisis Sir John adopted a fundamental principle: that if the situation had to be resolved through intervention by the Crown then this would be his intervention and not that of the Queen. He believed the Queen should not have to make highly political decisions in the Australian context. He believed that any intervention by the Queen would only take political passions in Australia beyond breaking point and prejudice for all time the connection between Australia and the United Kingdom through the monarchy. Buckingham Palace was aware of the Governor-General's attitude and accepted that it was the constitutionally appropriate position; the Palace had no desire to become involved.

Kerr realised that the Queen would be inevitably involved if Whitlam attempted to sack him on the basis of his intended actions. If Whitlam made such an approach to the Queen, she would be placed in the nearly impossible situation of having either to ignore her Prime Minister's advice about the Governor-General, or to accept it and remove him when he was on the verge of intervention himself. Whichever course she took would have been fatal. She would have had to intervene in Australian politics decisively on one side or the other, in favour of one political party or the other. This only strengthened the Governor-General's determination to conceal his dismissal decision from the Prime Minister until he effected it.[15]

Kerr was always confident about his position with Buckingham Palace and it is likely that if Whitlam had advised the Queen to remove the Governor-General she would have wanted time to consider it. Because Kerr as Governor-General took full responsibility for any intervention, he did not give Buckingham Palace prior notice that he was dismissing the Prime Minister. The Palace was told immediately afterwards. Under the Constitution the decommissioning could only be carried out by the Governor-General and Section 64 specifically vests this power in him, not the Queen. It is almost certain that in his correspondence to the Queen the Governor-General would have canvassed the option of dismissal as a reluctant last resort.

If Whitlam made the most grievous political misjudgement of his career, Kerr was nevertheless particularly adroit in concealing his 'checkmate' move from the Prime Minister. It was politics on a knife-edge for high stakes.

But it was also politics between a Governor-General and his chief adviser, the Prime Minister, on whose advice he traditionally relied. The Governor-General chose to dismiss his Prime Minister without giving Whitlam a choice; without telling Whitlam that his present course was unsatisfactory; and without seeking alternative advice from his Prime Minister. In this respect Kerr defied the conventions and traditions surrounding his office. He had an elaborate justification for his action in the dilemma which he faced. The crucial question is whether a Governor-General's deception of his Prime Minister on the issue of dismissal is warranted by his belief that his Prime Minister would try to dismiss him, with all the consequences that flowed from this.

Nobody will ever know what Whitlam would have done. There is a high to very high probability that he would have moved against Kerr. But in this situation definitive predictions are too hazardous. Kerr felt as certain as he could be that Whitlam would try to dismiss him—but there could never be sure knowledge of this point.[16]

By 11 November Kerr's actions and inactions had trapped him into an inescapable dilemma. Given his conviction that intervention was necessary, then the logic of his argument meant that it had to be performed by himself and with complete secrecy. But no Governor-General could act in this fashion without appearing to take sides in politics, without being accused of partisanship—one of the most damning accusations that could ever be levelled against the Crown or its representatives, whose political neutrality is essential for the system's survival.

Kerr decided to intervene in secrecy against one political party in a move that would give incalculable advantages to another political party. His decision enraged the deposed Prime Minister and was at the core of Whitlam's bitter attacks both that same day and throughout the election campaign, and of the Labor Party's later decision to boycott the opening of Federal Parliament on 17 February 1976. Whitlam's entire political strategy was based on his confidence in the Governor-General. He had built a political house upon quicksand and was engulfed in the trap he unconsciously set for himself.

The Governor-General found himself caught in a dilemma partly because of his faulty appreciation of the crisis and because of his belief in secrecy. Kerr successfully extricated himself but, in doing so, he used the office of Governor-General in a partisan way to an extent that it had never been used before. John Robert Kerr, the man who never went into politics, played his politics tougher and smarter than Gough Whitlam who had made politics his life.

# 2

# A MATTER OF TIMING

*I do not concede that there is any crisis requiring my intervention until the money runs out.*

Sir John Kerr to Senator Jim McClelland[1]

On the afternoon of 6 November 1975 Sir John Kerr had a twenty minute audience with Australia's Treasurer, Bill Hayden. Hayden gave Kerr a Treasury document explaining the alternative arrangements through the banking system which the Labor government was formulating in order to maintain funds to pay public servants and government contractors after supply was exhausted. The two men discussed the time left before supply ran out as a result of the blocking of the budget in the Senate.

Hayden said it would take another two and a half to three weeks before the government started to be depleted of funds that required parliamentary approval. He said the money would not run out evenly; no comprehensive exact date could be specified. The Labor government was completely secure of funds until about 27 November which would be the last pay day for some public servants and armed forces members. From this period new arrangements would be needed.

These were the crucial dates for the government. It knew, despite the alternative arrangements, that by this time moves to resolve the deadlock completely would have to be underway. On 6 November the deadlock was in its 21st day but funds were not exhausted and Whitlam was breaking no legal or constitutional provision by remaining in office. He still had supply and would have it until the end of the month. When the funds ran out the crunch would come. Whitlam's political strategy was to crack the Opposition ranks before this happened. Both government and Opposition were locked in a test of willpower as the public opinion polls registered a swing to the Labor government during the crisis.

Fraser had to hold firm; he had to maintain the unity of his party and in particular of his Senators and make it clear that they were prepared to go to the brink, to keep blocking the budget until the money ran out. Fraser had to prove to the Governor-General that he was immovable on this point and that his party was prepared to keep deferring the budget until there was no money left. This was a big political gamble for the Opposition because the opinion polls showed that it would probably be blamed for the adverse consequences. The polls sent tremors through the Liberal Party. They indicated that deferral of the budget was in itself a political liability for the Opposition and a major plus for the government.

The Morgan poll, taken a few days after the budget was deferred, showed the Labor Party up four points to 44 per cent and the Opposition parties down four points to 50 per cent. The *Age-Herald* poll, published on 30 October, showed that 70 per cent of people in capital cities believed that the budget should be passed compared with 25 per cent who supported the deferral of supply. At the same time 48 per cent said the Opposition was responsible for the consequences of budget deferment while only 40 per cent blamed the government. While 54 per cent believed Labor had a right to continue governing, only 44 per cent said it should resign or call an election.

Fraser had already adopted one fallback compromise. On 3 November Fraser had told Kerr that the Opposition would pass the budget if Whitlam agreed to hold a House of Representatives election in conjunction with the next Senate election which was due before I July 1976. Whitlam rejected this offer. He thought the trend of public opinion put him in a stronger political position than Fraser. He wanted a complete victory.

As the crisis continued into November, talk of compromise increased. Most of the Opposition backbench believed that the deadlock would end in a compromise, although the Opposition leadership never accepted this. The question for Fraser was whether he could hold the nerve of his party together on an action that had divided Australia and created a sufficiently negative response throughout wide sections of the nation to alarm a number of Liberal MPs and Senators. It was the most momentous game of political poker ever witnessed in Australian politics. Upon the outcome would depend the future course of development of the Australian parliamentary system itself.

Fraser held his party together until 11 November, the 26th day of the crisis, when he became Prime Minister. On this day there were another 16 days to go before the money squeeze started to bite. But the Governor-General did not wait. He decided to intervene at a point two-thirds of the way along the time scale that lay between the blocking of the budget and the exhaustion of supply. Nobody will ever know if there might have been a political compromise between 11 November and the end of the month. Instead, the Governor-General decided that it was time for a resolution of the crisis.

Towards the end of his talks with Hayden on 6 November, Kerr had surprised the Treasurer by asking him how Labor would go in a general election. Hayden replied in his normally pessimistic, but this time deadly accurate, fashion: 'We'd get done.' Hayden was sufficiently concerned after his conversation at Yarralumla with Kerr to visit Whitlam the same afternoon to tell him about it. But Whitlam was still supremely confident. He failed to realise that Kerr had set himself a D-day for decision—11 November—the same date Whitlam had also accepted for his own effort at resolution by calling a Senate election.

During early November one of the people thrust by events to the centre stage was the quietly efficient and ever reliable Chief Electoral Officer Frank Ley. Ley had the unenviable responsibility of organising all Australian federal elections. Anyone who wanted to know anything about an election spoke to Frank Ley. Whitlam was in close touch with Ley and was advised that the last practicable date for an election in 1975 was 13 December if the election involved the Senate, that is, if it was either a half-Senate election or a double dissolution election. While 20 December was not an impossible date on which to hold an election, it would create very severe difficulties being so close to the Christmas period with so many people on holidays. The crucial part of Ley's advice was that any decision on a 13 December election would have to be made on 11 November, in order to meet provisions covering Senate election writs.

There was nothing secret about this advice. The Opposition parties spoke to Ley and got the same advice, as did press gallery journalists. Another person who spoke to Ley was the official secretary to the Governor-General, David Smith. The Governor-General knew that if there was to be a resolution of the constitutional crisis through an election before Christmas, then that decision would have to be made by 11 November. This was the last possible date. If the Governor-General wanted to dismiss Whitlam and commission Fraser on the condition that he advise a general election before Christmas, then 11 November was the final deadline for action. This explains the timing of Kerr's intervention.

The Governor-General decided that a general election was needed before Christmas to resolve the deadlock. This was Kerr's text; this was where he took his stand. He said in his dismissal letter to Whitlam that there had to be a 'prompt' resolution of the crisis. Yet the crisis was in its 26th day with another 16 days left before supply was exhausted. Kerr dismissed Whitlam when the government still had supply. He thereby denied the government another 15 days, at the minimum, in which the Opposition might back down.

In his dismissal letter to Whitlam the Governor-General said that he had concluded there was no likelihood of a compromise. This was based on the firm assurances Fraser gave him that the Opposition parties would not relent and the fact that they had already maintained their stand for 26 days. But Kerr's conclusion was a highly political one based on an assessment of what was likely to happen, an assessment of an unprecedented political situation which was favouring the Labor government in the opinion polls. As a result of the Governor-General's assessment and his decision to act on that assessment, the Labor Party concluded that Kerr's intervention was partisan not just in its substance, but also in its timing. According to Jim McClelland, Kerr's intervention was contrary to statements he had made previously to McClelland, notably, that he would have no role to play until the funds ran out.

The determinant in the Governor-General's decision was his belief that the whole crisis should be resolved before Christmas. There was a parliamentary deadlock but no crisis of supply when he acted on 11 November. The only difference between a decision in mid-November and one in late November was that the former would produce an election before Christmas and the latter could only produce an election in the New Year. The actual date of an election was irrelevant to the passage of supply which would occur the moment Whitlam was dismissed and the Fraser caretaker government commissioned; the only difference would be in the period of the caretaker government.

That is, if the election was held before Christmas the caretaker government would be in office only a month, while if the election was in the New Year, the caretaker government would be in office for six to eight weeks. Because a caretaker government would receive a commission on limited terms, it was desirable to limit its tenure of office as far as possible. This was a major reason why the Governor-General wanted an election before Christmas. The other was to end the uncertainty and division within the community that had been exacerbated by the crisis and would continue until the deadlock between the House of Representatives and the Senate, and between the government and Opposition, was resolved.[2]

The Prime Minister also acted on a 11 November deadline. In seeking a half-Senate election from the Governor-General Whitlam was admitting that his efforts to crack the Opposition had thus far failed. He was now in a position of weakness in terms of the options available to him in the crisis. He was seeking a Senate election on a date by which supply would be exhausted. It is extremely doubtful whether any Governor-General would give an election to a Prime Minister without being first satisfied that supply was adequate until the election results were known.

Kerr himself had already looked into the prospects of a half-Senate election. It had been mooted for some time, well before the budget was blocked, and the Opposition was always confident that it could effectively abort a half-Senate poll. The coalition would simply get the non-Labor Premiers to advise the Governors of their states not to issue writs for the election, a power which appeared consistent with the Constitution.

The Governor-General was in Melbourne for the Melbourne Cup in early November and he stayed with the Governor of Victoria, Sir Henry Winneke. During Cup week, Kerr, Winneke and the NSW Governor, Sir Roden Cutler, who was also in Melbourne, discussed the prospect of a half-Senate election. They did this in the knowledge, based on public statements, that the non-Labor Premiers would be likely to advise their Governors not to issue writs for such an election. As a result of these talks, both Winneke and Cutler came to the conclusion that if their state governments advised them along these lines they would have to accept this advice even though it involved a breach of convention. In short, Kerr knew that any half-Senate election sought by Whitlam would be effectively aborted in a number of states.[3]

In summary, Kerr took two fundamental decisions that aroused the wrath of the Labor Party. First, he concealed from the Prime Minister his belief that the government would have to be dismissed if the deadlock was not resolved. Second, he timed the dismissal at a point well before the blocking of the budget exhausted the Labor government's supply.

Kerr would have transformed the whole situation if he had indicated just once, firmly and frankly to Whitlam, that another approach was needed to resolve the deadlock. If Whitlam had known that his tactics, ultimately, were unsuitable to Kerr, then the government strategy would have been reassessed and changed.

The Governor-General felt such an intimation would have resulted in his own sacking or in an effort to sack him. But if he had made his attitude clear to the Prime Minister right from the start, from 16 or 17 October—which would have been the appropriate time—then Whitlam would have been under great pressure to use other approaches or change his tactics as the crisis unfolded.

Kerr's acquiescence in Whitlam's tactics at the start locked the Governor-General into a role which he felt he had to keep playing. The longer the crisis continued, the more difficult it became for Kerr to tell Whitlam directly that his approach was inadequate and that it was insufficient as a means of resolving the deadlock. Finally, when Kerr struck, he exposed himself to the dual accusation of premature overkill. The reasons for his decisions lie in John Kerr the man, more than in John Kerr the Governor-General. Whitlam misjudged his man, but Fraser did not.

# 3

# THE KERR CONNECTIONS

*I believe the Governor-General will act some time tomorrow or the day after.*

Bob Ellicott, Liberal frontbencher, 10 November 1975,
speaking to his electorate council in Sydney

Sir John Kerr was Gough Whitlam's third choice to occupy the Yarralumla mansion of the Governor-General. Whitlam's first and second choices were, respectively, asking Sir Paul Hasluck to remain, and appointing the prominent businessman, Ken Myer. In either case, the course of history would surely have been different.[1]

Sir John Kerr's road to Yarralumla was a path over which he agonised for many months. He accepted only after receiving a number of special concessions from Whitlam concerning both the tenure of his office and its terms. From the start John Kerr was determined to ensure that if he became Governor-General the office would have its proper financial security and would assume a new perspective in the eyes of most Australians.

Gough Whitlam and Paul Hasluck had never been the best of friends in the political arena during the 1960s. Their relations deteriorated under the inflamed conflict over Vietnam and foreign policy generally. There was, for example, the infamous day when Whitlam temporarily lost control of himself and threw a glass of water in Hasluck's face. But their relations as Prime Minister and Governor-General were impeccable and solid.

Hasluck himself had had a vital decision to make in his capacity as Governor-General that had been crucial to the fortunes of the first Whitlam government. This was when he accepted the advice of his

Ministers in April 1974 and, for the first time since Federation, granted a double dissolution of Federal Parliament on a number of bills, not just one. This enabled the government to go to the May 1974 election with six bills on its 'double dissolution list'—bills to implement Medibank, reform electoral boundaries, give Senate representation to the Territories, and set up the Petroleum and Minerals Authority. Much of the Opposition and sections of the constitutional law fraternity argued that a double dissolution could only be granted on one bill. Hasluck's acceptance of the government's advice on this issue, backed by the weight of legal opinion, was vital for the consolidation of the Labor program through the historic July 1974 joint sitting of Federal Parliament.

Whitlam was perfectly satisfied with Hasluck and his conception of the role of Governor-General. In late 1973 the Prime Minister asked Sir Paul to stay on for another two years beyond the normal five year term for which, according to convention, most Governors-General held office. But Hasluck replied that he would be unable to do so, mainly due to his wife's health. In these circumstances, Whitlam asked Hasluck to provide a list of names of people whom he considered would be suitable successors, bearing in mind Whitlam's own thinking on this.

A short time later Whitlam received the list of eight names, three being Ken Myer, John Kerr and Frank Crean. Whitlam put definite parameters on the man who should be appointed. First, he wanted an Australian; he was determined to ensure than an Australian successor to Hasluck and Casey would cement this principle for all time. Second, he wanted a man who was still vigorous and able, not someone who was at the end of his career. This created particular problems because after serving as Governor-General a professional man could never return to his profession. Third, Whitlam wanted to end the practice of having former politicians appointed Governor-General and to ensure that no charges of partisanship could be laid against his appointee.

The man Whitlam approached was at the zenith of his career, the chairman of Myer Emporium Ltd, Ken Myer, who had publicly supported the Labor Party in 1972 and established a reputation for himself as a businessman, a prominent supporter of the arts, and a man with an interest in urban planning. Whitlam had a high opinion of Myer and believed he would be a distinguished appointment as well as a slap in the face for much of the Establishment. When Myer declined for personal reasons Whitlam returned to the 'short list'.[2]

In the interim two other suggestions were made to Whitlam and rejected. His private secretary Jim Spigelman said the former Catholic Archbishop of Sydney, Cardinal Norman Gilroy, would be a good appointment. Speechwriter Graham Freudenberg promptly observed that Gilroy was ineligible because he did not have a wife! Spigelman's case was that the Gilroy appointment would win votes for the ALP and enrage the Establishment which would be unable to criticise it. Meanwhile, the ALP and ACTU president Bob Hawke, said a fine appointment would be Sir Richard Eggleston, a distinguished lawyer and judge on the Commonwealth Industrial Court, a proposal which assumed an irony after the Whitlam government's sacking. During the constitutional crisis Eggleston declared that the Senate did not have the constitutional power to block the budget.

But Whitlam settled on Kerr. He had known Kerr for over 25 years from the Sydney bar, although from the time Whitlam entered politics he had had little contact with Kerr. Whitlam's thinking was that since Kerr was NSW Chief Justice the appointment would be seen as orthodox and impeccable. The Prime Minister spoke to Kerr in the last few months of 1974.

Kerr was then 59 and in the previous year had reached what was regarded as the summit of his career when he became Chief Justice of his state appointed by the Askin Liberal government. Before this Kerr had sat on the Commonwealth Industrial Court from 1966–72 and, along with his colleagues Mr Justice Fox and Mr Justice Gibbs, had been promised by Liberal Attorneys-General a place on the proposed Commonwealth Superior Court Bench when that court was established. This proposal was to create a new prestigious court to pass judgement on a series of matters within federal jurisdiction and to ease the burden on the High Court. But once Sir Garfield Barwick became Chief Justice of the High Court he opposed the concept of a Superior Court and the Liberals never proceeded with it. The pledge given to Kerr by the Liberal government of the day was a sign of both his ability and suitability to a conservative government. From September to February 1974 Whitlam kept his offer to Kerr a close secret. Even Margaret Whitlam, a long-time friend of Kerr's first wife, Alison, had no idea of the offer.

Kerr examined the Governor-Generalship from every possible angle, like an experienced lawyer evaluating a client's problem. There appear to have been two basic questions for the NSW Chief Justice—first, whether the office of Governor-General had sufficient substance for him to forsake the powerful position he already held and, second, his concern about the terms and tenure of the office. Kerr felt he still had a good ten working years left in him and told Whitlam that rather than accept a conventional five year term as Governor-General, he would like to have a period in the job of about ten years. Whitlam agreed and said that if Labor was still in office he would be happy to meet the request.

In order to meet Kerr's legitimate concerns about financial security, Whitlam introduced into Parliament the Governor-General Act 1974. Until this time the Governor-General's salary was $20,000 as laid down in the Constitution. There was no retirement pension, which had led the Prime Minister's Department to approve ex gratia payments in some cases to former Governors-General or their widows. As a result of their talks, Whitlam agreed to introduce a bill increasing the salary to $30,000 a year with a pension on retirement equivalent to that of a retired Chief Justice of Australia. These changes, which the Opposition readily supported, satisfied Kerr's financial concerns.

After considering the role of Governor-General and reading Hasluck's William Queale Memorial Lecture of October 1972 about the office, Kerr finally accepted it. But, as was proved later, he took the office with a determination to make it both more active and more meaningful. While Kerr was not a knight when Whitlam first approached him, he received his knighthood in early 1974.

When the Queen was visiting Australia in February 1974 the Prime Minister obtained her approval for the appointment and, before it was announced, rang the Opposition Leader Bill Snedden to inform him of the decision and to notify him of Kerr's desire to have twice the normal term. Snedden responded favourably on both counts. The Opposition Leader was on the verge of an evening press conference and it was Snedden himself, with Whitlam's approval, who announced Kerr's appointment on the evening of 27 February, evidence of the spirit of bipartisanship.[3]

Kerr was well-known to a wide number of senior Liberals and virtually all the Sydney legal community, in which he had played an outstanding role over 25 years. The Liberal Party was pleased about his appointment which was described by Snedden as 'the culmination of a brilliant career for an able, warm-hearted man'. Two of Kerr's former associates from Sydney, the man who opposed him in many industrial cases, the then Attorney-General Senator Lionel Murphy, and the man who had partnered Kerr as solicitor, Senator Jim McClelland, both endorsed the appointment. Murphy called it a 'magnificent choice' and McClelland claimed that Kerr's association with the groupers in the 1950s—which was resurrected after the sacking—was a purely legal one.

Once Kerr was in office Whitlam endorsed and supported his moves to build up the prestige of the position. He trusted Kerr, spoke with him on a wide range of political subjects, and gave the Governor-General virtually anything he wanted. The two men worked well and their relationship was closer and more friendly than that between Whitlam and Hasluck. After the dismissal, Whitlam told his senior colleagues that one of his major mistakes, apart from appointing Kerr in the first place, had been to trust him so much.

Kerr made a number of overseas visits and for the first time an Australian Governor-General went overseas in his capacity as head of state. His predecessors had made independent state visits in their capacity as Governor-General. But Whitlam, realising that the Queen could never travel overseas as Queen of Australia, built up the position of

Governor-General to a new status by ensuring that when Kerr travelled overseas he did so as Australia's head of state. The Governor-General visited Fiji and New Zealand, and in February–March 1975 went to Nepal for the coronation of the King, and later visited India, Pakistan, Afghanistan and Iran. Kerr surprised even Whitlam on his return by sending him a full report on the conversations he had had with the President and Prime Minister of India. Whitlam also approved an extensive visit by the Governor-General to the United Kingdom, Canada and Ireland, which was subsequently cancelled when the Senate denied supply. Kerr eventually went in December after the constitutional crisis was fully resolved.

John Kerr was a self-made man who believed that industry and progress should be blessed with their own rewards and he developed a rarefied skill for indulgence in the pleasures of office. He was even upset, after receiving an invitation from the Shah of Iran, that the Emperor of Japan did not extend a similar invitation after Kerr had entertained his grandson in Australia. The Governor-General also expressed his concern to Whitlam at the order of his knighthood which was a KCMG (Knight Commander of the Order of St Michael and St George), compared with his counterparts in Fiji, New Guinea and New Zealand who were all of a higher order, GCMG (Knight Grand Cross of the Order of St Michael and St George). These incidents highlight Kerr's determination to enjoy the office to the full and to insist that he receive all the necessary honours and entitlements which he felt should accompany it.[4]

Not long after he assumed office Kerr took the unusual step of inviting the entire parliamentary press gallery to Government House for a reception. As he mixed with journalists Kerr talked about his new job and how he could make it more meaningful. He discussed the sort of subjects that his speeches should cover and also to what extent he should espouse a particular line. One of the aspects discussed was whether he should canvass political issues. Later that night the press retired to the Wellington Hotel and fell into an argument about Kerr's apparent conception of his office. Some said it was desirable to see such an activist Governor-General; others warned against this trend and insisted that the office should be downgraded.

Kerr provoked the derision and tickled the amusement of a number of Labor members when he abolished the curtsy at Government House. Yet anyone aware of Kerr's background would have realised that he was a man of genuine substance and formidable skills whose ambitions transcended abolition of some of the more antiquated trappings. If Gough Whitlam had known the career of his Governor-General better he would have realised that Kerr would never be a cipher or allow the bonds of loyalty to prevail over either his duty or his self-interest.

It has now passed into legend that John Kerr was the son of a Balmain boilermaker and came from a family heavily committed to the Labor Party. He was educated at Fort Street Boys High in Sydney under the rigorous tutelage of headmaster Kilgour, who instilled in his students the notion that the glories of the world were not for idle silvertails but for the industrious, the clever and the curious. Kerr showed ability far above average even to gain entry to Fort Street, and he was a worthy product of the school that also turned out Dr H V Evatt, Sir Percy Spender and Sir Garfield Barwick, three lawyers like himself.

Kerr left Fort Street with a Leaving Certificate pass of three first class honours, three As and a B, sufficient to win him a scholarship to Sydney University. At this stage Kerr went to see Mr Justice Evatt, who confirmed his own thinking. 'Don't hesitate,' Evatt told the young Kerr. 'Do law and come back and see me when you finish.' So Kerr did law with the support of the boilermaker at Cockatoo Dock. He won nearly every prize at the Law School and finished with the University Medal.

He was admitted to the Sydney Bar in 1938 aged 24, on the verge of the outbreak of the Second World War which was to play a crucial role in his development. He joined the AIF and in 1942 was seconded to the Directorate of Research and Civil Affairs, which was placed under the personal control of the commander in chief of the Australian Armed Forces, General Sir Thomas Blamey. The directorate's chief function was to advise Blamey on affairs in Papua and New Guinea as well as the Pacific region. Kerr's link with the unit was through a brilliant and unorthodox colleague from his student days, Alf Conlon, who headed the unit and was a confidante not only of Blamey but also of the Labor Prime Minister John Curtin. Conlon left a marked impact on his colleagues in the directorate because of his intellectual ability and capacity to wield power through a shrewd appreciation of both politics and people. Kerr himself defined the purpose of the directorate as being to assist both Blamey and the Australian Army in relations 'of a slightly unorthodox character with outside institutions in this country and abroad'. The directorate was closely involved with the British military administration in Borneo as part of a long range plan to safeguard Australian influence in this area.

As the war ended Kerr was instrumental in the formation of the Army Civil Affairs Unit, out of which grew the Australian School of Pacific Administration whose primary interest was still New Guinea. By this stage Kerr's long connection with Evatt was bearing fruit and the latter, who was then External Affairs Minister, took Kerr with him to the United Nations in 1947 when the Pacific region was under discussion. Kerr played a major role in the formation of the South Pacific Commission, a new association of powers in the Pacific. At this stage Evatt pressed Kerr towards a diplomatic career but, after careful consideration, Kerr decided to return to the law from which he had been absent for about seven years. It was a turning point for him.

He returned in 1949, the year of Labor's debacle and the start of Menzies' long reign. Kerr himself was closely associated with the Labor Party but was increasingly suspicious about elements of the far left and the strength of the Communist Party. He returned to the Sydney bar a much wider and more experienced man, non-ideological, pragmatic and more sceptical. Over the next several years Kerr's career was tied to the upheavals of the Australian Labor Party and the trade union movement. He saw them both as an individual and as a barrister who made his reputation working with Jim McClelland in a series of cases for Laurie Short in a battle for control of the Federated Ironworkers Association, a battle which Short won. Kerr's legal activities brought him into close association with the men who ran the right-wing NSW Labor Party. Two of Kerr's colleagues at this time were McClelland and the federal secretary of the right-wing Federated Clerks Union, for whom he also worked, Joe Riordan—both Ministers in the Whitlam Labor government which Kerr dismissed from office over twenty years later.

It was in the early 1950s when he worked at the Sydney bar, that Kerr came into contact with a range of men who were all to exercise a great influence in the nation over the next thirty years. At this time Kerr worked on the same barristers' floor as Bob Ellicott, Gough Whitlam and Nigel Bowen. For some time Maurice Byers was also on the same floor. All these men, who cooperated together and struggled against one another at various stages of their careers, shared a common starting point at the Sydney bar.

In 1951 Evatt indicated to Kerr that he should stand at the double dissolution election against William McMahon in the Sydney seat of Lowe. But the Labor leader, in a characteristic change of mind, later tried to get Dr John Burton to stand instead. In this period Kerr's relations with Evatt gradually declined and he terminated his membership of the party forever in 1954 at the time of the split.

The fight in the trade unions saw Kerr develop close ties with the industrial groups which were formed to resist the communists. Kerr took many briefs for the 'groupers' which strained his relations with other ALP figures. When the Democratic Labor Party was formed heavy overtures were made to Kerr to persuade him to join it. According to his close friend, Jim McAuley, who committed to the breakaway movement, 'While it was disappointing to those of us who desperately needed help, his decision was not unreasonable. Kerr had a lot to throw away: would any use he could have been really have justified the sacrifice in a perfectly honourable commonsense view?' Kerr refused to join the breakaway group at a Sydney meeting attended by McAuley which Bob Santamaria was involved in organising.

The split left Kerr disillusioned with the now left-wing orientated Labor Party. He drifted away from his ALP associations and also from the right-wing faction with which he was particularly associated. Kerr began to direct his energies and ability into other channels. He became president of the Industrial Relations Society in 1960, the Marriage Guidance Council of NSW in 1961, a member of the NSW Bar Council in 1960 and its president in 1964. By this time Kerr was the epitome of the established lawyer, a man whose ambition and ability had carried him far and whose very professional and social environment brought him into extensive contact with senior figures in the Liberal party. Kerr had particularly good relations with a number of NSW Liberals, including the former president of the NSW division, John Atwill, who was president when Kerr was appointed Chief Justice of the state.

Approaches were made to Kerr in the 1960s about his standing as a Liberal Party candidate. Many colleagues had formed the view that he would have liked to have gone into politics as a Liberal. But the right opportunity never presented itself and Kerr also had to consider the sickness of his wife. However, Kerr had established a personal link with many lawyers associated with the Liberal Party including Garfield Barwick and Nigel Bowen. In 1966 he was appointed a judge on the Commonwealth Industrial Court and later received the undertaking from the Liberal Government that he would be appointed to the bench of the proposed Commonwealth Superior Court. In the same year Kerr was appointed a judge of the Supreme Court of the Australian Capital Territory and deputy president of the Trade Practices Tribunal.

As a senior justice he was high on the list for Federal Government appointments when they arose. He was appointed chairman of the Commonwealth Committee to Report on a Review of Administrative Decisions in 1968, and he worked very closely on this report with the Solicitor-General, Bob Ellicott. In 1970 he was appointed to chair the review of pay for the armed services and the following year was chairman of the review of parliamentary salaries. In 1972 he became Chief Justice of NSW, attaining the highest peak yet in his legal career.

As the result of a decision taken by Gough Whitlam, Kerr was to scale one more peak, the ultimate in Australia's social and political structure. The pattern of Kerr's career was that of a search for self-advancement in his profession and acceptance of his contribution and capacity within the corridors of power.

Three men who played key roles in the 1975 political and constitutional crisis had known one another for many years and were linked by kinship, the law, social position, intellectual attainment and political preference. They were Sir John Kerr, Governor-General, Sir Garfield Barwick, Chief Justice of the High Court since 1964, and Robert Ellicott, Solicitor-General 1969–74 and then a frontbench Liberal and a trusted

legal adviser to Malcolm Fraser. Many of the critical judgements during
the crisis were about individual character and personality and it should
be realised that these assessments were assisted because of the knowledge individuals had of each other.

Barwick and Ellicott were related to one another as first cousins.
They had enjoyed an association for many years, particularly when
Ellicott worked at the Sydney bar. They were professional colleagues, a
link which continued when they occupied two of the vital legal positions, Barwick as Chief Justice and Ellicott as Solicitor-General.[5] The
relationship between Kerr and Ellicott, on the other hand, went back to
the early 1950s when both men made their reputations at the Sydney
bar and worked on the same barristers' floor. In the early 1970s, when
Ellicott was Solicitor-General and Kerr was a judge on the Commonwealth Industrial Court, the two men saw one another quite frequently.
They collaborated on the report of the committee reviewing administrative decisions.

Kerr and Barwick had enjoyed a long and paradoxical relationship.
Kerr was a more worldly man than Barwick. With his more all-round
capabilities and diverse interests he probably saw himself as Barwick's
superior while recognising Barwick as a magnificent but narrow legal
technician. Barwick in turn regarded Kerr, according to a mutual friend,
as 'an unskilled dilettante on many legal problems'. The two men were
not close and colleagues suspected an element of rivalry, even dislike.
But Kerr, in one of the recurring characteristics of his career, sought
Barwick's esteem and approval.

Another interesting connection in the constitutional crisis was the
Whitlam–Ellicott relationship. Ellicott regarded himself as a student of
the law and an observer of men. He had watched Whitlam for many
years: from the proximity of the legal scene, from the distance of the
political arena and, as of December 1972, as Solicitor-General to the new
Prime Minister. During 1973 the two men had worked together on a
number of important legal questions. Ellicott had evaluated Labor's
latest Prime Minister before himself entering Parliament in 1974.

Ellicott was influential in the tactics followed by Malcolm Fraser.
When Whitlam threatened to 'tough it out' and to stay in office if the
budget was blocked, Ellicott tended to believe him. Fraser was also of
this view. Ellicott thought that Whitlam had a messianic view of himself
and that people who tended to cast themselves in the role of messiahs
were prone to crucify themselves. In politics they might erect a principle
for whose attainment they would try to 'crash through' anything.

Ellicott applied both his legal skill and his knowledge of Whitlam
and Kerr to the problem at hand. If he felt that Whitlam would remain
in office in defiance of the Senate, then he also felt that Kerr would
not endure this with acquiescence. Ellicott disagreed with Whitlam's

assessment of Kerr's character—that the Governor-General would not act against his Prime Minister. Ellicott's view was based on his knowledge of Kerr as a man and a lawyer. He could not accept that Kerr would allow himself to be relegated to the position of a mere figurehead, a constitutional cipher. He believed that in a constitutional crisis the time would come when Kerr would stand up; that he would repudiate toadyism by using the Governor-General's powers.

One of the most important days in the constitutional crisis was Sunday 26 October, although its full significance may defy revelation. It was ten days into the crisis and Whitlam, who was at Kirribilli House, had a phone conversation with Kerr in the afternoon. Kerr told Whitlam that he was concerned about stories appearing in the *Australian* which gave the impression that he would soon have to intervene in the crisis. He made it clear to Whitlam that he was embarrassed by such stories and as a direct result Whitlam went out of his way to criticise such headlines when he spoke next in Parliament.[6]

During their conversation Kerr asked Whitlam if he could consult with Barwick about the crisis. The Prime Minister immediately said no. Whitlam, well versed in this issue, offered three reasons for his refusal. First, he told Kerr that things had changed since 1914 when the Governor-General of the day, Sir Ronald Munro-Ferguson, had consulted with the Chief Justice Sir Samuel Griffith with the approval of the Prime Minister over the first double dissolution. Whitlam said that he no longer believed such a course was proper. Second, Whitlam said it would be dangerous for a Chief Justice to advise the Governor-General on any matter which could subsequently come before the High Court itself. Third, Whitlam said that the Australian High Court, unlike its counterparts in other English speaking countries, had no advisory role.[7]

Whitlam felt strongly on this issue. On no account did he want Kerr talking to Barwick, a man with whom the Prime Minister had never enjoyed good relations, whom he regarded as an arch constitutional conservative, and who was a former senior Liberal politician.

After his dismissal Whitlam launched scathing attacks on Kerr for seeking an opinion from the Chief Justice, who was just one of seven High Court judges. Kerr's decision to consult Barwick was a direct flouting of a direction given him on this precise point by the Prime Minister. The fact that Kerr's meeting with Barwick on Monday 10 November was contained in the Vice-regal notices on the morning of 11 November should have sent the death tremors through Whitlam. But it had no apparent impact on Whitlam's confidence.

Kerr's anxiousness to talk with Barwick as early as 26 October reflected his desire for outside or independent advice. It also raises the important question of Barwick's role in the whole crisis. Barwick in his letter to Kerr, and Kerr in his dismissal letter to Whitlam, went to lengths to stress that Kerr made up his mind on dismissal before he spoke with Barwick on 10 November. Barwick was advising him on a course that Kerr said he had already decided upon. A crucial question is whether the Governor-General spoke to the Chief Justice earlier. After the dismissal both Whitlam and McClelland were deeply suspicious of Barwick's role. They asked—if Kerr defied Whitlam's advice and spoke to Barwick once, then did he consult more than once? They asked whether Barwick had any role in shaping Kerr's decision, as distinct from confirming that decision?[8]

McClelland, after all, pointed out that Kerr was prepared to ring him at home to discuss the crisis. There is anecdotal evidence that Kerr canvassed speculation as to what he should do. For instance, at a Government House reception on the evening of Tuesday 28 October for people attending a public service Second Division seminar, Kerr stunned some public servants by asking them over drinks at the reception, 'And what do you think I should do?'

Whether or not Barwick helped to shaped Kerr's decision, as distinct from confirming that decision, may never be known.[9] Kerr's decision that he would have to dismiss Whitlam was the view held by both Barwick and Ellicott although they disagreed about the issue of timing. However Ellicott revealed considerable insight in predicting the precise timing that Kerr would adopt in the dismissal.

On the evening of 10 November Bob Ellicott addressed a meeting of his electorate council in Sydney. He was asked if he believed the Governor-General would act and replied he was confident that Sir John would intervene. 'I've known him for a long time,' Ellicott said. He was questioned about when the Governor-General was likely to intervene and said that, from his knowledge of Kerr, he believed the Governor-General would move to intervene 'some time tomorrow or the day after'. Ellicott was unerringly right. So was Malcolm Fraser. The Opposition banked on Kerr's action and it predicted Kerr's action.[10]

Fraser and Ellicott knew their man. The Opposition leadership was confident—even when the Liberal backbench and fringes of the party were in a tizzy—because of its assessment of Kerr and his reaction in the crisis. Just how much they knew is impossible to assess precisely. The line between knowledge and confidence was a fine one. And if the Opposition had knowledge of Kerr's thinking then how was this obtained?

Certainly Malcolm Fraser was most confident in the five days immediately preceding 11 November. On the evening of 6 November, in his office, he told a colleague that the Governor-General would ensure the issue was resolved by Christmas. When asked how this would happen if the deadlock continued, Fraser replied: 'The Governor-General will intervene and he will sack the Prime Minister.' Fraser was not just on the right track; he was precisely correct in judging how Kerr would act.[11]

The Opposition leadership acted on the assumption in the days immediately preceding 11 November that Kerr would intervene at this time. During the meeting between Fraser and Whitlam and their senior colleagues on the morning of 11 November Fraser was confident that Whitlam would never get his half-Senate election from the Governor-General.

The constitutional crisis is a classic study of the Opposition knowing more about the Governor-General, and judging him more accurately, than the government. The Opposition grasped that Kerr, the son of the Balmain boilermaker, had come full circle in his life, while the government clung to an outdated and false image of Kerr.

The Whitlam Labor government, 36 months old, fell on 11 November in a unique fashion. This was the day Kerr wrote himself into the history books and Whitlam out of them. The entire political crisis was sparked because Whitlam and Fraser worked on the same assessment: that if the Opposition succeeded in getting its election, Labor would be defeated. They were both right.

The crucial issue is to what extent the Opposition actually knew of Kerr's state of mind towards the end and therefore reaffirmed its course and determination. What was the key to Fraser's confidence? Was it knowledge or was it merely confidence based on accurate personal assessment and smarter legal experience? If the Opposition did have knowledge another two crucial questions follow: How was the knowledge obtained and did it predate the decision to defer the budget?

# 4

# THE SECURITY CRISIS

*This is the gravest risk to the nation's security there has ever been.*

Secretary of the Department of Defence,
Sir Arthur Tange, 10 November 1975

In the week before Gough Whitlam was dismissed as Prime Minister, security intelligence relations between Australia and the United States faced their gravest crisis. In the days preceding 11 November 1975 there were two major upheavals in Australia's system of government. The first was the political and constitutional crisis which covered the newspapers and engulfed the country. The second was a security crisis that centred on the United States communications base at Pine Gap near Alice Springs, and the cover of American Central Intelligence Agency (CIA) agents operating in Australia. Only the tip of the security iceberg was ever apparent.

One of the basic issues raised by the Labor Party in 1976 was whether the constitutional and security crises had been linked. And if they were linked, then how?

The day before Whitlam was dismissed, the CIA told the Australian government that the whole pattern of security relations between the two nations was in jeopardy. The issue was sparked by comments made by the Prime Minister at Port Augusta on 2 November when he indicated that the CIA had funded political parties in Australia and had been associated with the leader of the National Country Party, Doug Anthony. This subsequently led to revelations that the American who established the Pine Gap base in Australia, Richard Lee Stallings, was employed by the CIA, and that he had direct links with Anthony.

Whitlam's allegations, which attracted extensive press coverage at the time and provoked clashes in Parliament during the following week, had a deep impact on the intelligence community, the like of which experienced officers had never seen before. The extent of the reaction puzzled the handful of Labor people who witnessed it. But there was no doubting its existence, particularly on the American side.

The full extent of the CIA's alarm was revealed in a cable marked TOP SECRET, dated 10 November 1975 and sent from the ASIO liaison officer in Washington to the acting Director General of ASIO headquarters Melbourne, F J Mahoney. The Washington ASIO officer said he had been in contact with the chief of the East Asia division of the CIA, who had asked him to communicate with the head of ASIO back in Australia. The Washington officer then proceeded to describe the concern which had permeated the higher echelons of the CIA about events in Australia.

He documented the extensive diplomatic efforts made by the United States government to counter Whitlam's allegations as fast as possible. The cable referred to Whitlam's statement of 2 November about the CIA–Anthony connection and stressed that on 4 November the United States embassy had approached the Australian government and denied this connection. The embassy had rebutted suggestions that any United States government agency had provided funds to any Australian political party or candidate. This embassy approach had been to the deputy secretary of the Foreign Affairs Department in Canberra, Mr J R Rowland. At the same time the assistant secretary of the US State Department had visited the deputy chief of mission at the Australian embassy in Washington to deliver the same message along with a request that it be conveyed back to Australia.

The cable went on to say that on 6 November Whitlam repeated his allegations with wide press coverage in Australia 'such that a number of CIA members serving in Australia have been identified, Walker under State Department cover and Fitzwater and Bonin under Defence cover'. The cable continued: 'Now that these four persons have been publicised it is not possible for the CIA to continue to deal with the matter on a no comment basis.' The obvious reference here is to the revelations about Stallings. But the other three names were mentioned in an article in *Nation Review* of 7–13 November. Stallings was succeeded at Pine Gap by a former navy man, H Fitzwater, who in turn was succeeded by L Bonin. The Walker referred to is J D Walker, former CIA 'Station Chief' in Australia, based in the US embassy in Canberra.

The cable pointed out that on 7 November fifteen news agencies made inquiries of the Pentagon about the Stallings allegations. The Washington ASIO officer said that the CIA was deeply troubled and was wondering whether the public statements in Australia about Stallings signalled some change on Australia's side in bilateral security intelligence relations between the two countries. 'The CIA cannot see how this dialogue with continued reference to the CIA can do other than blow the lid off those installations in Australia where the persons concerned have been working and which are vital to both of our services and countries,' the cable read.

It referred particularly to the communications installation at Alice Springs, Pine Gap. The cable pointed out that on 7 November the director of the CIA, William Colby, publicly dismissed allegations that the CIA had taken any part in Australian politics. This was when Colby was questioned in Washington on the statements made a few days earlier in Australia by Whitlam. The cable referred to the chairman of the congressional committee making inquiries into the CIA, Otis Pike, a Republican, and indicated that the committee would now be looking at the recent statements coming from Australia.

The ASIO officer said the CIA now felt the need to talk to ASIO directly on this question and he specifically asked whether ASIO headquarters Melbourne had become involved in it. The cable went on to say the CIA was worried that Whitlam's attitude to security matters had changed. It continued: 'The CIA feels that . . . if this problem cannot be solved they do not see how our mutually beneficial relationships are going to continue . . . The CIA does not lightly adopt this attitude.' The ASIO officer concluded his cable by saying the Australian ambassador to the United States, who was then the late Sir Patrick Shaw, was fully informed of the contents of the message.[1]

The cable is clear evidence that the CIA believed its relations and operations with Australia were now in the gravest doubt. It was concerned about revelations involving CIA officers who had command of the Pine Gap base. It was worried about possible disclosures of the functions performed by this base. It was equally concerned that the cover of CIA operatives in Australia was now likely to be blown. It was worried about Whitlam's statements and whether the Australian Labor government had undergone any change of heart on the crucial issue of maintaining security secrecy. Finally, it appeared concerned about the reliability of its normal channels of communication with Australia.

The CIA felt that the situation in Australia was so unprecedented that it needed ASIO advice or information on what was happening. The cable implicitly confirms what the State Department had earlier denied—that Stallings had been employed by the CIA. The reference to other CIA operatives, Walker, Fitzwater and Bonin, two of whom had been in charge of Pine Gap, is an obvious indication of the agency's concern that these people might just be the first on its list of employees whose identity might be revealed. But the despatch of this cable and the CIA approach through ASIO proved to be a mistake. The contents of the cable make it clear that it was not meant for circulation outside

ASIO itself. But the acting Director General of ASIO, Mahoney, a former senior officer from the Attorney-General's Department in Canberra, sent it immediately to the Secretary of the Prime Minister's Department, John Menadue, who passed it to Whitlam's office.

The cable represented the culmination of a series of events that had begun in October 1975 when Labor staff began making their own investigations into the CIA's involvement in Australia. In particular they received a tip that Stallings may have been a CIA employee. Stallings had lived in Adelaide for some time and people there remembered him as a talkative man, surprisingly open about his role at Pine Gap and his intelligence connections. The Prime Minister's office was involved in this activity and believed the only way its information about Stallings could be authenticated was to ask the bureaucracy for a list of CIA agents who had operated in Australia. At this stage Labor people were working on the theory that Stallings may have handed over funds to political parties.[2]

Accordingly, Whitlam asked the Secretary of the Foreign Affairs Department, Alan Renouf, to supply a list of agents. Renouf did so and it contained several names but not that of Stallings. It was subsequently discovered that there was information held by the Defence Department about CIA employees that was not shared with Foreign Affairs. Defence was then asked and provided its own list, this one containing Stallings' name along with other names, all of whom were unknown to Foreign Affairs. In short Stallings worked for the CIA but the Foreign Affairs Department was not aware of it. Stallings was the officer in charge of Pine Gap from 1966–68 when it was under construction.

When Whitlam's office received confirmation of the Stallings–CIA connection, it already had the details concerning Anthony's house at 151 Kent Street, Hughes, in Canberra. In late 1966 the house was rented through a real estate agent to Stallings for about four months when Anthony and his wife, Margot, were living back in his electorate in northern New South Wales. At the time Anthony was unaware of Stallings' background and knew nothing of him. Anthony's involvement was strictly of an innocent nature although the revelations nine years later certainly proved to be an embarrassment for him. Anthony first met Stallings after the American had moved into his house. The two men were introduced by the Country Party member for the Northern Territory, Sam Calder, who brought Stallings to dinner at Parliament House. The Calders and the Stallings knew each other well in Alice Springs and he was introduced to Anthony as the man running the US defence establishment at Pine Gap near Alice Springs.

After confirming his information, the Prime Minister made his first CIA statement on 2 November, addressing an ALP rally of 500 at Port Augusta. Departing from his prepared notes he said: 'Every weekend he [Fraser] gets more and more desperate in his abuse of me. I have had no association with CIA money in Australia as Mr Anthony has. My wife has not received any $16,000 necklace for launching ships as Mr Sinclair's wife did. My family has not got superphosphate subsidies as Mr Fraser's has . . . No income tax troubles in my family. They have been able to get nothing on me. They are getting more and more desperate, these men who are subsidised by the CIA or overseas shipbuilders or the superphosphate people.'

Whitlam's comments received an extensive press cover and created a furore. The same evening Anthony sprang to his own defence saying: 'The Prime Minister must be losing his grip when he resorts to such fabrications. I am able to give the Australian people a categorical denial of Mr Whitlam's charge that my party has been supported by the CIA and overseas shipbuilders.'

The Whitlam–Anthony exchange took place on Sunday. On Monday 3 November the *Financial Review* carried a story by Brian Toohey naming Stallings and outlining his connection with Anthony through renting the house of the Country Party leader. This story caused a sensation in the US embassy, the intelligence community and the Defence Department. The situation was exacerbated the following day when the *Financial Review* carried another story by Toohey providing further details of Stallings' background and linking him with the Pine Gap base.

The head of the Defence Department, Sir Arthur Tange, was deeply alarmed at these revelations. Tange, a tough minded and able administrator under both Liberal and Labor governments, was privy to the most vital security secrets within Australia known only to a handful of men: the exact functions of the Pine Gap base and a fairly comprehensive knowledge of CIA operations in Australia. Tange himself, after a lifetime in the defence and diplomatic world, obviously had his own high level intelligence contacts with the Americans. It was clear right from the start by the concern Tange expressed, that Whitlam's comments and the Toohey stories had created an uproar within the CIA.

Tange contacted the Defence Minister, Bill Morrison, by phone to explain his concern and Morrison told him: 'If you want to see Whitlam about it, that's OK by me.' Tange subsequently spoke to the Prime Minister and told Whitlam that the Americans were worried about the CIA statements and the mention of Stallings.

As a result of this conversation Tange decided to approach Doug Anthony in an effort to dissuade the National Country Party leader from raising the matter himself in parliament. Tange was preoccupied by the issue. When he strode into Morrison's office at mid-morning on 4 November he brushed past one of the secretaries who said, 'Good morning Sir Arthur,' and snorted, 'You think it's good do you?' Tange told Morrison that he intended to see Anthony in an effort to kill further discussion on the security issue. But Morrison refused to allow it. He told Tange it would be improper for him as a departmental head to approach an Opposition leader on this sort of question. Morrison was quite firm on this point and said that if Anthony had to be approached he would do it himself and contact Whitlam's office beforehand to let them know what was happening.

That morning, before Question Time, Morrison went to Anthony's office and advised him to play down any follow-up to Whitlam's statements. The Defence Minister said this would be in the interests of national security as the Americans would become very concerned about public debate on the CIA. Anthony's immediate response was to point out that the issue had been raised by Whitlam not himself and that grievous allegations had been made about his involvement with the CIA. Anthony made it clear that he had not started this controversy and wanted to clear himself. Morrison replied that Anthony's response was a matter for himself but that it was important for public debate involving both Stallings and the CIA to cease as soon as possible instead of being drawn out.[3]

When Parliament sat, Anthony pursued the matter and asked Whitlam to prove that the American who rented his house had been a CIA officer. Whitlam said that Anthony confirmed the allegations about him in his question. The Prime Minister said of Anthony: 'It is inconceivable that a person who was holding the positions he did at that time and who has had a lifetime in politics—grew up with politics—and has practised it now in this parliament for some 20 years could have been so gullible.' The Prime Minister also quoted from the *Financial Review* editorial which claimed, with no substantiating evidence, that it believed funds had flowed into Australia from America with the purpose of influencing domestic politics. At the end of Question Time, Anthony made a long personal explanation outlining the innocent nature of his involvement with Stallings.

In his story on 4 November Toohey said that Stallings applied for and was granted permanent residence in Australia in late 1972. He quoted a person who described himself as a close friend of Stallings saying that the American 'absolutely worshipped the ground on which Mr Anthony walked'. Anthony made no effort to conceal that he and his wife formed a friendship with the Stallings and saw each other socially on many occasions. Meanwhile Tange was becoming deeply suspicious of Toohey's stories and the journalist's long-standing interest in the security services. The two had originally clashed in early 1973 when Toohey was on Lance Barnard's staff. He remained for only six weeks after Labor assumed office. On 5 and 6 November Anthony defended himself in letters and articles published in the *Financial Review* and the *Australian* saying that the Prime Minister was mud-slinging and trying to create the false impression that he had been associated with the intelligence service of a foreign power.

The next move occurred from the US side on the diplomatic front. On 6 November the *Australian* carried a story from John Raedler in New York quoting the State Department in an official denial that Stallings had worked for US intelligence agencies. On 8 November Australian papers carried reports that the director of the CIA, William Colby, had dismissed as ridiculous allegations that the CIA had taken any part in Australian politics. It was during this week that the United States embassy in Australia approached Foreign Affairs to deny the story and the State Department made a similar approach to the Australian embassy in Washington. In short, all diplomatic channels were used to kill the reports appearing in Australia.

The issue came to a crisis over the weekend of 8–9 November. It was precipitated by a Question on Notice from Doug Anthony to the Prime Minister which read:

> Has his attention been drawn to a report on page one of the *Australian* of Thursday, 6 November 1975, in which a United States State Department official is reported to have said that Mr Richard Stallings had never worked for any United States intelligence agencies? If so, will he provide substantiation of his claim that Mr Stallings was in fact an officer of the United States Central Intelligence Agency in 1966–67?

This question appeared on the Notice Paper on 11 November but had been circulated the previous Thursday. A draft answer was prepared by the Prime Minister's office, a copy being circulated to Sir Arthur Tange. The import of the answer was that Stallings had been a CIA employee and this fact had been confirmed with the appropriate sources in Australia who had been notified by the United States.

Over this weekend Tange made frantic efforts to contact Whitlam to ensure that this answer was not given in reply to Anthony's question. Tange rang Whitlam's principal private secretary John Mant in Canberra and asked Mant to contact the Prime Minister as soon as possible on this issue. Whitlam was in Hobart and staff with him could not see the urgency of the situation. But Tange redoubled his efforts with Mant, claiming that there was now a grave situation developing. The Defence head wanted the Anthony question answered in a different way that would not commit the government to direct revelations about Stallings and the CIA. At one point Whitlam's advisers were worried that Tange's approach could endanger Whitlam on grounds of misleading the Parliament.

On Monday 10 November Tange told a Whitlam staff member: 'This is the gravest risk to the nation's security there has ever been.'[4] He saw his Minister Bill Morrison and told Morrison that the Americans were gravely concerned about the present situation and that it should be played down as much as possible. Morrison agreed but could see little alternative to providing a direct answer to Anthony's question. A senior Labor source has described Tange's attitude at this time as that of a man who believed there was a real crisis looming between Australia and the United States at the security level. The real extent of US concern, which Tange was reflecting, was only shown at first hand in the CIA briefing of the Washington ASIO officer and the subsequent cable despatched back to Australia on 10 November.

It is axiomatic within intelligence communities that one of the greatest threats which a country such as the United States can make is that of withdrawing its intelligence swapping operations with another country. For a long time senior Australian officials and academics involved in this area have argued that this is a hold which the US has over nations including Australia. The CIA's belief that intelligence swapping between Australia and the United States was in jeopardy meant that relations were on the verge of breakdown. The 10 November cable from the Washington ASIO officer came direct from one of the most senior figures in the CIA, the chief of the South East Asia division, and obviously reflected the thinking at the very apex of that organisation.

Two main themes run through the cable: first, that continued open dialogue in Australia threatened to 'blow the lid off' US bases in this country, particularly Pine Gap, and second, that the revelation of CIA employees would destroy the trust and cooperation between the two services. The CIA was appealing to ASIO to see if that organisation knew what was happening. Implicit in this request was an understanding that the Australian organisation had obligations of loyalty to the CIA itself.

It is possible that the CIA had become aware of the fact that Whitlam's office had asked for a list of all CIA agents. It may have suspected that this indicated a change of policy on security or that further agents would be revealed during the unprecedented political crisis in Australia which was provoking attacks of a different dimension from normal from both political parties. It is also possible that the CIA may have fed on the paranoia of people within the Australian intelligence community who were alarmed at what was happening. Although it has always been assumed that the Russians know the function of Pine Gap, concern about the operating aspects of this base being revealed was a major force in the CIA's complaint. It is quite clear that, after the exhaustion of diplomatic channels, the American intelligence people felt it was necessary to make approaches through other channels such as ASIO.

Whitlam's longstanding suspicion of the intelligence services and the CIA was a documented fact. When the Prime Minister visited the United States in September–October 1974 his address to the United

Nations general assembly, regarded by both Whitlam and the Foreign Affairs Department as a major speech, contained a veiled but pointed criticism of the CIA. In this forum the Prime Minister warned against moves by states to bring about political or economic change in other countries through 'unconstitutional, clandestine, corrupt methods, by assassination or terrorism'. He said such approaches would turn 'quite quickly against even the most powerful nations who would seek to advance their cause by such methods'. The reference came at a time when the US government had admitted that it directly intervened in Chile in opposition to the Allende Marxist government and its purpose was clear enough.

When Defence Minister Morrison visited the United States in mid 1975 he held talks with Colby about the ambit of the CIA's activities in Australia. The official understanding between the two countries is that both are aware of the extent of the CIA's involvement.

On his visit to Washington the Prime Minister, speaking on the Meet the Press platform, declared his confidence in the integrity of the United States government by saying: 'My government knows what the United States is doing in Australia, and we know that nothing the United States does in Australia will be done except with our full knowledge and cooperation.' Despite Whitlam's confidence, a number of Australians previously involved in intelligence work believed that the real extent of CIA activity in Australia might not be known to the government.

The three main US bases in Australia are Pine Gap, Nurrungar (nearly 300 miles north-west of Adelaide), and North West Cape on the coast of Western Australia. The estimated cost for the Americans to remove Pine Gap from Australia—the base they were so worried about in November—and locate it elsewhere, is put at about $1000 million. Pine Gap and Nurrungar were critically associated with a series of secret US satellite programs that involved intelligence gathering and early warnings of tests and missile launches.[5]

Both the Whitlam Labor Government, and the Liberal-Country Party government before it, refused to disclose any of the functions of Pine Gap and Nurrungar. Only a handful of Ministers in any Australian government are ever provided with a briefing on the bases. During Labor's term of office it is doubtful if any more than five Ministers received such briefings. Those who certainly did include Whitlam, the former Defence Minister Lance Barnard, his successor Bill Morrison, the Foreign Minister Senator Don Willesee, and the former Minister assisting the Defence Minister, Senator Reg Bishop.

But it appears clear that the United States government has not kept the Australian government informed about all activities at the bases. In 1973 it appeared that Pine Gap, Nurrungar and North West Cape were placed on full alert on 11 October, five days after the Middle East war began and two weeks before the US general alert of 25 October. North West Cape was used on 25 October to communicate the US general alert to US installations and forces in the Indo-Pacific region. It was apparently only with this communication that the Australian government learnt that bases in Australia were involved in the alert.

An issue raised by Labor staff members is whether any of their Ministers possessed the technical expertise to grasp what bases really do. They are one of the most vital ingredients in the Australian–American connection, and also the one least discussed or understood. The extent of the US hold on Australia often manifests itself in peculiar ways. For instance, when he was Leader of the Opposition, Arthur Calwell indicated to the Americans whom he would appoint Defence Minister and Foreign Affairs Minister in a Labor government.[6]

The crisis in November 1975 involving the CIA was set against a backdrop of other security changes which may have affected it. In the previous two months the heads of Australia's two chief security organisations, the Australian Secret Intelligence Service (ASIS) and the Australian Security Intelligence Organisation (ASIO) had both been removed by a personal decision of the Prime Minister.

The change in ASIS would have had a direct bearing on the Americans since it was Australia's overseas spy service and heavily involved in liaison between Australia and both the CIA and British Intelligence Service. The very existence of ASIS has been held with the utmost secrecy in Canberra for many years even though its operations are known to a wide number of people, particularly those in the Foreign Affairs Department. It was formed in the early 1950s to act as an overseas covert intelligence gathering organisation and has from the time of its inception enjoyed very close relations with both the British and the Americans, often working for them in countries where their own presence would have been more difficult.

When Whitlam was Leader of the Opposition, successive Prime Ministers decided he should not be told about ASIS or its activities. He found out about the details of ASIS and also the operations of the Defence Signals Division (DSD) from the late Prime Minister of Malaysia, Tun Razak, in the late 1960s. Not only had Australian governments refused to inform Whitlam but some of Australia's leading public servants also advised the Liberal–Country Party government that the Leader of the Opposition should not be told. This is the origin of Whitlam's rigid insistence during his Prime Ministership that Opposition leaders should be fully briefed on security matters and that the government can assume their trustworthiness as alternative Prime Ministers.[7]

ASIS has operatives overseas in a number of countries including Singapore, Malaysia, Indonesia, Thailand, the Philippines, Japan, and in recent years has had a strong presence in Vietnam, China, Cambodia and Chile. It has liaison people in Washington and London but the thrust of its efforts is directed towards Asia. Its main job is to collect documentary intelligence—the sort of thing which would normally be one step beyond the role of a diplomat. ASIS officers operate with the benefit of a secret appropriation and frequently buy documents, information and people. ASIS agents normally work under Foreign Affairs cover.[8]

There are many reasons for the long-standing rivalry and bureaucratic tension between Foreign Affairs and the security organisation. These centre on the fact that one has to protect the other, competition as to whose information is the best, resentment that one lot of information is often purchased, and the fact that the head of ASIS has a responsibility to report to the Secretary of the Foreign Affairs Department.

During its three years of office the Labor government had a relationship of mutual diffidence with ASIS. One of the paradoxes was that the government placed few demands on the organisation, did not strain itself to discover the extent or effectiveness of its operations, and as a result only encouraged the service to keep even further to itself. But during the period of Labor rule there were three separate incidents which gradually brought the government's wrath down on ASIS, sufficiently strongly at the end to lead to the removal of its chief. Each incident related to ASIS forays into other countries. They were in chronological order and in order of importance to the Labor government: involvement in China, Chile, and Portuguese Timor.

One of Labor's first initiatives as a government was to establish relations with mainland China. When Australian diplomatic representatives were sent to Peking in early 1973 they were soon joined by an ASIS officer under embassy cover. The organisation had two people in China for a large part of 1973 with a conspicuous lack of success. They were withdrawn in either late 1973 or early 1974 at the government's insistence. The incident was not an important one as far as Labor was concerned, mainly because of the ineffectiveness of the operation. But it revealed the determination of ASIS to get its foot in a new door that had been closed for so long.

The Chilean involvement was more important. ASIS had two men in the country from either 1970 or 1971 when approval was given from the highest levels of the McMahon government. They were working on behalf of the CIA. Not long after Whitlam assumed office, he asked the head of the spy service for a list of countries in which ASIS operated. The Prime Minister immediately asked why Chile was one of them and instructed that Australia was to wind down its activities there. Whitlam specifically asked the director of ASIS, Mr T Robertson, to contact the Americans to ensure there was no confusion when Australia left.

However there was a delay of a few months in the Australian exit, which displeased Whitlam and which he personally pursued with Robertson.

The furore over Chile and the instructions to the organisation to vacate the field left a legacy of poor morale within ASIS. It was accentuated by criticism of ASIS from within the Foreign Affairs Department and those sections of the government that dealt with security matters. ASIS was seen as an ineffective organisation whose first loyalty was to the international intelligence community and whose friends in the British and American services were doing more than their share in helping their Australian counterparts by way of information and documents.

Robertson was removed as a result of ASIS activities in Portuguese Timor in late 1975 which were conducted without the knowledge of the Australian government. In early October the Foreign Affairs Department discovered through some of its officers in Darwin that an Australian citizen, Frank Favaro, a prominent figure in Portuguese Timor and the manager of a hotel in Dili, had been engaged on behalf of ASIS.

This issue had been previously raised in Parliament on 16 October when Victorian Labor Senator George Poyser asked the Foreign Affairs Minister, Senator Willesee, whether he had seen reports that the government had been asked to investigate alleged spying activities of its de facto consul in Timor, Frank Favaro. Willesee replied: 'Mr Frank Favaro does not represent the Australian government in Timor in any capacity whatsoever, either officially or, as the report claims, as de facto consul—a term which in itself is meaningless. He is a private Australian citizen who lives in Timor.'

Willesee was horrified when he later found out the real story and realised that he had misled the Parliament. Knowing the seriousness with which Whitlam regarded this offence he went straight to the Prime Minister and explained the situation. Whitlam was furious when he discovered that Robertson had hired Favaro as an operative in the midst of a highly localised and extremely dangerous political situation between Australia and Indonesia.

The affair was not without its ironies. Many Labor people, critical of the intelligence networks, wanted to know why ASIS did not have its own contacts in Portuguese Timor—an area close to Australia and certain to be in the forefront of political turmoil as a result of Portugal's decolonisation policies. Evidently ASIS belatedly thought along the same lines and tried to rectify the situation. The government subsequently received reports that Favaro had spoken openly about his activities and the self-styled Foreign Minister for Fretilin, the pro-independence political movement on the island, Jose Ramos Horta, knew that Favaro had been engaged. Whitlam discovered Favaro's activities in late October and, after a series of meetings with Willesee, Alan Renouf (the head of the Foreign Affairs Department), Menadue and other officials, it was agreed Robertson would be removed and replaced by the next man in line, Mr J Kennison, a career intelligence officer. Under the terms of Robertson's contract, he could be sacked at any time and the government had no hesitation in using its power in this regard.

The decision was a win for the Foreign Affairs Department in its rivalry with the security organisation, and in particular for Renouf who, as departmental head, should have been informed by Robertson when Favaro was hired. But the removal of Robertson, who worked closely with the Americans on a number of matters and in particular on ASIS involvement in both Cambodia and Chile, would have certainly come to the notice of the CIA and may have been an important factor in creating in their minds an aura of uncertainty about security in Australia. The Executive Council meeting which appointed his successor was attended by Whitlam, Morrison and the Governor-General. Whitlam told Fraser of the removal of Robertson and the reasons for it.

In a separate incident the Prime Minister also removed the head of ASIO, Peter Barbour, from his position in late 1975. Barbour, who gave up an MA scholarship on medieval German literature to begin work as an ASIO research officer, was appointed ASIO Director-General in 1970. Although ASIO was set up by the Chifley Labor government in 1949, with Mr Justice Reed its first Director-General, most of its career had been under the leadership of retired army officer Brigadier Charles Spry.

Its directive given by Prime Minister Chifley to Justice Reed read:

> The security service forms part of the Attorney-General's Department and the Attorney-General will be responsible for it to parliament. As Director-General of security, you will have access to the Prime Minister at all times. The security service is part of the defence forces of the Commonwealth and, save as herein expressed, has no concern with the enforcement of criminal law. Its task is the defence of the Commonwealth from external and internal dangers arising from attempts to sabotage and espionage, or from actions of persons and organisations, whether directed from within or without the country, which may be judged to be subversive of the security of the Commonwealth.

The directive also warned against actions that might be construed as being politically biased.

The extent to which ASIO subsequently followed this original directive and a subsequent one from Menzies given in similar terms is open to question. Its most famous involvement was in persuading a Soviet embassy official, Vladimir Petrov, to defect in a blaze of publicity which inflamed the anti-communist political atmosphere of the day and which Sir Robert Menzies cleverly exploited to win the decisive 1954 federal election.

Over the years ASIO came to reflect the preoccupations of Australia's successive conservative governments and maintained files on a number of trade unionists and some Labor members of parliament. Its activities passed into the folklore of the left in Australian politics and the 1971 ALP federal conference, the party's supreme policy-making body, recorded a tied 23–all vote on a move to make abolition of ASIO part of the ALP platform. The tied vote defeated the motion.

Not long after Labor assumed office, the new Attorney-General, Senator Lionel Murphy, was involved in one of the most sensational incidents in the history of Australian security. This was when Murphy staged his 'raid' on ASIO headquarters in Melbourne in the conviction that the organisation was withholding information from him on the activities of terrorists. Murphy only intended to visit the headquarters but on arrival found that his staff had arranged for a heavy Common- wealth Police presence. At the time the Yugoslav Prime Minister Bijeidc was planning a visit to Australia and the head of the Commonwealth Police told Murphy his security could not be guaranteed in the face of death threats. The Attorney-General's failure to give parliament ad- equate explanations for his action cost the Labor government dearly, and at the end of 1973 Whitlam nominated the ASIO incident as one of the most damaging for his government.

Despite reports at the time that Barbour would be sacked, he survived unharmed. ASIO also survived despite extensive reports that it would be destroyed as a domestic intelligence agency because other agencies would no longer cooperate with it in intelligence swapping.

In February 1975 Whitlam finally effected his long-standing objec- tive and established a Royal Commission on Intelligence and Security to be conducted by Mr Justice Hope of the Supreme Court of NSW. The terms of reference of the Hope inquiry, the bulk of which was to be conducted in camera, were as wide-ranging as possible with vast implications for the future of Australia's three main intelligence organisations, the Joint Intelligence Organisation (JIO), ASIO and ASIS. The terms of the Hope inquiry threw into the melting pot the future structure and operations of these three organisations and promised the most comprehensive review ever of Australian security and intelligence.

It is known that during his inquiries Mr Justice Hope became concerned about a number of aspects of ASIO's activities and efficiency. These appeared to provide ground for Barbour's removal. About Sep- tember 1975 the government became aware of an indiscretion Barbour had committed, of which the British were also aware. On receiving this information the Prime Minister believed that the Director-General should be transferred and he was appointed Consul General in New York. The move ended one period of uncertainty in relations between ASIO and the government and started another. Whitlam, in his conviction that a judge should head ASIO, appointed Mr Justice Woodward to the post.

Whitlam's decision to appoint a Royal Commission on Intelligence and Security offered the most significant opportunity for review and reform of the security services since their inception. But at the same time the change of personnel in ASIS and ASIO, together with the Stallings revelation, created the most vigorous upheaval within Australia's intelligence community and, more importantly, within the United States community.

The timing of this security crisis, and the previous experience of Sir John Kerr in security matters, has provided the necessary material for a pervasive conspiracy theory surrounding Whitlam's dismissal. But there is no evidence to sustain the theory. All the evidence suggests that security had no role whatsoever in Whitlam's dismissal. The security crisis and the concern of the CIA were never discussed at the meetings between the Governor-General and Fraser nor between the Governor-General and Whitlam. There is no suggestion that Sir Arthur Tange made any efforts to convey his profound concern to the Governor-General. The reasons for Kerr's action lie wholly within the parliamentary crisis.

The security crisis stands on its own. It is testimony to the importance of Pine Gap and the other bases in America's strategic position, the role of the CIA in Australia, the great sensitivity of intelligence and security relations, and finally, the failure of the Labor government to come to grips effectively with these issues.

# PART II

# THE FRASER EMERGENCE

# 5

# THE GENESIS

*I haven't had in some of you fellas for enough grogs.*

Bill Snedden to delegation of Fraser supporters
asking him to resign on 26 November 1974

The genesis of the elevation of Malcolm Fraser to the Liberal leadership can be pinpointed precisely to 5 a.m. on 15 November 1974 at the Canberra Rex Hotel. After a long night of self-debate, Tony Staley, parliamentary under-secretary to the Liberal leader, Bill Snedden, decided to resign his post in the conviction that Snedden was no longer suited to be leader and should be replaced. There was no doubt in Staley's mind that on the basis of intellectual capability, parliamentary performance and political strength, the rightful leader of the party was Malcolm Fraser. Indeed, he was the only leader.[1]

Tony Staley was not a force in the parliamentary Liberal Party. He was a relatively junior member, a backbencher who had spent four years in the House, a former political science lecturer at Melbourne University whose formal appearance often tended to conceal his disarmingly friendly disposition which many of his colleagues interpreted as both naive and boyish. Normally such a decision by a backbencher would be of no consequence in politics.

There are no permanent allegiances and few permanent friendships within the parliamentary arena. While a determined shift of attitude by a major powerbroker will always be important, Staley was not such a man. He probably commanded not a single vote within the party except his own. His decision was not sparked by any misdemeanour or political mistake by Snedden which Staley could point out to other Liberals to win them to his conclusion. It was a strictly personal decision based on an assessment of his leader over time. Nevertheless his decision was seminal in bringing Malcolm Fraser, then a frontbench Liberal but occupying no leadership position, to the office of Prime Minister just 56 weeks later. From the advantage of hindsight it can be said fairly definitely that, without Staley's decision, Fraser would not have won the Liberal leadership at the time he did and consequently would probably not have won it before the Liberals were returned to office.

The Opposition Leader, Bill Snedden, had made his first deliberate threat to force a new election in his speech to the Liberal Party Federal Council meeting on 13 October 1974. Measuring his words carefully, Snedden told the Canberra meeting:

> I recognise that the time may come when the people demand the restoration of sanity and good management to our economic and social life.

While stressing that the Opposition had no intention of forcing an unwanted election on Australia, he said it would nevertheless 'respond decisively when the public clearly demonstrates that a decision is required'. These were the words of a man in a position of political strength. To all appearances Billy Mackie Snedden had recovered from his defeat in the 18 May 1974 general election which he had precipitated by blocking supply to the Labor government. Only a few months afterwards, Liberals were already talking about that May election with a shrug of their shoulders: it had been an opportunity worth trying. The benefit of a few months' hindsight revealed it as an essentially correct political tactic blighted only by the tactical blunder of premature timing. This was the view of the Liberal leadership and wide sections of the party. Snedden was now giving every sign of directing his attention towards a new grab for power; this time a successful one.

The Liberal leader had escaped recriminations after his May defeat, because of two immediate factors. The first was the closeness of the margin. Snedden had cut Labor's majority in the House from nine seats to five and, with the support of the Tasmanian independent, Senator Townley—who later rejoined the Liberal Party—the Opposition could rely on thirty votes in the Senate, sufficient to deny passage to Labor's legislation and force another election at a time of its own choosing by blocking the government's money bills. The second factor was the absence of any leadership challenges within the party to either Snedden as leader or Phillip Lynch as his deputy. To all appearances they were now confirmed until after the following general election.

The most important political development in the post May 1974 election period was the dramatic slide in the standing of the Labor government coupled with a deteriorating economic situation. By October

Snedden was leading a party in a clear electoral ascendancy, built up over the previous months but not of the Liberals' making. Though Snedden had not won in May, every indication was that he would win next time.

In short, these external and internal political forces worked against criticism of Snedden's defeat. So much so that there was a lack of real post-election assessment by the Liberals of where they had gone wrong. It was business as usual. Snedden himself was convinced that the incompetence of the Labor government would deliver him office and his tactics were framed on this assumption. He spoke for most of the Liberals when he predicted in September that the government would lower its support 'to the irreducible minimum' because of its own actions.

But Snedden's position of strength was more apparent than real. Often he dismayed many of his own supporters with ineffectual public and parliamentary performances. There was continued discussion about his ability as a leader, particularly in comparison to Whitlam. In most cases these doubts about Snedden were latent, lurking beneath the political surface, leaving little sign of their existence and only making any appearance when there were new political currents to stir them. After nearly two years as leader, Snedden had some genuine achievements. It was unfortunate for him that they were often more subtle and less obvious than his weaknesses.

Snedden received a lot of credit for healing those divisions within the parliamentary party which had prompted the then Liberal federal president Bob Southey to assert after the 1972 election: 'I make only one reference to the recent past but I hope it will be understood. The personal ambitions and feuds inside the parliamentary Liberal Party since the death of Harold Holt have been deadly and destructive. That sort of conduct must be buried with the past.' Personal animosities always linger on in the heart; but by 1974 Snedden could point with justice to the fact that they appeared to have disappeared largely from the public stage. In August 1974 Malcolm Fraser himself acknowledged this: 'I think a great deal of credit must go to Bill Snedden for the unity and cohesion within the party at present.'[2]

Snedden also established new arrangements with the National Country Party (NCP) which represented a fresh brand of cooperation in contrast to their severed coalition after the 1972 election defeat. This had not been easy for him. Snedden and the NCP leader Doug Anthony had been involved in many public clashes at the Opposition's expense. The most notorious occurred in the May 1974 campaign when the two men clashed over Anthony's support for higher oil prices. Later Snedden privately blamed Anthony for costing him the election. But in the post election period Snedden persisted and finally succeeded in having a joint front bench established between the two parties as well as joint party meetings to form a full-scale coalition in Opposition. The aim was to have one coalition view on all matters, thereby creating a structure which maximised unity and minimised differences.

In his dealings with Liberal state branches and the non-Labor Premiers, Snedden largely managed to remove the hostility which had prevailed during John Gorton's Prime Ministership and, to a lesser extent, under William McMahon's administration. Admittedly he enjoyed the indispensable advantage of Opposition for this task, thereby being able to indulge the anti-centralists within the Liberal Party. Snedden introduced a system of summit meetings, which involved the regular coming together of state and federal Liberal leaders to discuss ideas and strategy.

Finally Snedden, like McMahon before him, took a major role in encouraging the party's organisation and grass roots to participate in the platform and policy review. In particular, Snedden supported the restructuring of the Liberal Party organisation in June 1974, which resulted in a larger federal secretariat designed to combine research, communications and policy support for the parliamentary party. The new federal director of the Liberal Party, Tony Eggleton, took charge of this secretariat in early 1975.

Snedden was a battler and a self-made man. He came from a lower middle class background in Perth, his father being a stonemason, two of his brothers apprenticed as stonemasons, and the other two starting off as butchers. From the age of eight he was a newspaper boy and in later years drew his first political consciousness from reading the papers he delivered. 'I was an avid reader of the newspapers I sold and I think I knew at the time where things were done and where decisions were taken and I wanted to be in that process,' Snedden said of his early days. 'I chose the side of politics early, too. It was a conviction that you ought to have freedom to do what you wanted to do and you ought to gain from your enterprise.'[3] He left school at fifteen in May 1942 but still aspired to greater things in law or politics.

Snedden worked first as a law clerk, then for the Commonwealth Crown Solicitor, joined the RAAF in 1945 and was later admitted to the University of Western Australia to study law without his matriculation. In 1948, aged only 21, he ran for the state seat of Boulder just for the experience because there was no hope of winning it. In 1949 he stood against Kim Beazley Snr in Fremantle in the federal election which brought the Menzies government to power. Snedden's ultimate goal was to run for the seat of Perth and he got his chance in the 1951 double dissolution election when he lost by just over 100 votes after a vigorous electoral battle. Already one of his main political characteristics was firmly in evidence—his doggedness. Although he had been defeated,

Snedden's West Australian experiences had brought him into contact with federal figures, people like Menzies and Holt, and meant that by the time he was 24 he had grounding in politics and campaigning.

But, after three electoral defeats, Snedden was uncertain about his future and finally went overseas where he worked as a public servant in the Immigration Department in Rome for over two years before returning to Australia. This time he left the west and moved to Melbourne on the path of further advancement. He became active in the party and within months had won Liberal preselection for the seat of Bruce. With his election to parliament, Snedden worked assiduously to turn Bruce into a safe Liberal seat and to establish his own credentials in the industrial and legal fields. His association with Harold Holt bore fruit in 1968 when he was appointed Immigration Minister.

After Holt's death he used the bond between them as an explanation of his decision to run for leader. It was at this time that Snedden came to national prominence. He risked extensive public and party ridicule in the statement which he prepared announcing his candidature for the leadership which said:

> Those who have urged me to submit myself to the choice of my party colleagues have said Australia's national leadership at this time requires the vital energy of a man on the wave length of his own era. Yet this leader must be a man of experience, background and imagination. Some of my colleagues have been kind enough to say I am such a man.

This was the most pointed indication so far of Snedden's ambition outstripping his ability and his lurch into delusions of grandeur.

From this time onwards Snedden became a compulsive leadership contender. He stood for the deputy leadership in 1969, the leadership again in March 1971, the deputy leadership in late 1971, this time successfully. Finally he was elected leader in December 1972 by one vote. Snedden's election as leader was not a ringing endorsement of him but more of a grudging admission that he was likely to be the best of an uninspiring group of leadership candidates.

En route to the top, Snedden had served as Attorney-General, Minister for Labour and National Service, and Treasurer. He gained a reputation as an acquiescent Minister. The most notable example was when as Labour Minister he announced that deflationary fiscal or monetary measures would not be adequate to halt wage-cost pressures, only to perform a volte face as Treasurer a few months later and introduce the very same measures to curb such pressures. In both cases he merely repeated the advice of departments with different views.

As a man Snedden enjoyed none of the advantages of birth or social status shared by so many of his colleagues. He had no family wealth to subsidise his advancement and indulge his interests; no natural affinity with the class allies of the Liberal Party, the captains of business and industry; no ruling graces instilled through an aristocratic upbringing. His experience of life—the stonemason's son who rose to power—shaped his view of politics. 'The reality of classes doesn't exist in our society. We have a more homogeneous society, so therefore how can we have deeply divided ideologies?' he said in 1972.

> I don't have any money. I live in a house that's got three bedrooms, occupied by myself and wife, by a daughter and another daughter and the boys are in the bungalow outside. We've got a lounge room and a sort of dining room and a sun room. Well you don't have gorgeous entertaining parties. It's fine for our friends but it's not something you socialise in. And for my wife, who has a rather similar background, it's more important for us to have personal friends in a real sense.[4]

Snedden often betrayed an honesty that bordered on the embarrassing in a man who sought to lead others. He once gave this description of meeting his wife, Joy:

> I met my wife on a tram. She used to catch the same tram, and I used to think she was a very beautiful girl—not a made-up girl, but a girl with a good bone structure—she was good looking. I used to hang around the tram stop until I saw her getting on and ultimately I talked to her. I talked to her and after a while I started taking her out. Once I started taking her out that was that. She comes from a like background to my own, a similar income strata.[5]

Snedden interpreted his own rise from obscurity to leadership as a vindication of the Liberal Party. It was proof that the Liberals had captured the middle ground in Australian politics, that they were the party prepared to encourage the enterprise and advancement of the little man. But some Liberals used it to highlight Snedden's deficiencies. After the November challenge, one Fraser supporter taunted: 'Look, Snedden has no breeding. Malcolm has.'

Although he saw himself as belonging to the progressive side of the Liberal Party, Snedden's record was not that of a political innovator. He brought few fresh ideas to the party he led. One of his most well-known quotations was when he told an interviewer in 1968: 'Politics is not a matter of class or ideology. Politics is largely a matter of sound and cautious administration.' Snedden was more preoccupied with the mechanics and cosmetics of politics. His efforts were directed towards smoothing divisions within the parliamentary party, promoting cooperation between the federal party and the states, improving relations between organisational and political wings.

Snedden's success in the party room originates in the great Australian ethic of mateship. During his time as a Minister, his office was often the scene for late night gatherings over a beer with journalists, ministerial staff and other Liberals. This was his modus operandi; a continually underestimated component in deciding a politician's party room vote is whether a contender is liked and respected. This was Snedden's forte. He made it hard not to like him. His qualities of affability and honesty were of high currency in the Liberal Party at the end of 1972. As a member and then a Minister Snedden gave support and loyalty to his leader. As a leader he expected and assumed in turn that others would give their loyalty to him. The notion of personal loyalty was at the core of Snedden's personal and political life. He once declared: 'I think the greatest quality a man possesses is loyalty.' It was this trait of Snedden's that led him to misjudge the strength of feeling against him within the party. He could never accept or really understand that he would be overthrown when he led the party as diligently and competently as he could. It was also this trait which left him stunned and embittered after he had been deposed as leader.

Snedden's approach to politics was invariably to seek and find the party consensus. When he selected his shadow Cabinet he tried to balance all interests in the party, even at the cost of ability. It was very rarely that Snedden attempted to use all the status and power which the Liberal Party surrenders to its leader to push a policy or political line. Snedden led through compromise rather than coercion in a party that was traditionally committed to powerful leadership.

A growing number of Liberals became dissatisfied over what they interpreted as Snedden's weakness. Ultimately one of the chief complaints about the leader was his tendency to shift his ground to reflect the consensus. What at one period was a political asset now became a liability. Many Liberals believed that Snedden had failed to develop and articulate the philosophical basis of Liberalism, that he was too prepared to bend with the wind and in consequence lacked the resolution and the ideas that should accompany leadership.

At the same time many members became alarmed at Snedden's unfailing capacity to trap himself with immortal exaggerations. In a ministerial speech in 1969 he predicted: ' . . . a great new age of Liberalism, the significance of which will at least equal that of the industrial revolution.' In 1970 he attacked moratorium marchers, calling them 'a mob of political bikies pack-raping democracy'. He incurred the anger of many Liberals after the 1974 election by refusing to admit at a Melbourne press conference that the Liberals had lost. What Snedden meant was that by denying Labor a Senate majority the Opposition had blocked their access to real power. But instead of explaining this, he left himself open to ridicule by refusing to admit defeat.

But Snedden's most memorable and costly exaggeration was made on Friday 15 November when he addressed a businessmen's lunch in Melbourne and was asked a hostile question about the Liberal leadership. At the end of his answer, attempting to be lighthearted Snedden replied:

> I'll tell you why I should be leader of the Liberal Party—I'm the best—that's why I should be. I can give leadership to my team and they will all follow me. If I asked them [Liberal parliamentarians] to walk through the valley of death on hot coals they'd do it. Every one of them trusts me. Everyone recognises my political judgement and, if I say something must be this, it will be. That's why I'm leader.

Snedden's comments amused some businessmen at the $50 a head lunch at Chadstone's Matthew Flinders Hotel. But it enraged a number of Liberal parliamentarians. This statement, made less than a fortnight before the November leadership challenge, cut too close to the bone. In it Snedden all too clearly revealed his need to overcompensate for his own inadequacies. The hallmarks of leadership—authority and perspective—were clearly missing. Staley said of this statement: 'A party leader can only insult the intelligence and sensitivity of his colleagues so much.'

In his media appearances Snedden was handicapped by a ponderous voice, a poor vocabulary and an ineffective wit. One of the surprising aspects about his career is that for a long time he was well regarded within the party for his impressive media image.

It was significant that the opposition to Snedden originated in the House of Representatives. These were the men who watched his performance every day in the House against Whitlam; they knew that Snedden was outmatched. This was reinforced by feedback from their electorates when parliament was in recess.

The bedrock concern about Snedden was that he was a loser—that he would be unable to return the Liberals to office for a long period of successful government. Some Liberals pointed out that it would be even more dangerous for the party if Snedden led them into the next election and won it on Labor's mistakes, which appeared likely. If this eventuated, they argued, the leadership weakness would become even more apparent in government and it would lead to a repeat of the Gorton years.

It was for all these reasons that when Tony Staley made up his mind, he was not alone.

Malcolm Fraser had always enjoyed a solid core of support within the parliamentary party. In the December 1972 leadership ballot after the defeat of the McMahon government, he was the third candidate to be eliminated after Jim Killen and John Gorton. That contest became a two man race between Snedden and NSW Liberal Nigel Bowen, with

Snedden winning by one vote in the fifth ballot after the fourth ballot had been tied, suggesting that someone abstained from voting. The election of Snedden, then 45 years old compared with Fraser's 42 years, suggested that Fraser might have lost his leadership opportunity for many years ahead.

Fraser was always regarded as a potential leader; but also as a man whose vaulting ambition, lofty arrogance and apparent disdain for many of his colleagues would have to be modified before he could assume the ultimate mantle. In particular Fraser's public repudiation of Prime Minister John Gorton, which precipitated Gorton's fall in March 1971, had raised such deep doubts about his character and such suspicion from so many Liberals that it appeared he would have to wait many years, certainly until Gorton lost his influence, before seriously looking at the leadership. Such was the conventional political wisdom which prevailed throughout 1973 and nearly all of 1974.

Tony Staley was one of the most unlikely coup leaders imaginable within the Liberal Party. Yet the decision he reached on the morning of 15 November led him directly into assuming this role and occupying the special position of public relations manager and confidante in Fraser's rise to power in the party. Staley was a theorist, a man who enjoyed philosophising, a trait which did not endear him to many of his colleagues who had a more practical and earthy experience of the world and a more cynical and mercenary approach to politics. He came from a wealthy Melbourne family which had immigrated to Australia in the pre gold-rush days and had firmly established itself in manufacturing and merchant business.

Staley had a sheltered and comfortable upbringing, following in his father's footsteps to Scotch College and then Melbourne University, where he graduated in law. At university he was active in the Student Christian Movement and for a period seriously considered the church as a career. Politics, along with religion and drama, were the young Staley's main interests, and at one time a visiting English actor told him to seek a career on the stage. He was prominent in the Liberal Club at Melbourne University and his student days modified the strong right-wing views he had held originally, the natural product of his family background.

At about the same time that Staley left university, he had a brief affair with the Labor Party, attending several meetings of the Parkville branch and joining the party before finally turning back to the Liberals with renewed conviction. Staley decided to study for his master's degree in politics, the first clear sign that politics was to dominate his other preoccupations, the church and the stage. He was offered a tutorship at Melbourne University. His practical interest in politics developed with his academic involvement and in about 1964 he joined the Liberal Party.

Staley quickly became secretary of the Croydon North branch, served on the state council and then on the state executive where one of the father figures of the Victorian Liberal Party, Sir Rutherford Guthrie, presided over his progress. Staley finally won Liberal endorsement for Chisholm, one of the safest non-Labor seats in Victoria, and his elevation to the House of Representatives became a formality. The Liberal parliamentary party which Staley joined was torn with bitter personality and ideological rifts as the Prime Ministership of John Gorton came under direct assault from within.

Staley had supported Snedden against Bowen in December 1972. But he harboured doubts, as did many other Liberals, about whether Snedden possessed the capabilities for leadership in such a difficult time for the party, its first experience in Opposition for 23 years, with Snedden being its fourth leader in the six years since the Menzies retirement. But Staley worked closely with the leader and his staff when appointed one of Snedden's under-secretaries in 1973—a natural springboard onto the party's front bench.

While Staley worked closely with Snedden, he also had a well-established relationship with Malcolm Fraser. The two men had met at the Melbourne Club before Staley entered Parliament. In 1971 Staley was on good enough terms with Fraser to discuss the latter's move against John Gorton and the young backbencher gave every appearance of enjoying Fraser's company and getting on well with him. When Fraser retired to the backbench after Gorton's downfall and his family moved back to the farm, Staley and another Fraser confidant, Victorian frontbencher Tony Street, shared Fraser's Canberra house during parliamentary sessions. Staley enjoyed discussing Liberal philosophy with Fraser and formed a close association with him during this period.

Towards the end of 1974 Staley went into hospital for a varicose veins operation and later went to the western district region of Victoria to rest and recuperate. It gave him the chance to reflect on his doubts about Snedden. They crystallised on the morning of 15 November 1974.

Staley's embrace of Malcolm Fraser contained all the zeal and agony of a religious conversion. He can still remember the exact time and place it occurred, just as those who have passed from the valley of darkness into light will always remember the moment. 'I wrote myself notes. It was something that had been going on in me for a long time. These things eat away at you,' he said later. Staley stayed up the whole night wrestling with his future before deciding to resign as Snedden's parliamentary under-secretary. He described his own actions and beliefs more in moral than in political terms. 'I acted on a very deep belief on the question of the leadership of the party,' he said later. 'I'm not prepared to be the sort of politician who won't stand up for his beliefs.' Likening the appearance of Fraser to that of the prophet, Staley said: 'Malcolm

Fraser has emerged as a man able to handle Australia's crisis.' After the unsuccessful November 1974 challenge he said that the Liberal Party had a responsibility to face facts, 'if there emerged a leader who met that crisis head on, who could stare disaster and crisis in the face'. Speaking further about Fraser he said: 'He is a big man. He is a man who simply commands respect. He is a man who has strong views— open to reason—but who has strong views and courage.' Staley said that what other people described as Fraser's aloofness was only 'the man's natural authority'. These comments illuminate the nature of the Fraser–Staley relationship, which some press gallery reporters were unkind enough to liken to that of a school prefect and his fag.

After his night of decision, Staley set about talking to his Liberal colleagues, at first cautiously and then with more enthusiasm when he found that many shared his own views. The following week Staley found a nucleus of Liberals who were prepared to make a similar commitment despite the political dangers involved. The pro-Fraser lobby centred upon two rooms in Parliament House. One was shared by the former president of the Queensland Liberal Party, Eric Robinson, elected to Parliament in 1972 representing the safe Gold Coast seat of McPherson, and by John Bourchier, a tough and direct man who held the very marginal Victorian seat of Bendigo, won in 1972 against the national swing to Labor. The other room was occupied by two West Australians, Ian Viner, a Perth lawyer elected in 1972 to the seat of Stirling, the most marginal electorate in the west, and his colleague Peter Drummond, elected in 1972 in the marginal rural seat of Forrest.

One of the first to discover the whisperings against Snedden and the likelihood of action was the party whip Vic Garland, also from the west. Garland himself had approached Snedden over the preceding weeks in his capacity as whip and warned the leader that the mood of the party was becoming increasingly restive. At first Snedden tended to reject Garland's warning, then he wanted the names of people involved and finally he grew angry with Garland. In fact, Garland himself was pro-Fraser and discussed the situation with Staley.

Staley spoke with Fraser's closest colleague, Victorian frontbencher Tony Street. Street was initially overwhelmed by the implications and, being a member of the executive, was plagued by doubts. He did not try to prevent Staley's activities but did not involve himself in them. Staley also approached the deputy Senate leader, Senator Ivor Greenwood from Victoria, who gave a positive response. Greenwood said the party had been waiting for someone to take a stand.

The strategy of the pro-Fraser core during this week was to widen the net and lobby members who could be trusted not to warn Snedden. The manoeuvrings were almost exclusively confined to the House of Representatives members, barely touching the Senate. The aim was to isolate Snedden and his loyalists—Don Chipp, Andrew Peacock, Jim Killen, John Gorton, John McLeay, Alan Jarman and Don Cameron.

From 20 November, Staley and his colleagues were canvassing the numbers available for a move to vacate the leadership in the party room. But they also wanted to persuade Snedden to resign. Options under review included a petition to the leader, a delegation asking him to reassess his position, or both combined with a party room challenge. By Thursday 21 November they were planning a party room challenge the next week.

The Senate was their weakness and they knew it. There were three big problems for the Fraser supporters in the Senate. The first was the influence still held there by the former Senator and leader, John Gorton, an arch enemy of Fraser. The second was the Senate whip, Senator Harold Young (SA), one of Snedden's strongest backers. The third and probably most important was the absence of Fraser organisers within the Senate.

For these reasons the Fraser camp arranged a meeting with the Senate Opposition leader, Senator Reg Withers, on the morning of Monday 25 November. Withers knew about the moves. He had been briefed on the Sunday flight from Perth to the east. But the Fraser push which had seized the House, had barely touched the Senate. Withers did not believe it would succeed.

The delegation that saw Withers on Monday comprised Staley, Drummond, Robinson and Viner. They outlined the support they had in the House and Withers in turn went through the Senators, making his assessment. The delegation left more encouraged than when it had arrived; it felt that Withers was sympathetic and noted his reservations about Snedden.

Staley first told Malcolm Fraser about the moves to make him leader on or about Wednesday 20 November. According to him, Fraser's response was, 'Oh my God, don't talk to me about it. I can't bear to think of this.' While Fraser did little or no lobbying during the remainder of the week, Staley kept him informed of the numbers. The lobbying for Fraser reached its peak in Parliament House on the following Monday afternoon and night. But while the House was sitting this day, the Senate was not. This meant that most Liberal Senators were still in ignorance of the move to replace Snedden.

At lunchtime on Monday 25 November, Snedden left Canberra for an interstate function and during the afternoon Vic Garland, after speaking to a number of Liberal backbenchers, felt obliged to notify the leader that there was a real possibility of a direct challenge to Snedden. Acting in his capacity as party whip, Garland went to see deputy leader Phillip Lynch and broke the news. Lynch was staggered and incredulous, but then made his own soundings. He tried to assess whether the whisperings would pass from rumour to rebellion.

That night a motley group gathered in Lynch's office, including Withers, Street, Garland and the South Australian frontbencher Dr Jim Forbes. It contained both firm Fraser and Snedden supporters, testimony to the fact that confusion was still the prevailing mood and hard alliances had not yet split the party. This group was not aware that a delegation would see Snedden the next day to ask him to resign. That was being decided by the inner core of Fraser supporters at the same time elsewhere in Parliament House.

The purpose of the meeting in Lynch's office was to determine first, whether there was a genuine challenge, and second, whether Snedden should be notified. Finally it was decided that Lynch meet Snedden at the airport in the morning to warn him of the danger. According to those present, it was decided not to contact Snedden that night because they were unsure where he was and, anyway, it was too late for him to address the crisis. It is significant that the response of Liberals who heard about a possible challenge was to assess the situation for themselves, and make their own judgements, rather than tell their leader.

Meanwhile, after talks in the Viner–Drummond room and elsewhere, the inner core of Fraser supporters decided that a six-man delegation would approach Snedden the next day, Tuesday, seeking his resignation as leader and informing him of the mood of the parliamentary party. It was decided that this would be followed up with a party room challenge as soon as possible unless Snedden heeded the delegation's advice.

The Fraser supporters had grown euphoric at the prospect of battle and were chancing their hand at a dangerous game. They had failed to make the sort of cast-iron head count that is fundamental if political leaders are to be deposed. A number of younger members from the House had offered their support—John Howard from NSW, Ian Macphee from Victoria, Mel Bungey from Western Australia, Kevin Cairns from Queensland and Ian Wilson from South Australia. Fraser also had the backing of a number of veterans including former Prime Minister Bill McMahon from NSW, William Wentworth from NSW, and Nigel Drury from Queensland, who had written to Fraser saying that he should be leader. The surge of support in so short a time had made the Fraser supporters over-confident and they over-played their hand.

Lynch met Snedden's plane from Sydney at 9.30 a.m. on Tuesday morning and took the Liberal leader straight into the Ansett VIP lounge. 'Bill, I've come here to get you before you go to the House,' Lynch said. 'There's a move against your leadership and it's serious. We'll need to work on it.' Snedden was one of the last Liberal members in the House of Representatives to discover the plot against him. There could be no more telling commentary on the state of relations between the leader and his party. His ignorance was a direct function of his fragile position and the willingness of those Liberals who knew, which by Monday included most members of the House, not to tell him until they had made their own assessments.[6]

Snedden was amazed when he found out about the move. He arrived at Parliament House twenty minutes later and went straight into a party meeting to finalise the Opposition's attitude towards government bills. It was at this meeting that most of the Liberal Senators found out about the impending challenge and the delegation that would be seeing Snedden asking him to resign. The word was quickly passed around the room. Snedden appeared cool under the pressure of his first face-to-face encounter with the men who sought to depose him. The leadership question was not raised at this meeting which dealt solely with legislation.

Just after the House sat at 10.30 a.m., Andrew Peacock, Don Chipp and John Gorton gathered at the side of the chamber to discuss how the Fraser challenge would be withstood. Snedden now found himself in a tricky parliamentary situation. He gave notice of a motion of no confidence in the Labor government for its economic mismanagement, which he intended to move at the following day's sitting. But Whitlam sprang to his feet, moved the suspension of standing orders and forced the Opposition leader to bring the debate on immediately. This was a parliamentary tactic always open to the government leader. Snedden, not fully prepared for the debate, had to launch his attack on the government at once.

The pressure on the leader in such debates is always considerable, but this time, on Snedden, it was infinitely greater than normal. Having just discovered that his position was under challenge, Snedden then had to display his leadership in debate on the floor of the House, one of his crucial weaknesses. His speech was a major disappointment; his Liberal opponents later described it as lacking preparation, delivery and sound argument. Whitlam walked out in disdain and left the deputy Prime Minister, Jim Cairns, to reply. For Snedden's challengers it confirmed their judgement. Labor members watching the debate had no idea of the impending eruption within the Liberal Party; that was still a party secret.

Snedden returned to his office and found that his staff had set an afternoon appointment for the pro-Fraser delegation. He rang Staley himself and insisted that the delegation come immediately. At noon Snedden received in his office the pro-Fraser lobby—Staley, Robinson, Bourchier, Drummond, Viner and R N ('Duke') Bonnett, the member for Herbert.

The delegation made three points to Snedden. First, that he had done a solid job in healing the previous divisions in the party and was respected for this. Second, that wide sections of the party no longer had confidence in his leadership. Third, that Malcolm Fraser should now replace him as leader of the party. The delegation reminded Snedden of a statement he made in the party room after the 1974 election—that when his moment came he would realise it and accept the party's decision.

Staley tendered his letter of resignation as the leader's parliamentary under-secretary, a letter which summed up the feelings of the rebels:

Dear Bill,

It is with great sadness that I write this letter because of my own personal regard for you. Despite the fact that I have immensely enjoyed my association with you, my view about the leadership of the party leaves me no alternative but to resign from the position of parliamentary secretary to the leader of the opposition. At the same time I believe your personal qualities, in particular your basic honesty and decency, have enabled you to play a crucial role in the history of the party. You were a healer when the Liberal Party needed healing.

Snedden had always believed that he could solve problems by getting people into his room, having a drink, and using his affable style to sort out a compromise. He told the delegation in a joking fashion, 'I haven't had in some of you fellas for enough grogs.' But this situation had gone beyond compromise. Snedden said that he would not resign. He defended his performance and told the delegation if it wanted to pursue the matter it could do so in the party room. Politicians who spend years seeking power will never resign at the first sign of trouble.

Snedden, although shaken, wasted no time in organising his counter-attack. Throughout that afternoon he saw a number of Liberals and worked solidly on the phone to bolster his support. Lynch, Gorton, Peacock, Killen, Don Cameron, Harold Young and Don Jessop all actively assisted him. Snedden spoke to Lynch and Withers throughout the afternoon to assess the situation in the House and Senate respectively. By 4 p.m. Snedden's backers knew that the challenge would be defeated. The heavy lobbying by the leadership group had intimidated a number of Liberals who had previously indicated their support for the pro-Fraser forces.

Malcolm Fraser had been interstate on both Monday and Tuesday and therefore absent from the lobbying. He returned to the House on Tuesday evening and spoke to a number of Senators that night including Withers. He later moved back to the House side and held further talks. At one stage Snedden received a message from a Liberal member that Fraser wanted to see him. He agreed but Fraser never came to his office. Later that night a dozen of Snedden's supporters gathered in his office for drinks, confident that they had demolished their opponents. Fraser left Parliament House that night knowing his chances were slim.

Staley had already approached the party whip Garland to seek a meeting of the Liberal Party for the following morning rather than a joint party meeting which would include the National Country Party. Garland took this request to Lynch, who conveyed it to Snedden. By early evening Snedden, convinced he had the numbers, wanted to force the test of strength himself if the Fraser forces retreated. The meeting of Fraser supporters that night broke up with a decision to re-convene in the morning to take their final decision on whether and how to proceed.

Next morning news of the leadership challenge was broken in the *Sydney Morning Herald* by Brian Johns and carried by most other papers in their second editions. The Liberal Party membership and organisation were stunned and the Labor Party delighted at the sudden disarray in the ranks of their opponents. It was like manna from heaven for Labor; then it was over within hours.

On Wednesday morning the Fraser forces met and decided to proceed with the challenge. The reasons were threefold. First, while they had strong support in the House they overestimated their support in the Senate. Second, too many people had made commitments for the issue not to be proceeded with. Third, the news had hit the press and the knife was already planted in Snedden; by this stage the challenge had a momentum and inevitability of its own.

In the party room Staley moved that the leadership be vacated and his motion was seconded by Bourchier. The debate centred on whether or not this vote would be an open or a secret ballot. While an open vote would favour Snedden, the Fraser supporters had to secure a secret ballot to have any chance.

Staley did not speak to the motion he moved. Gorton made a lengthy and effective speech asking the party room why there was any need to vote on such a proposition. 'After all, where is the challenger?' Gorton asked. 'Who is he?' Gorton then turned to Andrew Peacock and asked him whether he would be standing for leader. Peacock said no. Gorton then returned to his theme which, while not mentioning Fraser, involved a taunting of Fraser, whose supporters were moving for a leadership spill when Fraser himself had not declared his candidature.

Fraser said nothing throughout the party meeting. Snedden's supporters, including Killen, McLeay, Peter Durack from Western Australia and Peacock, argued over the form of the ballot with Fraser supporters. Finally, it was decided not to debate the merits of Snedden's leadership and that a secret ballot would be held on the Staley motion.

The vote on the vacation of the leadership was counted in the whip's office just opposite the entrance to the party room. While the loss of this motion was announced to the meeting, the actual voting figures were not given and this was to develop into a major bone of contention between competing factions. Snedden made a brief placatory speech declaring: 'There will be no blood on the floor.' He referred to the six-man delegation and said there would be no recriminations against them. As the meeting broke up Snedden was surrounded by well-wishers. Then he held a press conference to cement his image as a leader still victorious.

Looking relaxed and confident Snedden said: 'I am glad this is now finished. It will be finished. The matter will not arise again, ought not to arise again.' Snedden told the press he would now be in a stronger position because any doubts about the Liberal leadership had been resolved. Referring to both Staley and Fraser he said: 'I expect loyalty from these two men and unqualified loyalty from both of them.' Under further questioning Snedden repudiated any search for recriminations against either man: 'The future of Mr Fraser and Mr Staley will depend entirely upon their ability and their willingness to give loyalty to the elected leadership of the party.' He made it clear that Fraser would retain his frontbench post despite pressure on him to sack Fraser. Snedden ridiculed the challenge. He claimed the number of votes backing Staley's motion was as low as 10 out of 62.[7] The only Liberal who did not vote was Tasmanian Senator Reg Wright who was absent from Canberra at the time. Meanwhile Staley and the Fraser supporters put their vote as high as 25 or 26.

The Labor government moved swiftly to exploit the unsuccessful coup. When parliament assembled later that day, loud ironic cheers greeted Snedden when he entered the chamber. The Prime Minister in reply to a set-up question declared in a mocking tone: 'It was the universal opinion that nothing could suit the Government better than for the leadership of the Government and Opposition to remain in their present hands.' Recalling Snedden's statement of a fortnight before, the leader of the House, Fred Daly, one of Labor's most effective parliamentarians, said:

> Recent events in this once great party, if I might coin a phrase, indicate that many members are having second thoughts about walking through this valley of death even without the hot coals. In fact I would say that the honourable member for Wannon (Malcolm Fraser) is now an unemployed firewalker. I can also confirm that he will not be burnt at the stake.

The Labor government never let up on the Liberal leadership issue from this day until Snedden was finally challenged directly by Fraser four months later.

The November challenge came as a major blow to the Liberal Party which had been riding the crest of a wave. The party's organisation was surprised and hostile over the move. On Wednesday morning before the party meeting, Staley rang the federal president of the party, Bob Southey, to inform him. Southey immediately flew to Canberra. After the challenge Snedden moved to secure the complete backing of the organisation for his leadership. A meeting of the Liberal Party federal executive, arranged for Saturday 30 November in Melbourne, fully supported the leader and demanded that the parliamentary party act accordingly. Fraser's backers were very unhappy with the executive's decision. But the strategy they now adopted was low profile, biding their time until the bulk of the party fell in behind them.

Snedden himself appeared to become a victim of his own political rhetoric about the challenge. He not only claimed that only about a dozen people had voted for Fraser, he acted as though this was the case. In fact, Fraser had won 26 votes, almost entirely from the House of Representatives. This was a stunning result for him. Its significance was that by November 1974 Snedden had already lost a majority of Liberals in the House. It was true that he still enjoyed the support of the Senate, of the organisation, and probably of the party's rank and file, and that these groups within the party were baffled and outraged at the challenge. But over the next four months the base of Fraser's support would gradually spread out from the House of Representatives and seep right through the parliamentary party, winning extensive backing from the organisation and qualified endorsement from the party branches.

If Snedden had been a realist, he would have admitted to himself that the core of his support was fractured in November and worked solidly to win it back. But there was never any real sign of such an admission. By contrast the strength of Fraser's support had a profound impact on his supporters and on Fraser himself.

The immediate assessments of the unsuccessful coup by the press gallery were likewise astray. Almost without exception senior correspondents predicted that the challenge would increase tension within the party, weaken Snedden's position and destroy Fraser's leadership prospects for many years. While the first two points proved right, they were sadly amiss on the third. Due to a combination of factors Fraser emerged stronger, not weaker, from the November debacle. The coup leaders themselves, especially Staley, suffered heavy criticism and there was talk of removing his preselection. Staley however was careful to visit every branch in his electorate over the next few weeks explaining what he had done and the reasons for it.

On any assessment at the time the challenge had been a shambles. Yet in retrospect it is a landmark in Fraser's rise to power. Staley proved that commitment is a much underrated virtue in politics. Perhaps a more experienced politician with a more sophisticated appreciation of the difficulties involved in overthrowing a leader whose party was in the ascendancy, would not have tried. But Staley did and without him the unrest would have remained a dissipated and dispersed force, not channelled into political action. This is the historical function which he performed and which, on all indications, others were not prepared to accept. It involved placing one's political head squarely on the chopping block if success was not forthcoming.

Staley remained unrepentant after the challenge. While accepting the decision of the party, he said publicly it was inevitable that Fraser would emerge to lead the Liberals. This view was shared by the inner group of Fraser supporters who decided to change their tactics but not their long-term objective.

The challenge was depicted at the time as a combination of personal courage and political stupidity. The Snedden view that there were only 15 votes at most for Fraser prevailed for some time. It facilitated the accusation that the movers were wrecking party unity in a hopeless cause and provoking a dangerous revival of the personality friction that marked the Gorton years. Veteran journalist, Alan Reid, told his colleagues it was 'the most amateurish bid for power in thirty years'. Yet the fact was that, in securing 26 votes, the Fraser supporters came within seven votes of their objective in a revolt conducted in a political vacuum with no crisis to spark it and run by men who ignored every rule in the book of political powerbroking. The vote was a measure of powerful forces within the Liberal Party which, hitherto beneath the surface, were now revealed and given momentum. A new sentiment would engulf the Liberal Party.

Staley's aim after the defeat was to shield Fraser from the swell of bitterness against him, and to remove him from any complicity in the move. Under questioning that afternoon, Staley said that Fraser was told about the plan the previous week. After talking with Staley, Fraser released a statement in an effort to clear himself:

> I took no part in what occurred this morning in the party room. I asked no one for support, nor would I do so. What occurred was initiated by other people without my knowledge or encouragement. I believe however the party room has a right to express a view. It has done this and I respect its decision as always, and I support the parliamentary leader of the Liberal Party.

This statement appeared to contradict Staley's own remarks. Yet it was carefully drafted and Fraser claims that the move was 'initiated' by others without his knowledge, not that he had no knowledge at all. At the same time, Fraser made it clear he believed that the party room had a right to express its view on the leadership. While this was put in the context of supporting the party's decision on Snedden, it left the implication that the party was also free to reverse its stand whenever it liked.

Nothing better demonstrated the difficulty of keeping Fraser in the clear than an exchange on ABC television that night between Staley and Gorton. It was memorable television with Richard Carleton the interviewer:

Carleton: Mr Staley, Mr Fraser said this afternoon in his statement that what occurred was initiated by other people 'without my knowledge or encouragement'. It is difficult to understand how a man with Mr Fraser's political acumen could have been unaware of this. How did you manage to keep it secret from him?

Staley: He was unaware of it because we made the decision quite by ourselves and we told him only after we had talked to a number of people about the matter and he didn't learn until well into last week what we had in mind.

Carleton: He has known for a week or so?

Staley: Oh he knew. I can't remember exactly when. Some time late last week. He may remember when I first indicated my feelings to him.

Carleton: So for the last week at least then, there have been six people and Mr Fraser plotting against Mr Snedden?

Staley: There has been no plotting against Mr Snedden. This whole thing has been simply an expression of a deep view which a number of us hold about the leadership of the party. Now we lost today and we accept that decision.

Carleton: Mr Gorton, how close did Mr Snedden go to getting tossed in your estimation?

Gorton: I think he had about ten or twelve votes against him. I can't tell but ten to fifteen at the outside. But I am very interested to learn that he knew about this towards the end of last week. Did he ever say, for instance, that he wasn't interested, that he wasn't going to be the candidate?

Staley: Yes he did.

Gorton: Well why didn't he say so publicly?

Staley: When I told him that what we wanted—and I stress *we*—a very great number of us on the back bench—wanted, he said 'Oh my God, don't talk to me about it. I can't bear to think of this'.

Gorton: I bet he did. But did he say that he wasn't going to stand?

Staley: That was his . . . as far as we were concerned there was no . . . we weren't interested, we knew that his position would be that he was not a candidate.

| | |
|---|---|
| Gorton: | Then if he wasn't a candidate, were you going to muck up the Liberal Party and everything without having any head of your own to stand. He said he wasn't going to stand and Peacock said he wasn't going to stand. Who were you going to have? Yourself? |
| Staley: | Of course not. |
| Gorton: | Well then, who were you going to have? |
| Staley: | We were going to have him. Because we were going to draft him . . . |

Malcolm Fraser, when himself interviewed the same night by Michael Schildberger, took the same line:

| | |
|---|---|
| Schildberger: | Mr Fraser, did you err in your judgement yesterday? |
| Fraser: | It wasn't a question of *my* judgement, because I didn't initiate, I did not encourage what occurred yesterday. It was a decision by other people and they expressed the view. You know, people in the party room have a right to express a view if they want to express a view, and are determined to do it. That was their decision. |
| Schildberger: | But you didn't stop them? |
| Fraser: | They told me it was their decision, and it wasn't a question of me stopping them or not stopping them. I took no part in what happened in the party room, and it was their decision, it was not my decision. |
| Schildberger: | Do you think there should be another challenge of any sort? |
| Fraser: | No, I don't. |
| Schildberger: | And you won't initiate one? |
| Fraser: | I did not initiate one, I will not initiate one, and that is a definite and absolute statement. |
| Schildberger: | Mr Fraser, do you believe you would be a better leader than Bill Snedden? |
| Fraser: | I think Bill Snedden is the leader. I support him completely, and the question just does not arise and it would be presumptuous of me to make that kind of decision, make that kind of judgement. |

This interview, the first given by Fraser about the challenge, is illuminating. The thrust of the political tactics he was to pursue over the next year as aspiring Liberal leader, and then aspiring Prime Minister, are contained in these answers. Fraser maintains that he had nothing to do with the challenge; that it was totally divorced from him. Over the next four months he would go to extraordinary lengths to avoid accusations of complicity in moves to overthrow Snedden.

The public image Fraser cultivated was that of a man who acknowledged the supremacy of the party. If the party made a decision on the leadership, he would abide by it. If the party decided that a new leader was needed and believed he was the man for the job, then he would accept that. But all the time he was anxious to adopt a lofty and aloof pose: while prepared to accept the party's decision, he did not want to appear to influence that decision through lobbying and intrigue.

There was, of course, a dichotomy between the public and private images. In public Fraser never gave the slightest lie to his declarations of loyalty. Here was a man who believed in the proprieties of politics, that the way things were done and seen by others was vitally important, that all actions must be justified in terms of either the party or the national interest, rather than the baser instincts of ambition and self-gratification.

But what happened in private was another matter. Fraser was told on the evening of the challenge that there was a minimum of 23 votes for him and possibly more. The coup had transformed the political equation in Australia. The Fraser supporters accepted their defeat but they were determined to continue their efforts to change the leadership. They made this very clear to both the press and other Liberals that same afternoon. The Liberal party was now a house divided against itself.

# 6

# THE ECONOMIC CRISIS

*It was a fair budget, a humane budget, a confident budget. It was a great Labor budget.*

Gough Whitlam, 21 September 1974

$F$ew governments in Australian history have squandered their public goodwill after re-election so rapidly and so recklessly as the Whitlam Labor government, fresh from its May 1974 triumph at the polls. In May the Prime Minister created a record by being the first Labor leader ever re-elected; in the ensuing months his government was to create other records, most notably the highest unemployment and inflation for 40 years and the most dramatic reversal in economic policy in the shortest possible time.

The period from June to November 1974 is probably unique in the history of decision-making in Australia as the government moved from an orthodox deflationary policy designed to limit inflation, to an unorthodox reflationary policy designed to overcome unemployment and revive the private sector. These five months saw the three main components of advice to the government—the Treasury; Labor's own economic advisers; and its senior Ministers, Whitlam, Cairns, Frank Crean, Clyde Cameron, Bill Hayden and Tom Uren—all proceeding from different diagnoses of the economic problem to different solutions, operating on different value systems. The landmarks along the way were the 7 June Premiers' conference, the 23 July mini-budget, the 17 September budget, and the 12 November mini-budget.[1]

In this period economic policy was transformed. The cost was huge in blood and votes. The Cabinet severed its relations with the federal

71

Treasury. Treasurer Frank Crean was subjected to a cruel political execution by Whitlam. Relations between the Cabinet and the caucus reached their nadir. Whitlam's prestige and control over his government was largely demolished for a period that culminated in newspaper stories that he was about to resign, and relations between senior figures in the Labor government became deeply embittered. It was in these months that Labor confronted for the first time the real dimensions of the economic problem.

This in itself is the greatest single condemnation of the political strategy of Opposition leader Bill Snedden, who considered his economic expertise his major asset. Snedden picked for an election probably the second last month in which Labor could have won. The government won in May 1974, would probably have won in June but would almost certainly have been defeated in any July election, with a greater margin of defeat ensuing for each succeeding month to the year's end. If Snedden had restrained himself in April he could have blocked the September budget, forced the election at the end of the year instead of the middle, and been Prime Minister before Christmas 1974.

These months, when the government came under heavy pressure, exposed a multitude of Labor's chief deficiencies. It demonstrated the inadequacy of Labor's 27-man Cabinet structure and proved it unworkable. It also revealed for the first time a depth of animosity between the new government and the public service establishment which previously had been expressed only in occasional outbursts. Finally, it took a heavy personal toll on Labor Ministers, whose political ideology was dedication to the full employment ethic. Their enforced departure from this goal ravaged both the conscience of individuals and that of the party. The Labor government never recovered from this time of upheaval after its re-election. It probably could have recovered but that would have required a long period of quiet and sustained government management, which Labor never indicated was in its character.

In the 1974 campaign Whitlam argued that inflation was being beaten; now he had to live up to his words. On Friday 24 May, just six days after the election, Whitlam met the secretary to the Treasury Sir Frederick Wheeler and other senior Treasury officials at Kirribilli House, Sydney. Wheeler told Whitlam at this meeting that the March quarter consumer price index (CPI) of 2.4 per cent, which Whitlam had exploited during the campaign to prove inflation was being beaten, was just a mirage. Whitlam had known this during the campaign. Before the election, Treasury had told him forcefully that the economy would deteriorate. This was one of the main reasons why Whitlam accepted Snedden's challenge for a May general election. Realising that the economy would deteriorate, Whitlam decided to take a plunge before it did, trying to win control of both Houses of Parliament.

It was on 24 May that Wheeler put to Whitlam the economic strategy of the 'short, sharp shock'—a prescription of tough and orthodox anti-inflationary measures to restrain demand inflation. Wheeler wanted to dramatise a new deflationary policy in a way that would break the circle of inflationary expectations. Treasury wanted a tight money policy, a tough spending approach at the impending Premiers' conference, and an abandonment of the government's wage indexation plans, which Treasury believed would only worsen cost–push inflation.

The next day, 25 May, Ministers and officials met at Kirribilli House to formulate the Premiers' conference strategy. They were Whitlam, Cairns, Crean, Social Security Minister Bill Hayden, and Defence Minister Lance Barnard, who was still deputy Prime Minister. Officials included Wheeler, his deputy John Stone, Reserve Bank governor Sir John Phillips, and Professor Fred Gruen, an economic adviser to the Prime Minister's Department. This meeting confirmed the Treasury line as government policy.

At this stage Whitlam's two private economic advisers, Gruen and Dr H C 'Nugget' Coombs, supported the Treasury–Reserve Bank view. This meeting drew up a draconian policy package for the 7 June Premiers' conference, designed to impose severe restraint on the public sector. In order to show the bona fides of the government, it was decided to announce cutbacks in federal spending as a prelude to dishing out the same medicine to the Premiers.

Whitlam would announce a one per cent ceiling on the increase in the Commonwealth public service, abolition of the $28 million petrol price subsidy scheme, increased postal and telephone charges, reduced spending on airports and a cut in road grants. This amounted to an overall reduction of $240 million in federal spending. As a corollary to this, the states would receive no extra cash in additional revenue assistance during the 1974–75 year. Although when the Premiers came to Canberra in early June they wanted an extra $200 million from the federal government to balance their budgets, they got nothing. The squeeze was on.

The Prime Minister's 7 June speech at the Premiers' conference represented the high water mark of Treasury influence in the Labor government. Whitlam was full of vigour after his re-election and knew he had a mandate for action to curb inflation. The Prime Minister naturally turned to the Treasury for advice and they gave it forcefully and without real opposition from other areas within the government. Whitlam, reading a speech drafted by Treasury, said inflation was being fanned by a combination of excessive demand and excessive cost increases. 'Inflation must be curbed. The government is determined to curb it,' he told the Premiers. His speech reflected the Treasury 'short, sharp shock', which had as its chief aim the breaking of the inflationary spiral through a fiscal and monetary squeeze which would be deliberately dramatised. Whitlam said the public sector was trying to increase its spending faster than the availability of resources would permit. Foreshadowing a monetary policy characterised by high interest rates, Whitlam said the government adopted this course not from choice but in order to curb excessive private spending and to limit demand.

In a remarkable and prophetic section of the speech, which went almost unnoticed, his words revealed exactly what the Treasury was aiming at:

> It has for some time been easy to borrow money, invest in real assets such as property, and emerge with a handsome profit arising not from productive efforts but from inflation. When, as we will, we hear of some such ventures going badly wrong in the period ahead, we will know that the risk element has been reintroduced into such forms of investment.

Four months later came the spectacular financial crashes in the property market. While the Treasury may not have envisaged company crashes on this scale, it certainly expected that they would occur when its policy started to bite.

On 7 June the Premiers were not taken by surprise. On Monday 26 May the *Australian Financial Review* carried a page one story by Robert Haupt detailing the decisions reached over the weekend and the new thrust of policy for the Premiers' conference. Whitlam was furious and blamed John Stone for the leak. He even told Wheeler that Stone was not to attend any more meetings, but eventually modified this response. Stone himself was one of the chief originators and most forceful advocates of the Treasury line; he knew that it would result in a substantial increase in unemployment but believed that this was justified. Stone's argument was that in the long run unemployment could always be curbed, that governments knew how to rectify large-scale unemployment. He pointed out that, once inflation got over 20 per cent, the situation was entirely different—there was no certainty that governments could deal with this problem.

Throughout June and into early July the Treasury strategy prevailed. But the first signs of opposition towards it emerged in powerful areas of the Labor government, signalling a looming battle. The Treasury pursued its 'short, sharp shock' strategy and began to prepare the ground for another draconian economic package which would reinforce the 7 June punch. But outside the Treasury concern developed about the latest trend in economic indicators.

In June unemployment showed a massive increase in seasonally adjusted terms from 86,300 to 103,000. At the end of June the first signs of a downturn in the housing industry appeared and Tom Uren was notified by his department. A number of Labor Ministers became worried at Treasury's preoccupation with demand inflation when the latest indicators suggested it was on the wane. Although the government was unaware, there had been a severe contraction in the money supply, which was to have a catastrophic effect on the corporate sector. Both Treasury and the Reserve Bank had miscalculated the credit squeeze they were applying. The economic policy consensus began to disintegrate.

Whitlam believed it was impossible to conduct a review of the economy in the context of a 27-man Cabinet. He preferred a smaller, more efficient decision-making unit. Although there was an economic committee of Cabinet, Whitlam preferred to keep a tighter control over Ministers who attended economic policy talks. This was the origin of the 'kitchen Cabinet' which met on several occasions in mid-1974, usually at the Lodge, to discuss economic options. The 'kitchen Cabinet' which met at Whitlam's home on Monday 1 July comprised Whitlam, the new deputy Prime Minister Cairns, Crean, Hayden and the Labour Minister Clyde Cameron, a new addition to the group. A number of officials were also present including Wheeler, Stone, Coombs, Gruen and Brian Brogan, who was Cairns' economic adviser.

The Treasury emphasised the need to continue the credit squeeze and it was at this meeting that it pushed for a new mini-budget along tough and orthodox anti-inflationary lines seeking increases in indirect taxes and cutbacks in government programs. The Treasury warned that this could create unemployment ranging between 2.5 to 3 per cent or 180,000 jobless, another sign that it had underestimated the extent of the downturn which had already occurred. Clyde Cameron disagreed and said that unemployment was likely to go to this level anyway. Coombs generally supported the Treasury policies with one important proviso—the need to have employment support programs ready to absorb those people who lost their jobs as a result of the new measures. Both Cairns and Cameron held strong reservations about the Treasury recommendations. Cameron was opposed to them outright while Cairns expressed doubts. Both wanted an easing of the credit squeeze.

Cameron soon emerged as the most vocal and unremitting critic of the Treasury. He quickly drafted a set of economic proposals himself as an alternative to the Treasury line. These were contained in a letter Cameron wrote to Frank Crean in which he suggested a nine point program—the reintroduction of a federal tax upon unimproved land values of non-rural properties in excess of $100,000 value; a special tax on people owning more than a place of residence and one vacant block of land; a capital gains tax; adjustment of tax scales to assist low and middle income groups; re-introduction of import licensing; the elimination of sales tax on essential items; a review of the pricing arrangements of foreign-owned multinational corporations as well as Australian monopolies; and a tax on vacant office space. Cameron's proposals were thrown into the economic debate taking place in early July.

This was an important period, in which policy was in a state of flux and the first signs of shifting alliances and newly emerging positions began to occur. Cameron used all his political skill to discredit the Treasury; he started to release the unemployment figures every fortnight, leaked to the gallery first, and then issued in their monthly official form. Both Uren's and Hayden's staff prepared economic position papers for them indicating that the chief weakness in the Treasury line was its obsessive concern about demand when demand appeared to be falling off. This was the origin of the deep suspicions towards the Treasury which were harboured by senior Ministers in this period.

Brogan and Spigelman, Whitlam's private secretary, felt that behind its policy of reducing demand inflation by cutting spending, the Treasury was also aiming to reduce cost inflation by creating unemployment. Most of Treasury rhetoric centred on the first proposal yet it was clear that demand inflation was rapidly diminishing as an economic problem. Nothing was more calculated to arouse the hostility of elements within the Labor government than the suspicion that Treasury wanted to use unemployment as the instrument by which it could dampen wage increases.

It was in early July that the government began drafting plans for a new policy of wage restraint designed to curb cost pressures and implemented by applying in reverse the 'pacesetter' principle which it had established in the public service. Draft legislation was prepared that would apply a moratorium on public service wage increases through amendments to existing Acts. This proposal was tantamount to a wage freeze in the public sector and the idea was to implement this through legislative means and establish the basis by which wage increases would have to be scaled down in the private sector as well. This proposal was considered in conjunction with a rejection of the recommendations from the remuneration tribunal for pay rises of $5500 for all federal parliamentarians.

The 'kitchen Cabinet' met at the Prime Minister's Lodge on 15 July, a fortnight after its previous meeting. The same Ministers and officials were present. The Treasury pushed for an immediate mini-budget as the latest instalment of the 'short, sharp shock' and it put forward an economic package that would make any politician wobble at the knees.

This package subsequently went to a meeting of the full Cabinet on 22 July, one of the most vital Cabinet meetings of the Whitlam era. The proposals, which were discussed on the night of 15 July without any final conclusion, involved an increase in income tax ranging from one to six per cent on a sliding scale for incomes over $6000 a year; an increase in petrol excise by ten cents; increases in excise on tobacco and spirits; increases in postal and telephone charges; deferment of moves to abolish the means test on pensions; a cut in the immigration program; and deferment of the child care program. At the previous meeting Wheeler and Stone had told Ministers that the resulting unemployment would reach about 180,000. Gruen and Coombs supported the Treasury push although they queried the details. Cairns was relatively quiet and Whitlam had the impression his deputy agreed with the thrust. Hayden and Cameron in particular were unhappy with the package.

On 19 July Whitlam became more committed to the Treasury prescription with the release of the June quarter CPI showing a price rise of 4.1 per cent giving an annual inflation rate of 14.4 per cent. Crean said the prices outlook was very worrying and the government would not recoil from taking whatever further steps were necessary to curb inflation. The Liberal leader Bill Snedden claimed that Australia would have a 20 per cent inflation rate by the year's end.

On Saturday 20 July, Whitlam and senior Treasury officers Wheeler, Stone, and Bill Cole met at Kirribilli House to discuss the economic package. It was at this meeting that Whitlam asked irritably where Crean was and, when told that the Treasurer was in his car driving between Melbourne and Canberra, complained: 'Anyone would think this is a bloody banana republic.' The plan was that the Prime Minister himself, not the Treasurer, would announce the mini-budget to the nation to dramatise the urgency of the situation. Treasury was much in favour of this course.

The decisive Cabinet meeting lasted through the day and into the night of 22 July. Whitlam entered the meeting determined to push the tough Treasury line through the Cabinet. He was in a 'crashing through' mood. He knew the measures would be resented by the party and unpopular within the community but Whitlam believed that this was the time to grasp the nettle, that if Labor was not prepared to accept the tough option just after its success at the polls then it certainly would not do so later as the economy deteriorated even further. But, despite everything, Frank Crean was not prepared to fight for his department's submission, having either no heart in it or no stomach for the Cabinet battle.

As the Cabinet meeting continued, Whitlam found he was fighting a lone hand. Crean did not support the Treasury submission. Cairns said little to support it as the balance of Cabinet turned against it. Cameron tried to destroy it. Hayden argued that it would be the wrong remedy for the economy and was based on a faulty diagnosis. The bulk of the Cabinet, the Ministers who had not been privy to earlier talks, were alarmed at the political ramifications of the package and were not prepared to accept that it was the only option, the basis of Whitlam's argument.

Cabinet eventually tore the heart out of the Treasury submission by rejecting the income tax increases, the petrol excise rise, and reluctantly went along with the rest of the submission which paid for the biggest ever pension rise—up to $6 a week—which Hayden successfully carried through the Cabinet.

Whitlam was incensed and enraged, furious at his own failure to carry his Cabinet and contemptuous of what he regarded as his Cabinet's resort to expediency and its failure to face up to the long-range problems of government and economic management. Frustrated and beaten, the Prime Minister would have nothing to do with the economic package. He had no intention of reading the wreckage and left it to Crean. Whitlam was humiliated; a Prime Minister who had lost control of his Cabinet.

But the debate in the party room over the remnants of the package, on the evening of 23 July, showed that the backbench was even more distant from the Prime Minister than the Cabinet. A party room revolt just a few minutes before Crean was to deliver the speech nearly cut it in half once again. Only a vigorous last-ditch effort by Whitlam prevented a deeper humiliation at the hands of his party.

At 8 p.m. Crean stood up in Parliament and subjected himself to public ridicule by economic analysts who quickly realised that the rhetoric of his speech did not match its substance. While the 'guts' had been cut out of the Treasury submission, the actual text of the speech was the same as that drafted for the original measures. In short, Crean found himself echoing threatening warnings which the government itself no longer believed.

There were three conclusions of vast political significance from the fiasco of the July mini-budget. The first and most relevant in the economic context, was that Treasury had been completely eclipsed. It had sustained a major defeat from which it would take at least twelve months to recover, and then only partially. This defeat meant that the government had no economic policy; the July mini-budget was testimony to this. A policy vacuum was now created and the search for a new economic strategy began.

The second result was that the Prime Minister decided to axe Frank Crean as Treasurer. Whitlam had appointed Crean after Labor came into office acknowledging that he had been the party's economic spokesman in Opposition. But he had never been happy with the Treasurer. Crean never functioned in Cabinet in the fashion expected of a Treasurer, who traditionally had a vested interest in every single Cabinet submission involving spending of monies. Treasurers were usually resented by their fellow Ministers because, if they did their job properly, they were invariably 'axe' men. Crean was not cast in this mould. Most people in the Labor government got on with 'friendly Frank', who was most remembered for his statement to Parliament that Treasury advisers should be 'on tap' but not 'on top'.

Some of Whitlam's staff believed that Crean's weakness was the most fundamental problem with the Labor government. The economic decisions taken in 1973, particularly Labor's 1973–74 budget—its first—had sowed the seeds of disaster for the government by increasing spending without increasing taxes. This just revealed, in retrospect, how much the government needed a strong man in the Treasury. The events of July 1974 showed that they had precisely the opposite. In the Cabinet room on 22 July Whitlam, not Crean, was arguing the Treasury brief. The Prime Minister was no longer prepared to tolerate this state of affairs.

The third consequence of the July debacle was the profound impact it had on the Prime Minister. Whitlam's response to his defeat provides an illuminating insight into his character and techniques as a leader. The Prime Minister was not literate in economic matters. He had an understanding of economics but he rarely thought in economic terms and he never relished dealing with economics the way he dealt with other policy areas like foreign affairs, social welfare, legal issues or urban affairs. This created particular problems for Whitlam, who was a headstrong politician by instinct and whose great political strength was his fervent espousal of policies in which he believed, and his capacity to translate them into actualities. When it came to economics, Whitlam had to accept the advice of others. Unlike Hayden, who could meet his advisers on equal ground and wrestle with them in an intellectual sense over the economy, Whitlam was forced to trust his advisers. He seized the Treasury line after the election and fought for it with all the political strength he had. But when the battle was lost he had nowhere to go.

Whitlam took very little part in the search for a new economic strategy which occupied the mid-year. He became deeply introverted, not just on economic matters but on a whole range of subjects. One has only to look at the number of media interviews he gave during the mid-year period to realise that the Prime Minister was in introspective mode. Some people said he was sulking; others said he did not want to intervene in the economic debate until he had a policy to espouse. But whatever the reason, Whitlam retreated to the Lodge for many weeks and his government was left without strong leadership in a rudderless condition shifting from crisis to crisis, being discredited each day. Whitlam took out his wrath on both Crean and Hayden for failing to support him. Only much later, towards the end of the year, did he admit that the Treasury line mid-year had been flawed.

After the defeat of the Treasury line, the government abandoned its tentative plans for a freeze on public service pay rises; indeed it had no credibility to implement such a policy after the Cabinet had voted to accept the parliamentary pay rise in the teeth of Whitlam's opposition. The caucus endorsed this decision, once again despite Whitlam's every effort.

Throughout August Cairns and Hayden, together with their advisers, held a number of talks with academic economists, union leaders and other experts to determine the new direction of government policy. Hayden was concerned by the level of business confidence, which had slumped as a result of falling profits and rising costs. He believed that if the high rate of inflation continued then businesses would collapse. The tight money squeeze was only exacerbating the situation and there should be an easing of the money supply together with a program that would ensure wage restraint from the trade unions. Cairns and Brogan were pursuing a similar line.

Cairns told Whitlam that the Reserve Bank and Treasury were squeezing the economy too severely and that the tight money policy, combined with the effects of the 25 per cent tariff cut, was generating extensive unemployment. 'We're behaving like a kamikaze squad,' Cairns warned. He claimed the credit squeeze was too severe and must be eased. On Whitlam's advice, Cairns saw Phillips, the Reserve Bank governor, and asked him to ease credit.

The deputy Prime Minister was given full responsibility for handling the pre-budget talks with industry groups as a result of a decision by Whitlam. Cairns believed there was a surprising consensus among trade unions, manufacturers and the corporate sector. He felt that they opposed a tough budget, wanted the credit squeeze eased and would support a form of wage indexation.

The influence of Cairns was enhanced by a general economic paper written by Brian Brogan, his main aide. This paper was presented to a meeting of the caucus economic committee on 12 August. The meeting, which comprised about 30 members of caucus including several Ministers, was attended by Treasury officials as well as Coombs, Gruen and Brogan. Its intention was to allow the parliamentary party access to the broad parameters being developed as a prelude to the budget Cabinet talks.

This meeting examined two broad options which were available to the government when formulating its 1974–75 budget. One was similar to the Treasury line, which depended on the deflationary shock of higher taxes and cuts in spending to control inflation.

The other was the strategy outlined in the Cairns document presented to the meeting by Brogan, which argued that cost pressures and not demand were responsible for inflation and that a new economic package was needed to rectify this problem. Cairns said the budget should aim at a neutral to slight surplus, that it should restructure the tax scales to ease taxes at lower levels and increase them at higher levels. He supported wage indexation and the denial of extra pay rises sought by unions beyond cost of living adjustments. The Prices Justification Tribunal should not allow price increases based on excessive wage rises. Indirect taxes should be cut to lower the CPI. There should be a capital gains tax as well as a property tax so that the taxation burden would be shifted more to those who derived wealth from capital assets. Cairns also suggested the possibility of a new penalty tax on incomes which increased beyond a certain norm—he mentioned cost of living increases plus three or four per cent for productivity. He also wanted bank lending to be selective and channelled into housing and other essential areas.

These proposals had been distilled from the talks Cairns had conducted over the previous three weeks. He had been particularly impressed during discussions at the Melbourne Institute of Applied Economic Research by arguments put by Professor Ronald Henderson that a world recession was threatening. Henderson advocated penalty taxes on rising incomes and wage indexation. Professor Harcourt from Adelaide University had taken a similar line in support of a tough stand against excessive wage rises. Brogan supported using the tax system in an effort to restrain wage rises and this philosophy was at the core of Cairns' paper. The Treasury opposed manipulating the tax system in an effort to restrain wages.

So where was Whitlam? The Prime Minister was still leaving the development of an economic policy to his other Ministers. Cairns himself was enjoying the task. From the day he was elected deputy Prime Minister, he announced that he would take a greater interest in economic affairs. Ever since the July mini-budget, Cairns was in an unusual position where he made the running on the economy, relied on academic experts and devoted more of his public pronouncements to the economy. Never a good administrator and never a master of detail, Cairns was not burdened with the daily grind of work that faced the Treasurer Frank Crean. The portfolio of Overseas Trade allowed Cairns the time to turn his mind towards the debate over general economic strategy. By this stage Frank Crean had been relegated to obscurity.

The upshot, after a day of debate by the caucus economic committee on 12 August, was that the Cairns paper was fully endorsed as defining budget parameters. Crean voted for the package although it was substantially different from the Treasury case. At this stage the Treasury was arguing for a big budget surplus to curb demand as well as opposing wage indexation. Hostility within the party to Treasury was now so great that a number of caucus members attempted to move motions at this meeting specifically condemning the Treasury but these were dropped in favour of the definition of new policies. Ministers and members were unanimous in their rejection of efforts to curb inflation by creating unemployment.

The government was propelled in the Cairns direction by the gradual release of economic indicators suggesting that a big private investment slump combined with extensive cost increases was eroding the strength of the private sector. The day before the caucus meeting, the July unemployment figures were released. In seasonally adjusted terms the number of jobless rose 17,300 the previous month, taking the unemployment figure to 1.7 per cent of the work force. The demand for labour fell sharply and in seasonally adjusted terms vacancies fell by 21 per cent, showing the signs of an extensive slump. In the light of these figures there was no way the Labor Cabinet or caucus would accept a tough budget along the lines sought by Treasury.

The ideas articulated by Cairns laid the ground for the new economic policy prescriptions which the government would embrace in its budget. Cairns was assuming the role of influence which he publicly had preordained for himself two months previously on becoming deputy Prime Minister. In fact, he was filling a vacuum. By this stage Whitlam's failure to attend either the caucus economic committee or the pre-budget talks with industry leaders, had set the ever-receptive rumour mills of the national capital buzzing busily. The high profile of his deputy and the deterioration in the economy were leading a number of people to question Whitlam's leadership.

On 22 August the Sydney *Sun* hit the streets with banner headlines 'Whitlam to Quit Report'. This story, which was completely false, reflected the extent to which confusion within the ranks of the Labor government had permeated the community. Sydney was filled with rumours that morning about Whitlam's resignation. The editor of the *Daily Mirror* was stunned when a television network rang him asking if they could come out to film the historic edition being run off the presses!

Whitlam even joked about the story. But it was really no joke. There was something fundamentally wrong with the communications network in a government when such rumours could assume so wide a currency. The upshot was that a number of senior gallery journalists, anxious to improve their contact with the Prime Minister, sought unsuccessfully for regular background briefings. Journalists would see the Prime Minister occasionally but Whitlam was uncommunicative during this period to such an extent that the government was badly damaged.

Another major strand of economic policy being developed at this time was wages policy. Clyde Cameron had been fashioning an incomes policy since mid-1973 when his running battles over public service pay policy and criticism of the 'fat cats' became well-known. As early as December 1973 Cameron had proposed indexation of wages as a means of limiting the number of industrial disputes and achieving a more predictable system of salary increases, but indexation now assumed a new significance for the government in view of its belief that excessive cost pressures were the major factor in fuelling inflation and depressing the private sector. Indexation became inexorably linked with wage restraint. But this connection was not articulated in its strongest form until more than 12 months later when Senator Jim McClelland became Labour Minister.

One of the most significant changes in the distribution of power in the Labor government was the shifting of responsibility for preparing national wage case submissions from the Treasury to the Labour Department, Clyde Cameron's portfolio. On 29 July Cabinet decided to support indexation, in a major win for Cameron against Treasury. By this stage Whitlam, Hayden and Cairns all supported cost of living adjustments. The Cabinet agreed to indexation in the form of percentage increases to the minimum wage. This flat sum would then be applied to all other wages. But this was just the government's negotiating position and it was, in fact, prepared to accept indexation up to the average wage, at that time $119 a week.

The government would argue this case at the conference on wage fixing called by the president of the Arbitration Commission Mr Justice Moore. The government's wage package involved the commission's acceptance of quarterly adjustments, the formation of a tripartite body to compile a new index for adjustment, and a national conference each year to determine what variations in award wages were needed to reflect changes in productivity. Clyde Cameron said after the Cabinet meeting that no Minister had opposed indexation and that the government's aim was to eliminate the practice whereby unions sought wage rises in anticipation of future price increases. But Cameron was careful to say that in his opinion indexation was not necessarily anti-inflationary.

Both Spigelman and Brogan believed that the government needed to reach an accommodation with the unions to ensure that a structure was created for wage restraint on the basis of cooperation and not confrontation. Although there was no formal agreement or arrangement between the government and the unions, there was certainly an informal understanding between the ACTU president Bob Hawke and the government over the shape of the 1974–75 budget. In the week after the budget Cabinet meetings, Cairns briefed Hawke on the budget strategy. One of its foundations was the extensive tax cuts which were designed as a 'carrot' for wage restraint. The ACTU executive met in late August after the budget Cabinet and called for policies involving a reduction in direct and indirect taxes, wage indexation, strengthening of the Prices Justification Tribunal, and an easing of interest rates and pension increases—the directions of the coming budget.

On Monday 19 August federal Cabinet began its week of budget deliberations but the day was marked by bitterness directed towards the Treasury submission. The Treasury proposed cuts in government spending of $600 million and an increase in personal income tax of the order of $400 million resulting in a total withdrawal from the economy of $1000 million. The Treasury submission also referred to an overall budget surplus of $300 million, but this was where its document was potentially ambiguous. It was not clear to many Ministers whether this slight surplus was after or before the spending cuts and tax increases proposed by Treasury. Most of the Cabinet assumed that the surplus was after these measures had been taken into account.

During a break in the Cabinet meeting Uren's advisers, led by an economist from his department, Dr Mike Keating, calculated that the surplus after the fiscal recommendations would not be $300 million but $1300 million instead. That is, almost the entire Cabinet had misunderstood the extent of the budget surplus being proposed by the Treasury as a result of its submission. The Cabinet was absolutely incensed. Many Ministers believed that while the Treasury did not lie in its submission, it did seek to mislead the government and make the Cabinet more favourably disposed to its proposals than it would otherwise have been. This concern was superimposed on the dismay felt by most senior Ministers, including Whitlam, at the Treasury's failure to alter its economic line and cooperate with the government within the broad economic parameters defined by the Labor Cabinet. Treasury remained unmoved and unshakeable in its attitude.

The argument over the Treasury submission on the first day of budget Cabinet meant that Treasury would inevitably be cut off and isolated in the formulation of the budget strategy. Relations between the government and the Treasury reached a near breakdown. The fact that such a situation had arisen was testimony as much to poor ministerial direction as it was to Treasury intransigence. There was no Minister who made an effort with the Treasury and was firm enough to enlist its assistance for the general policy direction accepted by the government.

This had one important consequence in the drafting of the budget. There was virtually no restraint on government outlays, which were estimated to increase by 32 per cent with very big rises in education spending of up to 78 per cent, health 30 per cent, social security and welfare 38 per cent, cities spending 173 per cent, culture and recreation 44 per cent—to name only the big areas of increase. Overall the budget followed the Cairns parameters. Announcing it on the evening of 17 September Crean said: 'Crucial as the fight against inflation is, it cannot be made the sole objective of government policy. This government is committed to the program of social reform to improve the position of the less privileged groups in our society and to maintain employment opportunities.'

The government restructured tax scales to generate tax reductions of $430 million for low and middle income earners up to $10,500 a year. It also introduced a new series of taxes to slug the rich, including a capital gains tax, a surcharge on property income and the abolition of 'perks' for businessmen. The concessional deduction for education expenses was reduced from $400 to $150 for any one student. The key elements of the budget strategy were to secure the support of the trade union movement for wage restraint thereby curbing inflation. The government maintained its spending programs and increased the chief ones, tried to redistribute the tax burden, and moved to expand the public sector at the expense of the private sector.

As soon as the budget strategy was sealed, Whitlam re-emerged from his cocoon. He immediately set out to 'sell' it in his characteristic style. In major speeches during late August and throughout September Whitlam appealed to employers and unions to restrain wage and price demands. 'Quite bluntly, the Australian economy in 1974 just cannot absorb wage and salary increases of 20 per cent and 30 per cent without large increases in prices,' Whitlam said on 26 August at the end of the budget Cabinet week. 'Now this is a matter of involving all of us. It cannot be shrugged off as a problem for the government alone. We cannot solve this problem single-handed. We cannot solve it without cooperation and commonsense.' Whitlam embraced the new economic line of his government, in whose formulation he had acquiesced.

Labor's commissioned agency, ANOP, produced a poll on 7 September of the major east coast urban areas from Geelong to Brisbane, Labor's traditional strength, which assessed the government at 45 per cent and the Opposition at 51 per cent, a sharp turnabout since the May election result. On these figures Labor would be thoroughly thrashed in an election. The upheavals in the government and the deteriorating economic climate had transformed Labor's position.

But the budget, which had become known as the 'Cairns' budget, was put under review within weeks of its delivery. This was prompted by a number of factors. The government was alarmed at the extent of the credit squeeze, which assumed the proportions of a major political backlash when over-extended building and property developers suffered severe liquidity problems. On 19 August one of Australia's biggest building groups, Mainline Corporation, called in a receiver and threw into doubt over $300 million worth of building projects throughout Australia. It was just one of a series of developers in dire financial trouble. Many of these companies approached the federal government, both the Treasury and the Department of Urban and Regional Development, in an effort to alleviate their problems. The other big company crash was that of Cambridge Credit not long afterwards. In September the government moved swiftly to expand the money supply as a result of the severe contractions in the previous months. It was in this context that the question of devaluation of the dollar was raised.

On 17 September a large group met at the Prime Minister's Lodge to discuss a possible devaluation. The meeting comprised Whitlam, Cairns, Crean, senior Treasury officers, Austin Holmes from the Priorities Review Staff, Brogan, Gruen, Spigelman, John Taylor from the Prime Minister's Department, Harold Knight from the Reserve Bank, and John Menadue, whose appointment as the new head of the Prime Minister's Department had recently been announced.

Cairns favoured a devaluation based on advice from Brogan and Holmes and his argument reflected the concerns of the union movement about unemployment in import competing industries and the danger this presented to government–union cooperation. Holmes believed that without a devaluation the easing of the credit squeeze would merely drain off money into import spending. But the Treasury, with the support of Gruen, argued that all these points missed the main question which was still that of controlling inflation. The Treasury's view was still following a consistent pattern from earlier in the year. It opposed devaluation because it would only fan inflation.

However the strongest argument Whitlam's advisers exploited came from the Reserve Bank, an opinion not voiced at this 17 September meeting but held nonetheless. The bank believed that a devaluation was inevitable. This argument was not put strongly at the meeting, reflecting the traditional axis of support between Treasury and the Reserve Bank.

When the Lodge meeting broke up Taylor, Brogan and Spigelman went back to Spigelman's house. Menadue joined them briefly but then left. They were all upset at the outcome of the meeting and its failure to support devaluation. But a few days later Taylor and Brogan raised the issue with Whitlam when they accidentally bumped into him outside his office. 'Can we see you for a moment,' Brogan said suddenly. They went to Whitlam's office, where they were joined by Spigelman and revived the arguments in favour of devaluation. They were successful.

In the afternoon of Tuesday 24 September Whitlam called a snap meeting of senior Ministers which agreed on a 12 per cent devaluation of the dollar. News of the devaluation was leaked in Parliament House that night and some papers carried it as their front page story on 25 September. The media was aware of the decision before the London market closed.

Whitlam announced the devaluation as a triumph. It would boost the mining, farming and manufacturing sector and in particular curb import competition for the clothing, footwear and electrical industries. It would boost both rural and mining returns from overseas exports.

Bob Hawke welcomed the devaluation saying it would help the employment position, assist local industry and would not be inflationary. One of the side benefits of devaluation in Whitlam's mind was that it would relieve pressure on the government to restore higher tariffs. Whitlam espoused the low tariff economic approach championed by the chairman of the Industries Assistance Commission, Alf Rattigan, and on more than one occasion called himself a 'Rattigan man'. Whitlam had spearheaded the 25 per cent tariff cut in 1973 and was committed as a matter of principle to achieving a lower tariff structure in the long term.

The biggest casualty of this period of economic decision-making was Frank Crean; but while he fell towards the end, he was doomed from the start. From the time of the May 1974 election campaign Whitlam had been unimpressed with Crean, particularly on the hustings. Both Whitlam and Spigelman noticed how effective Cairns was during the campaign, particularly talking about the economy. The first indication Whitlam gave that he would remove Crean was in late June 1974 at the Lakeside Hotel in Canberra, at a luncheon arranged by the press gallery to farewell the senior correspondent from the *Age*, Allan Barnes. As he relaxed over a few drinks the Prime Minister gave a clear indication to both Barnes and his successor, John Jost, that Crean would go. From the time of the 22 July mini-budget Cabinet meeting, Whitlam was resolute in this view.

Jim Cairns adopted a high profile on the economy and was the most prominent advocate of a new budget strategy. Whitlam had an ambivalent attitude towards Cairns. He endorsed everything Cairns was saying about the future direction of economic policy, even though as Prime Minister he was not playing a direct role in the formulation of that policy. But at the same time Whitlam was irritated at the limelight Cairns was grabbing and the extent to which he was being projected as the architect of the new economic strategy. Two ideas fused in Whitlam's mind. He had already decided to push Crean out of Treasury. If Cairns wanted to do the talking on economics, then Whitlam reasoned that he should have the responsibility for economics. He decided to make Cairns Treasurer and put the pressure on him.

In late October Whitlam put his plans into operation. He told Cairns that he wanted to appoint him Treasurer. The deputy Prime Minister's initial response was to say he didn't want the job. But Whitlam was adamant. He even introduced Cairns to overseas visitors as 'Australia's next Treasurer'. Cairns was ambivalent but told senior officials in the Trade Department that he would be going. Whitlam broached the question with Crean and after a long discussion believed that he had talked Crean into accepting not just a move from the Treasury but retirement into the position of chairman of the Commonwealth Banking Corporation.

Whitlam was so anxious to remove Crean that he was prepared to have a by-election for the Treasurer's seat of Melbourne Ports, a reasonably safe Labor seat, but a risky move. It would have been difficult to hold. Whitlam believed that Crean would not accept any other portfolio apart from Treasury. Some of Crean's strongest supporters said he should resign to the backbench if Whitlam tried to move him and then gain re-election to the ministry through a party room vote.

Whitlam discussed his by-election plans with the Victorian Labor leader Clyde Holding and with the ALP president Bob Hawke, the man he wanted to contest the seat for the government. Whitlam asked the Minister for Manufacturing Industry, Kep Enderby, if he would move to the Overseas Trade portfolio which Cairns was leaving. He planned to shift the special Minister of State Lionel Bowen into the Manufacturing Industry slot.

From mid-October onwards rumours began to circulate about Crean's removal. At a press conference on 22 October Whitlam was asked: 'Is there any possibility of changes to your ministry in the near future in the light of the current economic problems? In particular, have you given any consideration to using Mr Crean's considerable talents in another portfolio?' Whitlam replied: 'I would want to discuss this with the Governor-General before I mentioned it in these wider circumstances.' A little later in the press conference Whitlam said that his answer had been 'purely facetious'. In fact, Whitlam was deadly serious.

However his plans were foiled in two ways. Firstly, Hawke decided he would not contest a Melbourne Ports by-election and told Whitlam this at Kirribilli House towards the end of October. Even more damaging for Whitlam was the leaking to the press of the story that Crean was about to be removed. Questioned on 1 November, the day the stories first appeared, Cairns denied that Crean was to be sacked and said he had not been offered the Treasury. Cairns then left on an overseas trip, a factor which was absolutely crucial to the subsequent course of events.

Whitlam was angry that his plans had come unstuck and that Hawke would not run. But he was determined to press ahead. It was here that Cairns' absence became important. Once the story was leaked, it became imperative for Whitlam to execute his plans. But this was impossible because the man he wanted to make the new Treasurer was out of Australia and arrangements had not been finalised with Crean. At this time Crean began to dig in and told Whitlam he would not accept the bank job and did not wish to leave politics. Whitlam's ministerial switch was in chaos.

The Opposition moved swiftly to exploit the position and began to probe Whitlam at Question Time on the floor of Parliament, asking him whether he had confidence in his Treasurer and challenging him to deny the strong reports that Crean would be moved from Treasury. To the ever-growing concern of the government backbench, Whitlam never once denied the stories or scotched the speculation. He said repeatedly that he would not respond to Opposition invitations to declare his support for his own Ministers. If he did this once he would be doing it all the time, Whitlam declared. Snedden, in a bad tactical mistake, started to ask Whitlam about the future of other Ministers, instead of concentrating his attack on Crean. During this period in early November the Victorian ALP came out strongly supporting Crean and so did Bob Hawke.

Whitlam was caught in a political dilemma. If he had confirmed Crean in his position, he would have settled the political controversy very quickly. But Whitlam saw this as bowing to outside pressure and abandoning his own judgement. Alternatively, while he did nothing and kept his options open, the issue became more explosive within the party and more damaging to the government. In retrospect it is clear that Whitlam never deviated from his plan to remove Crean no matter what the obstacles or who complained.

The situation was a political dream for the Opposition, even though it took some time to realise this. Eventually the Opposition gave notice of motion of no confidence in the Treasurer. This meant Whitlam was put squarely on the spot. In an unprecedented decision the Prime Minister refused to bring the motion on for debate, thereby avoiding having to declare his attitude towards Crean. Snedden gave notice of his motion on Tuesday 12 November and Whitlam avoided it the next day. There had been four such motions moved against individual Ministers or the Speaker of the House since 1964. Each one of them had been brought on for debate by the government the following day. 'Are they throwing him to the wolves or aren't they?' Snedden asked at his press conference called to attack the government on the issue. 'Will they state their confidence in him or won't they?'

This was too much for the caucus. The next day, 14 November, a five-man caucus delegation saw Whitlam in his office for more than an hour to tell him the dominant feeling of the party was that Crean should stay Treasurer. Some members were threatening to move a spill of all ministerial posts if Whitlam tried to shift Crean. The delegation was deliberately chosen to represent a cross-section of opinion from all states. It comprised Mick Young, Ted Innes, John Coates, Dick Klugman and Vince Martin. Whitlam gave no guarantee to the delegation and no indication of his plans. The intention of Crean's supporters was to let Whitlam know he would have a fight on his hands if he tried to move the Treasurer. They should have realised that Whitlam could never be intimidated.

When Cairns returned from overseas to find a major political controversy within the party, his initial reluctance to take Treasury was redoubled. But Whitlam told Cairns that the move would be going ahead. After Cabinet broke on Thursday 21 November Whitlam, Cairns and Crean stayed behind and discussed the situation. Cairns then left and Whitlam and Crean talked together privately. The Prime Minister simply told Cairns that Crean was being moved from Treasury and that if he did not accept the portfolio then it would be offered to Bowen. So Cairns accepted. After a long discussion with an unhappy Frank Crean, Whitlam announced that Cairns and Crean were swapping jobs.

Crean remained confident to the end that he would survive. On the morning of 21 November, the political correspondent of the ABC, Ken Begg, told Crean he would be going that afternoon but the Treasurer refused to believe it. His demotion was one of the most drawn out and agonising political executions seen in Canberra for some time. Contrary to reports Crean was not made a scapegoat for Labor's economic woes. Whitlam became convinced that Crean was too weak and ineffectual a man to be Treasurer at such a vital economic time. His central concern was to prevent any repeat of the chaos and fiasco which surrounded the open collapse in relations between the government and the Treasury in the run-up to the budget. Crean, knowledgeable and dedicated, lacked the political toughness that Whitlam wanted from his Treasurer.

In the end the changeover became a terrible political bungle which did severe damage to the government, caused personal agony to Crean, and provoked bitterness within the party. Yet there is little doubt it was necessary. One of the great myths that subsequently flourished about Crean's removal was that it resulted from his reluctance to endorse the overseas loan raisings.

Jim Cairns was now approaching the zenith of his political career. Whitlam had suggested in June, after Cairns had became deputy Prime Minister, that he might like the Treasury portfolio. Despite his later reluctance, Cairns nevertheless relished getting the job. He had displayed ability as a clever and communicative politician in the previous four months. But a number of highly placed people within the government were very dubious about the move. While they agreed that Crean had to go, they did not like the idea of Cairns as a replacement and believed it would prove a mistake. They said Whitlam should have looked to Hayden. In fact Whitlam had never considered Hayden and relations between the two men had deteriorated as a result of their differences over the economy.

During the Crean controversy the government was moving to review the effect of its economic strategy on the private sector. A vital development at this stage was the arrival of John Menadue as intended head of the Prime Minister's Department in place of Sir John Bunting. Menadue had worked on Whitlam's staff as private secretary from 1960 for seven years before moving to a senior executive position with the

Murdoch newspaper group. One of Menadue's closest associates was the former political correspondent for the Sydney *Daily Mirror*, Eric Walsh, who had worked for the Labor Party on the 1972 campaign and who became Whitlam's press secretary in office. For a long time Walsh worked on Whitlam to get Menadue into the government. He had the assistance of Whitlam's private secretary, Dr Peter Wilenski. Walsh was successful during the May 1974 campaign, when he finally got Whitlam to agree in principle to appointing Menadue as secretary to the Prime Minister's Department. The proposal was activated after the campaign and Menadue accepted the offer.

Whitlam's only problem was to find a position for Bunting but this was easily solved when John Armstrong retired as Australian High Commissioner to the United Kingdom. Bunting was given the vacancy and the Menadue appointment was announced on 23 August. Although Menadue did not officially succeed Sir John until 1 February 1975, he took up duty in late September as de facto secretary.

Menadue believed that the economic strategy needed substantial adjustment to provide more incentive and stimulus to private industry. In this respect Menadue disagreed with the shifting of resources to the public sector that was implicit in the September budget. He believed this strand of government policy would have to be reversed while maintaining the principle of wage restraint. Menadue was successful in persuading Whitlam to this point of view and the Prime Minister, having accepted this, made renewed efforts to consider yet another economic package.

The 'kitchen Cabinet' held a number of more informal meetings mainly attended by Whitlam, Cairns, Crean, Cameron and Enderby. These culminated in a meeting at the Lodge on Saturday 9 November with the main advisers involved being Menadue, Spigelman, Brogan and Gruen. They had the benefit of a number of working papers which had been prepared in the Prime Minister's Department under the guidance of Menadue and his deputy secretary Ian Castles, formerly from the Treasury. The upshot was a severe correction of the government's economic policy. On Sunday 10 November, after a meeting of senior Ministers and advisers, the Treasurer announced a major easing of the monetary squeeze. The government abolished completely the variable deposit requirement on overseas borrowings, which specified that a certain percentage of such funds had to be lodged with the Reserve Bank. It also moved to lower official interest rates and improve the liquidity position of private companies.

On Tuesday 12 November the Prime Minister, not the Treasurer, unveiled a new mini-budget in parliament. This last economic package set the seal on a complete reversal of economic strategy by the Labor government over the preceding five months. The package was an all-out attempt to woo the business community, which had gone into full retreat and was scaling down investment plans. Personal income tax was cut $650 million, which meant an increase of about three per cent in the take-home pay of employees on average weekly earnings. The new benefits applied mostly to middle income levels ranging from $6000–7000 and came on top of the tax cuts in the September budget. Company tax was cut 2.5 per cent, putting an extra $130 million into the economy. Whitlam somersaulted completely in his instructions to the PJT by notifying the tribunal that henceforth it should 'give particular attention to the problems of sustaining and stimulating an adequate level of private investment and of maintaining rates of return on capital which will induce new investment'. The government moved to protect the vehicle industry by increasing import duties and promised similar action for the textile industry.

Whitlam continued the September budget strategy by giving the trade unions tax cuts, and an inquiry to assess the viability of tax indexation along with extra industry protection, in return for wage restraint. He said the government would argue before the Arbitration Commission that the tax cuts should be regarded as compensation for cost of living increases in the December quarter. It would argue that wage indexation should commence with an adjustment for the CPI rise in the March 1975 quarter. It was in this speech that Whitlam emphasised for the first time the need to restore a healthy level of profitability to the private sector, an implicit admission that the September budget had failed in this respect.

The September budget, reinforced by the devaluation, the easing of the credit squeeze and the November mini-budget, provided a substantial boost to the economy. The Treasury assessment was that these moves had the potential to unleash a new round of inflation. The government's strategy was to hold the line on inflation, mainly through wages policy, and meanwhile revive the ailing private sector.

The mini-budget completed the full circle of economic policy for the Labor government. Its immediate political impact was to revitalise the Labor benches, transform pessimism into hope and, more importantly, give the government an invaluable political weapon of tax cuts to fling at its critics. Whitlam confidently predicted that the economy would turn the corner by mid-1975. But more importantly, the mini-budget put steel into the Cabinet and the party to cope with the weeks and months ahead over the Christmas–New Year period when unemployment would reach a new high.

Bob Hawke was of great assistance to the government at this time in leading the union movement along the path of cooperation. One of the most notable features of this period was that, despite rising unemployment, the fabric of government–union relations was maintained and was the basis on which a coherent economic strategy for wage restraint was formulated. Despite all the bluff and bluster made by Hawke on one hand and senior Ministers on the other—an inevitable part of their appeal to their own electorates—relations were never shattered the way many observers believed they would be.

The new rush to assist the private sector was continued in both December 1974 and in early 1975 and was embraced by both Cairns and Whitlam, who became its chief advocates. On the evening of 6 December Whitlam, Cairns and Enderby met at Kirribilli House and reviewed a series of measures designed to give the economy another boost. On 9 December Cabinet agreed to defer the next $500 million company tax payment—a move which would affect about 64,000 companies. At the same time it doubled the deduction for depreciation of plant and equipment, in an effort to stimulate investment. Cabinet moved in harmony with its new protectionist line to impose import quotas on a wide range of items. Whitlam also announced that a program of references would be sent to the Temporary Assistance Authority to report on the extent of protection needed for any industry facing difficulties. Both business and Bob Hawke welcomed the new moves.

In 1975, after Whitlam's return from Europe, the Cabinet held a two-day meeting over 28–29 January. It decided to abolish the capital gains tax in the budget, call a Premiers' conference to give the states more money, and review its abolition of the superphosphate bounty. Whitlam summed up the new outlook of the government when he told a press conference: 'We don't want to give anybody who's disposed to invest any discouragement whatever.' It was at this time that Whitlam announced the next new departure in federal policy, a move which had been inevitable since the new policy direction contained in the November mini-budget: the need for the government to curb its own spending program. The issue of government spending was henceforth to dominate the economic arena and the course of events throughout 1975. Labor belatedly accepted the need for cutbacks: the question now was not whether but by how much.

The government ended 1974 with the goodwill from its May election victory nearly completely exhausted. Its Ministers and its decision-making structure had both been found wanting. The real problems lay within Cabinet first and then the caucus. The government had completed a somersault in economic policy—but Australians faced a bitter economic legacy that would endure for some time. Labor's electoral standing was so low that a sustained and superb effort would be needed to recover. The proof of this was at hand.

# 7

## DEBACLE AND REVIVAL

*I believe a Prime Minister, in the nature of his office, has a special and, at times, over-riding duty to promote Australia's place in the world.*

Gough Whitlam, 11 February 1975

On 23 October 1974 the Queensland Premier Joh Bjelke-Petersen announced that his state would go to the polls on 7 December to consolidate the forces against socialism in Queensland and throughout the nation. Amid wild scenes in the state parliament the Premier said the election would allow Queenslanders to register their dismay at the policies of the federal Labor government. Foreshadowing his campaign theme Bjelke-Petersen said: 'The alien and stagnating centralist, socialist, communist inspired policies—call them what you like—of the Federal Labor government have been blindly supported by the Labor opposition in this House.'

The Labor leader, a relative unknown, Perc Tucker, said the big issue Labor had running for it was the Premier himself. 'Most of the people in the state hate his guts,' Tucker declared. He said the governing coalition was divided and that the main issues of the campaign would be state issues—public transport, decentralisation, aid to local authorities, jobs and price control.

The October announcement from Queensland meant that the federal government would sustain a solid month of Labor bashing in the sunshine state, something it could ill afford after such a demoralising six month period since its re-election in May. Whitlam's gut reaction was to join battle with Bjelke-Petersen and he was supported by Jim Spigelman and ALP federal secretary David Combe.

Whitlam's reasons for intervening in Queensland were sophisticated. He knew that the northern state was the Labor government's Achilles heel which had nearly cost him the 1974 election. An analysis of Labor primary votes across the states highlighted this. At the 1974 poll, under the two-party preferred system, Labor totalled an estimated 51.7 per cent nationally compared with 48.3 per cent for the Liberal–Country parties. A state by state breakdown of support for Labor under the two-party preferred system gave the following results: NSW 54.9 per cent, Victoria 50.6 per cent, Queensland 45.4 per cent, South Australia 52.5 per cent, Western Australia 48.5 per cent and Tasmania 55.4 per cent. Under the same system the swing to the Liberal–Country parties in Queensland was 4.1 per cent. Labor lost two Queensland seats, Lilley and Wide Bay. But it was in a precarious situation in five out of the six seats it retained. The swing required to lose them at the next general election was as follows: Dawson 0.7 per cent, Brisbane 0.9 per cent, Bowman 1.2 per cent, Leichhardt 3.4 per cent and Capricornia 4.8 per cent.[1]

Whitlam knew that Bjelke-Petersen would campaign heavily against the Federal Government throughout his state and the effect would be to weaken further Labor's popular base from which it would have to fight the next federal election. He reasoned that if the Premier was going to campaign against the Labor government anyway, then it would be far better for him to be opposed by the Labor government.

But Whitlam had other long-term reasons for participating in the state campaign. He wanted to defeat Bjelke-Petersen on the issue of obstructionism and demonstrate to the Queensland Premier that his refusal to cooperate with the Labor government on a range of programs was not only damaging Queensland but damaging his own electoral standing. If Whitlam's intervention was successful, it would be a clear warning not just to Bjelke-Petersen but to the Premiers of NSW and Victoria that they interfered with federal government programs and policies at their own risk.

Another factor in the Prime Minister's thinking was his sentimental attachment to Queensland. It was the state where he had first made his reputation as a big gun on the campaign trail. Through a series of coincidences Queensland, more than any other state, had determined his electoral fortunes and shaped his political career. It was in Queensland in 1966 that Whitlam, facing expulsion from the Labor Party, campaigned as de facto party leader and helped Dr Rex Patterson to a 'miracle' win in the Dawson by-election with a 12 per cent swing. He played a similar role in the Capricornia by-election in 1967 when Dr Doug Everingham won the seat. But even before this, it was in Queensland in the 1961 federal elections that Whitlam first proved his campaign mettle when he concentrated on the state and the theme of northern development, travelling extensively and building up a vast knowledge of the outback and western areas. Labor won eight seats in Queensland in that election and Whitlam established ties with the Queensland ALP which lasted for a decade.

But this time Whitlam's decision to travel north was the choice of a man in a weak position. Neither he nor his staff expected a Labor victory; that was in the realm of the impossible. The operation was designed to stop the rot. Whitlam's office treated it like a federal campaign. Whitlam spent three four-day weekends campaigning throughout the state. Contrary to later reports, the Queensland branch of the ALP welcomed Whitlam's presence; the only area which did not want him was Rockhampton, and he did not campaign there. Over the three weekends the Prime Minister visited Brisbane extensively, Ipswich, Cairns, Townsville, Weipa, Mt Isa, Gympie, Nambour, the Gold Coast, and inland centres such as Claremont and Emerald.

Although he was advised by Spigelman not to attack the Premier personally, Whitlam extended his criticism of Queensland's obstructionism to a strong attack on Bjelke-Petersen. He hammered the Premier on unfair electoral boundaries, on his close association with mining and oil companies, and declared that Bjelke-Petersen was a victim of his own obsessions. 'He's obsessed with Canberra, he is obsessed with centralism, he is obsessed with socialism and he is obsessed with state rights,' Whitlam told 400 people at the Toombul shopping centre. 'And his obsessions have blinded him to the needs of ordinary people.' But Whitlam failed to realise that this was counter-productive in Queensland where he was more unpopular than the Premier—despite Bjelke-Petersen's having been elected on only 19 per cent of the vote.

Whitlam resurrected the reputation of the former Liberal Prime Minister John Gorton and regularly told meetings that he had got no further with the Premier than had Gorton. Whitlam said that his problems with the Premier were a repeat of those faced by Gorton when Canberra tried to protect the Great Barrier Reef, ensure Australian ownership of resources and upgrade its Aboriginal affairs policy. He exploited the reluctant cooperation of the other Liberal Premiers—Sir Robert Askin, Dick Hamer and Sir Charles Court—as evidence of the lone course being charted by the Queensland Premier. 'Why should Queensland continue to be the odd state out?' Whitlam asked his rallies.

It was during this campaign that the first signs of a deep-seated personal hostility to Whitlam emerged from the electorate. On the Gold Coast, in Brisbane and in the country towns there were invariably demonstrations with placard carriers attacking his forthcoming trip to Europe, his purchase of Blue Poles, his recognition of Soviet sovereignty over the Baltic states and lost jobs through tariff cuts.

The worst demonstration occurred over the first weekend when Whitlam was mobbed by demonstrators leaving the Iluka Hotel in

Surfers Paradise. A tightly organised group surrounded his car and hurled abuse, calling 'commo rat', 'you filthy swine Whitlam' and 'get out of Queensland'. The car was jostled and one man smashed a heavy banner on its top. In nearly all the country areas, Whitlam came under sustained attack over the government's policies towards the rural sector and the abolition of subsidies, particularly the petrol price subsidy scheme.

Neither Whitlam nor his advisers foresaw the dimensions of the debacle. Queensland, which had in the previous century elected the first Labor government in the world, turned on Australia's Labor government and its leader with a vengeance. Labor polled 36 per cent of the vote, more than 10 per cent down on the previous state figure and a big drop on the 44 per cent the party recorded at the May federal election—just seven months before; its 33 state seats were reduced to 11 seats and even its state leader was defeated.

The result was unquestionably the greatest electoral blow of Whitlam's career. His involvement had been counter-productive and instead of winning votes he had lost them. Yet Whitlam still had cause to be grateful. If this result had been posted before the Labor government's budget had passed through the Senate, the temptation for the Opposition Leader Bill Snedden to force another election might have proved very great.

The Queensland result was a measure of Labor's failure on a variety of fronts. Both prices and unemployment were important, but so was the lack of attractive state leadership. Labor failed to get its message across. It was unable to counter the psychological climate Bjelke-Petersen had created, in which it became easy to discredit even the most laudable Labor initiatives. There were two obvious conclusions from this result. If the federal Labor government was to survive in office then it needed, first, a full three-year term to re-establish itself and, second, a hard examination to assess its mistakes and rectify them.

The Queensland defeat provoked the strongest criticism of Whitlam by a fellow Minister since Labor had assumed office. The Minister for Northern Development Dr Rex Patterson had traditionally been a Whitlam ally. But Patterson, who believed his seat of Dawson was as good as lost on these results, did some straight talking Queensland style:

> The great benefits of the federal Labor government's achievements in education, health and social services have been completely lost because of the large number of pinpricking policies which have been resented by Queensland and the north in general. Queensland, the most decentralised state in the commonwealth, is really a rural state. Its agricultural and mining resources earn huge annual export surpluses which are used to support the living standards of the great mass of people in Sydney and Melbourne. The pouring of millions of

dollars into heavily subsidised Sydney and Melbourne, the building of Albury-Wodonga, the establishment of cultural operations, the purchase of Blue Poles, makes no impression in the north. In fact, such actions only intensify the feeling of neglect when they are skilfully handled by anti-Labor forces. Down-to-earth grass-roots politics instead of airy-fairy, academic and theoretical mumbo jumbo policies, even if they are economically sound, are what is required in Queensland to restore confidence in the Labor movement.

Patterson said that almost each week policies were being implemented that were counter-productive to Labor in northern Australia. He pointed out that the abolition of the petrol subsidy was the kiss of political death to the city of Mt Isa. He nominated the reduction in the education tax deduction from $400 to $150, the abolition of freight rate subsidies, abolition of the free milk scheme, cutbacks in country air services, removal of the superphosphate bounty, and the abolition of tax concessions which were used as an incentive to increase productivity in high cost areas, as policies which had all cost Labor many votes. The situation was worsened by the federal government's mining policies which created deep distrust in the mining towns of Gove, Tennant Creek, Mt Isa, the Pilbara and the Bowen basin towns.

Patterson's complaint concerned both poor public relations and the essence of Whitlam's political strategy. It struck squarely at Whitlam's tactic, enshrined in the phrase 'cities strategy', which meant appealing to the urban voters and capturing the outer suburban seats in Sydney, Melbourne, Brisbane, Adelaide and Perth to win office. The truth was that Labor could lose office in the country.

The post mortems on the Queensland debacle revealed the great difficulty in getting the government to change its approach. The Labor Party federal executive met in Canberra on 13–14 December to review the position. The Queensland president Jack Egerton and secretary Bart Lourigan focused their comments on the Federal Government to ensure that the Queensland branch itself did not come under fire. Whitlam was at his pedantic best and vigorously defended Labor's policies, claiming the government's greatest critics were within the party, particularly the Labor Premiers. 'It is depressing to see Labor people taking up and using the arguments of the opposition against the government,' he told the meeting.

When the executive broke after midnight its recommendations included: that Ministers cooperate more closely with one another to avoid conflict; that the Prime Minister and Cabinet conduct a wide-ranging campaign to explain policies and legislation; and that in all states Ministers work in closer liaison with the Party machine. The trouble about such decisions was the lack of any machinery to implement them. After Labor lost office its secretary David Combe complained that the party had always accepted assurances from Whitlam and the government which were often worthless. Combe said that while the party could pass resolutions at federal executive level, nobody was ever responsible for their implementation. Whitlam would allow the party to make decisions but would then proceed in his own fashion regardless.

As early as October 1973 a three-man delegation comprising Combe, Don Willesee's press secretary, Geoff Briot, and Whitlam's then secretary, Eric Walsh, had gone to the Prime Minister's office for a discussion on measures to lift the government's image. It was at this meeting that Briot warned Whitlam just how much ministerial staff were damaging Labor by promoting their own Ministers at the expense of the government and that, when it came to press secretaries, Labor was not getting value for money. Whitlam had seemed bored for the first half hour of the meeting (he told the trio 'the government has only one thing going for it and you're in danger of wasting his time') but, as the delegation ignored his comments and kept at their argument, Whitlam began to take notice.

He was often critical of press secretaries himself but had never tried to formulate a better system. The trio also suggested a series of regular meetings between leading Ministers and Combe to discuss the government's image and tactics, another suggestion that was ignored. The irony of the debate about ministerial staff and press secretaries was that a move to give Whitlam veto power over such appointments had been defeated early in the life of the Labor government. In January 1973 Willesee had put a proposal to Cabinet that the Prime Minister should have such a veto but it was resoundingly defeated, a decision that would have disastrous consequences.

Whitlam's personal response to the Queensland debacle was extraordinary. He would allow neither the freshly revealed unpopularity of his government, nor the appeals from his own staff, the secretary of his Department John Menadue and his Ministers, nor the precarious economic outlook to dissuade him from proceeding on a 39-day overseas trip to fourteen different countries in Europe and Asia in the most widely publicised, heavily criticised Prime Ministerial visit for 30 years. The trip had been planned over twelve months before and was originally scheduled for June–July 1974, but had to be postponed when Snedden forced the double dissolution election in May 1974.

Throughout his three years in office Whitlam was his own Prime Minister, doing the job his way and not the way that either his advisers or the public would have preferred. Whitlam's persistence with his European trip, which everyone about him recognised to be a domestic political disaster the dimensions of which were only revealed as it continued, was a reflection of two fundamental aspects of his character. The first was his commitment as an internationalist intensely interested to the point of preoccupation in Australia's status in the world and its bilateral relations. The second was his determination to do the job his way and to insist that the Australian public accept him on his own terms. Such egotism is a dangerous trait in a politician whose survival depends on public acceptability, for ultimately the electorate was not prepared to have Whitlam as Prime Minister solely on his terms.

More than any other Prime Minister in Australia's history, Whitlam tried to break through the circle of political and social insulation in which Australia had been placed because of distance and geography. The Prime Minister himself had an abiding passion with foreign affairs, travel, the cultural and archaeological prizes of other countries; with meeting new leaders; with being a figure of substance both in the region and in the world, and with making Australia a nation of substance. The arduous itinerary of an overseas visit, which was physically exhausting to those involved, always seemed to recharge Whitlam's batteries and rekindle his spirit on his arrival back home. His initial visits, to Indonesia, New Zealand, Peking and Tokyo, to Washington and then Ottawa for the Commonwealth Heads of Government Meeting, to South-East Asia and then Washington again, attracted a growing amount of criticism. But it had been difficult to attack any as unnecessary.

However, Whitlam's visit to the United States during September–October 1974 had caused controversy over the way he travelled—a chartered Qantas 707 replete with food and drink for the official party, public servants and their wives, staff, security people and the dozen or so travelling press. Gradually the cost of such trips, the style of travel and the sightseeing stops became a political issue.

Whitlam only exacerbated the problem by going on the most costly and least necessary trip of all, seven days after the Queensland debacle. He visited Sri Lanka, Belgium, Britain, Ireland, Greece, the Netherlands, France, Italy, Yugoslavia, the Soviet Union, the Federal Republic of Germany, Pakistan and Bangladesh. He had intended to visit Malta but had to return to Australia instead. In his report to Parliament on 11 February after the visit, Whitlam said:

> I saw my mission as an essential part of my duty as head of government. The specious view was put forward that a Prime Minister's duty is to stay at home at a time of economic difficulty. Now, however serious our own problems and however acute my concern about them—and I trust my concern is not in question—I believe a Prime Minister, in the nature of his office, has a special and, at times, over-riding duty to promote Australia's place in the world.

The trip was ill-fated from the start. It was almost as though the gods had ordained that Whitlam was to be continually reminded of his absence from home. It took a cyclone to bring him back.

It was only late on Christmas afternoon at the Barclay Hotel, London, that the Prime Minister began to realise the devastation that had been wrought in Darwin by Cyclone Tracey. He spoke with his deputy Jim Cairns and his permanent head John Menadue back in Australia and early on Boxing Day summoned a meeting in his hotel suite to tell the Special Minister of State Lionel Bowen, who was travelling with him, that he would return to Australia. Whitlam was reluctant to abandon the trip, particularly in view of the criticism which the tour had already incurred in Australia. He felt that to abort it would be to validate the original allegations against the visit. It was therefore decided that Bowen and the rest of the party would continue on while Whitlam and some of his staff returned to Australia. In taking this decision Whitlam dismissed the one opportunity he had to call off the visit to the other European countries and to return to Australia, thereby at least reducing the political damage he was generating.

Whitlam arrived in Darwin on 28 December for an on-the-spot assessment, just as the Minister for Northern Development Rex Patterson was saying that $500 million would be needed to rebuild the city. The following Monday he chaired a Cabinet meeting at Kirribilli House in Sydney which laid the ground for Darwin reconstruction. It was at Kirribilli House that Menadue tried to talk Whitlam out of proceeding with the trip. The Prime Minister's staff had already told reporters when they left London it was not certain whether he would return, but Whitlam was determined. He made the long 10,000 mile flight back to Europe to pursue the odyssey.

Within a week another major disaster occurred in Australia. This time at the other end of the country in Hobart, where the bulk carrier *Lake Illawarra* rammed the city's lifeline, the Tasman Bridge, severing it completely and resulting in the deaths of twelve people. At a press conference at The Hague on 6 January the Prime Minister, tired from his long flights and irritated beyond belief at another disaster in Australia, momentarily lost his better judgement. In the gracious drawing room of the Hotel des Indes, with the Dutch Prime Minister by his side, he allowed himself to be needled by a Dutch journalist's suggestion that whenever he left Australia there seemed to be a disaster and that he must have felt like a farmer who went for a holiday only to hear that his barn had burnt down. Whitlam paused then angrily and curtly replied: 'No'. But when asked if he knew the reason for the accident, he launched into an amazing attack on the captain of the *Lake Illawarra*. 'It is beyond my imagination how any competent person could steer a ship into the pylons of a bridge,' Whitlam declared. 'But I have to restrain myself because I would expect the person responsible for such an act would find himself before a criminal jury. There is no possibility of the government guarding against mad or incompetent captains of ships, or pilots of aircraft.'

These statements provoked a storm of protest in Australia. To many people Whitlam's anger betrayed his conscience and the guilt which all the criticism of the trip must have evoked: that his rightful place was back in Australia not in Europe. The next morning in Paris Whitlam issued a statement of apology at 7 a.m. at the Hotel Crillon. A humiliating admission that the exhaustion and frustration of the trip was taking its toll.

It was only when they returned to Australia in late January that the Prime Minister's party realised the full extent of the public relations disaster the trip had been. A perusal of the newspapers during Whitlam's absence, particularly at the time of the cyclone and bridge disasters, is a sobering experience. No political leader could ever sustain this sort of criticism with impunity. Whitlam certainly did not and the European trip became a landmark in developing hostility towards the personal idiosyncrasies which marked his style of government.

A glance at the Brisbane *Courier Mail* of 4 January is sufficient to convey the damage that was done. The main page one story dealt with a court challenge by Darwin people over the federal government's handling of relief aid. Below the headlines was a huge photo of Gough, Margaret and daughter Cathy standing on the Acropolis with the Parthenon in the background under a heading 'And that's us in Athens'. The daily foreign affairs reports sent to Whitlam of the papers back in Australia could never convey the cartoons, the juxtaposition of stories and photos, and the overall impact of the trip.

A week after Whitlam returned, he faced one of the crucial tests of his Prime Ministership at the ALP federal conference at Terrigal, NSW. He was already planning a quick visit to Japan to sign the NARA treaty, then to Kingston, Jamaica for the next Commonwealth Heads of Government Meeting, as well as going to the Middle East. He also had to contend with the possibility of Snedden's forcing a mid-year election by blocking supply in April, as well as further economic difficulties facing the government. This was the pace Whitlam set himself; a pace that was too hot to last. A wiser politician, more aware of the currents of public opinion, less certain of his own ability to recover no matter what the opinion polls showed, would have stayed at home, tried to consolidate his government and to re-establish communication with the electorate.

Whitlam arrived back in Australia from the European trip with his leadership more in question than at any time during his Prime Ministership. One of the interesting developments during his absence had been the performance of Jim Cairns as acting Prime Minister. In this five-week period Cairns had given every appearance of emerging as an alternative Prime Minister in his own right. In Darwin during the crisis Cairns' humanity had shown through in a peculiarly appropriate Boxing Day statement:

> The people of Darwin have been magnificent. Most of them have lost their homes—often the result of a life's work—and no one is able to do more than search in the wreckage, moved by some hope of finding something of value, some link with yesterday. Some work feverishly or with calm application. Some have not yet emerged from shock. The morale and courage of the people of Darwin is high. It was an honour to move, often silently, among them and to try to share a little in their tragedy and their courage. The loss of Darwin is a national loss. Its cost must, and will, be shared by the nation.

The socialisation of Darwin's disaster was comprehensible and acceptable to the entire country.

Whitlam had failed earlier to have the ALP federal conference deferred until the middle of 1975. The February date meant that Whitlam would arrive at Terrigal when the economy was at its worst, unemployment at a new peak because of school leavers, and his image at an all time low because of the European trip. Terrigal would be the acid test of the proposition constantly put by the Opposition leader Bill Snedden: that the Labor Party would self-destruct in the midst of the economic crisis over which it was presiding.

The Terrigal conference was a species of animal very different from Labor Party conferences of the past. The 1975 conference was really the first for a generation with a Labor government in office. The 1973 conference at Surfers Paradise, held just six months after the election victory, was more of a celebration characterised by an indulgence in the long-denied spoils of office which overwhelmed any party friction. The 1975 conference would determine whether the party as a whole—Ministers, members, machine and trade union base—had the unity, tenacity and nerve to hold together. The fact that Terrigal was such a public and self-acknowledged test put everyone on their guard.

The most controversial issue would be that of Commonwealth–State relations given the tough stand being taken by South Australian Premier, Don Dunstan. Over the previous year Dunstan had become a vocal critic of the Prime Minister over state finances. On Sunday 16 June 1974 he had launched the most comprehensive attack on Whitlam and the Prime Minister's centralist philosophy. Addressing the South Australian ALP conference, Dunstan said that Whitlam was defying both the spirit and the letter of the ALP platform. This speech was a major effort to counter 'the new federalism', which was one of Whitlam's fundamental commitments. Dunstan said the Prime Minister was attempting to upgrade local government and give it access to federal revenue at the direct expense of the states. The Premier had warned that he would take his grievances to the supreme policy making body, the ALP federal conference.

The South Australian resolution on federalism which was put before the conference sought guarantees of adequate funds to the states with the proviso that 'the Australian government shall seek to involve and work in concert with state administration and work through state administration where this already covers the field concerned'.

ALP delegates assembled over the weekend of 1–2 February at Terrigal's Hotel Florida, the conference venue on the NSW central coast, and at other motels in the surrounding seaside area. During the previous two days the federal executive met to prepare the agenda. The spirit of compromise was in the air, irritated only by the sting of two-day-old sunburns. The mood was casual and relaxed and for two successive days federal executive delegates lunched shirtless by the poolside with press on that great Australian menu of steak and beer. Press photographers had a field day. The atmosphere made it hard to believe that Labor could be in a state of electoral crisis. On Sunday night the party president Bob Hawke arranged a dinner of state and federal leaders in an effort to defuse the issue of federalism.

This meeting, at Nino's Restaurant down the road from the Hotel Florida, opened the way for a compromise on the South Australian resolution. Dunstan heavily censured Whitlam for what he regarded as the breakdown of cooperation between the federal government and the state government. He praised the performance Cairns had given when Whitlam was away and the attitude he had shown to the Premiers at Kirribilli House. Dunstan claimed the basic principle of the South Australian item was 'non-negotiable'. It was resolved at this dinner to hold another meeting of the legal and constitutional committee during the week to consider the federalism platform and the conference agenda was arranged to have it debated at the end of the week. Whitlam was told by Lionel Murphy a little later: 'Look Gough, you can live with this. It is the best way to resolve the matter.' Thus the tone for the conference was set. The legal and constitutional affairs committee met in mid-week and a compromise resolution was drafted which was enough to satisfy Dunstan.

On the Monday morning Bob Hawke delivered a rallying opening address calling for an end to despair and a new determination. Hawke said that Gough Whitlam would remain leader of the party as long as he wanted to and predicted that the coming week would not provide the confrontation 'that some have expected and others hope for'. Hawke nominated three major mistakes of the Whitlam government—the economy, federal–state relations and communications between the government and the people. Hawke's address further cemented the tone of moderation which was to dominate the conference. It was a morale boosting speech and an effective one. Hawke declared the only way the party could prepare itself for the threat of another premature election was to throw its weight behind Whitlam.

The only area which the spirit of compromise did not touch was that of minerals policy. The Minerals and Energy Minister Rex Connor carried the conference with him in an acceptance of his hard-line policies committing the party to 100 per cent Australian ownership and control of coal, oil, natural gas, uranium and all other fuel and energy resources. Connor withstood an attempt by the West Australian MP Joe Berinson to soften this provision by seeking maximum rather than total local ownership. 'We either go for it in a proper way or we leave the bloody thing alone,' Connor said, effectively rebutting his critics.

The conference accepted a new economic platform presented by Jim Cairns and drafted largely by Brian Brogan and South Australian MP Chris Hurford. Cairns spelt out the new and positive attitude of the party towards the private sector, endorsed the need for further foreign investment in Australia, and secured party acceptance for a new department of economic planning.

By the second day of the conference, Tuesday 4 February, Whitlam had asserted his dominance. On the three major issues of the day—the development of Australia's uranium resources, the formation of the new economic planning department, and proposals to give the federal government power over prices, incomes and interest rates—the Prime Minister carried the conference with him on critical amendments. This was most noticeable when the party accepted the vesting of powers over prices and incomes in the federal government. This proposal, put by Whitlam and carried 41–5, followed strong warnings from the Victorian delegation that such a move could precipitate a major confrontation between a Labor government and the union movement.

The Terrigal conference had a number of enduring results for the Labor Party. It was, above all, a victory for pragmatism, for Whitlam, and for the notion that if governments are to remain in office they have to compromise the ideology of their platform. A successful Terrigal conference could never guarantee the government's survival; but it was a necessary precondition for survival. In a convincing demonstration of party unity, Whitlam was able to signal Snedden that the Opposition would be forced to fight every inch of the way to win an early election. Labor's strategy was to rely on that old political maxim: the best way to avert an election is to prepare for one. Labor's spearheads, Whitlam, Cairns and Hawke, had shown a willingness to admit the mistakes of the past. For the first time in history an ALP federal conference had declared its commitment to restore the level of private sector profits in order to revive the economy and its willingness to restrict the level of wages to achieve this, a considerable achievement.

Whitlam's keynote address was an exercise in keeping several political irons in the one fire. He assured the party there would be no reversing of policy, no reneging on the program, yet at the same time he bluntly told the conference that the level of wage increases would have to be lowered and that a redistribution of income was needed from wages and salaries to profits to stimulate the private sector. Whitlam made it perfectly clear that the politics of forcing an election in 1975 would be radically different from 1974. This time the government would not tolerate its term being cut—it would resist any move by the Opposition to force a new election. The Prime Minister maintained this stand to the day he was dismissed on 11 November ten months later.

Whitlam was now moving to exploit the differences between Snedden and Fraser inside the Liberal Party. He pointed to Fraser's record and warned that 'an entire apparatus of union intimidation' would be established if he became leader. In an effort to build up the threat from the right, a continuing tactic Whitlam used in dealing with Fraser, he declared 'trendyism has had its little day—the forces of the right have reasserted themselves with a vengeance'. The Prime Minister was already sharpening his knife for a possible fight to the death with Fraser.

In this speech Whitlam defined the political strategy he would pursue over the next year. It originated in Labor's political weakness and was designed to deny the Opposition the opportunity to strike down the government at its whim. 'He cannot commit them to bad conduct or compel them to good conduct,' Whitlam said, ridiculing Snedden's hold over his party.

> The irresponsibility of the Opposition injects a new poison, a further uncertainty into the Australian system. For our part, we are determined to work on the basic assumption of elections—that in 1974 the people elected us for a further three years and we have a mandate to carry out our program during the full term for which we were elected. Any other approach would be to succumb to the tactics and the propaganda of our opponents.

Whitlam would counter-attack an election-hungry Opposition.

For the Prime Minister the conference had been invaluable. In the space of seven days it had dispelled the doubts and uncertainties created by his European trip in a way that would have been impossible in such a quick fashion in any other forum of the party. His performance had given truth to the declaration Hawke made on the opening day that there would be no major confrontation. The victory of the Prime Minister and his senior Ministers, with the active support of Hawke, over the machine and those elements wanting to commit the government to more radical policies, was complete.

The conference also highlighted the decline of the left wing of the Labor Party. At no stage in the previous 15 years had the thrust of the left wing been so dissipated. Its one-time champion Bill Hartley was defeated on almost every issue on which he took a stand. The resolution from Jim Cairns seeking immediate recognition of the Provisional Revolutionary Government (PRG) in Vietnam was cast aside in favour of a compromise from Mick Young which called on the government to consider letting the PRG establish an information office in Australia.

Yet, for all the success of the conference, there was a distinct note of hollowness throughout. The price of Labor unity was high; the price of survival even higher. Labor's experience of government had transformed the party and troubled all those involved with it. Many principles it had cherished for so long had been compromised or abandoned. The decade of the 1960s was light years away for those Labor members who heard Jim Cairns tell the conference: 'We cannot have a socialist society until we have a society of socialists. We have few socialists in Australia and we have an even smaller proportion in the public sector than the private sector.' Whitlam himself tried hard to assure the conference that, despite abundant evidence to the contrary, Labor had not compromised its ideals. Yet, in the very week before the conference, federal Cabinet had abolished the capital gains tax which Labor had introduced in the previous budget and which was clearly called for in the ALP platform. The preceding months had been marked by a gradual reversal of the government's 25 per cent tariff cut made in 1973 as more and more industry references were sent to the Temporary Assistance Authority to increase protection levels.

The flight into pragmatism had taken a heavy toll on the party faithful. This trend in itself highlighted one of the chief reasons for the great and undiminished standing within the party of Rex Connor. He stood almost alone in the ministry as a man whose policies had not yet been checked or reversed, whose original policy direction was still being followed. Yet at the very time the conference was being conducted, Connor had already completed most of the overseas loan negotiations which would eventually lead to his own destruction.

The Terrigal conference, unlike conferences of the past, was almost totally devoid of new ideas and fresh directions for the party. If Labor had stayed in office longer, this failure of the 1975 conference would have been keenly felt. Ever since Whitlam became Labor leader in 1967, the ALP conference had become a watershed in the development of the party. The conferences of 1969 and 1971 were landmarks in altering the party's direction, rewriting its platform, and laying the basis for new programs on which the party eventually came to office. Terrigal did none of this. Its impact on the actual policies followed by the Whitlam government was close to zero. The conference in fact demonstrated the difficulty the party faced in an extensive rethink of its platform when it was preoccupied with the daily burdens of office. However a plus from the conference was the display of some new Labor men, Joe Berinson, Mick Young, and Victorian Senator John Button.

True to the finest Labor traditions, the Terrigal conference finished with a bang and not a whimper. Labor Ministers, members, staff and press drove out of Terrigal on Friday afternoon or Saturday morning for Canberra via Sydney. The 27 members of the Labor Cabinet had a late Sunday afternoon engagement in the Cabinet room at Parliament House and later that night the appointment of the Attorney-General and Labor Senate leader Lionel Murphy to the High Court was announced. It created a sensation within the ranks of both the government and the Opposition and was one of the best kept secrets during Labor's term of office.

The Murphy appointment had had its genesis in Whitlam's mind in late November or early December 1974. Whitlam had never enjoyed good relations with Murphy. They had been antagonists over many years and on many issues. During the 1960s Murphy had used all his influence and power within the left wing of the Labor Party to oppose Whitlam and discredit him. In government Whitlam, while recognising Murphy's substantial legislative achievements, always saw the Attorney-General as a brilliant but erratic man whose political actions were often unpredictable. In reviewing the first year of Labor's administration Whitlam described Murphy's 'raid' on ASIO early in the life of the government as one of its major mistakes.

Whitlam was obsessed about the importance of the High Court bench in passing judgement on a number of Labor's legislative achievements under challenge from the states. He was concerned to ensure that the Bench was not dominated by conservatives whose disposition would be anti-Labor. Whitlam had considered carefully the range of suitable appointees to the court. Some people had recommended to him Mr Justice Hope from the NSW Supreme Court. Whitlam had a high opinion of Hope and used him on a number of inquiries set up by the government. But his main concern about Hope was a doubt about his centralist credentials.

Towards the end of 1974 a senior Labor Minister told Whitlam he believed that Murphy would be interested in the court appointment caused by the death of Mr Justice Douglas Menzies. The idea interested Whitlam but he was initially cautious because of the controversy that had arisen over Junie Morosi and the proposal in early December for her to join the staff of Jim Cairns. The Senate had been sitting at this time and a number of questions had been asked about Morosi, who had been closely associated with Murphy for a number of years. Morosi's husband, David Ditchburn, whom Murphy appointed to a vacancy on the Film Board of Review, was the regional manager in Australia for Ethiopian Airlines, the company which employed Murphy's wife Ingrid as a public relations consultant, in return for which she received free overseas travel on the airline. Whitlam was worried that the Opposition might find a connection between Ethiopian Airlines and the Attorney-General. Whitlam speculated that if, for instance, it could be shown that Murphy himself had enjoyed free overseas travel with Ethiopian Airlines then his position would become difficult to defend. It was primarily for this reason that Whitlam in December deferred any decision about Murphy for about two months until after he returned from his European trip. But Murphy, while keen on the idea, still had some doubts. Before the Terrigal conference tentative agreement had been reached on the appointment between Whitlam and Murphy.[2]

The first person inside the party to suspect the impending appointment was Victorian lawyer and friend of Murphy, Senator John Button. On the Thursday night, 6 February, Button and Murphy spent four hours discussing the question. Button left with the impression that Murphy would go to the court although he still had reservations. After the Terrigal conference Button went straight to Jim McClelland's Sydney home where they worked out the strategy for getting McClelland into the ministerial vacancy to be left by Murphy. McClelland told Button that, if elected, the portfolio he wanted was manufacturing industry, then held by Kep Enderby.

Before the Cabinet meeting on Sunday evening 9 February Murphy had last-minute doubts. While the Ministers waited in the Cabinet room, Whitlam, Murphy and Cairns were in the Prime Minister's office discussing the move. At one stage Murphy called his wife to discuss the decision further with her. Whitlam said that Murphy should accept the position. Cairns took a similar line but added that Murphy could either take the position now or wait for Sir Edward McTiernan to retire from the bench. However Whitlam would have none of this and said Murphy had to make up his mind now. Whitlam then told Murphy, according to one of the three participants, that he could have the position of Chief Justice if the appointment was made in Labor's time.[3]

Whitlam stunned the Cabinet when he moved that Murphy be appointed to the High Court to replace Menzies. Once the shock passed there was support for the move; but there was one dissident. The vocal opponent of Murphy's departure was his long-standing colleague of the NSW left, the Minister for Urban and Regional Development Tom Uren, who made it clear he saw the move as bordering on betrayal. Uren insisted that his dissent from the Cabinet decision be officially recorded, a sign of resentment within the left.

The appointment of Murphy to the High Court was a highly debatable political strategy for Labor. It was doubtful if the pros outweighed the cons. The chief liability for Labor was that it appeared to surrender a Senate seat to the Opposition at the half-Senate election due before mid-1976. Before Murphy's appointment five NSW Senate vacancies would come up at this election and, given that NSW was Labor's traditionally strongest state, the party would normally expect to win three of these five seats. But the Murphy appointment would mean six Senate places would come for election and the outcome would be a three-all split between Labor and non-Labor. That is, the non-Labor parties could expect to be a Senate seat better off. In short, Labor prejudiced its chance of winning long-term control of the Senate, the key factor in Australian politics.

Labor entered the 29th parliament with 29 out of 60 Senators and needed to pick up only one extra Senator at the next election to take its numbers to 30 which, with the support of Liberal Movement Senator Steele Hall, would have denied the Opposition the numbers to block supply and force an election. In return for the Murphy appointment the Government obtained a judge on the High Court sympathetic to its own aspirations.

The Murphy appointment had a number of enduring consequences for the Labor government. It opened the way for the elevation to the ministry of Jim McClelland, then 59, who had been elected to the Senate five years before after a prominent legal career in Sydney. McClelland quickly established himself as one of the most articulate men and incisive minds in the Parliament. He failed by one vote to win election to the ministry in June 1974 and all the omens were that his late entry into politics would deny him a ministerial career. But on Monday 10 February 1975 McClelland defeated Joe Riordan 52–37 in the final count to obtain a ministry.

Whitlam gave McClelland the Manufacturing Industry job and switched Kep Enderby to Attorney-General, subject to one prior condition. This was that Enderby should proceed with the formation of the Australia Police, an amalgamation of the old Commonwealth Police, the ACT and Northern Territory Police Forces, and the Narcotics Bureau previously in the Customs Department.

The proposal was one of Whitlam's pet projects on which he would not compromise, despite opposition from within the party, civil liberties groups and other people concerned at the establishment of a monolithic repository of confidential information with an army of operatives to probe the lives of Australian citizens. Many Canberra police resented the amalgamation and strong pressure was put on their local member Enderby, who was in the unfortunate position of being the Minister responsible for the action. The Australia Police legacy stayed with Enderby to the very end. After he arrived home on the morning of 14 December 1975 from the central tally room realising he had lost his seat,

Enderby's phone rang at 1.30 a.m. The anonymous caller, obviously a policeman, crowed: 'You said if we were opposed to amalgamation of the police forces we could vote against it. That's what we've done, all of us.'

McClelland joined the Cabinet resentful of Whitlam. But after two or three meetings he changed and hitched his star to the Prime Minister. McClelland so impressed Whitlam over the next few months that, by the middle of the year, he had become one of the most powerful figures within the government.

The same caucus meeting also saw the elevation to the Senate leadership of Ken Wriedt whom Whitlam regarded as being one of his best Ministers. Wriedt was virtually an unknown when Labor won office in December 1972 and was given the Agriculture portfolio by the Prime Minister—a subject on which Wriedt freely admitted he knew nothing. But, unlike so many other Ministers who held easier portfolios, Wriedt displayed a thorough grasp of his subject, a solid administrative ability, sound political judgement and was able to establish good communications with the rural sector.

Whitlam defended the Murphy appointment vigorously and he pointed to the precedents already established by former Liberal–Country Party governments in this area. Whitlam told Parliament that Murphy was the fifth Attorney-General to become a High Court judge—his predecessors being Sir Garfield Barwick, Sir John Latham, Sir Isaac Isaacs, and Henry Bourne Higgins. He even quoted the number of British Attorneys-General who had been appointed Lords Chancellor this century.

On most accounts the Murphy appointment seemed a success for Whitlam. He removed one of his oldest rivals to the High Court, where Murphy could only benefit the Labor government. Murphy's departure created a NSW Senate vacancy to be filled. By a peculiar paradox this was to result in a major political plus for Whitlam and disaster for the Opposition leader Bill Snedden. Beyond this the Murphy appointment left a deep impact on the Liberals. After the defeat of the Whitlam Government many of them were still working against Murphy and prepared to lay money that he would not survive on the High Court bench.

# 8

# WHITLAM DEFEATS SNEDDEN

*It is only now that the federal leader of the Liberal Party is without power and without influence.*

Gough Whitlam, 19 February 1975

There is no greater ignominy for a political leader and no force so destructive as a pretender in the ranks whose aspirations are transparent. Such was the position in which Bill Snedden found himself after the Christmas–New Year season closed in January 1975. Snedden was a man who shunned personal clashes. But he possessed a brand of stubbornness that would never shirk a fight. At the end of January Snedden decided that the activities of the Fraser lobby and Fraser himself were all too obviously directed at presenting the party with an alternative leader. He resolved to confront Fraser directly on the issue and nail it once and for all. The confrontation that occurred was the only one between the two men during the entire leadership crisis period.

The Liberal Party shadow Cabinet met in Melbourne on 30 January. Snedden, having decided that after the meeting he would call Fraser aside for a private talk, carefully prepared his ground. Simultaneously and separately Fraser also decided that he must see Snedden. During the meeting he passed a note along the table to the leader asking for a discussion when the meeting concluded.

When the two met Snedden said he would not tolerate the continuing press stories speculating about the leadership. He said these stories were undermining the unity and leadership of the party. While they did not come directly from Fraser he knew their source. Snedden stressed that it was imperative that he have the loyalty of all Liberal parliamentarians, particularly Fraser. In the present circumstances it was hard to come to any other conclusion than that Fraser was preparing for another challenge. Snedden told Fraser that if he wanted to stay on the frontbench then he would have to make a public declaration of loyalty to the leadership and repudiate any suggestions that he was promoting a challenge. Snedden said he wanted such a declaration to be specific and for Fraser to spell out that he would not be a leadership candidate before the next elections. He had thought out beforehand a form of words which he suggested to Fraser.[1]

Fraser was caught unprepared by Snedden's tough line. He believed it was unreasonable and argued that he could not be expected to give such an all-embracing declaration. What if Snedden fell under the proverbial bus? Fraser denied that he was involved in any way with moves against Snedden. He said he would have no part of them. He reaffirmed his loyalty to Snedden but said that the demands Snedden was making on him were beyond what a politician could be expected to give. Fraser left saying he would consider the matter and consult a number of people in the party about it.

Fraser was worried by the Snedden ultimatum. At this stage Snedden still appeared to have a better than reasonable hold on the leadership and Fraser was anxious, as always, not to appear a saboteur. He was also deeply concerned at the prospect of being sacked to the backbench. But in another sense the Snedden stand gave Fraser just the sort of opportunity he wanted. It enabled him to consult widely in the party about a demand that had been placed on him. Implicit in all such discussions, even if it was never raised directly, was the question of the leadership itself. It meant Fraser could actively talk to members about the leadership without lobbying their votes, without being disloyal. He spoke to as many as twenty Liberal members and Senators during the next week and found that many of them believed that Snedden was being unreasonable and asking too much. One said: 'Fraser has been asked to give and say what no man can give and say.'

This provoked a tactical debate among the Fraser supporters. One view was that he should resign anyway—but Fraser rejected this saying he did not want to be tagged a wrecker. Following his previous resignation from the Defence portfolio during the Gorton years, such a move could have been highly dangerous. Some others wanted to use the issue to provoke another leadership challenge. But Fraser took the middle course. He decided to meet the bulk of Snedden's request. He would issue a statement as Snedden wanted, but not in the all-embracing terms sought by the Liberal leader.

Fraser saw Snedden in Canberra on 5 February 1975 and the two men talked about the form of words to be released in Fraser's name.

A few minor changes were made to the text, which both men accepted. It received extensive press cover the following day. Fraser said:

> At my initiative, last Thursday 30 January, and because of my concern, I discussed with Bill Snedden the continued and wrong press speculation that I am promoting a challenge to him as leader of the Liberal Party. As a consequence of the discussion I make this further statement. Bill Snedden has my full support. I repeat, as I have said on numerous occasions, that I supported the party room decision of last November and that I support the elected leader of the Liberal Party. Despite that, there has been continued widespread speculation that I, or colleagues of mine on my behalf, are promoting a challenge to Bill Snedden. That is not so. There is no contest. The issue was decided in November. No one to my knowledge, or with my consent or support, has done anything whatsoever to reopen the question. I make this statement to end speculation that my earlier statements were equivocal—they were not and are not. Those who seek to make them so serve the cause of the Labor Party. I will not advance that cause. Our need is for stability in the Liberal Party. Our purpose must be to work for the defeat of the Labor government at the earliest opportunity.

The one thing Fraser omitted to say was that he would not challenge Snedden in the future. This was pointed out the same day by John Gorton. While most newspapers ran this story 'straight', the lead on the Melbourne *Age* story said that senior Liberals believed that Fraser was still prepared to challenge Snedden despite his statement. Fraser himself contacted senior executives from one newspaper organisation asking for the story to be run 'straight'. Some of Fraser's closest supporters later interpreted this as a showdown between the two men which Fraser had won by still leaving his options open in his declaration of loyalty.

What Snedden wanted was personal loyalty in a genuine sense from Fraser and his close circle. Snedden came under extensive pressure during this period to use the authority of leadership to dump Fraser to the backbench. At the same time many Liberals, particularly NSW Senators Robert Cotton and John Carrick, urged Snedden not to sack Fraser, on the grounds that it would promote further division within the party. Ultimately Snedden accepted this argument. His whole career had been based on efforts to promote unity and defuse factions and he had no intention of changing the tactics of a political lifetime.

Snedden was driven by the high media profile Fraser had assumed over the previous six weeks and the continuing rumours within the party that the Fraser forces would strike again. Since the November challenge he had spoken to the six members involved, in an effort to secure their support or at least neutrality. One of them, 'Duke' Bonnett, had told Snedden the same day the delegation had seen him in November that he was with the leader anyway. After the challenge Snedden had made a brief trip to the United States to get a first-hand assessment of its economy, then he took a break at the Abrolhos Islands off Geraldton. The US trip left Snedden convinced that the international economic problems of inflation and unemployment were so great that Australia would not escape lightly.

In early 1975 Snedden's advisers, Tony Eggleton and Jon Gaul, reviewed how their leader could lift his performance—a requirement for his survival. It was decided that his private secretary, Dr Jack Best, the target of criticism from the parliamentary wing, would be replaced by Eggleton for a temporary period. Snedden's itinerary was rearranged to increase his impact, and plans were made for a series of public rallies in the major states to be attended by Snedden and other federal and state leaders. This was approved by the national campaign committee of the Liberal Party on 23 January. The campaigning program was designed both to boost Snedden's image and to maximise his options, notably for a mid-year election by blocking supply. The first rally was set for 16 February at Randwick racecourse in Sydney.

The program was approved by the shadow Cabinet meeting in Canberra on 5 February and announced on the same afternoon that the Fraser statement pledging support for Snedden was released. To many Liberals the two announcements were a strong indication that the decks were being cleared for a mid-year election. The national campaign committee meeting on 23 January had reviewed an extensive mid-term advertising campaign prepared by Berry Currie Advertising Pty Ltd, who handled the Liberal Party account. The aim of the campaign was to run a series of 'soft sell' television advertisements to market Liberalism and improve the party's image overall. It was at this meeting that the national campaign committee told all states that they should maintain a maximum level of readiness for a mid-year election.

On 10 February the Liberal Party rolled out another weapon that would occupy a formidable place in any election battery—a new economic policy. At a press conference Snedden released a 57 page document containing 33 specific policy initiatives in the most comprehensive assessment of the economy ever made by an Opposition party. In a document which bore all the marks of an election manifesto, the Opposition developed an argument already established as a vote winner: that all sections of the community could receive an increase in their incomes after tax at the cost of a cutback in public sector spending.

The hallmark of Labor's 1974–75 budget had been its refusal to restrain the public sector on the grounds that this would jeopardise Labor's program of social reform. The Opposition had no such qualms. It put the options bluntly to voters: they would have to accept a lower growth rate in public services as the price for getting a larger slice of the income cake and a reduction in unemployment and inflation. The Opposition pledged to stimulate the private sector by abolishing the Prices Justification Tribunal, instituting an investment tax allowance of 40 per cent for equipment which was on site by the end of 1976, abolishing permanently the capital gains tax and the surcharge on property income, as well as guaranteeing to the states a fixed proportion of income tax revenue. While the policy did not specify the extent of income tax cuts, it indicated they would be substantial in order to increase incentives for middle income earners.

The economic policy was open to criticism on the grounds that its proposals were not costed. There was no attempt to assess the cost of income tax reductions which would inevitably be expensive if they were substantial. The policy reflected Snedden's determination to hammer Labor on the economy and use it as the overriding issue in any election campaign. He was confident that, with the deterioration in the economy since the May 1974 election, the government would face an almost insurmountable task at its next trek to the polls.

The clearest sign that the Opposition was contemplating a mid-year election came from Snedden's public remarks. Indeed, it was a constant theme in his statements. On 3 February Snedden said in Hobart he would like to see an early election and predicted one could come from either the disintegration of the Labor Party or when the people were fed up with the government. Snedden told the Young Liberal Movement's national convention that many Australians now 'accept that only a change of government will provide the boost to confidence imperative for recovery'. Snedden said, 'This will be for the people to judge. Meanwhile, the Liberal and Country Parties will continue to provide positive and sound alternatives to the present government's failure of management and leadership.' Two days later, on 5 February when announcing the series of Liberal rallies, Snedden said he believed a change of government would be 'a delightful thing' for most Australians.

His strongest election statement came on 16 February at the Randwick racecourse rally when he demanded a federal election in front of 6000 Liberal supporters standing in the pouring rain. Snedden looked and sounded like a man on the campaign trail as he thundered out the coalition platform, attacked government policies on taxation, health, inflation, unemployment and foreign affairs. He told the cheering crowd: 'Soon we will look back on the Labor government as a temporary aberration—a bad dream—and make no mistake, we are going to get back. We are ready to fight and we know we will win. When it does come, the election will be a clear choice between individual enterprise and freedom and centralist-socialism.' In a direct challenge to the Prime

Minister, Snedden said: 'Mr Whitlam, if you believe the people of Australia want you in office, let's have an election.'

By this stage Snedden's tactics were too transparent. There was a hint of desperation in the bluster and bluff he directed towards the government about an early election. The political reality was that the issue of an early election would be determined by one man and one man alone, Snedden himself. Whitlam, who had been re-elected Prime Minister nine months previously, had no intention of calling a new poll. Snedden's implied threat to force another election through the Senate was designed to keep the pressure on both Whitlam and Fraser. He sought to whip up the climate of public opinion towards the election frenzy which he wanted.[2]

But Snedden was never able to execute his election strategy. Two formidable obstacles suddenly loomed, blocking his path and within a few days destroying his leadership credibility. The obstacles appeared in the form of the newly-appointed NSW Liberal Premier Tom Lewis, and Snedden's old and familiar adversary Gough Whitlam. The irony for Snedden was that the issue on which he sustained such damage was the very one on which the Liberals should have been able to reap a political harvest—the appointment of the Attorney-General Senator Lionel Murphy to the High Court. The federal Liberal Party was outraged at this move and believed the Whitlam government was trying to 'stack' the court. But before it had time to marshal its forces, Tom Lewis came in the night and drenched its ammunition.

The NSW Premier was involved in the issue by virtue of s15 of the constitution. This section provides that when a casual vacancy occurs in the Senate through the death or retirement of a Senator then both Houses of Parliament of the state which he represented shall vote on a replacement. In short, Tom Lewis as Premier and leader of the party which commanded a majority in both Houses of Parliament in NSW, could determine Murphy's replacement.[3]

It was a long-standing convention in Australian politics that Senators were always replaced with a new Senator of the same party. Such action had been automatic over the previous 26 years after the voting system of proportional representation had been introduced to the Senate, thereby ensuring that its numbers were always delicately balanced between the two major parties. In this period since 1949 the convention had always been observed by Labor and non-Labor Premiers alike, whether the vacancy was created through death, retirement, or elevation to a government post. The reason for the convention was simply that it promoted stable government and maintained the will of the people expressed at the last election. Everyone knew that, with the close balance of parties in the Senate, the flouting of the convention could mean a shift in the balance of power in that chamber.

After Snedden's decision to block supply in 1974 and force an election, the Senate became the major tactical focus in Australian politics. If state Premiers began to select the political complexion of replacements when Senate vacancies occurred, they would be assuming a potential power not just over the balance of parties in the Senate, not just over whether a bill became law by passing through the Senate, but over the survival of the federal government of the day which governed through the House of Representatives. This could only be done when Premiers decided to ignore the convention and use to the hilt the power which was theirs through s15. Often such an action might have only minor consequences but when it altered the balance of power in the Senate the implications were momentous. This is precisely what happened later in 1975 when the Queensland Premier Joh Bjelke-Petersen followed Tom Lewis and appointed a non-Labor Senator after the death in office of Queensland Labor Senator Bert Milliner.

Tom Lewis threw a bombshell into the federal political arena when he announced on Monday 10 February that Murphy would be replaced by a non-Labor Senator. Both the federal Labor and federal Liberal Parties were stunned. Whitlam had never anticipated such an action when he conceived and carried out the Murphy appointment. He called Lewis on the Sunday evening of 9 February to inform him about the appointment and the need for the vacancy to be filled. It never occurred to him that Labor might find itself left with only 28 Senators instead of the 29 elected in the May 1974 election.

Snedden was equally stunned. Lewis had made the decision without talking to him at all. It was a move which had far more federal than state repercussions. The vacancy was in the federal parliament and Lewis was embarking on a course that would breach 26 years of history in which the Liberal Party had observed the convention.

Tom Lewis, a new tough-minded Premier, stumbled into an abyss without watching his step. Lewis rang the Victorian Premier Dick Hamer on hearing about the vacancy and sought his colleague's advice. There was no doubt in Hamer's mind about the responsibilities of a state Premier in this position and he told Lewis to appoint a Labor Senator. But Lewis was more orientated to the style of a Bjelke-Petersen than a Hamer and, after thinking the matter over, decided to take the plunge by appointing a non-Labor man.

When Snedden held a press conference to unveil his economic policy he was infuriated to receive a barrage of questions about the Premier's move. Snedden replied abruptly: 'The convention has served us well—you never know when it could operate in a reverse direction. I believe the convention will be observed in the present case.' From the time Tom Lewis made his announcement, the merits or otherwise of the Murphy appointment was a dead issue. He had killed the political opportunity the federal Liberals were hoping to exploit in an awesomely effective way within hours of the Murphy announcement.

Whitlam recovered quickly from the Lewis shock and moved to exploit the disarray within the Liberals. Whitlam knew that Snedden was looking to force a mid-year poll through the Senate and he had been searching for an issue on which to confront and humble the Opposition Leader. Whitlam's standing at the end of January had sunk to its lowest ever—but he was now returning to Canberra and the parliament, the forum of his dominance. Whitlam never had any doubts about his abilities as a politician and parliamentarian. He had survived three Liberal leaders and regarded Snedden as a lesser opponent than any of his predecessors. Throughout his political career Whitlam had demonstrated a remarkable, almost Houdini-like capacity for resurgence. He had fought back from seemingly impossible positions to triumphs in a way that baffled commentators and defied the political norm.

At the end of the previous year relations between Whitlam and Snedden had reached their nadir. Politicians on both sides would testify that personal relations between the two men had deteriorated to the worst they had seen between a Prime Minister and a Leader of the Opposition. In December 1974 Whitlam referred with little less than contempt to 'snivelling, snarling Snedden' as part of a deliberate effort to denigrate the Opposition Leader and destroy his political standing. Snedden in turn became increasingly personal in his remarks, labelling the Prime Minister's European trip a 'caravanserai' and likening Whitlam to 'an ancient prelate traversing some of the lesser populated areas of the world'. This invective was a product, not just of personal differences, but of the war of nerves accentuated by the constant threat of a new election. Whitlam had set his sights on Snedden as the weak link in the Opposition line, the point at which Labor enjoyed its maximum advantage. He had this strategy verified by the Liberals in the November challenge and from that time embarked on a strategy to increase the internal tensions within the Liberal Party over the leadership. From December 1974 Whitlam constantly repeated that he was delighted to see Snedden remain as Opposition Leader and reaffirmed that the Labor government would see out its full three year term without being forced to an early election in the interim.

In his major address to the Terrigal conference Whitlam declared:

> Mr Snedden talks as though it were his prerogative to decide when the next election will be. That is a fantastic assumption for any leader of the opposition, but doubly fantastic for this one—a man with the shakiest hold on the leadership of his own party, a man who cannot commit his own Senators, on this issue or any other. The Australian people are being asked to contemplate the possibility of another

election for no better reason than that Mr Snedden's parliamentary colleagues are breathing down his neck.

Whitlam loved the office of Prime Minister and would not surrender it easily, certainly not to Snedden. He continued the direction of his attack on the Opposition Leader. As it became more and more successful during the session, he redoubled his efforts. Whitlam was to play a crucial role in the Liberal leadership struggle, a large part of which was to be conducted on the floor of parliament.

On 11 February the NSW Cabinet set up a three-man committee under the Premier to examine the legal problems involved in a non-Labor appointment to the Senate. On the same day the coalition parties in Canberra split over the issue. Country Party leader Doug Anthony supported Lewis saying his action was justified in view of the government's efforts to 'stack' the High Court. (If the Senate voting card for the previous May federal election was used by Lewis as a basis for filling the vacancy then the Country Party could argue that as number six on the ticket it should have preference over the Liberals in having its own candidate appointed). Anthony went on ABC television to praise Lewis for his courage. He told Lewis: 'If this is your decision, I will accept it and I will support you.' The other leading political figure who supported Lewis was the Queensland Premier Bjelke-Petersen who said: 'We have got to recognise that the Labor government is trying to destroy us as states. The appointment of Mr Murphy to the High Court proves that.' Bjelke-Petersen dismissed Snedden and the federal Liberals declaring: 'We have always been the ones to face reality.'

The next day Snedden reaffirmed his view that a Labor nominee should be appointed. In his first real move to dissuade the NSW Premier, Snedden rang Lewis and told him the convention should be upheld. The two men had a blazing row. Snedden told Lewis there was no point in putting a non-Labor person in the vacancy. He said the federal party opposed it. Snedden made it clear that any non-Labor appointee would be barred from the Opposition party room and effectively isolated. Lewis replied that he had no intention of changing his mind. He said the NSW party would back him on the issue and there was nothing Snedden could do about it.[4]

Meanwhile, hostility to the Lewis move mounted and was inexorably tied to criticism of Snedden for his failure to influence the NSW Premier. A number of well-known Liberals spoke out against the move with Gorton calling the Lewis plan 'crazy and mad'. The former Prime Minister said: 'It means you can have a majority one minute and have it taken away the next, quite regardless of the wishes of the people.' Queensland front bench Liberal Jim Killen warned that the whole process of democratic government was at risk. Liberal Movement Senator Steele Hall said the action of the Premier could lead to the destruction of parliamentary stability in Australia. Most newspapers attacked the Lewis move.

The Opposition parliamentary executive, at a meeting on the evening of 11 February, endorsed the principle that the convention should be maintained. Snedden was dismayed at the continued public statements by Anthony supporting Lewis after this time. Whitlam now branded the NSW action as 'an act of sabotage against the Senate, an act of sabotage against the clear will of the people of NSW, an act of sabotage against the constitution and an act of sabotage against the whole parliamentary system in Australia'.

The government Senate leader Ken Wriedt introduced a motion into the Senate to support the filling of casual vacancies to maintain the party status quo. This was designed to force the federal Liberal Party to either support Lewis or condemn his action in parliament. The feelings of the federal Liberals were revealed when the Opposition Senate leader Reg Withers moved an amendment to the Wriedt motion which still called on Lewis to uphold the convention and which was strong enough for the Labor Party to accept and endorse.

By Friday 14 February Snedden had become enraged with Lewis. All week in parliament Whitlam and his senior Ministers had used the issue to undermine the Opposition Leader and had linked this new breach of convention with Snedden's breach of convention in 1974 when he blocked supply to force an election. Snedden was particularly stung by a series of column pieces appearing on Friday and Saturday in which senior press gallery correspondents pinpointed the issue as one which verified the claims of weak leadership which Snedden's opponents within the party had made about him. Lewis and Snedden spoke to each other by phone on Saturday 15 February and this time the federal president of the Liberal Party Bob Southey was involved in an effort to mediate between the two men. This clash between Snedden and Lewis was even worse than before.

The following day, Sunday, the two men were to appear together on the same platform at Randwick racecourse—the first of several unity and campaign rallies. Snedden told Lewis it was nearly impossible for him to appear with the Premier. He said he would have to point out his own view, which would virtually amount to an attack on the Premier. Lewis would not tolerate this and at one stage it appeared the entire NSW Cabinet would refuse to participate in the rally. Southey, who was in Sydney on the Saturday, spent several hours on the phone to both men in an unsuccessful effort to resolve their differences. Snedden told Southey that the federal party could accept nothing less than a backdown by Lewis. Southey briefed Snedden that a softer approach was needed because of the danger of a direct split between the federal and NSW wings of the party. Snedden turned on Southey over what he interpreted as the federal president's failure to support both himself and the convention. Finally, a compromise was agreed upon, in which Snedden would state his own view and then say that under the constitution the appointment was purely a state matter in which he had no power to act.

Snedden reluctantly accepted this compromise, reasoning that an open split in the party would do nobody any good. Although the Randwick meeting was rescued, Snedden was angry that he did not possess the power to over-rule the Premier. He was equally angry that when he tried to bring pressure on Lewis, as everyone told him he should, the party president had different priorities. One of the unpublicised consequences was a falling out between Snedden and Southey. From this time onwards their relations were never the same. Southey believed that Snedden was becoming unreasonable and prone to projecting ulterior motives into anyone who disagreed with him. Snedden believed that Southey had tried to find excuses for Lewis instead of supporting his federal leader. This meant that the apex of the Liberal Party's organisation, hitherto one of Snedden's strengths, was now lost to him.[5]

A week later, when the Liberal Party federal executive met in Hobart, Snedden secured its support for the upholding of the convention, but, once again, the executive acknowledged the right of the state concerned to make the decision. By this stage the damage had already been done to Snedden.

Whitlam's parliamentary onslaught was in full flight by Wednesday 19 February. It was Snedden's most humiliating day. Whitlam demonstrated a remorseless attitude on the vacancy and was successfully needling his opponent. The Hansard read:

Dr Jenkins: Can the Prime Minister provide the House with any further information on the issue of the proper and democratic manner in which casual Senate vacancies are filled?

Mr Snedden: Come on Dorothy.

Mr Whitlam: I am glad that the Leader of the Opposition is here today because this is one of the matters on which he knows what ought to be done and refuses to do anything. Since last week . . .

Mr Snedden: Has not the honourable member any pride that he can think of a question for himself instead of doing just exactly what his leader says?

Mr Whitlam: The right honourable gentleman interjects about pride. Let me quote some of his portentous remarks of last Sunday. He said: 'I, Billy Mackie Snedden, have no power to determine who that successor will be. I have no power under the Liberal Party constitution. I have

|  |  |
|---|---|
|  | no power under the Australian constitution. I have stated my view clearly, frankly, without fear and without seeking favour. That is my view and I maintain it.' But let me go back to what the first leader, the founder of the Liberal Party, did in this matter. |
| Mr Nixon: | I rise on a point of order, Mr Speaker. The Leader of the Opposition also pointed out honestly what are the facts of the situation, which is more than the Prime Minister did on television on Sunday night. |
| Mr Speaker: | Order! The honourable member for Gippsland will resume his seat. I warn honourable members against taking frivolous points of order. The honourable member for Gippsland knows that that is a frivolous point of order. The honourable member for Gippsland will remain silent. |
| Mr Whitlam: | The first casual vacancy to arise after proportional representation was introduced in the Senate arose in December 1951. It occurred in Western Australia. A Labor Senator died. The Liberal Premier . . . |
| Mr Snedden: | Come on. Woof, woof! |
| Mr Speaker: | Order! Interjections will cease or I will take the appropriate action. That applies to every member of the House. |
| Mr Whitlam: | The right honourable gentleman seems to be more than usually hysterical. I have never known even him to giggle so much. He is going gaga. |
| Mr Speaker: | Order! The Prime Minister will address the Chair. |
| Mr Whitlam: | Let me reiterate: The first casual vacancy to occur after proportional representation was introduced in the Senate occurred in December 1951. It occurred through the death of a Labor Senator. The Premier of Western Australia at the time was a Liberal. The Liberal and Country League executive met shortly afterwards and carried a resolution agreeing to the appointment of an LCL candidate. The Premier, however, got the executive to agree that he should first consult the Liberal Prime Minister, Mr Menzies. He wrote to Mr Menzies on 20 December. Mr Menzies obviously gave him his view and as a result — |
| Mr Nixon: | I rise to a point of order, Mr Speaker. This is a clear abuse of the privileges of question time by the Prime Minister. Why does he not make a statement and let the subject be debated? |
| Mr Speaker: | Order! No point of order is involved. |
| Mr Nixon: | A point of order is involved. It is a clear abuse of privilege. |
| Mr Speaker: | Order! No point of order is involved. The honourable member for Gippsland will resume his seat. |

In his answer Whitlam said that all Premiers at the time agreed that a person of the same party should fill the vacancy and this had happened in all 25 subsequent vacancies. After further unsuccessful efforts by Snedden to take a point of order, Whitlam concluded:

> Mr Whitlam: There was nothing in the Liberal Party constitution to prevent Mr Menzies in 1951 telling the Liberal Premier of Western Australia the right thing to do. There was nothing in the Australian constitution to prevent the Liberal Prime Minister of Australia telling the Liberal Premier of Western Australia what to do in 1951. It is only now under this new Liberal leadership, leadership which the Liberal leader is always proclaiming, that the federal leader of the Liberal Party is without power and without influence.

This long exchange contains all the elements inherent in the explosive situation in the parliament. Whitlam's dominance was complete and each day he was well prepared, using the latest incidents available and the most recent comments by the Opposition to expose Snedden's vulnerability; the Prime Minister brought to bear all his fluency, his venom and his knowledge of parliamentary procedures as he leant across the table to taunt his opponents and then turned back to receive the endorsement of his own backbench, one foot on his own chair as he settled into a long answer. The extract reveals Snedden's frustration and impotence at Whitlam's attacks. It also indicates the constant stream of interjections coming from the Opposition. Another omen is the apparent failure of the Speaker to run the House with a firm hand.

The same day, when asked about Bjelke-Petersen's threat to deny Japan coal unless it imported more beef, Whitlam declared:

> As honourable members know, Liberal leadership has declined somewhat over the last two decades. The right honourable gentleman (Snedden) contents himself with inane interjections. Outside the parliament and inside the parliament he never says boo or moo to the Country Party leaders within the House, within the federal parliament or any of the state parliaments. It is an abysmal demonstration of national leadership.

Whitlam then announced that the government's Supply Bills would be introduced at the normal time thereby defying Snedden's implied election threats.

Throughout this period most Liberal backbenchers sat grimly in the House watching the parliamentary annihilation of their leader. One or two of the most well-known Fraser supporters were grinning during Snedden's most embarrassing moments as they realised that Whitlam was doing the job for them. The mood of Parliament House at the time was one of unpredictability fanned by constant crisis. Each day after Question Time reporters would mingle with Fraser supporters in the lobbies and in Kings Hall to reflect on Snedden's daily defeat in the House and be told that the leadership was 'only a matter of time'. A number of Fraser supporters established a regular rapport with senior newspaper correspondents and the psychology of crisis or, as it came to be known, the 'siege mentality' afflicting the leadership, was further exacerbated. The more it was written about, the more real it became.

By the weekend of 22–23 February it was clear that Snedden was staging his last fight as Leader of the Opposition. Both time and alternatives were running out for him. The essence of his task was to convince the voting public that it needed a general election in mid-year as much as Snedden did himself. An election with the prospect of elevation to the Prime Ministership now appeared the solitary option left for the Liberal leader. It appeared inconceivable that he could retain the leadership until the budget session of federal parliament.

Parliamentary performances have little or no impact on the public; but they have an enduring effect on the parliamentarians who witness them. One of Whitlam's greatest skills as a politician, perhaps his greatest, was his capacity to understand and absorb the issues of the day and translate them into invaluable political capital inside parliament. He had done this with vast success on the Senate vacancy, the constant theme being the failure of Snedden to stand up and be counted as a man of influence within his own party, within the Opposition coalition, and with state Premiers.

The next move had the aura of inevitability about it. The pro-Fraser backbenchers now began to turn against an early election, pointing to Snedden's weakness compared to Whitlam's strength and saying the Liberals could never countenance an election in these circumstances. Some even believed that if Snedden tried to persuade the parliamentary party to accept an election it would provide the stimulus needed to provoke a new leadership spill. Staley's prediction that Snedden would be replaced was looking more accurate every day. The Fraser forces had no set timetable; but they were more certain than ever that there was majority support to replace Snedden with Fraser at the right time and in the right way. A number of backbenchers and Senators who had opposed Fraser in November had changed sides.[6]

At this point Snedden called Staley to a meeting in an effort to stop the rot. Snedden confronted Staley reminding him of his pledge to accept the decision of the party room in November 1974. Snedden said that he did not believe Staley was abiding by this statement. He asked Staley to make a public declaration supporting him and warned that the constant leadership speculation was doing grave damage to the party.

Staley told Snedden his views were on the record. He refused to make such a declaration saying it would be dishonest of him and contrary to what he believed. He agreed with Snedden that grave damage was being done to the party and asked Snedden to resign the leadership. Staley denied that he had been lobbying against Snedden and actively working for Fraser. He claimed that a number of Liberals had approached him rather than vice versa and expressed their disenchantment with the leader.

The meeting proved abortive. But it was one of the few signs that Snedden was actively trying to bolster his position within the party. Jon Gaul was urging him to get out and win back the support which was gradually ebbing away. But Snedden was betrayed by his own nature. He never started running until it was too late. He made a fundamental political misjudgement about the strength of the Fraser forces. Snedden had no one working the parliamentary party in an organised way on his behalf. Yet the Fraser forces were waging a constant campaign, inside the party and with the press.[7]

The extent to which Snedden's position had been undermined was shown at the end of February when the Opposition singularly failed to exploit the amazing resignation of the Speaker of the House of Representatives Jim Cope.

This incident was a direct result of the inflamed passions and pressures on the floor of Parliament. A number of Labor Ministers, particularly Whitlam, Clyde Cameron and Rex Connor, were infuriated by what they regarded as Cope's inability to control the Opposition in parliament and his rulings from the Speaker's Chair which satisfied neither side. Whitlam felt that Cope was letting the Opposition disrupt Question Time in a deliberate campaign conducted by the three senior Country Party spokesmen, Doug Anthony, Ian Sinclair and Peter Nixon.

The issue came to a head at Question Time on 27 February by which stage the parliament had nearly reached boiling point. Two days before, Doug Anthony had been suspended from the House amid uproar as Whitlam continued his assault on the Opposition. On this fateful morning Liberal frontbencher Dr Jim Forbes accused Cameron of telling 'a monstrous lie'. Cameron asked for a withdrawal and a three-way exchange followed between the Speaker, Forbes and Cameron. Cameron, frustrated by what he considered Cope's lack of resolution, told the Speaker: 'Look, I don't give a damn what you say. I . . .' He was drowned out by Opposition members calling on the Speaker to name him—that is, move to have him suspended from the House. Cope called for order, asked Cameron to apologise three times and said finally: 'Is the Minister going to apologise?'

Before Cameron could answer, the Prime Minister declared 'No' in a loud voice, directly defying the Speaker. Whitlam had decided to precipitate the showdown with Cope. The Speaker immediately named Cameron whereupon Sinclair moved his suspension from the House—a motion which would normally be moved by the Leader of the House, Fred Daly, who had no intention of moving anything. When the question was put, Whitlam stood up, gathered his papers in a controlled fury and strode red-faced to the Speaker's Chair.

As the House broke into chaos, Whitlam angrily told Cope: 'If you lose this division you'll have to resign,' along with a few other choice words. None of his remarks could be heard by anyone but Cope. The Prime Minister then walked along the front bench and straight to the opposite side of the chamber to make certain that the government voted against Cope and that he did lose the division. The rest of the Labor Party followed. During the division former Prime Minister McMahon tried to take a point of order about Whitlam's conduct which he described as 'totally disorderly and appeared to be offensive and threatening to you, Mr Speaker'. When the division was concluded, Cope tendered his resignation as Speaker of the House and said he would give it in writing to the Governor-General. Snedden jumped to his feet and declared: 'Mr Speaker, that is a courageous act.'

While the incident sprang directly from the frustration of Whitlam and the government towards Cope, its roots were deeper. It reflected, and was partly the result of, the bitterness pervading the parliamentary arena stemming chiefly from the Opposition's cynical threat to force Labor to the polls and Whitlam's vicious response of attacking Snedden in an effort to crack open the Liberal Party. There was no clearer demonstration of this than after the division when Whitlam and Snedden, now openly contemptuous and antagonistic to each other, stood on the government side and hurled abuse back and forth for several seconds as members crossed the floor. That night the Labor caucus met and elected Victorian Labor backbencher Gordon Scholes as the new Speaker.

Snedden seized on Whitlam's defiance of Cope as a chance to grab the political initiative back from the government. After Cope left the Speaker's Chair, he told the House: 'We have just witnessed a matter the like of which has never occurred in the life of this parliament.' The Opposition moved a motion of censure against the Prime Minister when the Parliament next assembled on 4 March. Snedden attempted to turn Whitlam's own argument against himself. He said the Prime Minister could no longer argue in support of parliamentary convention when he had so spectacularly breached convention by defying the authority of the Speaker which was essential to the institution of parliament. Snedden told the new Speaker Scholes that he came to the Chair crippled in his authority.

Snedden's aim was to regain the initiative but the effect was the opposite. This was the day Whitlam put the final seal on Snedden's parliamentary destruction in a speech that revealed the extent to which the political battleground had become highly personalised. The Prime Minister said Snedden had to take responsibility for the uproar in parliament, that it was the logical end to the pattern of disruption established by the Opposition. 'He did it for the same reason that he does everything else: this embattled pygmy has to show his failing followers that he is a big boy after all,' Whitlam said of his opponent.

The psychology of crisis reached its peak in the Liberal Party on 6 March, the last parliamentary sitting day before a four week recess. During this week a Morgan Gallup Poll published in the *Bulletin* revealed that support for the Liberal–Country Party had fallen by four per cent to 48 per cent in the first fortnight of the parliamentary session and that support for Snedden's handling of his job had fallen five per cent to 28 per cent. That is, Snedden was retarding the electoral standing of his own party. On this final Thursday rumours about the Liberal leadership crisis reached a climax. Word was spread that there would be a special party meeting that day or the next to resolve the issue. One Liberal frontbencher—a known Fraser sympathiser, Tony Street—went to see Snedden on Thursday night and was later questioned by reporters following rumours that he had asked Snedden to resign. In fact he went to see the leader on a simple policy matter.

The claustrophobic and distorting atmosphere of Parliament House was taking its toll. The Liberal Party was displaying the classic symptoms of a political organisation with severe internal difficulties—an inability to capitalise on the weaknesses of its opponents. On any objective criteria the Opposition should have been riding high; it still had a decided edge in the opinion polls. Yet the election mentality which Snedden had fostered was now destroying him. He had provoked retaliation from Whitlam on a massive scale and forced his own supporters to judge him not in the fullness of time but in the immediacy of an election climate. Nobody in Parliament House would have dreamt that out in the countryside at large the Liberal Party was in a powerful electoral position.

When the House broke this night the preoccupation of the Liberals was no longer the prospect of an imminent double dissolution but the leadership question itself. This had now become the sole issue, the only issue inside the party. The press, encouraged by the more active members of the Fraser faction—now a permanent and identifiable feature of the party, growing stronger all the time—was ahead of the situation inside the party. The rhetoric used by the Prime Minister would have bounced off an Opposition Leader at ease with his party. But the combination of the internal difficulties which he faced and the external pressure led to a significant deterioration in Snedden's performance.

As the Liberals prepared to leave Canberra for a break it was clear that Snedden had lost any chance for an early election. His leadership was in tatters. The Fraser forces were already putting the machinery together for the kill.

# 9

# THE LEADERSHIP CHALLENGE

*They hate him and distrust him; but sooner or later they'll elect him.*

Mungo MacCallum on Malcolm Fraser,
27 December 1974

When parliament adjourned Malcolm Fraser already had the numbers to make him Liberal leader. The real question was how this support could be translated into votes inside the party room. In the previous fortnight there had been a decisive shift of attitude among Liberal leaders and senior party figures. The key events were acceptance by the deputy leader Phillip Lynch and by the two main figures in the NSW branch of the party, Senators Robert Cotton and John Carrick, that the leadership crisis had to be resolved through the party room; and secondly, the recognition by the Liberal Senate leader Reg Withers that Fraser appeared to have the numbers.

These Liberals along with their senior colleagues had held informal talks about the leadership issue which had resulted in the conviction that the crisis had to be brought to a head. In the atmosphere of the party at the time, this attitude amounted to a polite way of declaring one's support for Malcolm Fraser; he appeared to be the victor in a party room ballot.

Snedden's position and power base had eroded substantially since the previous November. In late 1974 he had carried with him the rest of the party's leaders with the presumed exception of Ivor Greenwood, nearly all of the Senate, most NSW members, and, in addition, he had enjoyed the complete backing of the Liberal Party organisation. In each one of these four vital areas he was now substantially undermined.

In November 1974 Staley had tried to persuade Lynch to join the rebel forces but the deputy leader had refused and instead had worked for Snedden. But Lynch, who was seen inside the parliamentary party and certainly saw himself as the 'honest broker' between competing groups, had enjoyed close relations with the Fraser camp from this time. It had been made clear to Lynch by Staley and other Fraser backers from late 1974 after the November bid that he was acceptable to Fraser as deputy. The same message was given to Lynch by Fraser himself in early 1975.

Lynch had always acted as a loyal deputy to Snedden and had told Snedden, as had Andrew Peacock, that he would never challenge him for the leadership. But Lynch now believed that Snedden's prospects for survival were limited. He concluded that the crisis would have to be resolved as quickly as possible, preferably in a behind-the-scenes fashion. He accepted that the consequences of this would be a change in the leadership and was most anxious to ensure that in any leadership challenge that he remained as deputy. Lynch felt that if Snedden survived it would be only by the narrowest of margins and would offer no permanent solution. In the meantime the party was slowly tearing itself apart and Whitlam was gaining strength daily.

The longer that Whitlam faced Snedden as an opponent, the more likely it seemed that Labor might actually recover and win the next election. For Lynch and the Liberal Party such a prospect was intolerable. Lynch had sound relations with Fraser. His office was down the corridor from Fraser's confidant, Tony Street, and sometimes Fraser would visit Lynch of an evening en route to Street's. The talk and the tide at the high levels within the party was turning against Snedden.[1]

One of the decisive differences between November and March was the shift of opinion in both the Senate and in NSW. This was symbolised in the reappraisal undertaken by the two senior NSW Senators, Cotton and Carrick. Both men, Cotton ever so tentatively and Carrick far more forcefully, supported a resolution of the crisis. Cotton's transition was similar to that of Lynch. He was a paradoxical figure over the crisis period with both the Snedden and Fraser camps claiming his support—but Cotton, like Lynch, favoured a resolution and that could only assist Fraser. Carrick and Cotton had worked together in the NSW organisation and then in Senate for more than 20 years. While Cotton was more of a front man with well-established ties to the Sydney business community, Carrick was more powerful, an idealistic but clever politician who held more sway with the NSW members and Senators and who took a considered long-range view of politics. Carrick became a dedicated but disguised Fraser supporter.

The changed outlook of Cotton and Carrick, who had supported Snedden in November, mirrored rather than inspired a rethink from the

NSW Liberals. There were no real 'kingmakers' for Malcolm Fraser. In the final analysis Cotton probably delivered no votes. Carrick carried more weight and those NSW Liberals who consulted him would have left feeling that a vote for Fraser was a sound decision. A number of his proteges in the NSW party, particularly John Howard, were heavily identified with the Fraser camp.[2]

Snedden made extensive efforts to use the party organisation to bolster his leadership but this tactic was now collapsing. He still enjoyed complete support from Tasmania and from the Victorian party president, Peter Hardie. But in NSW the party organisation swayed towards Fraser. Snedden had lost the support of the party's federal president Bob Southey following their dispute in February. Southey gave his undisguised endorsement to Fraser.[3]

The extent of the crisis within the party in early March was revealed by a prominent *Sydney Morning Herald* story that Fraser supporters were aiming to depose Withers as Senate leader in favour of Cotton. The story also predicted an early move against Snedden. When Jon Gaul discovered the report after the first edition of the *Herald* hit the street, he rang the paper's executive editor David Bowman, just after 1 a.m., complaining about the piece and saying that there was no threat to Snedden's leadership. The next day Cotton denied that he was involved in any moves whatsoever to secure the Senate leadership. One motive, used in retrospect to explain the floating of the story, was as a device to bring Withers firmly into line with the Fraser camp. The story illustrated the extent to which the Liberal Party itself was seized with the leadership question which was threatening to engulf some of the other leadership positions.[4]

This mood was partly a tribute to Fraser's media tactics during the 1974–75 summer break. The most famous example of his projection to the party and public had been a long profile on the leadership pretender by Trevor Hawkins in the *National Times*. The article was headlined: 'Watch out Gough, Watch out Bill, Malcolm still wants your jobs.' The thrust of the piece was Fraser's leadership ambitions as he philosophised about the qualities of leadership, declared himself as an early election man, and revealed the lighter, more relaxed side of his nature as he did wheelies down the gravel drive on a powerful motor bike and enjoyed cold beer and scotch in the homestead. The article caused a minor sensation in the party and nourished the speculation about a leadership change during February and March 1975.

When the parliament broke on Thursday 13 March, senior Liberals were looking towards a smooth and effective leadership settlement. But they got precisely the opposite. The Liberal leadership issue was given a massive kick along the next day, 14 March, by frontbencher Andrew Peacock. By mid-afternoon the airwaves were full of Peacock's comments made from Adelaide calling for a party meeting on the leadership. Peacock said it was 'totally unreal for the Liberal Party to continue to ignore stories about a challenge to Mr Snedden's leadership. Rumours and divisive speculation about the leadership are doing great damage to the party. Mr Snedden should call a meeting and ask for a vote of confidence so that speculation can be ended.'

Peacock's comments would pass into political folklore. They hit the parliamentary Liberal Party like a bombshell. From the moment they were uttered there was no way Snedden could hold out against a party meeting within the next few days at which his leadership would be put to the test. Peacock had shattered the fragile fabric of Liberal unity which was already falling apart. The background to Peacock's intervention and his motives became a talking point for years.

Two days before Peacock had spoken to four or five Liberal parliamentarians in Canberra who argued that the leadership crisis had to be resolved. Peacock told colleagues later that he had been urged to make a public statement that would force the showdown. Earlier that week Peacock and Fraser had bumped into one another at Old Customs House, Melbourne, and Fraser had suggested a lunch. Peacock in turn suggested they go to Florentino's, one of Melbourne's landmarks, where they would be seen, thereby rebuffing any conspiratorial interpretations. Despite speculation at the time, no deal was done at this lunch between the two men. While the leadership crisis was canvassed, there was no agreement on a joint Fraser–Peacock ticket to replace Snedden and Lynch. A large number of Fraser supporters, particularly Staley and members from NSW and Western Australia, were not prepared to tolerate a Peacock deal. Nor is there any claim that Fraser wanted one.

On the evening of 13 March—the day before his intervention—Peacock and one of his best Liberal mates, Don Chipp, had a major row over Peacock's intended statement. Chipp unsuccessfully urged Peacock not to make this statement. The next day Chipp failed in an effort to contact Snedden first and warn him.

Peacock dropped his bombshell on his arrival at Adelaide airport to campaign in the electorate of Sturt on behalf of the Liberal member, Ian Wilson. Snedden was also in South Australia this day near Millicent and was stunned when he heard the reports of Peacock's statement. Snedden's staff made furious efforts during the afternoon to contact Peacock to get him to ring Snedden. The two men made telephone contact about 6 p.m. that afternoon and Peacock told a dismayed and incredulous Snedden that he still supported him but believed the whole leadership crisis had to be cleared up. Peacock said that some of his statements had been taken out of context, but he told Snedden that the party was unable to continue with the present crisis. A devastated

Snedden finished the conversation still confused and uncertain as to why Peacock had gone public.

Snedden's adviser, Jon Gaul, had a blazing row with Peacock. Peacock told Gaul the party could not withstand such continued damage. He was highly emotional at the accusations already being made by many Liberals—that Peacock had betrayed Snedden. Gaul said it was hard to draw any other conclusion when Peacock was making statements calling for a party meeting. He said this would only play into Fraser's hands by giving the Fraser forces exactly what they had been seeking. Gaul went to Moorabbin just after midnight to meet Snedden who returned to Melbourne by light plane. The Liberal leader was deeply depressed and knew the leadership issue was blown open. The Fraser camp was delighted at Peacock's statement although many puzzled over his motives. The Snedden camp attacked Peacock bitterly. The self-styled Fraser coup leaders from November went into immediate operation.[5]

Lynch and others within the leadership group were appalled at the Peacock declaration and realised that any chance of effecting a behind-the-scenes leadership settlement was gone. It was now clear there would be a public bloodletting which would strain both the party and all of the leading participants and create lasting bad blood.[6]

Peacock's statement had taken events out of the control of individuals and given them a momentum of their own. Peacock, who up to this stage had not played a major role in the leadership crisis, now found himself under attack from Snedden's supporters and regarded with curiosity by the Fraser supporters, who had been hostile towards him in the past. That Friday evening Peacock's call was supported by both Withers and Greenwood. 'The thing has got to be resolved,' Withers declared. Greenwood, one of Fraser's earliest and most convinced supporters in the Senate, publicly declared: 'Andrew Peacock has said all that needs to be said. The issue needs to be cleared up—and the sooner the better.' By contrast an established Snedden supporter, Jim Killen, said he was mystified by Peacock's call. 'Anyone who wants to challenge should stand up,' Killen said. 'Moves for a confidence vote are a very curious form of political warfare. This is an incredible form of political extravagance.'

Lynch was propelled into action by the Peacock statement and some Fraser supporters suspected that Peacock was making a play for the deputy's position on a Fraser ticket. Lynch spoke to a number of Liberals in the next two days to confirm his standing as deputy. Peacock's statement pushed Lynch even further into the Fraser camp to ensure he maintained his position in any leadership change. By opening up the issue Peacock wrecked any chance of a quiet settlement and guaranteed an open contest. In this situation there was another possibility—that Peacock himself might stand for the leadership if Snedden was deposed.[7]

The reasons for Peacock's statement still remain the most debated feature of the entire leadership struggle. Why did Peacock, who had vigorously opposed Fraser's leadership push, apparently play into Fraser's hands by calling for a party meeting? One explanation is that Peacock believed a challenge was inevitable and tried to precipitate it early rather than late in order to protect Snedden. This theory is hardly sustainable since Snedden knew nothing of the plan. If this had been Peacock's motive, he would surely have told the man he was trying to save. The second theory is that Peacock sought to widen the crisis to include other leadership positions in an effort to become deputy in any general spill.

A third and more credible theory is that Peacock, sensing Snedden's weakness, was making his own play for the leadership. That is, Peacock realised that unless the current cycle was broken then Fraser would depose Snedden. So Peacock sought to precipitate events and give himself a chance of seizing the mantle. Peacock had always displayed a fine political touch in the past. But this time it deserted him completely.

On the Saturday morning Gaul and Jack Best gathered at Snedden's Melbourne home to plan the counter-attack. It is a sobering thought that it was only on this day, which proved to be six days before the party meeting, that Snedden really started to run hard and lobby members. It is a testimony to his misplaced faith in his political colleagues and to his inept political assessment of the strength of the forces opposed to him. Right to the very end, Snedden's political judgement was betrayed by his confidence in his colleagues as friends. He worked on the assumption they would not do to him what Brutus did to Caesar.

Contact men were set up in each state for Snedden—Don Cameron in Queensland, Senator Harold Young in South Australia, Senators Peter Durack and Fred Chaney in Western Australia, while Victoria was looked after by Snedden himself and state president Peter Hardie. Tasmania was virtually in the bag for Snedden. NSW was particularly weak with the main contacts being Alan Cadman and Bob Ellicott, who would fight an uphill battle.

Snedden was also busy preparing his keynote address to the Victorian Liberal Party conference at Bendigo to be held over the weekend. Beneath the facade of the Bendigo conference the overwhelming interest was the leadership question; Snedden and Fraser were now actively lobbying members. Snedden himself had a particularly poignant reminder of the growing connection between Fraser and Lynch. From his motel window he saw his deputy and the pretender to his leadership having a long and serious discussion in the courtyard of the motel. Snedden's communication with Lynch was now near breakdown point.[8]

The following day he delivered to the council meeting one of the most emotional and effective speeches of his career. Snedden declared:

> I am determined that this deliberate campaign to test the nerve of Liberal supporters will not turn me aside from the job in hand . . . I regret to say that some Liberals have buckled under in the face of this campaign of abuse and misrepresentation. Nothing could be more calculated to play into the hands of our opponents. If we as a party allow ourselves, our loyal supporters and the general public to be taken in by these cheap and transparent political tactics we will pay a heavy price. We cannot be defeated by Labor. We can only be defeated by ourselves. While I remain the leader we will go on, undistracted, undiverted, and we will win.

It was during this speech that Snedden repudiated the threat to block the government's Supply Bill in order to force a May election. This undertaking—to give passage to the government's Supply Bills—was designed to eliminate the pressure hanging over both the Labor government and his own party. Snedden later maintained that he never had any intention of forcing an election, despite substantial evidence to the contrary. But Snedden's staff saw this statement as a deliberate effort to knock down what many Liberals claimed was a crutch for their leader: henceforth, Snedden would seek to maintain the leadership on his own merits, not through any need to preserve stability due to a possible early election.

However Snedden was again responding to events far too late. By this time everyone knew an early election was inconceivable. Snedden was doing nothing more than recognising the political limitations which had been imposed upon him.

This speech was a last-ditch effort to counter the moves against him inside the party and his plea for party unity brought standing ovations as he publicly criticised the 'waverers'. It was the speech of a man who would countenance no compromise, no party meeting. Meanwhile the mechanics of Snedden's destruction were put together.

Victorian Liberal Senator Sir Magnus Cormack, former president of the Senate, former preselection opponent of Malcolm Fraser, long-standing supporter of John Gorton, mentor of Andrew Peacock, self-styled 'father figure' of the party, now assumed the centre stage. That night Cormack made arrangements for both Cotton and Withers to dine with him. Lynch had also spoken with Cotton about meeting to discuss the crisis and it was agreed that he should join the group. They were anxious to review the situation following Peacock's statement and the knowledge that something would have to be decided before the Opposition executive meeting in Melbourne on the Monday morning. Because of arrangements previously made, it was agreed to meet at Cormack's.

Lynch spoke with both Cotton and Fraser over this weekend and agreed that Fraser would also join the group. Withers arrived on a flight from Perth on the Sunday evening and had both Vic Garland and Senator Peter Durack with him. He rang Cormack from the airport who invited them all.

While it was assumed that the meeting was strictly private, the story had leaked to the press. By the time Cotton and Lynch reached Cormack's Toorak Road apartment, there were photographers outside. The photos the next day told their own story next to the news of the meeting broken by John Jost in the *Age*.

Cormack, in fact, had been having a busy weekend. Earlier that day he had enjoyed a drink with Peacock and told him that his statement was in the best interests of the party. But he did not tell Peacock about the gathering he had planned in the evening. The meeting at Cormack's was not a conspiracy. It could hardly be with Durack, a Snedden backer, in attendance. But this meeting reached a decision of immense importance: that a party meeting should be held as soon as possible and that the leaders should present themselves in a delegation to Snedden the next morning formally demanding he accept this.

Fraser's supporters merely had to point to Peacock's comments and seek a meeting to settle the question before more harm was done to the party. This was an eminently reasonable point of view, with which it was hard to disagree. Most of the talk at Cormack's was conducted on this level. There was a discussion about whether any spill could be confined to the leadership or whether it would be carried to all party positions. The consensus, not surprisingly, was that only one position was in dispute, that of federal leader. The Cormack gathering adopted this as its position. If the spill move spread, the person in most danger would be the Victorian Senate deputy leader Ivor Greenwood who had little power base and held his post through ability and his performances in the Senate. But Greenwood had already made his position clear to the Fraser supporters. He wanted the challenge to proceed and considered this so important that he was prepared to risk exposing his own position.

The Liberals despatched their drivers to buy dinner and then settled into steaks, chicken and Cormack's claret. If this meeting had not been held at Cormack's that evening, it would have been held elsewhere. It reflected a need on the part of the senior Liberals to assess the position in the obvious knowledge that the Fraser–Snedden clash was now only days away. Most participants assumed that Fraser would have the numbers in the looming ballot. They debated Snedden's defects and whether he could recover as leader. Most felt that he could not—and observed that his committee work, which was normally impressive, had been falling apart, a sign of the leadership strain.

Malcolm Fraser arrived at Cormack's about 9.30 p.m., after the others had finished their dinner. There were no overt declarations of support. Backing Fraser was strictly a business proposition, not a personal testament. As the night wore on, more claret was drunk and some of the participants seized the opportunity of having a crack at Fraser, the man they were going to make Liberal leader because there was nobody else. It was the last chance they would get. They broke at about 1 a.m. having decided that a delegation to seek a party meeting would assemble at Snedden's Treasury Place office the next morning at 9 a.m. Lynch contacted Greenwood so that the other three party leaders would be included in the group demanding the meeting.[9]

Snedden was informed of the Cormack gathering late on Sunday night when called by a journalist. Not until he read the morning papers did he realise the participants. He knew that he would be confronted with a demand for a party meeting.

At 9.20 a.m. Lynch, Withers, Greenwood, Garland and Cotton saw Snedden in his office and put two propositions to him. Firstly, they denied there was a conspiracy or a plot against his leadership and denied reports that this had been the main purpose of the meeting in Cormack's flat. Secondly, they told the leader it was essential to hold a party meeting as soon as possible in view of the current speculation to settle the leadership question. Snedden told the delegation he would consider its request and the Liberals then adjourned to Old Customs House in Flinders Street for their executive meeting.

Monday 17 March was St Patrick's Day and Snedden began proceedings by telling Doug Anthony that the Liberal executive would meet separately to discuss its problems. The meeting was then engulfed by a tactical battle between Snedden and Fraser. At this point Snedden, in the face of combined pressure from the other leaders, acceded to their request for a party meeting. But he would not accept the demands made on him by the Fraser forces, namely, that he seek a vote of confidence in his leadership. The arrogance of the Fraser push was breathtaking!

A number of Liberals, including Withers, Senator Margaret Guilfoyle, Jim Killen and Senator Peter Rae, supported the principle that Snedden as leader was not obliged to seek a vote of confidence in himself. Both Forbes and Rae specifically asked Fraser whether he was challenging Snedden for the leadership. Fraser avoided answering the question directly, implying that he would stand if the position was vacant and saying nothing could happen until the leadership had been vacated. Forbes clashed bitterly with Fraser, saying the party was facing a grave situation where its leader was under constant threat and that nobody could tolerate the leader of a political party having to subject himself to votes of confidence every three or four months.

Carrick spoke strongly for the Fraser line, saying that Snedden's approach was wrong and that people should not be forced to vote against him; it was up to Snedden to seek a vote of confidence on his own initiative. Snedden's tactic was sensible and appropriate. He said that if anybody was dissatisfied with his leadership and wanted to challenge him then it was up to them to do so. They could move the motion themselves. His aim was to flush out Fraser; to force Fraser to declare himself as a pretender to the leadership.

Snedden brought the issue to a head with a typed statement which he read to the executive:

> I have expected and assumed loyalty and confidence from each and all of you and I have given it to you. We have a shadow ministry. Each of you has been appointed by me. I have acted in accordance with the principle of the Westminster system of joint and collective responsibility. If any one of you has not been able to give me loyalty and confidence he should have told me. None of you have done so. I shall be in my office for the next fifteen minutes. If any one of you wish to see me privately I will be glad if you will do so.

Snedden then retired to his office.[10]

After some time Fraser and Lynch went to see Snedden. Fraser told Snedden that his approach was inappropriate and that, given the doubts about the leadership, he should seek a vote of confidence in himself. Snedden bluntly replied he had no intention of doing this. He said he had been elected in 1972 and 1974, and had been given another vote of confidence in November 1974. It was absurd to expect him to seek yet another one. Snedden was enraged that Fraser was still trying to conceal his hand. But Fraser and his backers felt it would have been a tactical mistake for Fraser to announce his candidature to Snedden. Fraser believed that if he declared himself at this time then Snedden was likely to sack him immediately and discredit him as being disloyal. Fraser, given his Gorton legacy, sought to avoid this at all costs.[11]

In fact, Fraser never declared himself until there was a party meeting agreed upon and even then he never admitted his supporters were moving to vacate the leadership.

At lunchtime Snedden faced a bevy of television cameras and newspaper journalists on the first floor of Old Customs House. He announced there would be a party meeting but went on to say that nobody had declared himself as a challenger. 'I told them that I had proposed we have a party meeting and they generally agreed that that should be done,' Snedden said. 'When we have that party meeting it should be an opportunity for anybody to challenge me in the leadership of the party. It will be the forum in which the challenge can be made. Whether there will be such a challenge I don't know. I want this over and done with and out of the way.' Asked if he would continue in politics if defeated, Snedden initially refused to answer but then added: 'I'm not going to lose; I'm going to win.' Asked why he had called a meeting when there was no declared challenger, Snedden said the notoriety and publicity surrounding the Liberal leadership had to be resolved. He said he would not be moving any motion at the party meeting.

One of Snedden's chief mistakes was to acquiesce in a party meeting to resolve the leadership before Fraser had declared his hand. Although it probably made no difference eventually, it put Snedden in a position which bordered on the absurd. Even more important was Snedden's failure to stand up to pressure from Withers and Lynch over the timing of the party meeting. It was in Snedden's interest to delay any party meeting as long as possible. His initial reaction was to hold the party meeting the following week on Monday or Tuesday. But his fellow leaders argued that this was unacceptable, that it would prolong the period of open dispute and that the meeting must be during the current week. Snedden finally succumbed and set the meeting for Friday 21 March, four days away.

That evening Malcolm Fraser was hounded by a number of journalists before he left the building. Fraser replied 'No comment' when asked if he would challenge Snedden at the Friday party meeting. 'You can ask as many questions as you like, but I'm not going to make a comment,' Fraser told reporters. 'No comment means no comment,' he said in reply to persistent questions. Fraser's refusal to be pinned down by the media reflected his earlier refusal to declare his hand at the executive meeting. Despite the fact that he was already lobbying members, that his backers were now planning their second challenge, that he had attended the meeting at Cormack's flat the night before to organise his leadership bid, that he had made it clear to Lynch that he would be acceptable as deputy, Malcolm Fraser still declined to stand up and be counted. This reflected the deepest fear in Fraser's political life.

Fraser was obsessed about preserving the facade of unity, which he was of necessity destroying. He was a creature of his past, above all, his public and destructive demolition of John Gorton's prime ministership carried out in the House of Representatives in 1971. The Liberal Party had a reservation about Fraser—that he was too divisive. So Fraser believed that any open declaration against Snedden could be counterproductive, that the 'wrecker' image which he had gained during the Gorton years might be revived. Jon Gaul bitterly complained that night that Fraser wanted a 'dream run' to the Liberal leadership; that he wanted to get the job without having to bear any of the odium of backstabbing that accompanied a political revolt. Fraser wanted to be drafted into the job or at least he wanted it to look as though he had been drafted into the job.

Right from the very start, from November 1974, when he had formulated tactics with Staley, the first and most fundamental principle was that Snedden should never be attacked. It was naturally difficult to attack Snedden anyway because the man was essentially so widely regarded for his integrity and good nature. But beyond this Fraser was anxious to justify all his actions in terms of a high political morality. This trait was highlighted after he became leader when all the vital decisions he took were depicted in terms of important principles, essential to the national interest. From November onwards Fraser had allowed his supporters to create absolute havoc within the Liberal Party while all the time pledging his loyalty to the Liberal leadership and never doing anything in public which would cause this loyalty to be questioned. More than anything else this political technique infuriated and eventually depleted Snedden, who could find no answer to it given the immense difficulties he brought on himself and his failure to judge its strength.

Fraser was lucky that his political operation fitted so neatly into the circumstances of the time. In a very real sense Snedden had lost support for his leadership by default. It had been a relatively simple operation for Fraser to occupy the middle ground. Fraser was well aware that he was now entering his most crucial week in politics. It would result either in his assumption of the Liberal leadership or this time, after a second unsuccessful challenge in five months, the worst setback of his career. He was still cautious, ever wary of overplaying his hand, of trying to seize the mantle prematurely.

That night Snedden authorised Gaul to give the Canberra journalists a briefing on the shadow Cabinet meeting because he believed the facts would discredit Fraser. Gaul went back to Noah's Melbourne with three journalists, briefed them over beers and said that after weeks of inaction Snedden was at last preparing to fight. Gaul complained that over the previous weeks Snedden had refused to confront the pro-Fraser forces.

The next morning Snedden tried to put together a political package that would torpedo Fraser. He tried to 'do a McEwen on Fraser'. It was, in effect, Snedden's decisive play—and it failed. Snedden tried to organise a collective veto on Fraser by several prominent frontbench Liberals. The intention was that a number of Snedden supporters would announce a veto on Fraser with the intention of destroying his leadership prospects.

The original plan was that a joint declaration would be made by Andrew Peacock, Jim Forbes, Peter Rae, John McLeay and Jim Killen. Such a statement would have split the Liberal Party wide open. It would have taken the present personality rifts into an entirely new dimension.

It would have both increased the stakes involved in Fraser's challenge and increased the risks to the political future of a number of frontbench Liberals. Those people making the declaration would be putting their political necks on the chopper.

On Tuesday morning two journalists waited in Snedden's office while the Liberal leader tried to put this package together. At lunchtime Gaul and the journalists went to a small restaurant not far from Snedden's Treasury Place office. The Snedden camp worked furiously to secure the collective veto. By lunch there was a fallback—the hope was for a joint veto by Peacock and Forbes. Snedden wanted them to make a television declaration that afternoon. The ABC put a camera crew on standby. Gaul spoke to Peacock from the restaurant in an effort to clarify the timing of any statement. But Snedden was asking for too much. By mid-afternoon Snedden was settling instead for open declarations of support. His original demand exceeded his strength. Professional politicians could not afford to veto themselves out of a ministerial job when it appeared that Fraser's chances were better than even money.[12]

Tuesday was the vital day in the leadership crisis week. If Snedden were to recover his position he needed a dramatic strike. But his 'king hit' never materialised. During the day Snedden also spoke to Lynch. He asked Lynch for a public declaration of support in his leadership. But Lynch refused. He said public statements would only harm the party in both the short and long term. Lynch told Snedden he would make no public statement opposing him but he was not prepared to make a declaration of support either. When he returned to Melbourne Lynch saw Snedden and reaffirmed his attitude.

Snedden and Lynch both worked out of their Treasury Place offices during the week and, although their rooms were only a corridor's walk away from one another, they only spoke on two or three occasions. The hostility between the two men was reflected in deteriorating relations between their staff.

Privately Snedden was very bitter about his deputy. He believed that Lynch should have stood with him and fought with him. He was later convinced that if both men and their offices had been working jointly to muster support he might have survived. In Snedden's view it was the job of the deputy to give loyalty to his leader and Lynch had failed to do this. Lynch in turn pointed out he had been loyal to Snedden while Snedden remained a viable leader. He believed the situation had altered fundamentally, that the party was divided, that it was being forced into a vote on Snedden's leadership and that he should not take sides in public. Lynch's stand was designed to maximise his strength regardless of the result. He was confident of remaining deputy no matter who won the leadership struggle. While he was neutral in public he was closely associated with the Fraser forces in private.[13]

Malcolm Fraser committed himself at 6.15 Tuesday evening. 'Mr Peacock has indicated publicly that the present situation cannot continue,' Fraser said in a four sentence statement. 'With others, I agree with him, and there is to be a party meeting to determine the issue. If through any circumstances the office of leader should become vacant, I would be a candidate. This is a right which in those circumstances belongs to every party member.'

Fraser, who handed the statement to journalists in his office, refused to elaborate. But that night he appeared on Channel 9's 'A Current Affair' and ABC's 'This Day Tonight'. In these two television performances Fraser predicted he would be elected leader. Asked if he had a good chance of winning Fraser said: 'I would have thought so but that's for the judgement of the party room. If I say "Yes, I'm supremely confident" somebody will say "Well that's that arrogant Fraser again".' During his interviews Fraser said he believed Lynch should remain as deputy. Asked if he was aware of moves for a no confidence motion on Snedden, Fraser replied: 'No comment.'

Fraser denied outright that he had been involved in any behind-the-scenes moves to depose Snedden and he used Peacock's statement as the trigger for all subsequent events. 'Somebody else made a statement. I didn't make a statement and we wouldn't be in this situation now if that statement had not been made,' Fraser said. 'The high hopes for February were for an election now or in May to get rid of this government. For some time those high hopes have disappeared.' Asked if he had been disloyal Fraser defended himself saying: 'It is not a question of that. It is quite possible and quite proper to support a person as a member of that person's team. But if the party room happens to say that position is vacant, then any member of the party has a right to stand for the position.'

These words reveal Fraser's obsession with process and appearances. Publicly he held to the very end that he was never associated with the moves against Snedden designed to vacate the leadership—moves inspired by his supporters with his full knowledge. Beneath Fraser's guise as the man of principle was a clever political operator who depicted the struggle in terms of a party room decision divorced from his own actions. The problem for Fraser's later career was that the public would weary of such hypocrisy. At the mid-point of the week Fraser looked and acted like a winner. His Tuesday night television performances were probably the best he had ever given and Snedden was still fighting a rearguard action.

The Snedden strategy came into effect on the Wednesday with a series of declarations of support for him. But the divisions in the party only widened further when Peacock, after announcing his unequivocal support for Snedden in any leadership challenge, declared that if the party leadership was vacated he would stand against Fraser in the leadership ballot. Killen adopted a similar position. Three other Liberal frontbenchers, Forbes, McLeay and Rae, declared themselves for Snedden.

In a particularly virulent statement Forbes declared:

> I am making this public statement of support for Bill Snedden because of the disgust and despair I feel at the devious, unscrupulous and utterly contemptible methods which have been used in attempts to undermine him. I had a similar feeling of disgust when identical methods were used to dispose of John Gorton. I remained silent then. I could not live with my conscience if I did so again.

The strongest single core of Snedden supporters comprised the Tasmanian branch. Rae warned that the situation in Tasmania was such that there could be a split in the Tasmanian Liberal Party if Fraser was elected. Over the previous months Snedden had developed a special electoral strategy based on Tasmania and had devoted a lot of his time to formulating policies to meet the unique circumstances of that state. One of his greatest allies was the Tasmanian Liberal leader Max Bingham and there was pressure building in the Tasmanian party to split away from the federal party if Snedden was deposed. Four of the five Tasmanian Liberal Senators, Rae, John Marriott, Michael Townley and Eric Bessell, all declared themselves for Snedden. 'I'm not aware of a single member or branch of the Liberal Party in Tasmania who has expressed support for a change of leadership,' Rae said.

Snedden also received an endorsement from the Victorian organisation. Peter Hardie was instrumental in having 61 out of 78 Liberal Party branches in marginal electorates express support for Snedden. At the same time the Young Liberal Movement threw its support behind the Liberal leader. Indeed, the only public note of discord for Snedden came when Lynch and the federal president of the party Bob Southey, after conferring with one another, released statements condemning open declarations of support from Liberal members—the very basis of Snedden's strategy.

After speaking with Southey, Lynch showed Snedden a copy of the statement he intended to release. Snedden was unhappy and suggested a number of changes, the bulk of which were not made. 'At a time when the party faces the prospect of polarisation, public declarations can only damage the prospect of unity,' Lynch said. 'I will not be drawn into a public auction by declaring what I believe is appropriate for the party room alone.' Southey's statement was in similar terms, a clear sign that the federal president was tacitly supporting Fraser.

On Wednesday the main numbers men in the Fraser camp, Robinson, Garland and Staley, estimated a minimum of 35 votes for a spill and possibly as many as 42 of the 64-strong parliamentary party. The decisive states for Fraser were NSW and Victoria, which contained 31 MPs and Senators. Fraser was expected to win at least 20 of these votes—the nucleus of his support. The Senate, so hostile to Fraser in November, had changed its complexion.

Snedden flew to Canberra on the Thursday evening and went to Withers' office, where he had talks with both the Senate leader and Forbes about the respective numbers. Snedden also spoke to Cotton on Thursday and assumed that both Withers and Cotton were supporting him.

The first ballot in the party room on Friday morning would be the crucial one. The Fraser supporters would have to move that the leadership be vacated. This was their only course given Snedden's sensible refusal not to seek a vote of confidence. The vote on the motion to vacate the leadership would provide the acid test of party support for both leader and challenger. Fraser needed 33 votes to secure a majority out of the 64-strong party room. In normal circumstances, if he secured this vote his success in the second ballot would be certain. Once the leadership was vacated, nominations would be called to contest the leadership and three people had already declared themselves as candidates, Fraser, Peacock and Killen.

But on Thursday evening and Friday morning Snedden decided that, even if he lost the first vote, he would still nominate in the second ballot. One reason for his decision was the curious statement to him by senior NSW Senators that they would vote against Snedden on the first ballot, but then support him on the second to prove conclusively he had the backing of the party. This was a most suspicious proposition which Snedden appeared to accept. Peacock and Killen did not know of Snedden's assessment and acted on the assumption that if the leadership was vacated then Snedden would not run again.[14]

On Thursday evening Fraser's supporters gathered at the Canberra Rex Hotel to decide that veteran NSW backbencher Bill Wentworth would move the motion. There were some last minute nerves. Former Prime Minister Bill McMahon said the Fraser camp was too soft, that the contest was a lot closer and that Snedden was gaining ground.

The Liberal parliamentary party was divided against itself, member against member, challenger against challenger. Snedden himself had been toughened by the week of crisis. He pledged, if re-elected, to exact retribution against any new whispers of rebellion. But this was an admission of his own weak position. Every Liberal remembered the previous November when, within hours of the abortive challenge, the threat to mount a new one hung over the party. Who was to say it would not happen again if Snedden was re-elected? Indeed, it was inevitable in the assessment of many Liberals that such events would only repeat themselves.

This gut feeling, the psyche of the Liberal Party, was one of the great factors working against Snedden. After an upheaval of the dimensions which the Liberals had seen in the previous six weeks, a preservation of the status quo would only leave Snedden with ever-greater problems as an ever-weaker leader. Too many Liberals believed that confirming Snedden in office would offer no resolution of the internal conflicts. This was a great admission of the inroads Fraser had made into the fabric of the party. There was only one conclusion for a number of realistic politicians: that the only solution was a change of leader. This was certainly a major factor in swinging both NSW Liberals and the Senate towards Fraser, a swing that meant the real difference between November and March.

When the party assembled at 10.30 a.m. Friday, Snedden opened the meeting and asked if there was any business. Wentworth moved that the leadership be vacated. Marriott then asked if Wentworth meant all the leadership positions or not. Snedden ruled that the only position involved was his own. John Gorton then moved an amendment to the Wentworth motion to extend it to include the other leaders as well as Snedden. Gorton was saying 'one out, all out' in an effort to broaden Snedden's support. Gorton's amendment was opposed by a number of people and a long debate followed. Greenwood bluntly told the party that Gorton was being mischievous, that he was trying to bolster Snedden by introducing other issues and appealed to the party to reject it. McMahon strongly supported Greenwood. Lynch then stood up and said that if Gorton wanted to widen the issue to include the deputy leader, he would invite the party to move a similar motion to Wentworth's applying to the deputy leadership. Finally, Snedden said he would treat the Wentworth motion as the motion before the Chair and regard Gorton's amendment as foreshadowing a later motion. He also indicated he would treat the Wentworth motion as a motion of 'no confidence'. From this the party assumed he would not run in the second ballot, if there was one.

Forbes, Killen, Robinson, Wright, Anderson, Missen, Marriott and Guilfoyle all spoke before Snedden's final statement. The voting was by secret ballot and the votes were counted in the Whip's office. The result was a clear win for Fraser and the leadership was declared vacant 36–28. Snedden announced the result, declared that he was no longer leader, and handed the meeting over to Lynch. Lynch immediately asked candidates who wished to contest the leadership to stand. Snedden, Fraser and Lynch were the only people standing. Lynch resolved a moment of confusion by saying he was not a candidate. Peacock and Killen pulled out when they saw Snedden stand to recontest the leadership. Peacock did not know of Snedden's intent until the votes were being counted from the Wentworth motion when Snedden told him that if he lost he would contest the next ballot. If Snedden had not run, Peacock and Killen would have divided his support among them but they had no chance of winning the extra support needed to defeat Fraser.[15]

In the second ballot Fraser was elected leader of the party against Snedden 37–27. Snedden made a short speech thanking the party for the honour of serving it and calling on Liberals to give full support to the new leader. Later that day Snedden said a new era had commenced for the Liberal Party. Events proved him to be right.

# *10*

## THE NEW LEADER

*There are three things in life, politics, business and family in that order.*

Malcolm Fraser, May 1975

$A$s the hot fires of rebellion and recrimination dwindled into ashes, Malcolm Fraser moved to cover the Liberal Party scars from public view. On the afternoon of his victory, the new leader met the press in Parliament House in order to legitimise the succession before the people and the party. The leader is dead; long live the leader. All day Fraser had avoided the blood on the floor as though he had never seen it. Now the only outward signs of his inner tension were his badly shaking hands as he read from notes before a packed audience of press. Fraser was flanked by party president Southey, deputy leader Lynch, Senate leader Withers, Senate deputy leader Greenwood, all of whom had maintained their positions in the upheaval, proof of their wisdom in moving to bring the leadership question to a head, testimony to the continuity and endurance of the Liberal Party.

Fraser moved at once to break the circle of self-destruction into which Snedden had manoeuvred himself. It was on this day that Fraser defined the political parameters that would guide him throughout his short stay as Leader of the Opposition. The following morning's papers were dominated by the considered declaration in his opening statement:

> I generally believe that if a government is elected to power in the Lower House and has the numbers and can maintain the numbers in the Lower House, it is entitled to expect that it will govern for the

three-year term unless quite extraordinary events intervene. I want to get talk about elections out of the air so the government can get on with the job of governing and make quite certain that it is not unduly distracted in these particular matters.

This statement was prepared in consultation with the other leaders flanking him. It recognised that the constant election mentality which Snedden had created had been a potent factor in destroying him. In order to consolidate his position Fraser sought to cool the political climate, to drain the pent-up emotionalism from it. He wanted to end the siege of the Labor government which had provoked Whitlam's massive retaliation. In the previous two months Whitlam had built up extensive support by depicting the Opposition as unfair, bloody-minded, and ultimately ridiculous in its constant election threats. Fraser wanted to minimise Whitlam's ability to exploit the 'obstructionist' tag against the Opposition. He was anxious to ensure that the Opposition could no longer be blamed for the government's mistakes and that Labor's actions would be assessed on their merits.

But Fraser's attitude was always double-edged. While he was determined to kill election speculation, which he diagnosed as damaging to the Liberals, he was still insistent on retaining his right to force an election through the Senate as Snedden had done.

In his opening statement to the press conference he said:

If there are questions when an election might be held or when someone might want to do something about it, I would not be wanting to answer that particular question or trailing my coat about what our tactics or approach would be. If we do make up our minds at some stage that the government is so reprehensible that an Opposition must use whatever power is available to it then I'd want to find a situation in which we made that decision and Mr Whitlam woke up one morning finding that he had been caught with his pants well and truly down. So there'll be no speculation as far as I'm concerned about the timing of an election.

This was Malcolm Fraser's 'Catch-22'. He sought to remove the threat of an election yet retain the capacity to force one. It was a classic move by a politician to defuse a difficult situation while retaining all his options. While Fraser's move to dampen election speculation was rooted in political consolidation, his move to maintain his option was rooted in political ambition. Fraser spoke quite often of his belief in the principle that governments should serve a full three-year term and there is no doubt that he genuinely espoused this principle. But it was never an over-riding political axiom, to which everything else would have to give way. Ultimately there were other factors which prevailed over this one. Fraser was a pragmatic man and his search for power continually triumphed over the elevation of abstract principles of political science, no matter how fundamental they were.

Fraser's previous record had shown him to be an election hawk. Just three days before, during the leadership crisis, Fraser pointed out that the party's inability to force an election reflected its internal weakness. 'The high hopes of February were for an election about now or in May to get rid of this government,' he said. 'For some time those high hopes have disappeared.' However one of the most detailed insights into Fraser's attitude towards an early election had been given the previous December, just a fortnight after the abortive November leadership challenge and after the government's budget had passed the Senate. It was also two days after the Queensland state election, where Labor had performed so disastrously. Fraser had been interviewed on 'This Day Tonight' by Paul Barber:

Barber: You seem to be suggesting though, underlying, that you would like an early election.

Fraser: I think everyone in Australia would. Because this is a wretched government. It is a bad government. There is enormous unemployment that's going to continue to mount, and many people are going to be hurt. You know, the Queensland answer is not just a Queensland answer, it's an Australian answer.

Barber: Supply has already gone through the Senate. Would you be in favour of obstructionist tactics by the Liberal and Country Party Senators, in order to force Mr Whitlam's hand, as it were.

Fraser: Well, I'd never be in favour of obstructionist tactics, but I'd certainly be in favour of any tactics in the House of Representatives and/or in the Senate, that would help to preserve good government and commonsense in Australia. Now, you know, it's easy to say if the Senate vote a certain way, that that's an obstruction. But the Senators are all elected, they are not a House of Lords, people appointed for life. They're answerable to the people of Australia and they're entitled to act as their philosophy and conscience determines and you know, we said that we believe that we ought to reflect in many ways the views of the people of Australia, and this is the view that Mr Snedden has taken. Where the message has come from Queensland, very plainly —

Barber: A yes or no question: Do you think we will see an election in Australia within the next six months?

Fraser: Well, yes or no, that's very easy. I certainly believe the majority of Australians would want it, and I believe the majority of the members of the parliamentary Liberal Party would want it, but what happens in four months' time—politics is an unpredictable world. From this moment on, I think

it would be an easy thing to say, yes there'll be an election,
but in four months' time, circumstances change.

This interview makes it clear that months before Fraser became leader, he was favourably disposed towards an early election. The import of these remarks is that the need to give the people a choice would over-ride the need to preserve governments in office for three years, a principle he neglected to mention in the interview. In late 1974 Fraser and his supporters used the early election lever as a political weapon against Snedden, who, having precipitated the May election, felt that, regardless of the government's poor standing, he had to wait twelve months before forcing another election. A big number of Fraser supporters were early election hawks and highly critical of the 1974–75 budget arguing that it should be rejected, thereby precipitating a November or December general election which everyone knew the Opposition would win. The fact that Snedden was unable even to consider this as an option was used against him inside the party. He had gone too early. He had shown bad political judgement. Now when he should force an election, he was unable to do so. If the Labor Party had made a realistic assessment of Fraser, based on his words and actions before he became leader, then it would have been less confident of the government surviving without an election throughout 1975.

John Malcolm Fraser, the successor to the Liberal leadership, unlike Sir Robert Menzies his friend and mentor, was born to the purple. He was the richest, tallest and most privileged man in parliament. Scion of a family established in the wool aristocracy of Victoria's western districts, Oxford educated, English cultivated, Fraser's political career was that of a man determined to achieve in public life the power and prestige which his birth and upbringing told him was his natural inheritance.

He was not in the contemporary tradition of Liberal leaders. Fraser came from a background which could genuinely be labelled rural aristocracy and he was the first man with such a history ever to lead the Liberal Party. His experiences of life had been nearly totally divorced from the mainstream of contemporary Australian society over the previous thirty years. If Fraser's social origins were the landed gentry, his intellectual origins were post-war Oxford.

Fraser's well-documented arrogance and sense of superiority was social rather than intellectual. No man with an ancestry like his could be otherwise. His grandfather Simon Fraser was born at Pictou, Nova Scotia in 1832 into an emigre Scottish family which had left the Highlands after the Jacobite rebellion of 1745. Fraser arrived in Australia in 1853, went to the Bendigo goldfields for two years before moving into business in Elizabeth Street, Melbourne. He became a produce merchant initially and then set up in business as a contract builder of roads, bridges and railways and was instrumental in building the railways from Echuca to Bendigo and from Port Augusta to Farina. Fraser's suggestion to use Bendigo gravel as ballast on the Echuca line, instead of the blue metal specified in the contract, enabled the company to clear £100,000 of which his own share was £30,000.

In the mid-1860s Simon Fraser began investing in big rural properties from Queensland to Victoria. In 1874 he moved into public life, winning the seat of Rodney in the Victorian Legislative Assembly where he remained till 1883, developing a reputation as a skilful debater and conspicuous supporter of crown and empire. In the 1880s he founded Squatting Investment Co and bought properties on the Dawson River. He became a director of the City of Melbourne Bank and survived the crash of this bank in the 1890s. In August 1886 he won a position in the Victorian Legislative Council representing South Yarra province and six years later became Minister without portfolio in the Cabinet. He was a member of the original Australian Parliament, being elected to the Senate in 1901 topping the Victorian poll, and remained in the federal parliament for eleven years. He supported the Canberra site for the federal capital and advocated private ownership of railways. Grandfather Fraser developed a reputation as a tough, shrewd and flamboyant conservative and at one time was grand master of the Loyal Orange Lodge. He was knighted in 1918, one year before his death.

Simon had three sons and one daughter. The sons were Simon jnr, a rowing blue for Melbourne University and representative for Australia at the 1912 Stockholm Olympics, a sportsman par excellence who died just before his father; Douglas Martin, who developed similar prowess as a sportsman and was killed in Darwin in 1942; and John Neville, an excellent scholar and sportsman who had two children, first Lorraine a daughter and then John Malcolm a son, later to become Australia's twenty-second Prime Minister.

John Neville Fraser was an achiever and set high standards for his son. He was a tennis blue and Melbourne University cricket blue in 1911, went to Magdalen College Oxford for two years, where he was again a cricket blue, served in the First World War, was admitted as a barrister but never practised, devoting most of his efforts to the land.

Malcolm Fraser's mother, Una, travelled to Melbourne for his birth at St George's Road in a house called Mowbray and then mother and baby returned to the home property, Nyang in the Riverina. The property was originally purchased by Simon Fraser about 1880 and was a huge area which had subsequently been cut off, with various slices sold to other settlers after the First World War. It was forty-five miles from Deniliquin and life there was, according to Fraser's mother, 'very very lonely'. To get to the township the river had to be traversed and this was not easy with a shaky makeshift bridge or a home-made punt that never worked when the river was extremely high or low.

Fraser's early years were spent on this property with his sister Lorraine, within contact of few other children and in the midst of what was literally the great Australian outback. A manager and jackaroo lived in the house along with an occasional nurse and governess for the children. Fraser's parents were established at the property from 1926 to 1943 when they sold Nyang and went to the rich western districts of Victoria to purchase the Nareen property, a magnificent 8072 acres with an old-style stately homestead whose verandah dominates the landscape. The young Malcolm received occasional tuition in Melbourne from a preparatory schoolmistress who had once educated Stanley Bruce. This tuition began when he was six or seven and lasted till he was ten. He then went to Tudor House in NSW as a boarder where he received his preparatory schooling.

Fraser's childhood is the obvious origin of the 'loner' tag he gained in politics. The loneliness and privilege, which were the hallmarks of his earliest years, were later revealed in a certain diffidence towards his colleagues in politics and a determination to pursue his own course. It was at Tudor House that Fraser first began a decade of mixing with his fellow man that was to continue at Melbourne Grammar and then Oxford; it was a rarefied form of social milieu. According to his mother, Malcolm the student was 'always conscientious and industrious, interested in most things and fitted in with what most people wanted to do'. Fraser did very well at Tudor House: he became a monitor in his final year, distinguished himself by winning a bevy of school honours including the proficiency prize, and became scout patrol leader, chief librarian and winner of the shooting cup.

In 1944 he began at one of Australia's most prestigious schools, Melbourne Grammar, which at that stage had already educated two former Prime Ministers, Alfred Deakin and Stanley Bruce. Melbourne Grammar was modelled on the English public school system; in those days its old buildings and beautiful gardens created an aura of stability which was only slightly compromised by subsequent building extensions. The headmaster was 'Joe' Sutcliffe, a World War I veteran who believed in iron discipline and the proper delegation of authority. Sutcliffe instilled the great spiritual virtues of the British tradition: a belief in God, faith in country, dedication to public service, and commitment to self-improvement.

Malcolm's earlier abilities at Tudor House were not displayed to the same extent in the bigger and more competitive Melbourne school. He was a diligent but not outstanding student and left little mark during his years there. According to Sutcliffe, Fraser was 'a difficult boy to get to know. He was shy and reserved, always polite, gentlemanly and correct.' He can never recall having to punish Fraser for any misdemeanour and even attributes to the student an appearance that was 'frightfully correct, giving him both presence and dignity'. Sutcliffe says: 'When I had him in the study, I felt as if I had to be on my best behaviour. He was very different from his father, who was a natural extrovert.'

Although Tony Street, one of Fraser's greatest political supporters, was head prefect two years ahead of Fraser, the boy who was later to become Prime Minister was never made a prefect himself. One of the ironies of the label 'the prefect' put on Fraser in his political life is that some of the people who use it say he is still trying to compensate for missing out at Melbourne. According to former school captain Ken James, it was decided that Fraser was too aloof and too remote to do the job of prefect well. Fraser was not a personality at the school in either an academic or athletic sense. He participated in all house sports as requested, according to the former captain of Rusden House, Ken McKaige. 'Anything he was asked to do he tried,' said McKaige, 'but he wasn't a volunteer.' McKaige says that Fraser was once asked to perform in a house boxing tournament—something he had never done before—but he went in and acquitted himself well, although losing.

Another school colleague, Peter Beer, says that even at such a conservative school as Melbourne Grammar, Fraser stood out as 'a nonconformist in his conformity'. He had a distinct English accent and, on one occasion when asked his name, young Malcolm replied 'Friser sar', much to the confusion of the teacher. According to Noel Austin, who taught Fraser Latin in the 1948 class, he left little impact on the school and was mainly regarded as a good steady student. Fraser matriculated with second class honours in English Expression, Latin and British History and a pass in English Literature and French. A solid but unspectacular pass. At no stage during his secondary schooling had Fraser given any indication that he would be destined for greater things. But the turning point of his life, the great seminal influence, came in the next three years at Oxford.

Fraser's family had always wanted him to follow in the footsteps of his father, John Neville. When they thought of tertiary education it was never in the Australian context, always in the British. His father wrote to the head of Magdalen College enclosing details of Malcolm's matriculation, pointing out that he had attended the college himself thirty years before and seeking a place for Malcolm in one of the slots set aside for overseas students. This was how Fraser got into the university. When he left Australia it was not even certain what course he would be studying. His parents assumed he would go on and do law, given his natural bias towards the humanities and the experience of his father. But not long after Fraser arrived, he wrote back saying he would be studying politics, philosophy and economics in the first real sign that he was interested in politics. It was at Oxford that Fraser developed his independence of action and maturity of mind. This would provide the inspiration for his move into politics and the intellectual backbone for the rest of his life.

Fraser found the gap between Melbourne Grammar and Oxford a tremendous hurdle. In his first week he was given Keynes' general theory to absorb and write an essay on. Two of his lecturers were A J P Taylor and Isaiah Berlin. But the men who influenced him most were two philosophy tutors, Harry Weldon and Gilbert Ryle. These men typified the strand of thinking at Oxford which had such a great impact on Fraser. Ryle had started life as a guards officer, studied philosophy and then in the Second World War had a high position in British intelligence. Weldon, while an academic before the war, had been personnel liaison officer to Air Vice-Marshall Harris during the war and was present at all the major conferences between the British and American commands over coordination of policy. These men were both intellectuals and men of action. Hardened in war they were pragmatic, non-ideological and only too ready to point out the mistakes Britain had made during the 1930s through weakness, misjudgement and self-indulgence.

Fraser attended Oxford when Britain was reassessing the mistakes it had made before the war and facing a new challenge from the communist sector in the post-war world. Fraser absorbed the lessons Britain had learnt and they became imprinted on his consciousness. This was his first real intellectual input. He was only nineteen when he arrived. It was in these years, through the study of history and absorption of the British experience, that he embraced the notion of community self-sacrifice for the national interest, the conviction that both leaders and their peoples must be ever vigilant to protect the fabric of their society from both within and without. He was convinced that the maintenance of private enterprise democracy needed both cleverness and toughness. This was when Fraser became a 'hard options man'. His conclusions are based on an interpretation of history which comes straight from the great historian Arnold Toynbee whom Fraser studied at Oxford and whose theme has centred on the rise and fall of civilisations, something which has always fascinated Fraser.

Toynbee's theme is that civilisations fall because of human weakness and decay from within, which Fraser has been warning against for the previous 25 years. The application of this theme is constantly changing but the theme itself always remains the same. Fraser has always said that Australians must be prepared to make the sacrifice of having a defence force adequate for their needs and survival. In his maiden speech to federal parliament in 1956 Fraser warned that the major choice facing Australians was whether they were prepared to make a sacrifice in personal consumption levels, that is immediate living standards, in order to build up the investment needed to develop the country into a stronger economic unit. During the days of Vietnam and national service, he saw the choice as being whether the sacrifice in men and blood in South-East Asia would be sufficiently forthcoming to hold the line of anti-communist forces. However it was in his Alfred Deakin Lecture, delivered in 1971 while he was on the backbench, that Fraser exposed these preoccupations most clearly. Referring to Toynbee, he said:

> His thesis can be condensed to a sentence, and is simply stated: That through history nations are confronted by a series of challenges and whether they survive or whether they fall to the wayside, depends on the manner and character of their response. Simple, and perhaps one of the few things that is self-evident. It involves a conclusion about the past that life has not been easy for people or for nations, and an assumption for the future that that condition will not alter. There is within me some part of the metaphysic, and thus I would add that life is not meant to be easy.

This is the diagnosis and from it flows the conclusion:

> The determination of people and political fortitude can be destroyed by the difficulties of foreign policy or by internal divisions and weaknesses. We need a rugged society, but our new generations have seen only affluence. If a man has not known adversity, if in his lifetime his country has not been subject to attack, it is harder for him to understand that there are some things for which we must always struggle. Thus people or leaders can be trapped to take the easy path. This is the high road to national disaster. There are many strands to the maintenance of will—a society that encourages individual strength and initiative, an understanding of events, ability to bear sacrifices, an understanding that there are obligations that precede rights and a belief that work is still desirable.

Fraser continued to adapt this theme. As Opposition Leader in 1975 he bluntly told Australians they would have to face up to the consequences of the debacle in Vietnam. He publicly advocated bringing thousands of refugees, men, women and children to Australia. He repeatedly warned the government there was no easy solution to Australia's economic problems. When as Prime Minister he repudiated his campaign promise to maintain wage indexation, saying that a 6.4 per cent wage rise in early 1976 was too much, Fraser justified himself by reference to the tough option. He said there was no easy way out and lived up to his self-imposed standards of leadership by not shirking the hard road but by facing up to it and telling the nation it also had to face up to it.

Fraser's application of his view of history to Australia's economic problems was set out in his ANZAAS congress address in February

1975—the most important speech he had given for four years and a speech which was designed to establish his credentials as Liberal leader. The origins of this speech lay in the abortive 27 November leadership coup. That night Fraser, Staley and the declared pro-Fraser supporters gathered for celebratory drinks, believing they had done so well in the ballot that self-congratulation was warranted. On this night they changed their tactics and decided to lie low inside the party and concentrate on building up Fraser as a national figure of substance and prestige. This resulted in a vigorous media campaign which subsequently alarmed Snedden.

One strand, culminating in the ANZAAS address, was to demonstrate that Fraser was a man of ideas and purpose, a statesman. A tremendous amount of work was put into the speech during the Christmas period by Staley and a colleague with whom he went to school, Melbourne University academic David Kemp, who subsequently became Fraser's speech writer in both Opposition and government. In political terms Fraser was again fingering one of Snedden's chief weaknesses: the party held a widespread belief that Snedden had no ideas for it and no direction in which to lead it. Fraser wanted to show that he had both. In a sense he was attempting to exploit the crisis of identity inside the parliamentary party.

The pretender to the Liberal leadership declared:

> There is little time now for the easy optimism and endless expectations of yesterday. We are locked in a battle for survival. I cannot guarantee success, but I do say that my view of the individual in society and the conflict between free and totalitarian forms of government, which might yet engulf Australia, is the only thing that continues to involve me in politics.

Fraser then defined the dimensions of the national crisis facing Australia. He nominated the legacy of Keynesian economics and the new-found power of the trade unions as the core of the present problem. Fraser said Keynes and the New Deal created great expectations in communities and changed the modus operandi of governments. For the first time governments could actually spend more than they collected in taxes and be praised for it. In the years after the war this was repeatedly done to strengthen inadequate levels of demand. But at the same time governments used this technique as the road to political popularity, promising to spend more and more money and buying off the votes of various interest groups in this fashion.

In Fraser's view governments have been debauched through this process and have lost the art of restraint. He sees this as the ultimate absurdity, when Keynesian techniques are applied for the wrong reasons and end up fuelling inflation through huge government outlays. This provided the basis for Fraser's most sustained criticism of the former Labor government—the huge increases it implemented in public spending in order to finance its program. Not only did this mean that the public sector expanded at the expense of the private sector but that individual and private incentives towards self-improvement were destroyed. The encouragement to individual betterment was removed. In Fraser's eyes this was the ultimate political sin.

Fraser sees in the growth of trade union power a fundamental challenge to the democratic system.

> I accept very plainly that parliament must govern with the general acceptance of the great majority, but the challenge of extra-parliamentary authority to the authority of parliament represents an essential challenge to our society which could spell the end of our democracy. The Australian parliament and the Australian community can only avoid this challenge at their peril. They will do so at the price of destruction of a free society.

In Fraser's view trade unions now have too much power as a result of changed circumstances and laws where companies and employers once had too much power. This underlines the need for a proper legal framework covering industrial affairs so that agreements and arbitrated decisions will be kept with 'proper consequences' for unions which do not keep them.

The origins of this view of history and the way governments should operate can be traced directly to Fraser's Oxford connection. It has remained with him all his life. For him the essence of national leadership involves facing up to the challenges of the modern world or, as he puts it himself:

> One of the worst sins of any government or of a political party is the mere pursuit of popularity. It is an old pursuit, older than the worst debauches of Caesar's in the Roman forum before the fall of Rome and the Caesars. Pursuit of popularity for its own sake brings only contempt. It may take a while in coming, but Australians know that to govern well a government must at times do unpopular things. A government can never be loved but it must earn respect, for without that a government will certainly fall.[1]

Malcolm Fraser's tragedy is that he is not Prime Minister during a crisis of truly momentous dimensions when his rhetoric would be consistent with the outside world. He is the apostle of hardship and self-sacrifice in the permissive society.

The intellectual atmosphere of the university confirmed the political biases of Fraser's upbringing. His experience of a Labour government in the United Kingdom only reaffirmed them. 'I hadn't really thought about politics until Oxford,' he said recently.

> I suppose you could really put it all down to Oxford. The university was strongly anti-Labour. If there was ever a need the Conservatives could always muster a majority. A lot of people at the university were highly critical of what socialism was doing to Britain. I remember going to the local dentist in Oxford and him sending me to London to see a specialist. He said my teeth looked as if they had always had a good dentist. He couldn't give them the time they deserved because he would only be paid ten shillings. I've always remembered that.'[2]

Fraser had never spoken of politics with his family or shown any real interest in it. But halfway through his course at Oxford he wrote home saying he was interested in politics generally and in the federal seat of Wannon in particular now that the local member Dan MacKinnon was retiring. It is a measure of the status of the Fraser name that his wish was soon converted into actuality. Fraser spent three years at Oxford from 1949–1951, graduating with third class honours to his Masters of Arts degree.

Fraser did not join the Liberal Party until he returned to Australia from Oxford and he immediately made inquiries about Liberal Party preselection. He joined the Liberal Party and not the Country Party because of his desire to be associated with a national, as distinct from a sectional, political party. This was a very real factor in Fraser's mind. By this stage he had set his sights on a political career and with typical arrogance and self-confidence aspired to reach the top position. Fraser's former school captain Ken James remembers clearly having dinner with Fraser one evening around Christmas time just after he returned from Oxford, when he would have been 21 or 22. As both men spoke about their future careers, James asked Fraser what he was going to do. Malcolm stunned him by replying that he was going to be Prime Minister one day. No matter what the challenge, Fraser has always assumed it to be within his capacity.

The clearest most recent demonstration of this was the way he put down a number of Liberals in 1975 who said the Liberal Party should be wary of coming to office with the economy in such a bad condition. 'I do not believe that men and women are governed by inexorable events beyond control,' Fraser said in his ANZAAS speech. 'When political leaders say the present situation cannot be helped, it is part of a world situation, they are expressing the futility of their own leadership when, if they were men of real stature, they would be saying "we can overcome".'

It was the local Liberal Party organiser in Fraser's electorate, a personal friend Brian Cowling, a neighbour and a farmer, who asked him to stand for preselection. Cowling was well aware of Fraser's interest. While three candidates entered the contest, it was really between former state president of the party and ex-Senator Magnus Cormack and Fraser. The preselection appears to have swung Fraser's way when the candidates were interviewed by the local committee and one of Cormack's supporters asked Fraser a difficult question about American monopolies, thinking he would know nothing about this field. But Fraser answered it well, according to one of those present, and demonstrated his maturity for the task sufficiently to become the party's candidate.

The young Fraser, still reserved and shy, who would shun debating nights at Oxford, found it very difficult to push himself onto people in the way that politics demanded. A colleague of Fraser, the then Minister for External Affairs Richard Casey, later Governor-General, advised him: 'It's no good you sitting here holding a daisy saying: "If you want me, come and get me". Politics doesn't work like that.' According to Fraser's mother: 'He found it difficult to stand on his feet and talk publicly, but he overcame this by sheer determination.' Fraser worked hard in the electorate and narrowly lost the 1954 general election for Wannon by seventeen votes after waiting ten days for the final results.

It was a case of second time lucky. The Labor Party split occurred before the 1955 election which Fraser won by five thousand votes. He has held the seat ever since. Despite rumblings at various times from both the Labor and Country Parties, it is doubtful whether his grip on the seat can be broken. Many locals in the electorate seem to share Fraser's view that he was born to rule and a number of them believe he has done nothing other than fulfil his 'manifest destiny' by becoming Prime Minister.

Fraser has always been concerned to consolidate his electoral base. When he was a Minister, he did not hesitate to hire extra secretarial staff at his own expense to ensure that he serviced the seat properly. As a rule, when he did the pubs in the electorate, he would come into the bar, put down ten or twenty dollars and shout everyone a drink. Every two or three months he would advertise his availability to interview people at the local hotel and a queue would form to air their electoral grievances.

Fraser's great affection has always been for his Nareen property, which is run by a manager and a number of farmhands. In Nareen itself he polled only 49 votes out of 130 at the polling booth at the 1972 general election, but he appears to earn the respect of those who work for him as well as those who work with him. The property itself is operated by two separate legal entities to maximise tax advantages. The land and buildings are owned by Fraser Properties Pty Ltd, valued at $640,683 in mid-1974. It showed a net profit of $480 after tax and its directors comprise Fraser and his wife, his mother Una and his father's estate. The other entity is Nareen Pastoral whose directors at September 1974 were Fraser, his wife, his mother, the Victorian Premier Rupert Hamer, Harry Sampson and Sandford Beggs, his wife's father. It is presumably through Nareen Pastoral that the profits are made. Over the last seven years Fraser has gradually transferred from sheep to Hereford cattle and the Nareen Pastoral Company has carried off a number of prizes.

Fraser's marriage to Tamara, daughter of Sandford Robert Beggs, on 9 December 1956 at St Johns Church Willaura, augmented his heritage. The family into which he married was even better established in the Victorian rural elite than his own. Tamara, or Tammy as she was called, was only twenty when they married and had led a very sheltered life in the western grazing district to that stage, having attended Hermitage Girls School in Geelong. On her first day in Canberra while her husband was in parliament, she spent her time at the War Memorial in tears because everything was so ghastly.

Right from the start she devoted herself to the private side of their life, being little interested in politics. 'My husband was already in politics when we were married,' she said in 1975. 'When the children began to arrive, we had a discussion and he said, "One of us has to be a politician, the other has to be a parent, and that's you." He was concerned that it had to be this way but we both agreed there was no alternative.' So Fraser took the high road to politics as his fundamental priority. Like Malcolm, Tammy is deeply attached to the Nareen property and the twelve-room showplace homestead is their spiritual home, so much so that Tammy declared in 1975 she would not be coming back to settle in Canberra while the Liberals were in Opposition. Now she has the Lodge.[3]

Fraser may have learnt slowly in parliament but he learnt well. In his maiden speech he called for a bigger, better, braver Australia. 'I am sure that I shall live to see the day when we shall have 25 million people in Australia and then we shall be able to look the world in the face far more boldly and play a more effective part in the maintenance of world peace and freedom,' he declared. Fraser applauded the Snowy Mountains scheme as a classic example of government action providing new spheres of enterprise and activity for private people. He expressed his support for the damming of the Ord and Fitzroy Rivers in Northern Australia in a massive irrigation project that would also be funded by the government. He called for a national communications plan, noting that when the Romans made their conquests two thousand years before, they always followed up their victories with the construction of highways. Finally he called for a national effort and self-sacrifice in the cause of economic development, demanding that Australians tackle this problem not as six separate states but as one national entity. He concluded:

'I was too young to fight in the last war, and I owe a debt of gratitude to those who fought in World War I and World War II. But I am not too young now to fight for my faith and belief in the future of this great nation, in which the individual is, and shall always remain, supreme.'

The notion of individual freedom has always been at the core of Fraser's political philosophy. His commitment as an anti-centralist is something which grew out of his experience as a politician and in his maiden speech he reflects the opposite trend. In his ANZAAS address Fraser declared at the start: 'Government is about people. Nations have no life but the life of their people. I reject utterly those concepts of the state that grant the state some superior status—a life or will of its own.' Malcolm Fraser is not a self-made man. But this has never prevented him from espousing the philosophy of a self-made man. He sees governments as a necessary evil, as arbiters between competing groups in society, as defenders of the social fabric and protectors of the national sovereignty. He believes governments are strictly limited in their ability to bring happiness to their people; that government programs and funds will never be the opiate of the masses. Fraser believes that too often in recent years governments, with their all-embracing remedies, have stifled both the freedom and incentive of the individual.

This is where Fraser and Whitlam are at opposite political poles. The former Labor Prime Minister saw the great purpose of his government as the promotion of equality, not of personal incomes, but equality of services which the community provides to all people through the government. This approach was based on the assumption that in contemporary society a person's real standard of living, his health care, educational opportunity and ability to enjoy the nation's resources, is increasingly determined not by individual income but by the range of community services. Fraser rejects this approach saying it is incorrect to perceive government as embodying some higher wisdom or the authentic voice of the community. He rejects the idea that government should have the dominating role in providing community services. The aim must always be to stimulate individuals to self-improvement.

Probably Fraser's greatest application of this principle was the school grants system he employed when Minister for Education and Science and the previously undisclosed political struggle he fought against the 'needs' principle espoused by the Labor Party and subsequently implemented when they came to power. Fraser was a vigorous and active Education Minister under both Gorton and McMahon. He introduced the system of recurrent grants covering running expenses for non-government schools in a major new involvement of the federal government in education.

In the run-up to the 1972 federal elections, education loomed as a major issue. The Liberal government strategy of recurrent grants to private schools was a major political effort to win the Catholic vote. Fraser saw it as such and this was one of the chief reasons he espoused it. The system gave flat across-the-board grants to all private schools based on a fixed grant per student, uniform throughout Australia. By contrast the Labor Party advocated a bigger outlay on education with different priorities. It wanted funds to be spent according to need with money being scaled down to the wealthy private schools and increased to the poorer ones. Fraser worked closely with the Catholic hierarchy, which was on his side. The leading Catholic bishops and archbishops, Young, Freeman, Knox and Stewart, all supported the per capita grants and had political fears about the needs concept. They felt that, although the Catholic schools would get more funds under Labor's program, this could provoke sectarian recriminations. Fraser worked assiduously through 1972 to hold this Catholic coalition together, bolstered by the Australian Parents Council, a parents group which heavily favoured the Liberal policy.

It was not until the campaign itself that the line cracked when Archbishop James Carroll from Sydney said there was no major difference between the per capita system and the needs basis and that people should not be worried by it. Carroll had been contacted by the ALP federal secretary Mick Young and by Eric Walsh and his comments were invaluable to the Labor Party. He was telling Catholics they need not fear the Opposition's policy, which was contrary to the impression the hierarchy had been fostering. Fraser's support for the per capita grant system represented a combination of both political expediency and principle.

The following year, in December 1973, Fraser spearheaded Opposition moves to block the Labor government's $694 million program for schools unless the per capita grant system was retained as the underlying basis, on top of which 'needs' grants would be given. This was one of the most extraordinary stances taken by the Liberal Party during its three years in Opposition and one in which Fraser played the dominant role. He was instrumental in persuading the Liberal executive to fight for the policy which he had introduced as Education Minister. Fraser was personally committed to this battle. The Opposition refused to pass the bill unless all private schools, even the most wealthy, received a flat grant. Whitlam was prepared to have a double dissolution election on the issue if necessary.

Fraser made the running for the Opposition so strongly that he had a major row with the Liberal Party's education spokesman Senator Peter Rae in the office of the Melbourne *Sun News-Pictorial*. Only a subsequent 'deal' between the government and the Country Party prevented a major clash which could have led to an election. The Liberal Party finished in the ignominious position of voting by itself supporting funds to wealthy private schools as Doug Anthony led the Country Party to the other side of the chamber to vote with Labor. It was the biggest parliamentary rift between the coalition parties in three years of Opposition. It showed the extent to which Fraser was prepared to dig in for his principles and defend his record.

As Prime Minister, Fraser has also displayed a grim determination to translate his commitment to federalism into practice. In his ANZAAS address he said Australia had to return to the true spirit and practice of federalism and in Opposition the Liberal Party agreed to give the states access to income tax to enable them to meet their responsibilities. In government he asked all Departments to assess which functions could be handed back to the states, and identify areas of federal–state duplication so inefficiency could be eradicated. This is a reversal of the trend followed by previous Liberal–Country Party governments in office and accelerated by Whitlam, the most centralist Prime Minister in Australian history.

Fraser spent eleven years on the government backbenches absorbing the practical lessons of politics and preparing himself for higher office. He was appointed Minister for the Army by Harold Holt in January 1966. Part of the reasons for his long period as a backbencher were his youth and the fact that other Liberals who entered parliament in the mid-fifties developed promise earlier. But Fraser soon proved he had the abilities of a first-rate politician and administrator. Unlike other Liberals, he was rarely 'snowed' by his Department. Almost from the start he developed the practice of 'going down the line' and seeking advice and making contact with a wide cross-section of the senior echelons. He always insisted in Army and in later Departments that things should be done his way and not theirs, unless there were overwhelming reasons for the opposing argument.

Fraser's career received a major boost when the man who promoted him to the ministry, Harold Holt, disappeared in the sea at Cheviot Beach on 17 December 1967. The next day Fraser, a junior Minister whose taste for ministerial authority had stimulated his ambition to exercise power on a more expansive scale, together with the government whip Dudley Erwin and the government Senate whip Senator Malcolm Scott, met in Parliament House Canberra to launch their efforts to make the then government Senate leader John Grey Gorton Prime Minister. After a month of political drama and intrigue, Gorton, an outsider at the start, was elected Prime Minister.

Fraser, who had worked tirelessly for him, was pulled from the Liberal ruck and given the important Education and Science portfolio, twelfth in ministry seniority and marking Fraser's rise to Cabinet status. For over two years Fraser enjoyed a close personal relationship with Gorton as a major powerbroker in the Liberal–Country Party government. His initial falling out with the Prime Minister began over Gorton's tactics of confrontation with the states, which Fraser believed was politically counter-productive. But the upheaval did not come until February–March 1971, the crucial flashpoint in Fraser's political life which dominated his approach to politics henceforth.

The incident which sparked the crisis was Gorton's refusal to discourage the political correspondent of the *Australian*, Alan Ramsey, from publishing a story claiming that the chief of the general staff General Sir Thomas Daly had told the Prime Minister that Fraser was guilty of extreme disloyalty to the army and had wrongly blamed the army on a number of issues, notably the civil action controversy in Vietnam. Gorton had discussed the story with Ramsey and had not denied it, thereby indirectly encouraging its publication. Fraser was then in an invidious position and believed that trust between himself and Gorton had been irrevocably breached. After consulting widely in the party Fraser set himself on a course of action designed to destroy Gorton as Prime Minister, the first step of which was his resignation from the ministry and refusal to serve in Gorton's government. Such a move would bring together all the anti-Gorton forces in one single thrust.

On 8 March Fraser went to Government House in the afternoon to resign his commission. The next day in parliament he rose from the back benches and delivered the best parliamentary speech of his career, detailing the whole controversy and saying of the Ramsey incident: 'I found that disloyalty intolerable and not to be endured.' He launched a controlled, reasoned and documented attack on Gorton and concluded by saying: 'I do not believe he is fit to hold the great office of Prime Minister and I cannot serve in his government.' After an inconclusive Liberal Party meeting that night, a second meeting was held on 10 March at which a vote of confidence in Gorton resulted in a 33–all tie and Gorton then voted 'no confidence' in himself, thereby voting himself out of the office of Prime Minister. He was replaced by Bill McMahon, who remained until defeated at the polls in December 1972.

Fraser spent five months on the backbench before McMahon re-appointed him to the Education and Science portfolio. But his actions in overthrowing Gorton led the Liberal Party to reassess the motives and character of the Victorian grazier. Gorton still had many supporters inside the party and Fraser's actions, coupled with his aloofness, led many Liberals to question his fitness for high office himself. People asked whether a man who could be so self-righteous and destructive in seeking his goals would ultimately do more harm than good to the party.

Fraser's political judgement was proved right in the incident: Gorton was deposed. But the Victorian Liberal also acted out of honour, his own personal sense of honour. Fraser was not prepared to be a cipher for Gorton or anyone else. Always his own man, he took a stand with a reasonable prospect of political success and with a determination to reject any Prime Minister who treated him with contempt and broke what he regarded as the rules of Cabinet solidarity and loyalty. This was the theme of Fraser's parliamentary speech. Five years later Fraser still refused to talk about these events to anyone but his closest confidants.

More than any other single incident this revealed the wild and turbulent side of his political nature. For Fraser is a man who, despite his talk of government stability, possesses the self-righteousness, determination and ruthlessness, to create political upheavals—always in the name of a great principle. The reason for Fraser's long silence about this incident is his belief, on reassessment, that he went too far, said too much and inflamed emotions inside the Liberal Party that scarred it for years. He could have achieved the same results in a less melodramatic way without doing such damage to his image inside the party.

Fraser learnt one of the chief political lessons of his life from this incident. A study of the Liberal leadership crisis and the downfall of Snedden reveals this. In his attack on Gorton, Fraser sought to justify himself, to let people know in detail his full and complete reasons for resigning. In doing so he publicly tried to discredit the Prime Minister with the inevitable consequences: an orgy of recrimination inside the party. He drew the lessons from this encounter, namely, that on this sort of personality issue there was a need for understatement, that at all costs one should avoid creating disunity and stirring latent hostility among senior party figures. This was why Fraser never touched Snedden, never criticised Snedden, only declared his loyalty to Snedden while at the same time saying he would accept the judgement of forces at work inside the party. Fraser was obsessive and meticulous about his conduct, about the way Snedden was deposed. He wanted to ensure that nobody would accuse him of repeating his tactics during the Gorton period. Above everything, he wanted to avoid the 'wrecker' label. It was this tactic which led to the discrepancy between his public and private actions. While in public Fraser was a model of shadow ministerial decorum, in private with his close circle he was a plotter and pretender for the Liberal leadership.

These political concerns dictated Fraser's approach in his early weeks as Opposition Leader when he sought to consolidate the reins of power. On the afternoon of his leadership win he established himself in Reg Withers' office. One of the first things he did was to call Tony Eggleton to see him and ask Eggleton to assist him as private secretary until he could gather staff. Eggleton himself, after serving so many Liberal leaders, was a symbol of continuity. Fraser also moved to pacify Snedden and those of his supporters who were anguished over his defeat and by the way it had been executed.

That afternoon Fraser saw Peter Rae and gave him a complete assurance that he would continue the policies Snedden had followed towards Tasmania. Rae and Fraser himself spoke to the Tasmanian Liberal leader Max Bingham to give him this personal reassurance, so that the threatened revolt in Tasmania was promptly quelled. The weekend after Fraser was elected, Bingham, Rae and the Tasmanian party president Don Wing met to review the decision and release a press statement which, while applauding Snedden's contribution in Tasmania, pledged Tasmania's support for Malcolm Fraser in view of his assurances to the state.

Fraser sought to heal the rupture in the parliamentary party following John Gorton's warning that it might disintegrate and Jim Forbes' resignation from the shadow Cabinet after the ballot. At his press conference Fraser said there would be a place for Snedden on the frontbench and expressed his hope that Snedden would take it. But sources close to Snedden claimed that afternoon the deposed leader would refuse to serve on the frontbench under Fraser. This was Snedden's initial gut reaction to the abrupt and bloody termination of a political career which hitherto had known only success as a result of hard work.

Over the next week Fraser held extensive talks with National Country Party leader Doug Anthony and his senior colleagues, the other Liberal leaders and the Liberal Party federal executive. In selecting his new shadow ministry Fraser was careful to promote Snedden supporters as well as rewarding the men who had made him leader. While he appointed Vic Garland, Eric Robinson and John Howard, all vigorous Fraser supporters, he also appointed Harold Young to the ministry and Jim Killen to the shadow Cabinet, the latter two being Snedden supporters. Other appointments to the shadow Cabinet included Tony Street and John Carrick, both solid Fraser supporters.

While Fraser was clever enough to extend the olive branch to consolidate his position, he never strained the quality of mercy the way Bill Snedden did. Fraser gave people one chance; if they failed, they were history. Snedden may have judged Fraser by his own standards but he made the third biggest mistake of his political career in refusing Fraser's shadow portfolio offer of Commonwealth–state relations. This was a new portfolio devised by Fraser, reflecting his high priority to re-establish a new federalism. Snedden saw the offer as an insult and said in his letter replying to Fraser: 'There is no clear job to do. It is not a position which fully utilises my capacity in the interests of the party.' Sources close to Snedden at this time, a few days after the leadership challenge, said the only portfolio he would accept was that of shadow Treasurer, then held by the Liberal deputy Phillip Lynch. Fraser accepted

Snedden's refusal and announced to his colleagues: 'The matter is closed.'

So Snedden, former Liberal leader, was consigned to the backbench and remained there until February 1976 when, having been denied a ministerial commission in the first Fraser government, he was elected Speaker of the House of Representatives.

Anyone who doubts the influence which Tony Staley had with Fraser should have those doubts dispelled by the composition of Fraser's staff. David Barnett, the head of the AAP bureau in the press gallery, was appointed press secretary mainly at Staley's instigation. Barnett was a not untypical middle class voter in the 1970s; he had voted Labor all his life until the ACT legislative assembly elections in September 1974. At this point his dissatisfaction with Labor over its economic dislocation caused a basic reassessment. Fraser's speechwriter was David Kemp, a colleague of Staley's from Melbourne University days, whom Staley had introduced to Fraser's office in late 1974 and who assisted Fraser in preparing his ANZAAS speech.

A mutual friend of both Staley and Kemp, another colleague from Melbourne University, Petro Georgiou, who was used as an informal adviser before Fraser became leader, was appointed to his staff as an adviser. Fraser's private secretary was Peter Cross who had already been a member of both the Liberal and Labor Parties, a diplomat in Djakarta, an economist and was recommended by the secretary of the Victorian branch of the party Dr Timothy Pascoe. When Cross left a few months later he was replaced by Dale Budd who had previously worked as private secretary to Fraser when he was Minister for Education and Science.

More than most Liberal parliamentarians, Fraser has an affinity with his coalition colleagues, the Country Party. This is natural. As a man of the land he shares their business problems, mixes with their supporters, knows their political techniques and gets on well with the Country Party hierarchy in Canberra, Doug Anthony, Ian Sinclair and Peter Nixon. For years Fraser fought a running battle in the Victorian Liberal Party against the progressive wing represented by the party president Peter Hardie and former party secretary Leo Hawkins, who were both dedicated to the view that the Liberal Party's aim should be government in its own right in Canberra just as it was in Victoria.

Fraser's view of the coalition is that of Menzies. When asked, after he became Opposition Leader, whether the Liberal Party could ever hope to govern in its own right he replied: 'I don't know what future you're talking about when you ask a question like that. The Country Party is the majority party in Queensland, it's a very significant party in NSW. If we want to govern we need partnership; if they want to govern they need partnership with us.'[4]

Menzies' advice to Holt in 1966 when he retired from politics was that the maintenance of the coalition was fundamental to conservative rule. This is Fraser's view. It is of crucial importance today when the Liberal Party has sufficient numbers in the House of Representatives to form a government in its own right without Country Party support. Under a different Liberal leader such a situation, which exposes the Country Party's vulnerability, could lead to all sorts of pressures for a major review of Liberal strategy. Under Fraser it almost assuredly will not.

Both as Prime Minister and Opposition Leader, Fraser cemented Liberal–Country Party links at the highest levels. Fraser is not the sort of man who seeks political advice far and wide. But he is a shrewd and clever politician who believes in consolidating his base like a rock. He did this by pacifying his opponents within the party during his first months as Opposition Leader. He then established a new structure of party decision-making in which the coalition operated as one unit and those men with real power numbered no more than ten. All the major decisions in Opposition originated from what became known as the 'leadership group'. This comprised Fraser, Lynch, Withers, Greenwood, Cotton, Anthony, Sinclair and Nixon. Decisions were cleared from this group through the shadow Cabinet and finally the party room. There was almost no way anything originating from the leadership group would be defeated for it represented a balance both between coalition parties and between the House of Representatives and the Senate.

While Fraser had better relations with Anthony and the Country Party, he gave every indication of being able to control them in a more effective fashion than Snedden. The first real test of coalition relations came when the Labor government decided to refer the case of Country Party Senator Jim Webster to the High Court following allegations that he was ineligible to remain in parliament because his family company fulfilled government contracts. The Country Party waged a 'boots and all' campaign when the government sought to have Webster's eligibility tested in the High Court. Both publicly and privately Country Party leaders sought to defend Webster and put strong pressure on the Liberals to back his case, seeking a general inquiry as to how many other members and Senators were involved before there was any High Court reference. But, after a meeting of the leadership group, it was the Fraser line that prevailed and a subsequent joint statement from Fraser and Anthony said the Webster case should go before the court as soon as possible.

This illustrated Fraser's modus operandi. There had to be a coalition view and he was not prepared to tolerate separate views from both parties. At the same time he proved that, unlike Snedden, he could stand up to Anthony and win, having already established in a wider framework a firm consensus on coalition rules. While Fraser remains Prime Minister the Country Party will always be influential in economic policy but never dominant. The reinstatement of the superphosphate bounty and other concessions to the rural sector after the Liberals were re-elected were not just Country Party commitments, they were commitments Fraser made when he presented a joint coalition policy speech for the December 1975 election. Unlike Snedden, Fraser would never have tolerated the damaging debate which marked the 1974 campaign as to who would be Treasurer in a change of government— Lynch or Anthony, Liberal Party or Country Party. While Fraser was prepared to give Anthony a significant trade and development portfolio, he always regarded the Treasury portfolio as the prerogative of the Liberals.

It is on foreign affairs and defence, one of his chief preoccupations, that Fraser takes a conservative stand within a conservative party. The starting point for his outlook is a deep scepticism about detente and a belief that the development of a multipolar world has only served to increase, not lessen, international tensions and the danger to middle-ranking powers like Australia. From his maiden parliamentary address to the present day, Fraser has called for a tough and vigilant approach to the world and has traditionally been a prime supporter of the forward defence concept which he defended vigorously during Australia's involvement in Vietnam. As Army Minister Fraser was a tireless supporter of US bombing of North Vietnam, an incessant critic of the Labor Party whose policies he claimed would only help the enemy and a fervent exhorter to the Australian public to pay the price needed for national security.

One of Fraser's most outspoken stands in Opposition was to oppose closer cooperation between the Liberal and Australia Parties following talks between Snedden and the convenor of the Australia Party, Gordon Barton. Fraser said the foreign and defence policies of the Australia Party were fundamentally opposed to those of the Liberal Party which were based upon the ANZUS treaty and defence cooperation with the United States. He said the differences between the two parties on foreign affairs were irreconcilable.

Fraser's attitude to foreign affairs is shaped by an unremitting and continuous suspicion of the Soviet Union. He is deeply worried about the prospect that Japan will be forced into closer commercial and defence arrangements with the Soviet Union and says that one of the major tasks of Australian diplomacy will be to prevent this. He is alarmed that the Soviets have not only gained the ascendancy in the strategic balance of terror but that they pose a significant threat to Australia, both through the Middle East and the Indian Ocean. He believes that the Labor government favoured the Arabs in the Middle East to stay on side with the Russians and has branded Labor's Middle East policy 'a euphemism to do what the Russians would want'. Before the Suez Canal was reopened he predicted:

> The main beneficiary is going to be the Russian navy's Black Sea and Mediterranean fleet, and that will link up with the Vladivostok Pacific Ocean fleet and the Straits of Malacca and the waters to our north are likely to become the highway for the Russian navy. That will give the Chinese a great feeling of insecurity and that results in instability.

Fraser is deeply concerned about the extent to which the Russian influence in the region will provoke a counter-response from China. During 1975 he was persuaded of the need to visit China to prove his credentials as a man of the time and accept political reality in the region. He responded to this and his office went to some lengths to get an invitation from the Chinese. Fraser planned to visit Peking during his winter recess trip overseas as Opposition Leader, a trip later abandoned because of the Bass by-election.

Fraser believes that Whitlam is a dilettante in foreign affairs, a man who has flirted around the edge of the problems but failed to come to grips with them. Despite substantial evidence to the contrary, he believes that Whitlam has failed to establish the closest possible links and friendships with countries in the South-East Asian region. This view was reflected in Fraser's first few months as Prime Minister. He made overtures immediately to the ASEAN grouping and even proposed that at its February 1976 meeting in Bali, Japan, Australia and New Zealand should also be present for wider talks on the region. The Indonesian Foreign Minister Adam Malik unerringly fingered Fraser's outlook, suggesting the new Prime Minister wanted to be seen to have better relations with ASEAN than Whitlam, and also sought to demonstrate to other people, notably the Americans, the extent of his influence here. Malik told other leaders that he would not have Fraser playing politics with ASEAN.

The essential difficulty for Fraser's foreign policy outlook is his determination to re-establish the ties with Australia's traditional allies, principally the United States which he believes the Labor government strained, and yet at the same time prove his credentials and win acceptance with the developing countries of the South-East Asian region. To the extent that these policies are incompatible Fraser has a diplomatic dilemma.

The extent of this dilemma is illustrated by just one section from his ANZAAS address when he declared that trade and foreign affairs must always be kept strictly apart and that resources diplomacy, as practised by the Middle East oil producers, will only plunge the world into another major depression. Fraser has solid convictions on this issue

171

but at the same time he is ignoring the newest and most potent force in world affairs, which nearly every developing country which has resources has already embraced. In the most superficial sense Fraser's lack of rapport with Australia's immediate neighbours was shown at the funeral in Malaysia for the late Tun Razak, which both Fraser and Whitlam attended. Australian officials had to spend some time persuading Fraser not to wear a top hat which he brought for the occasion.

Just after he became Opposition Leader Fraser seized the chance to attack the government over the fall of Indo-China and what he considered the government's pro-communist stand. Fraser argued that Whitlam's policies in South-East Asia, as in the Middle East, were designed to assist the Russians, Chinese and the communists in general. Eggleton warned that one of Fraser's problems was the tendency for the media to depict him as a hard right-winger on foreign affairs.

Malcolm Fraser is a living testimony to the notion of the power elite in Australian society. Throughout his life he has gravitated towards men who are wealthy or successful or both, like himself. This was by personal instinct as well as being an integral step along his path towards political fulfilment. Fraser's performance in 1974-75 is a classic case study of a man familiar with a labyrinth of powerful networks—public and private. No other Liberal can match Fraser's range of contacts at the higher echelons of the federal bureaucracy. After serving as Defence Minister Fraser enjoyed a close relationship with both Sir Henry Bland and Sir Arthur Tange, the two public servants who were his permanent heads in the job. When elected Prime Minister he brought in Bland as head of the Administrative Review Committee, which has the job of recommending cost-cutting measures throughout the bureaucracy. He has always maintained close relations with Tange, whom he regards as the best public servant he has met. Fraser deplored the public attacks which Whitlam and other members of the Labor government launched on the Treasury. He regarded the Secretary to the Treasury Sir Frederick Wheeler and his deputy John Stone as two of Australia's finest public servants. After Fraser became Prime Minister, Stone was instrumental in persuading him to take a tough line on wages. Fraser was a personal friend of a number of Australia's most prominent diplomats, including the late Sir Patrick Shaw, R W Furlonger former head of JIO, and K C O 'Mick' Shann.

When, as Opposition Leader in 1975, Fraser was planning the winter recess overseas trip that was later abandoned, he simply rang Shaw directly and asked him to make a number of appointments. Fraser's contacts are not just restricted to Australia. At this time he spoke directly on the phone to US Secretary of State Dr Henry Kissinger and also with another contact, the head of the US National Security Council General Brent Scowcroft. Fraser decided he would not visit the United States as

Opposition Leader unless he first secured an invitation for talks with President Ford—something never previously extended to an Opposition Leader from Australia and given only in the most indirect fashion to Prime Minister Whitlam.

Many of the public servants who served both Liberal and Labor governments are well known to him, men like Ken Jones, Secretary of the Education Department, with whom Fraser worked closely as Minister for Education and Science. He is also acquainted with most of the defence and service hierarchy in Australia after serving as both Minister for the Army and Minister for Defence in the late sixties. Fraser had no hesitation picking the head of the former government's Priorities Review Staff, Austin Holmes, to head the inquiry into Medibank which he established on coming to power. Holmes' Reserve Bank credentials were impeccable. After Sir Patrick Shaw died, Fraser ensured that Australia's new ambassador to Washington was a man he regarded as one of Australia's very best diplomats, N F Parkinson, someone with whom he had established close contacts over the years. As Prime Minister he retained John Menadue as his departmental head. Menadue in turn was previously a senior executive of News Ltd and worked for Rupert Murdoch, with whom Fraser was in contact through 1975.

The contrast with Labor is stark. Fraser believes the Australian public service is one of the best in the world. His relations with the bureaucracy have always been based on respect and trust. This is a world away from the almost total ignorance of the public service that marked the assumption of office by the Labor government. Whitlam's relations with the public service vacillated between deferring to the bureaucratic establishment and trying to introduce changes to get the right people to implement his policies.

In Opposition Fraser did not hesitate to talk with those senior public servants serving the Labor government who would talk to him. The most notorious example was his telephone contact with 'Mr Williams' in Treasury. 'Mr Williams' is the code name widely known around Parliament House for the senior public servant who gave Fraser information about the loans affair. Although most of the information on the loans was gathered by Lynch's office, Fraser did not hesitate to play a personal role himself.

Fraser's attitude towards the press was that of a man who had nothing to fear from a daily reporter. He had extensive contacts at the highest levels of the Australian media industry, two of them being Rupert Murdoch and Sir Warwick Fairfax. In mid-1975 Fraser attended board room lunches with both the Fairfax group and the Murdoch News Ltd group. On these occasions the prospect of an early election was discussed and Fraser indicated that he would not consider 'reprehensible circumstances' to exist until all major Australian newspapers were calling for an election. In short, Fraser decided very early on that he could not afford to force an election without the complete backing from all major papers and the papers themselves were made aware of this.

Fraser regarded the attitude of the papers as very important in his subsequent bid for power. He saw them as an integral part of the political process. They were an area where he had to protect himself and ensure he was on solid ground as a basic part of his job as Opposition Leader. More than any other political leader in recent years, he has recognised the influence of the media and the need for a politician to come to terms with it. He maintained a close dialogue with the highest levels of the industry throughout the year and particularly during the constitutional crisis and election campaign. He acted with a confidence based on the knowledge that reporters could not hurt him.

During the December 1975 election campaign, Fraser made it clear that he felt no obligation or need to hold regular press conferences if elected Prime Minister. Replying to the ABC political correspondent Ken Begg at the Sydney Journalists Club just after his campaign opening, Fraser said he had no intention of holding weekly press conferences and believed that any policy announcements should be made to the parliament not the press. This reflects his attitude both personally and politically. Malcolm Fraser is a very private man. Ever since the Gorton incident he has always shunned and declined opportunities to talk about himself. 'That is for others to judge,' is his standard reply which runs through interview after interview when he has been asked about himself. In a wider political sense he feels no particular affinity with the press and is deeply suspicious of a number of prominent press notably Richard Carleton, formerly with 'This Day Tonight', and Laurie Oakes, political correspondent for the Melbourne *Sun News-Pictorial*. He harbours a deep suspicion about the ABC, which was revealed in a number of incidents both before and during the 1975 election campaign.

Fraser's press secretary David Barnett made vigorous and successful efforts to ensure that he was accessible to senior press as Opposition Leader and this continued when he became Prime Minister. But despite this, Fraser's government, within four months of office, was showing signs of a conspicuous failure to explain its actions to the Australian people. This was symptomatic of Fraser's apparent failure to establish real rapport with the public, a communications problem which is likely to be one of the most intractable difficulties facing his government. A dangerous omen is the fact that Fraser is not a popular leader or particularly well-liked by the public, according to all the opinion polls.

Fraser supports stable government, gradual change, a strong private sector, a viable rural sector and as small a role as possible for government consistent with the demands of a welfare society. His political model is the founder of the Liberal Party and Australia's longest serving

Prime Minister, Sir Robert Menzies. Fraser himself regularly sees Menzies and does not think highly of his predecessors, who did not go out of their way to maintain contact with the founding father, the guiding philosopher.

Asked why he believed Menzies was Australia's greatest Prime Minister Fraser said when he was Opposition Leader:

> Because of the achievements that were introduced in his time. A health scheme that worked, a high level of home ownership and stability, a capacity for people to plan ahead, the longest period of full and continuous employment in Australia's history, a very great deal of social progress, a very large number of social welfare programs introduced. There was an aura of predictability and certainty. People could plan their futures knowing those futures would be secure. Now that's all ended. I'm not suggesting that you can return to the Menzies era because clocks don't get turned back. But while policies must change there are enduring principles.[5]

This is probably the clearest statement of Malcolm Fraser's political aspirations and indicates what he meant in his famous remark that he wanted to get politics off the front page of the papers. Predictability and certainty, as distinct from change and upheaval, are the virtues to which Fraser aspires and there can be little doubt that he has made an accurate assessment of the Australian electorate.

Fraser has a great faith and confidence in the future of the Australian mining and manufacturing industries. In his Alfred Deakin lecture he said Liberals should not be worried about company size or monopoly and he specifically defended an eight per cent rise in steel prices by BHP saying, while the rise was a 'pity', it was largely provoked through the industrial policies of unions. He went on to say that no one should question such a price rise made by one of Australia's greatest enterprises, BHP, 'a responsible firm which has given Australia the cheapest steel in the world'.

Unlike the Labor Party Fraser is sceptical about the capacity of government to eradicate social evils. Speaking about the government's role in social welfare Fraser has said: 'I sometimes think that there's some unrealistic talk in politics. Sure, you do what you can, what resources your country allows for those in special need. But if you talk about abolishing poverty I think it's unrealistic—you hold out a mirage. The poverty line shifts as the general wealth of the community grows.'[6] Asked whether he believed differences in wealth in the community were necessary to retain private and individual incentive Fraser replied: 'Within limits, yes. You've got to have incentive for people who want to start their own business or people who want to go on.'[7]

Like all politicians, Malcolm Fraser is far more than just a product of his ideology. His political career has always been a struggle between ideology and modernity; between trying to reconcile his conservative disposition on the one hand with the demands of popularity and vote winning on the other. He has always been aware that his right-wing image was never an electoral plus, always a potential danger and something which needed to be modified. To a considerable extent Fraser has succeeded in doing this, although he has never tried to bury his natural political inclinations.

This constant struggle between belief and presentation is always with Fraser. When he told the National Press Club on 31 July 1975 that a Liberal government would maintain relations with Peking he was proving he could adapt with the times; yet in the same breath he said some sort of arrangement would have to be made with Taiwan. Fraser has publicly advocated the appointment of trade unionists to government boards and even clashed with Snedden on this issue, which he saw as part of his efforts to develop a progressive industrial relations policy. Yet in talks in August 1975 with the vice-president of the Chemical Bank from New York he talked about jailing communist trade unionist Laurie Carmichael.

Fraser's approval of Menzies is well-known but when he became Opposition Leader he stressed that two other political figures he particularly admired were Franklin Delano Roosevelt and former Labor Treasurer Ted Theodore. Those men on the progressive side of the Liberal Party who worked to make Fraser leader, Staley, Macphee, Viner and Robinson, were all convinced that he was both shrewd enough and pragmatic enough to capture the middle ground.

Certainly Fraser's credentials as a leader have been established beyond dispute. His performance during the constitutional crisis and the political judgement he displayed testified not only to great leadership but to considered assessment accompanying it. Malcolm Fraser wants to be the greatest Liberal leader since Menzies. He has the chance.

# PART III

# THE BATTLE

# 11

# THE LOANS AFFAIR—
# THE CONNOR CONNECTION

*I have stood in the path of those who would have grabbed the mineral resources of Australia.*

Rex Connor, 9 July 1975

Reginald Francis Xavier Connor was the toughest and roughest man in the Labor Cabinet. For two and a half years he was virtually a law unto himself within the government. Few Ministers in Australian peacetime history have exercised so much power with so little check, so singularly, so secretly, for so long. The springboard of Connor's strength was his intimidation of the Labor Party caucus and his special relationship with the Prime Minister. A huge hulk of a man in the Irish–Australian political tradition, Rex Connor's philosophy was dominated by his commitment to the cause of Australian nationalism, forged in the early part of the century before the death of Henry Lawson, whose poems he read as a boy.

This was an old-style nationalism, whose fervour always surprised and sometimes embarrassed his colleagues, whose style was that of a bygone generation and whose political application always carried immense weight within the ranks of the ALP. When this nationalism was converted into a ruthless and long-range policy to maximise Australian ownership and control of the country's mineral and energy wealth, even if the cost was a loss of foreign capital, a fall-off in exploration, and deferment in development projects, Connor became the most reviled Minister in a reviled government. No other Minister came under such persistent and hostile criticism from industry as did Rex Connor, and no one replied in such a contemptuous and provocative fashion.

Connor was not just a big man physically; he was a man of genuine stature, a man who generated an aura, characterised by his drab suits, big braces, granite-like countenance, quick mind, pithy speech, a predilection to reel off statistics like a machine gun and whose old-fashioned style contrasted sharply with a radical espousal of modern and sometimes impractical schemes such as converting coal and natural gas to oil. Connor was never a warm and outward going man. The few close friendships he had were sealed with a stubborn loyalty that made them enduring. Those who crossed him knew they had taken on an opponent who was incessantly active and relentless in his search for retribution. Rex Connor saw himself as both protector of the national heritage and pragmatic business manager of its wealth. He saw Australia as a vital component in a world where vital resources and energy would be the barter through which some nations would become powerful and other nations would fall; Connor was presiding over one of the greatest structural changes in the Australian economy that was simultaneously accompanying large-scale changes in the pattern of international trade and distribution of the world's wealth. Like Whitlam he saw himself at a vital point on the stage of history.

The Connor family roots lie in Wollongong, where his great-great-grandfather, an Irish cobbler, settled in 1836; this is the city where Rex was born seventy-one years later, which he came to represent in two parliaments and which symbolised the preoccupation of his life. His politics was forged in contemplation of the great blast furnaces producing steel and of the surrounding coal mines of the NSW south coast, which ravaged the landscape and persistently reminded of Australia's mineral wealth. Rex always displayed intelligence and imagination. He was dux of Wollongong high school and afterwards worked in a local solicitor's office studying his way through his solicitor's admission examination. But Connor never practised. He went into business and then contracted to supply food to a local army camp. He joined the Labor Party in 1924 and, after the Lang upheaval in the NSW branch, became an active member of the left-wing faction that fought a bitter and sustained battle with the Lang forces during the 1930s. According to Mrs Grace Connor, Rex was generous and always willing to help others during the Depression. 'He gave them free legal advice, he gave them food and he gave them money,' she said. 'Wollongong people know how kind and generous he is.'

Connor's association with the anti-Lang faction was so strong that he even contested the federal seat of Werriwa against the official Labor Party and his political career was obviously retarded by the internal upheavals which characterised the party in the 1930s. After the unity conferences in the late 1930s, Connor rejoined the official party and, after serving as a local alderman during the forties, he was elected to the state parliament in 1950 where he remained for thirteen years. Connor became the lion of the left and, according to former colleagues, developed a deep contempt for the right-wing group which ran the state Labor Party. It was in the NSW parliament that the Connor legend really started.

His nickname 'The Strangler' is reputed to have developed from an incident with *Daily Telegraph* political roundsman Bert Birtles, when Connor took him in a headlock. One of the more famous Connor tantrums was when he ripped down a wall clock that constantly irritated him with its noises. While Connor had ambitions in state politics, he was never prepared to submit to the ruling clique and throw in his lot with them in the hope of promotion. But a chance came to switch to the federal arena when Vic Kearney, the sitting Labor member for the federal seat of Cunningham, which embraced Connor's state seat, retired. Connor won the preselection ballot and transferred to Canberra.

As a backbencher Connor was inconspicuous but formidable. While he appeared to adopt a low profile initially, he eventually attached himself to the rising star of Gough Whitlam and worked for Whitlam to succeed Calwell as leader. At the same time Connor displayed an awesome knowledge and technical knowhow in the mining and resources area, which amazed most of his colleagues and left his opponents astounded. Connor fell out with Whitlam after the 1969 election when he failed to win election to the shadow executive and blamed Whitlam to a large extent for his omission. But, despite differences between the two men at this time, Whitlam decided before coming to power that he would make Connor Minister in charge of the fuel and resources portfolio in his government.

Rex Connor was born on Australia Day in 1907 and was on the verge of his sixty-fifth birthday when sworn in as Minister for Minerals and Energy, being listed twentieth in the twenty-seven strong Labor ministry elected by the caucus. An unknown outside the narrow circle of Labor Party politics, after three months he established himself as one of the most influential and important Ministers within the government. A year and a half later when Labor was re-elected, Connor topped the ministerial ballot and was formally ranked number three in the Cabinet behind Whitlam and the new deputy leader Jim Cairns. During simultaneous overseas absences of both men he served as acting Prime Minister.

One of the most perplexing and faithful relationships within the government was that between Gough Whitlam and Rex Connor. The great paradox was that Whitlam, so outwardly urbane and modern, identified with and came to admire his Minister for Minerals and Energy. Whitlam was impressed with Connor's encyclopaedic knowledge of his portfolio and the technical details of the mining industry. At the same time the Prime Minister sympathised with and shared the nationalistic fire and determination of his Minerals Minister in setting out to regain Australia's birthright to her natural resources.

Most of all Whitlam saw Connor as a visionary; a man with a grand design which he began to implement immediately, just as the Prime Minister himself was doing on an even grander scale. He believed that this marked Connor out from the rest of the ministry, most of whom spent their early days scratching to pull the reins of office together. Finally, Whitlam could not fail to feel some affinity with the Connor style, the sheer strength of purpose, the conviction to plough ahead in the face of hostility. Resolution bred through years of working and waiting.

Another important factor in their relationship and in the power Connor subsequently wielded was that Whitlam had no experience or expertise whatsoever in the minerals area. This was a characteristic he shared with the overwhelming majority of the Labor caucus. In these circumstances it was difficult for the Prime Minister to pass harsh intellectual judgements on the Connor policies, just as it was difficult for the caucus to do anything but acquiesce when confronted with Connor's blistering bursts of facts, figures and technical terms. The Minerals and Energy Minister was protected because of the ignorance that surrounded him. 'Life is an equation in hydrocarbons,' was one of Connor's more famous cryptic quotes, indicating the style which his colleagues had to deal with.

The Labor government and Rex Connor had a totally different approach to resources compared with their Liberal–Country Party predecessors. Where there had been no single Department with overall responsibility for resources in the previous government, a new Department of Minerals and Energy was created under Labor with Connor as Minister and with one of Australia's best known public servants Sir Lenox Hewitt as permanent head. Hewitt had been Secretary of the Prime Minister's Department under John Gorton and was known for his espousal of the cause of Australian ownership of resources, his running fights with the Treasury and his skill as a bureaucratic infighter.

Connor's text was the ALP federal platform which he had largely written himself on the resources area. He saw his goal as the formulation of a national minerals and energy policy where the Australian government would decide the pace and direction of mining development and ensure there was maximum Australian ownership in the exploration, development and processing stages. Connor moved quickly. On 31 January 1973 he secured Cabinet approval that all mineral exports would be subject to export controls by the government. This gave Connor power to ensure prices were at reasonable levels but, more importantly, to determine the direction of mineral development through control over exports. The Minister insisted that both coal and iron ore producers operate as a group to ensure they obtained the best price possible and were not 'played off' against one another.

On 20 February 1973 Cabinet approved Connor's Pipeline Authority and the necessary legislation passed parliament in the autumn session. If it had been submitted any later the Opposition would have almost certainly blocked it in the Senate, but Connor moved too quickly for them. The pipeline, a massive project, was to link the north west coast of West Australia, the Palm Valley field in the Northern Territory and connect with the first stage, the Moomba-to-Sydney pipeline. Connor's grandiose plans for the pipeline envisaged it extending just less than 8000 miles and he claimed the substitution of natural gas for fuel oil would cut $450 million from Australia's import bill and cover the cost in thirty months.

Connor's legislation to establish the Petroleum and Minerals Authority was passed in July 1974 and he envisaged the authority would explore, develop, process and sell Australian petroleum and minerals. At the same time he withdrew income tax concessions from mining and oil companies, claiming they were mainly used for tax avoidance and were an inefficient form of assistance to the industry. Connor refused to approve new uranium export contracts saying the world market would peak in the 1980s, and eventually developed a framework for government–industry joint cooperation in mining the Northern Territory Ranger deposit. He undertook with the Japanese to hold a feasibility study into a uranium enrichment plant in Australia. In 1973 in a unilateral declaration Connor confirmed that the Australian government would acquire the resources of the North-West Shelf from Woodside-Burmah at the wellhead. He was furious at the massive area the overseas-dominated company had been given to explore. Connor believed an intensive drilling program was needed and was determined to ensure that the riches of the shelf were not 'handed away' to overseas interests. This statement was made without Cabinet approval, showing that Connor was already a law unto himself.

Contrary to everyone's impression, Connor was not anti-development. Just the opposite. He was fervently pro-development but he was rigidly determined to ensure that the development was supervised by the Australian government in the interests of Australians. The implementation of this policy led to a massive falling off in exploration programs and development projects both on land and offshore. As the industry fell more and more into the doldrums and development projects went begging, pressure on Connor and criticism of the Minister continued to mount. Connor believed he was a shrewd businessman and saw himself as preparing the ground for better returns on mineral wealth. He had a contempt for a large number of senior men in the mining industry and on one occasion called them 'mugs and hillbillies'.

Connor realised the central dilemma of his policies. This was where the overseas loan raising fitted neatly into the equation. The funds could be used to satisfy Connor's grandiose development program: the completion of the natural gas pipeline from Cooper Basin to Palm Valley on to Dampier and then Perth, including 84 miles of submarine pipeline; the petrochemical plant at Dampier to extract natural gas liquids for conversion into motor spirit; three uranium mining and milling plants in the Northern Territory; a uranium enrichment plant; the electrification of heavy freight rail areas in NSW and Victoria; upgrading coal exporting harbours at Port Kembla, Newcastle, Gladstone and Hay Point; research on coal conversion and solar energy; development of the North-West Shelf and assistance to the Cooper Basin natural gas consortium. If these projects could be funded through a massive overseas borrowing then Connor would satisfy his twin objectives of development and Australian control.

The search for overseas loan funds was not an aberration. It was the natural product of Connor's policies and objectives and of the limits within which he had to operate. He was given as much freedom in the search for overseas funds as he was in the development of his mining and energy policies. From late 1974, when Connor first began work on raising the loan funds, he became engrossed and then obsessed with the project until it finally dissipated his energy and nearly destroyed his health. Night after night he would remain in his office making international phone calls, taking or sending telex messages in an effort to finalise the deal.

Connor's motives were never hard to discover although they eluded the Opposition parties for many months, particularly when the first loan revelations were made. Defending his loan activities in parliament on 9 July Connor said:

> Throughout my two and a half years as a Minister of the Crown I have stood in the path of those who would have grabbed the mineral resources of Australia. I have no apologies whatever to make for what I have done. It has been done in good faith; it has been done in honesty. I fling in the face of the little men of the Opposition, the words of an old Australian poem: 'Give me men to match my mountains, Give me men to match my plains, Men with freedom in their vision, And creation in their brains.'

These words are as good a summary and explanation of Connor's motives and the philosophical basis to his policies as could be hoped for.

The first sign of Connor's active interest in overseas funds was a letter he wrote to Lionel Bowen on 16 September 1974 about money for his statutory authorities:

My dear Minister,

I refer to our conversation of today, when you informed me of the availability of certain loan funds from Barclays Australia Ltd, Merchant Bankers of Sydney.

I would be pleased to further discuss with them, through your good offices, the negotiation of a loan of $A240 million, for the general construction of projects by the Pipeline Authority and the Australian Atomic Energy Commission, both of which are statutory bodies under my administration.

My understanding is that funds would be available for a period of twenty years, at an interest rate of 7½–8 per cent, and with a brokerage payable at 1½ per cent. A further indicated requirement would be appropriate guarantee from the Australian Treasurer. I would appreciate your further advising on this matter. Yours sincerely,

(Signed)

R. F. X. Connor

Although nothing came of this effort, Connor was soon approached by his colleague the Labour Minister Clyde Cameron who said he believed the government could get access to extensive overseas funds. It was at this point that Labor was plunged into one of the most bizarre undertakings in our history.

Cameron's information came from an Adelaide builder, a Greek migrant, Gerry Karidis. The Labour Minister had known Karidis for some years but had lost track of him over the preceding three years until encountering him again at a ball in Cameron's Hindmarsh (SA) electorate in late September. 'I have had a very close association with the Greek community generally, and in a chief way with Mr Karidis,' Cameron said later. 'After the ball, he invited us back to his house for a drink. There were about twenty or thirty people there. During the night he told me he knew or believed he knew how the Australian government could get access to fairly large sums of money if the government wanted to borrow funds.' Cameron told Karidis he knew that Rex Connor was looking for large-scale overseas funds. He told the builder he would check the situation with the Minerals and Energy Minister.

Whitlam was overseas at the time in North America and Cairns was acting Prime Minister. Cameron raised the subject with both Connor and Cairns and asked the deputy Prime Minister whether he could see Karidis. As a result a meeting was held in Cairns' office comprising the deputy Prime Minister, Connor, Cameron, Karidis, his solicitor Tim

Anderson, and possibly Hewitt. Karidis was not certain of the original source of the funds but he had been told they could be raised by a close friend of his. His contact was an Adelaide-based opal merchant, Timbor Shelley, who travelled regularly to Hong Kong and the east. Shelley was familiar with the Hong Kong firm of Thomas Yu and Associates, importers and exporters, who also had some dealings in commodities. Thomas Yu in turn knew an Amsterdam-based businessman and dealer named Cranendonk, one of whose business associates was a Pakistani, Tirath Khemlani, the manager of Dalamal and Sons (Commodity) Limited, based in London, which dealt with fairly large sums in international trade.[1]

Khemlani first discovered the Australian government was interested in a loan in the third week of October 1974 when he was in Cranendonk's office near Amsterdam and a telex came in from Thomas Yu in Hong Kong to this effect. The figure being mentioned at this stage was $500 million and Khemlani's first response was 'unless I could be assured the Australian government would negotiate the loan direct through me, I am not interested'. Khemlani made it clear to Cranendonk that he could get the money and this message was conveyed back to Australia. Both Khemlani and Hewitt subsequently went to Hong Kong in November, where they held discussions about the loan. In early November Hewitt checked Khemlani's credentials with Charles Drover, a senior partner of Coward Chance and Company, who were the legal advisers of the Australian government in Britain for many years. On 11 November Drover sent a telex message to Hewitt saying that Johnson Matthey were the bankers for Khemlani's firm and they offered a good report about the firm. 'Dalamal do deal in fairly large sums. They invariably act as middlemen,' Drover said.

When he was in Hong Kong, Khemlani had talks with the opal merchant Timbor Shelley about his capacity to raise funds and as a result of these talks and Shelley's communications with Australia, it was decided that Khemlani would come to Australia. After business en route at Singapore, Khemlani arrived at Sydney airport on 11 November and was met by Shelley, Karidis and Anderson. He was taken to Canberra later that day and stayed at the Lakeside Hotel. After giving his hosts further assurances he could raise the money Karidis took Khemlani to Parliament House that afternoon and they went to Clyde Cameron's office. Cameron introduced Khemlani to Connor a few minutes later and their meeting initiated a long and fateful relationship for the Labor government. Connor examined Khemlani's references and explained to the Pakistani that the Australian government was interested in overseas funds and outlined their intended use.

Right from the start the main problem which bedevilled Khemlani's loan-raising efforts was obvious. According to the Pakistani he wanted a complete authority and letter of mandate to act on the government's behalf, thereby having a guarantee that when funds were mobilised they could be accepted. By the same token the government was never prepared to give such a guarantee until it was convinced the funds were mobilised. The failure of both sides to go far enough was a recurring problem at a number of stages when, according to Khemlani, the deal was close to being finalised. As a result of these initial talks with Connor and Hewitt, which covered the two days 11–12 November Khemlani was given a letter by Hewitt. The letter dated 12 November and signed by Hewitt said in part:

> . . . I am writing to confirm to you what was said by the Ministers at their meeting yesterday. The Australian government is interested in overseas borrowings of the magnitude you mention, up to a total of approximately $US4000 million, in blocks of $US500 million, repayable at the end of twenty years. The Minister has suggested that the availability of such funds for lending should be confirmed at this stage, whereupon negotiations on amounts and other terms and conditions could be commenced immediately between the principals . . .

While Khemlani did not regard this letter as satisfactory for his purposes he said he would try and raise the funds through a contact, Sheik Gassan. Khemlani left Australia immediately and did not return until 7 December. In the intervening month he says he did a great deal of work and saw many people in connection with the Australian loan. Khemlani communicated with both Karidis and with Connor during this period. On 1 December he notified Connor by telex that he had arranged the loan, that the first batch would be in $US500 million with the remainder to be completed over the next several months. Connor replied to Khemlani saying he was anxious to have negotiations finalised as soon as possible and indicating the government had expected things to be moving quicker. He said that both Hewitt and the Prime Minister were leaving Australia on an overseas visit on 14 December and he was keen to have the issue settled before then. Drover conveyed the same message to Khemlani in London. On 3 December Khemlani told Connor by telex he would bring the necessary documents to Australia and was confident the matter would be finalised by 9 December. Khemlani subsequently left for Australia.[2]

The Pakistani money lender was then involved in eight days of discussions in both Sydney and Canberra with Connor, Hewitt and a wide number of officials from the Departments of Minerals and Energy, Treasury and the Attorney-General. During this period there were continual delays within the government over the drafting of the loan agreement and other procedures required to finalise the loan raising. According to Khemlani, Connor asked him on a number of occasions to try to arrange an extension and he in turn spoke with Sheik Gassan to this effect.

It was during this period that Whitlam's involvement in the loan effort reached its peak. Although Whitlam never met or spoke to Khemlani himself, he was in close contact with Connor in this period and held extensive talks over the method and manner of the loan arrangement. Whitlam gave Connor complete support in his effort and turned aside contrary advice which was being put by both the Treasury and the Attorney-General's Department. By this stage it was abundantly clear to senior officers in both these Departments that Connor was engaged in a fantastic undertaking which was totally unprecedented in terms of Australia's loan-raising efforts.

The public servants whose job it was to organise overseas loans for Australia had a number of objections to the procedures now being followed. The first was Khemlani himself. Over the previous twelve months the federal Treasury had been approached by a multitude of 'funny money' men. These people claimed they had access to extensive funds in overseas markets and their claims had without exception been proved false after investigation. Treasury was convinced that Khemlani was such a man. It decided to make its own checks on him, first with Scotland Yard to see if he had a criminal background and to discover what information the British had, and secondly with the Morgan Guarantee Company of New York. While both reports cleared Khemlani, they indicated that he would not be able to raise the money. Later, on its own initiative, Treasury asked the Reserve Bank to send an official overseas to examine the bona fides of Khemlani. As a result of this visit the official concerned filed a report saying that Khemlani would not be able to obtain the $4000 million he originally offered or the $2000 million subsequently sought when the government reduced the sum.

The Treasury view was that the Australian government did not need an intermediary to raise its overseas loans: it had never used one in the past and it saw no need to use one now. This attitude was given precise expression in March 1975 when, in his capacity as Acting Treasurer, Hayden wrote in a letter replying to an approach to the government: 'The Australian government's international reputation as a prime borrower is such that it does not need to use any form of intermediary. In the past it has always confined overseas loan negotiations to dealing directly with principals; leading financial institutions in overseas capital markets.'

The institution Treasury often dealt with was the Morgan Stanley Company in New York. Treasury had a distinct preference for going to the well-established fund mobilisers in the market and was opposed to becoming involved with the consortium of other traders and commercial middlemen who claimed they had access to Middle East funds. The

Treasury was concerned that Australia's reputation as a borrower could suffer if its name was associated with someone like Khemlani and if he in any way had government authority to seek loan funds.

But Treasury's concern did not stop with Khemlani. It was amazed at the actual terms and conditions of the proposed borrowing. First, the Treasury was quite convinced that $4000 million was simply not available in the market. Second, it was convinced that it was not available over a twenty-year period, which was the time specified in Hewitt's letter to Khemlani. It knew that an eight-year period was the longest that anyone had recently borrowed in the US market, although in the Swiss market borrowing was often for fifteen years. But nowhere was it for twenty years.

Even more astounding was the proposal that the loan would be computed on the basis of a compound interest rate. This meant there would be no repayments until the end of the twenty-year period, when the Australian government would have to repay an amount, assessed on a compound interest rate of 7.7 per cent, of $US17,635 million or $A13,385 million, an astronomical figure. All previous loans raised by the Australian government had been on an ordinary interest rate with the interest repayable each year and the total of the loan at its expiry date. The Treasury had a practice of identifying 'funny money' men by their reliance on deals involving compound interest. It pointed out that if the Connor loan went ahead, Australia's total overseas debt, accumulated over the last fifty years, would triple.

The Treasury had objections to the proposed Khemlani commission. Commissions were normally paid for three purposes involving loans: managing, underwriting and selling the loan. It was not clear whether Khemlani would be doing any of these three functions. It was quite likely he would be doing none of them. He was, in effect, being paid a finder's commission. This sort of commission had never been paid before and the Treasury believed it should not be paid now, particularly since it was convinced Khemlani would not be able to find the money. Moreover, if other people were involved in managing, underwriting and selling the loan, then they would presumably seek a commission for doing this themselves. Under the draft agreement drawn up during the talks with Khemlani, it was proposed that he receive a 2½ per cent commission, a total of $100 million.

It was also proposed that this commission would come out of the loan being raised and, presumably, would be paid to Khemlani by the lenders themselves, the latter being quite contrary to normal practice. In his own statement Khemlani indicated that one of the reasons for this was to avoid having to secure parliamentary approval for the commission. But parliamentary approval is not necessarily needed for commissions in loan raisings. Finally, Treasury was concerned about the economic repercussions of introducing such funds into Australia. Both Whitlam and Connor rejected this argument when they defended the loan raisings on 9 July saying the funds would be introduced into Australia gradually.

The climax of this extraordinary venture occurred on 13 December 1974, exactly one year to the day before Gough Whitlam was defeated in the general election. It was Black Friday, Friday 13th. In the previous days the government's advisers had been busy preparing the draft agreement for the loan acceptance. It was then decided to proceed to the final stage and give formal Executive Council authority for the loan raising. The exceptional nature of the undertaking was recognised by everyone involved. During the afternoon senior officials from the Treasury, Attorney-General's Department, Minerals and Energy, and the Prime Minister's Department met at the Prime Minister's Lodge following an earlier series of meetings in the morning. The main officials involved in the talks, both at the Lodge and before, were Sir Frederick Wheeler, John Stone, Bert Prowse and Ian Hay from the Treasury, Clarrie Harders the Secretary of the Attorney-General's Department, the Solicitor-General Maurice Byers, and senior officials from the Attorney-General's Department, Andrew Menzies and Denis Rose. The main principals from the Minerals and Energy Department were Sir Lenox Hewitt and J T Larkin. John Menadue, who was then acting as the de facto head of the Prime Minister's Department, was also present. The Treasury and Attorney-General's officials drafted the Executive Council minute, despite the concern which they had previously expressed about the loan proposal.

Wheeler was an outspoken opponent of almost everything connected with the loan. At the meeting he argued strongly that the Treasurer's name should not be attached to the proposal and that the Treasurer should not have the loan authority vested in him. Whitlam and Connor conferred on the issue and agreed that Connor would be given the loan authority. The discussions continued into the night and the actual Executive Council meeting was not held until late.

The national executive of the Labor Party was meeting at the Lodge at the same time in another room. But Whitlam and the Attorney-General Lionel Murphy, both members of the ALP executive, spent most of their time discussing the loan-raising approval with officials and with Connor. Cairns spent a lot of time at the executive meeting and only went once or twice into the other room. At one stage Whitlam told him: 'We've decided to give Rex the authority, it won't be Treasury. We can't trust them.' Cairns, acting on the advice of his Department, expressed doubts about the proposal and suggested that the Premiers should be brought into the picture. But the others disagreed with him saying the government should try to get the money first and, if it got it, then bring the Premiers in.[3]

The Executive Council minute was signed by four Ministers: Whitlam, Cairns, Murphy and Connor. It authorised Connor 'to borrow for temporary purposes' $US4000 million and to determine the terms and conditions of the borrowing. Connor in turn could authorise other people in writing to borrow the funds on behalf of the Australian government. The explanatory memorandum attached to the minute, which normally explains concisely the purpose of the minute, said: 'The Australian government needs immediate access to substantial sums of non-equity capital from abroad for temporary purposes, amongst other things to deal with exigencies arising out of the current world situation and the international energy crisis, to strengthen Australia's external financial position, to provide immediate protection for Australia in regard to supplies of minerals and energy and to deal with current and immediately foreseeable unemployment in Australia.'[4]

There were a number of details about this minute which subsequently provoked heavy criticism. First, the memorandum failed to explain properly the real reasons for the seeking of the funds and to this extent represented a failure on the part of the government fully to inform the Governor-General. Second, although the phrase 'for temporary purposes' was used in both the minute itself and the memorandum, it appears quite clear that the funds were not being sought for temporary purposes in view of the big development projects they would finance. The significance of the 'temporary purposes' reference was that, in all other circumstances barring this one, the federal government had to seek the consent of the Loan Council for its borrowings. By inserting this reference, that legal obligation to consult with the state Premiers was avoided.

There was a well-established practice for the Commonwealth to consult with the Premiers on such loan matters. The normal procedure was that the Treasury, after investigating the proposed loan, would put the least favourable conditions before the Treasurer. Telegrams would then be sent to all Premiers seeking their concurrence for the loan to go ahead and giving details of the amount, rate of interest, price at issue and other relevant factors. Only when there was a clear majority of the Loan Council in favour of the proposal would it proceed. (Each state has one vote on the Loan Council and the federal government has two votes.) But on this occasion there had been no consultation whatsoever with the Premiers.

Although the loan was of momentous proportions, no written legal advice was provided. When he defended the authority in Parliament on 9 July the Prime Minister, choosing his words very carefully, said: 'The operation of the financial agreement was of course considered. The

former Attorney-General (Murphy) advised orally that, in the exceptional circumstances I have outlined, the borrowing could probably be
regarded as a borrowing for "temporary purposes".' The key admission
here was that the advice was only oral and not definite, and that the
borrowing was only 'probably' within the meaning of temporary purposes.

At a press conference on 15 July Whitlam claimed that no written
advice was ever sought or received. Whitlam also said oral advice was
given by both Byers and Harders and that he had acted in accordance
with that advice. On 20 May the Prime Minister said the government
would have sought the approval of the Loan Council 'if and when the
loan is made'. But the Opposition asked with justification why the
temporary purposes provision was included in the first place if the
intention was not to avoid Loan Council consultations. This is the origin
of the Opposition claim that the government was trying to circumvent
the Constitution.

The Governor-General normally attends Executive Council meetings. The usual practice is that, if he cannot attend, he is informed of
the meeting prior to it being held and the minutes of the meeting
(decisions) are conveyed to him immediately afterwards for his signature. On the afternoon and evening of 13 December, Kerr was at
Admiralty House, Sydney. That night he went to the Opera House to
see a performance of *Romeo and Juliet*. He was not notified that day that
an Executive Council meeting was taking place. Whitlam rang Kerr at
8 a.m. on Saturday to inform him that a meeting had been held and in
due course the minute was sent to the Governor-General for his signature.

Kerr signed the minute along with a second minute at the end of
January when the extent of the loan was reduced to $US2000 million.
Later, when the loans controversy erupted and it became obvious that
the 13 December minute was of highly dubious legality, the Governor-
General himself came under severe criticism for having approved it in
the first place. A number of newspapers were highly critical of his
acquiescent stand and claimed he should have been more vigilant in
scrutinising Executive Council minutes submitted for his signature.

This criticism must have left an impact on the Governor-General
and would presumably have made him more wary and meticulous in
his dealings with the government thenceforth. But Kerr never once
complained to Whitlam about any of the problems involved in the
Executive Council decision, either at the time or throughout 1975, as the
authority itself became the centre of a political storm. Despite later
efforts to argue that the loans authority was a factor in Whitlam's
dismissal from office, the Governor-General himself never considered it
was important enough to discuss with the Prime Minister. However a

number of senior Liberals believe that it was a significant event in shaping Kerr's later attitude. They argue that, just as the government was prepared to flout the Constitution over the loan raising, it was trying to do the same over supply.[5]

Whitlam and Hewitt, together with a large entourage, left Australia just after noon on Saturday 14 December for the epic European trip. According to Khemlani, the main reason for the breakdown in the loan arrangements on 13–14 December was the government's insistence that his commission be deducted at the lender's end. Khemlani claimed that he doubted whether the lenders would be prepared to do this for a commission of two per cent or more. However, after subsequent discussions with Sheik Gassan, Khemlani claimed that they were prepared to receive one per cent commission each, the equivalent of $US40 million. Finally Connor gave Khemlani a letter dated 16 December which the Pakistani could use to mobilise funds from the prime banks to the Union Bank of Switzerland in order to finalise the loan. Connor himself sent a copy of the Executive Council minute to the vice-president of the Swiss Bank to show the bona fides of the Australian government. He also sent a copy of the minute to Khemlani.

But the effort to mobilise funds through the Swiss Bank ended in fiasco. When Connor contacted the Union Bank of Switzerland, he received a negative response and officials immediately began to suspect that Khemlani had been 'leading them on'. They began to suspect that Khemlani had no money or chance of mobilising funds. On 21 December Connor sent a sudden telex to Khemlani which terminated relations between them and said the government was no longer interested in trying to raise a loan through him.[6]

Not long after, when Cairns was acting Prime Minister during Whitlam's trip, Wheeler impressed on him that Khemlani appeared to have been lying to the government. One Saturday morning Cairns convened a meeting with Murphy, Connor and senior officials. The acting Prime Minister said that Khemlani appeared to have misled the government and Wheeler had details of this. Not long after it was decided to cancel the $US4000 million authority.[7]

But this incident established the pattern with Khemlani. Relations were soon patched up and the cyclical process continued. In late January money was being raised through the Moscow Norodny Bank, then the Seattle First National Bank Switzerland. Gradually the net began to widen and a larger number of people became aware of Khemlani's activities, both banks and middlemen. A whole procession of people were unveiled in mid-1975 who had been involved in one form or another. A much greater number probably never came to light.

When Whitlam was overseas, the loan authority was revoked on 7 January in order to finance a German loan. It was reinstated on

28 January and the sum was lowered to $US2000 million. Khemlani returned to Australia and was in Canberra during 29–31 January. Throughout this month he had been in constant communication with Connor and other principals involved in the loan. The Pakistani was confident the loan would come to fruition at the end of January and, as a result, Connor's authority was reinstated. But once again the funds never materialised. According to Khemlani this effort came undone after Connor spoke to the Moscow Norodny Bank late one night, only to be told that the bank knew nothing about the funds.

Khemlani returned to Australia again on 25–28 February for further talks in Canberra with Connor and returned twice more after this on 4 March and then again on 22 March 1975. Connor gave him a letter dated 22 March which referred to funds totalling $US8000 million, which would come in two batches of $US4000 million each. There was regular communication between Connor and Khemlani up until 20 May 1975, by which stage the loan was just starting to become a public issue.

Throughout 1975 Connor was the moving force behind the loan-raising effort. He told Whitlam during the Terrigal conference in early February that the loan was coming along well. Whitlam left the pursuance of the matter completely with his Minerals and Energy Minister. He had only the vaguest idea of the extent of Connor's communication and what he was doing. One of the chief problems was that at no stage did the Prime Minister make Connor accountable to him for what was happening or make rigorous and regular checks to assess progress. He simply relied on Connor completely and gave him his head. By this stage both the Treasury and the Attorney-General's Department were playing no direct role whatsoever.

Treasury's efforts to monitor Connor's activities ran into a brick wall. On 31 December it drafted a letter addressed to Connor, which Cairns subsequently signed, trying to assess the liability of the Australian government in the event of Khemlani lodging a claim for expenses with the government. The letter contained the following passage: ' . . . I would be glad if you would arrange for copies of all relevant communications which passed to and from your office and your Department and Mr Khemlani on the one hand and the Union Bank of Switzerland on the other hand to be made available to the Treasury and to the Attorney-General's Department so that this follow-up action can be undertaken.' But Treasury never received any reply from Connor to this letter.

In a deeper sense the loans affair rose out of the fractured relations between the Government and the Treasury during the last six months of 1974 when they clashed over the direction of economic policy. Connor had a traditional distrust and contempt of Treasury's mandarins. His operating assumption, and that of many other Labor Ministers, was that

Treasury was being orthodox and obstructionist. Its stance on the loans issue was similar to that which it had adopted towards the economy in late 1974. Its advice had been disregarded once and would be disregarded once again. Both Connor and later Cairns assumed that Treasury was not simply tied by tradition to the established financial circles in New York; they assumed that Treasury officers were following not just their professional, but also their class instincts. Connor was backed by his permanent head Sir Lenox Hewitt, who had the chance to pull off one of the greatest ever victories against the Treasury if the loan was successfully raised.

But even more important was the suspicion in which the Prime Minister himself now held the Treasury. Whitlam threw in his lot with Connor in a scheme that was one of the most legally and financially dubious undertakings ever embraced in Australian history. He had gone from praising Sir Frederick Wheeler as a great public servant to damning him and wanting to get rid of him. At the Terrigal conference Whitlam had discussed with Cairns the question of replacing Wheeler as Secretary to the Treasury. At this time the Prime Minister was sympathetically disposed towards Hewitt for this position.[8]

On 9 July Whitlam defended his government's action in ignoring Treasury advice. He said:

> Throughout this affair, an assumption has been generated that non-acceptance of the Treasury viewpoint is itself improper. I can think of no concept more destructive of the nature of responsible government as we know it. Treasury is not beyond challenge either for its competence or, as the Solicitor-General's memorandum tabled today shows, its ethics.

Whitlam's reference to ethics referred to Wheeler's action in seeking a legal opinion on documents signed by Cairns without telling his Minister.

Throughout mid-1975 Whitlam and Connor argued that Khemlani had only been given a letter of identification. They said he had no authority, that he was not an intermediary or agent of the Australian government. This interpretation is severely called into question by the legal advice given by the Secretary of the Attorney-General's Department Clarrie Harders.

On 14 June Harders gave the Prime Minister a report on another critical loan issue—the letters which Cairns had sent to a Melbourne businessman, George Harris. Referring to this relationship Harders said: 'From the financial standpoint, the government's position would be basically the same as it was under the arrangements with Mr Khemlani.' That is, the obligation established between the government and

Khemlani was the same as that between Cairns and Harris, which later led to the sacking of Cairns from Treasury.[9]

The loan authority held by Connor was finally revoked when the government sought to raise $US100 million in the New York market. Whitlam later pointed to this and the government's triple A credit rating, the highest available, as an indication that the Khemlani exercise had not hurt it as a borrower.

Just before 20 May Wheeler told Cairns that overseas institutions would be alarmed at Australia's new approach to loan raisings through using people like Khemlani. He persuaded Cairns that something had to be done about Connor's authority. Cairns went into the House and mentioned this to Whitlam when the Prime Minister was sitting at the main table. 'OK but you've got to be the bastard, I'm not going to tell him,' Whitlam said to his deputy. Cairns slipped back to the front bench, mentioned the situation to Connor and the Minerals and Energy Minister agreed. Cairns told Whitlam a bit later that Connor had concurred in the withdrawal of the authority and the Prime Minister was amazed. 'Jesus, has he?' Whitlam declared.[10] On 26 May, the Prime Minister told the House: 'Not a cent has been paid to the gentleman. Not a cent has to be paid to the gentleman. Not a cent will be paid to the gentleman.'

The Executive Council meeting revoking the authority was attended by Whitlam, Connor, and the vice-president of the Executive Council, Frank Stewart. But it was not until 10 June at a press conference that Whitlam announced that no Minister no longer had any authority concerning overseas loans and that nothing was to be done without the authority of the new Treasurer Bill Hayden.

On 29 May Whitlam wrote a letter to all Ministers involved in loan raisings saying he wanted any further proposals referred to himself in the first instance. That is, it was only in May 1975 that the Prime Minister moved to assert himself in this area. But it was too late. The damage had already been done and a whole host of middlemen across the world had become involved in the Australian government's loan-raising activities.

Whitlam, in fact, never fully repented on what the government had done. During the July special parliamentary sitting day he said he was still prepared and anxious to borrow funds of the order with which Khemlani had dealt. Certainly Connor maintained contact with Khemlani after 20 May, either directly or through Karidis. When Connor was later dismissed, the vice-president of the Executive Council, Frank Stewart, even rang Kerr on the subject. Stewart claimed that while Whitlam had not given Connor approval to go ahead he had indicated that if the loan became viable then the government would take it up.

The loans affair had two significant consequences. It left Sir John Kerr suspicious of Whitlam. Kerr felt that he had been deceived, that his office had not been not treated with the proper respect and that Labor was prepared to bend the law to get its way. It also injected an uncontrollable electoral poison into the Labor government. The number of documents, the scope of the exercise, and its legal and financial gaps kept haunting Labor throughout 1975. No matter where Ministers tried to plug the cracks, new ones kept opening. Connor became obsessed about the proposal and it finished up destroying him. More than anything else the Khemlani affair proved that Labor was a bunch of amateurs and that 23 years in Opposition had been too long.

# *12*

# THE LOANS AFFAIR—THE CAIRNS CONNECTION

*If I have made a mistake in judgement, I accept the consequences.*

Jim Cairns, 5 June 1975, about
his letters to George Harris

**W**hile Rex Connor was the only Minister with Executive Council authority to pursue overseas loans, he was not the only Minister involved in this activity. Dr Jim Cairns was deeply interested in the prospect of recycling petrodollars—the reinvestment surplus generated by the historic 1973 OPEC oil price hikes. This interest only increased after the 13 December Executive Council meeting where the dimensions of the exercise left a deep impact on him. Cairns was sceptical about Khemlani but fascinated by the concept.

The Labor government was fated to have not just one, but two of its senior Ministers involved in loan raisings in a fashion that was ultimately to destroy them and bring inestimable damage to the government. Although the Cairns activities were peripheral to the main loan raising efforts under Rex Connor's responsibility, they proved to be even more fatal for the government in a public relations sense.

When Cairns went to the United States in November 1974, one of his prime aims was to talk about the shift in the world's investment funds from the western industrialised nations to the oil exporting countries. Cairns saw a number of officials in both the State Department and the US Treasury. He found a determination on all sides to ensure that such funds were reinvested back in the United States. But his impression was that the administration and the business circles connected with it shunned the notion of direct approaches to the Arabs. They wanted to work through the established banking channels and New York firms they had always relied upon in the same way that Australia's federal Treasury had relied upon the Morgan Stanley Company in New York.

When Cairns raised with these people the prospect of Australia getting large scale funds from the Middle East, he was ridiculed. But this trip only increased Cairns' interest in the loan question and did nothing to shake his belief that unconventional means should be used where necessary on either a government to government basis or through trusted individual contacts.

The person with whom Cairns became associated with loan raising efforts was a Melbourne businessman, George Harris, a socially mobile and adroit operator who had always aspired to win the respect of the ruling elite and whose colleagues claimed ultimately aspired to receive a knighthood. After the war Harris completed a dentistry course and later became a dentist at Pentridge jail before moving into business and establishing a number of important contacts through the Carlton football club of which he became president (he later had a stand at their ground named after him). A glimpse of the extent to which Harris used his contacts in high places is shown by his one-time business partner Lesley Nagy in a statutory declaration tabled in federal parliament. Nagy states:

> I have been introduced by Mr Harris to many important people. I was bedazzled by his familiarity with many important people. On one occasion when my wife and I were staying at the Southern Cross Hotel, Mr Harris took us to a private dining room where he was having dinner with Sir Robert Menzies, Dame Pattie, Mrs Jean Harris and two other couples whose names I do not recall. He also introduced me to Mr Ray Meagher. We had a luncheon meeting at the Southern Cross concerning our Melbourne property. Whilst we were in London Harris and myself were to go to Saudi Arabia, so I had to obtain a visa for that country. I found it very difficult to do so. So Harris took me to see Sir John Bunting, whom I had never met before. At that time it was a cordial visit and Sir John appeared to know Mr Harris very well. The following day, when we found that visas for Saudi Arabia were so impossible, we went to see Sir John Bunting again. We made no appointment to see Sir John Bunting—we just bowled in without an appointment. On the second occasion Sir John was not in but we had a discussion with his private secretary. George told him we had to go to Saudi Arabia and we needed a letter each from the High Commissioner to obtain our visas quickly. Later the same day we returned and spoke to the private secretary and were given a letter each. A copy of the letter concerning me is provided. Although I had met Sir John Bunting only once, the letter states 'Mr Nagy, who is of Christian faith, is well known to me . . . '

Jim Cairns first met George Harris in 1972 when Harris found out he was a Carlton football follower. On one occasion Cairns arrived back in Australia from Peking and went straight to the Melbourne Cricket

Ground for the grand final match with tickets provided by Harris. Cairns always assumed that Harris was an influential businessman, judging from his friends and his position. Once Harris took Cairns to lunch with Sir Robert Menzies immediately prior to a football game and they were subsequently joined by Liberal frontbencher Don Chipp.

In late 1974 contact between Cairns and Harris intensified and in December Cairns received a letter from Harris about loan raisings. Harris sought an indication that the Treasury and Reserve Bank would give their approval if he and his business associate, Lesley Nagy, could successfully negotiate overseas loans for Victorian state government authorities. They had already discussed this matter with senior people in the Victorian government whom they knew and who had indicated to them they could make investigations seeking overseas funds. This request from Harris received extensive attention in the federal Treasury. On 31 December a deputy secretary of the Treasury, Roy Daniel, submitted a minute to Cairns pointing out in some detail the danger of approaches of this nature.

Daniel's words were even more applicable to the loan raising efforts of Rex Connor. In retrospect they seem appropriate as the epitaph for the Labor government. Daniel said:

> Governments, if they are to retain respect and keep in good standing on the international capital markets, need to avoid allowing their names to be associated with any operators in these markets other than those whose reputation and standing are beyond question. Moreover, any negotiation by the government itself for an overseas loan could be quickly soured if it came to the notice of the underwriting group or potential lender that other parties were at the same time 'shopping' for funds on behalf of the government or with its backing, especially in the same market.
>
> Going beyond this particular case, I mention that previous Treasurers, including your predecessor, found it useful to adopt a general practice of having persons who approached them about possibilities of arranging overseas borrowings for the government or for government instrumentalities referred at least in the first instance to the Treasury, especially if they did not directly represent a major underwriting group or bank well-known to the government. Experience over the years has demonstrated that when tested, the propositions that come forward from what I might call the 'fringe' operators—and there is a surprisingly large number of them—almost without exception fall to the ground or are of a kind with which no reputable borrower, especially a government, should be associated. If you wish, I could give you a more detailed story in this regard, and I would of course be happy to talk with you on the subject at any time convenient to you.[1]

The Australian government received hundreds of approaches from mid 1973 onwards from individuals and companies offering to obtain loans from the Middle East. In nearly every case government inquiries found that the money could not be obtained. That is, out of the hundreds of such approaches none had ever been proved authentic. The Secretary of the Treasury, Sir Frederick Wheeler, and his senior officials had been thoroughly alarmed about the government's association with Khemlani earlier in December. Their advice to Cairns was summarised in the Daniel minute provoked by the first Harris approach. It was the strongest possible warning to the Treasurer to be wary of such people. A reply was sent from Cairns to Harris, drafted by the Treasury, informing him that any inquiries about loans procedures should be referred to the Department. This letter was also the basis for formalising a process to handle all such queries.

Daniel recorded the following 'note for file' on 12 January after speaking to the Treasurer's private secretary, Roger Freney, who spoke to Cairns:

> Mr Freney told me on Friday last that the Treasurer had agreed to a note he had prepared for circulation within the Treasurer's office pointing out the need for caution in relation to approaches by people claiming to be able to arrange overseas loans for the government. Mr Freney said that the Treasurer had agreed that such approaches should be referred automatically to senior Treasury officers.[2]

In summary, by early 1975 the Treasury had warned its Minister about any loan approaches from outsiders and had instituted safeguard procedures to handle them. But what the Department failed ever to counter was the unilateral administrative style of Jim Cairns and his naivety in dealing with people whom he believed were respectable businessmen and consequently beyond reproach. In March and April Cairns took steps which involved himself directly in loan raising efforts in a highly dangerous fashion.

The thinking of the Treasurer at the time and the mood of the government in which he operated is best described by Cairns himself when he later justified his dealings with Harris. Cairns told Parliament in June:

> We found that there were many individuals who came forward saying that they knew the location of funds. We were aware that the Saudi-Arabian Monetary Agency was a significant potential lender and we considered that it was desirable that these matters should be properly explored outside the conventional channels. So a number of individuals were interviewed, many of them—most of them, almost all of them—were found very quickly to be worthless; but some appeared to be somewhat different. In March a Mr George Harris, who was well known to me, to the former Prime Minister, Sir Robert Menzies, and to at least one or two members of the front bench today, told me he

was going to Europe and that while there he might be able to make some inquiries and give me information that might be useful. I considered that Mr Harris was trustworthy and therefore I furnished him with three notes.

Cairns said the Australian government had decided to investigate the possibility of obtaining investment funds from the oil exporting countries, funds which might not be under the control of established New York and European banking houses. This was the point of fundamental difference between the Government and the Treasury. The advice Labor got from the Treasury was that despite the change in the world economic situation, traditional loan raising sources should still be relied upon.

Harris and Nagy saw Cairns on Friday 7 March in his Canberra office at a meeting that was later to become the subject of one of Australia's major political battles. This meeting inaugurated a series of letters from Cairns to Harris which led to two successive upheavals—the dismissal of Cairns as Treasurer and then his dismissal from the ministry.

Harris left the Treasurer's office on 7 March with a letter which would eventually destroy the career of the deputy Prime Minister. In this letter Cairns authorised Harris to raise overseas loans for the Government and pledged a commission. But before this letter became public knowledge Cairns was first trapped by other letters which he gave Harris a few days later.

On Monday 10 March Harris saw Cairns in the Treasurer's Sydney office for another meeting and was given a letter on this date which read: 'The Australian government is willing to borrow funds from lenders overseas on terms and conditions suitable to us—J F Cairns.' The original copy of this letter had written across it, 'given to George Harris'. Later, on 15 April, at yet another meeting, Cairns gave Harris two more significant notes. The first one read:

TO WHOM IT MAY CONCERN

Recently I have been concerned that persons in Europe and elsewhere claim to represent the Australian government in negotiating loans. No such authority exists. The Australian government is interested in borrowing on favourable conditions and should any person be able to assist us we would be glad to hear from him. I am providing Mr George Harris, holder of Australian Passport No. G740206, and whose signature appears in the margin, with this letter so that he may make enquiries for me. If it is felt necessary to confirm the authenticity of this letter, then with the consent of Mr Harris, this may be done by contact with Sir John Bunting, Australian High Commissioner, London, or the Australian Ambassador to Switzerland in Berne, or direct with me by Telex AA62632 Parliament House, Canberra, Australia. In the event that he recommends that any funds are available and I am satisfied with the authenticity of such availability and the terms and conditions for lending are acceptable to me and the funds are in amounts sufficient for our needs, I would be pleased to take the matter up.

J F Cairns

The second note read:

Dear Mr Harris,

In the event that the Australian government or its representatives or nominees successfully negotiates the borrowing of overseas funds, introduced or arranged by you an appropriate commission would be paid to you or your nominees.

Yours faithfully,
J F Cairns[3]

Cairns said later in his defence that at this 15 April meeting he told Harris the letters created no legal agency between him and the government. According to Cairns the letters merely authorised Harris to make inquiries. If a loan resulted from his activities then he would be entitled to proper compensation.

It is significant that Cairns never told the Treasury that he was giving these notes to Harris; he acted unilaterally and without prior reference to his Department. Such ministerial discretion always exists— but Cairns had already been advised by the Treasury against such a relationship with middlemen to raise overseas funds.

The Treasurer's action flouted the advice he had received from the Treasury expressed in Daniel's minute of 31 December quoted above. Not only did Cairns not consult with his Department, there is no indication that he told anyone else of import within the Labor government that he had given these letters to Harris. Equally important was the fact that Cairns had no government authority to seek overseas loan funds through intermediaries. Despite his claim that no formal agency existed, later legal advice to the government was to the effect that an agency had been established through these letters. Moreover Cairns was not simply ignoring departmental advice; he was taking the precise course Treasury had warned against when it referred to the need for governments to avoid allowing their name to be associated with any operators in the market other than those who were institutional professionals.

Cairns, in fact, had made one important and formal loan-raising approach with the cooperation of the Treasury in early 1975. This was during his trip to the Middle East when he was accompanied by the Agriculture Minister Senator Ken Wriedt on a visit to Saudi Arabia,

Kuwait, Bahrain and Iran. Before the visit Cairns held talks with senior Treasury officers on the prospect of arranging loans directly through the Saudi Arabian Monetary Authority. Two senior officials, Bert Prowse, First Assistant Secretary from the revenue, loans and investment division and Ian Hay, also from this area, went to Saudi Arabia before the Treasurer's visit in an effort to hold preliminary talks. Although he had no prearranged appointment Cairns saw King Faisal just two days before the king was assassinated. Faisal said he was interested in long-term contracts with Australia in a similar fashion to the interest expressed in late 1974 when the Shah of Iran held talks in Canberra with government Ministers. Cairns wanted to arrange a $250 million loan through the Saudi Arabian Monetary Authority for use by the Australian Industries Development Corporation. The Saudis were offering funds at New York interest rates but the chief problem was that 50 per cent of the funds were to be in their own currency, ryals. Cairns said this was too much and before he left it was reduced to 33.3 per cent. Several weeks later he received a letter in which the ryals component was further reduced to 25 per cent.

Although the loan was never brought to fruition, this was the most concerted formal effort made by Cairns to raise overseas funds, conducted on a government to government basis in a direct approach to Saudi Arabia. Cairns believed it was a worthwhile try and could well open the way to further successes. But the Treasurer was never to have the opportunity again.

It was on 13 April that the Treasury's liaison officer in the Treasurer's office, Ed Shann, found a copy of the letter to Harris dated 10 March. Shann sent this to the Department and the Secretary to the Treasury, Sir Frederick Wheeler saw it on 14 April. Wheeler did not raise the matter with Cairns mainly because, in two of his most recent talks with the Treasurer, on 3 April and 10 April, Cairns had categorically stated that he had given no one any letters authorising them to borrow funds on behalf of the Australian government. The 10 March letter was not necessarily inconsistent with these statements.

However, on the evening of 22 April Wheeler received a phone message from the Treasury representative in London, Dr N W Davey, that George Harris had called on the Australian High Commissioner, Sir John Bunting, and had produced the 15 April letter signed by Cairns. Harris had said he was authorised to make inquiries on behalf of the Treasurer over possible loans to Australia. Later that night Wheeler rang Bunting, his old colleague of two decades at the top of the public service hierarchy in Canberra, and Bunting read the full text of the letter out as Wheeler wrote it down. The letter was the 'To whom it may concern' letter which Cairns said could be authenticated through either Bunting or the Australian Ambassador in Switzerland. At the end of their phone conversation Bunting agreed to send Wheeler a confirming copy. Cairns was away from Australia at the time, having left the previous day, 21 April, for the Philippines and a meeting of the Asian Development Bank. But on 2 May deputy secretary Roy Daniel told Wheeler that Bunting wanted urgent advice in the contingency that he was asked to authenticate the letter by people Harris had approached.

Wheeler saw Cairns the same day that the Treasurer returned from overseas. Cairns told him that he did not believe there would be any further developments in the Harris matter. But he made it clear to Wheeler that Bunting was to authenticate the letter if asked. Cairns told Wheeler that the letter was merely designed to enable Harris to 'ferret around in business circles' and do no more than identify himself. Cairns took a relaxed attitude to the whole question and believed there was nothing to worry about.

Wheeler felt the opposite. Wheeler and the Treasury had grave misgivings about the letter Cairns had given Harris. Wheeler was worried about reports Treasury had received that Cairns had issued Harris with two letters on 15 April, not just one. Wheeler told Cairns that any credentials given to Harris should immediately be withdrawn in writing. He wondered whether the letter had involved the government in a legal obligation towards Harris if he had been able to arrange any loan.

On 6 May Treasury obtained a copy of the second Cairns letter dated 15 April, in which he told Harris he would receive appropriate commission if the Australian government successfully negotiated an overseas loan introduced or arranged by Harris. At this point some Treasury officers believed there was a prima facie case that Cairns had involved the Australian government in an agency relationship with Harris. The Treasury was deeply suspicious of Harris. Senior officers suspected that Harris was trying to manoeuvre himself into a position to make a windfall gain from the government by acting as an intermediary or as instigator for a successful loan.[4]

As a result of his doubts, Wheeler then took a fateful decision which was to lead to the removal of Cairns as Treasurer and almost precipitate his own downfall as Secretary to the Treasury. It was a decision Wheeler took drawing upon his vast experience and an assessment of his responsibilities. Wheeler decided to seek a legal opinion on both the 15 April letters by Cairns to Harris without telling the Treasurer himself. This was an unprecedented move by a permanent head. Its intent was to establish the legal consequences of Cairns' actions; in effect, whether the Treasurer was guilty of a serious mistake. Wheeler believed he needed this legal opinion before he could take any further action. He had presumably concluded that there was no purpose in further talks with Cairns on this subject given the casual attitude and lack of concern displayed by the Treasurer in their previous talks.

On 6 May Treasury sought the advice of the Attorney-General's Department on the two Cairns letters. In order to maintain confidentiality and keep the authorship of the letters anonymous Treasury omitted the first two sentences of the 'To whom it may concern' letter and other specific details which could trace it to the Treasurer's own hand. Attorney-General's, of course, realised that the letters had been sent by the Treasurer anyway. At a meeting of officials between the two Departments on 9 May the Attorney-General's representative said it was difficult to give firm legal advice without knowing whether there were any additional oral instructions issued simultaneously with the letters.

The Secretary of the Attorney-General's Department, Clarrie Harders, had his own misgivings about the way in which Wheeler was seeking this legal opinion. The two permanent heads lunched together on 13 May and Harders expressed his doubts at the time. He suggested that if the Treasury was seeking an opinion on letters already despatched by its Minister then the most appropriate course might be to discuss this question with Cairns before seeking legal advice. Despite Harders' view, which Wheeler said he noted and considered, the Treasury Secretary still wanted the opinion before taking follow-up action. Harders then told Wheeler that he would have draft advice prepared.

In mid May Jim Cairns decided to make yet another overseas trip, this time to Paris for a meeting of the OECD. He was strongly advised against this trip before leaving by his colleague the Urban and Regional Development Minister, Tom Uren, and by his own economic adviser, Brian Brogan, both of whom said that he should begin initial work on the shape of the budget. Cairns went anyway and was absent from Australia during a critical period when his future was being sealed.

On the evening of 22 May the acting Treasurer, Bill Hayden, arranged for himself and Wheeler to see the Prime Minister over allegations made on the ABC's 'This Day Tonight' program about overseas loan operations involving Transia Corporation. In the previous month Sir William Gunn, one of the great power brokers in the Country Party in former years, a member of the Reserve Bank board and a shareholder in Transia Corporation, approached the government with a $US3.7 billion loan-raising proposal. Sir William rang the Minister for Northern Australia, Dr Rex Patterson, who passed the message on to the Treasurer. Cairns subsequently confirmed that the government was interested in raising the loan funds and this was conveyed to Sir William. On 20 April Wheeler telephoned Sir William and made it clear to him that the government was taking no action itself in connection with his proposal. But Transia Corporation was later referred to Rex Connor's office and conducted its subsequent dealings through Minerals and Energy. The loan was never finalised.

It was during this discussion on the Transia matter that Wheeler spoke about the general dangers of ministerial involvement with 'fringe' money operators. He had already pursued this theme with Whitlam in the past in relation to the Connor loan and Khemlani's activities. Wheeler now continued this theme and referred to the connections between Cairns and Harris and the need for the government to be wary about committing itself to such people. Wheeler made it clear he believed the government was taking a substantial risk in its dealings with Harris. A week later he was even more sure of this than ever.

Wheeler's doubts were confirmed on 28 May when he received the legal advice from Harders confirming what he had suspected all along. Harders said the Cairns 'To whom it may concern' letter implied an agency relationship between the bearer and the government. When this was considered with the second letter, the agent would be entitled to a reasonable commission for his efforts. Harders said his advice was given only on the documents and on the assumption that there was no further oral advice at the same time.

In the evening of that same day Wheeler gave Hayden and Whitlam two documents at a meeting in the Prime Minister's office. The first was the Harders opinion which he explained by going into the background of the Cairns letters, his own doubts and why he sought the opinion. The second document had come to him from the Trade Department, originating from the Australian Trade Commissioner in Milan, Italy. It read: 'Apparently a loan of $A500 million is being sought for Australia. Promissory notes to this effect, giving the terms as a 20-year compound loan resulting in a total repayment of $A2486 million and with the signature of Mr Connor on them, have been lodged with the small German bank Wurttembergische in Ulme.' All three men knew this was an obvious link with the Khemlani loan-raising efforts under Connor's guidance. Subsequently Connor denied the existence of this document.[5]

Whitlam was angry and concerned about these findings. The first document from Harders indicated that Cairns had exposed the government to great political danger. Whitlam was furious that Cairns had taken this action and consulted no one about it. The second report provided further evidence of the extent to which Khemlani's search for loan funds for the Australian government had permeated through Europe and appeared to be continuing unabated even though Connor's Executive Council loan approval had been revoked eight days before.

Within 24 hours Whitlam had decided to dismiss Cairns from Treasury knowing that the existence of the Harris letters would provide an irrefutable basis for his decision. Whitlam regarded the actions of his Treasurer as a gross breach of government propriety. At the same time the combination of warnings by Bill Hayden about the government's loan-raising efforts and advice by John Menadue resulted in Whitlam moving to pull the entire loan operations under his own control and to halt the almost reckless search for overseas funds.

On 29 May Whitlam, after further talks with Menadue, issued the following letter to the Treasurer, with a similar letter to the Minister for Minerals and Energy:

> Events this week show how imperative it is that before Monday I am personally familiar with all the papers relating to proposed overseas borrowings that have been under consideration since November last year but have not been concluded. Please let me have urgently copies of the documentation you have and copies also of documentation held by your Department. For the present I also want any proposals for further borrowings referred to me in the first instance. Except with my approval any current discussions (other than discussions on the pending $US100 million bond issue in New York) should be stayed for the time being. I have written also in the above terms to the Minister for Minerals and Energy.[6]

When Hayden received this letter in his capacity as acting Treasurer, he made immediate arrangements for a copy to be passed to Cairns who was still in Paris at the OECD ministerial council meeting. The letter was conveyed by a senior Treasury official, the first assistant secretary of the financial institutions division, Des Moore, who was a member of the Australian delegation to the Paris meeting. It was this approach which led to the gradual accumulation within the Prime Minister's office and Department of the documentation on overseas loan raisings. The letter was designed to end the government's loan-raising activities, consolidate its position in the face of political attacks from the Opposition and give the Prime Minister the chance to examine exactly what had happened and devise Labor's counter-attack.

But the letter is interesting in view of the controversy which later arose over Rex Connor's continuing dialogue with Khemlani after his authority had been revoked on 20 May. The sentence in the letter, 'Except with my approval any current discussions should be stayed for the time being', implies that Connor's loan-raising activities were still continuing and that their cessation would only be temporary.

The letter highlights the extent to which Whitlam had given his Ministers a free hand in conducting their own loan-raising activities in 1975. Whitlam had made virtually no effort since returning from Europe to review the ambit of the loan exercise and assess its progress. This letter is the first documentary instruction to Ministers to cease their activities, prompted in large part by the revelations involving Cairns. It also leaves the clear implication that, despite the revocation of Connor's authority on May 20, it was not until some days after this that actual instructions were given to halt loan talks and communications.

After the meeting in Whitlam's office on the evening of 28 May, Wheeler returned to the Department and prepared a message for transmission to Cairns in Paris, the text of which said:

Personal and Confidential and Immediate

For Treasurer

From Wheeler

1. As your private office will have informed you, the 'K' exercise has been greatly featured in the parliament and the press in recent days.
2. I now let you have as an attachment to this message the full extent of a letter which I received from Harders this afternoon.
3. Whilst with the acting Treasurer and the Prime Minister tonight on taxation matters inevitably I informed them both of the Harders letter.
4. I strongly advise that you take immediate steps to effect an immediate and complete cancellation of accreditations or authorisations (if any) given to George Harris.
5. I suggest that you telephone me.
6. Given all the circumstances I also strongly suggest that you telephone the Prime Minister without delay.[7]

The next morning Wheeler sent a copy of this message to Whitlam and received a telephone call from Cairns in Paris. During their phone conversation Wheeler repeated to Cairns the urgency of cancelling any authorisations he had given to Harris. The tone of Wheeler's telegram and his warning to Cairns to call Whitlam as soon as possible indicates that he was aware of the seriousness with which Whitlam viewed the Cairns–Harris connection.

But even at this stage Cairns seemed oblivious to the political danger about to engulf him. He told Wheeler that Harris was 'no problem'—a singular irony in view of the decision Whitlam had made to dismiss Cairns as Treasurer because of this very issue.

During their conversation Cairns told Wheeler that he proposed to do some personal investigation for himself about loan-raising matters when he travelled to Switzerland. He then asked Wheeler to give him the names of the banks and of other individuals who had come to the government's attention during the course of the Khemlani exercise. Wheeler told Cairns once again that he understood Harris was still in Europe and that the Treasurer should contact him as soon as possible to cancel any existing authorisation. This exchange had a macabre touch about it. While Cairns was still dreaming about a huge overseas loan, his political world was about to crash around him. Whitlam had decided to reshape his ministry.

# *13*

# THE CABINET RESHUFFLE

*Have we changed ships or are they just re-arranging the deck chairs on the Titanic?*

A senior Labor Party staff member,
on the Cabinet changes

On Tuesday 10 June 1974 Lance Barnard lost his post as deputy leader of the Labor Party and deputy Prime Minister to Dr Jim Cairns. The next night Whitlam came to Barnard's office to make peace with his former loyal deputy of the past seven years. The Prime Minister had given Barnard only token support in the contest for deputy and had made it clear that he was happy to work with Jim Cairns. It was agreed that when Barnard decided to leave the political arena a position with suitable status and reward would be found for him. The loss of the deputy Prime Ministership was a cruel blow for Barnard who had toiled diligently and inconspicuously to assist Whitlam to office only to be rejected by his party eighteen months after the goal was obtained. Barnard knew his best years were behind him and was clever enough to realise that his political career had almost completed full course—displaying a perspicacity all-too-rare among his colleagues.

After Labor had been returned at the May election, but before the ballot to decide the deputy leadership, Barnard had told his wife, Jill, that he had contested his last election. About the same time, when Whitlam, Barnard and Hayden were together at the Prime Minister's Lodge one night, Barnard told the others that he only wanted to stay on another year or eighteen months as deputy anyway. His health had not been good and in late 1973 he had an operation on his ear. In parliament his effectiveness was severely limited because of almost total deafness in one ear. But in June 1974 Whitlam had given him a commitment which Barnard knew would be honoured. For Lance Barnard it soothed the bitter taste of defeat and his own personal hurt at the fact that Whitlam offered him only limited support during the deputy leadership struggle.

The Whitlam–Barnard connection was one of the most successful in recent years in Australian politics. Both men were elected as leader and deputy in February 1967 with Barnard defeating Cairns by one vote for the deputy post. But their association predated these events. It was Barnard who first suggested to Whitlam, on Armistice Day 1959 when the two men were at the War Memorial, that the party leader, Dr Herbert Vere Evatt, was about to retire and that Whitlam should run for the deputy leadership in the ballot which would follow.

Barnard's great political quality was his loyalty: loyalty to his leader, loyalty to his party. For six years in Opposition Whitlam was the recipient of this loyalty when it was a critical necessity. In 1968 when Whitlam resigned the leadership Barnard could have won it himself with the support of both the left and the right. But he supported Whitlam's re-election instead, convinced he was unquestionably the best leader for the party. In the years following 1967, when the party was still divided and the style of Whitlam's leadership only inflamed the divisions, Barnard's support within the caucus and on the ALP federal executive was crucial to his leader.

All this changed in government. The man who had been so indispensable once now appeared readily dispensable. Barnard was a cautious but diligent Minister exposed early in 1973 as susceptible under pressure in parliament. Whitlam believed him to be a weak administrator and on more than one occasion strode the thirty yard corridor between their offices to march into Barnard's room and expend all his hostility on the Defence Minister for his handling of the VIP fleet, particularly his granting of flights to the Opposition. Whitlam's patience appeared to reach exhaustion point with his former deputy in May 1975. An incident at this time demonstrated the Prime Minister's intolerance towards his Ministers, the strength of his own dogmatism, and his determination to clean out the Cabinet, which was vented periodically in vigorous efforts to depose or retire the Minister currently in his sights. When Whitlam took a set against someone or finally ran out of patience with them, it inevitably meant the end for the individual concerned.

On Friday afternoon 16 May Whitlam and his staff flew to Maitland, NSW, for the opening of the E C Close Swimming Centre, staying the night at the Molly Morgan Motel. That evening a well-known right-wing activist, Michael Darby, approached the Prime Minister seeking approval for a team of private relief workers to join the RAAF flight to Guam the next day to pick up Vietnamese refugees. The flight was leaving Richmond base at 6 a.m. Saturday morning. Whitlam asked one of his staff to talk to Darby but made it quite clear that he did not want him or his private medical team on the plane. Whitlam himself believed that Australia should play a strictly limited role in accepting refugees from South Vietnam, whose government was now collapsing; he abhorred the fostering in Australia of those religious and political hatreds which originated overseas and were transplanted by migrant groups coming to a new country. The Prime Minister's staff contacted the Defence Department about Darby's request but made it clear that he was not to receive any assistance.

The following morning, when Whitlam and his aides heard the lead item on the ABC news announce that the Defence Minister, Lance Barnard, had interceded to allow Darby's medical team on the Guam flight, the Prime Minister smashed his arm in rage on the dashboard of the car they were travelling in and cursed Barnard loudly. By the time he arrived at the Williamstown RAAF base, he was so furious that he nearly terrified the Williamstown commander with the vehemence of his attacks on the commander of the Richmond base for letting the Darby team on board. Finally, he got Barnard on the phone from Williamstown and launched a virulent broadside against him. 'Do you know who he is?' Whitlam roared. 'That's the bastard that stood against me in Werriwa in 1974.' The Prime Minister only got more enraged when Barnard tried to excuse his action by saying that Darby claimed he had approval from Whitlam's office to board the flight. 'What if it had been a bunch of PLO terrorists? What if it had been the IRA? What if they'd been hijackers?' he demanded of Barnard. Whitlam's attitude towards the refugees was well-known and Barnard had transgressed the Prime Minister on an issue where Whitlam had acute personal feelings.

The Prime Minister was incensed that one of the government's arch opponents had been able to put a team of people on a RAAF plane without any scrutiny whatsoever, to build up an issue which Whitlam himself wanted played down as much as possible. When he settled back into his seat that morning, Whitlam said of Barnard: 'That's it, he's had it.' The Darby incident probably pushed Whitlam's patience with his former deputy beyond the breaking point. But, unlike his experiences with Frank Crean the previous year, Whitlam found that Lance Barnard was quite willing and anxious to leave the political stage.

Just two months before, in March 1975, Barnard had approached the Prime Minister and told Whitlam he was anxious to leave the political arena. A check was made in the Foreign Affairs Department at the time but there was no suitable post available. But several weeks later it was clear that Sweden was about to be vacated. Whitlam wanted to see Barnard leave and immediately put the proposition to him. His former deputy accepted it gladly. On Monday 26 May the Prime Minister discussed the move in Barnard's office and it was finalised the next morning in further talks between the two men. Barnard had originally hoped to receive a posting to one of the NATO nations or to North America but he was satisfied with Sweden where he was also designated Australian Ambassador to Norway and Finland.

The timing for the Prime Minister was important. The removal of Barnard would open the way for Whitlam to reshape the Labor Cabinet. The exit of such a senior Minister would automatically force a reshuffle of positions amongst the elected Cabinet members. It was a matter of Prime Ministerial discretion, without caucus guidance, as to whether the resulting reshuffle was extensive or only minor. Whitlam was determined to ensure it was far-reaching. Indeed, the Prime Minister's conviction that sweeping Cabinet changes were needed could have been a major motivating force in his desire to see Barnard go.

For a number of reasons the Prime Minister perceived this period as a likely watershed for his government. Just a few months previously Labor's fortunes had been at their lowest ebb with the strong prospect of Snedden forcing and winning a general election in the May–June period. But instead Snedden had been eclipsed by the Prime Minister in one of his most celebrated and characteristic victories and now Malcolm Fraser, the new Liberal leader, was still settling into the demands of office. Whitlam and Fraser, who had been leader for only two months, were gently sparring at each other from afar like two boxers in the first round of a long fight. The Supply Bills had gone through the parliament, giving the government a temporary reprieve from the worry of being forced to the polls, and, on any objective assessment, the likelihood of Fraser rejecting his first budget as Opposition Leader appeared to be remote. The Prime Minister's standing in his party was unrivalled and he was in a buoyant mood, refreshed from his three week overseas trip to the Commonwealth Heads of Government Meeting in Jamaica and meetings in Washington with President Ford and Secretary of State, Dr Henry Kissinger.

Whitlam had returned from overseas in mid May and the two set-piece caucus–Cabinet clashes later that month over both beach sand mining and government support for the wool industry only activated his energy and buttressed his determination to make extensive Cabinet changes. The political situation appeared favourable for any Ministerial changes which could be completed in the autumn and have time to settle and consolidate before budget talks began in winter. Another leader might have looked upon such a period in a different way and seen it as a time for consolidation. But Gough Whitlam did not; he saw it as the time for reconstruction of his government.

Whitlam had often told people that he would end up being the only Minister in his government over 60 years old, although he sometimes qualified this remark by including Rex Connor. Whitlam had repeated these comments to journalists as recently as the April–May Jamaica trip and when he returned home he began to turn his attention in this direction. Over the three years of Labor administration, one of the most intractable and frustrating problems Whitlam faced was that of his Cabinet. Contrary to the superficial view partly created by the 'It's Time' election campaign in 1972, the Labor government was not composed of bright young trendies. The average age of Ministers in the Whitlam government in 1973 was 53 years compared, for instance, with 46 years in the first Fraser government. This situation was not improved after the May election win when the only Ministerial change was to substitute Senator John Wheeldon from Western Australia, then 44, for the deposed Al Grassby, 47, making almost no difference to this figure. The youngest man in the ministry was Bill Hayden, who was 41 years old when re-elected to the Cabinet in May 1974.

Whitlam's long-term objective had always been to restructure his government and he saw this as an indispensable step in both governing effectively and producing the youth and new talent needed for Labor to be re-elected at the next general election. The Prime Minister was convinced that the generation of politicians that had come to power with him would have to be replaced during the life of the present government and their places taken by younger men in the lower ranks of the ministry and on the back bench. Whitlam himself was deeply dismayed by the caucus election results on 10 June 1974 in which the old Labor Cabinet was re-elected en masse. This meant that, instead of presenting a new image to the electorate after Labor's May success at the polls, it was business as usual with the same team. Whitlam believed the caucus result gave him little choice but to reappoint Ministers to their previous portfolios, which he did. Throughout 1974 and 1975, whenever a senior Minister incurred the Prime Minister's wrath, he would only become more determined to introduce a sweeping Cabinet reconstruction.

At the end of May a series of events occurred that prompted Whitlam to put his long-held plans into practice. The first was the Barnard retirement, the second the collapse of a move to force a spill of all Ministerial positions and the third the gross breach of propriety by Cairns in the form of the Harris letters, which gave Whitlam a powerful rationale for sacking the Treasurer.

Early in the same week that Barnard's appointment was being resolved, but before his exit was public knowledge, two young backbenchers began sounding out their colleagues about the possibility of a Cabinet spill. They were Victorian backbencher Race Mathews, elected in 1972 in the marginal seat of Casey, and South Australian backbencher Mick Young, elected in 1974 in the safe Labor seat of Port Adelaide. They were two of the closest backbenchers to Whitlam in the party. Mathews had worked previously as Whitlam's private secretary when he was leader of the Opposition and Young had become a national figure in his former capacity as ALP federal secretary from which he played a crucial role in the successful 1972 campaign before joining Whitlam's staff for a brief period prior to the May 1974 election when he entered parliament. The aim of the Mathews–Young exercise was to test the climate of the party on the prospect of a spill of all twenty-seven Cabinet positions and the re-election of an entirely new ministry. This meant, by definition, a spill of leadership positions and new elections for the leadership. Although Mathews and Young started the 'soundings' on their own initiative, Whitlam was soon told and fully supported their move while not lobbying any members himself.

The main obstacle to a spill move was always the fear of Cabinet Ministers that they would lose their position and the concern of one faction or another in the party that it might suffer. This is precisely what happened. Although many backbenchers were enthusiastic about the idea, the opposition proved too strong.

Two Ministers whose names were mentioned as likely candidates to be dropped to the backbench were the Postmaster-General, Senator Reg Bishop, and the Minister for Aboriginal Affairs, Senator Jim Cavanagh, both from South Australia. In was the Foreign Minister Senator Don Willesee who heard these reports and notified Bishop, who immediately contacted Cavanagh. Bishop, outraged, was determined to kill the move. He was particularly angry because Cavanagh and himself were two Ministers who had already indicated to their colleagues that they would not recontest their Ministerial positions in the next caucus ballot. But they did not want such a ballot precipitated before it was due, thereby cutting short their Ministerial tenure. Moreover the South Australian members of the Labor caucus had a strong tradition of working together as a cohesive and unified force in Ministerial ballots. This technique made them a significant factor in caucus elections and ensured South Australia representation in the ministry. Bishop believed that Young was violating this tradition. Sensing danger to their positions, the South Australian Ministers moved quickly to bring the matter to a climax before their opponents could muster sufficient support for a spill in the party room the following week. Bishop called a gathering of South Australian members and Senators in his office on the evening of Tuesday 27 May. When Young arrived, there was a rich exchange of language between the two men with Young admitting the whole move was now off anyway.

The uproar in the South Australian caucus put the final seal of defeat on any efforts to force a new-look Cabinet. A number of Labor members had expressed their doubts about the move, not because they were opposed to a reformed Cabinet, but because they were highly dubious about whether a new election would bring genuine changes.

The trouble with the Labor Cabinet was simply that the more changes were sought in it, the more it was likely to remain unchanged. The ballot system favoured existing Ministers exchanging votes to maintain their positions. Moreover, the caucus itself had always failed to reach a consensus on just which backbenchers deserved to be promoted in terms of ability. This had been the classic mistake in the June caucus elections after the May campaign, when a Melbourne Cup field entered the race for Cabinet positions and nearly everyone missed out. Furthermore, in May left-wing members of the caucus strongly opposed a spill recognising the weak position of their figurehead, the deputy Prime Minister Jim Cairns, and the strong possibility he would be deposed.

Despite all the grumblings about certain Ministers, the endless talk about the need for a 'new-look' Cabinet and the promotion of new ideas, the numbers were simply not on the board to do it. This incident showed that the party was still trapped in the shadow of the June 1974 re-election of the ministry en masse, a decision that demoralised the backbench, created a continuing locus of unrest within the party and yet offered a powerful deterrent to anyone contemplating another spill: it might happen again.

Whitlam was disgusted at the reluctance of caucus to accept a spill. He saw it as indecisive and soft-headed. He reasoned that if he, as leader with more to lose than anyone else, was prepared to accept a spill of Ministerial positions then caucus members, with everything to gain and nothing to lose, should certainly accept one. In typical fashion, Whitlam then decided that if the party would not accept a spill it would get the next best thing to one—an extensive, Prime Ministerially inspired, Cabinet reshuffle. The same men would remain in Cabinet but their portfolios would be altered.

The Prime Minister decided to make Bill Hayden Treasurer in place of Jim Cairns and Jim McClelland Minister for Labour and Immigration in place of Clyde Cameron. Given the history and status of Cairns and Cameron within the party, it was clear that this decision would shake the Labor government to its foundations and make both men his lasting enemies. But it would also be a major step towards cleaning out the old guard.

Whitlam had always treated Jim Cairns with great respect throughout their political careers, whether as allies or as enemies. In a wider sense he acknowledged the role Cairns had played in mobilising opinion against the Vietnam war and the special standing of Cairns as a symbol of the humanity and integrity of the Labor movement, which was always expressed in the strong support for him within caucus. Whitlam accepted the realities of power within the party after the May election and the elevation of Cairns to the deputy Prime Ministership. He was well aware of the political skill and economic innovation Cairns had displayed in late 1974 in making the budget strategy his own at a time when the Cabinet was in a state of abject confusion. Whitlam also perceived Cairns' ability as a communicator and admitted the success with which his deputy had conducted the administration during the Prime Minister's absence in Europe.

In politics nothing breeds contempt so quickly as an influential man whose power is failing him. The decline of Jim Cairns in the five months from January to May 1975 was one of the most discussed subjects within the political arena. It was canvassed in the House, in the lobbies and in the surrounding Canberra restaurants with little disguised contempt. Those people who had always disliked and opposed Cairns saw their arguments of years vindicated in his collapsed relations with the caucus, the traditional source of his support, in his unconvincing displays in parliament, a forum he normally handled with ease, and finally in the rupturing of his relations with those lifelines of Ministerial success—his own personal office, his department and senior advisers, and his party friends.

Those people who had always liked and supported Cairns were dismayed and baffled at the change which came over him. Long-time friends and confidantes of years, to whom his door had always been open, now found it shut. The case against him was put simply: here was a weak man with his weakness by his side.

The attractive figure of Junie Morosi had almost inevitably been by his side since she had begun to work for him in January 1975. Morosi was a gift for the scandal seekers who proved to be an extensive and powerful group; but beyond that, she assumed a definite political significance in her own right, not merely as a person whose presence was likely to create bad publicity for the Labor government. The Morosi factor is the crucial one in the equation leading to the downfall of Jim Cairns.

When she accepted the job on Cairns' staff, Junie Morosi was a well-known social acquaintance of several prominent Labor figures including Murphy, Grassby and Uren. But the decision by Cairns to introduce her directly into the processes of government alarmed both Murphy and Uren, who argued with Cairns in an effort to dissuade him from the appointment. Both of them were unsuccessful. As a person, Morosi represented a formidable combination of beauty, guile and toughness. She had survived the daily threat of death and hunger as a child in Manila during the Japanese occupation; had married and had three children by the time she was 18; had fought a court battle for their custody after separating from her husband; and been successful from among several hundred applicants for a Qantas ground hostess position in Manila. According to Morosi she had worked at that time on a five to ten year plan to leave the Philippines and settle with her sons in another country. She had transferred to Sydney with Qantas in 1962, fulfilling this objective. Through her contact with Lionel Murphy she had been appointed a civil marriage celebrant, one of the first women given this position. A few months later Al Grassby, the government's consultant on community relations, who had known Morosi for many years, asked her to come and work with him. This involved extensive travel, addressing migrant groups and examining migrant problems throughout the country. It had also brought Morosi into even closer social contact with some of the senior figures in the Labor government and it was in late 1974 that she was introduced to Jim Cairns.

Morosi's whole life had been a struggle for material and personal advancement. No one could have come so far without developing the skill to impress and ingratiate herself with people of influence. In December 1975 Morosi said: 'When I was 18, I found myself with three sons to support. I would starve if I didn't find some way to survive. The way of survival is to learn your rules you know, the rules of that establishment. Understand and succeed within it. And I did.'[1] After her appointment the Opposition parties had attacked the government because of her business connections. A number of Liberal backbenchers, including John McLeay and William Wentworth, had compiled dossiers on her business involvement in an effort to discredit the government by claiming she was guilty of fraud and business malpractice. Such criticisms had done Morosi little harm because the NSW Corporate Affairs Commission never found grounds on which to prosecute companies she had been associated with and some Labor members felt, at least at the start, that she was being victimised. But the Opposition had missed the real significance of Morosi—something that could not be splashed about in newspaper headlines. This was her powerful and permeating influence on nearly everything Jim Cairns did in his capacity as politician and Treasurer. When Morosi became the Treasurer's private secretary, she had had almost no experience of government, of economic decision-making or of the Labor Party. Yet, within a matter of days, she was in a position which appeared close to that of total command of the office. She had responsibility for making the Treasurer's appointments, arranging his movements, besides acting as friend and adviser. Her arrival led to an upheaval in Cairns' office.

The first rupture had been with the Treasurer's press secretary, Geoff Gleghorn. Gleghorn had expressed concern to Cairns about both the series of Morosi articles in *Woman's Day* and also about a large-scale Sydney press conference which a business associate of Morosi's, John Pola, had arranged for her with the purpose of rebutting some of the press stories at the time. Gleghorn was concerned that Pola appeared to be acting like a public relations manager for Morosi. The issue had come to a head at the ALP national conference at Terrigal NSW, in early

February 1975 when Pola and Morosi arranged for an exclusive interview to be given to Tony McRae from the Sydney *Sun* featuring both Cairns and Morosi talking about their personal lives. Gleghorn had not been consulted about the interview and only found out about it the night before when he was told by Morosi that it was not about politics but about women's issues. When the interview was in process in Cairns' Terrigal motel room, Gleghorn went to the door but Morosi refused to let him in.

The next afternoon, after the conference sessions had finished, a relaxed Prime Minister was mingling with a few journalists and shouting them drinks from the bar adjacent to the pool at the Hotel Florida, the conference venue. Whitlam and the journalists were sharing anecdotes when someone walked over with a copy of the Sydney afternoon papers. The banner headlines in the *Sun* read 'My love for Junie' and the story extensively quoted Jim Cairns talking about his feelings and relations with Morosi, including the memorable revelation: 'Surely you can't trust somebody in this world unless you feel something akin to a kind of love for them.' He spoke of the difficulties Morosi had experienced and reaffirmed his determination to stand by her.

This was the sort of phenomenon in politics with which Whitlam was ill at ease. The Prime Minister was a man of puritanical habit, who spent most of his time in the daily grind of political, policy and administrative work involved in his job. The spectacular and public relationship between Cairns and Morosi was something he found both baffling and amusing. But it clearly went against the grain as far as Whitlam was concerned. The curious thing was that, although Whitlam obviously disapproved of the Cairns–Morosi connection, he never made it a fundamental issue with Cairns by asking his deputy to change his personal staff.

Gleghorn and other Cairns staffers were aghast at the Sydney *Sun* story. When they arrived at Melbourne airport that afternoon, Gleghorn told Cairns he wanted to speak to him about the story but Cairns refused to talk. Gleghorn then said: 'Well in that case we might talk about my resignation then', trying to get Cairns into a discussion of the whole issue. But Cairns merely replied, 'I accept it.' A week went by and when Gleghorn went to Canberra he found that either Cairns or Morosi had given official notification of his resignation. Gleghorn then went to Cairns and said he had not yet resigned. Cairns replied that he thought Gleghorn had quit. Gleghorn told the deputy Prime Minister, 'If you want to get rid of me, you'll have to sack me.' Cairns replied, 'Well, you're sacked then.'

Gleghorn was not the only member of Cairns' staff to leave. At this same time the girl who had worked as Cairns' personal assistant since the early 1960s, Maxine Burgess, left his office as a result of differences with Morosi. Another member of the staff, Barbara Rosser, also left. Eventually there was virtually a full turnover of staff and over the next few months press secretary Neal Swancott was told his services were no longer required, as was economic adviser Brian Brogan when Cairns moved to the Environment portfolio. Many of the staff felt that the main priority became not loyalty to Cairns himself, but to Morosi. Morosi used the classic technique of consolidating power by controlling access to Cairns and many Labor members found he became an aloof and inaccessible figure. The irony of this was that in 1974 Cairns campaigned for the deputy leadership on the theme of building bridges to the caucus.

As 1975 had progressed, Morosi's influence had become more important. Often senior Treasury officers had to speak to her instead of the Minister and, when Cairns went to the Middle East, Australia's Ambassador to Saudi Arabia, Ian Haig, an expert on the area, had complained that he did not have enough time to talk to the Treasurer over policy issues. On all his overseas trips involving talks with Ministers and heads of government Cairns insisted that, wherever possible, Morosi also be privy to the discussions.

Parliament House gradually became littered with Morosi anecdotes. After returning from Paris in early June, Morosi claimed that Kissinger's speech to the OECD had followed up almost exactly the same themes discussed by Cairns. At another time she wanted to know who Milton Friedman was after the American economist had criticised Australian economic policy. Morosi did not shun all the press; indeed, she joined it herself when publicising her career and background for *Woman's Day*. It was always difficult for Cairns to complain about the exaggerated media coverage for Morosi when she was participating in it herself. Labor politicians shook their heads in disbelief at what was happening as the public were teased about the nature of the Cairns–Morosi relationship and innuendo in the papers soon had a rich dialogue to feed upon. In one interview Morosi said she was really interested in 'mental intercourse'. In another she said, 'I might have a far more sexual relationship with a man I don't go to bed with.'

Morosi bore final testimony to Cairns' political naivety. Anyone who had been even remotely associated with the course of Australian politics over the previous decade could not have failed to absorb the lessons of the Gorton years and the extent to which public controversy about the private life of a senior politician can erode his standing in the eyes of both the public and the party. Many Labor members were amazed at the way Cairns and Morosi insisted that the real issues involved in her appointment were the rejection of hypocrisy, sexism and double standards. To them and to the majority of the caucus, the issue was always the standing of the government and the effectiveness of Cairns as deputy Prime Minister.

Throughout March and April 1975 the Treasury Department became more alarmed about Cairns' performance. Its doubts were also shared by senior Ministers, including the Prime Minister. In April Cairns told parliament that government spending should be increased if this was necessary to find jobs for the unemployed—a strategy that appeared contrary to that already embraced by the government through the Cabinet Expenditure Review Committee which was taking a sharp knife to the public sector. In short, by May Cairns' political position was a fragile one indeed and Whitlam already had grave doubts about his deputy when he was presented with the Harris letters, which firmed his resolution completely. At a press conference in Canberra on 10 June the Prime Minister said these letters were the 'sole reason' for removing Cairns from Treasury. But it was the weakened position of the deputy Prime Minister within the party that made his removal so easy to implement.

The first real news of Whitlam's plans to change the ministry came on Wednesday 28 May when the Prime Minister called a meeting in his office of Ministers involved with the electorate of Bass, Lance Barnard's seat. It was attended by the Education Minister Kim Beazley, the Special Minister of State Lionel Bowen, the Transport Minister Charlie Jones, the Minister for Urban and Regional Development Tom Uren, and Barnard himself. The aim was to talk about government policy and programs in preparation for the Bass by-election. This was the same day that Wheeler informed Whitlam and Hayden about the agency relationship between Cairns and Harris. Whitlam subsequently rang Cairns, explained the legal opinions given on his actions and asked his deputy to return to Australia immediately. Whitlam told Cairns the reason for his return could be attributed to the need for a vote in the House the following week on a referendum proposal.

Cairns told the Prime Minister that he had already decided to return. The previous day in Paris he had held informal talks with both US Secretary of State Henry Kissinger and the Secretary to the Treasury Bill Simon on economic matters. He had also had breakfast with the UK Chancellor of the Exchequer Denis Healey who had impressed upon Cairns the need to maintain communication with the electorate when pursuing a policy of wage restraint. On the same day Cairns had spoken with Tom Uren by phone. Uren urged him to return to Australia as fast as possible, pointing out that the Barnard departure raised the possibility of changes within the government and expressing his own concern about the economy and the need to prepare for the budget. Uren, along with people from Cairns' office, had not wanted the Treasurer to go on his latest trip.

While Cairns was en route back to Australia, the news leaked within the Labor Cabinet about Whitlam's plans to remove him from Treasury.

Whitlam had told Barnard about his intentions and Barnard had mentioned this to a number of colleagues. Some of Cairns' friends within the party tried to contact him; when he reached Perth he took a call from Professor Harry Messel, who was working for Rex Connor, conveying a message on behalf of his Minister. The deputy Prime Minister arrived in eastern Australia about midnight on Sunday night and saw Whitlam on Monday morning, tired and exhausted from jet lag. At this meeting Whitlam was in a resolute and blunt mood. He simply confronted Cairns with the Harris letters and the Harders opinion, demanding that if Cairns had signed such letters he must resign. Cairns protested and defended himself to no avail. Whitlam was adamant and offered the deputy Prime Minister the Social Security portfolio, indicating a direct swap of portfolios between Cairns and Hayden.

Cairns left the Prime Minister's office an angry and disappointed man, convinced that he had been done an injustice. In an ironic twist of political fortunes he then went to see Barnard in an effort to persuade the Defence Minister against retiring from politics and consequently providing Whitlam with the need for a Cabinet reshuffle. Cairns told Barnard he believed it was wrong for him to leave at this stage. He said there would be a by-election in Bass, with a good probability of the government being defeated, and that at such a critical period it was inappropriate for a senior Minister voluntarily to leave the political arena. But Barnard had no intention of reconsidering the question. He wanted to go and refused to change his mind. Barnard himself was not unaware of the changed positions in which he and Cairns found themselves. Just twelve months before, almost to the day, Cairns had taken the deputy Prime Ministership from him when all he wanted was another year in the job before he would have been willing to stand down. Now Barnard himself was playing an instrumental role in events that would lead to the removal of Cairns from Treasury. Barnard was particularly struck at what he regarded as Cairns' insensitivity about his wife's health and the personal factor in his desire to leave politics. Lance Barnard had always resented Cairns for standing against him the previous year; now he was getting his satisfaction.

That afternoon Jim Cairns, after having a long talk with Morosi, decided directly and publicly to challenge the authority of the Prime Minister and his right, acknowledged in the caucus rules, to determine the allocation of portfolios to Labor Ministers. In the late afternoon Cairns' statement was issued in the press gallery boxes. It was the sort of statement that had the capacity to destroy governments.

> I have just returned from overseas, concerned with the need to concentrate all efforts on the forthcoming budget, to find there are proposals to appoint Mr Barnard to a diplomatic post and to make several changes in the ministry. If this were done it would cause the

distraction of a by-election and involve the risk of divisions in the party and government at a time when unity and teamwork are essential. I want it to be known that I am opposed to this course. We have been elected to govern effectively and I cannot accept any action which would result in the diversions of a by-election and the risks of divisions caused by Ministerial changes. We must work together now to form a budget in the national interest and thereby secure the interests of both the government and the people. We must not be diverted from this task.

There was once a time when this statement from Jim Cairns would have split the Labor Party wide open. That was when he had sufficient support within the caucus to back up his words with solid votes. But those days were over. Whitlam was only able to remove his deputy from the Treasury portfolio because Cairns no longer had enough support within the caucus to defy the Prime Minister. The issuing of this statement was another political mistake by Cairns, which left him with only two options: an ignominious backdown or complete resignation from the Cabinet altogether. He chose the former.

When caucus met the next day Cairns retreated and told the party room that, while he refused to leave his portfolio when Whitlam first put it to him, he was now prepared to accept the decision. Cairns said he wanted to act in the best interests of the party and that now was not the time to have it divided. He was heard in silence and applauded at the end of a short speech in which he repudiated his public statement of the day before. At this meeting NSW backbencher Joe Riordan was elected to the Labor Cabinet to fill the Barnard vacancy. Riordan won solid support from NSW members as well as from the right and centre groups to win in the final ballot 53–37 against John Coates from Tasmania.

On the Tuesday morning, news leaked that Whitlam intended to put Jim McClelland into Labour and Immigration and Lionel Bowen into Manufacturing Industry, the portfolio McClelland was leaving. These two Ministers, along with Hayden, would strengthen the economic policy area. Bowen would take responsibility for the Australian Industries Development Corporation which was previously under Cairns. The new Defence Minister was to be Bill Morrison, the twenty-seventh Minister on the Cabinet list, who was receiving a big promotion from the Science portfolio. Whitlam had always envisaged giving Morrison Defence and had spoken to him about the new portfolio a few weeks before.

During this week, Moss Cass, who knew that he was being moved from the Environment portfolio, had a long talk with Cairns and suggested that Cairns become the new Environment Minister. Cass pointed out that the environmental impact legislation which the parliament had recently approved gave the Environment Minister extensive powers over a number of development projects. The idea appealed to Cairns, who was not keen to accept the Social Security portfolio Whitlam had offered him. The deputy Prime Minister told Whitlam in the chamber on the Wednesday that he would like to take Environment. The Prime Minister was surprised and initially reluctant, wondering whether the portfolio was of sufficient status for the deputy leader, but he nevertheless agreed to Cairns' request.

During the week Whitlam contacted those Ministers involved in the reshuffle to inform them of their new portfolios. But there was one Minister he did not formally notify until late Thursday afternoon, the day before the swearing-in at Government House. This was Clyde Cameron, who was about to suffer the biggest setback in his political career. For three days Cameron had been reading in the newspapers that Whitlam intended to shift him from the Labour portfolio but he made no effort to contact the Prime Minister about these reports, waiting instead for Whitlam to speak to him. At 4.30 p.m. on Thursday, Whitlam's office rang Cameron's office to say the Prime Minister wanted to see the Minister. Subsequently Cameron rang Whitlam's office to speak to the Prime Minister but was not put through to Whitlam. Eventually a senior staff member from Cameron's office called back to say the Minister would be in his office if Whitlam wanted to see him.

Finally Whitlam was forced to walk from his office around to Cameron's, located in the new wing. It was the first time Whitlam had been to this office and the Prime Minister was uncertain which door to enter. Cameron's press secretary John Stubbs was suddenly startled to find the table and papers stacked against the door, which he never used, moving towards him along with a simultaneous banging on the door. Stubbs cleared the doorway to let Whitlam in and the Prime Minister then walked into Cameron's adjoining office where he stunned Cameron by telling him he would be appointed Minister for Science and Consumer Affairs. Cameron, like Cairns four days before him, refused to accept Whitlam's decision which meant a crushing blow to his political power and reputation. He told Whitlam during a bitter thirty minute meeting that he would think about the job overnight and see the Prime Minister before the swearing in on Friday. When Whitlam's office released a statement later that night outlining the shape of the new ministry, Cameron branded it as untrue. 'Senator J McClelland is not the Minister for Labour,' he declared. 'That position is still held by me.'

But once again, like Cairns before him, Cameron had only the choice of accepting the demotion or resigning from the ministry. Always a realistic politician he took the former course, suffered his humiliation and privately resolved that this was something he should never forget. But Cameron did come close to refusing the job. On the Friday morning when he arrived at his office he called his staff in and told them he would not accept the new portfolio and a number of them started clearing out the office in preparation for departure. Cameron finally changed his mind after a number of Ministers came to see him.

It is hard to avoid the conclusion that Whitlam deliberately set out to humiliate Cameron to an extent that went far beyond the removal of a Minister because of dissatisfaction with his performance. Dropping him to the Science and Consumer Affairs portfolio, previously held by the twenty-seventh and last man in the Cabinet, was interpreted as a blatant insult by Cameron and everyone in the party. Whitlam had an alternative course of action open to him but declined to follow it. This was to move Cameron into the Social Security portfolio after Cairns rejected it. Spigelman advocated this course to the Prime Minister without success. Certainly Cameron could never have complained about such a move and would have had no legitimate grounds for complaint. But Whitlam decided to amalgamate Social Security with Repatriation and Compensation under Senator John Wheeldon, thereby giving him an enormous burden.

Cameron and Whitlam had had a turbulent relationship over the years. Cameron was a curious mixture of principle and pragmatism, an intelligent man with great political skill who carried all his life the radicalism instilled in him from the poverty of his upbringing and the experience of unionism. He left school at 14 and worked as a fruit picker before entering the shearing sheds and joining the Australian Workers Union when he was 15 years old. Cameron became a life-long advocate of the land tax theories of Henry George, whose influence could still be seen in the policies he advocated as a Minister. He had a sense of humour and was a great story teller, which was a talent he used to entertain his friends and wreak vengeance on his enemies. He always displayed a capacity to needle people with his sarcastic, self-effacing humour.

In 1966 Cameron, a vigorous opponent of state aid for church schools, was one of the prime advocates of Whitlam's expulsion from the party. Yet after Whitlam's survival and success as Opposition Leader, the two grew closer together as Cameron realised that he would assume the portfolio of Labour Minister in any new Labor government under Whitlam. While Cameron never reached the highest levels of the Labor parliamentary party, he was a formidable power in the party machine. One of the decisive episodes along Whitlam's path to the Prime Minister-ship had been when Cameron turned against the Victorian left and worked out the 'nuts and bolts' of federal intervention into the affairs of the Victorian branch—the objective which Whitlam had sought for years. During their days in Opposition, Whitlam made his famous appeal to Cameron, asking him whether he wanted to go down in history as a footnote in a book written by Alan Reid or as the Labour Minister in a Labor government. Cameron chose the latter.

In government Cameron used all his energies to promote negotiated agreements between employers and employees, to give union members more say in the affairs of their union and to attempt to reverse the inequitable wages system in Australia. It was Cameron who coined the memorable description of public servants as 'fat cats', an indication of his hostility towards the middle and higher clerical grades in the Commonwealth public service who he believed were grossly overpaid. Cameron always argued for a compression of wage relativities which would improve the position of lower paid workers vis a vis their counterparts. He was always an advocate of heavier taxes on the rich who made windfall gains through capital assets. Throughout 1974 and 1975 Cameron had worked meticulously towards a system of wage indexation and this had been accepted by the full bench of the Conciliation and Arbitration Commission on an interim basis. The leadership group within the government, once it became convinced that wage restraint was fundamental to inflation control, saw wage indexation as an indispensable part of Labor's economic program. The great irony was that wage indexation was the very issue that led to Clyde Cameron's dismissal.

The day on which the Prime Minister decided to remove Cameron can be pinpointed as Monday 12 May 1975. Federal Cabinet met this day to discuss the federal government's attitude to the Amalgamated Metal Workers case before the full bench. The case was an acid test of the viability of wage indexation. Cameron supported the application by the metal workers, which would have meant the government arguing that the wages of turners and fitters should be equated with that of highly paid carpenters. In short he believed that the application related to a 'catch up' situation and that Australia's 600,000 metal workers should be granted a pay rise in addition to indexation. The most trenchant opponent of this argument was the newest Cabinet Minister Jim McClelland who, with his background in industrial law, argued that the government should ask the commission to reject the application and moved a motion to this effect. While Cameron was opposed by Whitlam, Cairns, Hayden and Crean, it was McClelland who spearheaded the argument against the Labour Minister. When it finally appeared he would be defeated, Cameron then produced a fall-back compromise motion which he had obviously carefully prepared before the meeting. The effect of this motion was to tie the government to a neutral stand in the wage case. The second motion was carried 19–6 in the Cabinet room. But Cameron was pegged back when the Science Minister Bill Morrison put and carried an addendum to the Cabinet motion stipulating that the precise form of the government's submission should be determined jointly through consultations between Whitlam, Cairns, Cameron and McClelland. 'We don't trust you, Clyde' was how one Minister summed up Morrison's additional motion.

The final Cabinet decision was a compromise which both Cameron and McClelland claimed as a win for themselves. But there is no doubt who the ultimate winner was. When the Prime Minister left the Cabinet room that afternoon he was deeply concerned about whether Cameron would fight for the maintenance of wage indexation with the tenacity required from the Labour Minister. Whitlam was tremendously impressed with the grasp of industrial issues and the skill with which McClelland argued for the maintenance of indexation. In Whitlam's mind McClelland had been talking in exactly the fashion he wanted the Labour Minister to talk. This was the Cabinet meeting which heralded the demise of Clyde Cameron and the rise of Jim McClelland who, elected to the Cabinet as recently as February that year, was to become one of the most powerful Ministers within the Labor government through hitching his political star to Gough Whitlam, the man he so bitterly criticised throughout 1974 and blamed for keeping him out of the Cabinet. Whitlam later told his colleagues, 'Cameron got us indexation, but can he maintain indexation?'. The Prime Minister's answer was 'No' and he decided to axe Cameron.

The other ministerial changes Whitlam made in his June reshuffle were the appointments of Riordan to Housing and Construction, Les Johnson from Housing and Construction to Aboriginal Affairs, Moss Cass from Environment to Media, Senator Doug McClelland from Media to Special Minister of State and Senator Jim Cavanagh from Aboriginal Affairs to Police and Customs. It was significant that the one senior Minister who had incurred extensive criticism and who was not moved was Rex Connor. The Prime Minister may have been disillusioned with Cairns, with Cameron, with Johnson, but he was still supporting Connor and Connor's policies.

The benefit of hindsight overwhelmingly suggests that Whitlam's Cabinet upheaval produced a better ministry, particularly at the higher levels. It laid the ground for the Hayden budget and was in all probability an indispensable condition for the production of that budget. In six short months Hayden was to show that he was the best economist in parliament and one of the best Treasurers for some years. Behind the Prime Minister, the front line of the Labor government now contained Hayden, McClelland, Bowen and Senator Ken Wriedt in the main portfolios. There was a definite awareness on the part of the Liberals that they were confronted with a more capable government.

Whitlam saw the reshuffle as the first stage in a two-stage reconstruction of his government. He would have liked both a caucus spill of positions as well as a reshuffle. Having failed to get the spill, he now set his sights on having one after the half Senate election which was due before 1 July 1976. He looked forward to this to complete the replacement of the old guard. In the more immediate future Whitlam saw the reshuffle as paving the way for the creation of an inner Cabinet comprising twelve or thirteen senior Ministers, which would become the real power centre of the government. The Prime Minister always believed that a twenty-seven man Cabinet was far too big for an efficient decision-making body.

But if the advantages of the reshuffle were great, then so were the liabilities. There was blood all over the floor by the time the Prime Minister had finished. Whitlam himself had shocked a number of Ministers by what they considered to be the insensitivity and delight with which he engaged in the changes. Throughout this week he was in a buoyant mood as he pursued his dominance over the government into new dimensions. But some Ministers believed the Prime Minister had been almost taunting them as he decided their fate.

The events highlighted the great difficulty facing the Prime Minister in forcing Cabinet changes. There were two broad strategies he could adopt. One was to work through the caucus and change the party rules to provide for an inner Cabinet of twelve, more frequent ministerial elections, and a new method of election. The second was simply to use his power as leader to encourage retirements, reshuffle existing Ministers and try to encourage the caucus itself into a spill of ministerial positions from the floor. Whitlam tried both these strategies at various times with some success and at some political cost.

In late 1974 the Prime Minister, in his determination to remove Frank Crean from Treasury, had been quite prepared to have a by-election at a time when the government's standing was very low. In February 1975 he had been prepared to provoke widespread criticism for appointing his old antagonist Lionel Murphy to the High Court. The political consequences of this had been counter-productive since it meant that at a half Senate election NSW would split 3–3 between Labor and non-Labor and the government would forgo any chance to win the state 3–2; indeed it had only been a matter of luck that the NSW Premier Tom Lewis had played into Labor's hands by appointing a non-Labor senator to the vacancy. In May Whitlam was happy to retire Barnard to an ambassadorship at disastrous cost to the government in the Bass by-election.

All these examples indicate that, despite his abilities as a Prime Minister, Whitlam lacked the political adroitness to work through party structures to achieve his aims.

# 14

## THE BATTLE FOR BASS

*The proposition that Lance Barnard should leave parliament at this time is preposterous.*

ALP national secretary David Combe, 29 May 1975

When Malcolm Fraser heard the rumour that Lance Barnard was retiring, he sent Tony Staley around the parliament house 'traps' to verify it. As soon as the story was confirmed, Fraser rang the federal director of the party, Tony Eggleton, about his first electoral test as leader. Fraser seized on the news with delight, unlike the Labor Party's chief strategists.

On the evening of Thursday 29 May, Eggleton's opposite number, David Combe, was drinking at the Canberra Rugby Union Club when he was rung by a journalist seeking his comments on the Barnard retirement. The next day they appeared on the front page of the *Australian* and revealed Combe's anguish: 'I cannot believe Mr Barnard would be sent to an overseas posting, thereby creating a by-election in Bass . . . Such a proposition has never been discussed with me or, to my knowledge, with other officials of the ALP.'

The Labor Party president Bob Hawke was not nearly so polite. Speaking from Geneva Hawke branded the move 'an act of lunacy'. A month later Labor's campaign manager in the by-election, Tasmanian Senator Merv Everett, declared in his official report that Bass was lost from the very start of the campaign.

Labor had held Bass through the Barnard family for 36 of the previous 41 years. It centred on the north-eastern tip of Tasmania taking in the towns of Launceston, Scottsdale, and St Helens. The seat was both metropolitan and rural with dairying and beef cattle combined with food processing, textile mills and the alumina refinery at Bell Bay. For many years during the sixties the seat could be classified as solid Labor with Barnard polling an estimated 64 per cent at the 1961 election and 60 per cent at the 1963 election under the two party preferred system. But by 1974 this vote had been reduced to 54 per cent, requiring a swing of only 4 per cent for Labor to lose.

As soon as the by-election was confirmed, Eggleton, along with Fraser's speechwriter David Kemp, flew to Tasmania for talks with the state party president, Don Wing. Eggleton wanted the campaign to contain all the ingredients of a federal election effort—extensive television, street walks, public meetings, visits to schools, factories and pubs, press conferences and talkback radio. Eggleton was determined to give Fraser a general election training program. It would identify his initial strengths and weaknesses. Kemp drafted an electorate profile with the details of the seat, its history, its interest groups and the areas where it had been hurt by Labor policies.

Despite the fact that Labor had forced the by-election, the Liberal Party was far better prepared for it. It had already endorsed a candidate, a retired army Lieutenant-Colonel, Kevin Newman, 41, who proved to be an impressive contender and well above average candidate. At the same time the Liberals had developed a far stronger party organisation in Tasmania than their opponents. The greatest irony of the Bass by-election was that Bill Snedden was not the Liberal leader to fight it, and that the man who deposed him reaped the benefit of his hard work.

After the May 1974 defeat Snedden had embraced what became known as the Tasmanian strategy. It was based on the assessment that Labor's stranglehold on Tasmania, where it held all five seats, could be thoroughly broken. Snedden worked closely with the Tasmanian Liberal leader Max Bingham and Tasmanian Senator Peter Rae to formulate a policy package for the state. The Tasmanian Liberals believed that Snedden was the first national leader in recent years to recognise the unique problems of their state. Snedden realised that the Liberals could win office at the next general election simply on the gains they could make in Tasmania. Snedden and Bingham developed a close working relationship which culminated in a weekend of Liberal rallies in Launceston in late 1974. About 5000 people were involved in the rallies and a march through the streets of Launceston, supposedly a Labor stronghold. Tasmania was on the move and the local Liberal Party was convinced that when Barnard retired his seat would change hands.

In stark contrast to the Liberals, Labor was totally unprepared. It did not have a candidate. Whitlam approached two Tasmanian Senators to run for Bass. First, he tried to persuade Senator Don Grimes, who was based in Launceston, to switch from the Senate and throw his hat into the ring for the seat. But when Grimes was on his way to Whitlam's office he suspected what the Prime Minister was going to ask him and said 'No' when he walked in the door. Whitlam made another unsuccessful approach to the former deputy Premier of Tasmania, Merv Everett, who was then in the Senate, and told Everett that if he lost he would get a government appointment. But Everett also declined.

The ALP preselection was a four-way contest between Barnard's former private secretary, Jim Brassil, his former electorate secretary, Gillian James, a Wynyard schoolteacher John Macrostie, and a Hobart schoolteacher Roger Hawkes. David Combe later described this contest in his official report to the federal executive:

> The Tasmanian conference was required to choose between a private secretary of Lance Barnard who was resident in Melbourne, an electorate secretary who was miffed because the private secretary and not herself had been given the nod by Lance, a bachelor schoolteacher who became the choice of the Tasmanian left when he dropped into the Launceston Trades Hall ('just to see what was happening') on his way to see a football match in Melbourne, and a late entering Hobart blow-in schoolteacher who in retrospect probably would have been the best choice of those offering.

Macrostie, 34, won the contest at the 170-member conference by gaining the united left vote which was designed to ensure Brassil's defeat. After formal meetings with the Tasmanian state executive, the Labor campaign committee held its first meeting 20 days before the poll. It was attended by a small group under Everett's direction, a number of ministerial staff members, Malcolm McFie from the ALP advertising agency Mullins, Clarke and Ralph, and the managing director of ANOP, Rod Cameron. By this stage it was too late for the party to formulate a strategy based on market research. It was agreed that the Labor campaign should be kept strictly local and any attempt to build up national issues or give it national significance should be resisted. This assessment was based on the assumption that the standing of the federal government was so bad that Labor could only lose such a debate with the Liberals. The intention was also to avoid giving the national media the opportunity of representing any adverse result for Labor in Bass as reflecting the general mood of the electorate.

In his official report later Combe said:

> We made the assessment that we had a candidate who, unlike his opponent. could be represented as a true local and that perhaps the people of Launceston were as parochial as they are often represented as being and, second, that the electorate of Bass had benefited so significantly from Australian government programs as a result of the successful pork barrelling of Lance Barnard that we may be able to invoke a favourable response from urging the electors to 'keep a voice

in Canberra'. This was the strategy which we pursued for the first two weeks of the campaign and one from which we deviated only in the final week when the Prime Minister's constant presence in the electorate made it impossible to avoid debate with the Liberals on broad national issues.

The Liberal strategy was exactly the opposite. Right from the start Malcolm Fraser tried to use Bass to seek a resounding vote of no confidence in the Whitlam government. He was in effect campaigning on national issues by focusing on how the policies of the federal government had hurt the electorate. He tried to use Bass as a microcosm of Australia; his battle cry was that Bass had a golden opportunity to lead the way for the rest of the nation in rejecting Whitlam and his socialist government.

Fraser opened his campaign on 11 June with an airport press conference, a luncheon address, and a speech in Launceston's main hall which was broadcast live on radio. Fraser was flanked by the leader of the National Country Party Doug Anthony, his own Deputy Phillip Lynch, and a bevy of front bench Liberals in a clear demonstration that the party was throwing everything it had into the by-election.

During the afternoon Fraser visited the Launceston Coats Paton factory and told people that 2000 workers had lost their jobs in the Bass electorate as a result of Labor's policies. The Opposition Leader attacked the Whitlam government for disunity, economic mismanagement and centralisation of power. Fraser exploited the recent upheaval within the government saying Whitlam had sacked Cairns 'because he wrote a letter' while protecting Connor who wrote a similar loans letter. He said the Prime Minister was 'only trying to kid people' about who was responsible for Australia's economic plight by changing his ministry and his Treasurer. 'We all know he's the one to blame,' Fraser said of Whitlam. At the same time the Opposition Leader developed standard political lines attacking Whitlam's personal style of government, his overseas trips, his purchase of Blue Poles, and the threat to freedom and jobs.

This was the constant electioneering technique Fraser used in the seven days he campaigned in Bass leading to the 28 June by-election. Fraser was impressed and relieved at the standard of the Liberal candidate Kevin Newman who proved to be an effective public speaker, able to meet and mix easily, with the stamp of success about him.

The difference between the candidates was shown at two separate meetings held at the Launceston railway yards. Every morning at 11.55 when the hooter sounded, the collection of rusty sheds marring the landscape would disgorge 500 blue overalled workers who would come from all directions and form one massive tributary flowing down a long driveway till it gushed across the road and into the Park Hotel. Both

Macrostie and Newman went to the railway yards with their respective leaders to marshal the dirtiest of the working class vote.

Big gum-chewing John Macrostie ('I'm a working class bloke') appeared tense and nervy before his fellow workers and tried to over-compensate by shouting at them. In all Macrostie's speeches he was desperately defending his preselection, living down the left wing label which the Liberals exploited, and trying to overcome his obscurity by promoting his status as a local Launceston lad. Macrostie told the railway men that one of the issues of the by-election was whether the working class was still the backbone of the Australian nation. Macrostie drew only a minority of workers back from the Park Hotel during their lunch break to hear him.

While Newman got no bigger crowd, his approach was certainly different. He told the workers he wouldn't be afraid to stand up to Malcolm Fraser if the issue was over the proper interests of the Bass electorate. Newman told the railway yard workers to stop listening 'to the bloody rubbish' of their pro-Labor unionist bosses. He assured them that if he was elected he would be down at the railway workshop after 28 June 'bloody often'. When he later went on to a businessmen's lunch, Newman immediately stopped roaring like a sergeant major and started talking like a colonel.

On 11 June Macrostie, just three days after his preselection, had asked well-known Melbourne journalist Laurie Oakes when he was going to stop 'reporting me like a spastic'. The next day the ABC's political correspondent Ken Begg had to stop an interview with Macrostie twice when the Labor candidate stumbled disastrously on questions such as 'Why should the people of Bass vote for you?'.

The Labor campaign suffered from a number of other major hand-icaps, the first being the local Labor organisation. In his report campaign director Merv Everett said:

> There was little enthusiasm for Labor's cause within the party itself. To me this indicates that at grassroots level the party is weak . . . there was a desperate shortage of manpower . . . some federal and state members were never seen . . . it was humiliating for me to welcome federal members from as far away as Western Australia to doorknock, while many Tasmanian members of parliament remained hidden. Again, personal donations from mainland members and branches contrasted with the almost total lack of Tasmanian financial support. In my view, the selfishness of many Tasmanian members of parliament is a disgrace. They have forgotten—if they ever knew—the relevance of the Australian Labor Party.

Combe himself described the local ALP organisation in Bass as 'atrocious'. He said in his report it showed itself to be unbelievably bad and, although charged with the responsibility of handling only few and minor aspects of the campaign, it was quite inadequate for that task.

The second major problem, according to Everett in his report, was the Tasmanian branch itself. 'I have never seen such a clear manifestation of inter-union hostility. One group was seen; the other group remained hidden.' The factionalisation of the Tasmanian party into a hardcore left–right freeze was revealed more starkly during the debate over the expulsion of Brian Harradine in the following months. Everett warned in his report that Labor would continue to lose elections in Tasmania while the union movement, Labor's real power base, was not fully behind the party. Combe himself criticised Labor members of the Tasmanian parliament for both their lack of cooperation and efforts to grab the credit when announcements were made to help Macrostie, such as the proposed maritime college for Launceston.

In the week preceding polling day, Whitlam spent four days in the electorate and took up Fraser's challenge to campaign on national issues. His change of tactic was partly provoked by the imminent South Australian state election of 12 July, which the Prime Minister was confident would result in a resounding Labor win. Whitlam compared the obstructionism of the Liberals in Tasmania, in South Australia and in the Senate and told the people of Bass they were the same everywhere. 'I can't remember where the Liberals were content to put a case so negative, so empty, so irrelevant, whether they were in government or in Opposition,' he declared. But during this week the Prime Minister's pessimism showed through. On two occasions he 'lost his cool', once when he abused a woman at length at a campaign meeting and the other when he got into a verbal brawl with a teacher at the matriculation college over recognition of the Baltic states.

At the conclusion of the campaign Graham Freudenberg declared: 'If the Labor Party holds Bass we will stay in government for another 25 years.' Despite his inexperience Macrostie made no blunders after the first few days, although as a candidate he was unable to match Newman. The Labor Party spent close to $20,000 on the campaign which Everett estimated to be about one-third of that spent by the Liberals. But, as was the case in the Queensland state election campaign the previous December, the result was far worse than expected.

Labor polled only 36.5 per cent of the vote compared with 57.6 per cent for the Liberals. That is, the Labor vote fell from 54 per cent in the 1974 federal election to 36.5 per cent 13 months later in the by-election. On these figures this seat, which had once been regarded as Labor territory and the Barnard preserve, appeared now to be fairly safe for the Liberal Party—indeed, Newman now needed a 10 per cent swing against him to lose it.

Bass was not so much a battle as a massacre. This by-election was merely the latest manifestation of Labor's dramatic electoral decline. On 28 September 1974 Labor had polled only 24 per cent of the vote at the Legislative Assembly elections in the ACT, a traditional Labor stronghold. The next month, on 19 October in the Northern Territory Assembly election Labor polled 29 per cent of the vote. Two months later in the Queensland state election it totalled 36 per cent of the vote. This was the same figure recorded seven months later in Bass at the other end of the continent. This was the clearest possible demonstration that, despite the local factors at work in the by-election, the chief influence was the unpopularity of the Whitlam government.

In pinpointing general reasons for the government's demise in Bass, Labor campaign workers nominated two issues: unemployment caused by tariff cuts together with high consumer prices, and a tendency on the part of the electorate to blame Canberra or the mainland in general for its problems. In fact, Labor's standing in Bass deteriorated further a month after the by-election when the federal government endorsed a 14 per cent increase in air fares between Tasmania and the mainland and a 40 per cent rise in ANL freight shipping rates.

In his campaign report Everett said disenchantment with the federal government was by far the biggest factor in the swing. He went on:

> It is clear that in two and a half years of government the Labor Party has failed to convince enough people that it is the right party for Australia. Its policies are not clearly outlined; their implementation is disorderly; the good is masked by too many politically inept incidents; the Australian government is still inexperienced in the practical art of politics and has not yet learned to handle power . . . no matter how much is done for identifiable groups—and undoubtedly Bass had been 'feather-bedded' for a long time—those groups do not necessarily judge the government in terms of what is done for them but rather in terms of the national image which the government projects. Basically, we are a conservative nation and Bass is a very conservative electorate. Labor's policies have failed collectively to win majority approval because they have, in my opinion, been pursued too quickly. The public has become bewildered and therefore politically frightened. I believe it is time to pause, take stock and then start again, but more slowly.

The ALP national secretary David Combe summed up what he believed to be the critical deficiencies in the government's approach which had produced this debacle. In his report to the federal executive meeting on 30 July Combe said:

> There is no doubt in my mind that the creation of a by-election in Bass epitomised the total breakdown of meaningful consultation

between the government and the party and initiated a chain of events which set the Australian Labor government on the inexorable path towards a new nadir in popularity—one which we have previously believed to be unattainable!

To this day, the true circumstances of Barnard's departure at that time remain a matter about which one hears inconsistent reports. But it matters not at all whether Barnard jumped because he wanted an ambassadorship, or whether he was pushed as part of the almost comic moves designed to provoke a 'spill'. It should not have been possible for him to leave at that time.

It would seem to be an elementary lesson of politics that a government does not contrive by-elections at times when its political fortunes are low, and anyone remotely in touch with the electorate in late May knew that we must be looking at a swing against us of 15 per cent in any by-election. It was obvious to any political realist that a by-election in Bass or anywhere else would have to produce a result so adverse to the ALP as to heighten the pressure on the LCP to block the budget and force an election upon us before the end of the year. Any of the national officers could have advised that Bass was unwinnable; any of the Tasmanian branch officers could have done likewise. None was consulted.

The fact is that Barnard should not have been pushed out, and if he insisted on going, it should have been made clear to him that he would go disgraced and unrewarded. It is just not good enough that people like Lionel Murphy and Lance Barnard, who are given the opportunity by party endorsement to reach positions of prominence in the government and the parliament of Australia, should be able to jump out into perk jobs without consultation with the party, and in so doing, to disadvantage the party in the parliament and/or the electorate.

Let it not be forgotten that Murphy's elevation to the high court has cost us the chance of gaining a Senate seat in New South Wales at a half-Senate election. This executive has an obligation to see to it that those who are prepared to sit in the parliament as representatives of the ALP should accept an obligation to leave the parliament voluntarily between elections only with the approval of an appropriate party authority. Otherwise rewards should be denied to them.

My objection to such a by-election being contrived without prior consultation with the party was made abundantly clear. My annoyance was not assuaged by the advice that we were not told lest the information find its way into the media. My only retort to such a proposition is that if the party's secretary cannot be trusted with such a decision, he should be removed from office . . .

The implications of the result for our future prospects in Tasmania are disastrous. The party must face the fact that it is now a distinct possibility that at a general election, we could find ourselves in a position where we hold no House of Representatives seat in Tasmania. I have already mentioned that the prospects for our state government in Tasmania are grim indeed.

The fact of the matter is that we can no longer go on finding excuses for adverse results in particular areas. For too long, we have tended to delude ourselves that special circumstances apply whenever and wherever a bad result is achieved in a limited area. In this way, in the past two years, we have explained away our reverses in Parramatta, the NSW local government elections, the ACT legislative assembly election and the Queensland state election.

Combe's report defined quite clearly the huge problems facing the Labor government. They were both national and regional. The overwhelming view of Combe and Everett was that the Bass vote reflected a national swing against the Labor government. This was an established fact. At the same time the Bass campaign had revealed the Tasmanian Labor Party was in an appalling condition, particularly at the grassroots level. It would take a matter of years for the necessary groundwork to revamp Labor in the island state.

For the Liberal Party the by-election had been crucial. After this test the Tasmanian Liberals became convinced that they could win the other four House of Representative seats currently held by Labor in that state. This was an assessment from which they did not waver. It converted the Tasmanian Liberals into a pro-early election party. Tasmania had joined Queensland as a state where Labor was not just in a weak position but where it was facing annihilation at a general election.

For the Liberal leader Malcolm Fraser the by-election had been a dream run. In a matter of three weeks Fraser had established the command over his party which can only come through electoral success. Tony Eggleton and a number of other Liberals had been apprehensive about how he would perform on the campaign trail against such an experienced opponent as Whitlam. But Bass wiped out these doubts completely. It was absolutely critical for Fraser in a personal sense and convinced him that he could take on Whitlam in a campaign and win. It gave him the indispensable confidence lift that any political leader needs in order to succeed on the campaign trail.

Bass also confirmed the correctness of the Liberal Party political strategy. It had run a campaign where the sole issue was the economy. Local issues were all used to reinforce this main theme, which had now proved its credentials as an election winner. Fraser also believed the Bass by-election showed the loans affair—and this was before Cairns was sacked from the ministry—was a major electoral liability for the government and had substantially destroyed its integrity in the public's mind.

Yet this massive boost to the Liberal confidence and psychology derived from a by-election which was forced by the government itself. Combe had correctly identified the complete breakdown in communications between the government on one hand and the party organisation on the other as the origin of the trouble. It was never rectified during Labor's term of office, except perhaps during the 1975 election campaign.

During the second week of the Bass campaign Tony Eggleton began to schedule meetings for Fraser with the Liberal Party national campaign committee. From this time onwards Eggleton's policy was to make the maximum preparations needed for an early election so that if Fraser wanted to block the budget he would be in the best possible position to do so. The Bass victory made Fraser and his party more hungry for an early election.

The Labor Party national executive met in Canberra on 31 July in a crisis atmosphere to review the government's standing. The executive had before it the Bass report from Combe and a second report from the NSW branch secretary Geoff Cahill saying that criticism of the federal leadership had now permeated all levels of the party. Cahill said that public disagreements between Ministers, the government's failure to communicate its program, and the perpetual crisis atmosphere made fundamental changes essential. But, it is a fact that despite all these criticisms, Whitlam remained both uncompromising and irrepressible. To all appearances it did not bother him.

A few days before the executive meeting Bob Hawke had declared on television he would give up drink if he became Prime Minister. Whitlam was unable to resist replying to this and when he arrived outside John Curtin House in Canberra on 31 July, he stood on the footpath and waited for reporters to interview him, an uncharacteristic habit. The following exchange occurred between Whitlam and Peter Harvey of Channel 9:

Harvey: Prime Minister, what are your hopes for this executive meeting?

Whitlam: Oh, you must realise Peter I'm very worried this morning. In my usual style I have a terrible hangover and I realise, of course, that to hold my position I've just got to undertake a very rigorous program of social drinking . . .

Harvey: Prime Minister, you don't expect any criticism from the state branches about this problem?

Whitlam: Oh I expect a wide-ranging, frank exchange of views. You know, where we all come clean about our failures.

Harvey: Do you think they may demand that you . . .

Whitlam: I mean this will be like an Alcoholics Anonymous meeting I expect.

Harvey: Well, indeed yes. You don't think that they'll be demanding that you drink more?

Whitlam: I fear so. They will. That's what I expect. I was in training. I've got a terrible hangover . . . that's why I'm giving this curbside interview . . . breaking the habits of a lifetime . . . pity the ABC missed out.

Despite all the premonitions of a major party row, the executive meeting went smoothly. A special committee comprising the party officers, Whitlam, and Ken Wriedt, was set up to review all the reports and recommend resolutions to the executive.

The final upshot was that the executive passed a number of motions along the lines suggested by Combe. It called on the Tasmanian branch to endorse the Labor candidates for the seats of Bass and Wilmot as soon as possible. The executive asked Combe to give urgent attention to improving the party organisation in Tasmania and these seats in particular. The executive also decided that in future no Labor members or Senators could retire from parliament in mid-term without direct party approval—a clear attempt to avoid a repetition of the Murphy and Barnard departures. Other motions passed were designed to lay the groundwork for the next Senate election due before July 1976 and also to require Ministers and members to spend more time at home and less overseas.

David Combe's report on the Bass by-election was one of the most hardhitting ever delivered by a federal secretary. Contrary to normal practice, it was not given to delegates before the executive meeting. Copies were distributed in the meeting and collected at the end of it. But this did not prevent one enterprising member leaking the report in full to the *National Times* where it received maximum publicity.

The clash between Whitlam and the machine reflected the belief in the party organisation that the Prime Minister was leading the party to electoral oblivion and holding by-elections along the way to confirm it. The left wing of both the caucus and the organisation was turning against the Prime Minister as a result of the Cairns and Cameron sackings and poor electoral results. To these people the words of the deposed deputy Prime Minister seven years before summed up the situation at that time. Cairns had asked of Whitlam: 'Whose party does he think it is—his or ours?'.

# 15

# THE CAUCUS

*I get through whatever I set my heart on.*

Gough Whitlam, 7 October 1974

**N**o single aspect of Labor's administration drew such fire from the government's critics and created such bewilderment among the public as the caucus system—the very foundation of the Labor Party. The three years of the Whitlam administration were marked by apparently never-ending conflicts between the Cabinet, the caucus and the Prime Minister. Such tensions were implicit in the Labor Party structure itself, which gave supreme and overriding power to the caucus when in practice it was the Cabinet or the Prime Minister who took the decisions. This was the constant dichotomy between the theory of power on one hand and its practice on the other; between the power balance ordained by the Labor Party rules and that ordained by the contingencies of office.

According to the party's rules and standing orders the caucus, which was 95 strong when the 29th Parliament began in June 1974, was able to exercise power of final approval over all Cabinet and Prime Ministerial decisions. This placed far stricter operating parameters on a Labor Prime Minister, in comparison with his Liberal counterpart where the party room possessed no veto power as such over Cabinet decisions. Within the Labor Party the only alternative to acceptance of absolute caucus sovereignty was resignation. Throughout the Labor government's period of office Whitlam and his Ministers, no matter how much they tried to manipulate or ignore the caucus, never questioned its powers.

In short the probability of caucus–Cabinet clashes was institutionalised into the Labor system. When the press wrote about caucus revolts it was simply the party room exercising its legitimate power, which it did not get a proper chance to use within the framework of government. This structural problem was exacerbated by the personality of the Prime Minister whose political instincts were towards centralism and elitism. He believed from the start that a 27-strong Cabinet was too cumbersome and unwieldy a decision-making body and adopted the stratagem of a Cabinet committee system to rationalise the decision-making process, narrow the number of principals involved, and maximise his own authority.

These traits were even more strongly in evidence when it came to the party caucus. Whitlam was always determined to ensure that the caucus did not commit the government in advance to any specific course of action. He adopted as an early article of faith that the caucus should not divert or repudiate the Labor government from the course to which he and his Ministers had committed it. Whitlam's deeply held personal view was that Ministers should never try to reverse a defeat they had suffered in the Cabinet by going to the caucus as a court of appeal. Nobody was ever more certain of incurring his displeasure than by adopting this course of action.

The Prime Minister's view of the caucus was also shaped by the sheer impracticality that such a big group, meeting once a week for 90 minutes on average, could have either the information or methodology to handle the complexities involved in government decision-making. He believed these factors in themselves disqualified the caucus from this role and wide sections of the ministry shared this belief. The upshot was that sometimes the principle of caucus sovereignty was acknowledged, sometimes it was given lip-service, and sometimes it was ignored.

For instance at its weekly Wednesday meeting during the parliamentary session, which was changed to Tuesday at the start of 1975, the bulk of time was spent with caucus approving government bills. When it came to major economic measures, such as the budget or the mini-budgets of July and November 1974, only token notice was given of caucus authority; the details were given to the party by the Treasurer at a special 7.30 p.m. meeting immediately preceding his speech to the parliament at 8 p.m. In these circumstances any assertion of caucus sovereignty became a near impossibility which members could only undertake at the price of destroying the standing of their government. This nearly happened in July when a caucus revolt came within three votes of torpedoing the government's mini-budget which the Treasurer Frank Crean had to announce to the parliament within minutes of the party room vote.

Sometimes the need for official secrecy eliminated even tokenism. For instance one of the most momentous decisions ever taken by the

Labor government, in both political and economic terms, the 13 December 1974 Executive Council authority for a $4000 million overseas loan raising, received no formal approval from either the Cabinet or caucus, most of whose members did not find out about it until months later.

Whitlam's approach to government normally assumed caucus acquiescence. The probability of caucus seeking to check Cabinet usually rested on three factors: the electoral impact of the Cabinet decision, whether caucus had been consulted in the first place, and the mood of the party at the time.

The sensitive issues with the party were those directly impinging on its electoral standing. Caucus members would always fight hardest when they saw a loss of votes in their electorate as a direct result of government decisions. The most stringent test they applied to Cabinet decisions was to assess their electoral impact and it was this consideration, more than any other, which sparked so many of the clashes. There was an inevitable and constant tension between Whitlam, with his commitment to reform, and his caucus, whose members had to bear the electoral cost of such reforms, particularly those involving income redistribution. Caucus operated against a backdrop of public opinion polls which usually showed Labor in a losing position. At the same time there was always a potential danger of caucus upheaval whenever the party believed that it had been bypassed. This was even more so when its exclusion could not be justified on grounds of budgetary or monetary secrecy.

Finally, the collective mood of the caucus was always a vital and intangible factor—its disposition at any particular time in the light of whatever political developments were current. During his great successes Whitlam was untouchable within the party room; at other times, when his actions had shaken the morale and popularity of the government, there was deep hostility towards him.

Superficially the caucus system appeared a liability in that it represented a 'free for all' style of decision making that was normally conveyed to the press in reasonable detail. In news terms the story was normally either 'Whitlam defeats Caucus' or 'Caucus rebuffs Whitlam', which meant that, regardless of who won, the Labor Party lost in media terms.

Yet the caucus system was, in effect, a highly sophisticated political machine which threw immense responsibility upon its own members, which gave intelligent backbenchers an avenue through which they could have a direct impact on government decisions, and which demanded considerable political adroitness from the party leadership.

The full caucus itself comprised an elaborate system of ten committees, which was revised to eight committees after the May 1974 election. The committees were economic, resources, welfare, urban and regional development, foreign affairs and defence, manpower and government enterprises, legal and parliamentary, and education arts and science. Most caucus members served on at least three committees. The frequency of committee meetings and their influence varied enormously depending upon the policy area, the committee chairman and the Labor Minister responsible for the subject.

The orthodox process that was supposed to prevail within the government was that all decisions went through a filter system. The first filter was the relevant caucus committee, where the Minister involved would present his draft submission. From here it would go to a Cabinet committee, then the full Cabinet, then finally back to the full caucus for ultimate endorsement. But throughout 1975 the filter that tended to be missing was that of the Cabinet committee, which was scaled down extensively by this stage. Overall, the caucus–Cabinet system raised a number of tricky problems for Whitlam and his Ministers.

The temptation for Ministers who were defeated in Cabinet to don their caucus hats and fight from the party room for a reversal of the Cabinet decision often proved too great. It destroyed the notion of Cabinet solidarity, which Whitlam was so anxious to build up. Whitlam insisted that if his Ministers were defeated in Cabinet then they should accept that defeat and not seek vindication through the caucus. Most Ministers did feel an obligation to support the Cabinet decision whenever they could. But on other occasions Ministers believed that the government's electoral standing was more important and felt justified in supporting party room moves to overturn Cabinet decisions. When caucus was asked to endorse a decision made by only a handful of Ministers, as distinct from the full Cabinet, then those Ministers not privy to the decision felt no constraints to support the Cabinet line.

The narrow re-election of the Labor government of 18 May 1974, with the loss of seats in both NSW and Queensland and the almost immediate drop in its popularity ratings after that poll, sharpened the edge in caucus–Cabinet relations. This was shown in the first major clash between the re-elected Prime Minister and the party. It occurred over the abolition of the $28 million petrol price subsidy scheme and was a classic study of small pence having big consequences.

Most city members of parliament gave little attention to the scheme. But it was a 'bread and butter' issue for the rural Labor member whose championing of the pork barrel matched that of the Country Party itself. In essence the scheme maintained equalisation of petrol prices in rural areas where there were huge transportation costs. Whitlam, a small group of Ministers and some of his senior advisers at the Kirribilli House meeting on the weekend after the 18 May election, decided that the subsidy scheme should be abolished as part of Labor's anti-inflationary drive.

The decision was formally announced by the Prime Minister at the 7 June Premiers' conference and nothing more was heard of the issue until 31 July, when the Attorney-General Senator Murphy told the caucus that he had not signed the papers giving effect to the abolition and did not support the move. John Fitzpatrick, representing the vast NSW electorate of Darling, moved for the issue to be referred to the caucus resources committee. But the caucus deferred a decision for a week. During the afternoon the government realised that there might not be another party meeting until after 1 August—the date from which abolition was to apply—and therefore called a special caucus meeting for the evening to settle the issue.

At this meeting rural-based caucus members led the fight to retain the subsidy but drew support far beyond the country group. They were spearheaded by the Minister for Northern Development Dr Rex Patterson, who argued that abolition would not only increase petrol prices in rural areas but would have a bad psychological impact for a government which was already branded as anti-rural. Fred Collard, representing Kalgoorlie, the biggest electorate in the world, warned in a powerful speech that he would probably lose his seat if the subsidy was abolished. Others speaking against the abolition included Tony Luchetti representing an inland NSW seat spanning the Blue Mountains, Len Keogh from the outer Brisbane seat of Bowman, Fitzpatrick, and Senators George Poyser from Victoria and George Georges from Queensland.

The Prime Minister was suddenly confronted with a major rebuff at the hands of the caucus over a decision taken and announced two months before. In a strong and emotional speech before the vote Whitlam swung the balance of the debate. He underlined the need to preserve party unity and emphasised that, if the decision was repudiated, promises given by the Australian government to the state Premiers by himself and Treasurer Crean would be publicly dishonoured. He said no government could survive blows of this nature to its credibility. During the debate Whitlam was supported by Cairns, Hayden, Crean and Cameron. In a bitter meeting Whitlam carried the party only 45–42, a narrow escape. In fact, the seats held by Patterson, Collard, Luchetti and Keogh were all lost in December 1975.

The real reason for the closeness of the vote was that the petrol scheme had taken on a symbolic value. Before the meeting members were circulated with a list of electorates showing 23 Labor seats that would be affected by higher petrol prices when the subsidy was abolished. For instance, in the Labor-held electorate of Leichhardt in north Queensland, there would be price rises of 21.4 cents a gallon at Weipa and 20 cents at Burketown. It was another blow to the rural sector, coming just two months after Labor had scraped back into office at the May general election despite massive swings against it in both the country and Queensland. At the 1974 election Labor had lost the country seats of Riverina and Hume in NSW and Wide Bay in Queensland and had just survived in other Queensland seats. At the same time the caucus resented the lack of any consultation over the scheme's abolition, which was presented as a fait accompli to the 7 June Premiers' conference, having never been endorsed by caucus.

A number of Ministers voted against abolition in the party room, highlighting that disputes were not purely along rigid caucus–Cabinet lines. Those sections of the ministry excluded from the original decision on this vote felt free to join other party dissidents in an effort to reverse the announced decision.

The subject to which caucus directed its most sustained attention was the Labor government's 1974–75 budget. The caucus set out to demonstrate that, contrary to popular traditions, a budget, even after it had been delivered by the Treasurer, could still be altered. The party's attitude towards the budget was generally hostile, not because of its overall economic thrust but because of a handful of measures which the party believed would create a public backlash. Declining support for the government only accentuated backbench hostility to some of the new measures. Its criticism was focused on three initiatives: the decision to reduce the taxation reduction claim for education expenses from $400 to $150 a year; the introduction of a surcharge on property income set at ten per cent of the tax on property income; and the levying of a capital gains tax.

The caucus economic and education committees met a fortnight after the budget and passed a motion calling for the interim restoration of the $400 concession pending a full government inquiry into the feasibility of replacing the concessional deduction system with a rebate system. The motion was passed on 3 October having been put to the joint committees by West Australian backbencher Joe Berinson. Most Labor backbenchers had been flooded with protest letters about the cutback in the education deduction and the Catholic church was using all the grass roots political pressure at its command to force a review of the decision. Berinson, along with South Australian backbencher Chris Hurford, believed that, until the government introduced a more equitable system of rebates, it should not incur the political odium of making changes to the system of concessional deductions which were only likely to be temporary anyway.

The Prime Minister was overseas at the time; when he returned, he set out immediately to scotch the moves to reverse part of the budget. At a press conference on 15 October, the day before the caucus meeting to debate the recommendation from the joint committees, Whitlam threw the prestige of his office against moves to restore the $400 tax deduction. 'I sometimes wonder who my colleagues believe elected a Labor government, who they think a Labor government should have first in mind,' Whitlam declared. 'I believe it will be rejected, as I strongly believe it should be.' In five minutes at this press conference Whitlam had transformed the education issue beyond its real merits into a test of strength between himself and the caucus.

The following day in the party room Whitlam moved that the lower deduction figure of $150 a year be accepted and was supported by both Crean and Wheeldon. The committee amendment moved by Berinson said the maximum deduction should be restored to $400 for the coming year and that the Treasury should be asked to consider alternatives to the present taxation deduction system such as a general rebate system. Whitlam carried the day with ease, by 53–26. But more significant was the general consensus that emerged during the debate over the need to reform the whole system of tax deductions. There was support for an inquiry along the lines recommended in the second part of the Berinson motion. This became the first assault by the Labor government on the system of concessional deductions, which would be radically reformed eleven months later in the Hayden budget.

But if caucus was unsuccessful in reversing the education tax deduction, it had a major victory on the controversial property tax. The impetus came at the party meeting on 25 September when Tasmanian backbencher John Coates, with the support of NSW Senator Arthur Gietzelt, moved that the tax apply only to people on incomes above a certain level. Treasurer Crean suggested that caucus committees review the proposal. On 2 September a joint meeting of the caucus economic and welfare committees recommended easing of the tax. The proposed changes would cut the number of people having to pay the tax from 1.3 million to 500,000. The tax, which had been originally suggested by Jim Spigelman, was opposed by both the Treasury and Crean because of administrative difficulties. Wide sections of the caucus saw it as electorally damaging and a number of Ministers agreed.

The following week caucus agreed to the committee's recommendations modifying the property tax but also rejected a move to scrap it completely. The changes meant that people with a taxable income below $5000 would be exempt altogether. The move to abolish the tax came from NSW member Paul Keating but it was defeated 48–29 with most members of Cabinet voting as a bloc against abolition. The modification of the tax was carried on the voices, indicating widespread support throughout the party from both Ministers and backbenchers. Whitlam was out of the country at the time but it is highly doubtful whether his presence would have made any difference to the outcome. The acting

Prime Minister Jim Cairns told a press conference that, while he preferred Cabinet decisions to stand, caucus had a right to exercise its will.

The property surcharge only operated during 1974–75 and was not renewed in the Hayden budget. It was one issue where the strength of feeling in the party prompted a rethinking of the issue by Ministers themselves. The caucus moves against both the education deduction and property tax shattered the notion that a budget was fixed once and for all when it was introduced into parliament by the Treasurer.

The caucus itself did not have to initiate action against the capital gains tax. The shifting base of Labor's economic policies moved rapidly after the budget and the tax was repealed in early 1975 as the chief thrust of economic policy centred on revival of the public sector.

Despite the rules he tried to enforce on his Ministers, there were times when even Whitlam himself was not prepared to accept them. The classic case was in July 1974 when both Whitlam and Cairns were outraged at federal Cabinet's decision to accept a $5500 pay rise for all parliamentarians and other pay increases for senior public servants and statutory officers. Cabinet voted 15–11 in favour of increasing the salary of parliamentarians to $20,000 annually. Whitlam believed that the government's credibility in arguing for wage restraint would be destroyed if it proceeded to accept pay rises of just under 40 per cent for parliamentarians. He had originally planned to use rejection of the pay rise for politicians as the first step in an overall wage freeze for the community. The Cabinet decision not only made this tactic impossible but undermined the government's capacity to appeal for wage restraint.

On 24 July Whitlam, Cairns, Hayden and Beazley all argued vigorously in the party room for a postponement of the rises. The decisive speaker for taking the money was the Leader of the House Fred Daly who told the party that, as far as most people were concerned, no time was ever right for a politician's pay increase. Earlier that morning Cairns had voiced his concern by saying, 'I don't think we can agree to a 38 per cent increase in parliamentary salaries and expect anyone else to demand anything less.' Whitlam told the party room that restraint on the wages front was essential. He wanted to go to the Premiers' conference on inflation and the Moore conference on wage indexation with solid backing for a policy of wage and spending restraint. The Prime Minister told the party that once these rises for parliamentarians and senior public servants were approved they would eventually flow throughout the public sector. He was rebuffed by the caucus 51–40.

The incident demonstrated that Whitlam himself could succumb to the tensions inherent in the Labor Party's decision-making process. On this occasion Whitlam broke his golden rule and, having been defeated in Cabinet on an issue which he regarded as being of overriding importance, both he and his senior Ministers did everything they could to have the move reversed by caucus. This issue was one of Whitlam's most important defeats in the party room in his last 18 months of government. But there was an ironic sequel to this debate which gave the Prime Minister the last laugh when Opposition Leader Bill Snedden attempted to win political capital by persuading the Liberal Party to reject the pay rise, which had to be approved by both Houses of federal parliament.

While the Liberals were procrastinating over this decision, Whitlam, in a presidential style initiative, called a press briefing to announce that if the Opposition disallowed the pay rise he would ask all state Premiers to assist the Australian government in a policy of wage restraint for federal, state and local government employees. The Prime Minister's announcement in the afternoon of 25 July made disallowance of the increases by the Opposition parties inevitable. So Whitlam won—with the Opposition's support, not that of his own caucus.

It was in July 1974 that the internal tensions within the party reached their most dangerous point. Both Cabinet and caucus were in a state of abject confusion over the economy, with advisers demanding tough action and the party running scared, unwilling to accept the consequences of strong action and unwilling to make personal sacrifices themselves. There was an atmosphere of panic, policy confusion and greater than normal caucus unpredictability.

The single most dangerous flashpoint in caucus–Cabinet relations occurred just before 8 p.m. on Tuesday 23 July 1974. At a special 7.30 p.m. caucus meeting called to approve the July mini-budget, just thirty minutes before Treasurer Frank Crean was due to deliver it, a caucus revolt came within a hair's breadth of carving the economic package to pieces. It was only an impassioned and powerful display by the Prime Minister that saved the government from an unprecedented humiliation.

Most caucus members were not formally notified until late in the afternoon that there would be a special meeting to endorse a sweeping package of economic measures thrashed out in Cabinet the previous day. This was despite extensive press headlines that morning about them. Senator Jim McClelland, not then a Minister himself, moved that those sections of the mini-budget dealing with the deferment of the means test abolition, postponement of the child care program, and increased postal charges, be removed from the speech.

McClelland argued on the grounds that Cabinet should not decide such major issues without reference to the party. He argued that, while decisions on currency values and tariffs had to be taken without prior caucus consultation due to their very nature, this was not the case with many of the items in the mini-budget. The caucus was still voting on the McClelland motion a few minutes before 8 p.m. as the House bells were summoning members to the chamber for Crean's speech. By this time the Leader of the Opposition and the press gallery had already been given copies of the Treasurer's text.

The vote, 40–35 against the motion, just avoided a massive crisis within the government. At least two Ministers who participated in drafting the Cabinet decisions, the Environment Minister Moss Cass and the Minister for the ACT Gordon Bryant, voted for deferral. This incident was one of the strongest expressions of caucus resentment over the lack of consultation in the three year period of the Whitlam government. If carried, the motion would have been an utter humiliation for Whitlam and the Cabinet.

These above episodes reveal a caucus which, after the 18 May election, was more active and ready to exercise its sovereignty than in the period before. But not all caucus differences were resolved by direct party room confrontations in one day.

The subtleties of the caucus system of government were revealed in salutary fashion by the dispute over beach sand mining on Fraser Island off the Queensland coast. This internal party struggle also provides a remarkable insight into how a minor administrative decision could be turned into a national debate involving the prestige of both the Prime Minister and Minister for Minerals and Energy Rex Connor. In November 1974 Whitlam, in reply to an earlier letter from Connor, gave the Minister authority to issue export permits to the Dillingham–Murphyores partnership on Fraser Island for the export of mineral sands. The Prime Minister also informed the Environment Minister Dr Moss Cass of the letter to Connor. The following month, on 13 December, Connor wrote to the company giving his approval—just four days before the Labor government's environmental impact legislation received the royal assent. This act would have required a full impact study before any approval for export licences could be issued. The 13 December approval given to the company by Rex Connor was not discovered by Moss Cass until March, three months later. From this time onwards efforts were made at both Cabinet level, the chief instrument of government, and caucus level, the chief instrument of the party—to have the decision reviewed.

The caucus committee on urban affairs, which also encompassed environmental matters, had a long interest in beach sand mining and became the initial avenue through which moves were made towards revision of the decision. As early as July 1974 this committee had passed a motion seeking information on all sand mining approvals, alternative sources of supply, and the feasibility of asking companies to fulfil their contracts from other non-sensitive areas. The committee met twice in early 1975 to discuss the way the approval of permits from Fraser Island could be reversed.

On both occasions the Environment Minister Dr Cass was present at the meeting and urged the committee to withhold any action in the hope that he could resolve the differences at ministerial level. Finally, at a night meeting on 22 April, the committee passed a motion which called for the Fraser Island export permits to be suspended pending a full environmental inquiry.

The next day in caucus the committee chairman, NSW Senator Arthur Gietzelt, raised the issue. It was not pursued when the Prime Minister told the party room that he had already specifically asked Cass and Connor to settle the question among themselves. But, after a number of talks, the two men failed to agree and the dispute was listed for Cabinet. Although the matter was intended to be resolved at the 12 May Cabinet meeting, the final submissions were not completed by this date. The next day Senator Gietzelt again took up the question in the caucus towards the end of the meeting and this time was successful in having the committee's resolution passed on the voices, although a number of people had left the room and others did not recognise the full significance of the decision. This in effect tied the party and the government to a position strongly favouring Dr Cass since the terms of the motion specifically referred to suspension of permits until the environmental study was made.

On Thursday night 15 May, Whitlam, now becoming exasperated beyond belief over the failure of his Ministers to resolve the issue, held a meeting in his office with both Connor and Cass which ended in fiasco. The Prime Minister launched a barrage of abuse on Cass. But this meeting failed to find any compromise and the question had to go to Cabinet at its next meeting on 19 May. On this day Cabinet examined opposing submissions from Cass and Connor in a two and a half hour meeting which never got beyond this item. By this stage the dispute within the government was well-known in environmental circles and was already attracting press coverage. It was seen as a test of Labor's credentials on the environment. At this Cabinet meeting both the pent-up tensions between senior Ministers and the growing hostility to Rex Connor, because of the loans affair and his own aloof and obsessive secrecy, were ventilated in one of the most heated meetings held during the last year of Labor's administration. It also marked a watershed in Connor's standing within the party. Ever since Labor's election in December 1972 he had operated as a law unto himself and got away with it. Now his authority was under assault.

Connor opened the Cabinet meeting with a long justification of his position; then Whitlam, the only other Minister involved in the November decision to give the licences, supported Connor. Whitlam attacked Cass bitterly, accusing him of disloyalty and branding him a failure as Environment Minister. When he finally got a chance to put his argument,

Cass was supported by McClelland, Bill Morrison, Hayden, Uren and John Wheeldon. At one stage, when Connor started interrupting Cass, he was effectively put down by Hayden who interjected angrily, warning Connor that Cabinet was sick of being bullied and bluffed by him. Towards the end of the debate it became clear that Cass had the numbers. But before the motion was put Connor rose to his feet, picked up his papers and stated baldly that he was prepared to resign over the issue. Whitlam then put Connor's motion to the Cabinet, as distinct from the Cass case, and declared it carried on the voices. The Cabinet broke up in a state of confusion.

Throughout that afternoon extensive lobbying took place within Parliament House to have the Cabinet decision overturned by caucus the next morning. But by the narrowest possible margin Whitlam and Connor carried the party with them, by one vote, 42–41, on a recount, only after a 'boots and all' effort with Whitlam opening the meeting by calling for support for the Cabinet decision and declaring that the government could not dishonour a commitment it had entered into with the company. Later that day at a press conference Whitlam revealed his personal antipathy for Dr Cass and sympathy for Connor. After attacking Cass he extolled the virtues of Connor: 'I think he has been a very effective and successful Minister. He's gone as far in asserting the national interest as the law allows.'

But the Cabinet meeting was proof that Connor's strength was on the wane. He carried Cabinet with him only because of a resignation threat—the ultimate weapon that, once used, quickly exhausts its own authority. The chronology of the Fraser Island dispute shows the results that could be achieved through clever use of the caucus system. The real point was not that the environmentalists had lost; it was that they had resurrected an administrative decision into a major issue which meant that the environmental lobby within the party was strengthened, not weakened. Moreover the crisis they provoked had far-reaching consequences. It threw into doubt Whitlam's own support for the environmental cause—something he previously championed—and was a significant factor in weakening Connor's position in the party.

Within a week of the Fraser Island dispute, caucus had its revenge with the most decisive rebuff of Cabinet in the three-year history of the Whitlam government. This was provoked by the Cabinet decision on Friday 23 May to lower the reserve price for wool during the new selling season from its current level of 250 cents a kilogram to 200 cents. This decision, which had been spearheaded by the acting Treasurer Bill Hayden, was based largely on the need to reduce the level of government outlays and minimise the deficit in the approaching budget. It was contrary to the case presented to Cabinet by agriculture Minister Senator Ken Wriedt, a submission endorsed by the caucus rural committee in the preceding weeks, for the retention of the reserve price at 250 cents. The Cabinet decision was leaked to the press and reported in the Saturday papers, much to the concern of Labor members in rural seats and to the wool industry itself.

There were extraordinary scenes in Parliament the following Monday when Bill Hayden as acting Treasurer defended the Cabinet decision against both the Opposition and the government backbench. Hayden eagerly took up the mantle of Treasurer while Jim Cairns was overseas. He told Parliament the cost of maintaining the 250 cents price had been $360 million to that stage. 'The Opposition has consistently asserted that there should be wide-ranging cuts in public expenditure and at the same time has given firm pledges to increase expenditure substantially in certain areas,' Hayden said. 'I repeat the challenge to the Opposition: where is it going to get the money and at whose expense in terms of cuts in programs affecting the rest of the community?' Hayden's comments were just as clearly directed to Labor's own back-benchers.

Throughout this day two struggles, one public, one private, were waged against the Cabinet decision. The Australian Wool Industry Conference warned the government that selling orders for the rest of the season would drop sharply if the decision was confirmed. The Country Party leader Doug Anthony predicted that Labor would lose at least four rural seats if the price support scheme was cut back to 200 cents. A big demonstration of farmers was planned outside Parliament House the next morning to coincide with the caucus meeting. Within Parliament House two young NSW backbenchers who had previously worked for the Bureau of Agricultural Economics, Bob Whan who held the seat of Eden–Monaro and John Kerin who held Macarthur, quietly lobbied Labor members and Senators to overturn the decision. By Monday evening they had the numbers to roll Cabinet.

The next morning Whan and Kerin were successful in a massive 52–29 vote, thereby confirming the reserve price at its existing level of 250 cents a kilo. The chief arguments used were that the decision would be the death blow for Labor's rural seats and secondly, a rejection of the economic arguments put by Bill Hayden. Whan argued that all current indications suggested wool prices would firm and claimed that the lowering of the floor price would reduce the value of the government's stockpile. In the event neither Whan nor Kerin survived the December 1975 election.

The caucus vote was an undisguised measure of party dissatisfaction with the politically inept nature of Cabinet decisions. Whitlam left Hayden to carry the brunt of the Cabinet defence. While Whitlam appealed to the party to reaffirm the original decision, this was no grand effort on the scale of the Fraser Island issue and was an ineffectual speech. Ken Wriedt, who presented the Cabinet recommendation to the caucus, said he had been placed in an invidious position and indicated his disagreement with it. This clash was a clear example of the Cabinet, with its mind fixed on a tight fiscal policy in anticipation of a tough budget, being pulled back into the realms of political reality by the caucus.

Caucus again demonstrated a more realistic attitude than the Cabinet in September when the question of parliamentary pay rises rose again. In March, the $5500, which had been disallowed the previous July, had been accepted, taking the pay level to $20,000. The September report from the Remuneration Tribunal, an independent salaries fixing body, suggested that parliamentarians' pay be indexed. This would have given an increase of $720 for the year backdated to 15 May. There was a heated debate in Cabinet over the report, which recommended an increase of 3.6 per cent—the consumer price index for the March quarter and the increase the Conciliation and Arbitration Commission made to award wages in the national wage case. The fact that the rises were based on indexation swung a number of people in favour of accepting them, including the Opposition parties.

But the Labour Minister Jim McClelland strongly opposed the rises in both Cabinet and caucus. After his defeat in Cabinet McClelland led moves in the party room to have the decision overturned and the caucus surprised many people by voting 46–28 to throw out the rises. Although he did not say so in the party room, McClelland claimed later he would have resigned if the increases had been endorsed. The real significance of this decision was the changed attitude of the caucus and a more realistic appreciation of the economic problems confronting the government. Unlike the previous year, the caucus was now prepared to set an example.

The party room was always sympathetic to policy issues which had an overwhelming effect on individual electorates. An excellent example was the November 1973 decision to amend Labor's first budget by reinstating income tax concessions for gold miners. The move was instigated by the member for Kalgoorlie Fred Collard, who wanted action deferred to enable a complete investigation of the proposal. Caucus accepted the vast political consequences for Collard's electorate and his motion was carried on the voices. In the same fashion caucus also accepted moves by the then Minister for Manufacturing Industry Kep Enderby to ensure that the government kept its promise of four weeks annual leave to all workers in the ACT and Northern Territory. Enderby was the member for Canberra, which at that time encompassed the entire ACT. Once again the caucus proved sympathetic.

The Labor Party's caucus system became the butt of jokes and ridicule throughout the period of the Whitlam government. Its defects were obvious matters of public knowledge; its strengths, because they were more subtle, often went unnoticed. Potential tensions existed at all times between the three power centres: the Prime Minister, the Cabinet and the caucus. The government belonged to no single one of them but to all of them in different strengths according to the issue.

Certainly the Whitlam government was not government by caucus. In three years caucus reversed only a handful out of hundreds of Cabinet decisions. The main ones were the reversal of the Cabinet 'do nothing' decision over Lake Pedder in Tasmania, reversal of the abolition of the gold mining subsidy in the 1973 budget, reversal of the property surcharge in the 1974 budget, reversal of the lowering of the price support level for the wool industry, and reversal of the 1975 Cabinet decision to accept parliamentary pay rises. This is a modest list and, given the 1975 election result, many caucus members might regret that they did not take a stronger attitude from the start.

On evidence it is impossible to draw any conclusion other than that the caucus was moderate and responsible, wary of the dangers it could provoke through disruption and reversal of policy, yet mindful of the electoral base it had to protect. On the whole, the 27-man Cabinet seemed to be a fair reflection of the party caucus. But some of the later decisions by the caucus, particularly on both the wool issue and the parliamentary pay question, demonstrated a more pragmatic and real-istic attitude than the Cabinet.

The caucus had a nearly impeccable record in the list of men it elected to the ministry to fill the casual vacancies which occurred after the 1974 election. They were in order, Wheeldon, McClelland, Riordan, Berinson and Paul Keating, a list which significantly improved the Labor government.

Despite upheavals there was never any sign that caucus meetings would degenerate into the self-destructive rabbles that prevailed during the Scullin Prime Ministership. Both Liberal leaders, Snedden and then Fraser after him, were always confident that the caucus tensions within the government would prove too great, particularly with high unem-ployment and inflation, and the Labor party would self-destruct. But this never happened and, although the caucus was always deeply concerned about the economy, it never lost its head.

A significant factor was the gradual defactionalisation of the caucus that took place with the election of new members in 1969, 1972 and 1974. The input of these people into the party gave it a more modern and pragmatic component and served to break down the rigid ideolog-ical freeze between left and right which had characterised it during the sixties.

Whitlam's record with the caucus was an impressive one with few reversals. But his tactics and approach to the party troubled even his greatest supporters. The Prime Minister operated as a confrontationalist; his technique was to build up issues beyond what they were and, by increasing the stakes involved, to make it harder for the party to alter the decisions. This was done with resignation threats, bluff and his own inimitable oratory. It reflects the fact that, despite the theoretical sovereignty of caucus, it was the Prime Minister and his Cabinet who nearly always steered the policy rudder of the Labor government.

# 16

# THE CAIRNS SACKING

*Perhaps I do wear my heart too easily on my sleeve.*

Jim Cairns, 9 July 1975

In May 1975 Malcolm Fraser's office was given a crucial tip—that information existed to prove that as Treasurer Dr Jim Cairns had authorised overseas loan raisings on his own initiative. They were told there was a letter held by a Sydney based company, Minerals Centre, that would prove this point. Fraser's office was told that Cairns had written a letter to a businessman, George Harris—and the Opposition leader's staff immediately launched a frantic effort to track Harris down. This occurred while Cairns was still Treasurer and before any Cairns letters to Harris had been made public.

It was Fraser's speechwriter David Kemp who made the connection between Harris and the Carlton Football Club. Further investigations revealed to Fraser that Harris was a good friend of the deputy Prime Minister. The possibility of such a letter began to sound feasible. Finally Fraser's press secretary David Barnett flew to Sydney on the morning of 4 June for a meeting with a Sydney businessman, Alexander Daniel Thomson. The firm was not prepared to hand over a copy of the letter to Barnett. But it nevertheless gave him a statutory declaration from Thomson containing a retyped version of the critical letter. Barnett flew back to Canberra and arrived at Parliament House towards the end of Question Time with full details of the letter which was to lead to unprecedented events four weeks later culminating in the sacking from the ministry of the deputy Prime Minister.

The actual letter read:

TREASURER
Parliament House
Canberra 2600

March 7, 1975

Alco International Pty. Ltd.,
6 Southam Court,
BULLEEN, Vic. 3105

Attention: Mr George Harris

Dear Sir,

The Australian government is interested in exploring available loan funds from overseas. In the event of a successful negotiation which may be introduced or arranged by you, and provided the interest rate for a term loan does not exceed 8% per annum in total, we would be prepared to pay a once only brokerage fee of 2½% deducted at the source to you and/or your nominees. We would need to be satisfied about the sources of the funds and the size of the loan would have to be appropriate to our needs.
Yours sincerely,

(Signed)

J F CAIRNS

The letter was sent on paper marked 'SECRET'. The only difference between the actual letter and the retyped version in the Thomson statutory declaration was the date, which Thomson specified as 5 March. Fraser was anxiously awaiting Barnett's return from Sydney as he sat in the chamber. The Thomson document was handed to Fraser who then showed it to his deputy Phillip Lynch. Cairns was then asked the following question:

| Mr Lynch: | I ask the Treasurer: Did he, in a letter dated on or about 5 March, offer a commission of two and a half per cent on any loan money arranged by the recipient of the letter or his company? |
| Dr J F Cairns: | The answer is no. At no stage did I offer a commission of two and a half per cent or any other amount or give any authority whatever to any person to do anything other than make inquiries. |
| Mr M Fraser: | No brokerage fee? |
| Dr J F Cairns: | No brokerage fee. Would the honourable member like to ask more questions? |

Lynch's office were convinced they had stumbled on to a major story. But Fraser was less certain; he thought the letter could be a furphy. 'Jim Cairns would never mislead the parliament,' he told his staff after Question Time.

However the following day in parliament Cairns revealed the existence of three other letters he had given Harris, one dated 10 March and two dated 15 April. It was as a result of these letters and their discovery by the government that Whitlam, as outlined previously, sacked Cairns as Treasurer this very week. Labor assumed at this point that the George Harris affair was over—but it was wrong.[1]

Throughout the public debate about Harris there was no mention of any letter sent by Cairns along the lines suggested in the Thomson statutory declaration.

The Opposition then decided its best option was to leak its latest information. So stories about the Thomson declaration and the Cairns letter appeared in both the Melbourne *Sun News-Pictorial* and the *Australian*. When asked by the *Australian* about the letter, a spokesman for Cairns said on 12 June: 'I am informed that no such letter was ever signed or sent.'

Yet just a few days earlier events were taking place overseas which would prove that the Harris letter was indeed genuine. Once again, the 'money trail' would ruin Cairns. The Australian embassy in Washington had been approached by a New York firm with a set of documents relating to loan raising activities by George Harris. A five page cable to the Foreign Affairs Department sent from Washington on 10 June documented the entire story, the centrepiece of which was the full text of the Cairns 7 March letter to Alco International, marked to Harris, suggesting a brokerage fee of two and a half per cent. Unbeknown to Malcolm Fraser, the Australian embassy confirmed the authenticity of the document he held. The cable to Australia from the First Secretary (Financial), Peter McLaughlin, was political dynamite.

The information had come to the embassy from the vice president of an American firm which had been negotiating with Harris. The company involved was Ivor B Clark and the approach was made through a Mr O Genena. According to McLaughlin, Clarks operated primarily as a real estate investment broker with offices throughout the United States but was 'not part of the established New York investment banking community'.

On 14 March, just seven days after Cairns signed the letter, Harris had held a meeting with representatives from Clarks and their associates. The McLaughlin cable said: 'According to Genena, Harris told the meeting that the letter of authority could be taken as authorising him to seek loan funds for the Australian government up to $4 billion. However, the government's immediate needs were not as great as that and after some discussion it was decided that Clarks would explore the prospects of arranging a loan of $1 billion.'

The cable said that Clarks were puzzled from the beginning at a two and a half per cent brokerage fee, which was at least double that usually required of a borrower of Australia's standing. As a result of the 14 March meeting, Harris appeared to settle with Clarks on a breakdown of commission in any successful raising which would give his company, Alco International, 45 per cent of the brokerage fee, Clarks and associate bankers 36.5 per cent with the remaining 18.5 per cent split between other parties.

Through their London contacts Clarks arranged a meeting on 20 March between Harris and his associate Lesley Nagy, and the directors of Morgan Grenfell, who agreed to sound out their sources in the traditional capital market and the Middle East. Not long afterwards Morgan Grenfell wrote to Harris and confirmed the doubts they expressed at the 20 March meeting—that loan funds could not be found anywhere at the interest rate specified. According to the McLaughlin cable, both Morgans and Clarks got feedback themselves from the market indicating that Harris had approached other possible sources in Europe well outside established banking houses.[2]

The Washington cable created deep concern within the highest levels of the Labor government. The day it arrived Whitlam rang Cairns informing him of the details and telling him that he would receive copies of the documents which would also be sent to the head of the Attorney-General's Department, Clarrie Harders, for a legal opinion. On 18 June the new Treasurer Bill Hayden received from Washington the actual documents Clarks had given the embassy and he passed them on to the Secretary of the Prime Minister's Department, John Menadue. After speaking with Whitlam, who was campaigning in Tasmania at the time, Menadue wrote to Cairns, then Environment Minister, enclosing copies of the letters, the main one being the 7 March letter to Alco International. On 25 June, Cairns replied to Menadue in the following terms:

> Dear John,
>
> Thanks for the documents relative (sic) to George Harris and Ivor B Clark Companies and others. Each of the letters given to Mr Harris have (sic) been returned to me and have (sic) been destroyed to prevent any possible misuse. Harris brought to an end in April his relations with Ivor B Clark Companies and the others. You will notice that all supposed arrangements were dependent upon a loan being accepted. I rejected the proposals made by Harris in April and he notified the parties accordingly.

The clear implication of this letter is that Cairns recovered and destroyed the 7 March letter to Harris. He said later that, had the House been in session when he realised he had signed such a letter, he would have immediately made a personal explanation to clarify the situation. Cairns subsequently told the House he had no recollection whatsoever of signing this letter to Harris on 7 March.

Meanwhile the revelation of yet another letter from the former Treasurer to Harris infuriated Whitlam. On the face of it, this letter not only seemed to establish an agency between the government and Harris—the offence for which Cairns had already been removed from Treasury—but specifically mentioned a two and a half per cent commission on any loan. It was not until Monday 30 June that Whitlam actually saw a copy of the letter. He realised at this point that there appeared to be a basic contradiction between the letter and Cairns' reply to Lynch in Parliament on 4 June. Whitlam decided at once that the issue must be brought to a head and he confronted Cairns over the differences the next day.

But the letter was not Whitlam's only worry about Cairns. The Prime Minister's determination was redoubled by his knowledge of recent events involving Philip Cairns, the stepson and electoral secretary of the deputy Prime Minister. Whitlam had seen recently a special report from the Auditor-General dealing with Philip Cairns' activities, which raised the most severe questions about the extent to which he was pursuing private and government business simultaneously on the government payroll.

In April the Fiji High Commission in Canberra was notified that two Arab representatives, Mr S Nassar and General M Galal, wanted to have discussions with government officials about investment opportunities in Fiji. The High Commission was told the Arabs would be accompanied by Philip Cairns on an official visit as private secretary to the deputy Prime Minister. On 7–8 May, talks were held in Suva between Galal, Mr Ian Richardson and Philip Cairns and a number of Fiji government Ministers and officials. Mr Nassar never arrived. Both Galal and Richardson were directors of an import–export company, Rawia International (Australia) Pty Ltd, incorporated in Melbourne a short time later on 20 May 1975. In the talks Cairns stated he was acting in his official capacity and the Fiji Ministers and nine officials were involved in the two day talks.

The discussions were exploratory, covering oil and sugar refineries, fishing and timber industries and access for Middle East airlines to Fiji. During the talks Galal said he and his associates could arrange for investments in Fiji once they assessed the needs of that country. He said it would be possible to arrange for investors in the Middle East, who would examine the question of setting up an oil refinery once they had further details from the Fiji government.

Philip Cairns made a number of visits to Fiji in this period. According to the Fiji government his second visit was on 19 June when he indicated that he was acting in an unofficial capacity and held further ministerial talks on behalf of Rawia International. In these talks Cairns advised that interests in Australia wanted to breed prime beef cattle in

Fiji. Subsequently the Cairns visit became the centre of a major political controversy in Fiji after it was reported that Jim Cairns had been dismissed and a series of allegations made about Philip Cairns' activities.

The import of the talks between Cairns and his colleagues on 7–8 May is demonstrated in a letter he later wrote on 19 May to the Fiji Minister for Commerce and Industry, M T Khan. The letter is written on official paper from the Treasurer's office:

TREASURER
Parliament House
Canberra 2600

May 19, 1975

My dear Minister,

I would like to thank you most sincerely on behalf of myself and my Minister, Dr Cairns, for your kindness during the visit just completed. I feel that the discussions held were most useful and I believe, sincerely, that results will be forthcoming in the very near future. I believe that the concept of the petrol refinery is of the utmost significance to Fiji and could have enormous benefits to your economy. Within hours of General Galal's return to Bahrain, no fewer than three offers were extended to build a petrol refinery in Fiji and I also believe that fairly substantial promises were made in reference to loan funds and grants to Fiji. I think that like myself, you must be enormously excited with the future and I believe that with the sort of assistance being extended, that you and your government will achieve what you all wish to achieve.

I will be returning to Fiji, unofficially, either the last week in June or the first week in July to have discussions at the western end on agricultural development with Ratu Osea, and I would like the opportunity of discussing this with you at that time. There is, I'm sure, a great deal that could be done in the immediate future to reduce Fiji's dependency on its sugar crop in the area of agriculture.

In closing, I would again like to thank you most warmly for the reception extended to me by yourself and your fellow Ministers on my recent visit.

Yours sincerely,

(signed)

(P. J. Cairns)
Private Secretary

When Philip Cairns was later reported denying that he told Fiji officials his visit was official, the Fiji Information Minister, Ratu David Toganivalu, replied that the minutes of the 7–8 May meeting recorded Cairns saying the visit was official. This is further substantiated by

Cairns' 19 May letter. In response to extensive criticism in Fiji, the government revealed that it had asked the Fiji High Commission in Canberra to make extra inquiries about Philip Cairns' visit. The reply was that it had official status.[3] Subsequently the Fiji Prime Minister, Ratu Sir Kamisese Mara, wrote to Whitlam seeking clarification of the status of the Cairns visit. The Prime Minister sent back a brief but devastating reply to the effect that Philip Cairns was in no way a representative of the Australian government, that his visit had no official status and that his activities were an embarrassment to the Australian government. The government was alarmed about the Auditor-General's report indicating that phone calls, accommodation and travelling allowance during Cairns' visit were costs on the government. At the same time the Auditor-General uncovered a payment that had been made to a woman in Fiji who had lived near Philip Cairns in Melbourne.

Philip Cairns' involvement in overseas loan raisings was revealed for the first time on 1 July when the *Age* ran a front page story about a company, Sunshine Migrant Services Pty Ltd, of which Cairns was a director. The company was trying to raise money for a land development near the Point Cook RAAF base. It was claimed that Cairns was involved in these efforts and the move had official authorisation. The *Age* story did not come as a surprise. For many weeks press gallery journalists had been tipped off by the Opposition to investigate the activities of Philip Cairns but the Melbourne paper was the first one to do so.

Whitlam now sought explanations from Cairns on two questions, the 7 March letter to Harris, and the activities of Philip Cairns. The Prime Minister called Cairns to his office after he returned to Canberra on Tuesday 1 July and set out the information he had, asking Cairns for complete explanations. The two men clashed during a 50-minute meeting in which Whitlam said that Cairns, now Environment Minister but still deputy Prime Minister, would be dismissed from the ministry unless he could provide satisfactory answers on both scores.

On this evening the Labor government headed towards the worst crisis of its three-year period in office. Whitlam had his mind set. He knew from the documents that the case against Cairns was watertight and that his deputy would be sacked the next day—the first time a Prime Minister had ever dismissed the deputy Prime Minister in Australian history.

At this stage the papers were being flooded with a torrent of new loan revelations coming from the London financier Harry Gilham, and a series of telex messages suggesting that Philip Cairns was involved in moves to raise a $US2000 million loan with both Gilham and Eric Sear Cowls. The papers also carried extensive reports on Cairns' efforts to raise money for Sunshine Migrant Service, whose purpose was to develop low cost housing near Melbourne. Whitlam realised that if

Cairns remained as deputy Prime Minister there would be further revelations likely to harm the government even more. At this stage the Prime Minister knew of Philip Cairns' activities in Fiji, although this had not hit the papers.

That evening Whitlam released a press statement foreshadowing Cairns' dismissal unless he gave a suitable explanation about the 7 March letter over which he appeared to have misled the Parliament. In reference to Philip Cairns, the statement said:

> I have also told Dr Cairns that Mr Philip Cairns' reported activities concerning housing projects in the Melbourne metropolitan area would make it possible for him to make a profit from his position on Dr Cairns' staff . . . I regard it as improper for ministerial staff to put themselves or allow themselves to be put in such a position. I have therefore asked Dr Cairns to give me a written explanation of this matter also tomorrow.

The following morning all papers carried front page banner headlines about the imminent demise of Cairns. Both the *Australian* and the *Australian Financial Review* saw in the impending dismissal of the deputy Prime Minister for misleading Parliament over loan activities, the reprehensible circumstances which Malcolm Fraser said were needed for the Opposition to block supply and force an election.

Throughout Wednesday Cairns' office was an embattled outpost. Cairns remained closeted in his office while his private secretary Junie Morosi sat in the outer office supervising all access to him. Cairns spoke to a number of his faction colleagues and both Tom Uren and Senator George Georges were important in persuading him that he should not resign.

Finally at 6 p.m. Morosi left Cairns' office and walked the one flight of stairs to the Prime Minister's office directly above to hand over the Cairns explanation. Attached to it was a statement from Philip Cairns about his business activities. In an extraordinary explanation Cairns said the 7 March letter to Harris was presented to him for signature but he rejected it because he found it unacceptable.

> I answered the question in Parliament on June 4, 1975 consistently with my recollection of these events. I answered the question as I did, believing that I spoke the truth, I have no recollection at all of having signed the letter quoted in your press statement and I have a clear recollection that I rejected it. I do not intend to resign from any position I hold because I answered the question in Parliament in the clear and sincere belief that what I said was true.

In his accompanying statement Philip Cairns said the company Sunshine Migrant Services Pty Ltd was not involved in profit making of any kind and there was no way he could have profited from his association with it. Cairns said he had one share to help the company achieve its objectives of low cost housing. Cairns also denied that he was to receive a share of the commission on an overseas loan being raised with Eric Sear Cowls. His statement continued: 'I did not intend to accept, nor would I have accepted, any commission on any overseas loan. I have not received at any time any remuneration outside my government salary and I have never used my position to further my personal interest or to obtain any personal gain or reward.'

Just after 7 p.m. a letter from the Prime Minister's office was delivered to Dr Cairns' office informing him that Whitlam was not satisfied with his explanation and, since he refused to resign, the Governor-General would be advised to withdraw his commission. Whitlam went to Government House at 8 p.m. and stayed there for 45 minutes. While he was there Dr Cairns completed and released a second statement to the press launching a bitter attack on Whitlam and claiming that he had been victimised. It was accompanied by a second letter to Whitlam:

> My dear Prime Minister,
>
> I am amazed at the receipt of your letter of 2 July and that you have taken the extreme action of advising the Governor-General to terminate any commission without the courtesy of informing me personally, although you are aware I am in the office below you.
>
> I reject your decision. It is arbitrary and unfair.
>
> You have twice held me guilty of wrongful action without any inquiry, each of which has had the most harmful consequences to me. You told me you were concerned alone about whether I had told the truth to Parliament. I have written to you that I told Parliament what I clearly and sincerely believed to be true. There is no proof to the contrary.
>
> Perhaps nowhere else in the nation could a person be so arbitrarily treated as I have been. Nowhere else would there be an absence of appeal or chance of defence.
>
> No person or government can pretend to stand for the rights of individuals and behave like this.
>
> I believe it is mandatory of you to give me the chance of being judged by my peers—the Cabinet and the parliamentary party—the matter must be put to them before any decision is made.
>
> J. F. CAIRNS

In his accompanying press statement Cairns attacked the Prime Minister saying:

> I have asked him to accord me the right of being judged by my peers—the Cabinet and parliamentary party. But although this request

was delivered to him in ample time before he went to see the Governor-General there is no reply. I believe there is extreme injustice in this case in which a Prime Minister has acted against his colleague closest in rank. This is not the way to victory for a Labor government. It is the way to defeat. After so many years of association with the Prime Minister, I feel nothing but extreme regret and sadness about the conclusions I am compelled to reach.

But Cairns' protest was in vain.

As Whitlam had demonstrated throughout the life of his government, once his mind was set on a ministerial change, he proceeded regardless of the consequences and cries of outrage. At the very time Cairns launched his bitter attack on the Prime Minister, the Governor-General Sir John Kerr was stripping him of his ministerial position. Whitlam was sworn in as Environment Minister pending the Labor Party's election of a replacement Minister. That night Cairns, his political career in tatters, left Parliament House by a rear exit with his constant companion Junie Morosi still by his side.

Cairns maintained an almost complete silence on his dismissal until the special parliamentary sitting day on the loans issue, 9 July. During his speech to the House he gave his own explanation of the Harris letter:

> On 7 March I had interviewed George Harris and Leslie Nagy in my office in Melbourne. They asked me to provide them with a letter offering a brokerage fee of two and a half per cent, provided that a loan could be arranged at a total cost of eight per cent. I made it clear to them that a loan could not be arranged under those conditions, that they would be wasting their time if they thought so, and that I would not provide any letter or other document making an offer of this kind. When I answered the question in this House on 4 June 1975 I had this clear recollection. I answered the question in accord with that recollection. This is still my clear and positive recollection of the matter.

At the same time Cairns tabled a statutory declaration from Nagy which substantiated his defence. Nagy made a number of allegations. He said during the meeting Cairns rejected the terms proposed by Harris, offered to give Harris another letter and called in one of his secretaries Karen Stegmar to take shorthand notes. Nagy says that Harris did most of the talking while Cairns objected to a number of points. When the girl was in the outer office typing up the letter, Harris stood next to her and spoke to her. Nagy claims that on two occasions paper was removed from the typewriter and destroyed. When the letter was completed the girl went into Cairns' office with a bundle of letters and returned a few minutes later handing a letter to Harris. Nagy says: 'I was pleasantly surprised at the terms of the letter as I had gained the impression whilst in Dr Cairns' office that he would not concede to most of our requests.' In subsequent interviews Cairns accepted the Nagy version of what had happened.

When the issue became a political controversy Karen Stegmar made her own statutory declaration detailing her recollection of events. According to her recollection, Cairns and Harris debated and argued about the letter for an hour and she was called in towards the end to take a letter which was dictated by both men but mainly Harris. They argued specifically over the two and a half per cent brokerage and, as far as she can remember, this was in the notes she took. When she was typing the letter she checked two points with Harris. She took this letter into Cairns' office for his signature and had it on top of another five or six letters. She said to Cairns: 'Can you sign the Harris letter first, it's on top and he's waiting for it.' Cairns looked at the letter for a few seconds, appeared to read it, and then signed it. But when the letter later became a matter of public controversy, Cairns could not remember approving it. When he spoke to Karen Stegmar by phone at this time he asked her: 'Did I actually sign it?' She assured him that he did.

In his speech to the Parliament Cairns reaffirmed his support for the government's efforts to explore the possibility of loan raisings through non-conventional sources. He stressed that in a wide range of talks with a number of people who approached him he always laid down two basic conditions: first, that the government gave nobody the right to act as its agent and secondly, that there would be no argument in advance to conditions such as interest or brokerage. But the deposed deputy Prime Minister asked Parliament whether he was not entitled to allow private individuals to make inquiries in the light of the December 1974 decision of the Prime Minister and other Ministers to work through Khemlani.

His speech was heard in almost complete silence in the House of Representatives. But what began as a strong and reasoned defence of his position deteriorated into an emotional attack on the media for victimising him and hounding his staff. Cairns alleged the media had spent hundreds of thousands of dollars both in Australia and overseas trying to damage both him and the Labor government. He said the Sydney *Daily Telegraph* had offered a sum increasing from $3000 to $15,000 to his secretary Glenda Bowden to write about his office and his life. He did not mention the articles Junie Morosi had written for *Woman's Day*.

Cairns defended his ministerial staff, the attractive women he had employed, saying they were 'more unfairly misrepresented about this nation than any other people in it'. He also defended the appointment of his stepson Philip to his personal staff, saying that if Philip had tried to use his position for personal gain he would have been dismissed immediately. He pointed out that the Prime Minister had previously dismissed him from the Treasury because of his loan activities with Harris. Cairns said: 'I ask this House: does it consider that I should pay any further penalty? How many Ministers or members are subject to the pressures which have been applied to me?' Several times Cairns told the House that it was true he did wear his heart too easily on his sleeve. He pointed out that he had no reason to disbelieve George Harris at any time when he dealt with him. If the decision of the government was that he should not be a Minister then he would accept it 'because I will not cease to wear my heart on my sleeve'.

Cairns' strong defence of his staff, his office and, by implication, his competence as Treasurer was timely. It was the very point at issue. Whitlam himself left no doubt about his own diagnosis of one of the chief problems. The following week, on 15 July, the Prime Minister announced at a press conference that henceforth he would assume veto powers on the appointment of any person to a Minister's staff. Whitlam said that in future new procedures would apply to all staff positions. Ministers intending to appoint staff would have to ensure they declared their employment history, academic attainments and pecuniary interests to ensure there would not be any conflict of interest situation. The new procedures were in addition to security clearances of ministerial staff by ASIO.

One of the great ironies of the Cairns dismissal was that his son Philip was so prominent. The last time Philip Cairns made the headlines was just after the Labor government was elected to office in December 1972. One of the very first actions for which it came under fire was the appointment by Cairns of his stepson to his staff. It was a story where the seeds of early and minor mistakes were reaped a thousandfold a few years later.

One of the Prime Minister's failures was his reluctance to take a tougher stand earlier with his Ministers on a whole range of issues, from the handing over of loan documents held by Rex Connor to the staff appointments of Jim Cairns. Whitlam's attitude towards his Ministers reflected the caucus structure of the Labor Party where Ministers held office not at the pleasure of the Prime Minister but by a decision of the caucus. Their power base was the party, not the Prime Minister. Throughout the loans controversy Whitlam always insisted that the Ministers involved take full responsibility—but such punishment came after the event, along with great damage for the Government. It was Whitlam's inability to act before the event—by laying down rules, by demanding documents, by checking progress, by controlling staff appointments—that led to so much political upheaval over the loans issue.

One of Cairns' major weaknesses was administration. Quite often he would sign a heap of papers on his desk with disarming speed and have them dispatched when other Ministers might still be examining them. As a result he frequently tended to accept departmental advice, even if that advice was contrary to his publicly known position on certain issues. For instance, when the Foreign Minister Don Willesee wrote to Cairns proposing the closure of trade commissions in South Africa, Cairns wrote back accepting the advice of his own Department and opposed the move. On another occasion he wrote back to Willesee, again accepting the line of his department, rejecting funds to assist refugees from Vietnam. The account of his office given by Ed Shann, a Treasury official who worked there, was that the filing system was not well kept and there were large numbers of loose documents awaiting placement on particular files.

Jim Cairns always reflected the dilemma of the man who, opposed to the system, suddenly found himself running the system. For all his tendency to accept advice on some occasions, on others he would simply go his own way. Every now and then his own odd, individualistic and sometimes charismatic way of doing things would break through the avalanche of paperwork and the bureaucratic straitjacket which over-whelmed him. The cynics labelled these occasions as the ones where nobody else got to him first. This is precisely what happened with the 7 March letter to Harris that led to his sacking. For the final and most amazing fact in an amazing story is that the Treasury discovered the existence of this letter, and warned Cairns about it. But the Treasurer never seemed concerned.

At a meeting on 3 April 1975 between Cairns, Wheeler and two other senior Treasury officials, Daniel and Prowse, Wheeler told Cairns about the letter and urged him to repudiate it as soon as possible in writing. Treasury had found out about the letter through their London representative Dr N W Davey who gave Wheeler the full details on 26 March. Davey was informed by a director of Morgan Grenfells that Harris showed them a copy of the letter signed by Cairns authorising him to seek funds for the Australian government with an undertaking to give him a two and a half per cent commission.

Wheeler presented Cairns with a minute on this subject at the 3 April meeting when Cairns told him that the Harris referred to was George Harris, that he had 'credentials' and that Cairns had told Harris that if he could get funds at less than eight percent 'we would be prepared to talk'. Wheeler's advice to Cairns to withdraw the credentials in writing was not followed.[4]

This omission of the deputy Prime Minister proved to be a charac-teristic and major mistake for him. Whitlam privately told a number of people that he never considered Cairns guilty of ignorance when it came to the letter. But, as Whitlam pointed out, this was not the issue—it was the Treasurer's performance and the fact that he had misled the Parliament.

Cairns was overwhelmed by the job and unable to cope. The final commentary on him comes from Morosi's husband, David Ditchburn: 'Dr Cairns annoys me,' Ditchburn said. 'He needs Morosi for emotional support. She dominates him completely. He is at the end of his career and Morosi is at her peak.'

But Cairns knew there was still a chance he could save his political neck. While his political head had been severed, it had not yet fallen. Whitlam's sacking of his deputy had immediately endangered the fabric of Labor Party unity. As Prime Minister, Whitlam could remove the ministerial commission held by Cairns but he could not remove Cairns as deputy leader of the Labor Party. This was the sole prerogative of the caucus. In the interim, until a caucus decision, Cairns was in the peculiar position of being deputy leader of the Labor Party but on the backbench.

On 3 July, the day after the dismissal, the Prime Minister sent telegrams to all Labor parliamentarians for a party meeting to be held on 14 July to elect a new Minister to replace Cairns and also vote on the proposal to establish an inner Cabinet. This caucus meeting would be vital to Labor's future. It would determine whether the party's unity would be maintained, at least publicly, in the face of the Cairns dismissal, or whether Whitlam's leadership would come under challenge because of his action.

Whitlam's unilateral action had placed him in a difficult position to win caucus endorsement of the Cairns dismissal. Cairns was both deputy leader and an elected member of the caucus executive. The party would have to vote first to vacate his position and then hold two more ballots. One would elect a new deputy leader and the second would elect a new Minister to the vacancy caused by Cairns' removal. The crucial vote in the party room for Whitlam would be the initial one on the motion to declare the deputy leadership vacant. If this vote was not carried then the caucus would effectively repudiate Whitlam's sacking of his deputy by reaffirming Cairns in his position. In these circumstances Whitlam would have two courses of action. He could either recommission Cairns as a Minister or declare the vote one of no confidence in himself and resign as leader.

The second crucial ballot for Whitlam would be the vote to fill the ministerial vacancy—assuming the deputy leadership was vacated. There was always a possibility that Cairns would contest this ballot along with several new ministerial aspirants from the backbench and even get elected. This would leave the Prime Minister in exactly the same dilemma.

Whitlam drew the obvious political conclusion. On Thursday 3 July he delivered what amounted to a public ultimatum to the party by saying that if the caucus confirmed Cairns in the ministry then Whitlam would not commission him. This amounted to a threat to the party to decide between Whitlam as leader and Cairns as deputy leader. It had to be one or the other. This was typical of the brinkmanship which was the hallmark of Whitlam's political style.

By this stage the standing of the Labor government had reached its nadir. The loans controversy had led to the sacking of the deputy Prime Minister, a major split in government ranks, a saturation newspaper coverage which could only lead the public to believe the government was guilty of at least incompetence and perhaps corruption and, at least in the view of wide elements in the media and the Opposition, to the establishment of those reprehensible circumstances that Malcolm Fraser had declared were necessary to force an election.

The Cairns dismissal came just five days after the devastating 28 June rebuff the government had received in the Bass by-election. Indeed, the critical mile posts in the government's downward path, symbolising its decay and the Opposition's strength, were the Bass poll on 28 June, and the Cairns sacking on 2 July.

This was probably the worst week of the Labor government. It suffered damage from which it never recovered either internally or in the public estimate. As the party now pulled together in a desperate effort to re-establish its standing, the chief tests were the 9 July special parliamentary sitting on the loan question, the narrow win of the South Australian Premier, Don Dunstan, in the state election on 12 July, and the Labor Party caucus meeting on 14 July to re-elect a new deputy.

# *17*

## STRUGGLE TIME

*My government's being smeared and it hurts.*

Don Dunstan

**W**hitlam moved quickly to bury the loans issue in the aftermath of the Cairns sacking. After a long debate about tactics, the Prime Minister adopted the risky option of trying to kill off the issue by recalling the House of Representatives for a special one day sitting to table all 'loan' documents and offer a stern wall of defence.

The day after the Cairns sacking, on Thursday 3 July, a council of war was held involving Whitlam, his staff—John Mant, Freudenberg, Michael Delaney and David Solomon—and from the Prime Minister's Department, John Menadue, Geoff Yeend and Brian Johns. Some argued for a royal commission—the line taken by both the Opposition and the media—as the best way to redeem the government's good name.

But Whitlam was dubious about this tactic. The dangers in a royal commission were obvious. The Opposition would hire the best lawyers in the country on a day-by-day basis, producing more and more documents and revelations that would discredit Labor. The shadow of Vladimir Petrov was hanging over these discussions. Whitlam, with his mind's eye on the past, perceived the extent of the public relations disaster that a royal commission could be. He probably realised that the government could not survive a full disclosure of the entire loans controversy. At this stage nobody at the meeting knew the full extent of Connor's activities; how many people he had contacted, and for how long.

The idea of recalling Parliament appealed to Whitlam. It was the forum where he remained supreme. To use one of Whitlam's favourite phrases, the Opposition could 'put up or shut up'. So the special sitting was set for Wednesday 9 July. But there was a catch—the government failed to realise that while it could recall the House, the Opposition could recall the Senate. This is exactly what happened.

Freudenberg and Delaney began work on Whitlam's speech for the sitting. But a fundamental problem remained—to fathom out exactly what Connor had done. The intention had been to table as many documents as possible; to come 'clean' with everything; almost to swamp the media with a paper avalanche. Menadue did most of the work in gathering the papers and deciding what would be tabled. But Menadue and Whitlam had to rely on Connor's word that they had the relevant papers. Whitlam was determined to stand by Connor. But he needed Connor's support to make a credible defence. Menadue and Whitlam's staff were extremely worried about whether Connor would come 'clean' with the Prime Minister. This led Whitlam to secure an assurance from Connor in writing that he had got everything of importance involving the loan effort.

The special sitting was strictly a holding operation for Labor. This was a crucial period for the Prime Minister. The left wing was throwing its support behind Cairns to persuade him to seek re-election to the ministry at the caucus meeting on 14 July. Such a move would be a direct challenge to Whitlam's leadership. Cairns did not have sufficient caucus support in his own right. But there was another way the anti-Whitlam forces inside the party could strengthen their hand. This depended on the outcome of the South Australian state election on Saturday 12 July. If the Dunstan government lost this election, the blame could be laid squarely at the door of the federal government over the loans issue and, according to wide sections of the caucus, at Whitlam's door for bringing the issue to a head by sacking his deputy.

Don Dunstan was the most charismatic political leader in Australia. He stood alone among Labor politicians since the Second World War in implementing the reformist policies of the Labor Party, making them work and receiving popular endorsement for them over a sustained period. Dunstan had transformed South Australia from one of the most conservative states in the federation to the most socially progressive, and his reputation inside the party was unassailable. Dunstan was one of Labor's most precious jewels.

Throughout the early part of 1975 Dunstan had begun looking for an election issue. He had been advised on this by both his own staff and the ALP national secretary David Combe who had climbed to his position through the South Australian branch. In December 1974 Australian Nationwide Opinion Polls (ANOP) conducted a long-term study for the South Australian party as a basis for its electoral planning. Combe then urged Dunstan to go for an election as soon as possible. The research suggested that there was a very big margin, about 14–15 per cent, between Labor's support at the federal and state level in South Australia. But the unpopularity of the federal government would affect Dunstan and hinder his chances the longer he prevaricated.

In an act of ideological dogmatism and political stupidity, the South Australian Liberals played into Dunstan's hands. The issue which precipitated the election was the proposed Commonwealth–state railway agreement in which the federal government would assume control of country railways. Dunstan was delighted with the agreement, which he regarded as one of the best financial deals in South Australia's history. He said that, when parliament approved it, he would be able to abolish the five cents a gallon petrol tax which his government had previously levied to balance its budget. Dunstan said that if the Opposition parties combined in the Upper House to reject the agreement he would call an election. Secretly, the Premier wanted to see the agreement defeated so he could go to the polls.

On Wednesday 18 June the Upper House obliged him. Dunstan was staying at the Lakeside Hotel in Canberra having come to the capital for a Premiers' conference the next day. He conferred with his Cabinet by phone, consulted with Whitlam, and told an impromptu press conference that the state election would be held on 12 July. He expected to be returned and thought the worst possible result would be the loss of one shaky seat, thereby having his majority in the House of Assembly reduced from five to three. But Dunstan's main hope was to break the Opposition's power in the Upper House, the Legislative Council, where the Liberal Party had thirteen members, Labor six and the Liberal Movement one. The Premier was confident of securing ten Labor members out of twenty-one in an expanded Upper House after the election, with the Liberal Movement holding the balance of power.

The strength of Dunstan's position, given the poor standing of federal Labor, was a remarkable tribute to his abilities as a politician. But not even Dunstan had bargained on the media's hue and cry during the course of his state campaign over the sensational loan revelations, the sacking of Cairns, and the calling of the special one day sitting of federal parliament. Day after day the Premier could barely get onto the front page of the Adelaide *Advertiser* which was saturated, as were all other papers, with the loans saga. The state Liberal leader Dr Eastick began to campaign solely on federal issues, arguing that a vote for Dunstan was a vote for federal Labor.

By early July Dunstan was in trouble because of developments in Canberra. If caucus met two days after Dunstan's defeat at the polls to vote on the Cairns sacking then anything, absolutely anything, could happen. There was already a strong residue of hostility towards Whitlam from the South Australian party following the ruthlessness of his axing of Clyde Cameron from the labour ministry.

Fortunately for Whitlam the 9 July loans sitting was an anti-climax. While a number of important documents were tabled, they represented only a minority of those held by Rex Connor on the loans affair. The Prime Minister used all his forensic skill and debating bluff to carry the government through. Whitlam ignored or brushed aside all the chief criticisms from the Opposition: that the Executive Council minute of 13 December was an attempt to circumvent the Constitution and the states by use of the 'temporary purposes' formula to avoid seeking Loan Council approval; that the government had destroyed Australia's reputation as an international borrower; that it had displayed incredible stupidity and naivety in using Khemlani as an intermediary; and that its proposals for $4000 million worth of development projects were an economic pipedream. Fortunately for Whitlam, Cairns delivered an over-emotional speech which was counter-productive to his political interests.

The Opposition parties moved to initiate a new inquiry when the Senate endorsed a motion from Reg Withers to call eleven of Australia's leading public servants, including the Treasury head Sir Frederick Wheeler, the head of the Minerals and Energy Department, Sir Lenox Hewitt, and the head of the Attorney-General's Department, Clarrie Harders, before the bar of the Senate to question them about the loans affair. But Whitlam would have none of this. The government instructed all the public servants to claim privilege and to refuse to answer questions from the Senate. This was a direct confrontation between the parliamentary and executive wings of the government in which the executive prevailed when the public servants, after being called by the Senate, obeyed their ministerial instructions and refused to comment. Whitlam had pulled the curtain down on the loans affair as hard as possible and he was determined not to let it up again.

Combe went to Adelaide for the South Australian campaign and was alarmed at Dunstan's electoral situation about ten days out. At this time Labor was facing the prospect of defeat. Combe proposed that the federal party pay for a series of 'call-backs' which ANOP could do on its original study, to devise tactics in the remainder of the campaign. The research drew three main conclusions: first, there was a significant shift away from Labor; second, that the state government was the recipient of hostility generated by the federal government; and third, that most people believed the only question was not whether Dunstan would win but how much his margin of victory would be. The risk was that voters, assuming Dunstan would be re-elected, would vote against him.

The party drew two conclusions from the results. First, to convince the public that Dunstan's government was in grave danger, and second, to distance Dunstan from the federal government. A number of prominent state Ministers, including the Transport Minister Geoff Virgo, the deputy Premier Des Corcoran, and the Mines and Energy Minister Hugh Hudson, all wanted to attack the Whitlam government. But while they were too hawkish, Dunstan in turn appeared to be too soft.

On the afternoon of Monday 7 July, the start of the last week of the campaign, Dunstan changed his strategy completely and preparations were made for the Premier to record two new advertisements. In both, Dunstan warned that his government was being smeared by his opponents. He said that the state Labor government was in no way responsible for the mistakes made by the Whitlam government in Canberra. He reaffirmed that the 12 July poll was a vote for South Australia and not for Australia as a whole or for Canberra.

Dunstan rang Whitlam to explain that the campaign strategy was being altered and that it directly implied criticism of the federal government, in order to disassociate the state government from the hostile attitude towards Canberra. Whitlam said he understood the change of tactics and appreciated Dunstan contacting him.

The thirty-second advertisement was the most powerful—with its text reproduced in papers as well as run on radio and television. The longer advertisement dealt with a list of Dunstan's achievements and then towards the end began to 'off-load' the federal government.

The election result was a cliff-hanger. Labor held 23 seats compared with the combined Opposition parties who also totalled 23 seats (Liberals 20, Country Party 1 and Liberal Movement 2). The balance of power was held by the independent member for Port Pirie, G E Connelly, who later rejoined the Labor Party. The Dunstan government had scraped back into office by the skin of its teeth.

The South Australian win not only returned Dunstan to office but was crucial for Whitlam as well. The caucus gathered two days later to re-elect a new deputy Prime Minister and confirm Whitlam's decision to sack his deputy. On the eve of the meeting the ACTU and ALP president Bob Hawke openly condemned Whitlam for his ministerial veto on Jim Cairns. Hawke claimed that Whitlam had to accept any decision by the party to restore Cairns to the ministry saying: 'The caucus is supreme not Mr Whitlam'.

The two logical front-runners for the deputy leadership, the Treasurer Bill Hayden and the Minister for Manufacturing Industry Lionel Bowen, both declined to run. Hayden did not want the job; Bowen knew he could not win it. The contest was a race between two of Labor's old guard, the Education Minister Kim Beazley and the Overseas Trade Minister Frank Crean. In an unusual move on the eve of the caucus ballot, Whitlam entertained the entire party at the Lodge for supper from 7 to 10 p.m. on the Sunday. A number of left-wing members staged a boycott of the function.

The party room debate was marked by a direct confrontation between Whitlam and Cairns. The Prime Minister outlined the sequence of events concerning Cairns' letters to Harris and referred to the Auditor-General's investigation of Philip Cairns. Cairns in turn made a lengthy defence of himself. He said Whitlam had placed the party in a difficult position and had refused to allow it to make a free choice. He said Whitlam should have come to the caucus first before he had dismissed his deputy. But instead of that, he had acted unilaterally and put the party in the position of having to accept his decision or repudiate it. Cairns said that in these circumstances it was impossible that justice could be done, let alone appear to be done. He appealed to the party to try to make a free choice to resist the pressures applied by the Prime Minister. Cairns said that he had always answered questions in parliament honestly and if he had ever misled parliament it was never deliberate. He was supported by Doug Everingham, Moss Cass, Tom Uren and Queensland Senators George Georges and Jim Keeffe.

Whitlam spoke first, followed by Cairns and then a number of his supporters. Both Everingham and Cass called on the Prime Minister to retract his 'Cairns or me' declaration and allow his former deputy a place in the ministry. When Whitlam summed up the debate, he raised the question of Philip Cairns' activities in Fiji and said that he had been negotiating with the Fijian government without Whitlam's approval. But at no stage of the meeting did Whitlam reaffirm his veto over Cairns. Towards the end Senator Georges called out to Whitlam to clarify his attitude on this crucial point but the chairman of caucus Senator Bill Brown ruled the question out of order.

The vital caucus vote on Whitlam's motion to declare the deputy leadership of the party vacant was carried on the hands 55–33. The former Treasurer Frank Crean won a lacklustre ballot for the deputy leadership by defeating Kim Beazley 47–33 after preferences were distributed. The contest was one between two 'caretaker deputies', neither of whom was regarded as potential successors to Whitlam. Crean, obviously enjoying his endorsement by the party following his humiliation at the hands of the Prime Minister the previous year, told a press conference his job would be to improve teamwork and communication in the government. He endorsed Hawke's criticism of Whitlam for his one-man style of government.

Nine backbenchers stood for the ministerial vacancy, including Jim Cairns who fought to the very end to regain his place at the risk of defying Whitlam's authority. Cairns received a solid core of left-wing votes but the anti-Cairns (pro-Whitlam) vote proved too strong. One of the most capable backbenchers in the party, Joe Berinson from Western Australia, was elected to the vacancy at his fifth try and was appointed Environment Minister, the portfolio previously held by Cairns. Berinson received nineteen of the twenty-two preferences from NSW candidate Paul Keating after Keating's elimination, thereby assuring his election.

With the successful negotiation of the loans sitting day, the preservation of the Dunstan government, and the avoidance of a major party upheaval over the Cairns sacking, the Labor Party had survived the most dangerous period of its existence. Although its electoral position was still appallingly low and offered a permanent temptation to Malcolm Fraser to force an election according to his whim, Whitlam and a number of his senior Ministers were still confident the government could pull through. Whitlam believed the worst was over. Labor now turned to the task of devising a sound and responsible budget with Hayden as Treasurer. But, despite Whitlam's confidence, Labor was not to recover from the loans affair or from the electoral damage that it had visited upon the Government.

# *18*

## THE BUDGET AND REPLY

*The age of 'me-tooism' in Australian politics has ended.*

Allan Barnes in the *Age*, 18 August 1975

From the Bass by-election huge pressures mounted throughout the coalition parties for an early election. The National Country Party was committed to blocking the budget and forcing an election. The Liberal Party organisation, state branches, strong elements in the Liberal frontbench and the parliamentary party were all in favour of an early poll. But nothing could be decided and the assessments could not begin until Labor's new Treasurer Bill Hayden introduced the 1975–76 budget. This was the budget which would have to be blocked and the instrument through which an election would be forced by denying supply. The content of the budget would therefore be crucial in deciding the political repercussions involved in denying it to the people in return for an election.

Unlike the previous year, the government had both a clear economic strategy and machinery established through which it could be effected. The process by which the Hayden budget was produced, in comparison to the previous year's budget, was a measure of the extent to which Labor had come to terms with government.

In early 1975 Menadue had impressed upon Whitlam the need for a new Cabinet committee which would be the vehicle for reducing government spending. In February the Prime Minister announced the formation of the Expenditure Review Committee of Cabinet comprising the Prime Minister, his deputy, the Treasurer, the Minister for Social Security, the Labour Minister and the Minister for Urban and Regional

Development. Throughout 1975, Cabinet submissions involving the spending of funds were cleared first through this committee and went to the full Cabinet with a recommendation. This Cabinet committee was serviced by a committee of officials which, in the prelude to the budget, was given the job of recommending large-scale cutbacks throughout the public sector. The budget strategy, based on the need to restrain the government sector and stimulate the private sector as the first step in a gradual recovery, was the natural product of over six months of effort.

Before the full Cabinet met to discuss the budget, the Expenditure Review Committee held a week of meetings in which it drew up two main options. One was for spending cuts designed to give a budget deficit of $2780 million; the second was a much tougher program, resulting in a deficit of about $1000 million less than this. Before the budget talks, Hayden told the Cabinet that more than $2500 million would have to be pruned from spending programs of federal Ministers and that a budget with a deficit around $2500 million was desirable.

It was only as a result of work by the Expenditure Review Committee that the Labor government was able to make substantial inroads into the public sector and successfully reduce the spending programs of its 27 Ministers. During the week of budget discussions in late July, the tough line pushed by the Expenditure Review Committee Ministers, notably Hayden and McClelland, carried the day. In most spending areas the increase in government outlays was less than the inflation rate. Defence increased 10.6 per cent, education 14.2 per cent, social security 30 per cent, urban and regional development 18 per cent, while funds on housing declined by 10 per cent. The major new increase in the public sector was for the Medibank scheme.

The knife taken to the public sector meant a big scaling down in outlays to schools, colleges and universities, and the 1976 year saw the deferral of the triennial programs in the education area. Pensions were tied to rises in the consumer price index rather than wage movements, thereby dampening the level of their increases. Abolition of the means test was deferred for those aged 65 to 69. A ceiling on public service growth was put at an operational level of 1.5 per cent in the coming year and administrative savings were implemented through requiring members of parliament and public servants to travel economy class not first class on air flights. Tight restrictions were placed on the use of government cars, overseas travel and office equipment to point to the government's bona fides in this area.

The receipts side of the budget was prepared in talks between only three Cabinet Ministers, Whitlam, Crean and Hayden. Unlike the previous budget, the government was able to maintain secrecy on its taxation changes. In order to keep the deficit to a reasonable level, big increases in indirect taxes were approved in the most politically damaging part of the budget and also one which would fan inflation. Duty on beer rose by the equivalent of four cents a glass, on cigarettes by about six cents an average packet and on spirits by about one cent a nip. A decision to levy $2 per barrel on the production of crude oil meant an almost immediate rise in petrol of more than six cents a gallon. At the same time a new export duty was imposed on coal at the rate of $6 per tonne on coking coal and $2 per tonne on steaming coal—the work of Treasury, not Rex Connor, who later got the steaming coal duty abolished. Company tax was reduced by 2.5 per cent to 42.5 per cent.

The budget's innovation lay in the reforms to the personal income tax system, which involved the government's acceptance of the recommendations of the Asprey Committee to alter the tax scales to reduce the excessive marginal rates of taxation. Hayden called it 'perhaps the most revolutionary change' since Australia's inception of that system. The existing system of concessional deductions for private expenditure on health, education, insurance and dependants was replaced by a flat minimum rebate of $540. For a spouse the rebate was set at $400; for children at $200 for the first child under 16 and $150 for other children. The previous system depended on the notion of taxable income which was obtained by subtracting the value of various concessional deductions such as insurance, medical costs and so on from total income. Under the Hayden system, tax was paid on total income. If this tax totalled $1000 then an individual with no dependants could simply claim a basic rebate of $540 and actually pay $460 tax. This represented a sweeping change in Australia's tax system.

Hayden said the two chief advantages of the new tax system were the reduction in the marginal tax rate and a more equitable system of taxation deductions. In summary the system meant 500,000 people would be freed from tax entirely, about three million wage earners on average incomes would have an extra $5 a week and that taxpayers with dependants would be favoured over those without them. Those people paying more tax would be married couples without children who were both working, single people claiming a high rate of non-dependant deductions, and wealthy people with few or no dependants.

The tax reforms were the work of a small committee set up by Hayden and headed by Professor Trevor Swan from the ANU. Besides Swan, the other guiding force on the committee was a senior official, Daryl Dixon. Dixon was well aware of the views of the ACTU industrial advocate, Rob Jolly, that unless the present tax scales were reformed the trade union movement would reject indexation. The Swan committee had two essential choices—the Mathews committee report which called for full personal income tax indexation or the Asprey committee report which recommended new tax scales to reduce marginal tax rates. The committee eventually came up with the compromise of the Asprey report combined with the rebate system.

Swan argued that the existing forms of taxation deductions were of no help to poor people. Being unable to afford extensive expenditure on insurance and other items they received hardly any deduction. Moreover, as Whitlam constantly pointed out, the higher one's income the greater the taxation deduction one received. Swan and Dixon won the support of the Secretary of the Treasury Sir Frederick Wheeler for their tax package. But Treasury was by no means unanimous and senior officers such as John Stone and Bill Cole were very dubious about the proposals. But the group secured the support of the deputy secretary of the Prime Minister's Department, Ian Castles, who sold the idea to John Menadue who in turn convinced Whitlam. The tax reforms became the chief reform of the budget and the main political weapon for Whitlam and Hayden.

In both his budget speech and address to the National Press Club the following day, Hayden said there were tentative signs of economic recovery and the government's strategy was to find a middle way—'a line along which we can achieve sound and sustainable growth while at the same time bringing inflation down gradually over perhaps two or three years.' This is the most precise summary of the Hayden strategy. For success it needed two vital commodities, both of which were likely to be in short supply to the Labor government—time and goodwill.

But, as most commentators accepted and as the Opposition privately admitted, the budget had the stamp of responsibility. It would give no help to the Opposition parties if they decided to block the budget and could well create new political problems for them. The deficit in the Hayden budget, which later became the focus of so much controversy, was $2797 million overall, based on a growth in spending of 22.9 per cent (half that of 1974–75) equivalent to 30.5 per cent of GDP.

On 11 August, just over a week before the budget was delivered, the Opposition leadership assembled with advisers, academics and businessmen to review the economy and prepare a coherent economic strategy. This meeting was vital in the subsequent economic policy adopted by Malcolm Fraser. It was attended by Fraser, Anthony, Lynch, Sinclair, Cotton, Harry Edwards, Garland, Street, Nixon, Peacock and others. Academics included Professor Warren Hogan from Sydney University and Professor Don Whitehead from La Trobe University, along with an academic economist Ainslie Jolly from Lynch's office. A number of businessmen were present including Rod Carnegie, chairman and managing director of CRA, and David Block, Sydney businessman and member of the Mathews committee. The meeting, organised by the Liberal Party secretariat, included Tony Eggleton and Ian Marsh from the secretariat and advisers, Stephen Vaughan from Fraser's office,

Andrew Hay from Lynch's office, and Michael Baume, the endorsed Liberal candidate for the seat of Macarthur.

There was extensive discussion of the Mathews committee report at this meeting. The Labor government had set up the committee in December 1974 under Professor Russell Mathews from the ANU. Its task was to examine the effect of inflation on the level of taxation paid by individuals and to assess the merits and practicability of tax indexation. The terms of reference on the personal tax side were quite sweeping.

But the committee had a second paragraph in its terms of reference. This was added chiefly at the instigation of Jim Spigelman, then Whitlam's private secretary, after talking with a business colleague, David Block. As a result of these talks Spigelman became convinced of the need for a thorough review of the company tax provisions and he was responsible for adding the second paragraph in the terms of reference. This paragraph was quite specific and asked the committee to examine other ways of valuing company stock for taxation. Although he did not know it at the time, Spigelman was giving the Opposition parties a massive kick along with their economic policy and political platform.

The Mathews committee report in May 1975 claimed that the private sector in Australia was in a state of economic crisis and recommended indexation of taxes at both personal and company level. But the government claimed the cost was too great to accept the recommendations. At the 11 August meeting Carnegie and Block argued persuasively on the need to implement the Mathews committee recommendations, particularly on the company tax side. This meeting was important in convincing Fraser and Lynch that the Mathews recommendations, quite apart from their economic merits, had the strong support of the business sector. They saw both economic and political advantages in accepting them. Lynch's office, particularly Jolly and Hay, were advocates of the Mathews proposals. Fraser himself was determined to ensure that the restoration of business confidence was given top priority in the Opposition's economic policy. The meeting broke up with no clear conclusions but with the Liberal leadership giving qualified endorsement to the Mathews committee recommendations.

The Opposition found the Hayden budget more difficult to attack than it had expected. Hayden had made substantial inroads into the public sector and also moved to ease the tax burden. Fraser's initial response was to damn the budget as vigorously as possible and he claimed that the changes to the system of taxation deductions would only destroy incentive by discouraging individuals towards self-help.

Fraser and Lynch now began to formulate their budget reply. Lynch's office prepared a draft which backed the full Mathews proposals for personal income and company tax while making deep cuts in government spending. Fraser's initial response was to keep his options open. But Lynch's office argued that this was the time for the Opposition to take a firm attitude. Both Warren Hogan and Michael Baume, a former director of Patrick Partners, also endorsed the Mathews proposals. So Fraser shifted his ground and agreed to deliver a detailed speech that would commit the Opposition parties to tax indexation. Fraser also decided, on his own initiative, that the Opposition should spell out where it would cut government spending.

Fraser's budget reply on 26 August was his most important policy statement as Opposition Leader. His election campaign speech, delivered two months later, originated with the ideas accepted in this reply. It was the most comprehensive reply to a budget in Australia's history. At this point Fraser put into practice his repeated claim that he wanted to win power on his own positive merits and not on sufferance. This speech was a landmark for the Liberal Party and represented a massive change of strategy compared with the Bass by-election. In Bass Fraser made virtually no promises. Now he pledged himself to an economic blueprint which would commit the Liberal Party during the full three years of its first term. Moreover this blueprint was a radical departure for Australian governments or the Liberal Party.

Fraser promised to implement tax indexation for both individuals and companies, the essence of the Mathews report. He said this would be done over a three-year period with the first start in a new budget. The Mathews committee estimated the cost of these proposals, at present prices, as $2500 million. In his budget speech Hayden said the government could not even consider them because of the cost. Fraser also called for an extra $500 million cut in income tax on top of those in the Hayden budget and special incentives to the private sector, which would cost another $500 million.

In identifying public sector cuts Fraser said there should be a zero growth rate on the commonwealth public service. Savings would stem from the abolition of the Media Department, the Prices Justification Tribunal, the Australian Legal Aid Office, the Australia Police, as well as special economies in the Department of Urban and Regional Development. He foreshadowed suspension of advances to the AIDC and the Australian Housing Corporation, the Pharmaceutical Corporation would be sold, the Overseas Trading Corporation and the Australian Government Insurance Corporation abolished, the National Capital Development Commission cut back, employment training schemes would be means tested, the regional growth centre program abolished and uranium exploration by the Australian Atomic Energy Commission abandoned.

While Fraser said this would produce economies of $1000 million, the federal Treasury could only find savings of $560 million when asked for an analysis by Hayden. So Fraser would have to cut back much further. But, even beyond this, he would have to maintain similar cutbacks for the next three years to introduce the Mathews committee report.

The principles which Fraser accepted amounted to a detailed radical program of economic change that not only struck at the political philosophy of the Labor government but was significantly different from the prescriptions of the federal Treasury. It was also a clear departure from the direction, if not the rhetoric, of former Liberal–Country Party governments. From his luxurious position as political front-runner, Fraser could have afforded to stand aloof and refused to commit himself. But he took the opposite course and chose to commit himself to the hilt to prove his mettle.

His reply was a clever political document. But it also contained risks—the risks of cutting off options. Fraser successfully upstaged Labor by his decisive support of tax indexation, which had been demanded by both the trade union movement and the private sector. It meant that Fraser could legitimately say that the Liberal Party, rather than the Labor Party, was in accord with the demands of the trade union movement on the fundamental question of indexation of taxes, which the unions said was necessary for the long-term survival of wage indexation.

Fraser rejected the classic political practice which both Liberal and Labor governments had used over the previous fifteen to twenty years to win votes. This was the interest group technique. One of the features of the Whitlam era was the fostering of community and pressure groups which pitched their demands to the government and in turn received both funds and support for their activities. One of the chief reasons for Labor's ascension to office was that it won the backing of a whole series of interest groups, teachers, pensioners, consumers, artists, academics, migrants, working mothers and working women, public servants and a number of small groups who saw benefits for themselves through Labor's platform. To all appearances Fraser only followed this specific approach in respect of business and the rural sector.

In return for the massive boost to the private sector with tax cuts and indexation for individuals and companies, along with the restoration of subsidies for the business and farming communities, a Fraser government would have to hit the public sector harder than it had ever been cut before.

These commitments by Fraser in August 1975 are the origin of the major dilemmas which confront him in government. For he has been elected to power, although the public never recognised this, on a truly radical program involving a major redistribution of wealth more far-reaching than that proposed by Whitlam in December 1972. To implement this program will require both extensive political skill and courage, as well as effective communication with the electorate. Fraser confirmed that he would lead the party in different directions from his predecessor Bill Snedden. He was reversing the well-established political practice of the Liberals in expanding the government sector and winning the votes of the public through this process. One has only to look at the expansion in the commonwealth public service under both Gorton and McMahon to grasp the break with the past.

In August 1975 Fraser was in a situation where the economic prescriptions offered to him coincided with his own political bias towards small government. He was putting into operation the principles he had espoused at the National Press Club in Canberra on 31 July. On this occasion he said: 'I do not see the next Liberal government as restoring the pre-1972 status quo. There is no going back in politics . . . whatever have been the failings of the past, they should not be seen as setting a pattern for future Liberal governments.' On his own admission Fraser aspired to lead the party in different directions from Holt, Gorton, McMahon and Snedden.

The budget reply Fraser devised in August 1975 gave the Australian public a real choice at the next election between two parties offering quite different programs and solutions in fundamentally different spirits. Fraser was fulfilling the logic of his background and hardening the choices and sharpening the contrasts in Australian politics. The age of me-tooism in Australian political affairs was over for some time.

# PART IV

# THE CRISIS

# *19*

# FRASER'S DECISION

*At this stage it's our intention to allow the budget passage through the Senate.*

Malcolm Fraser, 21 August 1975

Two days after the Hayden budget, Malcolm Fraser gave the strongest possible indication that it would be passed. Beneath the bluster of his political attacks this was the unmistakable message Fraser conveyed to both the press and the public. After the budget was delivered, Fraser conferred with the Opposition leadership group including Anthony, Lynch, Withers, Sinclair, Nixon, Greenwood and Cotton. On 21 August the Opposition Leader was interviewed on the ABC by Richard Carleton. Fraser said of the budget: 'At this stage it would be our intention to allow it a passage through the Senate.' His announcement was clearly premeditated and he read from notes during part of the interview, being very careful about the precise words used.

Fraser's intention was to kill off speculation that the Opposition might try to force an early election by blocking the budget. It was in the interests of the Opposition parties that any decision on an election should be kept secret until the time of execution. In this sense the move was a sound political tactic regardless of whatever course Fraser later followed.

'I'm not one of those who believe that any means are justified by the ends,' Fraser said in the interview. 'I think the way things are done are just as important as what is done and that's one of the great criticisms I've got of the present government . . . just taking a grab for something isn't a way to go about business in politics.'

These comments were similar to the remarks Fraser made the day he was elected Liberal leader. They were to haunt him throughout the rest of the year, particularly when the Opposition eventually decided to force an election by blocking the budget. But on the evening of 21 August it appeared that Fraser was seriously thinking that the budget should be passed. He appeared relaxed after making the announcement, as though a weight had been taken from his mind. That night press secretary David Barnett indicated clearly to senior correspondents that Fraser's thinking was that the budget should pass.

A major factor in the Opposition Leader's mind at this stage was the technical difficulty in getting an early election. Fraser was worried that the Labor government would hold up the introduction of the budget so a vote was not taken until late November. This meant that after the normal five or six week interval before an election, January would be the earliest possible date. But, because of the practical difficulties involved in holding an election at this time, the earliest polling day would be in mid-February and temporary supply would be needed until this date. Most newspapers played up Fraser's comments after conferring with his office and the next day's headlines announced the election threat had been called off.

A number of senior Liberals believed the Opposition should wait until autumn 1976 and use the Labor government's Supply Bills to force the election they wanted, the same way Snedden had done in May 1974. At this stage it was widely accepted within the Liberal Party, particularly among House of Representatives members, that the real question was not whether Fraser would force an election but when. They claimed the very weakness of the government's electoral position made an early election, before Labor's three-year term expired, almost inevitable. On this day, 21 August, the much-heralded election threat appeared to have been postponed, not repudiated.

Doug Anthony, however, was determined to make sure the issue was kept alive. The National Country Party wanted an election and Anthony had made this clear to Fraser, pointing out that the party was confident of making gains for the coalition in the countryside. The same day that reports of Fraser's comments appeared in the press, Anthony indicated the qualifications contained in those comments and asserted that the question was still an open one. This was the opening shot of a campaign before the campaign. The next seven weeks comprised a series of political skirmishes in which the Opposition sought to establish solid justification for budget rejection.

But while the Opposition prevaricated, the Prime Minister launched what became known as 'the strategy of survival'. On 2 September Whitlam told the party room: 'With Snedden I was impatient; with Fraser I am being patient,' in a cheery reminder that he still remained Australia's best political executioner. Whitlam sought to exploit the psychological impact of the budget within the Labor Party. In the short term, the budget had restored hope to a previously demoralised Labor caucus. Under the spearhead of the Prime Minister, the desperation that had pervaded the government benches a few short weeks previously had given way to a grim determination to survive.

Whitlam set his heart on changing the image, if not the nature, of his administration. The policy was one of battening down the hatches to ensure that Fraser found no sudden trip-wire which he could label 'reprehensible' and manipulate as the rationale to spring an election. For the first time during his Prime Ministership, Whitlam embraced the need for consolidation and told his colleagues: 'It has taken us nearly three years to learn how to govern. But we have learnt.'

The mood of the party was to close ranks and avoid any damaging confrontations, either among Ministers or between the Cabinet and caucus. The economic strategy in the budget, based on the premise that Labor's programs must be sacrificed in an effort to control inflation, became dominant. While the spirit of reformism was not dead—the tax reforms in the budget proved this—it was thoroughly in check, with a moratorium on new government initiatives requiring money.

Whitlam himself remained as irrepressibly optimistic as ever. He was resorting to his old election technique of psyching himself into a winning position as a prelude to psyching others into the same frame of mind. While his standing within the party was diminished, it still remained unrivalled. During this period Whitlam sought to increase his public appearances and carefully picked the issues on which to attack Fraser. He was given valuable political capital when both Fraser and Anthony put the pro-communist tag on Fretilin, the independence party in East Timor. Whitlam warned that nothing was more calculated to encourage Indonesian intervention. The government also exploited to the hilt reported remarks by the Opposition spokesman on social security Don Chipp that Medibank would be disbanded when the Liberals came to power. Fraser heavily censured Chipp for what he regarded as a major political blunder and from this time on resolved to dump the Victorian from the front bench.

Whitlam was now in a similar political position to that of February–March earlier in the year when he was faced with an election threat from Snedden but on that occasion he had had one great asset which was now missing: an Opposition Leader whose position was under challenge.

The Prime Minister's political approach was highlighted in an interview with Richard Carleton on 28 August, in which he announced he would hold the next half-Senate election in May or June 1976, conveying a 'business as usual' message. Whitlam declared he would have no trouble with Fraser on the hustings. 'Give me a campaign and I'll beat him or anybody else the Liberals put up,' he said. While such comments bordered on foolish bravado, they were also an important element in Whitlam's efforts to present his government as strong, confident and on the way back. Whitlam predicted there would be no early election, saying Malcolm Fraser had a better sense of propriety than his predecessors and realised that when he was in power the same weapon could be turned against him. Whitlam stressed the importance of preserving the three-year term of an elected government and declared that the present Labor Cabinet was 'very much better as the result of the changes that I made'.

Fraser's dilemma centred on the constitutional propriety and long-term political consequences involved in forcing an election by blocking the budget in the Senate. The Opposition had taken unprecedented action in this direction the previous year when it precipitated the 18 May double dissolution election by refusing to pass Labor's Supply Bills in the Senate. A repetition of that decision would confirm it as an acceptable political tactic and would have an enduring impact on the future of democratic government in Australia. It would open the way for the Senate to force the elected government to the people on two separate occasions each year when the government sought supply funds for its program. This would insert a new element of instability into the political system, the future impact of which would be difficult to assess. Having been used by one party against another, it would undoubtedly become a feature of the system.

Fraser spoke often about the importance of the principle that elected governments should serve a three-year term. But while he regarded this principle highly, he always believed there were other factors to be taken into account and that it was not an over-riding concept. Probably the best summary of his views was given in an interview with the author in August 1975. When questioned about his attitude towards the convention, Fraser replied: 'To speak as a political philosopher for a moment I think the convention is important. But ultimately the survival of Australia is the only thing that matters and it's not a convention that's been preserved inviolate over the years.' In short, Fraser believed that, if the government were sufficiently bad, the Opposition was justified in forcing it to the people.

From late August Malcolm Fraser, despite his statements on the Carleton program, began to talk and act like a man searching for election issues.

On 28 August the Liberal Party's federal executive met in Canberra. The Liberals were enthusiastic about Fraser's budget reply, which was well received by local branches and business groups. Fraser stressed the technical problems involved in an early election, particularly over the setting of a polling day. But he was anxious to get feedback from each state division and went around the table with all state presidents reporting.

The most hawkish state was Queensland, with good reasons in view of the electoral position in the north. The Queensland president John Moore said he believed the coalition could win five of the six Labor seats in the state. The only doubtful seat was Oxley held by Bill Hayden. Moore said there would be strong support from Queensland for an early poll. He could not see problems with a backlash against it. The Tasmanian president Don Wing said his state was completely operational for an election campaign and, in the light of the Bass by-election result, believed it could win the remaining four Labor seats in Tasmania. Wing said there would be strong support from Tasmania for an early election.

The South Australian president Trevor Griffin said there was a favourable climate in his state, one of Labor's strongest areas, and pointed out that support for the federal government was a lot lower than support for the Dunstan government. The party expected to win one seat, Kingston, and possibly another one, Grey. The situation in NSW looked good. The party secretary in that state Jim Carlton believed the Liberals could win four seats in NSW: Cook, Barton, Evans and Phillip. On Carlton's assessment there were another four doubtfuls which they might win, Macquarie, Macarthur, St George and Eden–Monaro. Carlton himself was opposed to an early poll forced on the budget, mainly because of the propriety and practical consequences of such an action. But the NSW president John Atwill gave qualified support for an early election from the outset and became more certain as events unfolded.

The Victorian president Peter Hardie missed this meeting and was represented by Victoria's country vice-president Joy Mein. Victoria was the division strongly opposed to any election on the budget and expressed no support for the idea at this meeting. The West Australian division took an optimistic view of the electoral position and believed that in any campaign Labor was likely to lose two or three seats—Tangney, Swan and Kalgoorlie.

Overall it was a 'gung-ho' mood. Most divisions wanted an election because they could smell victory and Fraser was left in no doubt that the result would be a foregone conclusion. Only Victoria was seriously wary. Of the two coalition parties the National Country Party was even more certain of its ground than the Liberals. On 4 September Anthony became the third party leader in succession to appear on the Carleton program and he tipped a bucket of petrol on the early election fires. Anthony said he supported the form of words Fraser had previously used and commented: 'That gives plenty of scope to take other action if circumstances should warrant it.' Anthony went on:

> I think there is a very strong feeling throughout the community that there ought to be an election and that the only way to do it would be

by opposing the budget. There is certainly a groundswell developing
and I don't think anybody can deny that . . . I personally want to get
rid of this government as soon as it's practical to do so. But . . . it
would be quite unwise to push for an election if you didn't have the
support of the electorate.'

But Anthony did not let matters rest there. He argued that there
was a sense in which the Opposition parties had a direct responsibility
to force an election: 'I think there is a degree of lack of responsibility
on the part of the Opposition if it doesn't act with the powers that are
given to it under the constitution, if it thinks it can correct the circumstances of Australians who are being hurt by the ineptitude and the
mess that the present government's creating.'

Anthony's position throughout this period was one of continuing
pressure for an early election. While ever Labor was in office there was
always a danger of it passing an electoral redistribution to weaken the
power base and parliamentary strength of the Country Party. Anthony
knew that Labor could only lose ground in country areas at any election.
But he wanted to avoid repeating the mistake of 1974 when the Liberals
failed to make gains in the cities. Anthony's comments set the mood
which dominated federal politics in the next six weeks. He had given
the early election a momentum which it never lost.

His comments reduced Fraser's 'form of words' on 21 August to
tatters. The early election question now became a matter of constant
debate and review, in the press, in the parliament and in the electorate.
This helped to create an atmosphere which poisoned personal relations
and set in train forces which would undermine the institution of parliament itself.

Fraser now hit the warpath. On 10 September he tabled a letter in
federal parliament from Hayden to Whitlam which had been leaked to
him. The letter mentioned the possibility that early appropriation might
be needed to cover both the Regional Employment Development (RED)
Scheme and Medibank following the entry into the scheme of some
non-Labor states. Although the letter was purely of administrative
import, Fraser maintained both publicly and privately it showed the
Hayden budget was shonky. Some Liberals privately claimed that this
might even be an 'extraordinary circumstance'. On Monday 15 September, interviewed for the 0–10 Network by Bill D'Arcy, Fraser went on
to say he believed that speculation about an early election could encourage business confidence because businessmen might think there was
going to be a change of government. He then confused his original
position even more in the following exchange:

Question: You are still in favour of the present government running
its full term?

Answer:   I don't think that can be said, no, because the government is so unpredictable. Nobody knows what's going to happen. There could be another loans affair, they might get rid of another Treasurer . . . I believe really that the sooner there can be responsibility returned to government, the better. But you've got to balance that against the constitutional practices, or the conventional practices which have generally determined how long governments will last.

Fraser went to Queensland on 22–23 September, visiting Brisbane and Rockhampton on what was billed by the local Liberal Party as 'the first shot in the coming election campaign'. He used this trip to both assess and encourage grassroot support for an early election. Addressing a big rally in King George Square, Brisbane, Fraser widened his election options completely. He told a large crowd that the Prime Minister, in seeking a definite statement of intention from the Opposition, was asking for a blank cheque: 'We would not give Mr Whitlam a blank cheque for one day, let alone for two months. How could we when his credit is so low?'

The next day in Rockhampton Fraser got an even stronger response, addressing six hundred people at a street meeting in Labor's remaining Queensland stronghold. He said he was finding right around Australia 'very large numbers of people are asking me to hold an early election', and that after two days in Queensland he believed there was a reasonable majority who wanted an election as soon as possible, 'maybe an overwhelming majority'. Obviously testing the Queensland climate he called to the crowd: 'How many of you want Labor to continue?' drawing only a few isolated calls. But he was greeted with loud cheers of approval in response to the question: 'How many want them dismissed?'

After the rally John Moore drove Fraser to the airport to catch his plane. From the time of this two-day visit to the northern state, the Queensland Liberal Party began election preparations. Moore was sure that Fraser would block the budget.

On 23 September Anthony renewed his own calls for an election. He suggested that if the Opposition did not force an election on the budget it could not expect to have the confidence of the people in another two years when an election was due—that is, failure to block the budget would undermine the coalition!

On 22 September Fraser had attacked the government and said the fundamental reason for talk about elections was the mismanagement of the Labor Party. 'If Mr Whitlam had governed well nobody would talk of elections,' Fraser declared. The previous week on 14 September in his electoral broadcast he had said: 'I have never promoted speculation about elections. I have sought to end that speculation. The Opposition is not casting around for a pretext in relation to an election.'

Fraser was now involved in exactly the same sort of political operation that Snedden had played in early 1975, the only difference being that he was a cleverer politician. From the start Fraser insisted that the Opposition would make no decision until the very last moment, just before the Senate voted on the budget. This kept his options open. It also maximised the time he had to build a groundswell of support for an election. Fraser's actions in this period highlighted the dichotomy in him between the tough politician pushing for an election and the conservative posing as statesman expressing his concern that democratic conventions be upheld.

These two views were irreconcilable. They were at the core of the confusion which Fraser's statements caused during this period as first one view became predominant, and then the other. As a result Fraser began exposing himself to more and more charges of political weakness, of refusing to commit himself, and of always shifting his ground. This was inevitable given the fact that he felt it was impossible to make a decision before it was time to vote on the budget in the Senate.

But Fraser's judgement was proved right because important events did occur on the weekend before the vote which affected the Opposition's attitude. Fraser never wanted to appear to be grabbing for power; if he blocked the budget he wanted to do so in response to a groundswell of support. The very process by which he assessed this support was calculated to arouse it.

The techniques being used by Anthony and Fraser were of a nature that no political system could sustain with impunity. Gough Whitlam, whose fighting instincts reached their peak in a crisis, retaliated. If the Opposition was prepared to threaten established convention, then Whitlam was prepared to do the same to defy them.

This point is fundamental—the origins of Whitlam's response sprang directly from the experience of his government.

In early 1974, when Snedden had decided to block supply and force an election, Whitlam gladly accepted the challenge. The political climate in April 1974 was most unusual. Both the Opposition Leader and the Prime Minister were confident of winning a general election. One of Whitlam's prime motives at the time was to seize the chance offered and try to win control of both Houses of Parliament. Whitlam had advice from Treasury in early April indicating that the economy would deteriorate. He decided the government would have a much better chance of a total victory at the polls in early 1974 rather than at the end of 1975. In short, he joined the double dissolution battle in an effort to prevent the Opposition from being in a position to do the same thing again—and he just failed.

If Labor had polled a few thousand more votes in Queensland it would have won five Senators from that state, not four, and totalled an overall Senate strength of 30, not 29. In this situation, with Steele Hall supporting the government, the Opposition would have been unable to force an election.

As the government's standing fell throughout the remainder of 1974 and 1975 with a deteriorating economic situation, Whitlam knew he would need a full three-year term if he were to survive. He decided he would firmly resist any move by the Opposition to repeat in 1975 its 1974 tactic of forcing a poll. Whitlam made his position clear as early as the Terrigal federal conference and there is no sign he wavered from it. When Snedden threatened a poll in early 1975 Whitlam retaliated and played a major role in destroying the Liberal leader. Now he retaliated again but in a different fashion.

On Friday afternoon 12 September Whitlam drove from Canberra to Goulburn to speak at the new College of Advanced Education. This was when he first foreshadowed the strategy which ended two months later in his dismissal from office. In his address the Prime Minister said:

> There are no laws applying to a situation where supply is refused by an Upper House, no laws at all. There is no precedent in the federal parliament and the last state precedent was in Victoria in 1947. And there is in fact no convention because people never used to think it could happen, so it's never been discussed. And accordingly one can only say that there is no obligation by law, by rule, by precedent or by convention for a Prime Minister in those circumstances which are threatened, to advise the Governor-General to dissolve the House of Representatives and have an election for it.

Whitlam argued that in Australia, as in all other parliaments based on the British tradition, the Prime Minister was entitled to remain in office while he had a majority on the floor of the Lower House. He added the Governor-General could get advice from the Prime Minister alone. This was a view which Whitlam floated for political reasons at Goulburn. It was to become the text he later used to defy the Senate.

Whitlam's declaration made it clear that there would only be a general election at the cost of the worst political and constitutional crisis in Australian history.

His stand was a threat that held not just for the government's budget but for supply in 1976 as well. The basis of Fraser's political strategy had always been that the Opposition could only successfully force an election if the act itself did not become a dangerously counter-productive political issue. Whitlam had now spelt out that if the Opposition forced an election it would simultaneously precipitate a constitutional crisis that would not only become the centre of national attention but dominate any resulting election campaign. Whitlam was inserting a new and unknown factor into the political equation with which the Opposition would have to wrestle. Henceforth, it would be a courageous Opposition that committed itself to blocking the budget and plunging into a constitutional abyss where the initiative would lie with the government.

Whitlam had taken no firm decision on tactics at this stage. His Goulburn statement was a political manoeuvre to make the Opposition think twice before acting. It was also a sign that the politics of desperation, which were always at hand following the constant rejecting of government legislation and the threat to its survival, were now dominant.

This statement by Whitlam reflected a completely different view of the Australian parliament and system of government from that of the Opposition. The Prime Minister was asserting the supremacy of the House of Representatives over the Senate, regardless of the specific provisions of the Constitution. The political strategy he suggested had one massive assumption as its linchpin: that the Governor-General would act only on the advice of the Prime Minister and not without his advice.

Over the following five weeks Whitlam's office discussed a number of possible strategies if the Opposition moved to block the budget. There were many options. One was to go into a double dissolution immediately. Other options available were: to seek a half-Senate election; a House of Representatives election together with half the Senate; or a House of Representatives election alone. Alternatively they could 'tough it out', meaning that the government would call no election but use political tactics in an effort to crack the Opposition Senate blockage.

Eventually Whitlam moved towards two firm options on which his opinion seemed to fluctuate. One was to 'tough it out' and remain in office, and the other was to respond to any deferral or rejection of the budget by seeking a half-Senate election. In late September Whitlam met the editor of the *Age*, Graham Perkin, at a social function and indicated to Perkin that he would almost certainly call a half-Senate election if the budget were blocked. Perkin conveyed this to his political correspondent John Jost who had originally asked him to find out, and Jost subsequently wrote a story to this effect.

The half-Senate election option was very complex but opened up a number of possibilities for the government which would deeply trouble the Opposition. The key to this option for the government was its legislation to expand the size of the Senate from 60 to 64 Senators without any increase in the size of the House of Representatives. This came about because of legislation to allow both the ACT and Northern Territory to elect two Senators where they previously had no Senate representation. This was controversial legislation since it would under-mine the Senate's claim to be a state's house with its own separate method of election and term of office: the territorial Senators would be elected for three years only, being elected initially at the next Senate election and thereafter at each House of Representatives election in a completely different fashion from the rest of the Senate. Yet the bills giving effect to these provisions had become law when they passed the joint sitting of federal parliament in July 1974, being bills on which the 1974 double dissolution was granted. The Opposition had opposed them every inch of the way and saw them as inconsistent with the notion of the Senate as a state's house. This legislation was currently under challenge in the High Court by the non-Labor states but Whitlam was hopeful it would be upheld and territorial Senators elected at the next Senate poll.

Whitlam was obliged to call an election for half the Senate before mid-1976 so that the Senators elected could take their places on 1 July that year—as provided by the Constitution. If the Territories legislation were ruled valid, then 36 Senators would be elected at this election, comprising the normal 30 representing half the Senate, four territorial Senators, and two more Senators as a result of casual vacancies in NSW and Queens-land. The casual vacancies had arisen because of the retirement of Lionel Murphy in early 1975 and the death in June 1975 of Queensland ALP Senator Bert Milliner. The respective state governments had appointed replacements for Murphy and Milliner pending the election of two new Senators at the next Senate poll. This meant that under Section 15 of the constitution there would be an election for six Senators (instead of the normal five) from these two states at the next Senate poll.

According to the constitution the normally elected 30 Senators would take their places on 1 July 1976. But the other six Senators would take their places in the Senate immediately after the election. This was the provision in the legislation regarding territorial Senators and it was also the provision of Section 15 regarding vacancies. In short, a remark-able situation existed. This opened up the possibility for a newly constituted interim Senate which would sit for a brief period from the time of the half-Senate election results until 1 July 1976, when all the elected Senators from the states, five from each, would take their places. The prospect, which terrified the Opposition and appealed to the gov-ernment, was that Labor had a chance, although only a remote one, of winning control of the Senate during any such interim period before July 1. If Whitlam called a half-Senate election early, in late 1975 or early 1976, then Labor would have time to pass laws through any interim Senate in which it had the numbers.

The mechanics of this chance were quite simple in the Territories. The best result Labor could expect in the Northern Territory was to win one out of two Senate places. The best result it could expect in the ACT was to win one Senate place and have former Prime Minister John Gorton, running as an independent, win the other Senate place. Whitlam's office had been in a dialogue with Gorton for some time and was very interested in this possibility. Gorton would be a vote for Labor on the crucial issues: he had pledged to pass both supply and the government's redistribution of electoral boundaries. In NSW and Queensland the Senator who took his place immediately and became part of the interim Senate was the sixth one elected, the last one. This would be a matter of pot luck. Labor would win the sixth spot in NSW providing it was outpolled overall by the Opposition but still had sufficient votes to have three Senators elected. In Queensland, where Labor was certain to be outpolled by the Opposition, it would win the sixth place providing it mustered sufficient votes to win three Senate places. If Queensland split 4–2 against Labor then the non-Labor parties would almost certainly win the sixth vacancy.

This Senate strategy had some appeal to Labor. By a conjunction of events there was a very remote chance that it could win control of the Senate, although this still depended on the High Court judgement on the Territories legislation. While overall the prospect of Labor winning control of the Senate for an interim period seemed unlikely, there was yet another reason for favouring the half-Senate strategy. This was based on the premise, proven in 1974 and accepted by most Labor people, that the Labor Party would pick up ground on the Opposition during the actual period of an election campaign. It was in Labor's interests to prolong the campaign period, particularly it if had a favourable issue.

In these circumstances the strategy became one of holding a half-Senate election as a prelude to a House of Representatives election. If Labor won Senate control in the half-Senate election, the budget could be passed and the deadlock resolved. But if it did not, it would almost certainly pick up ground in a half-Senate campaign with the main issue being the blocking of the budget and its support would be at a much higher plateau from which to enter a House of Representatives election, if there were no other alternative.

Fraser and Anthony were aware of the half-Senate option and were alarmed at the possible consequences. There was one way they could attempt to nullify its effect. Under Section 12 of the constitution, writs for Senate elections were issued by the Governors of each state after a request from the Governor-General. If the non-Labor state governments advised their Governors not to issue the writs then they could prevent the Senate election being held in their states. If this action were taken it would be unprecedented and once again represent a fundamental breach of a constitutional convention. But it would not necessarily prevent an election being held. If Whitlam wanted a half-Senate election then he could proceed to hold one in the Territories and the Labor states where the state governments did not prevent the issue of writs.

In summary, in late August and early September, as Fraser's D-Day for decision approached, Whitlam's response focused on two main strategies. One was to 'tough it out', which appeared a short-term move but not a viable long-term strategy if the Opposition didn't buckle, since supply would eventually expire. The other was to use a half-Senate election, either by itself or as the prelude to a House of Representatives election.

In this period the government used every means at its disposal to discredit any Opposition move to block the budget. The Minister for Manufacturing Industry, Lionel Bowen, stirred a large controversy when he claimed that the Governor-General could give the Royal Assent to the budget bills even if they had not been passed by the Senate. The Attorney-General, Kep Enderby, claimed that the Senate had no power to reject money bills and that it would be defying the constitution.

In this political warfare the shadow Attorney-General, Senator Ivor Greenwood, released the opinion of two leading barristers, whose legal advice the Liberal Party had sought. The opinions were from former Attorney-General, T E F Hughes QC from the Sydney Bar, and from S E K Hulme QC of the Victorian Bar, senior counsel with wide constitutional practice. Both counsel indicated their advice was not about the propriety of the use of the Senate's power, it was only concerned with the legality of the question. The two counsel said the constitutional position was beyond doubt and that the Senate was legally entitled to reject the money bill. They said a Prime Minister advising his Governor-General to assent to a bill which had not passed the Senate would be acting contrary to the constitution.

In this period the Opposition, through seeking legal advice, established to its own satisfaction the view that the Senate was fully entitled in law to reject or to defer the budget. The Liberal Party based its subsequent actions upon this rock. While there was extensive debate over whether this power should be used and strong opposition in many quarters to its use, there was no doubting the existence of the power, as far as nearly all constitutional lawyers were concerned.

However a totally new and subsequently crucial factor had been introduced into the political climate with the events that followed the death in June of Queensland Labor Senator Bert Milliner, which had created a vacancy in the Senate. As was the case with the Murphy vacancy earlier in the year, the parliament of the state nominated a replacement. The NSW Liberal Government under Premier Tom Lewis had eventually settled upon an independent, Cleaver Bunton, to replace Murphy, rather than a Labor nominee. This had been a clear breach of convention. Now the Queensland Premier Bjelke-Petersen had the same decision to make. Although the Premier initially indicated that a Labor man would be appointed, the Labor Party itself was never confident of this, particularly after the early breach of convention by Lewis. But not even the most cynical were prepared for what happened.

The appointment was vital for the Labor government because of the strong pressure within the Opposition parties to defer the budget by the use of their Senate numbers. After Milliner's death the Liberal–National Country Parties had 30 Senators, the Labor Party 27, with the remaining two places occupied by South Australian Liberal Movement Senator Steele Hall and the independent appointed by Lewis, Senator Cleaver Bunton. The last place would now be determined by Bjelke-Petersen.

The numbers on the crucial issue of blocking the budget were actually 30–29 against Labor. This is because both Hall and Bunton supported Labor on the budget, taking its strength on this issue to 29 compared with the non-Labor strength of 30. This was where the Queensland decision was fundamental.

If the Queensland government followed convention and appointed a Labor Senator then the Senate would be tied 30–all on the budget. This meant the Opposition parties had a negative majority; they could negate bills and defeat them. But this was all they could do. They would not have a Senate majority and would not be able to pass motions in the Senate. In short, they would not be able to defer the budget. The only way the Opposition could defer the budget in the Senate would be if it maintained its 30–29 absolute majority or even increased it. This would only happen if the Queensland Premier appointed an anti-Labor Senator; a Senator who would not vote with the Labor Party. This is precisely what happened.

The only way Malcolm Fraser was able to defer the 1975–76 budget was because Bjelke-Petersen appointed an anti-Labor Senator to replace Bert Milliner. It is highly debatable whether Fraser would have been able to force an election or would have tried to force an election without a clear majority in the Senate, which was delivered him from Queensland. Senator Albert Field who was appointed to the vacancy never voted on the budget. But if his place had been occupied by a Labor Senator instead, then the Opposition could not have passed the motion deferring the budget which was repeatedly passed during the crisis period. This was the origin of Steele Hall's incredibly emotive, but nevertheless accurate, statement that the Opposition denied the budget 'over a dead man's corpse'.

After Milliner's death the Queensland Labor Party nominated Dr Mal Colston as its replacement. But Bjelke-Petersen refused to accept Colston and asked the Labor Party for a list of names of possible replacements, which it refused to provide. The Premier later described how he came to select Field for the vacancy:

> A number of people, some wrote to me, some rang. In the first instance Field rang the office. I didn't speak to him. My secretary told me that another chap had contacted us and said that he's quite happy to stand, got his name and address, and so on. That's how we contacted Field, and we chose Field ultimately out of quite a number of them. I didn't know him. I asked my secretary to ring him. I said: 'Who is he?' He gave me his background, and I said: 'Well, he sounds a true-blue Labor man,' and I said to Stan Wilcox my secretary: 'Give him a ring. I'll talk to him.' I said: 'You understand; you know what'll happen to you?' He said: 'You can't tell me anything that will happen to me, after being in the Labor Party and a Labor Party member for 37 years. Naturally I know that they'll take some action against me, perhaps in court, all sorts of things. But look, I'm happy to serve. I'm a Labor man, I represent the average Labor man in the community and I want to serve our state'.

Field was sworn in as Australia's newest Senator on 9 September in the face of a massive government walkout. All government Senators except the Senate leader Ken Wriedt walked out as the acting Usher of the Black Rod escorted Field into the chamber. Wriedt sat stiffly at the main table with his back to Field when he was administered the oath of office amid rows of empty benches. Field later confirmed that no Labor member or Senator spoke to him that day.

A french polisher by trade, Field said he would spend more time concentrating on unemployment than on issues such as abortion and homosexuality. 'I don't think homosexuality should be spoken about in the Senate,' Field said after his first day in the chamber. 'It brings the homosexuals too much out into the open. I guess they can't help being what they are—and you never know who is one—but they were certainly much quieter before people started talking so much about them.'

Right from the start Field left no doubt about his politics. He made a farce out of the Queensland Premier's claim that he was a Labor man. 'Mr Whitlam will never get a vote from me,' he said at Sydney airport en route to Canberra. Field said he would support any attempt by the Opposition to force an early election and would oppose the government on any contentious issue. He criticised Whitlam for calling the Queensland Premier, who is a practising Lutheran and Sunday school teacher, a 'bible-bashing bastard'. Field said this was 'the last straw' for him as far as Whitlam was concerned.

On Field's first day in the Senate the government moved to question his eligibility to sit. Queensland Labor Senator George Georges claimed that Field was still a member of the Queensland public service at the time of his nomination and that since no Senator could hold an office of profit under the crown he was ineligible. Eventually Field was given a month's leave on 1 October after being served with a High Court writ by a Labor Party member challenging his eligibility. The critical point is that Labor was left one Senate vote down after Milliner's death.

Fraser had an achilles heel when it came to forcing an election. It was the small group of Liberal parliamentarians who believed for various reasons that the Opposition parties should not reject supply. On 11 September the two independent Senators, the leader of the Liberal Movement Senator Steele Hall and the NSW independent Senator Cleaver Bunton, both announced they would vote in the Senate to pass the budget.

The fact that the two independent Senators, one leading a party on the Liberal side of politics and the other a self-styled 'political neuter', reached this conclusion was a major plus for Labor. Hall became an outspoken critic of the Opposition parties on this issue and was involved in extensive behind-the-scenes efforts to encourage Liberal Senators to refuse to block the budget. Bunton, whose appointment by Tom Lewis had caused such a furore earlier in the year, had developed close relations with Hall. He had also, during his short time in the Senate, become more sympathetically inclined towards the government than the Opposition. A former mayor of Albury, he found when walking to Parliament House on his first day that a white Mercedes pulled up next to him and Gough Whitlam offered him a lift. Whitlam, who had an abiding interest in the cities and growth centres, had got to know Bunton when he was mayor.

In this situation, if Fraser intended successfully to defer the budget, he could not afford any defections from his own side. But it was a well-known secret that a number of Liberal Senators had grave doubts about forcing an election on the budget. The same situation had applied in April 1974 when Snedden forced the double dissolution. But this time there appeared to be a greater number of Senators with graver doubts.

The most prominent was Victorian Senator Alan Missen, elected in 1974 and an advocate of social and legal reform. Missen's views on the Senate were set out clearly in an article he wrote in the July 1975 edition of the *Higher School Certificate* magazine in Victoria. In this article he argued that, while the Senate had the power to reject supply, it should be avoided at all costs. Missen claimed that the Opposition move to force the 1974 election had been disastrous. He pointed out that, without this interruption, the government's term would have expired at the end of 1975 anyway. Missen said that an Opposition should define quite precisely the extraordinary circumstances prevailing if it was using them to block supply. He concluded that the power 'should be used only in the most stringent of situations'.

While Missen was an intelligent and courageous man, he had no wish to become a political martyr, a figure in the history books who had sabotaged his party for a principle. His private view was always that he would never vote against the decision of his own party. What Missen tried to do instead was to encourage and foster a group of Liberal Senators around him who would give strength to their position through numbers and increase their chances inside the party room of dissuading the party against blocking the budget.

Most Liberal Senators prided themselves on their independence. While some were close to Missen, others decided the matter for themselves. But the chief Senators who opposed blocking supply were, besides Missen, Senator Don Jessop from South Australia, Senator Neville Bonner from Queensland, Senator Eric Bessell from Tasmania, and Senator Condor Laucke from South Australia. They were a collection of men in a tiny minority in a situation where the logic of the political climate was against them; their fragile efforts were eventually torpedoed. But they were a factor that Malcolm Fraser could ignore only at his own peril.

The first outward sign of their views came on Saturday 13 September when the *Adelaide Advertiser* carried a short letter from Jessop reading:

> Sir. It is strange that such prominence was given to Senator Hall's statement that he would not help to force an election. His speech was obviously prompted by inaccurate press reports that a head count of Liberal Party members indicated they wanted an election this year. I have not been approached by the press on this subject and, to my certain knowledge, neither have many of my colleagues. It is my view that the appropriation should be allowed to pass and only in extreme circumstances would I agree with the rejection of a future supply bill.

When gallery reporters had the letter pointed out to them, it assumed national importance. This was close to a public declaration by Jessop that the budget should pass, at the very time when both Anthony and Fraser appeared to be looking for reasons why it should not pass.

Fraser was in New Guinea at the time but when he returned he promptly rang Jessop to discuss the letter and the budget with him. As a result of this conversation Jessop issued a statement on 17 September through the Liberal Party secretariat saying: 'All my letter was doing was restating the position taken by Malcolm Fraser on the first day he took office and which he has reiterated on many occasions since. It is likely there will be no vote on this issue until the end of November. Exceptional circumstances may yet arise before then.' This statement, following his talk with Fraser, was a significant backdown from Jessop's letter. It showed Fraser's determination to ensure his options were kept open.

At least two Senators who had doubts—Peter Baume (NSW) and Condor Laucke—made approaches to Fraser and held talks with him on the question. Another House of Representatives Liberal who did this was Ian Macphee, who believed the Opposition should not force an election on the budget. Fraser himself initiated talks with both Missen and Jessop and he had a number of telephone discussions with Missen as well as seeing the Victorian Senator in his office. Throughout September and early October Missen was optimistic that the budget would be passed and that moves to reject it could be countered through a strong stand by a number of Senators. This proved to be both wishful thinking and bad political judgement. But it was a genuinely held view.[1]

While there was opposition to an early election from some Senators there was also support for it from other significant areas. The Senate leader Reg Withers was a hawk. Withers, a sophisticated political opportunist, saw no reason to throw up the chance of defeating the Labor government. Two other prominent Senators who came to support an early election were John Carrick from NSW and Peter Rae from Tasmania. Both men had been opposed to forcing the 1974 election but this time they had a different view. Carrick's decision was typical of that of many senior Liberals. Although he was generally opposed to the Senate's use of its money power, he believed as a matter of principle that the Labor government was beyond redemption and had to be removed as fast as possible. This was an argument to say the end justified the means.

Peter Rae, who spoke against the 1974 decision in the Opposition executive, was also encouraging other Senators to go along with it in 1975. Rae believed the government could not recover and that it was better to offend against constitutional convention rather than allow it to remain in office. He saw forcing the election as the lesser of two evils.

Through late September and early October the majority of the Liberal frontbench came to similar conclusions for various reasons. From the time the budget was first introduced some of Fraser's closest colleagues, men like Garland and Robinson, were strong advocates of blocking the budget and were confident that Fraser would grasp the nettle. Others like Ellicott and Greenwood had virtually convinced themselves the government was guilty of flagrant illegalities and deception over the loans affair and was unfit to hold office. By early October Cotton and Lynch felt an election was almost certain. All the time the Country Party and its trio of shadow Ministers, Anthony, Sinclair and Nixon, were egging Fraser on.

The fact is that there was no lobby for restraint, no really powerful faction within the coalition arguing against it. As the probability of an election increased, Steele Hall tried to highlight the stand of the doubting Liberal Senators. He wrote a vivid and dramatic letter to Fraser summarising the arguments against blocking the budget and sent copies to all Opposition members, Senators and the press. Hall wrote:

Dear Mr Fraser,

I am concerned about the continuing uncertainty regarding your position and that of the Liberal Party in regard to a possible rejection of supply in the Senate. There are almost no limits to the complexities which are now being discussed as a possible result of such action . . .

I urge you in the immediate future to state your position clearly in support of the previously accepted conventions which underpin our obviously fragile parliamentary democracy. I believe Labor will be defeated whenever a general election is held. In this event, it is very important that the manner in which you assume office should have the long-term approval of most Australians. We ought not to underestimate the ability of the electorate to recognise shabby behaviour . . . I hope you will at least consider my prediction that if you take, or attempt to take, the Prime Minister's office by the device of a vote in the Senate, your leadership capacity will automatically degenerate to the disadvantage of the Liberal Party. It would be extremely difficult to develop a popular base for your leadership in a community which contained the bitter and growing discontent of Labor supporters who believed the ballot box had lost its democratic function . . .

If you 'assemble' your members in the Senate to reject supply you will consciously destroy the stability of Australian politics which we as Liberals have grown to expect under our administrations since 1949 . . . As I pointed out publicly in Melbourne recently, Labor has governed for less than twenty-five per cent of the time since Federation. It is our side of politics which is likely to be disrupted for much longer periods by a hostile Senate.

This letter was directed not so much to Fraser but to the Liberal Party Senators upon whom he would have to rely to block the budget. It echoed all the doubts and suspicions held by the wavering Liberals. Hall himself had tried to persuade Missen and his supporters to make a public declaration spelling out their views but this had never come to fruition. Despite their sincerity, the political tactics they pursued were based more on misplaced optimism than the harsh realities of Liberal politics at that time.[2]

The only way these Liberal Senators could have changed the course of events would have been to make a pre-emptive declaration. If they had all come out jointly with a strong statement, immediately following Fraser's comments on 21 August, they might have had a chance. But by saying nothing they allowed to build up the inevitable pressures for an election which just made that prospect more likely. There was very little chance of their being able to swing the party room the day before the Senate vote when it had a unanimous recommendation from the shadow ministry to defer the budget. In order to prevail they had to act together, forcefully, and early in the piece before the pressure mounted. But they were not prepared to do this and gradually crumbled, victims of the subsequent course of events which took on a momentum of their own.

By early October it appeared fairly certain that the 'reprehensible' circumstances which Fraser was seeking were not likely to occur. Whitlam and his government were in a clear ascendancy on the floor of parliament and gave no sign of making the fatal mistake which Fraser was searching for. The ACTU congress in Melbourne had gone smoothly and had been a major victory for Bob Hawke. Despite inevitable loopholes, the line on wage indexation had been held and the bonds of government and trade union cooperation maintained.

But the scent of victory was in the nostrils of the majority of the parliamentary Liberal Party, the shadow ministry, the party organisation and the state divisions. Fraser was under immense pressure and, while he had not yet made up his mind, the prospects of an early election were strong, certainly in comparison to the situation at the end of August.

By this stage Fraser was aware of the polling work conducted by the Liberal Party federal secretariat. Polls conducted in September by the party increased the early election momentum. There were indications that support for the party was near an all-time high. When asked how they would vote at the next election, of those polled about 57 per cent indicated a preference for the Liberal Party. When asked how they would vote at an early election forced by the Liberals this figure was between 53 and 54 per cent. That is, the act of blocking the budget would only lose the Opposition about 3.5 per cent of votes and they would still be in a position to win well. This poll, which was conducted on a telephone basis in Sydney and Melbourne, was just the final one in a series conducted by the party over the previous twelve months. It was consistent with other national polls being published. The party had found from past experience that its sample, although by telephone, was still fairly accurate.

It was in this atmosphere that the Federal Council of the Liberal Party met at the Lakeside Hotel in Canberra on the weekend of 11–12 October with the federal executive meeting on the Friday before. The Appropriation Bills would come to a vote in the Senate the following week and the council meeting would be an invaluable opportunity for party notables from all areas to put their views to Fraser. The executive meeting was a vital one. This time assessments and opinions were given in the knowledge that they were a direct input for a decision that would have to be reached within days. Each state president outlined the electoral position and the views of that state on an early election. The seat assessments varied little from the last meeting on 29 August. The hawks were the three outlying states of Queensland, Tasmania and Western Australia. Both NSW and South Australia supported an early election. Only three speakers opposed an election at the executive meeting and the chief opponent was the Victorian president Peter Hardie.

Hardie would not have a bar of rejecting the budget. He spoke at length, emotionally and forcefully. He said the budget itself had not offered the political ammunition which the party had originally expected; that it had all the hallmarks of being a responsible budget and a genuine effort to deal with the economic problem. Hardie severely questioned whether the Liberal Senators would be prepared to reject the budget. As a close friend of Missen, he was aware of the grave doubts harboured by a number of Liberal Senators and of Missen's confidence that they would be able to hold out.

Hardie argued that by blocking the budget the Liberals would be throwing away the rule book and would almost certainly face a similar fate themselves when they were in government at the hands of a hostile Senate. He said the future complexion of the Senate was a worry with both the DLP and Gorton having a good chance of winning election and possibly holding the balance of power. Finally he warned that the move would create dangerous divisions within the community and was likely to provoke massive industrial unrest from the trade union movement. Hardie's line was supported by the president of the Young Liberals, Chris Puplick, and the head of the women's section of the party, Beryl Beaurepaire.

Hardie's speech was so vigorous that Fraser said he would come back to him on it. From the tone of the Victorian president, there was grave doubt whether he would even accept a decision to force a poll. At a later stage in the meeting Fraser asked Hardie whether he would support the decision made by the parliamentary party. The Victorian president initially declined to answer; finally, he said that Victoria would abide by any decision.[3]

It was during the executive meeting that the 'clinching' event occurred in shaping Fraser's decision to block the budget. In mid-afternoon news came through that the High Court in Melbourne had handed down its judgement declaring that the Labor government's law entitling the ACT and the Northern Territory to elect two Senators each, was valid. The court split 4–3 on the issue with Justices McTiernan, Jacobs, Mason and Murphy upholding the legislation while the Chief Justice Sir Garfield Barwick and Justices Gibbs and Stephen ruled it invalid. It was a day on which the Labor Party was thankful Lionel Murphy had been appointed to the High Court.

The decision meant that Whitlam could call a half-Senate election with the option of constituting the interim Senate before 1 July comprising the four Territorial Senators as well as Senators filling the casual vacancies in NSW and Queensland.

This decision had great consequences for the Liberal Party. There was now an outside chance that the Labor Party might be able to control the Senate for a short period. The Liberals were horrified at this possibility. It meant that the government would be able to pass into law every bill which had been blocked in the Senate. There were two in particular that would have vast repercussions. The first was the Labor government's electoral redistribution which it had now embodied in the form of bills based on the new electoral law passed at the 1974 joint sitting; this was designed to minimise differences in the size of electorates from a twenty per cent variance to a ten per cent variance. The redistribution would adversely affect the National Country Party and assist both the Liberal and Labor Parties. Both the coalition parties condemned it and believed that it would give a considerable advantage to the Labor Party.

The second area of concern was the reforms to the electoral system being proposed by Labor's Property and Services Minister, Fred Daly. This would introduce optional preferential voting, which would favour the Labor Party in seats that were three-way contests between the Labor, Liberal and the National Country Parties. But even more important was the provision that required the declaration of the source of campaign funds for each party. The Liberals were vigorously opposed to this and determined to stop it at all costs. While this view was very strong within the organisation, it was also a powerful factor at the parliamentary level. Senior Liberals within the party's organisation estimated that this legislation would cut their campaign funds by 50 per cent. It would be a major deterrent to a large number of companies and organisations which supported them. Such support would be made public under Daly's proposals.

In summary, as the Liberals saw it, if Whitlam secured control of an interim Senate he could pass legislation that would help Labor towards a long tenure in office. The electoral redistribution would assist Labor at the next House of Representatives poll; the electoral reforms would assist Labor vis-a-vis the Liberals in any election campaign.

There were two distinct periods in the federal executive meeting that afternoon at the Lakeside—before and after the High Court decision. Some Liberals changed their attitude towards an election on the basis of this decision, including Fraser's adviser and speechwriter David Kemp, the federal president Bob Southey, and the NSW Secretary Jim Carlton, to name only three. It had an influence on Fraser and significantly shifted his mind towards the early election option.

The fact that Whitlam only had an outside chance of controlling an interim Senate did not matter. Even if Whitlam's chances were only ten to one, they were still too strong for Fraser and Anthony. Both men were convinced they had to eliminate this as an option altogether and ensure that Whitlam had an absolutely zero chance of gaining control of the Senate. The best way to achieve this was by forcing a general election instead. The Liberals knew that if they blocked the budget Whitlam might call a half-Senate election anyway. But they had doubts whether he could secure such an election in circumstances where the budget was being deferred pending a general election. The Liberals knew that if they did not block the budget then Whitlam would be fully entitled to call the Senate election anytime he liked before 1 July. They were not comforted by Whitlam's statement that in the normal course of events he would not hold the election until May or June 1976.

The shift in Fraser's attitude towards an early election was shown on Sunday 12 October in his keynote address to the party's federal council. Once again Fraser's tendency to dress his actions with the clothes of principle were obvious. In this speech he said his decision was not one between expediency and principle but one between 'two heavy and conflicting principles'. The first principle, on which he placed 'very great weight' was that of continuity of government and the notion of a three-year term for an elected government. The second principle, which he spent twice as long explaining, was the obligation of an Opposition to the people of Australia in the face of a government doing grave damage to the community. Fraser went on:

> Many people are being hurt. People who are retired, who thought they had adequate savings to look after themselves, after three years of Labor find they are utterly dependent on the government. They are destroyed until they die unless the situation can be redressed. Have not the small businessmen, thousands of whom are seeing their live-lihoods wiped out at this moment, the right to ask us to act? Of course they have. It is a major obligation on us as a political party to take these facts into account. The incompetence, the damage, the failures of the worst government in our history cannot be ignored.

There were very few Liberals who, after this speech, had doubts about whether Fraser would take the plunge.

Fraser's staff insisted that no final decision had been taken and this was unquestionably the case. But Fraser was on the edge and it would take a considerable political force to get him to turn back at this point. The question now was to tie up the loose ends in preparation for the move. There were two chief problems here. The first was to ensure that the Senate was on side and would hold. The second was to do every-thing possible to ensure that if Whitlam decided to call a half-Senate election following the deferral of the budget, he was effectively coun-tered.

On Monday 13 October the council meeting passed a motion calling on state governments to do everything in their power to prevent

Whitlam calling an early half-Senate election and thereby ever constituting an interim Senate. This was a direct appeal to the non-Labor
Premiers to ensure they refused to issue writs in these circumstances.
Both the Queensland Premier Joh Bjelke-Petersen and the NSW Premier
Tom Lewis had already said that they would instruct their Governors
not to issue writs. The West Australian Premier Sir Charles Court was
expected to take a similar stand. The Victorian Premier, Dick Hamer,
told the press that the issuing of writs was a power for the state
government and not the federal government and that it did not necessarily follow that they would be issued when the federal government
wanted an election.

Throughout the conference period Fraser spent his time in a side
room where a procession of Liberals walked in and out to see him. He
stayed in close contact with Opposition Senate leader Withers, who had
doubts about the Senate on the Friday but appeared much more confident on Monday, 13 October. On the Saturday morning Fraser had a
private talk with Hardie and stressed that he regarded the three year
principle as important and had not yet made up his mind. But unbeknown to these three men, another decisive event was to occur which
would eliminate their worry about the doubting Liberal Senators.

The origins of this final and fateful move came on Wednesday 8
October when the *Melbourne Herald* published new loan revelations from
Khemlani. One of its reporters, Peter Game, had followed Khemlani
around the world for several weeks and had taped more than thirteen
hours of interviews with him. The story quoted Khemlani saying he still
had approval from Rex Connor to raise $US8000 million for the Austra-
lian government. The real significance of the story was Khemlani's claim
that Connor had continued his efforts to raise overseas funds after the
executive council authority was revoked on 20 May.

According to Khemlani, he had been in contact with Connor in the
past ten days and Connor had wanted to meet Middle East representatives about the loan. When questioned about letters written by the
Treasurer Bill Hayden to all middlemen revoking any authorities issued
by Ministers, Khemlani said: 'I have received no letter, and anyway,
when Mr Hayden said something similar last June, Mr Connor told me
not to worry and to go ahead.'

The Opposition immediately seized on these new loan allegations,
the timing of which was impeccable for them, coming just a week before
the Senate vote on the budget. The deputy Opposition Leader Phillip
Lynch was told about the substance of the *Melbourne Herald* story before
Question Time that morning and before the paper hit the street. In
parliament Lynch asked Whitlam: 'Is there any authority outstanding
for any money lender, intermediary or agent to raise a loan for the
Australian government? If so, what are the details? Are any of your

senior Ministers presently involved in major overseas loan raising?' The Prime Minister replied: 'No.' Subsequently the *Melbourne Herald* appeared with a splash story headlined 'Khemlani tells—I've Got Connor Go Ahead'.

The allegations were incredibly damaging to the government. Suddenly it appeared that Labor's involvement in overseas loan raisings was about to haunt it again at the very time that its survival depended on presenting a solid front without any weakness. The Opposition aimed to exploit the revelations as the 'reprehensible circumstances' needed to force an election. The onus was now squarely on Connor and the Labor government to defend themselves before the day was out.

Rex Connor was not in Parliament House this day. He had been in hospital for some time and was recuperating at home. Whitlam told John Menadue to ensure that Connor put out a prompt statement clarifying his position in regard to Khemlani's claims. Late in the morning Connor's departmental head Jim Scully and his press secretary Bob Sorby went to the Canberra suburb of Deakin where Connor was staying and drafted a statement. There were further talks at the house the same afternoon between Connor, Menadue and Scully over the text of Connor's defence.

Malcolm Fraser moved quickly to exploit the latest Khemlani connection. He said the statements by the London-based money broker indicated that the government was still to tell the whole story about its overseas loan raisings. Khemlani's statements were completely inconsistent with an answer to a Question on Notice which Whitlam gave Lynch on 2 September. The Prime Minister's answer on this date read: 'I am advised that there were no further negotiations with Mr Khemlani after 20 May 1975 when the Executive Council authority was revoked.' In short, if Khemlani was right, Whitlam himself had misled Parliament based on advice from Connor. Fraser and Lynch both felt certain that Connor had continued negotiations with Khemlani after 20 May on Whitlam's authority. They were well aware of Whitlam's comments in his 9 July speech to parliament when he said: 'If the opportunity presents itself with reasonable chance of success, we shall try again.'

But the Opposition was not aware of another incident on 9 July which was of significance to the present debate. When Rex Connor delivered his long and famous defence of himself to the House of Representatives on this day, he read from a text which was later incorporated in full in the Senate Hansard by the government Senate leader Ken Wriedt. The second last paragraph of this text reads: 'The Executive Council authority of 28 January was rescinded on 20 May to permit of the finalising of a $100 million loan to Australia in New York. Matters have not been further pursued with Mr Khemlani.' Yet this paragraph, with its crucial last sentence, was never spoken by Connor in the House of Representatives. Although it was in the text, he omitted it from his speech.

That evening Connor released his statement:

> My authority to pursue the question of loan raisings was revoked on 20 May last to enable a $100 million Australian loan to be raised in the United States. I have never proceeded on any basis other than that authority. I have persistently abided by the decision of 20 May and have rejected any endeavours to further involve me in loan-raising matters. I have since 20 May made clear that anyone interested in loan matters should deal with the Treasurer. Specifically I have had only one telephone discussion with Mr Khemlani since 20 May which was initiated by him, about 11 June. I indicated to him then that I was in no way authorised to discuss loan matters with him, and such matters were under the control of the Treasurer. I have also received one telephone message from Mr Karidis which involved Mr Khemlani. This message was from Athens on 12 August in which it was stated that discussions were then proceeding with certain bankers who wanted to come to Australia that weekend and asked whether I would be interested in pursuing the loan matter further. I repeated that I was not and that the matter was one for approach to the Treasurer.

This was a comprehensive denial of the Khemlani allegations. It was so comprehensive that if anyone could verify contact between Connor and Khemlani about the loan after 20 May then Connor's position would be untenable. There was one man close to Connor who was deeply concerned about the wording of the statement. This was Connor's press secretary Bob Sorby. When Sorby saw the statement he rang Jim Scully and asked whether it should be released in its present form. Sorby was worried by the wording and had doubts whether the statement was completely accurate. But he was reassured and it was released. Connor announced he had instructed his solicitors to issue writs for damages against the *Melbourne Herald*.[4]

Connor's statement and his appearances on television that night appeared to rebut the *Melbourne Herald* story. The Minister revealed that Khemlani sent him a telex in mid-June in an effort to further the loan negotiations but said that he had ignored the message. Connor said that he had not spoken to Khemlani since he took a call from the money dealer in mid-June. The Minerals and Energy Minister appeared on national television from his sickbed and ridiculed Khemlani's claim that they had spoken in the last ten days. Connor said he was in Canberra Hospital at the time. In his fighting political style he branded the claims as absurd and untrue. 'It's a patent political ploy of the worst possible type. A despicable ploy,' Connor said.

It is difficult to fathom why Connor's prepared statement contained the wording it did. Perhaps the Minister, who had been sick for some time, did not have a full grip of the situation. Perhaps the two public servants with him, Menadue and Scully, were unaware of the full ambit of his loan-raising efforts. This seems likely since Connor conducted them in the utmost secrecy, relying mainly on his Canberra landlady, Joan Taggart, and Karidis. It should have been obvious that at such a critical period Connor's statement had to be firstly, completely accurate and, secondly, as strong a rebuttal of Khemlani as possible. The government would be placed in a fatal position if the statement could be exposed as inaccurate. Yet this is what happened.

Those people familiar with the overseas loan episode should have been more wary. For instance, just after he became Treasurer, Bill Hayden sent letters to all the middlemen who had had contact with the Australian government informing them they had no authority on the government's behalf and that it was not interested in loans. Hayden also wrote to Connor asking him to send a letter to this effect to Khemlani. Connor wrote back saying Khemlani had been informed that the government was no longer interested in loans. But he never wrote a letter and therefore had no documentary proof of having notified Khemlani that he had no mandate and the government no longer wished to communicate with him. Whitlam had had the same experience as Hayden. Whitlam wrote to Connor on 13 June asking him to confirm that he had terminated all talks with Khemlani and anyone else involved in loan raisings. Connor wrote back on 18 June giving this assurance. But at no stage did the Prime Minister, his office or his department seek a copy of the letter to Mr Khemlani to this effect. If they had, they would have found that none existed.

This in itself is a commentary on Whitlam's style as Prime Minister. It is certainly an argument against those who claimed that Whitlam was too head-strong and too dominating a leader. The loans affair, from start to finish, demonstrated precisely the opposite. The reason the government came close to the brink of disaster in mid-year was because the Prime Minister gave a free rein to Rex Connor: he delegated the entire task of raising the $US4000 million loan to the Minerals and Energy Minister and in doing so abdicated his own responsibility as head of government.

It is permissible for a Prime Minister to err once; but Whitlam made precisely the same mistake, on the same subject, with the same man, twice. The Prime Minister gave Connor a free hand in the middle of the year when pulling out of the loan deal, just as he had given him a free hand at the start of the deal. It would have been easy for Whitlam to insist that Connor send a letter to Khemlani, thereby being absolutely sure. Yet the Prime Minister never insisted; he merely accepted at face value Connor's advice and found himself in the embarrassing situation of having to tell Parliament that previous assurances he had given the House were incorrect because he had been misled by Connor.

While Connor's statement on the evening of 8 October seemed to bolster the government in the face of the latest loan allegations, it was a defence conceived without proper preparation and could be easily shattered by Khemlani himself. Certainly the *Melbourne Herald*, faced with a writ, had a vested interest in proving the authenticity of its story. The next morning, 9 October, the *Herald* reported that Khemlani was flying to Australia to see Connor in an effort to conclude the loan. It appears that by this stage Khemlani himself was in big financial trouble, according to overseas reports.

The money dealer arrived in Sydney on the morning of 10 October in a tan safari suit and went straight to the Sydney Hilton for talks with his business associate Allan Crawford. The press, the government and the Opposition were all anxious to see whether Khemlani could produce any evidence of his continuing negotiations and dialogue with Connor which he claimed occurred after 20 May, in particular whether he could produce the telex he said he got from Connor in mid-June.

The *Melbourne Herald* made arrangements for Khemlani to travel to Melbourne over the weekend so it could examine his documents. On Sunday afternoon at the Liberal Party federal council meeting, the *Melbourne Herald* correspondent, John Monks, found out from his head office the essence of the story his paper would be carrying the next day and told Fraser and Lynch that the *Herald* would back its original story with proof. Fraser, who was already almost inexorably heading towards blocking the budget and forcing an election, had his confidence boosted by the knowledge of a new political plus for the Opposition.

Of all the fantastic and extraordinary events which occurred during Labor's three years in office, there was probably nothing more remarkable and ironic than the conjunction of incidents on Monday 13 October. The Opposition shadow Cabinet was due to meet this day to decide whether the coalition should force an election. Yet at the very same time the *Melbourne Herald*'s story plunged the government into a new crisis which could only end with either the dismissal or resignation of Rex Connor. The *Herald* carried a statutory declaration from Khemlani which said:

> I have read a copy of the statement of Mr Connor of October 8. Much of what Mr Connor said in this statement is not correct.
>
> In his statement, Mr Connor has said that he had only one telephone conversation with me after May 20. I say that I had at least twenty telephone conversations with Mr Connor between May 20 and the middle of June about problems I had run into with the negotiations for loans for the Australian government.
>
> In his statement, Mr Connor has said that he told me by telephone on June 11 that he was in no way authorised to discuss loan matters

with me and that such matters were under the control of the Treasurer. I say that he has never said these things to me. I also say that I have never had any doubt at all that he personally wanted me to continue my work in raising loan monies and to keep him advised of progress.

I have not received from Mr Connor either directly or indirectly any notification that my authority to negotiate loans for the Australian government has been revoked. On the contrary, it has been clear from my dealings with Mr Connor since May 20 that he personally has continued to work for the raising of loan monies.

During the period between May 20 and the middle of June, I communicated directly with Mr Connor by telex on many occasions. Now produced and shown to me and marked with the letters 'TK1' is a bundle of copies of the said telexes. In the middle of June it became apparent to me that there were problems in making sure that communications between Mr Connor and myself were kept confidential. I then advised Mr Connor that whilst I would continue to keep him advised of progress with the loan negotiations, I would not contact him directly unless this was necessary. From this time onwards, I have communicated with Mr Connor mainly through Mr Gerry Karidis who has had the confidence of both Mr Connor and myself . . .

In September I did believe that a loan for $US4 billion would be made because all conditions laid down by the lenders and by Mr Connor, of which I was aware, had been satisfied. I was then advised of a further requirement as to the verification of the availability of the funds and I have been and still am engaged in work directed to satisfying this requirement.

The *Herald* published eighteen telex messages with its statutory declaration. This was only a small number of the telexes Khemlani had with him. But of the eighteen messages all were from Khemlani to Connor except one—the crucial one in political terms. This was an outward message from Connor to the money man dated 23 May, three days after the loans authority was revoked. But the inward messages contained acknowledgments from Connor, one of his closest friends Joan Taggart, and one of his secretaries named Jill.

Connor's 23 May message was in response to one the same day from Khemlani indicating he was trying to mobilise funds through a prime bank in Frankfurt and suggesting that Karidis leave to meet him on Saturday. Connor replied: 'Attention Mr TH Khemlani: Response your telex of 0310 of today. I await further specific communication from your principals for consideration. From RFX Connor.'

It was obvious as soon as the *Melbourne Herald* arrived in Canberra that Connor would have to resign. Whitlam was in a situation where he had absolutely no political choice or room to manoeuvre. The Prime Minister had twice sacked Jim Cairns because of information he had received concerning Cairns' loan-raising activities. In both those cases the Prime Minister had a more flexible range of options than he had now. Whitlam had been very clever to protect himself in his parliamentary answers, stressing all the time that he was being advised by Connor. When the advice subsequently proved wrong as it did this Monday, he could say the responsibility was Connor's.

Whitlam saw Connor for half an hour in his office during the afternoon and said that he would have to resign. Throughout 1975 Whitlam had left the entire loan question in Connor's hands in an extraordinary abdication of Prime Ministerial responsibility. While there is no sign that Whitlam gave Connor definite approval to keep negotiating after 20 May, all the signs point to Connor having the tacit approval of the Prime Minister at least up until early June. If Connor could get the funds then the government would take them.

That evening as he left Parliament House, Connor was surrounded by journalists and was forced to push his way past them to get into his car. Government morale, which had been gradually building up over the previous two months since the Hayden budget, was destroyed at one blow. There was not a single Labor member or Senator who did not believe that the Opposition parties would now block the budget and force an election. The Opposition shadow Cabinet met but Fraser indicated no decision should be made until the Connor incident was completely resolved.

When the Labor Party caucus met on Tuesday 15 October, it voted 55–24 to accept Connor's offer to resign. The Minister told the party room he regarded himself as responsible to the caucus and any decision about his future should be made by the caucus. Connor told the party room he intended to resign from Cabinet about Christmas time anyway because of medical advice and his recent illness. He made no effort to attack Whitlam or to claim Whitlam was implicated through knowledge in loan-raising efforts after 20 May. But some of Connor's supporters wanted him to use Whitlam's letter to him of 29 May, which contained the suggestion that loan-raising activities were continuing up to that time. The caucus defeated a move by South Australian backbencher Martin Nicholls that Connor should be suspended pending a royal commission into the loans affair. Hayden and Jim McClelland opposed this motion. Tom Uren made a spirited defence of Connor inside the party room and claimed that he was being made a scapegoat.

The party accepted a motion moved by Mick Young and amended by Clyde Cameron which read: 'That Rex Connor's offer of resignation be accepted with regret, and that we place on record the party's admiration for the assiduous and dedicated manner in which Mr Connor has sought to implement Labor's policy to preserve Australian ownership and control of its energy and mineral resources.' As soon as the caucus broke, Whitlam made swift arrangements to present a solid front in Parliament that afternoon. The Governor-General accepted Connor's resignation and Wriedt was sworn in as Minister for Minerals and Energy.

When the House sat at 2.15 p.m. the Opposition, spearheaded by Fraser and Lynch, put into effect the last strategy it would adopt on the loans affair: trying to implicate Whitlam himself and force him to resign, in the manner both Cairns and Connor had been executed.

Malcolm Fraser decided quite firmly in his own mind that the Opposition would force an election when the Connor incident came to the boil. Whether he would have plunged into the same unknown waters without the Connor resignation will never be known. But all the signs suggest that he would.[5]

Fraser's speech to the Liberal Party federal council and the talks he held over the weekend immediately preceding the Connor upheaval indicate that he was already far advanced along this course. The real significance of the Connor resignation was not in shifting the balance with Fraser but in making it impossible for those Liberals who had genuine doubts about blocking supply to dissuade the party out of this course of action.

The timing of Connor's exit was perfect for Fraser. All the arguments he used against the government in July, at the time of the Cairns sacking, were given fresh credence once again. The two most senior men in the party next to Whitlam, Cairns and Connor, had both been driven from office as a result of the government's loan activities. Few Opposition Leaders in history have been given such invaluable political ammunition to use against a government to argue that it was unfit to hold office. The overwhelming majority of the Liberal and National Country Party parliamentarians favoured blocking the budget. Those who were waverers had their minds made up by the Connor resignation. Those who were committed opponents of blocking the budget had their arguments all but destroyed.

It is again a hypothetical question whether Missen and his group of Senators could ever have forced the coalition parties to pass the budget by refusing to obstruct it in the Senate. All the indications are that they would not have succeeded if Fraser and his leadership group were committed to an early poll. But the Connor resignation made absolutely certain they would never prevail in the party room.

That evening Whitlam made a television address to explain the reasons for Connor's resignation and to try to hold together the shattered morale of his government. One could hardly imagine a greater contrast between the Connor departure and that of Jim Cairns three months previously in July. Whitlam said he was forced to act because of a departure from the fundamental principle of parliamentary government: that the parliament must be able to accept assurances given to it by Ministers. The Prime Minister made the point that Connor had resigned not because of his loan negotiations but because he misled parliament. Describing Connor as 'a great Minister and a close friend', Whitlam said that at no time had there been any allegations of 'improper conduct, of dishonest conduct, or reprehensible conduct, of illegal or corrupt conduct by any member of the government'.

That afternoon Fraser's leadership group met to discuss the government's Appropriation Bills then in the Senate. It was unanimously decided that the Opposition should use its numbers in the Senate to delay the bills and force the Whitlam government into a general election. Fraser and Withers were meticulous about the way this should be done, particularly in view of Whitlam's publicly stated remarks that in these circumstances he would not feel obliged to call a general election but would seek either a half-Senate election or try to remain in office and 'tough it out'.

The Opposition decided it would not reject the budget. Rejection would mean that it lost its control over the money bills and the only way supply could ever be obtained would be for the Labor government to reintroduce the bills into the House of Representatives, where it had a majority, and pass them. This would give Whitlam substantial room to manoeuvre.

The Opposition would move instead to defer the budget bills, using the same technique it had applied in 1974 when forcing the May double dissolution election. In deferring the bills the Opposition would pass a motion in the Senate delaying the passage of the budget until Whitlam sought an election. Once the election was obtained, the budget would pass. In short, the Opposition would use its Senate strength to blackmail the government into an election. It would never pass or reject the budget; it would simply defer the budget until its prime condition was met. To pass such a motion, the Opposition needed a clear majority in the Senate. It had the required numbers 30–29 over Labor, without the vote of Senator Field who was then on leave of absence and given that the other two independents, Steele Hall and Cleaver Bunton, would vote with Labor.

The decision to defer rather than reject had two political advantages. First, the wavering Liberal Senators saw a substantial difference between deferment and outright rejection of the budget and would be more prepared to accept the former rather than the latter. But the second and more fundamental reason for deferral originated with Whitlam's threat to remain in office. Fraser and his leadership group assessed this possibility very carefully before taking their decision. Fraser realised that if Whitlam tried to remain in office after the budget was blocked it would be essential for the Opposition to have control over supply in the Senate; if a constitutional crisis threatened involving the Governor-General, then

Fraser himself would be in a position to obtain supply through the Senate. If the budget was rejected he would have no such power.[6]

So from the very start the Opposition planned for the contingency that eventually happened. It believed that if Whitlam tried to remain in office the Governor-General would eventually have to dismiss him and commission a new government. It would be essential for the Opposition, as the potential new government, to be in a situation where it could guarantee supply through the Senate as a prelude to giving the Governor-General the advice he wanted, namely, a general election.

That evening Fraser spoke with senior newspaper executives from at least two of Australia's three major newspaper chains and informed them that he had decided to force an election. The next morning's papers contained front page reports based on leaks of the Opposition's decision. Almost without exception the press supported Fraser's decision to force an election and the *Sydney Morning Herald* and the *Age* adopted the unusual practice of running part of their editorial on page one, giving full backing to the Liberal–National Country Parties. Fraser was particularly pleased with the editorial in the *Age*, which he regarded as the most independently minded and influential newspaper.

On page one the *Age* editorialised:

> We will say it straight and clear, and at once. The Whitlam government has run its course; it must go now, and preferably by the honourable course of resignation—a course which would dispel all arguments about constitutional proprieties, historic conventions and 'grabs' for power. It must go because it no longer has the degree of public support and acceptance that permits governments to govern effectively.

The Opposition Leader now had satisfied the condition he set in mid-year for an early election: the support of Australia's major newspapers. The next morning the Opposition shadow ministry met briefly and Fraser put the proposition decided by the leadership group. He went right around the table seeking the opinion of every member. They all replied 'Yes' with the exception of Senator Margaret Guilfoyle, who betrayed the confidence of the Opposition parties' belief that the government was there for the taking when she replied, 'Yes please'. The die was now cast: all that remained was to secure the formality of party room endorsement.

There were two party meetings that day on the Opposition side of parliament. During the morning the Liberal Senators met and had an extensive discussion about the imminent deferral of the budget. It was clear to Missen at this meeting that there was no way he would be able to prevent the party from this course of action.[7]

The main Liberal and National Country party meeting began with a minor uproar when it was realised that Missen was not present. Some feared he might be boycotting the meeting as a prelude to repudiating the decision. But Fred Chaney found him in the dining room totally unaware that the meeting was on. Fraser addressed the joint parties, announced the recommendation from the shadow ministry, and told the party room that he wanted a unanimous decision on the issue so there would be no misunderstanding about anyone's position. Fraser realised this was vital, for he anticipated a long struggle with Whitlam that would test the nerve of every member of both sides of parliament.

A number of members spoke in favour of the decision, including front bench Liberal Jim Killen who in the past had been a vigorous critic of the Senate's use of its power over money bills. But Killen told the party room he believed the use of such power was fully justified in the present circumstances to force the Labor government to the people. Only two people stood out against the move—Missen and Don Jessop.

Missen delivered a lengthy, cogent and tense speech outlining his objections to the deferral of the budget. He said the Senate's power should only be used in the most extreme circumstances and that in the present situation the Senate should not overplay its hand. He argued that governments should expect to remain in office for three years and that once they were cut down there were dreadful dangers that the community would become polarised and that henceforth the party which had been forced to the polls would merely wait for the chance to do exactly the same to its successor. Missen said he believed the government would probably disintegrate anyway. He pointed out that the Liberal Party had indicated to the government that it could ordinarily expect to remain for three years, that Labor had proceeded on this basis, and that the Opposition should see how the Hayden budget worked. Missen also warned about the industrial repercussions of such action. He said there was a danger of severe divisions developing in the community if the industrial movement believed its government had been sabotaged in office.

The clear import of Missen's speech was that he disagreed with the decision and reserved his position.[8] After he had finished speaking and while the party meeting was continuing, Lynch quietly asked Missen to have a private chat with him. The two men left the party room through the door to the office of the Opposition Leader and chatted together in Fraser's office for a few minutes. Missen told Lynch that while he had grave doubts about the decision he would not repudiate the party or go against it in a unilateral revolt. When the two men re-entered the party room Lynch spoke briefly to Fraser and the Opposition Leader said, 'Thank you, Alan. We have a unanimous decision.' The only other note of discontent was Jessop who spoke briefly setting out his doubt. But Jessop indicated he would adhere to the party room decision.

That afternoon Malcolm Fraser called a press conference to explain his decision to the nation. Fraser used three main arguments to support his case. First, that the Whitlam Labor government was the most incompetent and disastrous in Australian history. Despite Australia's basically strong economy, the country had been brought to the brink of disaster with the highest unemployment since the great Depression and the worst prolonged inflation ever. Second, he branded the Hayden budget an admitted failure even though it had been introduced only eight weeks before. Fraser said the estimated deficit of $3.5 billion, compared with the deficit figure of $2.8 billion when the budget was introduced, was proof of failure.

Finally he attacked the government's loan raisings, saying they had been marked by a long record of scandals, attempts to evade the constitution, and the removal of two men who were acting Prime Minister when Whitlam was overseas. Fraser said: 'We are dealing with a chain of improprieties which constitute one of the most extraordinary and reprehensible episodes in Australia's political history.'

The following exchange then took place during a bitter and tough press conference with gallery reporters:

Question: Will it be acceptable to you if the PM calls a half-Senate election?

Fraser: The House of Representatives must go to an election.

Question: Under those circumstances, what would you do?

Fraser: After this statement the ball will be in the Prime Minister's court. Let him say what he will be doing but he should take the House of Representatives and half the Senate at least to an election.

Question: What are the constitutional options open to you if he doesn't?

Fraser: Let's see what happens when the Prime Minister has made his decision about whether he'll behave with propriety in one of the remaining acts that he will be able to do of service to Australia.

Question: Mr Fraser, can you force the Prime Minister to a double dissolution?

Fraser: We can get the House of Representatives to an election. Yes.

Question: How?

Fraser: When we know the Prime Minister's other moves, our other moves will also be revealed.

Question: This is the second time in eighteen months that you have threatened to reject money bills in the Senate to force an election. Why should the people of Australia think that this is none other than another attempt by the Opposition to take power?

Fraser: I suggest that you read this morning's newspapers.

Question: On 21 August you said your intention at that time was to pass the budget through the Senate. Could you tell us precisely what's happened over the last seven weeks to make you change your mind?

Fraser: Over the last seven weeks the budget has been an admitted failure on two counts as I mentioned in the statement, and in addition to this it is the totality of the government's action for which it must be brought to account. The most recent of its actions concerns the resignation of Mr Connor, and I think that you all know about that or as much as anyone else does . . .

Question: Mr Fraser, how soon after you become Prime Minister will you be able to get jobs for school leavers, homes for young people, restore the savings of the aged and shore up the life's work of small business men?

Fraser: The country has, I believe, been so severely damaged by the present government that it would take a full three year program of responsible government to restore the situation to one that we would like to see.

This press conference contained the vital ingredients involved in the Fraser decision. He placed stress on the newspapers because he was keen to see the move depicted as a response to a popular feeling. Knowing there was a major battle looming with Whitlam, he was resolute from the outset. Finally, he made it clear that it would take three years to 'right' the economy, even though he was denying this to the Labor government.

Fraser's decision to block the budget was, on his own admission, probably the most difficult of his political career. He assessed the prospects and consequences carefully, of both going and not going at that time, weighed the feelings inside his own party, within the Senate, within the organisation and among the state branches. He thought through Whitlam's likely response and, along with Ellicott, made a judgement of the Governor-General.

The record shows that this was both a momentous and faultless decision on Fraser's part. It was superb politics, as subsequent events were to prove. But the manner in which Fraser reached his decision raised the most fundamental question about his techniques as a leader. Ultimately his bid for power, and his belief that there was a justification for that bid, triumphed over his concern about constitutional proprieties. Fraser, like a number of his senior colleagues, believed his action was justified to get rid of a government that he saw as corrupt, dishonest and ineffective.

Fraser's decision confirmed one of the great paradoxes of the Whitlam years: that the conservative parties cast themselves in the role of constitutional radicals. By their actions in successive years both Snedden and Fraser had changed the future ground rules of Australian politics so that henceforth any government which did not have a Senate majority would be in danger of being forced to the polls twice a year. This was a drastic change which might not necessarily favour the non-Labor parties, who normally spent more time in government than in Opposition.

The strength of this view was highlighted on Saturday 11 October before the Connor resignation when eight of Australia's leading law professors publicly declared themselves against the blocking of the budget. They were Professors Geoffrey Sawer, Lesley Zines, A Castles, Colin Howard, J Stone, R Sackville, I Shearer and Garth Nettheim. The letter signed by the first four read:

> The rejection of the budget by the Senate in the present circumstances would be a constitutional impropriety of the first order. It would be likely to do irreparable damage to the parliamentary system as we have known it. It would be an act which future generations will have cause to regret . . . The strict letter of the constitution has to be read subject to a great many unwritten rules, which are extremely important in making the whole system work . . . One example may suffice: The Queen has the power, conferred in the clearest terms by Section 59 of the constitution, to disallow any Australian law within one year of it being assented to by the Governor-General. But it would be unthinkable now for the Queen to exercise that power. The unwritten rule in question in the present situation is the convention that the control of the supply of money to the government, which determines the government's continued existence, should rest with the Lower House. Only the Lower House, where governments are made, should have the power to break them . . . Governments have to put up major money bills at least twice year. If they have to run the gauntlet of an election threat every time they do so, orderly government and rational long-term decision-making will become impossible . . . The reduction of an ultimate constitutional sanction—if indeed it should ever be used at all—to the level of a routine political tactic is a debasing of our constitutional system and the democratic values it is supposed to protect.

325

# 20

## THE CONSTITUTIONAL CRISIS

*The Governor-General takes advice from his Prime Minister and from no-one else.*

Gough Whitlam, 17 October 1975

Only when it became obvious that the budget would be blocked did the Prime Minister decide his tactics. He moved instinctively. He would 'tough it out' with all the determination he could summon.

The Labor Party caucus met at 7 p.m., a few hours after Fraser's press conference, and Whitlam received overwhelming party endorsement for his stand. The Prime Minister told the caucus he wanted the Senate to vote on the budget and would continue referring the bills to the Senate until it voted to either accept or reject them, instead of merely deferring them. Meanwhile the government would remain in office and defy the Senate's move to force a general election. Whitlam reserved his right to call a half-Senate election at a later stage or after the budget was rejected. Only two people opposed these tactics. They were the Leader of the Government in the Senate Ken Wriedt and the Minister for Social Security Senator John Wheeldon, both of whom argued for a double dissolution instead.

That evening Whitlam delivered a fighting address to the nation, televised nationally, attacking Fraser for repudiating his earlier statements and declaring:

> I make it clear that the government will not yield to pressure. We will not yield to blackmail. We will not be panicked. We will not turn over the government of this country to vested interests, pressure groups and newspaper proprietors whose tactics would destroy the standards

and traditions of parliamentary government. The business of government will go on.

Australia's constitutional battle had been joined.

The clash between the government and the Opposition during the constitutional crisis was very much a public one. From the start this was the greatest confrontation between the two Houses of Parliament since Federation. On Thursday 16 October, as soon as the House sat in the morning, Whitlam moved a long motion of confidence in his government and a condemnation of the Senate for its threatened action. He said the Senate 'cannot, does not, and must never determine who the government shall be'. He said that under the system of responsible government on the Westminster model, the House of Representatives, through which the government was chosen, held financial paramountcy over the Upper House. 'The convention has been clearly established that the Senate, which has no power to originate or amend money bills, shall not block or reject them either,' Whitlam declared as he launched a bitter attack on his opponents.

> It is because this government has attempted to make this parliament the instrument for reform, for long overdue change, for progress, for the redistribution of wealth, for the uplifting of the underprivileged, for the reduction of the privileges of great wealth and deeply entrenched vested interests, an instrument towards equality of opportunity for all Australians, that our opponents and those vested interests have from the very beginning, as Senator Withers revealed, embarked on a course to destroy this government at the earliest opportunity. But what they are really doing is destroying the very basis of parliamentary democracy in our country . . . It is the Senate which is on trial . . . It is the Senate which must face the people. Again, in the indelible words of Senator Steele Hall, it is the Senate, the Liberal Party and the Liberal leader which, by the course they are now attempting, have sown the seeds of their own destruction.

Whitlam saw the Senate as the greatest obstacle to stable government and the legislative program of a reformist government. It was only a short step from his statements in the parliament to his later declaration on 19 October that he would 'smash the Senate's power for all time'.

This was the first ingredient in the Prime Minister's political misjudgement. His comments about convention were true and his predictions about the difficulties parliamentary democracy would face if the Senate succeeded were probably also true, although only time will tell. But Whitlam's mistake in trying to break the Senate was to ignore that, under Section 53 of the constitution, the Senate had the power to reject or defer money bills. This was the law. The Opposition in the Senate had the constitution on its side.

Whitlam, by his stand, was really trying to force upon history his own interpretation of the relations between both Houses, an interpretation at variance with the powers conferred by the constitution. If he won, then in practical political terms, the Senate might never attempt to defer money bills again. But if the Opposition held out in the Senate, with the force of law behind it, then Whitlam would be in trouble. This was where the Prime Minister took his greatest gamble and staked the future of his political life. If events went this far then the key person would become the Governor-General Sir John Kerr.

Whitlam knew Kerr well. He was always confident, right from the start, that Kerr was sympathetic to his position and understanding of what he was trying to achieve. The Prime Minister's tactics were sound, providing the Governor-General continued to acquiesce in them despite the consequences.

This raised the crucial question as to the role of the Governor-General. By convention and tradition, the Governor-General always acted on the advice of his Ministers and not without that advice. But once again, under the Australian constitution, under the strict letter of the law, the Governor-General had immense powers. For instance under Section 5 he could appoint times for the holding of parliament as he thought fit and in the same way dissolve the House of Representatives on his own initiative. Under Section 64 the Governor-General appointed his Ministers who 'hold office during the pleasure of the Governor-General'. In short, the Governor-General had the power to decommission Ministers and dissolve the House of Representatives and this function was vested in his office, not the Queen's.

In the formulation of his strategy Whitlam dismissed these factors. It was inconceivable to the Prime Minister that the Governor-General would embark on a course of major action in defiance of his government. This would be a breach of all the conventions surrounding his office as well as being calculated to inflame political passions beyond control. Whitlam made two incorrect assessments. The first was that Sir John Kerr would remain acquiescent throughout, and the second that these constitutional powers of the Governor-General would never be invoked.

The Prime Minister was quite vocal in his view of the Governor-General's role. On 17 October when interviewed on 'This Day Tonight' by Richard Carleton, the following exchange took place:

Carleton: Sir, must Sir John Kerr accept your advice whatever advice you give him?

Whitlam: Unquestionably. The Governor-General takes the advice from his Prime Minister and from no one else.

Carleton: And must act on that advice?

Whitlam: Unquestionably. The Governor-General must act on the advice of his Prime Minister.

Carleton: There is no tolerance here, he must do . . .

Whitlam: None whatever.

Carleton: Fine. Well obviously there is dispute in the community, but your view is quite plain.

This was the cornerstone of Whitlam's strategy and if it did not stand then his strategy would collapse. Sir John had to remain solid for the Prime Minister; he had to act on Whitlam's advice. This was the second main area of the Prime Minister's misjudgement.

His third mistake was pushing his half-Senate election option further and further into the background. A fortnight before the budget was blocked it appeared likely that Whitlam would call a half-Senate election when this happened. But after the Opposition's announcement, Whitlam said he would remain in office and not call a half-Senate election for some time. On 17 October, two days after the announcement, he said he would only call a half-Senate election when the Senate rejected the budget. By 21 October, Whitlam was announcing in the House that he would tender no advice to the Governor-General for either a House of Representatives or Senate election until the crisis was over and the budget passed.

This pattern of statements reveals that over the first week, after the deferral of the budget, Whitlam took an increasingly tougher stand in favour of remaining in office and not seeking a half-Senate election. The political tactic behind this was to kill dead any Opposition hope that the government would cave in. The Prime Minister deliberately cut off any hope of a government concession and then kept referring the budget back to the Senate, all the while documenting the hardship which would result from continued refusal to pass it. Whitlam knew very well the great doubts shared by a number of Liberal Senators over the deferral. He aimed to crack the nerve of the Liberal Party.

The real weakness of Whitlam's position was that he did not cover himself in the event that his strategy was unsuccessful. What happened after a few weeks if the Opposition remained firm and the Prime Minister did not have time to call a half-Senate election before supply ran out? What were Kerr's options in such a situation? According to Whitlam's approach the Governor-General would have to accept either a government remaining in office without supply or a Senate election being held with supply expiring before its conclusion.

One of the fundamental requirements on any Governor-General before granting a Prime Minister an election was to ensure there was adequate supply for the period up to the return of election writs or declaration of the poll. This was axiomatic. It was a convention binding on all Governors-General and Viceroys who did their job properly. Yet Whitlam embarked on a strategy where, if there were no quick resolution of the crisis, Kerr would have to accept a situation where the government ran out of money.

In retrospect it is clear, and it was clear to a number of Liberal Party strategists at the time, that if Whitlam was to have a half-Senate election he had to seek it immediately. If his initial response after the deferral of the budget had been to advise the Governor-General on a half-Senate election then it would have been possible to have the election, which was due before July 1976, before the exhaustion of money. The sole issue of this election campaign would have been the deferral of the budget and this would have maximised Labor's electoral opportunities. If Labor lost this poll and the Opposition continued to defer the budget then Whitlam would have had to accept a general election.

The real alternative to this half-Senate strategy was to 'tough it out' as the Prime Minister did for as long as possible, building up Labor's electoral position all the time and then, when the money was nearly depleted, to call a general election. These were the two viable strategies facing the Labor government. The half-Senate strategy was aimed at winning control of the Senate through exploiting budget deferral. The 'toughing it out' strategy was aimed at cracking the Liberal Senators by building up pressure against them. If either strategy failed then the fall-back position would be a general election.

However Whitlam did not see it this way. He rejected a general election absolutely. His own instinctive response was to 'tough it out' and, if this failed to break the Opposition, to seek a half-Senate election late in the crisis with the knowledge that supply would not last until polling day, let alone the election results. If Whitlam was forced into this fall-back position he would be in peril. This is precisely what happened. The fact that it did reveals a failure of political strategy and judgement on the part of the Prime Minister and his advisers.

The crisis immediately provoked violence in the country and bitterness in parliament. Thousands of people demonstrated in Melbourne in the opening days. On Thursday 16 October several thousand people demonstrated on the lawns opposite Parliament House. The worst incidents occurred in Hobart on 17 October when Fraser was howled down by a jeering and hostile crowd of 4000 people in the city's Franklin Square. Punches were traded between pro- and anti-Fraser demonstrators, Tasmanian Liberal Senator John Marriott and other Liberal supporters scuffled with demonstrators, and Fraser was surrounded by uniformed and plain-clothes policemen all day. On the same day in Brisbane 5000 people attended a huge Labor rally in King George Square to hear Bill Hayden tell them that the government would not surrender.

This was the start of the political campaign, in which each side tried to discredit the other as the prospect of hardship through the depletion of government monies was continually emphasised by Labor Ministers.

The question of who was to blame was at the core of this debate. If the electorate shifted decisively one way or the other then the side being blamed would face enormous pressure to concede.

Hayden initiated this line of attack in Parliament on 16 October predicting that, as a result of the Opposition's action, a major economic collapse was threatening. He predicted the failure of a big number of corporate sector enterprises, an upsurge in unemployment and deepening of the recession. The Opposition absorbed Labor's attack and retaliated. In Parliament on 16 October Malcolm Fraser, in reply to Whitlam's motion of confidence, said that there was a universal call around the nation for an election. In particular, Fraser sought to expose Whitlam as a hypocrite. He quoted the Prime Minister's own words when he was Opposition leader in 1970 debating a Liberal budget. Whitlam had said: 'If the motion is defeated, we will vote against the bills here and in the Senate. Our purpose is to destroy this budget and to destroy the government which has sponsored it.' That is, Whitlam himself was prepared to take the precise action for which he was now attacking the Opposition. Fraser hammered the Prime Minister's duplicity, the economy and the loans affair.

But it was the next day that the Opposition's own strategy and hopes were revealed when Liberal frontbencher Bob Ellicott released a press statement on the Governor-General's powers. This statement was virtually ignored at the time; it received very little press cover but its thinking was central to Fraser's decision to defer the budget. Ellicott's view of the Governor-General's powers and responsibilities was diametrically opposed to that of the Prime Minister. His statement was the Liberal Party text. It proved to be one of the most prophetic statements in Australian politics:

> The Prime Minister is treating the Governor-General as a mere automaton with no public will of his own, sitting at Yarralumla waiting to do his bidding.
>
> Nothing could be further from the truth. It is contrary to principle, precedent and common sense. The Governor-General has at least two clear constitutional prerogatives which he can exercise—the right to dismiss his Ministers and appoint others, and the right to refuse a dissolution of the Parliament or of either House.
>
> These prerogatives, of their very nature, will only be exercised on the rarest occasions. They have been exercised in the past and the proper working of the Constitution demands that they continue. One only has to think of extreme cases to realise the sense behind them, e.g. the case of an obviously corrupt government.
>
> The maintenance of the Constitution and of the laws of the Commonwealth require that the government has authority from Parliament to spend money in order to perform those functions. A government without supply cannot govern. The refusal by Parliament

of supply, whether through the House or the Senate, is a clear signal to the Governor-General that his chosen Ministers may not be able to carry on. In the proper performance of his role, he would inevitably want to have from the Prime Minister an explanation of how he proposed to overcome the situation. If the Prime Minister proposed and insisted on means which were unlawful or which did not solve the problems of the disagreement between the Houses and left the Government without funds to carry on, it would be within the Governor-General's power and his duty to dismiss his Ministers and appoint others . . .

The Governor-General is entitled to know:

1  when it is that the Government will or is likely to run out of funds under the current supply acts; and
2  how the Government proposes to carry on after those funds run out; and
3  how the Government proposes that the disagreement between the two Houses should be resolved . . .

If he is informed by the Prime Minister that the Government proposes that a half-Senate election be held and that by this means (as a result of the election of territory Senators) the Government hopes to have a majority in the Senate the Governor-General will need to be satisfied:

i  that having regard to the proposed date of the election, the Government will have sufficient supply to carry on until the result of that election has been ascertained
ii  that the election is likely to resolve the difference between the two Houses by giving the Government a majority in the Senate . . .

If the Governor-General was not satisfied that the Government would have supply until the election results in the territories was known he would only have one option open to him in the interests of good government. He is entitled to and should ask the Prime Minister if the Government is prepared to advise him to dissolve the House of Representatives and the Senate or the House of Representatives alone as a means of ensuring that the disagreement between the two Houses is resolved.

If the Prime Minister refuses to do either it is then open to the Governor-General to dismiss his present Ministers and seek others who are prepared to give him the only proper advice open. This he should proceed to do.

After he released this press statement Ellicott sent a copy to the Governor-General's official secretary David Smith. One of the perplexing questions is whether Government House asked for the statement or Ellicott sent it on his own initiative. Ellicott has told his colleagues that Government House gave him an indication it was interested in the opinion. But Government House said that Ellicott simply sent it to them.

On 6 November the Attorney-General Kep Enderby asked Kerr whether he had sought the Ellicott opinion and the Governor-General replied that he had not.

The Opposition took up Ellicott's assessment and ran with it. On Sunday 19 October Fraser told a 12,000 strong cheering rally in Melbourne that the Governor-General might have to intervene to resolve the crisis. Fraser said he expected that Sir John would act 'quite soon' to break the deadlock. The same weekend Ellicott appeared on the television program 'Federal File' and repeated the substance of his opinion saying that if Whitlam maintained his position, the Governor-General would have no option but to withdraw his commission. This Opposition line received extensive media treatment and some papers carried banner headlines declaring 'Fraser says Kerr must sack Whitlam—pressure on Governor-General to end crisis'. Whitlam and his Ministers were incredulous at the Opposition claim that the Prime Minister could be dismissed from office. The main question in Whitlam's mind was always whether or not Kerr would concur in his tactics. But the Prime Minister never appeared to give serious consideration to the possibility of his dismissal.

Throughout the crisis period the Solicitor-General Maurice Byers provided Whitlam's office with a large number of drafts replying to the Ellicott opinion. But when Freudenberg and other Whitlam staffers were preparing the Prime Minister's parliamentary speeches they made only minor efforts to include detailed rebuttals of the Ellicott view based on Byers' drafts. Freudenberg tended to think that Byers was engaging in legal rivalry with his old associate Ellicott by trying to shoot down his opinion. At no stage did Whitlam's office believe that the Ellicott opinion was central to the debate. Unlike the Attorney-General's Department, it believed that Ellicott's remarks were peripheral and that the question of withdrawing Whitlam's commission was simply not an issue. They could not have been more wrong.[1]

Kerr and Whitlam seemed to engage in apparently friendly banter at the outset of the crisis. On one occasion the Governor-General said to the Prime Minister in a jovial fashion: 'I believe you'll be out to see me shortly.' Whitlam replied in similar vein: 'Not next week, not next month, not next year.'

On the evening of 16 October at the Government House dinner for the late Malaysian Prime Minister Tun Razak, there was an exchange which assumed much significance. Whitlam jovially told Kerr that the whole situation revolved around who could sack whom first. Kerr interpreted this as a sign that Whitlam was prepared to sack him if he bucked the Prime Minister.[2]

On the morning of Monday 20 October Whitlam was at Government House for an Executive Council meeting and the swearing in of Labor's latest Minister, Paul Keating, as Minister for Northern Development, and of Rex Patterson as Agriculture Minister. This followed the Connor resignation. Whitlam saw Kerr for about ten minutes after the meeting and the Governor-General sought the Prime Minister's consent to hold talks with the Opposition Leader about the crisis. Whitlam readily agreed. He saw no problem with this. Whitlam was prepared to have Kerr talking with both leaders because he was confident of the Governor-General. This was a fateful decision. It transformed Kerr's role in the crisis and put him into touch with both leaders on a regular basis.

By the same token Whitlam had conveyed to Kerr, spiced with suitable displays of joviality, the importance of the Governor-General relying on his advice. As time went on and Whitlam's reliance on the Governor-General became more important, a number of people close to the Prime Minister became convinced that he would sack Kerr if the Governor-General did not cooperate. From an early stage in the crisis this was Kerr's own view.[3]

It was during this period—the week following budget deferral—that Whitlam explained the government's plan for alternative arrangements for supply to the Governor-General. John Menadue, as Secretary to the Prime Minister's Department, had been involved in this assessment. Soon after the first vote in the Senate deferring the budget, a special ad hoc Cabinet committee was established to study how the government could continue paying its employees and government contractors. The committee comprised Whitlam, Crean, Hayden, Enderby and Wriedt. Most of the preparatory work was done within the Treasury and the Attorney-General's Department, with Menadue playing an important role. When Whitlam explained the alternative funding through the banking system to Kerr, the Governor-General expressed no objection at all despite the huge ramifications.

These measures were one of the most curious aspects of the whole crisis. In seeking to pay both its own employees as well as government contractors, the government was attempting to find a partial solution through the banking system that would avoid practical difficulties involved in the blocking of the budget. This in itself appeared to be an admission of the Ellicott argument, which was that a government could not continue without money.

Yet the alternative arrangements could never be regarded as an adequate substitute for supply and could not cover the wide ambit of programs which supply funded. Moreover, such measures in themselves were contrary to the political purposes the government was aiming at, namely the breaking of the Opposition deadlock. The chief argument to achieve this was the threat of chaos. The more the government assured people they would be paid, the less was chaos threatened and the more was pressure on the Opposition to back down reduced.

The Prime Minister himself was furious with Crean when, on Sunday 19 October the ex-Treasurer said of the budget blockage: 'If it continues there will have to be unconstitutional things done to stop the system breaking down.' The one axiom on which Whitlam insisted about the alternative arrangements was that they had to be legal and constitutional. The Prime Minister wanted to be absolutely certain that there was no way he could be accused of acting illegally, thereby putting the Governor-General under pressure to dismiss him. Senior Attorney-General's officials, as well as the Solicitor-General, were told that they had to examine the arrangements from every point of view to ensure there was no illegality. This was done and it forced the Treasury to modify its original proposals.

Whitlam was always a determined politician but during this crisis the vehemence with which he took his stand seemed to transcend even his well-known determination. A number of Labor members who were close to the Prime Minister reported that they had never before seen him so committed and so relentless in his pursuit of a political goal. The Prime Minister's speeches in parliament at this period reflected his state of mind. On 21 October Whitlam rejected the Senate's message deferring the budget and moved in the House that a message be sent to the Senate asking it to pass the bills without delay. The Prime Minister said:

> This is an issue not just for this present government and for me; it is a principle of fundamental importance for all future governments and Prime Ministers and for Australia . . . Not for the first time is government of the people for the people by the people—and in our case, by the people's House—at stake. In the words of Lincoln when he was trying to avert the greatest constitutional convulsion in the history of democracy, let me say to the Leader of the Opposition and his followers: in your hands and not in mine rests this momentous issue. You can have no conflict without yourself being the aggressor. You have registered no oath to destroy the constitution, while I have the most solemn one to preserve and defend it. The Leader of the Opposition maintains that all that is required for Australia to avoid the evil consequences of his own actions is for us—the elected government—to cave in. Of course, if Britain had caved in in 1940 a great deal of inconvenience would have been avoided. But the destruction of British parliamentary democracy would have only been postponed. We will stand up for the rights of this House and the rights of the Australian people. We will not surrender.

The previous evening Whitlam said when interviewed by Michael Schildberger: 'I've never been so certain of anything in my life as I am, that the Senate's money power will be broken as a result of this crisis.

No future Australian government will ever be threatened by the Senate again, with a rejection of its budget or a refusal of supply. Never again.' Whitlam always believed in crashing through. Now he was trying to crash through the Senate. These sorts of comments led a number of Liberals, including Fraser, to believe that Whitlam was becoming irrational. But while this claim was incorrect it was nevertheless true that Whitlam's sheer dogmatism was to a certain extent clouding a more hard-headed long-term political assessment of the crisis.

On the evening of 21 October Fraser received his invitation to Government House for his first session with Kerr, left at 7 p.m. and returned at 8.30 p.m. This meeting became a matter of major controversy when Fraser returned to Parliament House. A number of journalists were told by authoritative non-Labor sources before the meeting that Sir John had been upset about the prominent media treatment given statements by Opposition leaders saying he had to intervene and dismiss the government. On hearing of these rumours during the night, Fraser's office firmly denied them and the Opposition Leader spoke with senior newspaper executives as well as the Governor-General's official secretary David Smith, to ensure that stories of this nature were denied and did not appear.

The real significance of Fraser's first discussion with Kerr was revealed the next day on Wednesday 22 October when the Opposition changed its public stand. After conferring extensively with his leadership group, Fraser announced on television that night that the Opposition parties would abide by any decision reached by the Governor-General.

Fraser said the Opposition would consider 'very deeply' any advice tendered by Sir John. This was widely interpreted at the time as the first step in a backdown by the Opposition. But it was not. It was designed to cover all Fraser's options. If the Governor-General intervened against the Opposition then Fraser would have already prepared his ground for a backdown and would be in a better position to accept such a defeat, particularly inside his own party and in terms of public opinion. But it was also signalling the Governor-General that the Opposition believed he had a role and they would acquiesce in it without trying to tell him what to do. Fraser was deferring to the Governor-General's judgement— a smart stance. Fraser remained confident that this judgement would be in his favour. But henceforth Fraser avoided making public declarations about what the Governor-General should or should not do.

Whitlam's own statements about the Governor-General could be interpreted in two ways. In the early part of the crisis the Prime Minister attacked the Opposition, accusing it of intimidating the Governor-General. 'It is unthinkable that in Britain the Queen would dismiss a Prime Minister having the confidence of the House of Commons,' Whitlam declared in parliament. When he made these statements, Whitlam believed he was both defending Kerr from outside pressures as well as defining his own view of the Governor-General's position. The other interpretation of his comments was that put forward by the Opposition—that Whitlam was trying to reduce Kerr's role to that of a puppet.

As the crisis moved into its second week, Labor appeared to be well on top. Right from the start Bob Hawke had used all his efforts to prevent the threat of nationwide strikes. The industrial movement had fallen behind the political wing of the party in a massive display of support. Telegrams, letters and donations poured into the party, lifting the morale of the Prime Minister and his colleagues. Even more important was the response which individual caucus members received from their electorates over the weekend. They were sure after returning to parliament on Tuesday 21 October that the issue of 'who's to blame' was running Labor's way. At every opportunity both Whitlam and Fraser were flying interstate to address major rallies in a desperate effort to sway public opinion their way. But that part of the fight conducted on the floor of parliament always belonged to Whitlam.

Over previous months the Prime Minister's reputation inside the party had fallen from its earlier heights. But he recovered more quickly each day from 16 October and the deferral of the budget. Any other political leader would almost certainly have accepted the budget blockage and gone to the people for an election. But Whitlam, imbued with a sense of historical mission and possessing boundless confidence in his own abilities, would not have a bar of this. He put into practice the threats he made in September. In the space of a week, from the evening of Monday 14 October when it became clear that Connor would have to resign and the Opposition would halt the budget, Whitlam carried his party from the depths of depression to a dangerous over-confidence. While there were a few Labor members and Ministers apprehensive about his tactics, the overwhelming majority became confident that Labor would win the deadlock.

The government's parliamentary onslaught reached its peak on Thursday 23 October when Whitlam let Question Time continue nearly half an hour beyond its normal 45 minutes. The government set out to demolish the claims made by the Opposition that deferral of the budget would have little impact on the economy.

Hayden began by saying that without the budget a flow of funds equivalent to about one-eighth of gross domestic product was being cut off each month. He said the service sector of the economy was already being affected: restaurants, motels. Consumers were now hesitating to purchase consumer durable goods. Fred Daly told the House that members' travel would be curtailed and tight restrictions would apply to all use of official cars. He said the withdrawal of all travel facilities might be necessary. The Education Minister Kim Beazley said that pay for Northern Territory schoolteachers would expire in three weeks, as would allowances for 73,000 tertiary students and 13,000 aboriginal children. The Minister for Northern Australia Paul Keating warned that Darwin reconstruction work would cease in four weeks. This would mean a large section of the workforce would have no income. The Agriculture Minister Rex Patterson said that meat exports would stop because the government could not pay meat inspectors. The Housing Minister Joe Riordan said apprenticeship allowances would stop and payments under the RED scheme would be exhausted.

The government concentrated its attention in both the ACT and Northern Territory—the crucial areas in any Senate election. Whitlam finished Question Time by announcing that the CPI index for the September quarter was only 0.8 per cent, caused by the introduction of Medibank and consequent removal of the health services section of the index. This was a parliamentary blitz which deeply concerned wide sections of the Liberal backbench. By this stage a growing number of Liberal members and Senators believed that a compromise was inevitable to resolve the deadlock. In an effort to shore up his own supporters and turn the attack back to the government, Fraser called a press conference the same afternoon. The conference was marked by further bitter exchanges between the Opposition leader and gallery journalists. The type of pressure that Fraser had to bear and his relentless determination to stick at his course was revealed during this press conference:

Question: You said if the Prime Minister is forced to an election. What do you think will happen to make this happen?

Fraser: If a government can't govern, if a government can't gain funds, it will have to go to the people for a verdict. And Minister after Minister has got up at Question Time and said they can't do their job because they are running out of money.

Question: Are you surprised at the backlash against your decision to block the budget?

Fraser: I've not had great evidence of a public opinion backlash.

Question: What do you think of a public opinion poll which showed that 55 per cent of people don't want an election?

Fraser: That same opinion poll shows that a great number of people don't want this present government to continue.

Question: Senator Steele Hall has characterised your position as a sleazy road to power over a dead man's corpse. How do you react to this criticism from a man of self-professed Liberal principles who supported you for the leadership?

Fraser: I was not aware that Senator Steele Hall had a vote for my leadership.

| | |
|---|---|
| Question: | In your last press conference you talked about universal support for an election. Where does that universal support come from? |
| Fraser: | There is a good deal of support for an election all around the country. |
| Question: | You said universal Mr Fraser. Would you say universal business? Universal trade unions? Universal from the populace? What is your source? |
| Fraser: | There is a great deal of support from many different sections of the Australian community for an election. |
| Question: | Have you requested the government's permission to speak to the Treasurer or the Reserve Bank about how seriously the economy is going to be damaged? I heard your shadow Treasurer this morning and he dismissed this as unimportant . . . I ask you how seriously have you addressed yourself to this problem? What do you think is going to happen? How much are you going to put us through and for how long? |
| Fraser: | We are not putting the economy through the wringer . . . |
| Question: | Mr Fraser, sorry, I don't want to interrupt this, but would you answer the first question: how seriously have you addressed yourself to this problem and have you sought any official advice? |
| Fraser: | The question of whether or not the economy is being hurt rests entirely in the hands of the government, because in the proper course of events the Prime Minister ought to have ordered an election before this. If anyone is hurt it is because he has refused to do so. |
| Question: | Do you have any conscionable problems about the actions you have taken and the consequences for Australia? |
| Fraser: | The action we have taken is right to remove from Australia the worst government since the beginning of Australia. |

By this stage it was clear that the actual issue of budget deferment favoured the government even though Labor's overall electoral position was still weak. It was in this context that the Opposition searched for an issue that would firstly discredit the government and secondly maintain the unity of its own members.

There were four main attacks launched by the Opposition on the government during the crisis period. The first was the claim that a front bench Labor member had 'leaked' documents to the Opposition, the second the claim that Hayden should resign because he briefed Bob Hawke on the budget, the third that the government had conspired with the firm ACTU–Solo over its crude oil allocation, and the fourth an effort to implicate Whitlam directly in the loans affair through information provided by Khemlani.

The Opposition had mixed success on these issues but was never able really to damage the Government. Fraser demonstrated his weakness for political overkill on the issue of the 'leaked' letter. This document was openly given to Lynch by Frank Crean after the senior Liberal requested to see it. Fraser's allegations about this perfectly normal transaction severely embarrassed Lynch, who apologised profusely to Crean about them. But the Opposition still had its hopes set on the loans issue. In late October Khemlani returned to Australia and wanted to clear his name by appearing before the Senate. But, after extensive examination of his documents, the Opposition decided not to pursue this course. This was the end of the loans affair and the attempt to implicate the Prime Minister.

The full extent of Labor's strength on the supply issue was shown in a *Herald–Age* poll published on 30 October which showed that 70 per cent of people in capital cities believed the budget should pass and only 25 per cent believed it should be blocked. A total of 44 per cent believed Labor should resign and call a general election compared with 55 per cent who said it should continue to govern. More people blamed the Opposition for the crisis than the government.

The national executive of the Labor Party met in Canberra the day this poll was published, to review the government's tactics. The majority of executive delegates supported a half-Senate election immediately and Whitlam came under pressure to call one. However a number of delegates, notably the Queensland secretary Bart Lourigan, Victorian delegate Bill Hartley, and the Foreign Minister Senator Don Willesee were adamantly opposed to a Senate election. The national secretary David Combe and the Prime Minister, although they did not express their views inside the executive meeting, were both thoroughly opposed to a Senate election. The most vocal and outspoken advocate for a Senate poll was the party's national president Bob Hawke. Hawke argued that in normal times the government stood little chance in any election but in the current climate there were abnormal factors working to assist it and the opportunity should not be lost.

Whitlam was still confident that the constitutional crisis could be resolved without an election and believed the Opposition parties would crack. David Combe endorsed the assessment of the ANOP managing director Rod Cameron, who was employed by the party for marketing purposes. Cameron argued that Labor should not confuse support on the question of budget deferral with its general standing in the electorate at any poll, saying the two issues were quite separate. In short, Combe was being advised that, despite the mood of euphoria, the party was still facing defeat at any imminent election. Despite the Senate election hawks within the party, Whitlam and Combe were still against one. The

Prime Minister wanted to see Fraser beaten on the constitutional issue and therefore permanently weakened for the future.

At this stage of the crisis the Governor-General became more active. On 30 October Kerr held his second round of talks with both Whitlam and Fraser. Whitlam and McClelland attended an Executive Council meeting at Government House just before noon and stayed on for lunch with the Governor-General. The three men, old colleagues for many years, chatted about the crisis during most of the lunch period. Kerr and McClelland shared a bottle of wine and at one stage the Governor-General looked up at the Prime Minister and then, nodding towards McClelland, asked 'Well how's he going?' The Prime Minister paused and then replied: 'Good, bloody good, but he gets a bit histrionic at times.' The three men briefly discussed Fraser and the manner and the method of his inevitable backdown. Both Whitlam and McClelland left Government House that day resolutely confident that they would emerge the victors from the crisis.[4]

In the afternoon the Governor-General saw both Hayden and Fraser separately. This gave the Treasurer a chance to brief Kerr on the government's alternative arrangements for supply.

In this atmosphere the coalition parties held a summit meeting in Melbourne on Sunday 2 November to review the crisis. It was attended by federal and state Liberal and National Country Party leaders. The upshot of the meeting was that the Opposition would maintain its stand in principle but approach the Governor-General with a compromise in an effort to show its bona fides to solve the crisis.

The meeting began at 2 p.m. at Treasury Place and lasted for just over three hours. In a communique issued later, the meeting expressed 'absolute determination to let the people be the judges through a general election'. The meeting also discussed the possibility of the Prime Minister seeking a half-Senate election and the Premiers gave undertakings that they would advise their Governors not to issue writs for such an election. Although there was growing concern at the apparent increase in the Labor government's popularity, the federal and state non-Labor leaders expressed their full backing for Fraser. In this way the Opposition Leader maintained a united front. After the meeting Fraser said that Whitlam's proposal to remain in office and make alternative arrangements for supply was 'the way to establish a dictatorship'.

Monday 3 November was the false dawn of an end to the crisis. Fraser went to the Governor-General's Melbourne office and spent 35 minutes outlining a new compromise position. He said the Opposition would pass supply immediately on the clear understanding that a House of Representatives election was held at the same time as the next Senate election, which was due before 30 June 1976. This would give the Prime Minister at least six months grace before having to face a general election. 'I make this proposal because I believe that common sense, reason and a concern for the people of Australia must prevail,' Fraser said. In offering this compromise the Opposition was not abandoning the principle of using the Senate to force a general election. Fraser, in fact, was extending the time period in which Whitlam could wait before calling such an election. In this offer there was a distinct concession for Whitlam – he could say that his own tactics had won his government another six months.

This proposal originated with the Victorian Premier Dick Hamer, who believed Fraser was in danger of painting himself into an uncompromising corner. From his own point of view Hamer had a state election looming and would prefer to hold it when the Labor government was still in office. But the compromise was exceptionally timely. The Governor-General was now actively trying to find common ground for a settlement between Whitlam and Fraser.

Over the weekend 1–2 November Kerr himself had spoken to both Whitlam and McClelland separately and floated his own compromise proposal. This was that the government agree to hold a late Senate election, thereby guaranteeing never to constitute the interim Senate, in return for which the Opposition would pass the budget. This was a compromise clearly in Labor's favour: it would be interpreted as a victory for Whitlam and a defeat for Fraser, but it would still give Fraser something out of the whole upheaval, since he would be able to claim he had saved the danger of an interim Senate, which was one of the main reasons the Opposition blocked the budget in the first place.[5]

One of the most intriguing questions raised by Fraser's compromise is whether he had knowledge that the Governor-General himself was suggesting a compromise. In this case he would have been anxious to show his own credentials as a conciliator. But, regardless of this, the Liberals concluded from the overall situation that a compromise offer was in Fraser's interests.

When news reached Canberra on the afternoon of 3 November about Fraser's offer, the government was more than ever convinced it was on the road to victory. The Labor Party interpreted the offer as a concession stemming directly from the adverse public reaction which had met Fraser's efforts to force an election.

Whitlam's staff were initially worried by the offer and were concerned that an outright rejection might make them appear unreasonable. But Whitlam himself had no doubts. Still convinced he was in a position of strength, the Prime Minister said he would never succumb to blackmail from Fraser. Whitlam was looking for a complete backdown from the Opposition. He believed that he could crush Fraser. Whitlam misjudged his position. At this stage Whitlam's position was that he would not hold a half-Senate election and he would not accept Fraser's compromise. He was still aiming to 'tough it out', now more certain than ever that the Opposition would back down. By contrast Fraser had put himself forward as the advocate of a 'reasonable compromise' and he maintained this position during the rest of the crisis period. There is no doubt that Whitlam's defiant and confident rejection of Fraser's offer was a turning point in the crisis.

During this week the Governor-General began seriously to consider that he would have to dismiss Whitlam. From as early as September, well before the budget had been deferred, Kerr had discussed his role in a crisis with some of his old legal colleagues from Sydney. One of them can distinctly remember the Governor-General saying that the situation could arise where he might have to dismiss his Ministers. While Whitlam never considered this possible, the Governor-General always considered it possible. But the Governor-General, like the Prime Minister, and along with most observers, believed there would be a political settlement of the crisis without his intervention. His talks with Whitlam hardly ever encroached on the possibility of a half-Senate election.[6]

Whitlam's position with the Governor-General was always that he would never seek a general election in response to the Senate's black-mail. Kerr's discussions with Whitlam were, as far as is known, conducted within these parameters. The Prime Minister said publicly after his dismissal that the Governor-General never put it to him that he should resign or seek a general election. The Governor-General, according to Whitlam's public statements later, only put one proposal to him during their talks: this was the compromise suggestion on the timing for the half-Senate election mentioned above.

It appears from this evidence that the Governor-General acted during the crisis in one of two ways. The first explanation is that he realised right from the start that he might have to sack the Prime Minister and therefore decided that he must keep this secret from Whitlam because of possible retaliatory action. The second explanation is that the Governor-General was a victim of his own weakness; that he was sympathetic to Whitlam's position and went along with it only to find that his options ran out over time. Eventually he believed the only option left was to dismiss the Prime Minister and that, once again, he could not give prior warning of his intentions for fear of Whitlam's response.[7]

Sir John Kerr held his final round of talks with the leaders on Thursday 6 November and these discussions betrayed the direction in which events were moving. He saw Whitlam during the morning and the Prime Minister repeated his stand. He was as solid as ever. When Fraser saw Kerr, the Opposition leader impressed two fundamental points on the Governor-General. The first was that, contrary to statements made by the government, the Opposition would not alter its course; its Senators would remain firm; and it would keep deferring the budget no matter how many times Whitlam submitted it. Secondly, Fraser told the Governor-General that in the Opposition's view the alternative arrangements being proposed by the government to maintain supply were likely to be both illegal and unconstitutional.[8]

After Kerr's talks with Fraser, Government House contacted both the Treasurer's office and the Attorney-General's office and made appointments for both Hayden and Enderby to see Kerr in the afternoon to explain both the substance and the legality of the proposals. Enderby took two documents to Government House with him, both joint opinions from himself and Byers. The first dealt with the legality of the alternative arrangements while the second was a draft opinion on the original Ellicott statement about the Governor-General's powers.

The government had been examining the legality of its alternative arrangements for some time. Whitlam had made them a matter of major political controversy when he said on 31 October that he could stay in office without the budget and still manage to pay the public service, the armed forces and government contractors. 'If it comes to the crunch, it is probable that the government can govern without the budget,' he said. Whitlam went on to say that this was 'not the regular, the easy way to do it'.

Both Fraser and Anthony were incensed by this declaration and attacked the government on the floor of parliament on 4 and 5 November demanding to know how the government could obtain alternative funds without defying parliament. Two Labor Ministers were themselves concerned about the government's course of action and expressed these doubts during meetings of the ad hoc Cabinet committee. They were Hayden and Wriedt, who had grave doubts whether the measures would satisfy the Governor-General. The plan was that all federal departments would give their employees documents stating the amount due to them for the preceding pay period. This would be called a 'Certificate of Indebtedness'. A similar document would be issued to suppliers of government goods and employees in statutory authorities. The workings of the system were explained in the joint Enderby–Byers opinion:

> The Certificate will contain an endorsement to the effect, as is the case in law, that it is neither a cheque nor a negotiable instrument . . . The Certificate will show as the relevant amount a sum equivalent to gross pay less PAYE tax instalments and superannuation and DFR and DB contributions.
>
> The employee will present his Certificate to a bank (whether government or private) and will enter into a contract of loan with that bank for an advance equal to his net salary . . . The government will announce the introduction of legislation to enable it to pay interest to

the bankers and give an undertaking, subject to legislation being passed, to pay interest at a rate to be struck.

When the appropriation bills have been passed the banks will be paid direct sums equalling in total what they have advanced the various employees and suppliers. These payments will discharge the employees' obligations to repay their various loans except for interest, which latter obligation will also be discharged by the government should its interest legislation pass the parliament . . .

Under the proposal no money is withdrawn from the Treasury either directly or indirectly. The constitutional provisions relating to parliament's control of expenditure by the executive are observed both in letter and in spirit. Nor does the proposal contemplate nor allow the doing by indirection of what may not be done directly. The proposal and its effectuation are, in our opinion, clearly constitutional.

Before Enderby went to Government House he tracked down Whitlam and told him the Governor-General wanted to see him. Enderby said he would be taking the legal opinion on the measures. 'You're absolutely sure it's legal now, aren't you?' Whitlam asked. The Prime Minister knew it would be fatal for him to take an illegal action at this stage. Enderby replied, 'Don't worry. I've never seen Maurice [Byers] stronger on anything.'

The second document Enderby took was requested by the Governor-General himself. On the morning of 22 October Whitlam spoke to Kerr about the Ellicott opinion, which the Governor-General had apparently read. It was on this occasion that Kerr asked to speak to the government's legal advisers himself and, when Whitlam declined, he asked for an opinion from the law officers on the Ellicott opinion. The Labor caucus was meeting at the time and Whitlam called Enderby to the back of the party room. 'I've just been speaking to the Governor-General,' Whitlam said. 'He's got a copy of the Ellicott opinion. He thinks it's bullshit but wants an opinion on it from us.'[9]

Whitlam told Enderby to have the opinion drafted and to give it to him so that the Prime Minister could deliver it to the Governor-General personally. Talks were then held among the government's senior legal officers to draft a reply for the Governor-General. The main people involved were the Solicitor-General Byers, the Secretary of the Attorney-General's Department Clarrie Harders, and a first assistant secretary in the Department, Pat Brazil.

When Enderby realised on 6 November that he would be seeing the Governor-General that afternoon, he asked his Department for this second opinion anyway to give Kerr an indication of the formal advice on this subject which Whitlam would be submitting to him later. A number of drafts of this opinion had been prepared. But there were three things about the earlier draft opinions with which Enderby did not agree.

First, he wanted to improve the style and language of the document. Second, the opinion admitted that Section 53 gave the Senate the power to refuse supply, a proposition with which Enderby did not agree. Third, the draft conceded the existence of reserve powers to the Governor-General, something else with which Enderby did not agree. He wanted to get the opinion redrafted so its central argument, which was a rebuttal of Ellicott's view that the Governor-General had a duty to dismiss his Ministers if supply was exhausted, was clearer to understand.

The Attorney-General saw the Governor-General for about twenty minutes. The two men discussed the alternative arrangements and Enderby strongly emphasised that they were completely legal and gave Kerr the opinion from himself and Byers to document this argument. They then discussed the role of the Governor-General in the context of the second draft opinion which Enderby had for Kerr. Enderby said he took the Whig view of history and did not accept the argument that the Governor-General had reserve powers.

The Attorney-General said he believed that Liberal Senators were looking for an excuse to abstain and that they would go to water. 'That's certainly not what Fraser tells me,' Kerr replied. The Governor-General appeared quite convinced on this point and most confident that the Opposition would not retract from its present stand. This was obviously impressed upon him by Fraser during the morning.[10]

The two men discussed the Ellicott opinion and Enderby gave Kerr his draft opinion on this matter. He crossed out Byers' signature and told Kerr that there were sections of the document relating to the Senate's power and the reserve power of the Governor-General with which he disagreed. The Governor-General asked Enderby on what basis he was giving him the document. The Attorney-General replied: 'You can regard this as background but it shows the line of advice which the Prime Minister will be giving you.'

The Prime Minister never submitted the formal opinion to the Governor-General before he was sacked. It is not known whether Kerr ever read the draft opinion Enderby gave him on 6 November. It was a lengthy document, just under thirty pages, but it contained substantial arguments to rebut the case put by Ellicott. It referred to Section 61 of the Constitution saying:

> That Section 61 affords no ground for the conclusion that, upon the Senate deferring or rejecting supply solely to procure the resignation or dismissal of the ministry possessing a majority in the Representatives, His Excellency is constitutionally obliged immediately to seek an explanation of the Prime Minister of how he proposes to overcome the situation. Nor do we agree with the suggestion that were the Prime Minister unable to suggest means which solve the disagreement

between the Houses and left the government without funds to carry on, it would be His Excellency's duty to dismiss his Ministers.

Byers argued that other constitutional provisions notably Sections 64, 28 and 5, did not offer a guide as to when the 'abnormal reserve powers of dismissal of a ministry and consequent dissolution of the Representatives should or may be exercised or even that they still exist. This is the field of convention and discretion.' Byers said it was not correct to think that the exercise of these powers was demanded when supply was threatened.

He pointed out that, according to one of the pre-eminent authorities in this area (Dr Jennings, *Cabinet Government*, 3rd ed. 1969), no government has been dismissed by the sovereign since 1783 when George III sacked Lord North. Other dissolutions given in the dominions in the last 170 years were, with one possible exception, granted because Ministers could not govern with the existing Lower House. Byers continues: 'We have referred to forced dissolutions only to indicate that their very rarity and the long years since their exercise casts the gravest doubt on the present existence of that prerogative.' The opinion then quotes Asquith in his memorandum on the King's position of which Jennings said: 'So far as it goes, is uncontrovertible.' Whitlam had read Asquith's memorandum very closely and embraced it fully:

Nothing can be more important, in the best interests of the Crown and of the country, than that a practice, so long established and so well justified by experience, should remain unimpaired. It frees the occupant of the throne from all personal responsibility for the acts of the executive and the legislature. It gives force and meaning to the old maxim that 'the King can do no wrong'. So long as it prevails, however objectionable particular acts may be to a large section of his subjects, they cannot hold him in any way accountable. If, on the other hand, the King were to intervene on one side, or in one case—which he could only do by dismissing Ministers in de facto possession of a parliamentary majority—he would be expected to do the same on another occasion, and perhaps for the other side . . . He would, whether he wished it or not, be dragged into the arena of party politics; and at a dissolution following such a dismissal of Ministers as had been referred to, it is no exaggeration to say that the Crown would become the football of contending factions.

Byers concluded by saying that Section 57 of the constitution was provided for the resolution of deadlocks and that this also applied to money bills. He said that, to the extent that Ellicott proposed a reserve power of uncertain existence which denied effect to this constitutional provision, then he was wrong. Overall, this document Enderby gave Kerr contained a number of powerful arguments against the course of action which the Governor-General adopted five days later. It also documented the rarity of such an action. The import of Byers' opinion was that, while the dismissal power might exist, it should not be used.

Hayden saw the Governor-General at 4.30 the same afternoon and gave Kerr another document prepared by the Treasury explaining more fully the alternative arrangements through the banking system. Hayden explained the practical operation of the scheme and briefed Kerr on when supply would run out: a few days before the end of November. The same day Treasury officers met representatives of the banks in Canberra to discuss the alternative arrangements with them. The details of the proposed scheme were outlined and while the banks gave no firm commitment, they responded favourably and seemed confident that the scheme was viable. The following morning Whitlam spoke with the governor of the Reserve Bank, Harold Knight, and was assured by him that the scheme was quite feasible and should work. The Prime Minister also spoke to the chairman of the Commonwealth Banking Corporation, Professor Fin Crisp, who assured the Prime Minister that the Commonwealth Bank saw no problems. Don Dunstan gave similar assurances with his state bank. The real question was whether some banks could afford to stay out if enough of them cooperated with the government.

However Malcolm Fraser was determined to ensure that the alternative arrangements never got off the ground. He spoke personally with people at the highest levels in most of the private banks warning them that the government's proposals were subverting the parliamentary institution and saying he believed they were illegal. This was a theme which Fraser never left. He told person after person during this period that the government was on the verge of committing a major illegality. Fraser himself sought high-level legal opinions on the government's proposals, one from a distinguished lawyer, Keith Aitken QC. 'As I understand the position, it is beyond the legal capacity of the commonwealth to give the banks any guarantee that those funds will be paid back,' Fraser said on 6 November. 'When you've got a desperate government that's done so many desperate things, they're bound to go over the brink.'

In response to a combination of Fraser's urgings and their own concern, two major banks, the Bank of NSW and the Commercial Banking Company, sought separate legal opinions on the proposals and actually sent these to the Governor-General. The opinions argued that the government was on very shaky ground. Kerr's official secretary David Smith received them on 11 November, by which stage they had been overtaken by events. The government was confident both the National Bank and the ANZ would cooperate. It was also optimistic about the Bank of NSW although Fraser himself, who enjoyed excellent top level contact in this bank, was always confident that it would not cooperate.

The Governor-General himself was unhappy about the government's arrangements for alternative supply. Although he had never complained to Whitlam about them or expressed his disquiet, Government House sources said immediately after the sacking that the Governor-General believed the government was breaching a fundamental proposition by seeking to remain in office without parliamentary appropriation. But the measures themselves, while adding to the conviction that the deadlock would continue, do not appear to have been instrumental in any way in either the timing or nature of Kerr's subsequent action.

Although the polls were against him and the Prime Minister appeared as confident as ever, Malcolm Fraser now believed he would prevail in the constitutional crisis. The Opposition parties set their sights on Tuesday 11 November knowing that a decision would be needed this day if there were to be an election before Christmas. The Liberal leadership was confident Kerr would intervene.

On the evening of 6 November Fraser said in his office that he believed the Governor-General would intervene by dismissing Whitlam and have the crisis resolved before Christmas. Doug Anthony told a senior gallery journalist the next day he believed that Kerr would intervene. Bob Ellicott told a Liberal Party gathering in Sydney on the evening of Monday 10 November that the Governor-General would intervene in his judgement either the next day or the day after.[11]

On Sunday 9 November Fraser continued his role of seeking a 'reasoned compromise'. He was at pains to do everything possible to indicate that he would make concessions to resolve the deadlock. That afternoon Fraser announced he was willing to meet Whitlam to discuss a solution to the crisis based on a House of Representatives election. It was a calculated political ploy to show that he was the man of reason and Whitlam was intransigent. But unbeknown to Fraser, the Prime Minister had finally changed his tactics.

On 9 November Whitlam moved decisively from his long-standing 'tough it out' position towards a half-Senate election. The previous week, on the Thursday, the Prime Minister had held a long discussion with Frank Ley about election dates and realised that if there were to be a Senate election before Christmas he would have to call it on the following Tuesday. After four weeks Whitlam had failed to crack the Opposition. He now felt obliged to move into an election situation to increase the pressure. The political correspondent for the Melbourne *Sun News-Pictorial*, Laurie Oakes, rang David Solomon, Whitlam's press secretary, on the Sunday evening after he heard Fraser's offer to meet with the Prime Minister. Solomon contacted Whitlam and they decided it was in the government's interest to accept the offer. This was a shock for Fraser's press secretary David Barnett, who said when he was putting out the statements he didn't think Whitlam would respond.

Once he was committed to the meeting, Whitlam needed a bargaining counter and this became an immediate half-Senate poll. Whitlam released a statement that evening saying he would be happy to meet Fraser and his colleagues Lynch and Anthony at 9 a.m. on Tuesday 11 November immediately before the regular party meetings.

The timing was very important for the Prime Minister. In the week just concluded, rumours that the Opposition would back down had reached a new peak. During the crisis both Missen and Jessop had spoken out in the party room against continued deferral of the budget. Jessop had spoken privately to Fraser about what he considered to be the adverse electoral climate in South Australia.

In the Opposition lobbies frontbench Liberals were openly dissociating themselves from Fraser's course of action. The overwhelming majority of Liberal members and Senators believed that the Opposition would have to back down and accept a compromise. A number of Fraser's closest supporters on the backbench were already trying to assess the extent to which his leadership would be undermined by a defeat. The Opposition Senate leader Reg Withers was working hour by hour to keep his Senators in line. There was strong pressure from the Victorian division of the party for Fraser to back down. On the evening of Fraser's first meeting with the Governor-General, the Victorian party president Peter Hardie flew to Canberra and spent a long time in Fraser's office arguing with him that compromise was the only way out. As Fraser sat at his desk Hardie went through reason after reason why the Opposition should abandon its course. Newspapers which had been favourable to Fraser at the outset, notably the Melbourne *Herald*, had swung around during the crisis and appealed to the Opposition to pass the budget.

It was probably only the great leadership ethic in the Liberal Party which had allowed Fraser to continue his course of action for so long. No Labor leader could have done it; the caucus would have revolted long ago. But the position taken by most Liberals was that, while they believed a compromise essential, it was Fraser's job as leader to reach this decision for himself and not their job to impose it on him. It was a remarkable testimony to Fraser's strength of purpose that, in the face of all these pressures, he continued his course.

Whitlam set the meeting between the leaders at a time just before the party room meeting. This was to maximise pressure on Fraser to concede. But he underestimated Fraser's strength within his own party. Whitlam decided before the meeting that he would adopt the compromise position originally suggested by the Governor-General. That is, he would tell Fraser the government was prepared to hold a late Senate election and never constitute the interim Senate if, in return, the Opposition passed the budget. If Fraser refused this deal then Whitlam would call an immediate half-Senate election.

The Prime Minister was in Melbourne all day Monday as a prelude to the Lord Mayor's Annual Banquet that night. During the afternoon Whitlam saw Bob Hawke, the state Labor leader Clyde Holding, the state party chairman Peter Redlich, and the secretary Bill Tracey. The Victorians had been Senate election hawks for a long time and their urgings, combined with the Tuesday meeting with Fraser, confirmed Whitlam's decision on a half-Senate election.

That evening Whitlam offered Fraser, Peacock and McMahon a lift back to Canberra on his VIP flight. It was the only way Fraser could return to the capital in time for the next morning's meeting. Fraser and Whitlam spoke briefly on the flight, neither showing any knowledge of the events which were to engulf them the next day. Whitlam and Freudenberg went straight to the Prime Minister's Lodge just after midnight to discuss Whitlam's speech that morning following the motion of censure of which Fraser had given notice. 'How was Malcolm?' Freudenberg asked his boss. 'He seemed cheerful enough,' Whitlam replied. The two men then worked over Whitlam's speech, still confident that their position was sound, still sure they would emerge victors from the constitutional crisis, and still convinced the Governor-General would not act against them.

But Whitlam's doom had already been sealed at Yarralumla the previous evening, Monday 10 November. Just a few hours before, when Whitlam was at the Lord Mayor's Banquet, the letter dismissing him from office was being typed at Government House. The linchpin of Labor's strategy had dropped out of the political woodwork.

Sir John Kerr had reached a decisive conclusion in the previous week. When he was in Melbourne for the Cup, he had conferred with the Governors of NSW and Victoria who both agreed that, if so advised, they would not issue writs for a Senate election. Kerr then dismissed a Senate poll as a solution. There were two problems with it. First, supply would run out before it was held and secondly, there was no guarantee it would solve anything.

Some time after his final round of talks with the political leaders on 6 November, Kerr contacted the Chief Justice of the High Court, Sir Garfield Barwick, to seek his advice. Kerr first asked Whitlam as early as Sunday 26 October whether he could discuss the crisis with Barwick and the Prime Minister refused. Kerr's conversations on 6 November suggest he was well advanced in his view by that stage. The Governor-General made arrangements for Barwick to see him at Admiralty House, Sydney, on the Monday. Barwick came early in the morning and then left, only to come back again for lunch. It is thought that, after their early morning meeting, Barwick brought with him to lunch the letter that was later released publicly.

In this letter (Appendix II) from Barwick to Kerr, the Chief Justice says the Governor-General invited him to give legal advice on the decision he had already reached to withdraw Whitlam's commission. In a remarkable opinion, Barwick said that once Kerr was satisfied the Labor government was 'unable to secure supply', he had a duty to dismiss it. There is no suggestion that the Governor-General should wait until there is no longer supply for the government, no suggestion that if dissatisfied with the Prime Minister's approach the Governor-General should seek fresh advice. Barwick suggests in a far-reaching opinion that the elected government of the day in Australia has to be regarded as being responsible to both the House of Representatives and to the Senate. This is a basic alteration in the system of responsible government which has applied since Federation where, under the constitution, it has always been assumed that as far as choice, control and dismissal of the executive government is concerned, the House of Representatives is the primary House. Barwick's view is at odds with this position and implies by logical extension that whenever a government controls only one House, and thus only enjoys the confidence of one House, an election is needed.

But a crucial section of Barwick's letter was where he said, in relation to the Prime Minister and the options of either advising a general election or resigning, if 'he refuses to take either course' the Governor-General had a responsibility to withdraw his commission. The key word here is 'refuses'. The Prime Minister could only refuse if he had been asked. According to Whitlam's later public statements on numerous occasions, the Governor-General never asked him. Whitlam may have said this to Kerr in stating his position, indeed this was his position, but the Governor-General never offered his Prime Minister a choice by putting the question and allowing Whitlam to refuse.

With Barwick's backing, Kerr knew there was no danger of his action being declared illegal. He had the support and confirmation of the Chief Justice. After he returned to Canberra, the Governor-General had a letter to Whitlam prepared and a general statement explaining the reasons for his decision. Much of the typing was done Monday night.

On Tuesday morning at 9 a.m. Whitlam, Daly and Crean met Fraser, Lynch and Anthony in Whitlam's office. The Prime Minister said he wanted both the budget and the electoral redistribution passed in return for holding a late Senate election. Otherwise he would use his option of calling an immediate half-Senate election. As the Senate election was being discussed, Fraser asked, 'Are you sure this is the only option?'

The Opposition Leader appeared confident throughout the meeting that the Governor-General would never agree to Whitlam's request for a half-Senate election. Replying to questions during the meeting, Whitlam said he would not be seeking temporary supply to cover the period of the election.[12] The meeting broke with the Opposition trio clearly rejecting Whitlam's compromise offer. Fraser, Lynch and Anthony conferred briefly after they left Whitlam's office and Fraser called the Prime Minister at 10.05 and confirmed this with him saying, 'There'll be no deal.' The constitutional crisis had now reached its decisive point. Whitlam was approaching Kerr to seek an immediate half-Senate poll.

Both Daly and Crean were alarmed at the great confidence Fraser displayed during the meeting. But Whitlam was still confident. He returned to his office and began preparations to draft a formal letter to the Governor-General requesting a half-Senate election on 13 December. Whitlam tried to arrange a meeting with the Governor-General through his Department but there was a delay. He rang the Governor-General himself about 10 a.m. and Kerr said he had not been able to talk earlier because of trouble with one of his grandchildren. The Prime Minister told Kerr he would be seeking a half-Senate election and wanted to notify the Governor-General that he wished to announce this to the party room. Kerr consented.

The Prime Minister strode into the party room and announced his decision to the caucus, reporting on his meeting with the Opposition leaders. The Prime Minister received the full backing of the party room, which was delighted at the decision. For some days backbench pressure had been building up on Whitlam to call a half-Senate election. The mood of government optimism now reached its zenith. Whitlam's staff believed a Senate election would be another turn of the screw on Fraser. The government would keep the House of Representatives sitting throughout the entire period of the election, campaigning on one issue, Senate deferral of the budget and its drastic consequences.

Enderby told Whitlam just before the party meeting that he had to go to the War Memorial for the Remembrance Day ceremony. For a brief moment Whitlam wondered whether he should go himself but then realised he would not have time. Enderby and Kerr stood next to one another as the national capital commemorated the eleventh hour of the eleventh day of the eleventh month. That year it had an extra significance. The Attorney-General led the Governor-General down the steps to his car at the end of the ceremony and then turned expecting to shake hands with Kerr. But the Governor-General climbed quickly into his car, looking the other way and failing to acknowledge the Minister whom he would dispatch from office two hours hence.

As soon as the Labor caucus broke, the news quickly spread of the Senate election decision. It was carried on all radio stations and afternoon newspaper journalists phoned it through immediately. But while the mood was one of relief now that a decision had been made, combined with optimism in the government lobbies, the situation was very different on the other side of the House.

After Fraser and Lynch had completed their meeting with Whitlam, they both went back to Fraser's office before the joint party meeting. Both men knew the decision hour was now at hand. In a few hours they would know whether the crux of their policy, their assumptions about the Governor-General, were correct or not. If Kerr gave Whitlam his half-Senate election then it would be with the full knowledge that supply would be exhausted well before the results of that election. It would be a clear indication that the Governor-General concurred in Whitlam's tactics and it would eventually mean they would have to concede and accept a political compromise.

It was imperative for the Opposition at this crucial stage that its resolution be maintained. Its prospects of success would be destroyed by a crack in the party room. Because of this danger, Fraser and Lynch decided not to report to the party on their talks with Whitlam or even tell the party that the Prime Minister was seeking a 13 December half-Senate election. They feared any chance that this news might provoke a debate which, leaked to the press, would shatter the fabric of their unity.

Fraser, tense and emotional, began the party meeting by saying his wish was that there should be no discussion on the decision taken by the Opposition parties a month before. The party, although concerned by the situation, accepted this. Fraser said everyone was carrying a great burden and appealed to the party to stay firm for the moment till events sorted themselves out in the next few hours. A little later, when Doug Anthony spoke to the meeting, he told them: 'We must stay firm. The next twenty-four hours are the most vital in the entire history of our parties.' Most Opposition members and Senators left the party room having no idea that the Prime Minister was calling a half-Senate election.

Journalists waiting in Kings Hall were incredulous when they spoke to Liberal members after the meeting and found they knew nothing about the election. 'Fraser's been too scared to tell them,' some people began speculating immediately. A few minutes later Lynch held a briefing for journalists in the Whip's office. Newspaper, radio and television reporters crammed into the small office. Lynch smiled as they all came in. He opened the briefing by saying he was afraid it would be an anti-climax. It had been a routine meeting and he went through the business. There was no discussion of the crisis. Lynch said that both Fraser and Anthony spoke to the party room briefly but there had been no discussion on the crisis. The deputy leader parried a series of questions. Did he know the Prime Minister was seeking a Senate election? Had the Opposition parties been told this? Why not? 'We believe events will work themselves out,' Lynch told journalists. 'We believe the present course is sound for reasons which will become apparent to you later.'

From this comment by Lynch, it seemed clear that the Opposition was very confident that the Governor-General would deny Whitlam his half-Senate election and come to another conclusion, in its favour. Two senior Liberals told the political correspondent for the Melbourne *Sun News-Pictorial*, Laurie Oakes, that same afternoon, that they had known in the morning what Kerr would do. Both Fraser and Lynch subsequently denied they had any prior knowledge of Kerr's action.[13]

But from their words and actions they were both very confident that Whitlam would be denied his half-Senate election. At morning tea that day Labor members called out to their Liberal counterparts 'We've got you now' and this statement reflected the overwhelming feeling of both parties, with the exception of the inner group of Liberal leaders. The Liberal backbench was despondent and still convinced that a political compromise was inevitable.

The House of Representatives sat at 11.45 in the morning and Fraser spoke to his motion of censure against the government. His motion attacked Labor for intending to remain in office without supply, failing to call a general election, and attempting to defy and reduce the power of the Senate. Attacking Whitlam, the Opposition Leader declared: 'He believes that he alone is the constitution; that he alone is the parliament.'

But the debate had an aura of anti-climax in view of the Prime Minister's half-Senate election decision. Whitlam had an appointment at Government House at 1 p.m. which he made during his earlier telephone discussion with Kerr. But before the Prime Minister left Parliament House, Fraser's office was rung by Government House and his private secretary Dale Budd took the message. The Governor-General wanted to see Fraser about ten minutes after his appointment with the Prime Minister. This could only mean one thing.

The parliamentary sitting was suspended for lunch just before 1 p.m. A few minutes earlier Whitlam left the chamber and returned to his office before leaving for Government House. Fraser's staff miscalculated and the Opposition Leader arrived at Government House before the Prime Minister. Fraser went inside and his car was parked around the side of the house adjacent to the lake so Whitlam would not see it.

A few minutes later Whitlam arrived in his car, got out and went in to see the Governor-General. Before he had time to hand his written advice to the Governor-General for a half-Senate election, Kerr asked the Prime Minister if he would hold a general election. When Whitlam said he would not, the Governor-General handed him the letter withdrawing his commission (Appendix III). Whitlam left abruptly and went straight back to the Lodge. After Whitlam's departure, the Governor-General commissioned Fraser as Prime Minister, the first Prime Minister in Australian history lacking the confidence of the House of Representatives. Fraser was commissioned on the understanding that he would first secure supply, and second, seek a general election thereby allowing the deadlock to be decided by the people. The Opposition Leader, who had been waiting in another room while Whitlam was decommissioned, received his Prime Ministerial commission about twenty minutes later.[14]

Whitlam arrived at the Lodge about 1.15. He immediately summoned his senior Ministers and advisers. Freudenberg and Mant drove out together and heard on the radio news that there would be a half-Senate election. Already the non-Labor Premiers were saying they would not issue the writs. As the two staffers walked to the door, they saw Whitlam sitting alone in the summer room eating his lunch and Freudenberg gave him the 'victory' sign with his fingers.

Whitlam declared 'I've been sacked' and both Freudenberg and Mant laughed. 'I'm serious, the letter's over there,' Whitlam said pointing to the bench. The same procedure was followed repeatedly as Crean, Enderby, Combe, Daly and John Menadue all arrived to be told the same news. They either laughed or just looked incredulous. 'The bastard's sacked us,' Whitlam said as they arrived.

The stunned Labor camp tried to prepare itself for the afternoon but, after such a shock, it was not easy to think clearly. Labor made two fatal mistakes. The first was that Whitlam had no knowledge at all that Fraser had been commissioned Prime Minister. He failed to appreciate that the government had already effectively changed hands. This meant that Fraser himself now had the problem of getting supply through the Senate.

The second mistake was the failure to call Wriedt or another Labor Senate leader to the Lodge. There was nothing deliberate about this; it was a mere oversight made in the 40 minutes the Labor Party had to pull itself together after its leaders had suffered the biggest shock that anyone in politics could ever experience. Most people at the Lodge were too sickened, sorry, amazed and confused about the dismissal to think through their present tactical position.

Whitlam said it was imperative for the party to introduce a motion of confidence on the floor of the House and, after having proved it had a majority in that chamber, to reapproach the Governor-General. Most of the time was spent in devising a form of words to reaffirm the confidence of the House of Representatives in Whitlam and the request that he be recommissioned Prime Minister. The Speaker of the House Gordon Scholes, who attended the Lodge lunch-time gathering, would convey this message to the Governor-General. There was no discussion about the critical factor of supply at this meeting. Yet this was where the new Prime Minister was vulnerable. Whitlam's oversight here was fatal—again.

The Governor-General's statement explaining his action was released in the press gallery boxes at 2.05 (Appendix D). He said the deadlock had to be resolved as promptly as possible and that the Prime Minister had either to resign or call a general election. Because Whitlam had refused to do this he was being dismissed and a new caretaker government commissioned which could guarantee supply and recommend a double dissolution.

There were a number of inconsistencies and arguable points in the Governor-General's letter. First, at no stage had he ever indicated to Whitlam that a prompt solution was needed and he had in fact waited until the twenty-sixth day to intervene. Second, he had never previously indicated to Whitlam that after supply was blocked, he had either to advise a general election or resign. According to the Prime Minister the Governor-General gave the opposite impression. Third, at no stage did the Governor-General indicate to Whitlam that a half-Senate election would not be suitable. Fourth, the Governor-General said he was satisfied there was no chance of a compromise although the majority of members within the Liberal Party believed there would be a compromise. Fifth, the Governor-General said a Prime Minister who could not obtain supply could not govern—but supply had not been exhausted. Sixth, although the Governor-General said he made up his mind before consulting with the Chief Justice, the argument he put relied heavily on that contained in Barwick's letter of the previous day. Seventh, although the Governor-General said the Prime Minister refused to resign or call a general election, Whitlam himself said he was never asked this at any stage during the crisis. Eighth, the secrecy and swiftness with which the Governor-General moved indicated he was not anxious to give Whitlam any choice. Ninth, the Governor-General said he would be surprised if the law officers did not agree that he had the power to dismiss a ministry—yet he already had a draft opinion on this very subject indicating the law officers believed such a power should not be used. Tenth, the Governor-General put himself in a position of installing a minority leader as Prime Minister, ignoring a vote of no confidence in Fraser and delaying a meeting with both Whitlam and Speaker Scholes to express the view of the House of Representatives. Eleventh, he accepted a double dissolution on advice from Fraser, the grounds for which were the 21 bills which the Liberal–National Country Parties had blocked in the Senate. That is, Fraser secured the dissolution on Labor's proposed legislation, which he himself had opposed.

In summary, the Governor-General's overall conduct put him in a position where the accusation of 'political partisanship' could be levelled against the Crown. His exercise of the ultimate power arising from the use of the Senate's money power, which can be used twice a year, is

357

certain to change the nature of the office of Governor-General and provoke a new assessment as to what sort of person should fill it.

Kerr's decision had vast consequences for the Australian parliament. It represented a great assertion of the Senate's power in relation to the House of Representatives. Ultimately Kerr had put the principle that a government should resign when denied supply by the Upper House above the principle that the government of the day should be determined by the balance of forces in the House of Representatives.

Another question is how did Sir John know that Fraser could or would accept a commission on the terms in which it was given, that is, to guarantee supply and seek a general election. He was confident enough of this to have Fraser at Government House immediately Whitlam was decommissioned. Had he spoken to Fraser about this before? Had he asked Fraser whether he was prepared to accept a commission on these terms? Had he asked Fraser whether he could guarantee supply? If he had asked these questions recently, then Fraser would obviously have prior warning of his action.

Alternatively had Fraser, acting on Ellicott's advice, already indicated to the Governor-General that he was prepared to accept a commission on these terms and conditions? Certainly, the confidence which Fraser and Ellicott had over the previous week, that Kerr would intervene, proved to be deadly accurate.

The Senate sat at 2.00 after the lunch break. The change of government was never announced in the Upper House. The government Senate leader Ken Wriedt walked into the chamber and spoke briefly to his opposite number Reg Withers. The Liberal leader was careful to say nothing about the change of government but said cryptically: 'I think we can all go home tonight.' At about 2.10 Wriedt took a message from his private secretary that the government had been dismissed and the manager of government business in the Senate Doug McClelland went out of the chamber to try and confirm this.

By 2.15 the Labor Senate leaders knew for a fact that the government had been deposed. They were in a nearly impossible position when they discovered this, with the Appropriation Bills just about to be introduced 75 minutes after Whitlam had been decommissioned. Wriedt was in the position of securing supply for the Fraser government, not the Whitlam government. The bills were declared urgent and the president of the Senate put the motion. They were carried on the voices.

The deadlock was over and the budget was passed. Labor had lost the only real opportunity it had to foil the Governor-General's dismissal, by attempting to delay the granting of supply to the Fraser government, one of the conditions on which Fraser received his commission.

This sequence of events was amazing and would be unbelievable if it had not actually occurred. No Senators had been called to the meeting at the Lodge during the lunch break when Whitlam planned his tactics. Similarly, at the lunch-time meeting there was no thought given to either the Senate or the passage of supply. Events had moved too quickly for the Labor leaders to keep up with them. They did not realise that Fraser was Prime Minister and that his prime concern was to secure passage of the Supply Bills.

If Labor had realised, it could have used a number of parliamentary devices in the Senate to delay a vote on the Appropriation Bills. Moreover, it is possible that the President of the Senate, Justin O'Byrne, a Labor Senator, could have suspended the Senate sitting on his own initiative. According to J R Odgers, in *Australian Senate Practice*, there is clear precedent for the President to suspend sittings of the Senate at his own discretion. The Liberal–National Country Parties, of course, had a clear majority on the floor of the Senate and Labor was only capable of delaying the passage of the budget, not preventing it. But this could have created severe problems for Fraser and any attempt by O'Byrne to suspend the sitting certainly would have, because of events taking place in the House of Representatives.

The House of Representatives met at 2.34 and Malcolm Fraser announced he had been commissioned to form a government. Fraser said he had accepted the commission and given an assurance that he would secure supply immediately and then advise the dissolution of both Houses of Parliament. His government would act as a caretaker government and would make no appointments or dismissals or initiate new policies before the election. The Prime Minister made this announcement more than ten minutes after supply had been passed.

After explaining the position, Fraser then moved that the House adjourn. He was defeated on the floor of the House 64–55. The Leader of the House Fred Daly then moved suspension of standing orders to allow Whitlam to move a motion. Daly put the question immediately and it was carried 64–54. Standing orders were then suspended. Whitlam moved that the House of Representatives express its want of confidence in the Prime Minister and called upon the Governor-General to commission himself to form a government. Whitlam spoke for about a minute and his motion was carried by 64–54 once again. The Speaker Gordon Scholes announced that he would convey the message of the House to the Governor-General as soon as possible. The House was suspended at 3.15 until 5.30. Prime Minister Fraser had been defeated in every division.

Scholes contacted Government House seeking an audience with the Governor-General but was told that Sir John could not see him until 4.45, which was ninety minutes after the House broke. Whitlam also sought an audience with the Governor-General and was told he could call at 5.00. Meanwhile Fraser left Parliament House just before 3.30, by which stage the first group of hostile demonstrators was gathering outside. He was jeered and abused by demonstrators and Labor staffers shouting 'fascist' and pounding the car as he drove off. From this time onwards, a large crowd quickly gathered to demonstrate against the new government and in support of the Labor Party. Whitlam and a number of former Labor Ministers came on to the stairs of Parliament House just after 4.30 to speak briefly to the crowd. But at the same time a microphone and podium was set up on the front stairs to allow the Governor-General's official secretary David Smith to read the proclamation dissolving both Houses of Parliament. The Governor-General had refused to see either Whitlam or Scholes until the parliament was dissolved.

A few minutes later David Smith arrived dressed in a formal black jacket to read the proclamation dissolving parliament. Smith's words were completely drowned out by cheering demonstrators chanting 'We want Gough' and waving makeshift banners. Behind Smith to his right was the tall figure of the former Prime Minister, red-faced and tense, surrounded by both Labor and Liberal politicians, staff people, journalists, and a big crowd of more than a thousand people gathering on the steps and spilling on to the road. Police were everywhere trying to clear a path up and down the front stairs. When Smith finished, he pushed his way out of the crowd and Whitlam took over the lectern and microphones. Whitlam, decommissioned and sacked as Prime Minister three hours before, turned his controlled fury on his opponents Fraser and Kerr. He launched the Labor campaign which would continue as a crusade for the next four weeks.

Measuring his words, the former Prime Minister declared to the cheering crowd 'Well might we say God save the Queen, because nothing will save the Governor-General.' As the cheers went up, Whitlam continued, 'On Remembrance Day 1975 Malcolm Fraser will go down in history as Kerr's cur. Maintain your rage and enthusiasm. You will have a Labor government again.' A new battle was joined.

That night, while Fraser and the Liberal Party celebrated their rise to power, Labor members and supporters drowned their sorrows at a number of wakes around Canberra, the most notable being at Charlie's Restaurant. Throughout Australia, in all capital cities, people marched in protest at the controversial and historic sacking of the Whitlam government and the way in which it was effected. Trade unions threatened retaliatory action despite a plea for restraint from Bob Hawke, who flew to Canberra in the afternoon. That night a meeting of the Commonwealth Labor Advisory Council called on trade unionists to donate 'a day's pay for democracy'.

At a press conference that evening Whitlam declared: 'I am the twice elected Prime Minister of Australia—there is a caretaker at the moment.

There is no elected Prime Minister.' Meanwhile Fraser defended the Governor-General at his press conference, saying: 'The Governor-General was left with no alternative. He has acted in accordance with his duty under the constitution and withdrawn Mr Whitlam's commission.'

Regardless of the circumstances and upheaval, Fraser was Prime Minister, sworn in on 11 November. He had obtained not just the election he wanted. He had obtained the office of Prime Minister as a prelude to the election. He began the campaign itself with a massive advantage which only the authority of office can bring. Whitlam on the other hand was disadvantaged to a similar extent. But the campaign proved to be a mere formality.

# PART V

# THE AFTERMATH

# 21

## THE CAMPAIGN

*This was the campaign that didn't matter.*

A Labor staffer, 12 December 1975

The Labor leader and his advisers held a series of meetings at the Prime Minister's Lodge from breakfast time onwards on 12 November to plan the basic strategy of Labor's campaign. The party believed from the start that it had a chance of winning the 13 December general election. Because Labor people were so affected by the sacking of their government they saw this as casting a long and dominating shadow over the period running up to polling day. The conventional wisdom within the party was that the sacking was an electoral asset for them— that it gave the ALP more chance of being re-elected on 13 December than if the party was still in government and facing a general election on the same date.

Throughout the constitutional crisis Labor had campaigned on the constitutional theme and depicted Fraser as a man who would do anything for power. Now Labor would vary this tactic. It had an event which would be seen as an obvious injustice; a clear demonstration of the consequences involved in Fraser's actions. In short, the Labor Party would base its campaign on the constitutional issue. As the campaign progressed and the Fraser government announced its own policies then Labor would come in behind and attack them in an effort to make political mountains out of the inconsistencies and unanswered questions on the economy.

The meeting decided that the main components of Labor's campaign effort would be Whitlam and the former government's two main economic Ministers, Hayden and McClelland, backed by the ALP president, Bob Hawke. The breakfast meeting discussed the possibility of a series of debates between members of the old government and the new: Whitlam and Fraser, Hayden and Lynch, McClelland and Street. Labor advisers had to rely on their own 'gut' feeling about the effect of the dismissal. No one dreamed at the time that, instead of being a political plus, it was precisely the opposite for them. Labor had no market research on the dismissal.

The reality, of course, is that Labor had nothing else to use as a campaign peg. Labor's dilemma was highlighted by the chief of its marketing organisation ANOP, Rod Cameron, in a memorandum he had sent to Whitlam's office on 21 October. This note was written during the early stages of the constitutional crisis as the current of public opinion was moving in Labor's direction and the first signs of pressure emerged within the party for a snap half-Senate election. Cameron wrote:

> I believe there is some confusion in the minds of many Labor Party people I have spoken to recently that is operating to equate the new-found apparent reaction against the Opposition's stance with an increase in the likely vote for Labor in an early election. The two are by no means any more than marginally related. I would suggest that voting for Labor is by no means the same thing as supporting an emotional bandwagon movement which is for the preservation of the democratic system as we know it. It would appear as if Labor and general media communications efforts are doing very well to help the success of the latter. However, I would urge you strongly not to assume that such support automatically transfers to a vote for Labor in a 1975 election.
>
> Labor has, *little by little*, lost support in the last eighteen months to a situation where it would, assuming no campaign, receive about 40 per cent of the vote in an imminent election. Undoubtedly, the present 'constitutional crisis' has won Labor some votes: undoubtedly Labor would win more over a campaign. Not enough, however, to win an election. We are too far behind to expect to achieve a winning result in six weeks.
>
> All the research evidence points to the fact that Labor gained considerable ground over the month or so campaign period in April–May 1974. Perhaps as much as two to three per cent. All the research evidence suggests that in the past Labor has run a better campaign than have the conservatives. But to come from a situation between 35 per cent and 40 per cent in late October to a winning situation in mid-December, whether for a half-Senate election or not is, in my opinion, just not on . . . I have just seen the third Liberal ad in the current series (the one featuring a quote from Gough) and regard it as the best piece of Liberal communications I have seen from them in three years. I think we should assume that the conservatives will make

it harder for Labor to maintain, to the same extent, its customary campaign advantage.

Moreover, the major issue, as I have suggested previously, is 'competent government'. In a strictly election oriented campaign, rather than the pre-season effort we have at the moment with both sides playing under different rules, Labor may hope to divert some attention away from competent government as an issue. It is unlikely, however, to be able completely to defuse it. We cannot hope no matter how impressive Gough will be on the campaign trail, no matter how skilful we can make the communications effort to defuse in a short period a year's worth of constant, repetitious reinforcement of the incompetent government theme. Other things being equal, we have a show of doing it in six months—not in six weeks.

There are always two strands to an election campaign. One is the paid campaign which is reflected chiefly through media advertisements. The other is the campaign waged by the leader, which ideally should strengthen and spearhead the former. The two strands of Labor's campaign were planned at the Sydney meetings on 14 and 16 November. The party's advertising agency, Mullins, Clarke and Ralph, was given its brief at the Friday meeting and returned on the Sunday to explain concepts and layouts to the national campaign committee.

The aim was to incorporate a number of themes in the campaign, the underlying strategy being that of 'rule breaking', 'unfair play', and 'stability of government'. The party recognised that this theme was based to a large extent on emotional feelings which, while strong in the period immediately following the 11 November sacking, were certain to dissipate over time. Even Whitlam could only maintain the rage of the community for a small period. It was too much to expect that it could be sustained until polling day. Combe recognised this but argued strongly that there was no alternative central theme. This view was summarised in another memorandum after the campaign by Cameron:

To have campaigned on 'its record' Labor would have won no ideo-logically uncommitted votes. It was not a credible theme. Labor's record in totality, rightly or wrongly, was perceived by the community as one of mistakes rather than of achievements. Labor had a very big plus—Medibank—which by late 1975 had become solidified as indeed a most impressively perceived achievement. However, Medibank, and to a lesser extent, the Australian Legal Aid office, were the only achievements that could be used in a three week campaign . . . If Labor's achievements and record and entire social program had not been effectively communicated in three years of government, it is folly to expect to be able to communicate it in three weeks of a campaign. Thus to attempt to divert as much attention away from the reality of the perception of general and economic mismanagement must have been the underlying aim of the campaign.

367

A number of Labor people disagreed with this strategy and they were successful in the last ten days of the campaign in having fresh emphasis placed on Labor's abilities to handle the economy in contrast to the caretaker government.

The analysis of Labor's position by its own strategists was similar to that of the Liberal Party. This was one of the chief reasons why the Opposition had forced the election in the first place. Anyone who studied the opinion polls over the life of the Labor government and was familiar with the patterns of political behaviour knew that Labor could win an election only with the help of a miracle. Some Labor people thought the dismissal might be the miracle they wanted. It was only in the last week of the election campaign that they realised it was no electoral asset to Labor whatsoever.

Whitlam began campaigning almost immediately, now that the burdens of office had left him. He visited South Australia, Melbourne, and Tasmania before flying to Cairns on the weekend of 22–23 November for a meeting in the heart of the Leichhardt electorate.

Everywhere the dismissed Prime Minister went, there were huge crowds unprecedented in a modern Labor campaign. Whitlam had money thrust into his hands as people mobbed him on stages and platforms in each state he visited, in every electorate, in each city and town. Right from the start Labor strategists knew the crucial question was whether the crowds simply reflected committed Labor voters mobilised into action, or whether they represented a widespread mood of outrage that would affect the behaviour of swinging voters.

The Labor campaign received a momentous official launching on Monday 24 November with a dual opening in both Sydney and Melbourne. An estimated 30,000 people gathered beneath Sydney's summer skies in the Domain as Whitlam launched the Sydney 'leg' backed by a huge banner reading 'Shame Fraser Shame'. But the Sydney meeting was just a warm-up for one of the most momentous political meetings in Australian history. A total of 7500 people were packed into Festival Hall Melbourne that evening in preparation for Whitlam's Melbourne opening, the address that would be televised live to the nation.

This was not an ordinary policy speech. Whitlam made no new promises, no new undertakings. It was a manifesto, a political polemic designed to rally the mood and spirit of the Australian people to the crisis of democracy which Whitlam claimed the nation now faced, and to fan a sense of outraged injustice at the fate which had befallen the Whitlam government, the first Labor government since the start of the Menzies era in 1949.

Whitlam declared:

Men and women of Australia, the whole future of Australian democracy is in your hands. The decision you make on 13 December goes far beyond who shall govern Australia for a few months or a few years. It goes to the heart of how Australia is to be governed into the twenty-first century . . . Remembrance Day 1975. Remember that day. Mr Fraser's day of shame—a day that will live in infamy . . . Our opponents have deliberately and wilfully sown the seeds of a terrible division. To confirm them in the power they have usurped would be to confirm and deepen for all time the division they have created . . . Above all I appeal to those thousands and thousands of my fellow Australians who hitherto have voted otherwise and have supported other parties, but who have always supported in their hearts and minds the far greater cause—the cause of democracy, the cause of the Australian way, the cause of Australia herself. For that is what is at stake in this election . . . let us all make sure that 13 December 1975 is recorded for all time as the day when the Australian people asserted for all time that parliamentary democracy would survive in Australia for all time. Let us make sure that government of the people, by the people, for all the people, through the House of the people, shall endure in this nation forever.

Whitlam summarised the achievements of his government and appealed for a reaffirmation of the mandate. Several times during his speech he had to stop in the face of a mounting crescendo by the crowd chanting 'We want Gough'. But the crowd was restrained during the television address in comparison to the emotional tumult afterwards as the footstamping and chanting engulfed the hall and Whitlam was dragged along the edge of the stage by more and more people wanting to shake his hand. At the Festival Hall rally, as in every single campaign rally attended by Whitlam, the strains of *Advance Australia Fair* opened the meeting—one of the most popular decisions of the Labor government according to research which had been done by the party. After the speech the crowd sang and chanted for fifteen minutes to the words of *Waltzing Matilda* and *Click Go the Shears*.

Whitlam staffers later declared that the Festival Hall opening was the greatest political rally they had ever witnessed. While a series of Labor notables, including Crean, Dunstan and Hawke, received massive ovations as they 'massaged' the crowd for the climax, the night belonged to Whitlam who received one of the most emotional and sustained ovations of his political career. No one in the Labor camp could not but think the party had a definite chance of victory after the opening day. Whitlam then began his trip to South Australia, Perth, the Northern Territory, and back to the eastern coast via Brisbane.

But the signs of a massive debacle for the Labor Party also appeared from the start. The news of the first public opinion poll came at the end of the first week of the campaign when Whitlam was addressing a Brisbane rally in King George Square. The Morgan poll taken over the weekend 22–23 November showed support for the Liberals at 48 per cent compared with Labor support at 42 per cent with the Others category at ten per cent. The McNair poll taken over the same weekend and released at the end of the first week of the campaign showed the Liberals at 51 per cent, Labor at 42 per cent, with seven per cent in the Others category.

Many Labor staffers refused to believe these polls and were certain that they overestimated the strength of the coalition vote. After the solid start to Labor's campaign, its optimism was gradually destroyed as more poll figures were released over the following three weeks making it clear that the trend against Labor was both widespread and deep.

The Whitlam dismissal was a significant boost to the campaign of the Liberal–National Country parties. Fraser was now in the role of caretaker Prime Minister not Opposition Leader: the most unique position of any political leader in any campaign in Australian history.

Fraser had the full resources of government at his command and was able to use them, not to defend past government policy, but this time condemn it. He became both an active and a very political caretaker. In his first day in the job Fraser claimed that the Labor government had suppressed details showing the full extent of Australia's economic predicament. On the second day the caretaker Treasurer Phillip Lynch asked his department to examine ways government spending could be cut after 13 December and also how Labor's tax reforms could be altered.

Fraser had a number of advantages stemming from the office of Prime Minister. He was now in office trying to stay there, which was a much easier political task than being an Opposition Leader attempting to win office. Fraser was able to speak with the authority of the nation's leader and not as the pretender to leadership. He was able to announce decisions and appear surrounded by the trappings of office. He could use the bureaucracy to claim the Labor government was both incompetent and misleading, and he did this very cleverly.

The change of government helped the Liberal Party enormously in the election plan it had mapped out. Fraser could effectively argue that everything he said about the Whitlam government was correct. The Governor-General had proved it: he had been forced to dismiss Whitlam to uphold the Constitution. While Fraser did not make this point so bluntly, it was underlying nearly every speech he gave during the campaign. It gave him great assistance in depicting the Labor Party as dishonest, inefficient and willing to subvert the constitution to stay in power.

It was in these first days of office that Fraser once again demonstrated his capacity for political overkill. The former Treasurer Bill Hayden announced he would take legal action over reports published in some newspapers in which Fraser alleged Hayden had stolen Treasury documents. Hayden denied that he had stolen any papers and said the only documents he took with him were his personal papers. Hayden challenged Fraser to specify what documents he had taken and explain just where the Labor government had suppressed economic indicators. The extent to which the caretaker government was prepared to use its position to discredit the Whitlam government brought sections of the public service close to an open revolt. One of the great ironies was that the controversy centred on the Treasury, the department with which Labor had clashed more frequently and more bitterly than any other section of the bureaucracy.

On Wednesday 12 November, the three top Treasury officers, Wheeler, Stone and Cole, briefed senior Ministers on the economy, indicating that signs of a recovery were present. However after this briefing Fraser seized front page headlines with his accusation that the economy was worse than the Labor government had publicly admitted. In subsequent days Wheeler himself expressed concern to the caretaker Treasurer Phillip Lynch about the way the Treasury's assessments were being manipulated for political purposes. Relations further deteriorated when Lynch's office asked the Treasury for long-range policy advice on Labor's tax reforms and forecasts of government spending for 1976–77. None of this material was needed for the government's caretaker role prior to 13 December.

The Liberal–National Country Parties were already acting as a fully fledged government in their own right. Two senior second division officers in Treasury complained to Wheeler about the request and eventually the Secretary called a senior officers' conference to discuss relations with the caretaker government. Wheeler told the meeting the Treasury had an obligation to meet requests of the caretaker government unless they involved digging up 'political dirt' on the Labor Party. But a number of officers objected to this view, saying the information sought from Treasury would be used for political purposes anyway. Some officers even asked Wheeler to seek clarification of the caretaker guidelines from the Governor-General. Finally, the Treasury revolt began to assume an open form with a meeting of nearly a hundred middle-ranking officers which resulted in a letter being sent to the Governor-General complaining about the actions of the caretaker government and seeking clarification of its guidelines.

Fraser returned to the economic attack however in the first week of the campaign, this time using figures from the OECD. The Prime Minister said he had received advance information on the OECD forecasts showing that Australia's inflation rate during 1976 was expected to be second only to that of Britain. He later put this estimate at 15 per cent. Fraser's statements clearly embarrassed the OECD which was subsequently contacted by Labor staff people. Hayden himself accused Fraser of breaching trust with the organisation and hinted that the Treasury's assessment of Australia's inflation rate in the coming year was 10–12 per cent.

Fraser's comments set the direction of the Liberal campaign—but in another twist to the campaign, Fraser was confined to bed with the flu and unable to deliver his policy speech on the evening of 25 November. Fraser's speech was rescheduled for Thursday 27 November at the Dallas Brookes Hall. He was photographed with Phil Lynch and Doug Anthony by the bedside talking over campaign tactics.

The Labor Party revealed the weakness of its own position when most of its strategists became convinced that Fraser's illness would only assist the government. Normally a sickness such as this during an election would be a major blow. But in the 1975 campaign it meant that the Labor Party was unable to move on to stage two of its campaign tactics: criticism of the Fraser policies, which had to await the policy speech. It was already clear towards the end of the first week of the campaign that the constitutional issue was beginning to die.

Fraser's policy speech accentuated this process. Its twin themes were a new economic program to boost business profitability and the private sector, combined with a bitter attack on the dishonesty and incompetence of the Whitlam Labor government. The core of Fraser's program was taken straight from his reply to the budget the previous August. This was the promise to introduce tax indexation for individuals and companies. In addition to this Fraser promised a 40 per cent investment allowance, suspension of quarterly tax payments, extra protection for Australian industry, abolition of the Prices Justification Tribunal, and a new home savings grants scheme. Fraser's speech was pitched to the business sector with a strong reaffirmation of the private enterprise ethic. He promised an end to jobs for the boys, waste and extravagance in government spending, and 'international safaris' by members of parliament.

The new Prime Minister wanted a return to the Menzies era of peace and security without the upheaval of reform. 'On 13 December we can start helping all those people who have been harmed by Labor,' Fraser declared. 'We have heard about a fair go for Labor. A fair go for the most hopeless government in our history? A fair go for a man who had to be sacked because he was prepared to damage the nation rather than face the people? They've had a fair go. What about a fair go for Australia?' Fraser received a strong and enthusiastic reception from a packed crowd which distinctly lacked the emotional fervour that marked Whitlam's opening. Fraser's speech was a strong and confident start, only 16 days out.

The Liberal campaign was the best prepared and researched in its history. One of the first advertisements run on both television and in newspapers headed 'The Three Dark Years', contained a series of flashing reminders of almost all the indiscretions, mistakes and upheavals that marked the Labor government: the Khemlani loan, the Cairns sacking, the Crean removal, rises in cigarettes, spirits and petrol, Philip Cairns, record unemployment, the increase in interest rates, the Connor sacking, the ASIO raid, the Gair affair. They were all featured in a devastating fashion. The Liberals maintained a saturation newspaper and live media advertising campaign which Labor could never match.

At the same time Fraser was determined to ensure that he did not repeat the same mistakes made by his predecessor, Bill Snedden, in the 1974 campaign. The Prime Minister's chief campaign advisers were the Liberal Party director Tony Eggleton, his press secretary David Barnett, and Snedden's former press secretary Jon Gaul, who was hired for the campaign. The role of the Canberra press gallery in the 1974 campaign had already passed into legend. The gallery had caught Snedden out very badly on several issues and in disagreements between himself and Doug Anthony, which had been a vital factor in creating the image of incompetence and disunity that cost the Liberals so much in such a close election. Fraser was determined not to make the same mistake. Each day of the campaign he held an opening media session with television and radio journalists, which allowed Fraser to say what he wanted and convey his political arguments. Press conferences with newspaper reporters were held separately and the general purpose of such conferences was normally to probe policies a lot deeper. But Fraser refused to spell out the details of his policies, thereby denying either the press or the Labor Party a chance to attack him. It was a clever and solid political strategy, which was conducted successfully throughout the remaining two weeks of the campaign.

Fraser showed the hard line he would take with the press at his first conference held in the backyard of his South Yarra home on 26 November when he was recuperating from his illness:

Question: Do you anticipate the inflation rate next year will be higher or lower than the rate this year?

Fraser: It's going to remain at a very high rate. It's going to remain at one of the highest rates in the Western world.

Question: The ex-Prime Minister has said ten per cent. What does the present Prime Minister say?

Fraser: Well I'm saying that the ex-Prime Minister is talking a great deal of nonsense.

Question: Is it true that Treasury estimates inflation for this year 1975–76 to be ten to twelve per cent?

Fraser: If so, I haven't heard of it. Is that your estimate?

Question: Well that's what I heard.

Fraser: Well it's wrong.

Question: If you're able to say that that Treasury estimate is wrong,

| | |
|---|---|
| | will you tell us the correct Treasury estimate of inflation for the next financial year? |
| Fraser: | No, you're only repeating your question. |
| Question: | In August, you indicated that as your alternative to the Labor budget you would spend an extra $1000 million and would cut government spending by that amount to maintain the deficit at $2800 million. Now that the deficit is estimated to be $4000 million, do you still aim to maintain it at $2800 million, if you're elected on December 13? Do you still aim to spend the $1000 million you said you'd spend? |
| Fraser: | The best thing would be to wait for the policy speech on Thursday night. |
| Question: | Will the answer—as to the level of the deficit you'll aim for and what cuts in government spending you will make—be in your policy speech? |
| Fraser: | Not in the precise terms you asked the question, no. |
| Question: | When will you answer those questions precisely? |
| Fraser: | The answers will be plain enough in the policy speech itself . . . |

The Prime Minister got on top of the press from the start and stayed there. Only a politician enjoying a big margin in the public opinion polls could have afforded to engage in the 'stone-walling' strategy Fraser adopted. But it was clearly the right strategy at the time. Fraser's aim was to ensure that he was not trapped into making a mistake the way Snedden had in 1974. Two of the crucial areas where Fraser refused to be pinned down were the future of Medibank and the Labor government's programs which would be abolished to finance his new policies.

In order to bolster his refusal to give details, Fraser even claimed the policy proposals in his speech could not be costed. He said only that the implementation of tax indexation, which the Mathews Committee estimated to cost $2500 million, would be financed by the elimination of the Labor government's waste and extravagance. But he refused to specify what areas of the public sector would be reduced in the great transfer of resources from the public to private sector which he was proposing. The radicalism of Fraser's program received almost no media attention, simply because he refused to be drawn on it.

A journalist from the *Washington Post* who was in Australia during the campaign was amazed at Fraser's success at avoiding questions. 'Nixon would never have got away with it,' he declared after a Sydney press conference in the second week. Fraser said that while Medibank would be retained it would be changed and refused to give a guarantee that the main features of the scheme would be preserved. He also refused to say when the means test on pensions would be abolished or from what age. He refused to give a commitment on the national compensation scheme and said that while legal aid should remain, the means by which it would be provided needed review. When questioned whether his policies would only increase inflation, Fraser gave bland replies typified by the following: 'One thing we must remember is that a higher level of business activity—a reversal of the downward trend in business investment—is necessary to provide jobs for the people of Australia. If people are trying to suggest that policies which are designed to create jobs for Australians are wrong, well I find that rather surprising.' So pronounced was Fraser's refusal to answer questions that in the last week of the campaign Whitlam tried to seize this as an issue in itself.

In the last ten days of the campaign Fraser barely generated any news but simply maintained his attack on the Labor Party and hammered in broad outline his policies to revive the economy and restore economic security. The government was working on the assumption that the constitutional issue would die for the Labor Party. It was right. But beyond this Fraser was convinced that Labor was following the wrong strategy. He was delighted the longer the Labor Party stayed on the constitutional theme and refused to fight on the economy.

Throughout the campaign the *National Times* published a series of polls on the attitude of swinging voters and how they saw the main issues. The poll was based on surveys taken in the three weekends before polling day, that is, 19–20 November, 26–27 November and 3–4 December. Those swingers who saw economic management and inflation as the major issue totalled 21 per cent, 30 per cent and 37 per cent successively over those weekends. Those who saw the breaking of rules and conventions and the sacking of the Prime Minister as the main issued totalled 41 per cent, 32 per cent and 27 per cent successively. This survey work was commissioned by the paper from ANOP. Swinging voters shifted from the constitutional issue to the economy as the major issue.

Over the weekend of 29–30 November, after Fraser's policy speech, the Labor Party moved its focus more onto the economy. The advertising agency prepared a new series of ads featuring Hayden and McClelland, in an effort to prove that Labor was better equipped to fight economic problems than the government. Labor's chief problem was to seize back the political initiative. One option was the issuing of challenges to the Liberal leaders for a round of debates between Whitlam and Fraser, Hayden and Lynch, and McClelland and Street. Labor strategists reasoned that if the debates were held they would win; if they were not held, the Liberals would be discredited. Labor was hoping to secure the services of British compere, David Frost, as a moderator. The debate scheme was enthusiastically supported by Combe. But Freudenberg and eventually Whitlam were not happy and it was abandoned. It is almost certain that Fraser would have declined to appear in such debates.

Whitlam foreshadowed the shift in Labor's campaign on Sunday night 30 November addressing a Queanbeyan rally, when he linked the constitutional issue and the economic issue together saying they were 'one and the same'. He said: 'The onslaught on the constitution, the onslaught on parliamentary democracy was the necessary prelude to the greatest onslaught on social programs in health, in schools, in hospitals, in cities ever experienced.'

On Monday afternoon, 1 December, Whitlam held a major press conference in his Martin Place offices to hammer Fraser on the economy. It was the day Whitlam tried to grab back the campaign initiative. Four days before he had rung Freudenberg early in the morning after reading Fraser's policy speech, excited by the possibilities it presented for counter-attack. Whitlam argued that a Fraser government would demolish Labor's achievements in the fields of education, health, welfare and the cities. But the quotes he used from Fraser's economic statement failed to substantiate the allegation. In one of the worst performances of his career, Whitlam failed in both a strategic and public relations sense. He failed to find a credible line of political attack against Fraser and spent a large part of his press conference reeling off figures, refusing to answer questions and then issuing a 13 page statement to substantiate his arguments when the conference was finished.

From this time on Labor was fighting a losing battle and each public opinion poll only showed an increasingly desperate position. At the end of the second week the Morgan poll had Liberals 53 per cent, and Labor 42 per cent, while McNair had the Liberals at 55 per cent and Labor at 38 per cent. The party, while accepting it was facing defeat, did not accept the magnitude of defeat being suggested in the polls. In the last week of the campaign Morgan showed the Liberals at 55 per cent and Labor at 41 per cent, while McNair had the Liberals at 53 per cent and Labor at 40 per cent.

Three days before polling day Whitlam received a phone call from John Menadue, who was now head of the Prime Minister's Department under Malcolm Fraser. Menadue was anxious to stay on in the job if Labor was defeated but thought he should clear this with Whitlam who had originally appointed him. Whitlam told Menadue he could see no problem with this and said later he regarded it as a vindication of Menadue's appointment in the first place.

On the evening of Thursday 11 December Whitlam addressed his last Melbourne rally at Moorabbin Oval, in the marginal Liberal electorate of Hotham. Although Labor had been written off, more than 20,000 people crammed into the stand and went crazy when Whitlam arrived and left the field. The Labor Party still saw Melbourne as its main hope of picking up seats and the Moorabbin meeting only confirmed the core of Labor's campaign debacle: that the committed were more committed than ever. The trouble was that Labor had completely lost the swinging voters who had carried it to power in 1972 and re-elected it in 1974.

On Friday 12 December Whitlam addressed his last campaign rally in Hyde Park, where he accused the Liberals of trying to incite campaign violence. In a characteristic fashion the leader ended his campaign with a bitter attack on both Sir John Kerr and Malcolm Fraser and returned to his original theme saying that the election would decide the future of parliamentary democracy in Australia.

At lunchtime Gough and Margaret Whitlam, together with their staff and the journalists who had covered the campaign with them, went to the traditional end-of-campaign lunch. It was held in the Papillon Restaurant in King Street, Sydney. Towards the end of the lunch Whitlam began talking about the candidature of his son, Tony Whitlam, who was running in Fred Daly's old seat of Grayndler. 'Why the bloody hell he'd want this sort of life, I just don't know,' Whitlam told two journalists. 'I didn't suggest it, he just wants to do it.' It was one of the few remarks Whitlam had made about the futility of going into politics in Australia. It summed up the mood of the former Prime Minister, who knew he was staring defeat in the face.

Whitlam's speech writer Graham Freudenberg, who was on his last election campaign, his ninth, delivered a short and emotional speech that summed up the ethos of the Whitlam group. Freudenberg praised Whitlam for his performance in the campaign which he compared with the quality identified by Hemingway as 'grace under pressure'.

Freudenberg concluded:

> You have shown, not for the first time but particularly during this campaign, that great quality which is one of your most but one of your many admirable qualities—grace under pressure. Some of us have been with you for many years, others have been for some years, some have been throughout this campaign. But the qualities you have shown are the qualities that we know are yours and yours alone, the qualities of the greatest living Australian and the greatest Australian who has ever lived. It has been a privilege for all of us to be associated with you throughout this campaign. It will be our honour and privilege to be associated with you in continuing the growth and greatness of the nation that we love under the leadership of the man we love.

# 22

## RESULTS AND AFTERMATH

*I and my wife sometimes wonder 'Is it worth it?' but we always
decide it is.*

Gough Whitlam, 28 August 1975

$A$t 11 p.m. Gough Whitlam walks through the door of the Belconnen
High School Hall, central tally room for the election results. A crowd of
television cameramen, radio reporters and newspapermen engulf him
as he pushes his way into the hall with press secretary David Solomon
by his side. There are 1500 people crammed into the hall which is set
up like a theatre with great arc lights spanning the vast cinemascope
screen of a tally board which covers every seat and state in Australia.
The floor is packed with press benches, phones, empty beer cans; at the
rear are three multistoreyed television commentators' booths. Along the
side are black screen computers which at command flash up in green
digits an instant analysis of seats and swings, documenting an ever
unfolding and deepening political tragedy for the Labor Party and its
leader.

This is the end of the road for Gough Whitlam; the end of nine
years of struggle and dedication to revamp and revive the Labor Party,
pull it to office, struggle against the most sustained campaign of obstruction and criticism which any government in Australia has ever faced,
only to be dismissed from office by the Governor-General. Tonight the
Australian public has deserted Whitlam en masse and his reputation as
a popular leader has been destroyed.

Whitlam stands on the right hand side of the tally board, not
glancing at it—there is no longer any need to—while a ring of thrusting,
bristling microphones surround his face as journalists push desperately

378

against their fellow journalists to record his words. David Combe watches from the side, his face white and grim. At one side, away from the raucous glare of the media, stands Margaret Whitlam and long-time loyal speechwriter and friend Graham Freudenberg. As Whitlam enters a cry of 'We want Gough' begins, a pathetic and cruel reminder of yesterday.

Whitlam, tense but in full control of himself, simply says:

> We've lost a very great number of seats and the Liberals have won a very great number of seats. Let me congratulate them on their success. Let me also say how much my colleagues and I appreciate the magnificent spirit shown by the Labor movement during the past couple of months. I'd like to express in particular my profound regret at losing so many colleagues who were in the prime of their political life, and whose contribution to this country's political life has been interrupted. The vote at the moment is 44.6 per cent and I suppose later votes will bring it down to 43 per cent.

In characteristic fashion Whitlam confronted defeat in the face, made no effort to shirk its dimensions or hide from its consequences.

Did he intend to stay on as leader? 'Let me think about that and discuss it.' Gone is the conviction and arrogance of yesterday. Why did Labor lose? 'It's the general fate of any government in a time of recession and particularly a reformist government.'

Referring to the main theme of the campaign Whitlam says that 'there are very serious implications for Australian democracy' in Labor's defeat. Responding to Solomon's move to close the questioning, Whitlam and his group move to the side of the tally board and then walk along behind it and out the exit on the other side of the hall. The two tall figures, Margaret in a long batik dress and Gough in navy sports coat and grey pants, briefly acknowledge the cheers of the tally board workers high above them on the scaffolding before police gently guide them into a white commonwealth car. A black car carrying Whitlam's staff follows and crashes its bottom on to a drain to the jeers of hecklers who call out across the dark playground: 'Hey, who won mate?'

The press and pundits in the tally room knew who had won even before 9 p.m. The first figures went up on the tally board at 8.25 p.m. From the first few hundred votes on the board, the swing was there, in every seat in every state with an inexorable uniformity. At 9.30 p.m., when just on 3.4 per cent of the vote was counted, the swing against Labor was 2.3 per cent, the swing to the Liberals 5.7 per cent.

This is no 1974, when the result was a knife edge, shifting to Labor and then moving back to the coalition, gluing everyone to the board and forcing them to make analysis after analysis. The mood is one of anti-climax. The result is certain; only the dimensions of the landslide are to be determined. As the night progresses what looks like a solid defeat begins turning into a massive debacle, worse than 1966, the worst defeat ever. One Labor staffer says: 'After 23 years in exile we end up with this.' David Combe, near exhaustion after running the month long campaign, looks glumly at the board. Earlier that day on the tarmac at Canberra airport Combe told reporters: 'I've got to be a realist about it. But it's not going to be as bad as the polls indicate.' But it is.

Whitlam spends the night at the Lodge, a private night not a public night, unlike the victories of 1972 and 1974. Political leaders always share their joy with the electorate but only the most crass try to share their sorrow. Family and staff gather in the white house on Adelaide Avenue where Whitlam has lived the last three years. There are about 25 people in all: daughter Cathy, son Nick and his wife Judy, son Stephen and his wife Sheena, and the staff—Freudenberg, Solomon, Mant, Delaney, Lorraine Dwyer, Evan Williams, Canberra driver Bob Miller and his wife, Sydney driver Terry Hudson and his wife, and the girls from the office. The group spreads out along the back terrace, Whitlam's office, the lounge and the drawing room. Two computer visual display units have been set up in the Lodge with staff from the electoral office to man them, allowing Whitlam to get feedback from the central computer. There are four television sets, including one in the study, and a number of extra phones installed for the occasion.

Gough and Margaret have been working since 6 a.m. visiting every polling booth in the Werriwa electorate getting sunburnt and covered in dust in the process. This is an election day ritual, something they have done every election since Whitlam first entered parliament in 1952 representing the backblocks of Australian suburbia. But as the results come in, immediately there is a profound sadness and shock. Whitlam and his senior staff are stunned at the extent of the swing against them, particularly in the outer metropolitan seats of Sydney and Melbourne to which Whitlam has traditionally pitched his appeal. Even though defeat was not unexpected, its reality is still demoralising.

At 10 o'clock there is discussion about going to the tally room. The staff suggests a form of words for the leader, conceding defeat. At 10.45 the white car glides slowly out of the Lodge past the guard, who is more philosophical than anyone else. 'I've been here since Menzies' time, I've seen them all come and go,' he says.

Later that night at the Lodge Whitlam said: 'I guess I'd better give it away,' referring to the leadership of the Labor Party which he had held since February 1967. On this evening Whitlam believed his credentials as a political leader had been revoked by the Australian electorate. This was his gut reaction which continued for some days.

The Liberal Party has made extensive preparations for its anticipated victory. The fifteenth floor of the Southern Cross Hotel,

Melbourne, is completely booked for a celebratory rally. More than $1000 worth of champagne—Great Western and Veuve Cliquot—Scotch whisky and Danish beer is provided. Federal Liberal Party director Tony Eggleton, who has run a campaign as smooth as clockwork, is living up to his reputation on the final night.

Malcolm and Tamara Fraser begin their day at the Warrnambool polling booths in Fraser's Wannon electorate, which he has held since 1955. Unlike Whitlam, who travels his electorate by car, Fraser needs a light plane to swing round the Victorian western districts to Portland, Casterton and Hamilton. The Frasers fly home to vote at Nareen near their property and about forty people wait outside a small bluestone hall built in 1870 to meet them. Fraser is relaxed and confident and enjoys a quiet lunch at his property, one of the last opportunities he will have for solitude before becoming the real, as distinct from caretaker, Prime Minister.

That afternoon the Frasers fly to Melbourne to their South Yarra home where they watch the early results on television. At the Southern Cross, Eggleton has arranged for about fifteen colour television sets to be set up with a computer hook-up to the central tally room in Canberra to give an instant account of the vote. Malcolm Fraser knows by 9.30 the trend is too uniform and too big to be reversed.

At 10 p.m. Malcolm Fraser and Tammy arrive at the Southern Cross as crowds gather to cheer and security men race to their sides, link arms and prepare a path for them through the packed foyer. Fraser stops to acknowledge the pleading microphones thrust towards him. 'All the work, all the jobs are ahead,' he declares. 'All the problems are still to be solved.' But tonight is the night to celebrate.

The Frasers eventually fight their way into the lift and go straight to the fifteenth floor. This is the cream of the establishment in Australia's most establishment city, Liberals almost to a man. John McEwen is there, former Country Party interim Prime Minister, along with all the Victorian Liberals, Phillip Lynch, Andrew Peacock, Ivor Greenwood, former Premier Sir Henry Bolte, and a host of new faces, faces of the new Liberals who have won seats in the House of Representatives.

Fraser, whose drinking habits have become famous over the previous two months, is only seen with soda water or ginger ale. Tony Eggleton receives congratulations from everyone and candidly admits that the margin of victory is greater than the Liberals expected. But the talk is all of Fraser and his year of extraordinary success, one of the most startling this country has ever witnessed. Fraser talks of everything he likes best, fishing in Alaska, his friends who perform aerial tricks in their light planes, trail-bike riding, cars, and the future.

But politics is ever present. Fraser's election predictions have all proved to be right. The coalition has won not only government in the

House of Representatives, but a clear, safe majority in the Senate, just as he said it would. Moreover the swing against Labor extends from its traditional strongholds through the suburbs to the country, again just as Fraser said it would. He thanks all the Liberal workers at the Southern Cross who are manning the video machines and feeding out results. Tammy Fraser, who said a few days before she didn't want to live in a communist country, says: 'I'd like to hug everyone who voted Liberal.'

Just before midnight Fraser takes a congratulatory call from Gough Whitlam just as he had received a congratulatory call from Whitlam the previous March, the day he was elected Liberal leader. Fraser calls his electorate and then calls his sister in Rome. He and Tammy leave the Southern Cross at 2.30 a.m. and arrive downstairs only to find their official car is missing. By this stage all the celebrators and demonstrators have left. He gets a lift home with the police and they come in and share a few drinks with him. For Malcolm Fraser the long haul is over. Another one is about to begin.

Election night in the central tally room in Canberra is becoming a showbiz spectacular. It is Australia's own version of Hollywood. The working press consoles itself with the thought that future elections will all be recorded by computer and the tally board will become unnecessary. Television panellists make their way down to the main floor for a break between their commentaries. Bob Hawke in a sky blue shirt and safari suit admits defeat at 9.30 and goes over to talk to John Gorton who has been thoroughly defeated in the ACT Senate race. John Singleton of the Workers Party has model Maggie Eckhardt on his right arm and a bottle of white wine in his left. It's a perfect television commercial.

The deposed Attorney-General, Kep Enderby, who has lost his Canberra seat, puts on a brave face realising that the tragedy transcends personal concerns. Bill McMahon gulps down champagne as he stands under a television light pole for an interview. Doug Anthony arrives in the tally room to cheers and hisses. The result is a mixed one for the National Country Party as it returns to government but with a weaker influence in the coalition than before. Harry M Miller spends his time talking with Doug and Margot Anthony.

Bill Snedden smiles at the victory which he believes should have been his. This time all the election pundits are right, Malcolm Mackerras, Max Walsh, David Butler. Down in the front stalls near the tally board are Mick Young, David Combe and the rest of the Labor front line tapping pocket calculators and making endless phone calls.

People drift away from the tally room at about 1 a.m. The Liberal victory celebration is in Melbourne and this time Labor has nothing to celebrate. There is no party at David Solomon's that will go to dawn, just a few isolated wakes around the town. A few people gather at Mungo MacCallum's on the other side of the lake. Xavier Herbert, author of *Poor Fellow My Country* who declared himself for Labor during the campaign, is bent over his walking stick stricken with sorrow. Graham Freudenberg stands speechless, shattered.

Where is the Governor-General? His private secretary David Smith says: 'No, Sir John isn't here tonight, he's in Sydney spending the evening privately with friends. He'll be back in Canberra tomorrow. I might come down to the tally room soon for a look.' But he didn't.[1]

Labor lost 29 House of Representatives seats. Its 65–62 majority was transformed into a 36–91 deficit. Its three seat majority in 1975 was converted into a 55 seat Liberal–National Country Party majority after the election. Fraser received the biggest mandate in Australian history in the 13 December poll. The governing coalition gained a stranglehold on the Senate, a key factor in ensuring that Fraser will have an uninterrupted term. The new Senate totalled 64 Senators compared to the previous 60, resulting from the election of two Senators each for the first time from both the ACT and the Northern Territory. Labor's Senate strength remained at 27 while the coalition figure rose from 30 to 35. The other Senators were Liberal Movement leader Steele Hall who was re-elected and Tasmanian independent, Brian Harradine. Leaving aside the independents, the Government had a Senate majority of eight, which ensures that it will have a majority for at least six years following the 1975 election.

The following table shows the extent of the fall in Labor first preference votes compared with previous elections and with its other big defeat in 1966.[2]

|  | 1966 | 1969 | 1972 | 1974 | 1975 | % Swing |
|---|---|---|---|---|---|---|
| Labor Party | 39.98 | 46.95 | 49.95 | 49.30 | 42.8 | −6.5 |
| Liberal Party | 40.15 | 34.77 | 32.14 | 34.95 | 41.7 | +6.8 |
| Country Party | 9.84 | 8.56 | 9.44 | 10.78 | 11.2 | +0.4 |
| DLP | 7.31 | 6.02 | 5.25 | 1.42 | 1.3 | −0.1 |
| Australia Party |  | 0.88 | 2.42 | 2.33 | 0.4 | −1.9 |
| Others | 2.72 | 2.82 | 1.26 | 1.22 | 2.3 |  |

This table reveals the basic story of the election, the switch of votes from the Labor Party to the Liberal Party and the eclipse of all the smaller parties with people voting for major parties at a time of crisis. Although Labor is in a worse position than after the 1966 election, it won a lot more of the vote than in 1966. In two party preferred terms Labor polled about 44.5 per cent in the 1975 election compared with 55.5 per cent for the Liberal–National Country parties.

In the 1966 election Labor polled 43.1 per cent in two party preferred terms compared with 56.9 per cent for the coalition. That is, Labor's performance in 1975 in terms of votes is quite definitely better than in 1966. But in terms of seats Labor has 36 after the 1975 election in a

127-strong chamber compared with 41 after the 1966 election in a 123-strong chamber. In his report on the campaign to the ALP national executive, the national secretary David Combe said:

> After the 1966 reverse, the ALP achieved at the following election, and within less than three years, an increase of 7 per cent in our primary vote and came within an ace of winning government. It is not unreasonable to expect that a similar improvement can be achieved between 1975 and 1978, if the whole party sets its sights on regaining government at the next House of Representatives elections. Should we achieve a swing of similar proportions at the next House of Representative elections, this would give us a primary vote to 49.8 per cent—equal to that which we gained in 1972 when we were returned to office after a quarter of a century on the opposition benches.

Labor's disastrous performance in terms of seats reflects the fact that once Labor's vote drops below 47 per cent it loses a lot of seats by a small margin. But a factor suggesting that recovery need not necessarily be long is that the number of swinging voters is increasing. Election swings of the order of five to nine per cent are becoming the rule rather than the exception in a number of marginal metropolitan seats, as each election thousands of young people join the electoral role. This offers the Labor Party some encouragement for the future.

In two-party preferred terms the swing against Labor at the 1975 election is slightly worse than when assessed on first preference votes for each party. While the last column of the preceding table shows a swing against Labor of 6.5 per cent this is estimated to be about 7.2 per cent in two party preferred terms. The swing against the government took place throughout Australia, in all states and territories.

|        | NSW  | VIC  | QLD  | SA   | WA   | TAS   | ACT  | NT   | NATIONAL |
|--------|------|------|------|------|------|-------|------|------|----------|
| % ALP  | 45.4 | 42.0 | 38.7 | 42.6 | 40.1 | 43.4  | 48.2 | 43.6 | 42.8     |
| % Swing| -7.3 | -5.9 | -5.3 | -6.1 | -6.2 | -11.7 | -7.4 | -1.9 | -6.5     |

These figures show that Labor was not spared anywhere. The swing against Labor occurred on a substantial level, regardless of whether the state concerned had a high plateau of support for Labor in the first place or whether it had already swung substantially against Labor in 1974. Although Queensland had the lowest swing at 5.3 per cent, this took its Labor vote to the lowest level of any state.

Labor's traditionally strongest state, NSW, although recording a substantial swing against Labor, still had a better vote than anywhere else with the exception of the ACT. In Victoria, where Labor won two Melbourne seats in the 1974 election, there was a strong anti-Labor movement which resulted in a large number of marginal seat losses.

This swing took the seats of Holt, Henty, Diamond Valley, Casey, La Trobe and Isaacs, all of which Labor had won at recent elections.

The huge swing against Labor in Tasmania, which followed an earlier swing against the government in 1974, resulted in the loss of all the remaining four House of Representatives members from Tasmania. Labor now faces a long period of reconstruction in the island state.

In Queensland only the former Treasurer Bill Hayden held on in the teeth of the anti-Labor move. Labor lost five seats in the northern state: Brisbane, Bowman, Dawson, Leichhardt and Capricornia. In the previous 1974 election it lost two seats, Lilley and Wide Bay, making a loss of seven of the eight Queensland seats Labor held on assuming office in 1972. The Queensland swing was smaller because it came in two parts. The first one was an anti-Labor swing of 3.2 per cent in 1974 and this was followed with 5.3 per cent in 1975. In a sense both Queensland and Tasmania led the way for Australia. The rest of the nation caught up with them in 1975 by swinging to the non-Labor parties.

Labor was close to being wiped out in Western Australia, losing four of its five seats and retaining only Fremantle. This was an even better result than the West Australian Liberals were predicting before the coalition parties forced the election. In South Australia Labor minimised its losses to one seat, Kingston. But its 42.6 per cent vote was proof of the extent to which the Dunstan government was handicapped by being associated with the federal Labor government.

Labor lost eight seats in NSW: Barton, Cook, Eden-Monaro, Evans, Macquarie, Phillip, St George and Macarthur. The 7.3 per cent swing here, the most populous state with the most seats, was fatal to the government. One encouraging feature for the Labor Party is that a swing of a few percentage points back will mean the return of a number of these seats. The swing against Labor was in both urban and rural areas and makes a stark contrast with the results from the 1974 election on a city-country breakdown.

| | Metropolitan | | | Non-metropolitan | | | National total |
|---|---|---|---|---|---|---|---|
| | Inner | Outer | Total | Provincial | Rural | Total | |
| % Swing 1974 | +1.6 | −0.2 | +0.8 | −0.5 | −3.0 | −2.2 | −0.3 |
| % Swing 1975 | −6.4 | −8.0 | −7.2 | −6.5 | −4.9 | −5.7 | −6.5 |

This is an illuminating table, particularly in view of the electorate strategy pursued by Whitlam since he became Labor leader in 1967. The above breakdown is devised by the Commonwealth Electoral Office after dividing all federal electorates into four categories. The table shows that in 1974 there was an overall swing to Labor in the cities made up of a solid swing to Labor in traditional ALP seats and a very slight swing against Labor in outer suburban areas. By contrast the countryside moved against Labor in 1974 with a three per cent swing in rural areas.

All this changed in the 1975 election. The biggest swing against Labor was in the cities. It was most pronounced in the outer suburbs, the precise areas that Whitlam had formulated his entire political strategy to capture. In these seats the anti-Labor swing was eight per cent. But at the same time there was a big anti-Labor swing of 6.4 per cent in the well-established city areas where the majority of seats would be regarded as Labor or fairly safe Labor.

When the two elections, 1974 and 1975, are viewed together there was a combined swing against the Labor government in both city and country. While the country swing was spread over both elections the cities turned against the Government with a vengeance in the 1975 election to make up for their continued support in 1974. These trends, revealed by a geographic breakdown of the vote into urban and rural areas, were consistent throughout the nation and reflected in all states.

### % Swing against ALP in 1975 election

|            | Metropolitan | Non-Metropolitan | Total  |
|------------|--------------|------------------|--------|
| NSW        | - 7.6        | - 6.7            | - 7.3  |
| Victoria   | - 6.4        | - 4.5            | - 5.9  |
| Queensland | - 6.2        | - 4.4            | - 5.3  |
| SA         | - 7.4        | - 2.7            | - 6.1  |
| WA         | - 7.5        | - 3.9            | - 6.2  |
| Tasmania   | -11.5        | -14.1            | -11.7  |
| ACT        | - 7.4        |                  | - 7.4  |
| NT         |              | - 1.9            | - 1.9  |
| National   | - 7.2        | - 5.7            | - 6.5  |

The swing against the ALP was also uniform regardless of whether the seat was a safe or marginal one for the government. The national swing against Labor in its safe seats totalled 7.7 per cent, in its fairly safe seats 7.1 per cent, and in its marginal seats 7.3 per cent. The same pattern was apparent for the Liberal Party. The swing to the Liberals in their safe seats was 8.1 per cent, in their fairly safe seats 6.1 per cent, and in their marginal seats 8.9 per cent.

The heavy swing against Labor was of more long-term significance in the Senate than in the House of Representatives. While Labor has a very remote chance of recovering its deficit in the House in one election, it cannot do this in the Senate. NSW was the only state in which Labor was able to break even with the non-Labor parties and win five out of ten Senate places. In Victoria, Queensland, South Australia, Western Australia and Tasmania it won only four out of ten positions. In the two territories Labor and the non-Labor parties won a Senate seat each. It will take the Labor Party at least two if not three normal half-Senate elections in which to make up this deficit of Senate places, that is, of course, without the prospect of any double dissolution. Even if Labor won the 1978 House of Representatives election, it would still face a hostile Senate which could force it to the people twice a year in the same way the Whitlam government was eventually defeated. This situation could even apply at the 1981 general election.

The Fraser landslide was important in altering the shape of the parliamentary Labor Party, the caucus. The party lost some of its younger Ministers who would have played an important role in either government or Opposition. Even more important was the group of Labor backbenchers who were defeated. They comprised by and large a younger, better educated, socially-progressive and economically rationalist component in comparison to the overall caucus. Many of them comprised the vanguard of the future: elected in 1969, 1972 or 1974, they had altered the complexion of the party and in particular, had largely defactionalised it from the left–right freeze that was so destructive at various stages of the 1950s and 1960s. These people were John Kerin, Bob Whan, Max Oldmeadow, David McKenzie, Race Mathews, Tony Lamb, Richie Gunn, John Coates, John Dawkins, Joan Child (the only woman in the House in the twenty-ninth parliament), and Ray Sherry.

The consequences of a Labor defeat were discussed on Thursday 11 December by both David Combe and John Mant. Both men knew the party was facing defeat and wanted to talk over the problems that would dominate the following week. They were certain that Whitlam's initial response would be to stand down and that this would only be more pronounced with the margin of defeat. They also felt that any sudden decision of Whitlam's made in such an atmosphere could be disastrous for the party, chiefly because there appeared no logical successor from within the caucus. Hawke seemed to be the most capable alternative, but he was not in parliament.

On Sunday 14 December Whitlam's staff gathered at the Lodge for lunch to give their leader as much encouragement as possible. But Whitlam himself believed he should stand down. After such a defeat he did not think he was the right man to lead the party through three years of Opposition up to the 1978 election, by which stage he would be 62. Whitlam believed his final political task should be to leave the Labor Party in as good shape as possible after the defeat, ensure it did not lurch into recriminations, and try to have the best man available replace him as leader.

That morning Whitlam called Bill Hayden, who was hanging on to a narrow lead in Oxley. He put the leadership proposition to Hayden, who in turn made it clear he was not interested in the job at this stage; indeed he was uncertain whether he would be interested in the future. Hayden was the only man in the caucus that Whitlam seriously considered had the potential and capabilities to assume the leadership. Hayden's refusal made it obvious to Whitlam that he would have to remain as leader for some time.

That afternoon Whitlam saw Bob Hawke and David Combe at the Lodge to discuss the party's future. Whitlam explained his views to Hawke in the light of Hayden's attitude and said that in his opinion Hawke was the best man to replace him. If Hawke could get into parliament quickly and win the acceptance of the caucus then he might be in a position to take over the leadership before the next general election. Whitlam was prepared to stand down for Hawke in eighteen months time. Later the same day Hawke confirmed that he would stand for parliament within the next three years. On Sunday night Whitlam issued a press statement hinting at the understanding he and Hawke had reached in the afternoon. At the same time Whitlam put his own future squarely in the hands of the Labor caucus. The statement read:

> The president of the party Mr Bob Hawke and I met today to discuss the rebuilding of the Labor movement. In the immediate future, we place ourselves at the disposal of the will of the party, to ensure that whatever arrangements are made about particular people, the high purposes of the ALP and those who believe in its cause shall continue to be served for the good of Australia and her people. Each of us is ready to serve in any capacity which the Labor Party chooses.

The next day 15 December the Labor Party was engulfed by recriminations, almost all of them directed towards Whitlam. At one moment all the pent-up hostility of the last three years, all the anger at Whitlam's sackings, taunts, arrogance and occasional contempt of his colleagues was let loose. Clyde Cameron declared that Whitlam would only remain leader 'until the next caucus meeting'. Crean, stung at reports of a Whitlam–Hawke deal, declared there was no logical line of succession in the Labor leadership and that the party would decide it. While Crean made no public announcement, he indicated he would contest the leadership against Whitlam.

One of Whitlam's proteges in the party, Lionel Bowen, who had fallen out with the former Prime Minister in recent months, was also determined to run against Whitlam. Senate leader Ken Wriedt, once one of Whitlam's closest associates in the Cabinet, was now bitterly critical of Whitlam and believed the former Prime Minister was guilty of poor tactics during the constitutional crisis. Jim Cairns attacked Whitlam's presidential style of leadership and called on the party to build a team and not rely on an individual. Cairns included Hawke in his criticism saying Hawke was similar in style to Whitlam. Don Dunstan reaffirmed that he was not anxious to go into federal politics and wanted to stay in South Australia. From Sydney NSW Labor leader Neville Wran criticised Whitlam for sacking his senior Ministers. From Perth Labor leader John Tonkin said Whitlam's arrogance was a major factor in the loss. On this Monday journalists could not find one good word for the former Prime Minister from anyone except Bill Hayden and Kep Enderby. At the same time Hayden announced he would not be a leadership candidate.

But this picture soon changed. The NSW and Victorian Labor Party branches supported the new Whitlam–Hawke axis. Nevertheless it was clear to Whitlam by mid-week that, if he wished to gain re-election, he would have to repudiate any suggestion of a deal with Hawke and any claim that he would only be a caretaker leader.

The former Prime Minister announced that he wanted to lead Labor at the 1978 elections and, despite solid forces against him, Whitlam was expected to be re-elected when the party met on 22 December. The previous day the left-wing caucus group met at Ken Fry's Canberra home to review their strength and tactics. The main problem facing the left was that, while there were plenty of votes against Whitlam, there were not many votes for Crean, the candidate they intended to support.

The strength of the anti-Whitlam forces was shown in the party room the next day. Whitlam was most anxious to have the leadership ballot held this day to confirm him in his position. But both the left and the right wings supported a motion from Tom Uren to have the ballots deferred until 27 January. This would leave matters on the boil for another month. The left wing mounted an unsuccessful campaign to persuade Hayden to stand when Whitlam told the press he would not contest the leadership if Hayden ran.

In the meantime the party divisions which had formed the previous week became more pronounced. Mick Young, who had Whitlam's support, Paul Keating and Kim Beazley who had the support of the right wing, and Tom Uren who had the support of the left wing, were the main candidates for the deputy leadership. NSW Senator Jim McClelland joined forces with the Whitlam camp to run against Ken Wriedt for the Senate leadership. Contrary to original expectations, the four week delay worked to Whitlam's advantage simply because the more people looked for alternatives to him the more they realised there weren't any. In this period Whitlam did surprisingly little lobbying for himself and the Labor Party as a whole remained more concerned with its own internal troubles than criticising the Fraser government.

When the caucus met on 27 January Whitlam was overwhelmingly re-elected. He polled 36 votes, easily defeating the other two contestants, Frank Crean who collected 11 votes and Lionel Bowen 14. But the main feature of the ballot was the discipline and strength of the left-wing vote. While the left could not stop Whitlam they succeeded in putting his critics into the other three leadership positions. Ken Wriedt decisively beat Jim McClelland 38–25 for the Senate leadership. Tom Uren, a spearhead of the party's left but a man who had also worked closely with Whitlam over the previous five years, won the deputy leadership 33–30 against Paul Keating who collected the right-wing vote. This was a classic case of the left outmanoeuvring the right. The left got some of their supporters to vote for Paul Keating to ensure that the third last man eliminated was Young and not Keating. They believed that, if Keating had been eliminated before Young, his votes would have gone in a bloc to Young, who would have defeated Uren. But with Young going out first, his votes were not as well controlled; they split between both Keating and Uren, thereby ensuring Uren's election as deputy. The final devastating win for the left was in the Senate deputy leadership where their candidate Senator Jim Keeffe beat Jim McClelland 38–25, the same vote recorded in the Senate leadership ballot when McClelland was also defeated. The strength of the left and the extent to which they knew their exact number of votes reflected a more factionalised caucus than before. It could also be an omen of the future.

One of the significant results of the party meeting was the caucus decision to elect its leaders and executive every eighteen months, which meant they would come up for re-election half way through the life of the parliament. Contrary to press reports Whitlam believed this was a desirable move. He saw it as fundamental for the party to have this sort of flexibility in turning over the Cabinet or shadow Cabinet. One of the greatest single problems Whitlam had in government was trying to restructure his ministry. The change in party rules went a major way to rectifying this difficulty. At the same time the party also elected a number of new faces to the shadow Cabinet. The prominent ones included Ralph Willis, Don Grimes, Mick Young, John Button, Chris Hurford, Gordon Scholes and Peter Morris.

For Gough Whitlam there was a new constant in Australian politics. This was his unremitting campaign to attack the Governor-General publicly and never speak to him again privately. Whitlam spurned all those in the Labor Party, notably Bob Hawke, who claimed that Labor should not conduct a vendetta against Sir John Kerr.

Whitlam's attitude was that if the Labor Party did not preserve the memory of what happened on 11 November 1975 then no one else would. The former Prime Minister argued that Kerr's action had such fundamental consequences for the future of Australian democracy and was so essentially contrary to the spirit of his office that it must never be put to rest. On 9 February he attacked Kerr on the ABC with a new vigour in his first onslaught since the election result. 'Sir John deceived me,' Whitlam said. 'Sir John deceived people that he's known, he worked with, for decades, like Jim McClelland or Joe Riordan.'

On Monday 16 February the Labor caucus spent over 90 minutes debating whether it should boycott the official opening of parliament the next day by the Governor-General. A motion by Mick Young to leave the decision to each individual was narrowly defeated. But the next morning the caucus endorsed the wishes of its leader and decided to boycott the opening en masse.

More than 800 demonstrators jeered at Sir John when he arrived for the swearing in ceremony to open the thirtieth parliament. No Labor members went into the Senate for the Governor-General's speech, in which he outlined the policies of the Fraser government. The opening was the most bitter in Australian history. In the Senate Tasmanian independent Brian Harradine occupied the centre table chair that belonged to the Opposition Senate leader Ken Wriedt, saying he was acting to represent the Opposition forces. In both the House of Representatives during the swearing in and later in the afternoon, Sir John was subjected to snipes and sustained criticism over his dismissal of the Whitlam government.

Speaking to a motion nominating Gordon Scholes as the Labor Party's choice for Speaker against Bill Snedden, Whitlam said the reserve powers of the Governor-General had to be defined and curtailed if parliamentary democracy were to flourish. He said the previous November the Speaker had been insulted by the Governor-General and treated with contempt when Sir John Kerr had refused to see him before dissolving parliament. In the following weeks the Governor-General came under sustained criticism from a number of Labor members, notably Whitlam and Jim McClelland. On Thursday 4 March the Attorney-General Bob Ellicott told parliament that after studying Whitlam's comments there was a 'prima facie case of seditious libel' against him for remarks he made about the Governor-General. Events in the first three months of 1976 only confirmed that Kerr's action in 1975 had made him a symbol of disunity and a partisan political personality.

Malcolm Fraser did not have to assume the reins of power on 14 December. He was already Prime Minister and the only difference was that his caretaker status had been removed. On Sunday Fraser held talks with his permanent head John Menadue, the chairman of the Public Service Board Alan Cooley, and with both Doug Anthony and Phillip Lynch. Signalling a slower and more cautious approach to government than that adopted by the reforming Labor government in December 1972, Fraser said: 'If we do things the right way, we're much more likely to make the right decision.' He pledged to serve the nation in cooperation and understanding and to preserve those reforms introduced by the Labor government which improved the lives of the people.

Four days later Fraser announced the new 24-strong Liberal–National Country Party ministry which comprised an inner Cabinet of twelve. After the Prime Minister, Cabinet Ministers in order of seniority were: National Resources and Overseas Trade Doug Anthony; Treasury Phillip Lynch; Primary Industry Ian Sinclair; Administrative Services Reg Withers; Environment, Housing and Community Development Ivor Greenwood; Industry and Commerce Robert Cotton; Employment and Industrial Relations Tony Street; Transport Peter Nixon; Education John Carrick; Foreign Affairs Andrew Peacock; Defence Jim Killen. Fraser dropped from the ministry Bill Snedden, Don Chipp and Tasmanian Senator Peter Rae. He appointed Bob Ellicott, who had played such a fundamental role in the constitutional crisis, as Attorney-General. Fraser rewarded a number of his leading supporters during the leadership struggle against Snedden: notably Carrick, John Howard who became Minister for Business and Consumer Affairs, Vic Garland who became Minister for Posts and Telecommunications, Ian Viner who got Aboriginal Affairs, and Eric Robinson who was appointed as Minister for the ACT. Fraser also appointed Kevin Newman, who was elected to parliament in the crucial Bass by-election so important to Fraser, as Repatriation Minister. There were seven Country Party Ministers out of 24, three out of twelve in the Cabinet. The ministry contained three fewer places than the 27-man Labor ministry.

Fraser also substantially restructured a number of public service departments. He abolished the Department of Urban and Regional Development, symbol of Labor's commitment to improving the cities and the most original bureaucratic creation of the Labor government. A number of departments were merged to form the Department of Environment, Housing and Community Development. The same process was applied to form the new Department of Business and Consumer Affairs—strange bedfellows—under John Howard. While Fraser retained John Menadue as his permanent head, he quickly used the axe on the other two permanent heads who had been associated with the former Prime Minister, Dr Peter Wilenski, a career public servant who headed the Labour Department and Jim Spigelman, Secretary to the Media Department. While Fraser did not make Tony Staley a Minister because he felt this would have exposed him to criticism for merely promoting his own supporters, he indicated to Staley he would get the first vacancy. Fraser's overall approach carried the hallmarks of his own conservatism. Six of the twelve Cabinet Ministers had farming backgrounds and their preoccupations like Fraser's were mainly with administration and management as distinct from new ideas.

In his first three weeks as the elected Prime Minister Fraser showed his real style in government. There could have been no greater contrast than with the first several weeks of the Whitlam government. Whitlam moved quickly, saturated the press with government activity and deliberately created a sense of drama, of newness, of achievement. Fraser said nothing, he announced virtually no new policies at all, his Ministers were conspicuously quiet and the Prime Minister gave every intention of trying to play down political developments.

'The Prime Minister will hold a press conference in due course,' David Barnett told gallery journalists in the week before Christmas. Fraser moved to create an aura of calmness and stability, virtues which he believed had been conspicuously lacking from Australia's public life under Labor. Studies of long-term significance were set in train. A three-man committee was set up to review the entire operations of the Medibank scheme, to ensure funds were being effectively utilised and to recommend changes needed. Sir Henry Bland was appointed chairman of the Administrative Review Committee to examine the public service operations and programs, and to recommend cutbacks.

In a host of minor ways Fraser revealed his own political and personal predilections. As a traditionalist he restored the British honours system and *God Save the Queen* as anthem. In deference to the cause of Australian nationalism he maintained the Order of Australia and *Waltzing Matilda*, *Advance Australia Fair* and *Song of Australia*. This gave the nation four anthems and two systems of honours. As a prosperous country squire he hired a butler; not any butler but the Government House butler. Demonstrating his commitment to restraint and his scepticism towards the media, Fraser abolished press secretaries for most Ministers and told them there were to be no leaks from Cabinet. When there were leaks, particularly the publication of a cable to Australia by the ambassador to Indonesia Dick Woolcott, the Commonwealth Police were called in. It was not the first time or the last. Finally, at the parliamentary opening reception hosted by Sir John Kerr, Fraser cut out the champagne and lobsters in favour of lamingtons, tea and orange juice. The excesses of the Labor government were clearly condemned.

The most crucial early decision of the Fraser Government was the reversal of the previously high profile pledge to back wage indexation. This revealed Fraser's political nature. It showed him as a mixture of both pragmatism and conservatism. Fraser was not terribly concerned about repudiating a key section of his policy platform if other factors came into play. He believed that the government was elected by the people in an act of trust to take the best decisions possible at any given time, rather than be tied to a specific set of promises. He claimed that dogmatism would inevitably lead to bad government. 'Measures which seem appropriate at one stage can sometimes, indeed must, be superseded by new knowledge, new events,' Fraser declared.

# 23

# THE IRAQI AFFAIR

*If you are dismissed or forced to resign I shall resign immediately.*
Gough Whitlam to David Combe, 1 March 1976

On Sunday 16 November 1975, five days after Whitlam's sacking, the Labor Party national campaign committee met at the NSW headquarters, Sussex Street, Sydney. Australia's political climate had rarely been so hot. A few days later the first of the campaign's letter bombs exploded. Hayden and Fraser exchanged charge and counter-charge about the Labor government's suppression of economic details. The ALP was suddenly in Opposition and facing a general election campaign; six days before, it had been in government and gearing up for only a half-Senate election. Labor had never expected a general election, never planned for one. The first and most pressing subject discussed at the campaign committee meeting was money or the lack of it as far as campaigning was concerned.

The certitudes and conventions of years had been called into question by the dismissal. In this climate of desperation, Labor's search for campaign funds led it into exactly the same trap that had ravaged the Whitlam government and brought it to the brink of destruction.

On 13 December 1974 the former government embarked on a wild and fantastic project to raise $US4000 million from the Middle East to finance its development programs. Almost a year later, to the very day, it embarked on an equally dubious effort to raise $US500,000 from the Arab nations to finance its campaign for re-election. On both occasions the party delivered its reputation and political livelihood into the hands of untried, unknown, and what proved to be unreliable, middlemen whose job it was to 'clinch the deal'. In government the party chose a Pakistani money dealer Tirath Khemlani; in Opposition it chose a right-wing extremist Henri Fischer.

The campaign committee was told that the party had $250,000 from the federal organisation in addition to contributions from each state branch for its own advertising. South Australia had $120,000, which was a hefty sum for that state. NSW said it had $80,000 which was totally inadequate and which it later increased to $100,000. Federal officials were convinced the NSW branch was saving its funds for the state election campaign. Victoria said it had $40,000 but at the end of the meeting this was revised under pressure to $150,000. Victoria also had a state election campaign imminent. But despite these reports, the party was determined to conduct an adequate campaign, even though it would cost a lot more. At one stage there was discussion that people could mortgage their houses in an effort to raise funds.

Once again, as ever, the Labor Party was bedevilled by the problem of campaign funds. Even though it had received extensive private and union donations during the period of the constitutional crisis, they were not adequate for a full-scale campaign effort. Nevertheless the meeting decided to double the federal budget spending to $500,000. It did not answer the question: where was the money coming from?[1]

During the lunch break over sandwiches Victorian delegate Bill Hartley grabbed the national secretary David Combe and said he thought he could raise more money himself. Hartley told Combe he was confident substantial funds could be raised for the party from Arab sources in the Middle East. If Hartley went to the Middle East he should be able to arrange it. Combe mentioned his conversation with Hartley to Whitlam. The three men subsequently went into another office where they discussed the question. Hartley was thinking of Iraq, one of the richest oil producing nations.

Both Whitlam and Combe vetoed any overseas trip by Hartley. They said that Hartley's movements would certainly be monitored by security. Not only was he a Senate election candidate but he was also a well-known Labor Party identity. They were convinced that if Hartley went, security would have him under observation from the time he left until the time he returned, as well as checking on whom he saw. It was then that Whitlam suggested that arrangements could be made through the Scarf Foundation and the Scarf group of companies.

Reuben F Scarf is a well-known Sydney entrepreneur of Arab descent with wide Middle East contacts. He was chairman of the Scarf Foundation and involved with a number of companies that had extensive dealings in the Arab world. The Scarf Foundation was the chief buying and selling agent in Australia for a number of Arab organisations, including the Iraqi State Trading Corporations. Whitlam had known Scarf for some time and was aware that his organisation conducted nearly all of Australia's trade with the Arab countries, that it had been encouraged by both the Departments of Foreign Affairs and Overseas Trade. Scarf himself was sympathetic to the Arab cause and had excellent contacts in this area. In 1973 Whitlam had made a short speech on Australia's Middle East policy at Scarf's Sydney home which had been taped and subsequently taken to the Middle East and played to high level people in the ruling parties.

The upshot of this talk between Whitlam, Combe and Hartley was that Hartley was authorised to establish a meeting with Scarf so that Whitlam and Combe could explain their financial requirements. Hartley was familiar with Scarf's operations and knew that Henri Fischer, an employee of the Scarf Foundation, was its chief Middle East contact. Hartley rang Fischer first from the ALP office but could not reach him. He then rang Scarf asking where Fischer was but did not discuss the subject of funds with Scarf at all. Hartley got Fischer about 4 p.m. and, after a brief conversation, Fischer came into the city to see the Victorian delegate.

When the trio left Sussex Street that afternoon Whitlam went to his Darling Point home, Combe went to a media meeting at Balmain to discuss campaign advertising and Hartley went to Fischer's apartment. He briefed Fischer fully during the afternoon about the party's keenness to find Middle East funds for the campaign. Fischer drove Hartley to Sydney airport, where the Victorian delegate rang David Combe and gave him a rundown on the discussion. He gave Combe Fischer's Sydney phone number and address and the national secretary then rang Fischer himself. Fischer told Combe it was Scarf's idea that he should have carriage of this matter for the Labor Party since he normally looked after most Middle East transactions for the Foundation. Fischer asked whether a meeting that night between himself, Whitlam and Combe would be suitable. Combe rang Whitlam to check and to tell the Labor leader about Fischer. 'I may know him and can't place him,' Whitlam said of Fischer. 'Perhaps I do know him.'[2]

Whitlam's driver collected Combe at Balmain that evening and the leader and national secretary drove to the eastern side of the city. They went to flat 139, 23rd level, Blues Point Towers, 14 Blues Point Road— Fischer's apartment. They spent about thirty to forty minutes talking with Fischer, who had obviously been made aware of his job by Hartley. Fischer said he would be going overseas in a few days to make arrangements for the funds. There was no discussion of the money at the meeting. Whitlam spent some time talking about the derivation of Fischer's name and giving an historical summary of events in the Lebanon leading to the civil war in that country. Fischer gave his own version of the background to the Lebanese situation. Supper consisted of some nuts and a bottle of good German white wine. Whitlam restricted himself to one glass and Combe and Fischer shared the rest. As they were leaving Whitlam said to Fischer, 'Well you've met David now; you'll be able to keep in touch with him from now on.'[3]

Both Whitlam and Combe were left with the impression that Fischer had a wide knowledge of affairs and people in the Middle East. But they knew only vaguely of Fischer's peculiar background and connections with the radical right in Australian politics. Fischer had worked variously as a caterer, in the advertising section of the *Sydney Morning Herald*, and at the Olympic Games in Melbourne in 1956. He had travelled extensively in Europe, Africa and Asia, and in 1965 had launched a journal called the *Australian International News Review*. This was later described in *Quadrant* as 'an unpalatable organ of the totalitarian right'. According to Albert Moran, who wrote an article on Fischer in the 20 July 1967 issue of *Honi Soit*, Fischer's journal dealt with apartheid, Rhodesia, South Africa, the communist 'infiltration' of the Liberal Party, the 'creeping socialism' of the Country Party, anti-Semitism, fluoridation and racism. Fischer was an outspoken opponent of Edward St John who held the seat of Warringah for the Liberal Party from 1966 to 1969 and who was a prominent critic of apartheid.[4]

Bill Hartley himself was aware of Fischer's right-wing background and had even made some efforts to investigate it. But Hartley had little knowledge of any right-wing political activity continued by Fischer since 1967. In the previous five years Fischer had built up an expertise on the Middle East and was a key figure in Scarf's operations in that part of the world. Hartley knew that Fischer was an anti-Zionist and, along with a number of people, noticed his anti-Semitic comments. However he thought that Fischer might have moderated the vehemence of his right-wing outlook.

Just a few months earlier, in August 1975, Hartley, Fischer and the president of the Australian Union of Students, Ian MacDonald, had dined at the Bacchus Restaurant in Canberra and MacDonald had severely questioned Fischer on his political views, particularly his support for apartheid. Hartley felt after this meeting that Fischer had probably moderated his views in the last several years. At a later date Whitlam was also able to recollect Fischer and put him in a right-wing context. But in November 1975 Whitlam, Combe and Hartley were all prepared to trust Fischer's credentials with the Scarf Foundation and his obvious knowledge of the Middle East for the highly sensitive and politically dangerous task of raising a big sum of money for the ALP.

If the first indiscretion of the party was to seek the funds, the second was to use Fischer as an intermediary. His background suggested that if things went wrong he would feel no allegiance or sympathy for the

Labor Party. He had spent most of his life in politics fighting against the policies espoused by the ALP.

There was never any suggestion that conditions would be attached to the money. Whitlam and Combe believed that it would be raised in the Middle East, that it would be a substantial sum and that it might come from one or a number of countries in that area. It would be Arab money. Both men entered the arrangement believing the party badly needed the funds and that the donation could be kept secret. Right from the start the only people who knew would be Combe, Whitlam and Hartley. There was no intention of telling anybody else or having it recorded in the party's books.[5]

There was no way this donation was going to be directed through either of the two fund-raising channels used by the Labor Party. The first channel was the party's official funds which the ALP officers administered or, in practical terms, left the national secretary to administer. The second channel was the fund controlled by the Labor leader. This was the caucus trust account and Whitlam said in March 1976 that it was administered by the party leader, deputy leader and one of the accountants in the caucus. 'Everything that comes in, including cash or bank cheques, is put into a bank account,' Whitlam said. 'It is audited. Everything that goes out is by cheque, signed by two people. The butts, the statements, the audits are all kept.' In short, the main burden of administering funds fell on the party's national secretary, whose efforts were supplemented from the leader's fund.

The reality of fund raising within the Labor Party was that most people in the party and on the national executive didn't want to know about it. For all the executive's talk and breast-beating after the Iraqi affair broke, this sort of incident was the direct product of long-established party practices. In the past party secretaries had hunted long and hard to find funds wherever they could and many campaign donations were given secretly without members of the national executive ever knowing the source. David Combe had to assume full responsibility for raising the $500,000 needed as mortgage for the construction of the party's national secretariat headquarters, John Curtin House. When this subject was raised at an executive meeting, it was moved that the secretary take charge of the matter. The rest of the executive was not interested. Similarly, the $72,000 donation from the Murdoch group in 1972 was not made known until two years later.

It was always assumed by those involved that the money from Iraq would not be recorded in either of the two official funding channels. The Labor principals involved believed the funds would enter Australia through the Scarf group of companies and there would probably be a direct payment from the companies to the Labor Party's advertising agency.[6]

A few days after the arrangement was finalised, Fischer flew to Melbourne to see Hartley, who was one of the most well-connected people in Australia with Arab sources throughout the Middle East. Hartley had visited the area on numerous occasions over the past several years and had a subtle appreciation of Middle East politics on a country by country basis. Few people in Australia could match his knowledge of the area. Hartley gave Fischer three letters which he said might be of assistance to him during his talks in Baghdad. It was clear well before Fischer left that this would be his first point of contact. Hartley's letters were addressed to the Vice-President of Iraq, the Minister for Youth and Friendship and Chairman of the Revolutionary Command Council, Naeem Hadad, and the head of the Palestinian Liberation Organisation (PLO), Yasser Arafat, all of whom were personal contacts of Hartley. His letters conveyed a very firm and highly political account of the events leading to the dismissal of Gough Whitlam from office and installation of the Fraser government. Hartley described this as a coup which the Labor Party was anxious to reverse with popular support at the coming election.[7]

After their initial meeting on the evening of 16 November, the next time Combe saw Fischer was a breakfast meeting at the Macleay Street Travelodge on the morning of 19 November. Combe was surprised to hear from Fischer and thought he would have been overseas by this stage. At their meeting Fischer showed Combe an article from the magazine *Scope*. This concerned an incident at an Australian airport involving a visiting Iraqi who got involved in a scuffle with a customs official when he was being body-searched. The incident had received extensive coverage in Baghdad and, according to Fischer, had strengthened anti-Australian feeling among important people in the country. Scarf had written to a number of leading politicians about the incident including Whitlam, Crean, Cairns, Willesee and Fraser. Fischer told Combe he believed the Iraqi involved had been physically assaulted and he wanted Whitlam to issue a statement condemning this.

Combe subsequently spoke to Whitlam by phone and he and Fischer met the Labor leader in Whitlam's Martin Place office before lunch. The Sydney *Daily Mirror* had just hit the street and carried a story about the latest opinion poll indicating Labor was in trouble. Fischer attacked Rupert Murdoch in front of Combe and Whitlam. They were surprised by the vehemence of his remarks and the fact that he was inclined to see events in terms of a Murdoch conspiracy.

Fischer made his complaint to Whitlam about the airport incident. Whitlam in turn rang the Secretary of the Foreign Affairs Department Alan Renouf and Renouf read out the file on the subject to the Labor leader, including his previous reply to Scarf's letter. He also read Willesee's reply to Scarf. Whitlam then dictated another letter for Scarf.

The letter noted the latest reports about the incident and said that if these allegations were true they were serious ones. The Labor leader said he would have a full investigation made of the matter if he was re-elected to office. The letter was immediately typed up by a secretary in Whitlam's office and he signed the letter and handed it to Fischer to convey to Scarf. Combe and Whitlam assumed at the time that Fischer might well make his own photocopy of the letter and take it with him when he went to the Middle East, particularly Iraq. It would be a tangible sign of Labor's sympathy.[8]

Fischer left Australia about 23 November and went straight to Baghdad, the capital of Iraq. It appears he saw Naeem Hadad and had an audience with the President and one of his closest associates from the Ba'ath Socialist Party. According to reports Fischer waited three days and was then recalled to the palace where he was told that Iraq agreed with the view of its Australian comrades 'that there had been a grave coup d'etat engineered by imperialism, the CIA and Zionism'. Shortly afterwards Fischer spoke to Hartley from Kuwait, saying the visit had been successful and everything was being arranged.[9]

The next contact Combe had involving Fischer was when Fischer's wife Diana called the national secretary about late November or very early December and told him that Fischer was due back immediately. No indication was given on the phone whether the mission was successful. Combe had a firm practice of not discussing the fund raising by phone. Soon afterwards Fischer called Combe and the two men met for breakfast again at the Macleay Street Travelodge. Fischer told Combe that he only needed to go to one country. He had guarantees from the Ba'ath Socialist Party of Iraq and the sum would be $500,000. He did not say whether this would be Australian or American dollars. Fischer told Combe whom he had spoken to in Iraq; Combe believed Fischer and felt certain the money was coming. But Combe wanted to know when. It would be very risky to spend funds until he actually saw the money. Fischer said not to worry and that Iraq would be sending out emissaries to finalise the deal. Combe replied that it would be hard to proceed until they arrived.[10]

On 2 December Fischer went to Melbourne with an Iraqi colleague Mustaffa Nakishly who had returned with him from Baghdad to Australia. This evening the Labor Party was celebrating the third anniversary of its election to office on 2 December 1972. Fischer and the Iraqi went to the celebratory ball and later to the Commodore Motel with Hartley and several Labor people. At this stage Fischer was talking of a $500,000 donation for the party but was implying there was no ceiling and the funds could go beyond this. Efforts were made the same night to have the visiting Iraqi Nakishly meet Gough Whitlam, who was in Melbourne for the celebrations, and the two men met very briefly.

A few days later Fischer rang Combe again saying there was a delay with the emissaries. The British embassy in Baghdad would not issue them with visas for entry into Australia. Fischer asked Combe if Whitlam could use his influence to get the visas issued. Combe said that would be impossible. Other arrangements would have to be made. Finally on 6 or 7 December Fischer told Combe that the Iraqis established an elaborate subterfuge which allowed them to enter the country. On 2 December the Australian embassy in Tokyo informed Canberra that two Iraqi foreign ministry officials wished to visit Australia with the declared object of holding talks to establish an Iraqi Consulate-General in Sydney. The Foreign Affairs Department cabled back giving Tokyo instructions to issue the visas and saying it would welcome the visit.[11]

The Iraqi ambassador in Tokyo was unable to contact Fischer with the flight details so he notified the editor of the Arabic language paper *Ell Telegraph* Peter Indari and told him to ensure someone was at the airport to meet them. The Iraqis arrived at Sydney on 8 December. One was carrying a diplomatic passport and the other an official passport. They were subjected to normal entry formalities and customs checks, except that on Foreign Affairs' advice they were given diplomatic privileges and not subjected to selective search procedures. A Foreign Affairs official was at Sydney airport to meet them and was promptly given the 'brush off'. The two men who had entered Australia under false pretences were Farooq Abdulla Yehya and Ghafil Jassim, prominent figures in the Ba'ath Socialist Party of Iraq. Fischer and Indari took the Iraqis back to Fischer's apartment.

Fischer had called Hartley at 6.30 that morning asking him to come to Sydney to meet them and that afternoon Combe, Hartley, the two Iraqis and Indari gathered at Fischer's apartment. Fischer was very concerned at Indari's presence because the editor knew nothing of the money and security was vital. Combe gave the Iraqis an outline of developments in Australia which led to the sacking of the Whitlam government. While one of the emissaries spoke rough English the other one had practically no English at all, although they appeared to have a better capacity to understand the language than articulate it.

The Iraqis left in the afternoon with Indari, who showed them around Sydney. They were booked into the North Sydney Travelodge, where they stayed until their departure on 10 December. At one stage Foreign Affairs established phone contact with them about discussions concerning the Consulate in Sydney. But the Iraqis said they were not interested. Questions dealing with the establishment of consular missions by Iraq in Australia were in the hands of the Egyptian embassy. The Iraqis were in Australia to see friends.

By this stage Combe had already spoken to the managing director of the Labor Party's advertising agency, Malcolm McFie. He wanted an increase in Labor's advertising effort, newspaper, radio and television, throughout the last week of the campaign. The groundwork for this was laid in the week before 8 December. As soon as he knew the Iraqis were coming to Australia to finalise the donation, Combe gave the agency the go-ahead and from 8 December extra ads were run above the original plans; these would be financed by the Iraqi money. These included the television ads done by John Gorton and the double page newspaper spreads which appeared in the last few days of the campaign.

On 9 December Indari showed the Iraqis around Sydney and that evening took them to dinner at the Sheik's Tent restaurant at Bondi. On the same morning Fischer rang Combe and asked if the Iraqis could see Whitlam. Fischer said they regarded this as very important and were anxious to see the Labor leader. Combe rang Whitlam late in the afternoon and put the proposition to him. The Labor leader was dubious at first.

Whitlam said the earliest time he could possibly meet the two Iraqis was breakfast in Canberra on Thursday 11 December. Combe conveyed this message back to Fischer who was very unhappy. The Iraqis were expecting to see Whitlam soon and Fischer told Combe that if they did not meet him quickly then 'the whole deal will be off'.[12]

The national secretary called Whitlam again. He told the Labor leader the situation was obviously urgent or he wouldn't bother calling him back and risking the possibility of Whitlam 'grinding his teeth' over the issue. Combe impressed upon Whitlam the urgent need to meet the Iraqis. The Labor leader agreed and said he could meet them at breakfast the next morning. He had a 9.30 appointment in town so the meeting would have to be brief. Combe called Fischer back and he was delighted. Fischer said his wife Diana would be happy to provide breakfast for the group at Flat 139, 23rd level, Blues Point Towers, 14 Blues Point Road— Fischer's apartment.

Combe arrived at Blues Point Towers at 8.15 on the morning of 10 December. At 8.30 Whitlam had still not arrived. Combe began to worry. He was terrified the Labor leader might not turn up. Combe gulped down a number of orange drinks while he waited. He didn't have Whitlam's home phone number on him. He rang the leader's Sydney office to get it and was just about to dial Darling Point when Whitlam arrived.[13]

The Iraqis appeared genuinely overwhelmed by the Labor leader, who took off his coat, sat down and talked about the Middle East. Whitlam said he had not visited the Middle East as Prime Minister but was hoping to make an official visit in this capacity in 1976. If so, he would certainly visit Iraq. Whitlam also made it clear that he would visit Israel. He said it was his long-standing practice on travelling to the Middle East to ensure that he visited both sides. If he went to Arab nations then he would also go to Israel.

Whitlam stressed the three fundamental points that provided the basis for the Labor Party's Middle East policy both in government and in Opposition. These were the insistence that Israel withdraw from its occupied territories, that a separate state be established for the Palestinian people, and that Israel's sovereign rights be fully accepted and recognised.

The Labor leader spent about 30 or 35 minutes at most at the breakfast. He arrived at 8.45 and left at 9.20 to keep an appointment he had at AWA House in town at 9.30. At no stage was the money discussed. But the meeting was in the context of the Iraqi donation and Whitlam's very presence at that time was because of Fischer's insistence that the funds might not go ahead unless he came.[14]

After Whitlam left, Fischer told Combe the transaction would be finalised in Tokyo. Fischer and the two Iraqis were flying to Tokyo that afternoon and Fischer dropped Combe off at his hotel after the breakfast meeting. By this stage the $500,000 was already being spent in Labor Party campaign advertising. The poll was three days away.

That night the Labor Party held its nationally televised Candlelight Vigil for Democracy on the lawns outside Parliament House Canberra. Nearly ten thousand people gathered in the twilight holding candles as the most impressive of Labor's national figures addressed the crowd— Bob Hawke, Don Dunstan, Bill Hayden and the star of the evening, Gough Whitlam. Before the vigil Whitlam's staff held a briefing in his office.

At the conclusion of the briefing Whitlam called Combe into his room and said, 'How did we go this morning, comrade?' Combe told the leader that everything was fine. For the first time he told Whitlam the sum was $US500,000. The former Prime Minister knew by then that the source of funds was the Ba'ath Socialist Party in Iraq. It is likely that Combe mentioned this to Whitlam a few days before, when they were discussing the subject.[15]

Nothing happened until late January. Combe had not spoken with Fischer since 10 December, the morning he left Australia with the two Iraqis to finalise the transaction. Combe had rung Fischer's Sydney apartment on numerous occasions and never received an answer. Finally Fischer's wife, Diana, picked up the phone and told Combe that she had been away for some time. Fischer had not returned to Australia since 10 December. Combe felt the first twinge of doubt and of the worry which would wrack him for the next six weeks. He later discovered that Fischer and the Iraqis had not travelled straight to Tokyo as they had said. They went via Hong Kong to enjoy some of the delights of the East. When they arrived in Tokyo the election was over. Labor had been thrashed and all the Australian papers were saying that Whitlam's leadership was in danger. Hawke was being mentioned as a possible successor and all the Arab nations knew Hawke was fervently pro-Israel.

Diana told Combe that Fischer would not leave Tokyo until the money was finalised. If Whitlam stayed leader everything would be fine. But by this stage Combe was deeply worried as there were important figures in the ALP caucus committed to destroying Whitlam's career. What if Whitlam didn't hold the leadership? On the night of 27 January, the day the caucus re-elected Whitlam leader, Combe received a call from Fischer in Baghdad. Fischer seemed in a highly agitated state and much less confident about the transaction being finalised. He was buoyed up by the news that Whitlam had been re-elected. Perhaps everything would be all right. But after this phone conversation, Combe knew there was a genuine problem about getting the money.[16]

On 28 January Combe told Whitlam there had been a hold-up with the money. At the national executive meeting held at the end of January, Combe told Hartley privately that the money was needed before the end of the following week in order to pay the Labor Party's advertising agency Mullins, Clarke and Ralph. Combe knew the money was not required for another fortnight but he was giving himself a week's grace.

Hartley had had a similar experience to Combe. He had been on holidays for the first three weeks in January and in the brief contact he had with Fischer sensed that the intermediary was worried. On one occasion Fischer asked Hartley to send a report from Australia which he could show to the Iraqis saying that the people were on the verge of a revolt and would overthrow the Fraser government!![17]

Fischer had gone from Tokyo to Baghdad in an effort to secure the money. After talking with Combe at the executive meeting, Hartley sent a telex to Fischer asking Fischer to ring him. He received subsequent telex messages and phone calls from Fischer telling him that the matter was now before the Revolutionary Command Council of the Ba'ath Socialist Party and that a 'positive decision' was expected. The key date was Saturday 7 February when the council of the party was meeting to decide the issue. Hartley impressed upon Fischer that the party now had to meet deadlines as a result of its campaign debts and that it needed the funds urgently. Combe was worried over exactly what Fischer meant by the words 'positive decision'. Did Fischer mean that he was expecting an approval of the money or did he simply mean there would be a decision one way or the other, meaning that it might be negative. By this stage Combe was suffering from chronic insomnia and was deeply worried about the success of the transaction.

Fischer arranged to leave Baghdad on the Sunday and then contact Australia with the details of the decision. On Friday 6 February Combe flew to Sydney for a meeting with McFie. The agency had only seven days left to meet their commitments with deadline day being 13 February. Combe was a good friend of McFie and decided he would tell him the whole story. He gave McFie a guarantee that no matter what happened the party would not let the advertising agency go into liquidation.

Combe spent all Sunday afternoon and night waiting for Hartley to ring him. The arrangement was that Fischer would call Hartley when he had the decision from the 7 February Baghdad meeting. Combe waited all night until Hartley finally rang at 6 a.m. Monday with the news that Fischer was now going to London and emissaries would be sent from Iraq to London to finalise the funds. Hartley gave Combe a telex number and a phone number for Fischer in London. He said that according to Fischer the money should be cleared by the end of the week. Combe rang McFie to give him the details. McFie was now almost beside himself with worry and believed that under NSW law it was possible he could go to jail if he was not able to meet his commitments.[18]

On Monday 9 February Combe called Fischer in London and both he and McFie spoke to the intermediary. Fischer told them not to worry. He said that Iraqis would be coming to London to finalise the matter and everything was fine. The decision had been made.

Combe had planned to take holidays from the Tuesday and go on a cruise on the Russian ship *Leonid Sovinov* up the east coast of Australia and then to Fiji before returning to Sydney. He had family commitments and was anxious to go on the holiday. Although McFie was not keen for Combe to leave, the national secretary decided to go on his holiday as planned in view of Fischer's latest assurance. But from the time Combe set foot on the boat, the whole Iraqi issue started to blow.

Just after Combe left, McFie had lunch with the NSW state secretary Geoff Cahill and told Cahill about the dire financial plight of the party. This was a fateful move. Cahill now entered the picture and began to launch efforts to save the advertising agency and this necessitated his contacting a number of Labor notables, including the Queensland secretary Bart Lourigan. From this time on, the question of the financial indebtedness of the advertising agency and the party began to circulate.

McFie contacted Combe by ship radio before the cruise reached Brisbane and told Combe that he would have to get bridging finance to save the agency. Combe left the ship at Brisbane and flew straight back to Sydney. He went to the Mullins, Clarke and Ralph office and McFie told him he needed $250,000 urgently.

Combe then rang Whitlam and put four propositions to the Labor leader. First, the party could borrow the money from the trade unions. Second, it could get the funds 'under the counter' from the Tammany Hall branches. Third, the party could allow the agency to go into liquidation, in which case the ALP itself would be sued. Fourth, Combe could approach the Commonwealth Bank in an effort to negotiate a loan. Both Whitlam and Combe agreed on the fourth alternative and the Labor leader gave Combe his approval to proceed on this basis.

Combe was no stranger to the Commonwealth Bank. He had arranged a loan through the bank to finance the new national headquarters of the Labor Party, John Curtin House; he went straight to his contact in the bank who had helped him on this matter. Combe explained the full situation to the bank and then held talks with senior officials. While approval further up the line would normally be required, they were prepared to authorise the loan. The bank indicated the sort of letter which the party would need to sign to secure the funds. The letter was drafted, signed by Combe and then sent to Whitlam for his signature. Combe spoke to McFie and told him the money was coming through the Commonwealth Bank.[19]

Still confident that Fischer would produce the funds from Iraq, Combe flew back to Brisbane to rejoin his cruise. McFie spoke to Fischer himself once again and was reassured that the money was coming.

However once again the undertaking fell apart as soon as Combe reboarded his ship. The bank found that the party needed to open a trading account in order to obtain the loan and that other signatures would be needed for this. The assistant national secretary of the party Ken Bennett found that he had to take responsibility for the matter. Bennett contacted the senior vice-president of the party Jack Egerton and then the party president Bob Hawke about the $250,000 loan. Bennett had no choice. There had been a misunderstanding in the talks Combe had held at the bank. The signatures, at least of the officers of the Labor Party, were needed to establish a trading account and allow the loan to proceed. This was the first either Hawke or Egerton had heard of the proposed loan. They demanded to know the whole story.

When the *Leonid Sovinov* reached Cairns, Combe made a precautionary phone call to McFie in Sydney to make certain things were working smoothly. McFie was out and he spoke with his wife, who said that Combe should ring Ken Bennett. This was the warning signal that something was wrong and Combe immediately called Bennett to see what had happened. Bennett explained the problem with the Commonwealth Bank and the fact that Egerton and Hawke were now aware of the whole situation.

Combe rang Hawke and the party president told him there would have to be an urgent meeting of officers to review the situation. Neither Hawke nor Egerton would have a bar of the Iraqi money. They believed that while everything possible had to be done to save the agency, the party would have to live with its debt and find other ways to finance it. Hawke told Combe he would support him in the impending political crisis that would follow revelation of the Iraqi money. But the party president said Combe would have to come back. 'If you don't, it will be very hard for me to support you,' Hawke warned.

Combe then rang Hartley. The Victorian delegate told him he had just received a cable from Fischer saying the funds were coming and everything was fine. Two Iraqi emissaries would be arriving in Australia on Monday 16 February to seal the deal. In the space of a few minutes Combe realised that the Iraqi donation had been killed dead at the Australian end and yet he was being told by Hartley that it would be proceeding from the Iraqi end anyway.[20]

On 15 February the Labor Party officers met at Bob Hawke's Melbourne home. The meeting comprised the party president Bob Hawke, the vice-president Jack Egerton, John Ducker and George Whitten, as well as the national secretary David Combe. Ken Bennett also attended the meeting. Combe delivered a briefing on the effort to secure funds from Iraq explaining that himself, Whitlam and Hartley were the only people with any knowledge of the affair and pointing out that the party expected to get $US500,000 and campaign spending in the last week had been on this assumption. Hawke was horrified by the revelations. All the officers were angry that they had not been informed and claimed that such undertakings should never have been entered into on the basis of Arab money.

Combe told the meeting he accepted responsibility as national secretary for what had happened. He explained what a mental and emotional burden the previous weeks had been, waiting for the money to arrive as the deadline for the advertising agency crept closer all the time. He told the officers he was preparing to resign and said that he wanted and hoped to have the opportunity to resign rather than be dismissed.

Hawke told Combe he shouldn't be thinking in these terms. The national secretary replied that he could not be expected to think in any other way after a misdemeanour of this magnitude. 'It's not a misdemeanour, it was a grave error of judgement,' Hawke told Combe. The secretary told the officers that he was not prepared to carry the 'can' for either Whitlam or Hartley, who had also been involved. But at the same time he said he would not have either or both of these men having to 'carry the can' for his own actions.[21]

It was at this meeting that Combe enunciated the political principle of equal culpability. This was absolutely crucial to the subsequent course of events inside the Labor Party, at both the national executive meeting and the caucus meeting. Combe was in fact saying 'one for all and all for one'. This was the position which Whitlam, Combe and Hartley subsequently adopted and it was one of the main reasons why all of them survived and the threat of a major split within the Labor Party, of far-reaching dimensions, was avoided.

Hawke and Combe enjoyed a special and close relationship, which went back many years. Over a series of controversies Hawke had always supported Combe and Combe in turn had acted as an important apologist for Hawke on many occasions within party ranks, particularly the parliamentary party. Hawke saw the ties between himself and Combe not just as personal ones but in terms of their positions as national president and national secretary of the Labor Party. He was prepared to go to extreme lengths to fight for Combe and to ensure that Combe, who was directly responsible to the national executive, retained his post and was not sacrificed because of the Iraqi connection.

Hawke's attitude to both Whitlam and Hartley was very different. The party president was very critical of Whitlam initially and the consensus at the officers' meeting was that Whitlam could never survive as leader in the face of these latest revelations. It was assumed that he was a walking political corpse. Hawke was openly hostile towards Hartley, who was the most public and committed supporter of the Arab cause within the Labor Party as well as a prominent figure within the left wing, which had withdrawn its support from Hawke and was fighting to ensure he never became Labor leader.

During the course of the meeting Hawke argued that a national executive meeting should be held immediately so the Iraqi issue could be killed off. At this stage there had been no public revelations about the donation. Hawke said the executive should meet to scotch the Iraqi deal at once and then make a public announcement that an Iraqi offer had been made and was refused. He later claimed this would have killed the story before it got out of control and did so much damage. 'But the silly bastards wanted to keep the whole thing quiet,' he said.

There were three main results stemming from the meeting at Hawke's house. First, the party would not accept the Iraqi money and Combe was instructed to tell this to the Iraqi emissaries who were supposed to arrive in Australia the following day, 16 February. Second, the national executive meeting was brought forward from 14 April to 21–22 March with the purpose of reviewing the whole Iraqi involvement as quickly and as quietly as possible. Third, the meeting provided information which was subsequently conveyed to other Labor Party figures and then leaked to the press.

The following morning Bill Hartley sent his secretary Gail Cotton from Melbourne to Sydney to meet the Iraqis arriving to finalise the donation. They were supposed to arrive on QF2 but there was no sign of them and, when Gail Cotton checked the passenger name list, their names were not on it. She contacted Hartley, who then spoke with Combe. From this time on the Labor Party was convinced the money would never arrive. Combe had his last communication with Fischer when the supposed intermediary called him at 1.45 on the morning of

17 February. Fischer wanted to know whether the Iraqis had arrived on the flight the previous day. Combe assured him they had not.

Fischer was in a very emotional state and appeared to be frightened. He said a number of things to Combe which did not make sense to the national secretary. Fischer said there were 'other people given assurances by the Iraqis'. He said the story would break in New York, where they were going to hold a press conference. When Combe seemed puzzled, Fischer said that Hartley would understand. This was Combe's last communication with Fischer. The national secretary returned once more to his holiday cruise knowing that the Iraqi deal was dead and a national executive meeting was scheduled to debate the whole question.

The story now broke into two separate strands. One centred on Fischer and his activities in Europe; the other centred on internal intrigue within the Labor Party in Australia. Both strands led to separate newspaper organisations obtaining details of the Iraqi donation from different people quite independently.

It is impossible to say what pressures Fischer was under and what his motives were at this time. He had attacked Rupert Murdoch vehemently in front of both Whitlam and Combe and accused the newspaper proprietor of being pro-Zionist. But from reports, Fischer contacted Murdoch on 17 February at about the same time he made his last telephone call to Combe. He subsequently met Murdoch in London on Friday morning 20 February.

It appears that Fischer drafted a lengthy statement in subsequent talks with Murdoch over three to five days documenting his meetings with Whitlam, Combe and the Iraqis during the previous December. The allegations were astounding and obviously the basis of a huge political story. The Murdoch group subsequently began to check out the details. Murdoch took a hand in checking the facts claimed by Fischer and in preparing the story for publication.

Meanwhile in Canberra the political correspondent of the Melbourne *Sun News-Pictorial*, Laurie Oakes, was working on the story. Oakes spoke to a number of people in the party, including high-placed sources in the NSW branch. He discovered strong criticism of Combe and, when the first details of the Iraqi story were given to him, disbelieved them. But subsequent checking proved the basic outline of the story. Oakes had his facts sufficiently confirmed by Tuesday 24 February to file copy. The *Sun Pictorial* had a 'dummy run' to confuse its competitors and to conceal that it had a major political story.

However, the Murdoch organisation discovered on Tuesday evening, before the Melbourne paper published, that the *Sun* had the Iraqi story and intended to run it. There was a fatal security leak in the organisation of the Melbourne paper. Murdoch moved immediately and ordered that the *Australian* be held to run the story. After some hasty work, the *Australian* was remade and came out with the Iraqi story under the by-line 'By a special correspondent'. This story was based on the information which Fischer gave Murdoch and which was contained in the document he had drafted. Murdoch was the special correspondent.

The Melbourne story was leaked to Laurie Oakes for internal political reasons, revealing a number of cross-currents and animosities within the Labor movement. The Oakes story was damaging to Whitlam and even more damaging to Combe, with its fifth sentence incorrectly suggesting that Whitlam's involvement came very late in the picture: 'Mr Whitlam is said to have become involved when the gift did not arrive on time and temporary financial arrangements had to be made.'

The Labor Party was reeling on Wednesday 25 February when the story appeared from two separate organisations and quite obviously from two separate sources. In a few short hours the gradual consolidation which had characterised the party over the previous four weeks was destroyed. Whitlam faced a hostile round of questioning that morning from the Labor Party executive. This was followed up with an even tenser exchange in the caucus room. The party rejected a motion from a Whitlam supporter, Chris Hurford, which said in part that no member of the parliamentary party was involved and that a final statement would await the return of the national secretary and meeting of the national executive.

The party accepted a motion moved by Mick Young calling for the national executive to investigate the issue fully and report back to the party as soon as possible. The motion also endorsed the principle that no Australian political party should accept overseas funds and that all campaign donations should be made public. The Young amendment was carried 35–25 in a clear display that the caucus either disbelieved its leader or was not prepared to accept his statements on the subject. The passage of this motion was a major rebuff to the former Prime Minister and a sign of the ground-swell against him.

At a lengthy press conference Whitlam pulled down the information screen as far as possible and said virtually nothing about the allegations. He admitted meeting the Iraqis on 10 December, which was the main meeting featured in the newspaper stories. The Labor leader subsequently denied sections of the story in the *Australian* saying he had made arrangements to seek funds from the PLO, and that he claimed Hawke would never lead the Labor Party.

Whitlam's performance this day infuriated his party colleagues, who said that his reluctance to issue a comprehensive statement on the allegations implied his guilt. The following morning the papers were full of reports that Whitlam would either resign the parliamentary leadership or be deposed in a party room revolt. The former Education

Minister Kim Beazley, former Treasurer Bill Hayden, and former Minister for Manufacturing Industry Lionel Bowen, were all mentioned as possible successors.

Yet it was Whitlam's refusal to talk which was very important in saving him. If he had given a full account of his deep involvement on the first day, the caucus might have been provoked into immediate action. By refusing to talk and accepting the caucus resolution, Whitlam left the issue in the hands of the national executive which would then report back to the party. He gained valuable time.

Within hours of the allegations the Prime Minister Malcolm Fraser moved to exploit them and to compound Whitlam's difficulties. The Prime Minister's office was the source for newspaper stories which first appeared the following day saying that the Australian government was told that Iraq was prepared to pay one million dollars to the Labor Party. The government was told that half of the money had already been paid. This information came from a Sydney businessman who was in London at the time. This information was later used as justification for the involvement of the Commonwealth Police, which helped to turn the tide of Labor Party support in Whitlam's favour.

Subsequently newspaper articles appeared alleging that the Prime Minister himself had been the source of stories that $US500,000 in Arab funds had actually been transferred to Australia. When questioned on this matter in parliament, Fraser refused to confirm or deny it. Meanwhile on 25 February the assistant national secretary Ken Bennett confirmed that the Labor Party was in substantial debt. This debt was later put at about $A350,000 or $US500,000, the precise amount which the party was expecting to obtain from Iraq.

By Friday 27 February, the anti-Whitlam forces within the caucus believed they had the numbers nicely tied up. Whitlam's arrogance at the executive meeting on the Wednesday and his refusal to make a detailed statement had persuaded wide sections of the party of his guilt and convinced his arch enemies that they had a perfect issue on which to swing the execution axe. Hayden came under extensive pressure to run for the leadership and a number of party members claimed he would succumb. But Hayden showed no sign of wavering or of withdrawing his support from the leader and told people privately he hoped that Whitlam survived.

The allegation against Whitlam was squarely put: he had compromised his party and a possible future government by accepting funds from one of the more notorious Arab nations. He had exposed himself to blackmail if re-elected, on the threat that the campaign donation might be revealed. Even more important he had tarnished his own reputation in an area where his previous credentials had always been impeccable. Whitlam had always left the clinking of the cash register to experienced

Labor Party 'bagmen', particularly his former staffer Richard Hall and former national secretary Mick Young. As both Opposition Leader and Prime Minister, Whitlam accepted that an integral part of his job was mixing on a social level with people who were likely to give money to the Labor Party. But he had never publicly compromised himself in the way that was implicit in the Iraqi deal.

Whitlam was always clever enough never to meet with or speak to Khemlani but he broke this golden rule with the Iraqi project, in which he had been involved from the moment of its inception and which he had continually endorsed throughout the campaign and into the new year. 'This matter would never had proceeded if I had scotched it at the outset, as I could have done,' Whitlam admitted after the story was told. 'I am culpable and I accept responsibility.'

At the end of the week the acting party president Jack Egerton told all Labor leaders, officers and members to cease public statements on the Iraqi affair. The national executive meeting was pulled forward to Friday 5 March and the party president Bob Hawke, away at the time, made immediate preparations to return. Before Hawke left Jerusalem he spoke to Murdoch by phone about the Iraqi contribution. At the same time Hartley went on a series of radio and television programs claiming that there was a conspiracy being mounted to destroy Whitlam by the combined influence of the CIA, Israeli intelligence and elements of the Labor Party.

Hawke held a press conference at his Melbourne home on Saturday 28 February. After the press conference Hawke entertained a number of journalists in his house and by the poolside speaking to them at length about the Iraqi affair. A number of Murdoch journalists were present and on the afternoon of Sunday 29 February a senior Murdoch journalist who had attended Hawke's home despatched to that day's news editor Phil Cornford a long memorandum which later became the subject of controversy in so far as it alleged that Hawke had made non-attributable comments highly critical of Whitlam's leadership.

At his Saturday press conference Hawke said that it was in the party's best interests if the substance of discussions at the Friday executive meeting were made public. Asked if the affair would cost Whitlam the leadership, Hawke told the press conference: 'That's a matter for the executive and the caucus. I'm not saying anything about it in advance.' When asked if Whitlam's credibility was now destroyed even if he were proved innocent, Hawke replied: 'Well the question of Mr Whitlam's leadership or credibility or otherwise is a matter which may or may not emerge out of the meeting. I am not going to comment in advance.'

The *Australian*'s memorandum was sent from its Sydney office to the Canberra office where the head of bureau, Warren Beeby, was assured that the quotations were accurate. They were used as the basis for Beeby's page one story the next day, which had banner headlines 'It's the end for Whitlam'. The first few sentences of the story were based on Hawke's non-attributable remarks as transmitted by the senior journalist; Hawke later complained to the ethics committee of the Australian Journalists Association that this was grossly inaccurate reportage. A second story on the front page of the *Australian* that morning reported that support for Whitlam had slumped dramatically in his home state NSW and there had been a corresponding increase in support for Hawke. The story quoted comments from the NSW secretary Geoff Cahill supporting its headlines.

In the next four days support swung dramatically back towards Whitlam inside the parliamentary Labor Party. This was a direct result of widespread hostility throughout the Labor movement at what it regarded as the 'over-kill' being used by both the Murdoch press and the Prime Minister Malcolm Fraser. On Friday 27 February, the Commonwealth Police interviewed officials of the Labor Party's advertising agency Mullins, Clarke and Ralph about the agency's business relationship with the Labor Party and the receiving of funds from overseas sources. The Attorney-General Bob Ellicott told parliament that the police approach followed information given to him that the two Iraqis might have been associated with a breach of the foreign exchange regulations. This followed Fraser's previous briefing to gallery journalists saying he had information that another $500,000 had actually arrived. On 25 February, Commonwealth Police impounded the diaries of police officers who accompanied Whitlam during the 1975 election campaign.

These actions gave Whitlam just the type of political ammunition he needed to send a few volleys in the government's direction and move on to the attack himself. The Opposition Leader said the Commonwealth Police were being compromised and corrupted by the government for party political purposes. Whitlam claimed that at no stage had the government given any substantial reason for these activities of the Commonwealth Police except hearsay and rumour, all of which had subsequently proved false.

The Russian ship *Leonid Sovinov* berthed at Sydney Cove on the morning of Monday 1 March, and David Combe was escorted by a strong police unit off the liner into a waiting car and taken to Whitlam's Parliament House office. The Labor leader was angry with the assistant national secretary of the party Ken Bennett, who had not provided him with a report of the officers' meeting at Hawke's house. One of the first things Whitlam said to Combe was, 'If you are dismissed or forced to resign, I shall resign immediately.' Whitlam told Combe that a number of Labor people had suggested to him that the national secretary was prepared to dump him but, after further talks with Labor officers notably Jack Egerton, Whitlam said that he knew that this was not true and understood Combe's position. The Labor leader himself now accepted the principle of equal culpability, meaning in political terms that he and Combe would almost certainly stand or fall together.[22] Whitlam showed Combe the story on page one of the *Australian*, which he claimed was based on comments made by Hawke. The Labor leader had been leaked a copy of the ten page telex message which had been sent the previous afternoon from the *Australian*'s office, allegedly based on Hawke's press conference and the subsequent talks at his home. Whitlam, taking the report at face value and not knowing of Hawke's vehement assertion that this was an inaccurate account, criticised the party president to Combe. Whitlam and the national secretary then had a general discussion about the tactics they should adopt at the national executive meeting on Friday.

By mid-week moves were well under way to ensure that the national executive reached a decision which would not result in a major party eruption. On Wednesday 3 March, Hawke spent the afternoon and evening at Combe's Canberra house and the two men discussed in detail the type of decision the executive should make. As the day wore on Hawke came to the conclusion that he should play a constructive role at the executive rather than attempt to discredit some of the principals he disliked.

Eventually Hawke and Combe decided that the final executive resolution should make four main points. The first was that the trio involved in the Iraqi money, Combe, Whitlam and Hartley, should be condemned and the reasons for that condemnation should be clearly spelt out. Second, the executive should acknowledge that fund-raising procedures needed to be revised to remove the burden from the shoulders of the national secretary and parliamentary leader. Third, that both the Fraser government and the Murdoch press should be specifically criticised for misrepresenting the issue and using false information. Fourth, the executive should restate the party's position on the source of campaign funds, in particular stress that the Labor Party was the only party which supported the disclosure of campaign sources.

Hawke spoke to Whitlam on three separate occasions this night from Combe's home and the three men had a solid outline of the recommendations which the officers would place before the executive meeting. Hawke subsequently spoke to Egerton and Combe conferred with the NSW delegate John Ducker. On Thursday morning the South Australian secretary George Whitten went to Combe's Canberra home for further talks on the recommended motion the officers would put. On Thursday night at the Canberra Rex the party officers met and were joined by Whitlam when parliament adjourned. The final recommendation from the officers was rewritten by Hawke on Friday morning, based on three days of consultation.

The executive met on the third floor of John Curtin House on Friday 5 March. Exceptional measures were taken to keep the working press away from the meeting and newsmen had to wait in the downstairs foyer or on the footpath outside. All Friday was spent hearing lengthy reports from Combe, Whitlam and Hartley on the full details of the Iraqi money. Questioning of these principals continued on Saturday morning. After it was concluded, the officers' resolution was put before the meeting. But this resolution had been amended once again, largely by Hawke, and it contained a section declaring that Hartley was unacceptable to the executive. The officers' resolution was moved by Egerton and was to be seconded by Ducker. But a number of points of order were taken and a long debate followed in which it became clear that a majority of the executive was opposed to the move against Hartley and this form of words was then omitted.

There were four amendments subsequently moved to the officers' motion. The first came from the Senate deputy leader Jim Keeffe, who wanted a more generalised and shorter motion. The second amendment came from the Tasmanian branch, moved by the Tasmanian branch president Neil Batt with the support of its real inspirer, the Labor Senate leader Ken Wriedt. This was the 'axe' motion. Its import was to declare Hartley unfit to be a national executive delegate, to seek a specific report from the party officers on the future of the national secretary David Combe and to ask the caucus to decide the fate of Whitlam in view of his involvement in the affair. The third amendment was moved by South Australian delegate Mick Young and seconded by NSW Senator Arthur Gietzelt. This motion was tougher on the three principals, Whitlam, Combe and Hartley, but it did not contain a number of points which the officers believed should be in the executive resolution. It did not mention that no money had been received, that no law had been broken and that the party put too much burden on both the national secretary and parliamentary leader in fund raising. It did not attack the Fraser government or refer to the particular circumstances during the campaign in which the money was sought.

Both Keeffe and Batt withdrew their motions in favour of the Young–Gietzelt motion. During a break in the executive, this motion was subsequently revised and appeared in the form of a new motion moved by West Australian secretary Bob McMullan. A long debate then followed on the respective merits of the officers' motion and the alternative motion, which had been refined throughout Saturday. Whitlam spoke strongly for the officers' motion saying the specific charges and the errors of judgement should be clearly spelt out. Hawke gave a brilliant speech in support of the officers' motion, going through it point by point, explaining why it was a more comprehensive and better resolution. Eventually it was agreed that sponsors of the two motions would meet in an effort to find a compromise. When this happened, Hawke made only token concessions on a number of words and the original officers' motion was then unanimously endorsed by the executive.

The full text of the resolution read:

> The Australian Labor Party in Opposition and in government has been the only party in this country to espouse disclosure of sources and the public funding of election campaigns. This practice, adopted in several overseas countries, is necessary on two grounds. First, these measures guarantee substantial equity between parties in terms of their broad electoral support to present their policies to the people. Secondly, they serve to eliminate the possibility of influence or attempted influence by those making contributions secretly to party campaign funds.
>
> Labor in government twice introduced legislation for these purposes. Contrary to the public interest, the legislation was twice defeated in the Senate by the vote of the Liberal and National Country Parties which have been historically beholden to wealthy private and privileged interests from which they receive massive financial support. In this context particularly, the national executive, having heard reports from the other officers and the national secretary, the federal parliamentary leader and Mr Hartley, can only condemn in the strongest terms the action of the three latter persons in the matter of a proposed gift of funds from Arab sources for the 1976 election campaign.
>
> At no time did the Australian Labor Party officially engage in any negotiations, nor will it, to receive funds from any such source. This applies to past elections as well as future elections.
>
> The principles, policies and programs of this party are not up for sale or auction and yet the initiation and endorsement of such a proposal put the party at risk of this charge. There is no suggestion that they would involve themselves in such compromise. The grave errors of judgement were, first, the suggestion being made by Mr Hartley on November 16 1975, and entertained by Mr Whitlam and Mr Combe; second, the non-communication of the proposal to the officers and the executive; third, the action of Mr Whitlam and Mr Combe in signing a proposed letter of February 11 1976, to the Commonwealth Trading Bank on the basis of this proposed transaction.
>
> Four points should be made clear from the evidence now available to the national executive. One, no money in fact was received. Two, none of the three persons involved stood in a position to profit personally from the proposed transaction. Three, none of the three persons directly talked on this matter with the two Iraqis who visited Australia on December 8–10 1975. Four, no breach of the law was committed or intended. We would point out that this error of judgement now condemned by the national executive could be attributed in considerable measure not only to the extraordinary circumstances

of the recent election but to the excessive pressures and responsibility which have been allowed by the party and the national secretary for the raising of election campaign funds. We believe that this should be an item of separate consideration by the national executive and ask the officers to prepare proposals in this area for our next meeting. Just as our principles, policies and programs are the exclusive property of the appropriate organs of the party, so are the decisions as to the leadership and direction of the party. The national executive deplores and condemns the concentrated attempts by the media generally and the Murdoch press in particular to interfere in, and manipulate, our affairs. The totally unprincipled campaign by the Murdoch group against Mr Whitlam has appropriately been made a matter of legal action.

Similarly, we deplore and condemn the blatant attempts by the Fraser government to interfere in, and misrepresent, this issue for its own party political advantage. The government had fed fake information to the press and the Attorney-General has abused his office by involving the Commonwealth Police in a personal political vendetta. We call upon all sections of the Labor movement to support the drive for financial support which must now be initiated by the officers to enable us to discharge our obligations. The national executive has a direct responsibility for the appointment and tenure of the national secretary of the party. Whilst all concerned have equal culpability in this matter, the national secretary has in all other respects served the party well in his office. We are confident he will continue to do so. We urge all members of the party, constituent sections, branches and affiliated unions, now to close ranks and to concentrate upon the task of attacking and defeating the Fraser government which has already demonstrated its contempt for the welfare of the mass of the Australian people.

The Executive finally broke at noon on Sunday after meeting for nearly two and a half days in a marathon session. The above resolution was similar to that canvassed by the officers on the Thursday before the meeting. It was the product of a long and searching inquiry by the executive, which found that grave errors of judgement had been committed by the three principal figures involved. But the executive showed the way by taking no action against David Combe the national secretary, the one of the three people involved who held his position at the executive's pleasure.

Bob Hawke gave a long press briefing on Sunday 7 March in which he explained the main details of the Iraqi affair and said under questioning he believed Whitlam should remain parliamentary leader of the Labor Party. Hawke had played an instrumental role throughout the executive, and the days immediately preceding it, to ensure that the executive not only investigated the matter completely but produced a motion that would be acceptable to wide sections of the party without provoking a new split or upheaval. Whitlam took a number of documents with him to the executive meeting which would have been damaging to Hawke if released. The Labor leader was quite prepared to retaliate and to take on anyone who tried to move against him. But a rupture of these dimensions was avoided and the ground laid for a swift burying of the Iraqi affair.

Whitlam survived as leader in the caucus meeting on Wednesday 17 March despite the resignation from the front bench of the former Education Minister Kim Beazley. One of the most notable aspects of the affair was the strong groundswell of support for Whitlam among the rank and file. The Labor leader enjoyed a new popularity at the grass-roots level since his dismissal from office on 11 November and this strong support increased during the Iraqi controversy. At the same time there was growing hostility to the role played by the ALP president Bob Hawke, once again from Labor branches. But while Whitlam was strong at the branch level, his reputation within the parliamentary party seemed to be so thoroughly damaged that recovery was impossible.

In the days immediately following the Iraqi revelations, Whitlam had seriously considered resigning the leadership of the parliamentary party. The fact that he successfully retained it bore witness to the absence of a genuine alternative leader, to the party's support for its own in the face of sustained pressure, to the questionable tactics of both the newspapers and the Fraser government, and finally to the mounting of a smooth political operation to ensure that the Iraqi affair did not split the party. Gough Whitlam survived as leader but was permanently handicapped politically. Whitlam has always maintained that when he leaves politics it will be of his own volition and not of anyone else's. There must be a good chance that he will resign the Labor leadership some time in the next two years from early 1976.

The Iraqi affair highlighted the lack of public accountability of political parties in fund raising. The ALP national executive was careful to state that the Labor Party had consistently supported public disclosure of sources of campaign funds. The former Labor government drafted bills to this effect which were defeated in the Senate by the Liberal–Country Parties. The Prime Minister Malcolm Fraser has consistently opposed the declaration of campaign fund sources. He has been strongly backed in this opposition by the Liberal Party organisation, which believes it would be gravely handicapped by such declarations, which would inhibit a big number of its contributors.

For all the indiscretion involved in the Iraqi affair, the fact is that political parties are far more likely to be compromised by domestic donations than by overseas donations. Governments have a greater sway over local affairs than they do over international affairs.

The former secretary of the Victorian division of the Liberal Party, Leo Hawkins, recently admitted that people and companies who make extensive donations to political parties, whether they are unions contributing to the Labor Party or companies contributing to the Liberal Party, are looking for a 'pay off'. Hawkins pointed out that such pay offs can come in many ways. Some might be specific, a tangible decision from the government which will benefit the company. Others might be more general, such as policies affecting a special interest group or sector of the community. But the expectation is always there and the pressure is always greater when the assumed obligation is one to an organisation that lies inside, rather than outside Australia.

It is difficult to see just what the Iraqis would have gained from such a donation. Admittedly, they could have used it as a tool of blackmail to push Australia to a more sympathetic pro-Arab anti-Israeli stand in the Middle East and in the United Nations. But it is more realistic to assume that the donation would have had none or only the most marginal impact on the thrust of Australian foreign policy. There is no sign that Whitlam wanted to alter policy. That was made abundantly clear to the Iraqis.

The full story of the Iraqi affair still rests with Henri Fischer and the new twist that was given to it in early March 1976 when Fischer disappeared from his hotel room in Singapore. One aspect of Fischer's character seems clear from discussions with everyone who knows him: his genuine dedication and almost fanatical commitment to the Arab cause. One of the perplexing aspects of the affair was Fischer's motive in changing sides and, after working as an intermediary for the Labor Party, leaking his story to the newspapers in a way that not only discredited the Labor Party but did huge damage to the Arab cause in Australia. It has been confirmed that Fischer was not paid any money for his story. According to all reports, however, it was Fischer who approached Rupert Murdoch and spoke with him over several days, building up a forty-page dossier on the affair which was later used as the basis for the stories.

When Fischer was travelling to Australia he had a bodyguard, Douglas Sinclair, with him. Reports in the *Sunday Times* newspaper in early March claimed that a previously unknown figure in the Iraqi affair, Tito Howard, said he 'rescued' Fischer from his Singapore hotel. Murdoch provided Fischer with a bodyguard after publication of the first story, when Fischer told Murdoch that he feared for his life and the man he most feared was Tito Howard. Fischer was subsequently seen leaving the back entrance of his hotel in Singapore with the same Tito Howard, the man whom he had convinced Murdoch and his bodyguards was after him.

But when the *Sunday Times* tracked him down, Tito Howard gave a different version of the story. Howard claimed that when he went to see Fischer in London there were two bodyguards with him and at one stage Fischer gave him a piece of paper which said: 'I've been kidnapped. As soon as you leave please destroy this note.' Howard claims he arranged with Fischer to trail him back to Australia via Singapore. At this stage Howard employed a Chinese karate expert to help him get Fischer out of the Singapore hotel. Howard claimed that the two men dressed in white jackets took a food trolley to Fischer's floor of the hotel where they got Fischer out of his room and took him down to Howard's room. Howard claims that Fischer paid him $2000 for helping him.

As this book goes to press Fischer is reported to be on his way back to Australia and Diana has moved out of their Blues Point Towers apartment.

# 24

# THE WHITLAM YEARS

*The qualities you have shown are the qualities that we know are yours and yours alone—the qualities of the greatest living Australian.*

Graham Freudenberg to Gough Whitlam, 12 December 1975, at the lunch ending Labor's election campaign

Although he has been denying it, the Whitlam era in Australian politics is almost assuredly at an end. Not even Gough Whitlam, with his Houdini-like capacity for political revival and his Banquo-like capacity to return and haunt his opponents, is likely to survive the recent blows to his reputation, self-image and electoral standing. In the space of four months Whitlam has been the first Prime Minister in Australian history to be dismissed from office, has suffered the worst electoral defeat ever, and been the anchor man in a scandalous effort to pull half a million dollars from Iraq into his party's campaign fund.

Any one of these incidents would have been sufficient in itself to terminate the career of most politicians. Whitlam's ability to survive them all, at least for an interim period, is testimony to his remarkable standing even in defeat.

The basic question surrounding Gough Whitlam now is whether in the future he can still play the role which he always played in the past—that of an initiator of new ideas with both the personal drive and popular following that is so fundamental to the translation of ideas into actuality. Only the most optimistic or foolhardy could answer 'yes' to this query. For each one of the three blows he sustained between November 1975 and March 1976 struck at different points in his makeup, and overall left him perilously close to being the 'lame duck' leader which he always scorned and forever claimed he would never tolerate.

The Kerr sacking left him glorious in defeat; as his career's most monumental political misjudgement of both a situation and another man, it was also witness to his great fighting qualities, his genuine radicalism and his role as a populist symbol of Labor reformism.

The 13 December election defeat represented the premature termination of the Whitlam government, five years short of the eight-year reign which Whitlam envisaged, with half of Labor's reformist policies introduced, half of them aborted and hardly any of them ingrained into the community. This torpedoed the Whitlam image as a great vote winner and convinced him for some time that the Australian people had revoked not only his Prime Ministerial commission but his credentials as a political leader.

The Iraqi campaign funds affair did him both less damage and yet more damage than the two earlier blows. It made little difference to Labor's opponents; but its greatest impact was among the party faithful and supporters. They could readily forgive Whitlam for losing an election forced on him by the Opposition. But they could not forgive such a massive indiscretion, which seemed partly to justify the vilification heaped on him by his political enemies.

Within the ruthless political world of the Labor Party Whitlam survived as leader for only one reason: there was no heir apparent, no credible alternative acceptable to the party. There were only Whitlam's contemporaries, men who had been tried in government after a long period in Opposition and were not even regarded by their closest followers as adequate successors. Whitlam is now a permanently crippled political leader, a man whose defeat at the polls and whose personal role in the Iraqi affair will never leave him or the voting public.

This in itself is a huge irony. For, just before his dismissal from office by the Governor-General, Whitlam was convinced he would prevail in the constitutional crisis and that his arch opponent Malcolm Fraser would be left permanently handicapped. It may well be, indeed it is likely, that Whitlam's main political task will now be to hand over the reins of the Labor leadership to the man most able to return the party to office.

Today's Australians will never see another politician like Gough Whitlam. He was a freakish political product, of a species never likely to reproduce. An innocent in the ruthless milieu of head-counting who rose to lead the party on his ability alone, an intellectual with a sympathy for the aspirations of the working man but no real roots in the trade union movement, a dedicated Australian nationalist at home who was his country's first genuine internationalist abroad, the most fervently centralist Prime Minister in the nation's history leading a strictly federalist party, a man personally committed to racial equality, civil liberties and social progress with the most highly developed sense of elitism within one of the most democratically structured parties in the world and, finally, a politician who spent years persuading the Labor Party to seek power through pragmatism only to lose office because he proved unable to display pragmatism himself. The paradoxes never end. Whitlam's ultimate indiscretion involved the seeking of campaign funds from a despised power when his whole career had been characterised by a meticulous approach to fund raising and a subtle appreciation of foreign devils.

In a very real sense Gough Whitlam's vision of himself was too large and egocentric for the country to handle. He was eventually rejected because he lost contact with the electorate, the silent majority to which his program was pitched but which insisted on different priorities from those Whitlam offered. While he constantly reaffirmed his faith in the wisdom, decency and common sense of the Australian electorate, he tended to interpret these qualities in terms of his own vision instead of what they really meant. Like some men who see themselves as embodying the forces of history, Whitlam came undone at the grassroots. Dictators can afford such a luxury but politicians in a democratic country cannot.

Whitlam himself exercised an incomparable influence on the policies and style of the Labor government. Hence it was inevitably characterised by drama, excitement, reform, upheaval, and excesses which spelt destruction. There is no easy way to assess the Whitlam record.

His successor Malcolm Fraser branded the Whitlam government the worst since Federation and there are many captains of industry prepared to endorse this exaggeration. The difficulty is that Gough Whitlam defied all political custom. He turned the conventional wisdom on its head and made it look stupid. No Australian Prime Minister ever ruled with the flamboyance, the panache, the vigour or obvious enjoyment that he did. Despite his model of Menzies, the two men were worlds apart in spirit. Menzies believed in the settlement of time, the serenity of government, of measured and controlled movements, of waiting for opportunities and striking your opponent when he was weak. Their greatest difference was Menzies' commitment to stability and Whitlam's commitment to change. Whitlam began his reformist policies with a rush that ended only in electoral oblivion. He was the Prime Minister who could not wait, even for the election result, even for the caucus meeting in December 1972. Whitlam broke tradition from the start with the two man government run by both himself and Lance Barnard systematically knocking down the pillars of the established order, the China bogy, the national service legacy. If the pace was too fast, if Labor tried to do too many things simultaneously without properly explaining and 'selling' them to the public, then Whitlam must shoulder the main responsibility. He was always the man in a hurry, anxious to keep that appointment with the history books, determined to ensure that his administration would not slip into the Menzian slumber.

Whitlam's philosophy of reform was that, once a compromise was made, once the spirit and pace of reform slackened, it was quite likely lost forever. After the May 1974 re-election success he defended the extent of change arguing that, while some people might have been alienated, a bigger number applauded the implementation of the program. He believed the only reason Labor was re-elected was because it achieved so much so swiftly in the first eighteen months. And he was right. There is no doubt that in three years his government was responsible for more reforms and innovations than any other government in Australian history. They would never have been so broad in concept and so firmly executed without his hand on the political rudder.

At home Whitlam involved the central government in the affairs of the people. The two great achievements were Medibank and his education funding policy to schools and tertiary institutions. The 'needs policy' appears to have ended a century-old sectarian debate which divided the community, member against member, school against school, and political parties both within and without. The Grants Commission was the first step towards a restructuring of power and responsibility among levels of government and gave local government a status it had never previously enjoyed. The Whitlam policies offered a new deal for pensioners, aboriginals, students and women. But, more than any of these groups, it was the migrant communities, or at least the bulk of them, who responded to Whitlam and identified with him as they had done with no other major political figure.

The Prime Minister kept his pledges on the cities and established a new department which took an active role in urban development, establishing land commissions to lower land prices and formulate a viable growth centre program. The Whitlam government established community health centres, gave land rights to aboriginals, embarked on a comprehensive preschool and child care program, developed a national hospitals plan, established a legislative framework to ensure environmental protection, and in the Hayden budget introduced major tax reforms substituting flat rate rebates in place of the inequitable system of concessional deductions.

The government's big minus, Whitlam's real achilles heel, was the economy. Gough Whitlam, a lawyer and parliamentarian, was never at home with economic and financial issues. He was never the economic literate that Bill Hayden was and, unlike his last and best Treasurer, failed to think political problems through in economic terms.

Thus one of the Labor Government's most significant tactical errors, in which Whitlam's lack of leadership was notable, was the 1973–74 budget, its first budget in office. At that time Whitlam enthusiastically supported and proudly endorsed the policies of new and huge government spending initiated by Labor. In particular he pointed to the government's record in supporting better wages for women, better conditions for the public service and, as a result, higher wages for private sector employees. Yet these very moves were sowing the seeds of future economic disaster.

Labor came to office on a multitude of promises, which in power became commitments. It is probably true that the Labor Cabinet could not have repudiated its spending promises in the first year and in its first budget. But having proceeded, it should have accepted the consequences and increased taxation in the first year, thereby covering itself against an inflationary momentum. It singularly failed to do this despite advice to this effect. In the first year too many Labor Ministers, with no previous experience of government, refused to accept the notion of the 'tough option'. Labor had promised not to raise taxes, so it would not raise taxes. Malcolm Fraser was never guilty of this sort of thinking and demonstrated within days of his election that campaign promises are only kept as long as the government of the day believes they are suitable.

In summary, Labor's first and most successful year, 1973, was the very year in which it was betrayed by its false sense of security. Labor refused to face up to the realities of the economic climate it had inherited from the McMahon government. If McMahon had been re-elected, he would have applied an economic squeeze very early to correct inflationary pressures. Whitlam's uncertainty with the economy was fused with his other chief weakness: an inability to act as a good manager and build up an effective team. Admittedly, men like Clyde Cameron and Rex Connor were not the easiest individuals to mould into a smoothly working unit. But Whitlam's own character and style militated against the spirit of harmony and united direction which was so important, particularly in such a big Cabinet. When the 1974 election campaign began, Whitlam tried at first to ignore inflation as an issue but eventually he swung into it. He embraced the Treasury line with new-found vigour after his electoral victory and was enraged when the rest of his Cabinet colleagues rejected the Treasury prescriptions. Whitlam was at a loss on the economy when he had no policy to champion and in this period of uncertainty he left the formulation of that policy to other Ministers, notably Jim Cairns.

This was Whitlam's pattern on the economy. He relied first on the Treasury, then on Cairns, next on his new permanent head John Menadue, and finally on his favourite Treasurer Bill Hayden, all the time shifting his ground as one strand of policy proved inadequate and the search for another began. The Prime Minister's dilemma was that the economic battleground was not one of his own choosing nor of his liking. It was natural that he came to rely on others.

The damaging change of Treasurers which Whitlam precipitated was the product of his own uncertainty and his fickleness with his colleagues. It is a documented fact that Whitlam alienated the overwhelming majority of the senior men with whom he worked, right and left, young and old, old friends or old enemies. The list is a long one: Cairns, Cameron, Connor, Crean, Beazley, Cass, Wriedt, Bowen and Patterson. All of them were alienated after working in close proximity with Whitlam. This is a list which goes beyond political reasons and enters into personal ones.

According to some of them Whitlam lacked an appreciation of the merits of introspection and sensitivity. How, they asked, could he proceed with the Tony Whitlam exercise? With the long drawn out political agony of Frank Crean? With the gathering around him of favourite Ministers for a few months and then abandoning them for others? How could he be so self-righteous about the loans affair, after sacking both Cairns and Connor, and claim he was utterly blameless himself? His sacking of Clyde Cameron in mid-year to the humiliating portfolio of Science was hard to interpret as anything else but deliberate vindictiveness.

Whitlam seemed genuinely surprised when he discovered that the advice given the government by the Treasury and Reserve Bank in 1974 was astray. He seemed to lack a touch for financial matters and this streak of naivety was shown during the loans affairs. All the indications are that when the initial loan authority was issued to Rex Connor in December 1974, Whitlam failed to appreciate the political dangers inherent in the scheme and the way the matter was being approached. From the time the loan revelations began he had no choice but to fight a long, defensive operation as best he could and uphold the original decision which he privately admitted was a mistake. On the loans affair Whitlam appeared as both a devious and weak leader. Devious because he put the entire onus of responsibility and hence the consequences on the shoulders of Rex Connor when he himself was a party to the original Executive Council minute on 13 December; weak because he never insisted that Connor be regularly accountable to him for his loan-raising activities either when they were underway or when they were supposed to have been terminated. The same trait was again evident in his indecisive attitude towards the Cairns–Morosi connection which was so damaging to his government.

In the end Whitlam's complex and larger-than-life personality tended to become a central, even dominant, issue in itself. He could be absolutely impetuous, such as when he resigned the Labor leadership in 1968 and just regained it by four votes, such as when he stood on the front steps of Parliament House and branded Fraser 'Kerr's cur'. He could be politically foolish such as when he predicted in 1966 that he was destined to lead the party, or when he made successive efforts to get Crean, Murphy and Barnard out of politics even when the direct repercussions of such moves would damage his government. He was capable of ruthlessness when he sacked Cairns as Treasurer and could display an almost physical pleasure in taunting his Ministers during the mid-1975 Cabinet reshuffle when many Ministers did not know where they would end up.

Yet on other occasions both small and large gestures indicated his concern for other people—staff members, journalists or politicians of either side. In 1975 he asked McMahon and his family back to the Lodge for lunch—a Whitlam courtesy probably sparked by the fact that as Leader of the Opposition for six years he was never asked there himself.

One of Whitlam's great qualities has been his prodigious capacity for work and his apparently inexhaustible reservoirs of energy—assets which those people close to politics know are incalculable. Blessed with a remarkable constitution, he has always spurned the twin delights of the Members Bar and female companionship, in both of which so many of his colleagues have sought solace from the strain and loneliness of political life. No one ever prepared himself so diligently, so rigorously for the Prime Ministership. Overseas trips established his standing with world and regional leaders and familiarised him with the international scene he loved so much; long hours at home preparing policy, mapping out strategy and seeking changes in the party's structure laid the basis for the 1972 election victory. In office Whitlam worked without respite and, unlike most other politicians, had virtually no relaxations or diversions from the daily grind.

Yet the reverse side of the coin was that he expected recognition from others of his talents and continually tried to seize the mantle of greatness, being unable to wait for others to bestow it upon him. This is one of the central themes of his career: so anxious was he to depose Arthur Calwell that he nearly blew the chance; so convinced was he that he and he alone knew the right course for the party when he was leader that it nearly rejected him; so sure was he after the December 1972 election that the people would endorse Labor's policies that he mistook a limited mandate. Whitlam's tendency to see himself as embodying the forces of history became even more pronounced when he assumed the office of Prime Minister. He wanted to be Prime Minister on his own terms, not on the terms set out by the electorate.

As Labor leader and Prime Minister Whitlam made no concessions from what he considered his duty. He refused to concede the Australian public its well-known prejudice against Prime Ministerial travel overseas, insisting on going frequently and for a long time and even returning to Europe after coming home to visit cyclone-ravaged Darwin. Eventually his personal style of government and preferences became issues in themselves exploited by Malcolm Fraser around the nation in the form of Blue Poles, aid to the arts, his photo in government offices, overseas travel, and appointing his wife to government boards—trivia on which the electorate thrives. But electoral damage that no politician could afford.

He berated and abused the caucus, and on crucial issues would intimidate it into submission by putting his own prestige or position on the line, thereby increasing the stakes involved. Where he could not do this in Cabinet he would grind his teeth in anger at a rebuff. Whitlam's philosophy was that of political confrontation. For a long time he had massive success through indulging in this strategy. 'When you are faced with an impasse you have got to crash through or you've got to crash,' he once declared in a frank admission of his own tactics. This was both his weakness and his strength. Normally his ability was so great that 'crashing through' succeeded, but this type of operation did great damage to his government. His regular declarations of 'I'm the greatest' and anxiety to compare himself with Curtin and Menzies only proved counter-productive to the goals he sought. Eventually his 'crashing through' days reached the situation where an irresistible force met an immovable object in the form of the Australian constitution and Whitlam was sacked. Perhaps the very success of his own brand of tactics ultimately betrayed his better judgement.

Whitlam stands as one of the great creative politicians in Australian history. He had that rare combination of both creative vision and the ability to turn that vision into political reality—the indispensable mix that marks out the great man from the masses.

The son of a distinguished federal public servant and lawyer, with a great love of the classics, he spent twenty years of his life in the western and southern suburbs of Sydney trying to devise policies to improve the lot of the average Australian. His political career is remarkable for its consistency of views and nearly every central theme underpinning his strongest ideas can be traced back over twenty or thirty years. His preoccupation with referenda to modernise the constitution, his obsession with involving the central government directly to improve health, education, and urban environment of the people, his opposition to military involvement in South–East Asia, his commitment as a centralist, all go back over decades. His political career was always spectacular, marked with crisis and counter-crisis. If Whitlam eventually came to harbour a great and implicit faith in his own political capacity, it was forged in the battle itself. No man walked so close to the brink. He constantly came to the precipice of defeat only to avoid it through his own efforts and those of his colleagues and move on to a new battleground.

None of his party critics could have accomplished the internal reforms within the party in the 1960s which he wrought, played such a seminal role in revamping the party's policies and returned it to office the way that Whitlam did. Nobody else could have withstood the Snedden challenge in 1974 so ably, demolished Snedden before he could force an election and finally, nobody could have defied the Fraser Senate for five weeks so strongly and almost successfully as Gough Whitlam did. It is a chronology next to which those of most other politicians assume pygmy-like proportions.

Yet the house so carefully constructed fell to pieces. Three major problems bedevilled the Whitlam government. The first was that it was elected to office on a reformist program to expand the public sector in an economic situation that required precisely the opposite treatment. Labor never came to terms with this problem. Whether it could have eventually under the Whitlam–Hayden–McClelland axis is a moot point.

The second major problem was the failure of Labor's senior Ministers to handle the task facing them. Despite their achievements, Crean, Cairns, Cameron and Connor were overwhelmed by the course of events and their own ministerial inexperience. Unlike Ministers in today's Fraser government they were not managers, were not used to dealing with and utilising a public service. They made abundant errors concerning personal staff appointments, excessive secrecy, failure to explain what they were doing. Philip Cairns, Morosi and Khemlani were just the obvious examples. In addition to this they had a Prime Minister prone to making excessive misjudgements of a fatal nature. The shonky 13 December loans approval to avoid the constitution and the seeking of funds from Iraq are again the obvious examples.

The third major problem facing the Labor government was the political sabotage to which it was subjected. History was cruel to Whitlam in that he won two House of Representative elections, in 1972 and 1974, but never controlled the Senate, the chamber which twice struck him down, the second time fatally. The facts are that Labor was not swept into office in December 1972 despite all the euphoria of victory. Its win was a limited one giving a nine seat majority without control of the Senate. The subsequent actions of the Whitlam government and the constant reaffirmation of the mandate by the Prime Minister did not reflect the real political balance of power. The truth was that Labor spent three years in office without having real power, in the sense of controlling the parliament. In its three years Labor sought supply six times. On only one of those six occasions did the Opposition parties not consider denying that supply. That was in autumn 1973. The Liberals talked a lot about blocking the 1973 budget but did nothing until the next occasion in autumn 1974 when they forced the double dissolution election. Even though Labor was returned there was more talk about blocking the 1974 budget only six months later. In autumn 1975 Snedden revived the election threat and might well have blocked supply had he not been deposed as leader. Fraser then blocked the 1975 budget, the first opportunity he had to vote on supply. The Opposition Leader in the Senate Reg Withers, admitted in 1974 that the Opposition had been looking towards forcing an election since early 1973. The fact is that the Labor government was given two eighteen month terms by its opponents.

The Senate's power over money bills has been confirmed in a legal sense and cemented as a political tactic. The constant threat of being forced to the polls became a built-in factor in the decision-making process of the Labor government. More than any other single influence, this disrupted the pattern of government and made sound administration a near impossibility. It is true that bad government breeds contemptuous Oppositions; but it is equally true that in the Australian context contemptuous Oppositions can breed bad government.

The Whitlam years were marked by a dangerous breakdown in constitutional conventions, without which the democratic system cannot survive. Not only was the Senate's power over money bills reduced to a political tactic; the convention that Senate vacancies be filled by an appointee of the same political party was breached. The convention that state governments should accept the calling of a Senate election by the Prime Minister was also breached. A whole new range of opportunities for harassment and obstruction against the government of the day has been established. The way is now open for political parties, working through state Premiers of their own complexion, to 'stack' the Senate, even alter its balance of power in a fashion that can decide the future of government bills and even the tenure of office of a government itself. The way is similarly open for parties, again working through state Premiers, to decide whether or not they will have a Senate election when the Federal Government wants one. Events over the past three years have clearly altered the pattern of Australian politics and tilted the system towards instability.[1]

# APPENDIX I

## Chronology of Events

**1974**

| | |
|---|---|
| 18 May | Labor government re-elected |
| 10 June | Jim Cairns elected deputy leader of the ALP and becomes deputy Prime Minister |
| 23 July | Labor government introduces its mini-budget |
| 17 September | 1974–75 budget |
| 12 November | New mini-budget introduced by Whitlam |
| 21 November | Cairns' appointment as Treasurer announced |
| 27 November | Fraser supporters fail in move to depose Snedden |
| 7 December | Queensland state election win for non-Labor parties |
| 13 December | Executive Council meeting authorises Connor to raise $US4000 million loan |
| 14 December | Whitlam leaves for five week European trip |

**1975**

| | |
|---|---|
| 7 January | Connor's loan authority revoked |
| 28 January | Loan authority re-instated at $US2000 million |
| 3 February | ALP federal conference at Terrigal begins |
| 9 February | Cabinet appoints Lionel Murphy to the High Court |
| 10 February | Jim McClelland elected to ministry; Ken Wriedt becomes Labor Senate leader; NSW Premier Lewis |

|                | announces that Murphy will be replaced by non-Labor Senator |
|----------------|---------------------------------------------------------------|
| 27 February    | Cope resigns as Speaker after clash with Whitlam |
| 3 March        | Gorton announces retirement from federal parliament |
| 7–10 March     | Cairns gives George Harris the loan letters |
| 14 March       | Peacock calls for Liberal leadership issue to be resolved |
| 21 March       | Fraser overthrows Snedden as Liberal leader and says governments can normally expect to remain three years in office |
| 20 May         | Government revokes $US2000 million loan authority |
| 30 May         | Lance Barnard's retirement from politics is reported |
| 6 June         | Cabinet reshuffle. Cairns is replaced as Treasurer and Cameron as Labour Minister by Hayden and McClelland respectively |
| 28 June        | Bass by-election in which Labor suffers a heavy defeat |
| 2 July         | Cairns sacked from ministry |
| 9 July         | Special parliamentary sitting day on the loans affair |
| 12 July        | Dunstan just wins South Australian state election |
| 14 July        | Crean elected deputy Labor leader and becomes deputy Prime Minister |
| 19 August      | Hayden budget announced |
| 26 August      | Fraser's reply to the budget |
| 9 September    | Senator Albert Field sworn in to replace Labor Senator Milliner |
| 10 October     | High Court decision upholds Labor's legislation to give Senate representation to the Territories |
| 14 October     | Connor resigns and Fraser decides to block the budget and force an election |
| 16 October     | Senate defers budget and Whitlam stays in office |
| 11 November    | Governor-General dismisses Whitlam and commissions Fraser as caretaker Prime Minister |
| 16 November    | Whitlam, Combe and Hartley agree to seek Arab funds for campaign |
| 10 December    | Whitlam has breakfast with the two Iraqis |
| 13 December    | Fraser elected |

**1976**

|            |                                                              |
|------------|--------------------------------------------------------------|
| 27 January | Whitlam re-elected Labor leader with Uren as his deputy |
| 7 March    | ALP's federal executive condemns Whitlam, Combe and Hartley for trying to raise Arab funds |
| 17 March   | Caucus meets and there is no leadership spill |

# APPENDIX II

## Letter from Sir Garfield Barwick to the Governor-General on 10 November

Dear Sir John,

In response to Your Excellency's invitation I attended this day at Admiralty House. In our conversation I indicated that I considered myself, as Chief Justice of Australia, free, on Your Excellency's request, to offer you legal advice as to Your Excellency's constitutional rights and duties in relation to an existing situation which, of its nature, was unlikely to come before the court. We both clearly understood that I was not in any way concerned with matters of a purely political kind, or with any political consequences of the advice I might give.

In response to Your Excellency's request for my legal advice as to whether a course on which you had determined was consistent with your constitutional authority and duty, I respectfully offer the following. The constitution of Australia is a federal constitution which embodies the principle of ministerial responsibility. The parliament consists of two Houses, the House of Representatives and the Senate, each popularly elected, and each with the same legislative power, with the one exception that the Senate may not originate nor amend a money bill.

Two relevant constitutional consequences flow from this structure of the parliament. First, the Senate has constitutional power to refuse to pass a money bill; it has power to refuse supply to the government of the day. Second, a Prime Minister who cannot ensure supply to the Crown, including funds for carrying on the ordinary services of government, must either advise a general election (of a kind which the constitutional situation may then allow), or resign. If, being unable to secure supply, he refuses to take either course, your Excellency has a constitutional authority to withdraw his commission as Prime Minister.

There is no analogy in respect of a Prime Minister's duty between the situation of the parliament under the federal constitution of Australia and the relationship between the House of Commons, a popularly elected body, and the House of Lords, a non-elected body, in the unitary form of government functioning in the United Kingdom. Under that system, a government having the confidence of the House of Commons can secure supply, despite a recalcitrant House of Lords. But it is otherwise under our federal constitution. A government having the confidence of the House of Representatives but not that of the Senate, both elected Houses, cannot secure supply to the Crown.

But there is an analogy between the situation of a Prime Minister who has lost the confidence of the House of Commons and a Prime Minister who does not have the confidence of the parliament, i.e. of the House of Representatives and of the Senate. The duty and responsibility of the Prime Minister to the Crown in each case is the same: if unable to secure supply to the Crown, to resign or to advise an election.

In the event that, conformably to this advice, the Prime Minister ceases to retain his commission, Your Excellency's constitutional authority and duty would be to invite the Leader of the Opposition, if he can undertake to secure supply, to form a caretaker government (i.e. one which makes no appointments or initiates any policies) pending a general election, whether of the House of Representatives, or of both Houses of Parliament, as that government may advise.

Accordingly, my opinion is that, if Your Excellency is satisfied in the current situation that the present government is unable to secure supply, the course upon which Your Excellency has determined is consistent with your constitutional duty.

Yours respectfully,

(Garfield Barwick)

# APPENDIX III

## The Governor-General's termination of Whitlam's Prime Ministership

11 November 1975

Dear Mr Whitlam,

In accordance with Section 64 of the constitution I hereby determine your appointment as my chief adviser and head of the government. It follows that I also hereby determine the appointments of all of the Ministers in your government.

You have previously told me that you would never resign or advise an election of the House of Representatives or a double dissolution and that the only way in which such an election could be obtained would be by my dismissal of you and your ministerial colleagues. As it appeared likely that you would today persist in this attitude I decided that, if you did, I would determine your commission and state my reasons for doing so. You have persisted in your attitude and I have accordingly acted as indicated. I attach a statement of my reasons which I intend to publish immediately. It is with a great deal of regret that I have taken this step both in respect of yourself and your colleagues.

I propose to send for the Leader of the Opposition and to commission him to form a new caretaker government until an election can be held.

Yours sincerely,

(signed John R. Kerr)

# APPENDIX IV

## Statement by the Governor-General on 11 November

I have given careful consideration to the constitutional crisis and have made some decisions which I wish to explain.

**Summary**

It has been necessary for me to find a democratic and constitutional solution to the current crisis which will permit the people of Australia to decide as soon as possible what should be the outcome of the deadlock which developed over supply between the two Houses of Parliament and between the government and the Opposition parties. The only solution consistent with the constitution and with my oath of office and my responsibilities, authority and duty as Governor-General is to terminate the commission as Prime Minister of Mr Whitlam and to arrange for a caretaker government able to secure supply and willing to let the issue go to the people.

I shall summarise the elements of the problem and the reasons for my decision which places the matter before the people of Australia for prompt determination.

Because of the federal nature of our constitution and because of its provisions the Senate undoubtedly has constitutional power to refuse or defer supply to the government. Because of the principles of responsible government a Prime Minister who cannot obtain supply, including money for carrying on the ordinary services of government, must either advise a general election or resign. If he refuses to do this I have the authority and indeed the duty under the constitution to withdraw his commission as Prime Minister. The position in Australia is quite different from the position in the United Kingdom. Here the confidence of both Houses on supply is necessary to ensure its provision. In the United Kingdom the confidence of the House of Commons alone is necessary. But both here and in the United Kingdom the duty of the Prime Minister is the same in a most important respect—if he cannot get supply he must resign or advise an election. If a Prime Minister refuses to resign or to advise an election, and this is the case with Mr Whitlam, my constitutional authority and duty require me to do what I have now done—to withdraw his commission—and to invite the Leader of the Opposition to form a caretaker government—that is one that makes no appointments or dismissals and initiates no policies, until a general election is held. It is most desirable that he should guarantee supply. Mr Fraser will be asked to give the necessary undertakings and advise whether he is prepared to recommend a double dissolution. He will also be asked to guarantee supply.

The decisions I have made were made after I was satisfied that Mr Whitlam could not obtain supply. No other decision open to me would enable the Australian people to decide for themselves what should be done. Once I had made up my mind, for my own part, what I must do if Mr Whitlam persisted in his stated intentions I consulted the Chief Justice of Australia, Sir Garfield Barwick. I have his permission to say that I consulted him in this way.

The result is that there will be an early general election for both Houses and the people can do what, in a democracy such as ours, is their responsibility and duty and theirs alone. It is for the people now to decide the issue which the two leaders have failed to settle.

### Detailed Statement of Decisions

On 16 October the Senate deferred consideration of Appropriation Bills (Nos. 1 & 2) 1975–1976. In the time which elapsed since then events made it clear that the Senate was determined to refuse to grant supply to the government. In that time the Senate on no less than two occasions resolved to proceed no further with fresh Appropriation Bills, in identical terms, which had been passed by the House of Representatives. The determination of the Senate to maintain its refusal to grant supply was confirmed by the public statements made by the Leader of the Opposition, the Opposition having control of the Senate.

By virtue of what has in fact happened there therefore came into existence a deadlock between the House of Representatives and the Senate on the central issue of supply without which all the ordinary services of the government cannot be maintained. I had the benefit of discussions with the Prime Minister and, with his approval, with the Leader of the Opposition and with the Treasurer and the Attorney-General. As a result of those discussions and having regard to the public statements of the Prime Minister and the Leader of the Opposition I have come regretfully to the conclusion that there is no likelihood of a compromise between the House of Representatives and the Senate nor for that matter between the government and the Opposition.

The deadlock which arose was one which, in the interests of the nation, had to be resolved as promptly as possible and by means which are appropriate in our democratic system. In all the circumstances which have occurred the appropriate means is a dissolution of the parliament and an election for both Houses. No other course offers a sufficient assurance of resolving the deadlock and resolving it promptly.

Parliamentary control of appropriation and accordingly of expenditure is a fundamental feature of our system of responsible government. In consequence it has been generally accepted that a government which has been denied supply by the parliament cannot govern. So much at least is clear in cases where a ministry is refused supply by a popularly elected Lower House. In other systems where an Upper House is denied the right to reject a money bill denial of supply can occur only at the instance of the Lower House. When, however, an Upper House possesses the power to reject a money bill including an Appropriation Bill, and exercises the power by denying supply, the principle that a government which has been denied supply by the parliament should resign or go to an election must still apply—it is a necessary consequence of parliamentary control of appropriation and expenditure and of the expectation that the ordinary and necessary services of government will continue to be provided.

The constitution combines the two elements of responsible government and federalism. The Senate is, like the House, a popularly elected chamber. It was designed to provide representation by states, not by electorates, and was given by Section 53, equal powers with the House with respect to proposed laws, except in the respects mentioned in the section. It was denied power to originate or amend Appropriation Bills but was left with power to reject them or defer consideration of them. The Senate accordingly has the power and has exercised the power to refuse to grant supply to the government. The government stands in the position that it has been denied supply by the parliament with all the consequences which flow from that fact.

There have been public discussions about whether there is a convention deriving from the principles of responsible government that the Senate must never under any circumstances exercise the power to reject an Appropriation Bill. The constitution must prevail over any convention because, in determining the question how far the conventions of responsible government have been grafted on to the federal compact, the constitution itself must in the end control the situation.

Section 57 of the constitution provides a means, perhaps the usual means, of resolving a disagreement between the Houses with respect to a proposed law. But the machinery which it provides necessarily entails a considerable time lag which is quite inappropriate to a speedy resolution of the fundamental problems posed by the refusal of supply. Its presence in the constitution does not cut down the reserve powers of the Governor-General.

I should be surprised if the law officers expressed the view that there is no reserve power in the Governor-General to dismiss a ministry which has been refused supply by the parliament and to commission a ministry, as a caretaker ministry which will secure supply and recommend a dissolution, including where appropriate a double dissolution. This is a matter on which my own mind is quite clear and I am acting in accordance with my own clear view of the principles laid down by the constitution and of the nature, powers and responsibility of my office.

There is one other point. There has been discussion of the possibility that a half-Senate election might be held under circumstances in which the government has not obtained supply. If such advice were given to me I should feel constrained to reject it because a half-Senate election held whilst supply continues to be denied does not guarantee a prompt or sufficiently clear prospect of the deadlock being resolved in accordance with proper principles. When I refer to rejection of such advice I mean that, as I would find it necessary in the circumstances I have envisaged to determine Mr Whitlam's commission and, as things have turned out have done so, he would not be Prime Minister and not able to give or persist with such advice.

The announced proposals about financing public servants, suppliers, contractors and others do not amount to a satisfactory alternative to supply.

Government House,
Canberra. 2600.
11 November 1975

# ENDNOTES

## Chapter 1

1  This assessment of Kerr's decision at this time was based on interviews with Government House sources in January and February 1976. It was confirmed when Kerr released his memoirs *Matters for Judgment*, Macmillan, South Melbourne, 1978, refer pages 298, 308–311.
2  Graham Freudenberg, personal interview, February 1976.
3  I have modified the original text to remove any unintended implication that Kerr took his wife's advice on this issue. Refer Kerr, *Matters for Judgment*, pages 258, 309–11 and 329–32 for verification of Sir John's conviction that if he indicated his intentions to Whitlam then he would be sacked by the Prime Minister. Also, pages 388–89 where Kerr dismisses this incident as a 'myth' and quotes McAuley in his favour. My information was based on an interview with Whitlam in February 1976. Refer Whitlam, *The Truth of the Matter*, Penguin Books, Ringwood Victoria, 1979, pages 155–56, where Whitlam says that a person present during the discussion related it to a friend who related it to him when he was in Hobart the following weekend. According to Whitlam, McAuley's comments did not constitute a denial of the conversation.
4  Gough Whitlam, personal interview, February 1976. Whitlam also referred to this discussion in *The Truth of the Matter*, pages 92–93. However there is a fundamental difference between Kerr and Whitlam over both the timing and substance of this conversation. In *Matters for Judgment*, pages 246–47, Kerr gives a very different account of his position.
5  In this paragraph I have directly attributed this version of events to

Whitlam, who was my source. Kerr's own version has this idea originating with Whitlam, not with himself.

6   I have added this revised assessment in the final sentences of the paragraph. Kerr's own version in *Matters for Judgment*, pages 246–47, has him telling Whitlam that this Prime Ministerial proposal would create an 'uproar' and records his own worry that Whitlam might recommend this course of action.

7   This paragraph is based on personal interviews with Gough Whitlam in February 1976. It appears to be verified by Kerr's own version in *Matters for Judgment*, pages 309–11, where Kerr says that he decided his duty was to 'keep silent about my thinking' and that Whitlam was 'not entitled to receive a running report on how I was wrestling with the problem'.

8   Gough Whitlam, personal interview, February 1976. Whitlam's own version of this exchange is given in *The Truth of the Matter*, page 83. Kerr provides his own more detailed and different version in *Matters for Judgment*, pages 270–72. Kerr points out that he disagreed with Ellicott's thesis in terms of the timing (acting immediately to dismiss Whitlam) although he obviously agreed with its substance. Whitlam was not aware of the critical distinction Kerr made between timing and substance in evaluating the Ellicott opinion.

9   This account of the Kerr 'compromise' was based upon personal interviews with Whitlam in February 1976 and McClelland in January 1976. The proposal was confirmed by Kerr in *Matters for Judgment*, page 288. However Kerr points out that neither leader was very interested in the proposal. Significantly, Kerr says that when he put his proposal he did not indicate to either leader whether he agreed or disagreed with their basic stance.

10  Based on interviews with Government House sources in January 1976 and with Gough Whitlam in February 1976. In the subsequent accounts of Whitlam and Kerr there is at least one significant difference in their versions of this vital exchange. Kerr reports in *Matters for Judgment*, pages 358–59 that Whitlam replied, 'I must get in touch with the Palace at once.' Whitlam claims in *The Truth of the Matter*, page 110, that he said 'Have you discussed this with the Palace?'

11  Government House sources, personal interview, January 1976. This view of Kerr's assessment of Whitlam is confirmed completely in Kerr's *Matters for Judgment*. But Whitlam denied comprehensively any intent or plan to sack or replace Kerr, refer *The Truth of the Matter*, page 111.

12  Government House sources, personal interview, January 1976.

13  ibid.

14  ibid.

15  Kerr offers his own explanation of this position in *Matters for Judgment*, chapter 20.

16  Whitlam denies that he would have sacked Kerr, refer *The Truth of the Matter*, page 111.

## Chapter 2

1   Jim McClelland, Senate Hansard, 18 February 1976

2   Refer John Kerr, *Matters for Judgment*, chapter 18, for his own explanation for the timing of his intervention.

3   Gough Whitlam, personal interview, February 1976. Refer Whitlam, *The Truth of the Matter*, page 133

## Chapter 3

1  Gough Whitlam, personal interview, February 1976.

2  ibid.

3  Gough Whitlam, personal interview February 1976; Bill Snedden, personal interview, February 1976.

4  Gough Whitlam, personal interview, February 1976.

5  Barwick later played down his association with Ellicott saying that 'we have seen very little of one another throughout our lives . . . we have never worked on a case together'. Refer Garfield Barwick, *Sir John Did His Duty*, Serendip Publications, Wahroonga, 1983, page 75.

6  Whitlam records in his book that this conversation took place a week earlier, on 19 October 1975. Refer Whitlam, *The Truth of the Matter*, Penguin, Melbourne, 1979, page 90.

7  Gough Whitlam, personal interview, February 1976.

8  Kerr answered this question directly. In Kerr, *Matters for Judgment*, chapter 21, he makes it clear that there was no earlier dialogue with Barwick during the crisis before a phone call on 9 November which led to their consultations on 10 November. Barwick also confirms that there was no such dialogue, direct or indirect. However Barwick reveals that there was a discussion between the two men at a 20 September dinner at which stage the outlines of a potential crisis were apparent. According to Barwick, Kerr could envisage a serious situation developing. He asked Barwick whether he could see any way in which the High Court might become involved. Barwick replied that the matter appeared to be for the Parliament not for the Court. Barwick advised Kerr that the issue might land on his table. Kerr then asked Barwick if the Chief Justice would be prepared to advise him if the need arose. Barwick replied that that would depend upon the circumstances but says that 'I left the door open for the Governor-General to approach me'. Refer Barwick, *Sir John Did His Duty*, pages 73–75.

9  Barwick entertains the notion that he may have influenced Kerr. He says: 'To the extent that he respected and accepted my opinion, it can be said that I had some influence in his pursuit of the course on which he had decided.' Refer Barwick, *Sir John Did His Duty*, page 94.

10  Bob Ellicott, personal interview, February 1976.

11  The colleague referred to in the text is myself. The word 'colleague' was used as a journalistic device to enable me to convey the essence of what Fraser told me. I saw Fraser in his office early on the evening of 6 November after his final session with the Governor-General. I had earlier spoken with Whitlam the same day who assured me that Kerr was 'rock solid' and would act only on his advice. I was surprised by the deep confidence Fraser displayed and even more by how explicit he was in predicting Kerr's actions. The conversation was on the basis of non-attributable background and only the two of us were present. Fraser stressed that Kerr wanted the issue resolved by Christmas. He was quite firm on the point that Kerr would intervene and equally firm that Kerr would dismiss Whitlam. I left puzzled by the great confidence both leaders displayed realising that one of them must surely be mistaken.

## Chapter 4

1   I read the full text of the cable in January 1976 and took selective notes for use in the book. The full text of the cable was published some years later, refer Desmond Ball, *A Suitable Piece of Real Estate*, Hale and Iremonger, Sydney, 1980, pages 169–70.
2   Interviews with Whitlam Government advisers, January 1976. These interviews provide the material for the following account.
3   Bill Morrison, personal interview, February 1976; Whitlam Government advisers, personal interviews, January 1976.
4   Whitlam adviser, personal interview, January 1976.
5   I have deleted those sections of the original text which drew upon the then current literature to assess the functions of the bases because far more recent material is now available.
6   Personal interviews with Labor advisers, January and February 1976
7   Gough Whitlam, personal interview, February 1976.
8   This overview of ASIS was written in early 1976 and has not been updated to reflect the changes since then.

## Chapter 5

1   Tony Staley, personal interview, January 1976.
2   Malcolm Fraser, unpublished interview with the author, 16 September, 1974.
3   Billy Snedden, interview with John Edwards, *Australian Financial Review*, 4 May, 1972.
4   ibid.
5   ibid.
6   Bill Snedden, personal interview, January 1976; Phillip Lynch, personal interview, February 1976.
7   Snedden subsequently claimed that he did not know the November vote but suspected the number for a spill was a fairly low figure.

## Chapter 6

1   The account of economics and politics in this chapter is based upon public documents, published assessments during the Whitlam years and a series of interviews conducted during the first three months of 1976. Those interviewed for this chapter included Gough Whitlam, Dr Jim Cairns, Jim McClelland, Kep Enderby, Bob Hawke, Dr Peter Wilenski, Jim Spigelman, Dr Brian Brogan, Michael Delaney, Geoff Briot, Eric Walsh, David Combe.

## Chapter 7

1   Figures based on Malcolm Mackerras, *Elections 1975*, Angus and Robertson, Sydney, 1976.
2   Gough Whitlam, personal interview, February 1976.
3   Jim Cairns, personal interview, February 1976.

## Chapter 8

1   Bill Snedden, personal interview, February 1976; Malcolm Fraser, personal interview, February 1976; Tony Staley, personal interview, March 1976. While the author believes this is an accurate account of the meeting, Snedden's version did not include asking Fraser to forgo being a leadership candidate before the next elections.
2   During our interview Snedden claimed that he had no intention of forcing a mid-year election in 1975.
3   This constitutional provision was removed by referendum after Malcolm Fraser came to office.
4   Bill Snedden, personal interview, February 1976.
5   Bill Snedden, personal interview, February 1976; Tony Staley, personal interview, March 1976.
6   Eric Robinson, personal interview, March 1976; Tony Staley, personal interview, March 1976; Vic Garland, personal interview February 1976.
7   Bill Snedden, personal interview, February 1976; Tony Staley, personal interview, March 1976; Jon Gaul, personal interview, March 1976.

## Chapter 9

1   Phillip Lynch, personal interview, March 1976; Andrew Hay, personal interview, March 1976; Tony Staley, personal interview, March 1976.
2   John Howard, personal interview, March 1976; Tony Staley, personal interview, March 1976; Reg Withers, personal interview, March 1976.
3   Peter Hardie, personal interview, March 1976; Ian Macphee, personal interview, April 1976; Tony Eggleton, personal interview, April 1976.
4   Peter Bowers, personal interview, April 1976; Jon Gaul, personal interview, April 1976.
5   Bill Snedden, personal interview, February 1976; Andrew Peacock, personal interview, April 1976; Don Chipp, personal interview, April 1976; Jon Gaul, personal interview, April 1976; Tony Staley, personal interview, March 1976; Eric Robinson, personal interview, March 1976; John Howard, personal interview, March 1976.
6   Phillip Lynch, personal interview, March 1976.
7   ibid.
8   Bill Snedden, personal interview, February 1976; Jon Gaul, personal interview, April 1976.
9   Vic Garland, personal interview, February 1976; Tony Staley, personal interview, March 1976; Phillip Lynch, personal interview, March 1976; Malcolm Fraser, personal interview, March 1976.
10  Bill Snedden, personal interview, February 1976.
11  Bill Snedden, personal interview, February 1976; Phillip Lynch, personal interview, March 1976.
12  Jon Gaul, personal interview, April 1976.
13  Bill Snedden, personal interview, February 1976; Jon Gaul, personal interview, April 1976; Phillip Lynch, personal interview, March 1976; Andrew Hay, personal interview, March 1976; Brian Buckley, personal interview, March 1976.
14  Bill Snedden, personal interview, February 1976.
15  Andrew Peacock, personal interview, April 1976.

## Chapter 10

1    Malcolm Fraser, the *Age*, 21 May 1973.
2    Malcolm Fraser, interview with Sally Wilkins, the *Age*, 24 May 1975.
3    Interview with Gwen Mosley, the *Australian Women's Weekly*, 9 April 1975.
     Interview with Paul Kelly, the *Australian*, 29 March 1975
4    Unpublished interview with Paul Kelly.
5    Interview with John Edwards, *Australian Financial Review*, 28 June 1972.
6    ibid.

## Chapter 11

1    Documents tabled in House of Representatives, 9 July 1975.
2    ibid.
3    Jim Cairns, personal interview, March 1976.
4    Documents tabled in House of Representatives, 9 July 1975.
5    Gough Whitlam, personal interview, February 1976. In his memoirs Kerr
     says that the circumstances of this meeting were a 'great shock', that he
     believed it was not a valid Executive Council meeting, that he felt that
     legal errors were made in the official minute and that the Attorney-
     General's advice was 'probably wrong', refer Kerr, *Matters for Judgment*,
     chapter 15.
6    Documents tabled in House of Representatives, 9 July 1975.
7    Jim Cairns, personal interview, March 1976.
8    Jim Cairns, personal interview, March 1976; Jim Spigelman, personal inter-
     view, March 1976; Bob Sorby, personal interview, February 1976; Andrew
     Hay, personal interview, March 1976.
9    Documents tabled in House of Representatives, 9 July 1975.
10   Jim Cairns, personal interview, March 1976.

## Chapter 12

1    Documents tabled in House of Representatives, 9 July 1975.
2    ibid.
3    ibid.
4    ibid.
5    ibid.
6    ibid.
7    ibid.

## Chapter 13

1    Channel 9 interview, 28 November 1975.

## Chapter 16

1    Refer chapter 12.
2    Refer documents tabled in House of Representatives, 9 July 1975.
3    ibid.

4    ibid.

## Chapter 19

1    Alan Missen, personal interview, April 1976.
2    Steele Hall, personal interview, April 1976.
3    Peter Hardie, personal interview, March 1976.
4    Bob Sorby, personal interview, March 1976.
5    Assessment based upon interviews with Malcolm Fraser, Phillip Lynch, Tony Staley, David Barnett, and Tony Eggleton.
6    This point was confirmed in interviews with Staley and Withers.
7    Alan Missen, personal interview, April 1976.
8    ibid.

## Chapter 20

1    Gough Whitlam, personal interview, February 1976; Graham Freudenberg, personal interview, February 1976; Michael Delaney, personal interview, January 1976; Kep Enderby, personal interview, January 1976.
2    This incident is related in full in chapter one.
3    Whitlam staffers, personal interviews, January–February 1976. Also, refer chapter one for Kerr's assessment.
4    Gough Whitlam, personal interview, February 1976; Jim McClelland, personal interview, February 1976. Also, refer chapter one.
5    Refer chapter one for a more detailed account of this compromise proposal.
6    Refer chapter one.
7    For Kerr's own explanation see his book *Matters for Judgment*, Macmillan, South Melbourne, 1978.
8    Based upon a personal discussion with Fraser the evening of this meeting.
9    Kep Enderby, personal interview, February 1976.
10    ibid.
11    The comments by Fraser in his office on 6 November were made to the author.
12    Gough Whitlam, personal interview, February 1976; Malcolm Fraser, personal interview, March 1976.
13    Fraser has subsequently confirmed that before the joint parties meeting that morning he took what has been described as 'the most momentous call' of his career. It was from Kerr. Fraser's revelations about this call are contained in Philip Ayres, *Malcolm Fraser, A Biography*, William Heinemann, Victoria, 1987, pages 292–94. According to Fraser, Kerr asked him four questions, the answers to which Kerr needed to know before he dismissed Whitlam. He asked whether Fraser would be prepared to accept a caretaker commission, advise an election and guarantee supply. The biographer notes that Fraser 'now felt sure of the outcome'—that he would be commissioned after Whitlam's dismissal—but that he did not yet have 'knowledge' of this.
14    Refer chapter one for the account of the exchange between Whitlam and Kerr.

## Chapter 22

1   Election night descriptions have drawn on articles in the *Age* by Ben Hills and Sally Wilkins on 15 December and in the *Australian* by Janet Hawley on 15 December.
2   This table and all others following it are based on figures provided by the Commonwealth Electoral Office.

## Chapter 23

1   David Combe, personal interview, March 1976.
2   David Combe, personal interview, March 1976, Bill Hartley, personal interview, March 1976.
3   David Combe, personal interview, March 1976.
4   Summary drawn from the *National Times*, 29 February 1976.
5   ibid.
6   ibid.
7   Bill Hartley, personal interview, March 1976.
8   David Combe, personal interview, March 1976.
9   Bill Hartley, personal interview, March 1976.
10  David Combe, personal interview, March 1976.
11  Bill Hartley, personal interview, March 1976.
12  David Combe, personal interview, March 1976.
13  ibid.
14  Gough Whitlam, personal interview, February 1976; David Combe, personal interview, March 1976.
15  David Combe, personal interview, March 1976.
16  ibid.
17  Bill Hartley, personal interview, March 1976.
18  David Combe, personal interview, March 1976.
19  ibid.
20  ibid.
21  ibid.
22  ibid.

## Chapter 24

1   A referendum passed during the Fraser years on 21 May 1977 changed section 15 of the constitution to require that casual Senate vacancies be filled by a candidate of the same party as that of the vacating Senator.

447

# INDEX